Call Me Sergeant Rock: How a Boy Becomes a Man in Vietnam

Strategic Book Publishing and Rights Co.
12620 FM 1960, Suite A4-507
Houston, TX 77065
www.sbpra.com

Paperback
ISBN: 978-1-62516-221-2

Hardcover
ISBN: 978-1-62516-842-9

Table of Contents

CHAPTER 1

Thirteen Men out of 143 (A Guardian Angel)

"How many do we have now?"

Sergeant Chuck Lewis said, "Thirteen."

We now had thirteen men. We had 143 — the largest the company had ever been in my year in Vietnam. *Where are all of our men now?* It was January 9, 1968. I was an old man now. I had a birthday while in this country called Vietnam. I am twenty-one-years-old, but my mind thinks like a forty-year-old soldier. I have had to learn so quickly. I do not expect to have another birthday, nor do I expect to live through the night. Thirteen of us cannot fight three regiments of North Vietnam Regulars (NVR, also known as NVA or North Vietnam Army) with 2,000 men in each regiment.

I had always wondered if a person who is really afraid of being killed at arm's length could be perfectly still and quiet. The enemy is only a few feet away. *Can they see my silhouette? Can they smell me? Can they hear my heart beating?* The rain is down to a sprinkle. We are sitting in our wet, muddy foxholes, holding our breath. I am answering my own question; I *can* be perfectly still when danger is near. The raindrops and the sweat are running down my face, causing my eyes to burn. I don't budge. My heart is beating so loud that I think the NVA are going to hear it. My chest feels like it is going to explode. My stomach is sick. I need to vomit, but I don't dare. My head feels like it has been run over by a freight train. My temples are pulsating. The NVA are moving past us. We can see their legs and their rifles between the trees and bushes. They are within ten feet of our position. They are walking parallel to our position. I close my eyes tight and start to pray again. I believe in God with all of my heart and soul, but I know that it is time for Chuck and me to go to heaven tonight. My family will be devastated. My wonderful wife will be heartbroken. God has a plan for all of us; I just hope that He gives my family and wife the ability to go on in life after my death.

I look at Chuck, my best friend, and notice that he is praying also. He finishes his prayer and looks at me. His eyes tell the story. He knows that this will be our last night on earth. Chuck also knows that he and I will be in Heaven soon. He glances at me again and tilts his head as if to say, "We just said the same prayer, and thank you for being my friend." Chuck and I always know what the other is thinking.

I look at Chuck again. He is concerned that the enemy will come through the tree line at any second and kill the rest of us. We don't move a muscle. We keep holding our breath, sometimes for so long that it seems like we will pass out. I cannot tell if I am hearing my heartbeat or Chuck's. Our skin has been in the water for such a long time that it is white and wrinkled. The leeches are crawling up our boots. Chuck looks at my boots and nods his head at me. I'd already seen the leeches. He looks down and sees leeches on his pants. He does not move. I don't move. I think, "Let them bite. It is better than being shot."

It is raining much harder now, but this is good, because the NVA cannot hear us breathing. We still don't dare move. The rainwater is now about three inches deep in our foxholes. We have taken off our helmets to sit on them, trying to keep our butts out of the mud. This only gives us relief for a little while. The water is soon eight inches deep and rises above the helmets that we are sitting on. We don't bail water for the risk of being heard. "Here comes something," someone whispers.

Our bodies tighten up with fear. I look at Chuck, and he looks back at me. We have never been so afraid. *Are the NVA coming in now to kill the rest of us?* I hear the noise getting closer. I whisper to Chuck, "Get ready buddy; this could be it for us."

A soldier busts through the tree line and the bushes, coming toward us. We lift our rifles and aim in the direction of the noise he made. My finger is on the trigger, ready to fire. I take another deep breath and wait for a second. If I squeeze off a round now, the gooks will surely know we are alive (*gook* is the term we use for anyone who wants to kill Americans, usually of Vietnamese descent). I look up. He is one of our soldiers. We are relieved. We hear a scream from somewhere in the rice paddies. The NVA are ripping off rings, watches, and wallets from another wounded soldier. This ripping off of items, as we found out later, is exactly what they were doing with no mercy.

Chuck Lewis says, "Ten seconds."

I know what he means. He is trying to figure out how long it takes for the sound to get to us after we see the flash from the rifle. This time it is fifteen seconds. Chuck's wrong. They are farther away than he thought.

Chuck moves in toward me really close. "How many of those guys do you think we will see in Heaven tomorrow?"

Again, I know what he means. He does not think we will make it through the night. "Half of them, maybe more, but don't let your team know what we are talking about," I told him very quietly.

Three more of our men come running to our perimeter. They have no weapons. They are ripped, torn, and bleeding. They are white with fear. "That is seventeen now," Chuck says.

I acknowledge him with a nod. Chuck and I both know that without more men, we don't stand a chance in a real battle. "Do you think the angel will greet us?" Chuck asks.

"Do you mean the angel we saw yesterday?"

"Yes."

"Maybe God and the angel have another plan for us. Why would we be saved this morning if He didn't have a plan?" I asked.

Chuck looked at me with a half grin and a small glimmer of hope. "Maybe you're right."

This mess that we are in now all started the day before. The company was heading north toward the DMZ (demilitarized zone). We were in a valley in Khe Sanh (pronounced *Kay-Saun*). Soon everyone else and I would call this place Death Valley. But for now, it was just another God-forsaken place.

Although I carried a map, I was never notified where we were on a big scale. For instance, in the States, you may get a map of California showing all of the cities. Here in Vietnam, we got a very, very small portion of Vietnam — just enough for grid coordinates. The squad leaders were given another map once the company moved from an area that was no longer on the map. Knowing the overall destination was for the higher ups. Platoon leaders and squad leaders only knew the immediate destinations and usually never more than a week at a time. This was done on purpose, for security reasons. Other companies did it differently.

I oriented my map, and we moved out. Our platoon was first, and my squad was pulling point duty (point is the first person or group leading, usually the first to make contact with the enemy). I was pulling point for my squad. Normally, a squad leader is not supposed to pull point, but if I was going to keep the respect of my men, I needed to take my turn. Pulling point was very lonely most of the time, and very dangerous. The point man would move far from the rest of the squad in case he ran into a trip wire, an ambush, or a sniper. This way, he would be the only one killed or wounded. When I pulled point I was very careful, constantly looking for trip wires and any movement in the jungle (the bush). In the six months I was in country, I had developed a great deal of esteem with my men. I believed that pulling point on this particular day would be easy, because we had not been shot at in over a week. I was looking forward to an easy day. I liked that every once in a while.

As we were walking along, right there, smack in front of me, were five NVA. I opened up and hit the ground. They were in a huddle, looking at what appeared to be a map. I fired off two magazines from my rifle. To my surprise, all of them were on the ground. Three dead and two wounded. The captain saw the bodies and congratulated me. One of the bodies we thought was dead blinked his eyes. He was not dead. He was lying on his side with both his hands under his head. The captain said, "Shoot him again."

This puzzled me somewhat. Usually the captain wanted the prisoners for interrogating. One of my men shot him with his rifle at point blank range. With a strong voice, the captain said, "Now roll him over."

He had a .45 pistol under his head, clinched in his hands. *How did the captain know?* He made another good decision, as he had done so many times before. If we had rolled the NVA over before killing him, he would have killed one of us, maybe more. "Sergeant Rodgers, your kill, your yield," the captain said.

In our company, it was an unwritten law that if you got the body count, you could keep everything on the body except important papers. One of our guys got what was worth $2,000 off of one NVA. I thought, "What will I get for the five I killed?" I could hardly wait. Of course, I was entitled to the five AK-47 weapons. Three were new and two were almost brand new. I had shot a hole through the stock of one of them. That was the rifle that I really wanted. Now it was time for the big moment that I was waiting for — the search. A couple of men helped turn the pockets inside out and lay the findings next to the bodies. There it was, all laid out on the ground, every pocket turned inside out. Yes, there was all of my treasure — one dollar and thirty-seven cents. *What bad luck,* I thought. Chuck Lewis jokingly said, "Can I get a loan?" then slapped me on the back. "Maybe we will have better luck tomorrow."

Little did he know that our luck was about to run out. Actually, I was tired of killing and fighting. I wished that we would never see another NVA, gook, or VC (Viet Cong or Victor Charlie) again. I knew that was an impossible wish, because locating the enemy, engaging in battle, and finding out how many troops they had was our job. Finding large groups of the enemy was the specialty of the 196th Light Infantry Brigade.

It was time to set up the perimeter for the night. We formed a big circle, sort of like the covered wagons would do in the western days of cowboys and Indians. We would dig foxholes to accommodate three to four men per hole. We had 143 men. Therefore, we had about forty-one foxholes. Each hole would be from two to four feet deep depending on the softness of the ground and, of course, how tired we were.

Chuck, Emerald, Brant, and I were in one hole; my three other men were in the next hole. I would always keep Emerald with me, because he was much more afraid than most soldiers. He was a really nice guy, but he worried all the time about being killed. We had a very good night — no rain, no snipers, no snakes, no mortars, and no rocketing. It even seemed like there were fewer mosquitoes than usual.

We slept in until seven o'clock. We ate our C-ration breakfast and did the usual moaning and complaining about the big hump (hiking for a long distance, usually up hills) we were about to make. The hump was to be across one half mile of rice paddies, and then up through the mountains for ten klicks (a military klick is one kilometer, or .62 miles). At least we were going to get out of the Khe Sanh Valley. We called it Death Valley because of all the soldiers that had given their lives there. There was talk about something called the Tet Offensive. It seemed pretty quiet — no bombs going off from far away and no snipers. Maybe it was a little too quiet.

"Gooks in the open!" someone yelled.

The gooks fired a few shots at us. They started running through the rice paddies. The radio sounded off, "This is Annihilator Three-Three. All platoons get on line!"

The company lined up, 143 abreast, keeping about ten meters between individuals. We started firing our weapons at the five

NVA that ran through the rice paddies. We started advancing. Two NVA were still running, but three were dead. Chuck said, "Can you believe this? We have over one hundred men, and we cannot kill five gooks."

We both knew that when everyone is shooting on full automatic, it is very hard to hit a moving target. I would rather be shot at with a full automatic weapon than with one shot at a time when the shooter can take his time and aim. This was not a movie; it was real. In the movies, a full automatic shooter hits his target twenty times before he runs out of bullets. It does not happen that way in real life.

We passed a dead body, then another. We were almost running by now. We were still in the rice paddies and in the open. "What is this?" we wondered. It was a river, thirty feet wide and appearing to be four feet deep. It cut right in front of us. The river looked like it ran for miles. On the other side of the river was an embankment about twelve feet tall. This was spooky; something was wrong.

Chuck and I looked at each other with our mouths open. I told Chuck to start praying. He already knew why I was so worried. This could be an ambush. The gooks would have to have a lot of guts to set a trap for us when we were now 143 men strong. *But wait a minute, what if they were more in number?* If they had 300, we could handle it. If they had 1,000, we were in trouble. The mortars started going off, and they were not our mortars. The .50-caliber machine guns started pounding the earth around us. The rounds were missing us, but the dirt and mud were peppering our eyes. The rockets started hitting. It sounded like 10,000 bombs going off at the same time. The concussions from the rockets and mortars were throwing us up against the rice paddy dikes. The oxygen was being removed from the air. We were choking, and we could hardly see. We could not retreat, for we would be even more in the open. We were still in the rice paddies. We had to attack immediately. We had to get through the river and over the straight-up embankment to knock out the

.50-caliber machine gun. I gave the word to my small group of men to advance.

We jumped in the water, and my RTO (radio telephone operator) went out of sight. He was drowning. He was carrying the weight of all of his rations and a radio that weighed about twenty-eight pounds. This weight was too much for him. We were in seven-foot-deep water. Chuck and I grabbed the RTO and pulled with all of our strength. We got him out of the water. He was alive.

We made it to the other side of the river, but we had no place to go. The NVA with the .50-caliber was above us. The ear-pounding sound stopped suddenly. We looked back across the river and saw twenty or so of our wounded men. They were reaching out to us for help, but we were fifty or more meters from them. Three men from another squad ran out to help, but the .50-caliber shot them, not to kill, but to wound. Now they were also begging for our help. I was dying inside. I called for artillery support, but our radio had been drenched from the river. We needed to, at least, get to the gooks with the .50-caliber who were torturing our men by intentionally wounding them and not killing them. Our wounded soldiers' faces were showing fright like no other. One of my men had a grenade launcher. "Warner, I want you to fire just over the bank and the trees to knock out the fifty."

Warner had a look of despair. "Do you want to do it or what?"

My tone showed him that I was not going to take any lip.

"Yes, sir."

I tell him to fire it almost straight up. He keeps pounding the vicinity of the .50-caliber. The deafening and ground-pounding noise started again, but at least we had stopped one of the .50-calibers. Now we could kill some gooks. Now we could reach the top of the embankment. We had to call in artillery at the tree line. We could see lots of flashes from the rifles being fired at the tree line. "Hey Chuck, it looks about 500 meters away," I told him.

"The radio is still dead," Chuck said.

I looked at the tree line again. "Look, look, look! The tree line is advancing!"

How can a line of trees move forward? "Give me the binos (binoculars)."

I look through the wet lenses and try to wipe them before taking another look. I cannot believe my eyes. I see, now, how the tree line is advancing toward us. It is what looks to be 2,000 NVA with tree branches stuck all over them for camouflage. They are almost in complete unity, shooting and reloading, as they move forward. "Chuck, take a look."

He looks and says, "Help us, God!"

They are like many ants. We are going to be slaughtered, I was thinking. Emerald looks over the top of the embankment. "Oh, God!" he said.

We slide back down to the edge of the water. I get my seven-man squad to huddle up. Emerald says, "We are going to die. Aren't we, Sarge?"

His look was horrifying. A squad leader is supposed to always tell his men they are not going to die and that there is a plan for their safety. We all knew that this was going to be the end. We all knew that we were going to die today. "Yes we are, Emerald," I said as I looked him straight in the eye. "Do all of you believe in God? And don't B.S. me now, it's too late."

They all said that they did. "Danny, would you say a prayer?" Chuck asked.

I nodded my head and began the prayer. "Dear God, we know that we are going to die in the next few moments, but before we go, please help our men across the river. Make their suffering stop. Please let us die with dignity and let us die quickly. Amen."

Each man said, "Amen."

The sky lit up like a flash from an atomic bomb. It was a rocket that landed right in the middle of the suffering men across the river. To my surprise, none of the men were crying any longer. Their faces were now calm as they drifted off to their deaths. I felt as if a great load had been lifted from my shoulders. Now I thought, *Did I do the right thing?* It seemed as if I prayed for many to be killed so a few could live. I think that my mind was getting mixed up.

I have to show strength for the sake of the men, but I am actually weak. If my men knew that I had to pray for guidance, almost hourly now, they would be overly concerned about my ability to lead. Sometimes, I just wished that someone else would tell me exactly what to do about these mixed feelings that I have. I look up to the heavens and pray, "God, please sort out my feelings and keep giving me your directions."

"I don't want to give these gooks the satisfaction of killing us here where we cannot shoot back," I told my men. "Drop everything but your rifles."

We dropped our packs, starlight night vision scopes, all C-rations, canteens, and sleeping gear. Our rifles were not working because of the mud and sand that was lodged in them. We found a couple of AK-47s (the weapon of choice for the NVA, a very durable rifle) lying next to a few dead gooks. Evidently, we killed a few.

"Let's head down the river," I said.

We jumped in the water. It was seven feet deep in some places and four feet deep in others. The rounds (bullets) started hitting all around us again. The mortars started going off in the water. They spotted us for sure. I swore I could hear the bullets bouncing off of my helmet. If we could just make it to a place where we could get out of the river, we could start firing back. This way they could kill us all at the same time. But our instincts told us to keep moving. Emerald grabbed me. "Sergeant, will you shoot me now?"

He asked not in panic, but in a request-like manner, like when we would ask for a trade of C-rations. I thought it would be easier on him if I did kill him, but I didn't. "You save a round for yourself, and for sure. Don't be taken alive."

Emerald said, "See ya in Heaven."

This was out of context for Emerald. But what wasn't out of context today? We heard a voice say, "I know the way out."

"What?" I asked.

"I know how to get us back to the other side," he said again.

He was a sandy-haired guy, about six feet tall. He was leaning up against the side of the dirt bank next to the river. He had nothing but his Army fatigues — no weapon, no ammo, no canteens, and no helmet. He was holding one hand on his leg. He was wounded.

I said once more, "What did you say?"

He leaned forward. "I know the way out of here, but you need to help me. I can barely walk."

Without me giving an order, two of my men got on either side of him for support. "We have to head downstream a little farther."

He nodded his head in that direction. Chuck looked at me and shrugged his shoulders. "I have never seen this guy in our company before. Have you?"

"No, but if he really does know the way out, we will put him in for a medal and give him the biggest party that he has ever seen. Let's move out," I said.

We started moving again, but the shelling and the machine gun fire was too intense. We had to take some kind of a stand to get some of the firepower off of us. We pulled off to the side while still keeping most of our bodies in the water. We started firing back, all of us at the same time. I was thinking that we could not make the NVA any madder than they were at the moment. We all knew that we were not going to kill any of them. We just wanted a few of them to take cover and slow their firepower down. The M-16s (our rifles) were jamming again. "Start using the AKs," I said.

The gooks' rifles that we had picked up a few minutes ago were working perfectly. "Now move!" I yelled.

We started down river again. The sandy-haired guy said, "There!"

It was the prettiest sight I had ever seen. It was a river running at a ninety-degree angle to the river that we were in now. The river, if we make it, will eventually take us through the rice paddies and to our perimeter we had set up the night before. This new river was only about four feet deep in most places, but the walls were a foot taller. We were now heading away from the enemy. The NVA could not see us, except for when one of us stood up too far. The NVA were searching to see where we were in the river. They were pounding the river in front of us with mortars. They would drop two, then move fifty meters closer to us. They were walking them in toward our position. We advanced. "The second explosion you guys hear in front of us, run as fast as you can past it," I said to my guys.

This is something we were taught not to do. Always move away from artillery and take cover. However, on this occasion, Chuck and I figured out the NVA plan. After a half hour, the explosions were far behind us. We made it to the tree line where we had spent the night before. We saw a few more men and our friend, Baby Bird, from the mortar platoon. We never knew Baby Bird's real name. The end of his nose was hanging off. He had cuts on his head, and he was as white as a ghost. "Hey Baby Bird, glad to see you," I said.

He didn't respond. He was in shock. I found out later that the entire mortar platoon was wiped out, except for a few men. Baby Bird was always with the captain. I asked another soldier if the captain was still alive. He nodded his head. I was relieved. The captain would know what to do. I wanted to tell the captain to give the guy who saved us a medal. I looked behind me and the sandy-haired guy was between two of my men, leaning against a four-foot-tall rice paddy dike. My other men were on the other side, still laying half in and half out of the water. As I looked over my fine bunch of men, I thought they looked more dead than alive. The captain came walking up to us from the direction of our perimeter, where we had been the night before. He was still very strong-looking, not straggly-looking as we were.

He grabbed Chuck and me, and with a big hug, he said, "I thought everyone was dead. How many you got?"

"Seven, the same as I started with, plus one more," I said.

The captain, with a slight twist of his head, asked, "How did you guys get back, Sergeant Rodgers?"

"Sir, you need to give this man a medal. He saved all of us."

I turned to summon the sandy-haired guy to bring him to the captain, but he was gone. The two men that were lying against the bank beside him said, "He did not go anywhere, honest, Sarge. He never moved from this spot."

Everyone shrugged their shoulders as I looked at every man. He had vanished. Chuck and I, and all of my men, looked at each other with utter amazement. Our mouths were wide open and not saying a word. This sandy-haired soldier was truly our guardian angel. My mind was racing again. God had saved us. I don't know what God's plan was for my men and me, but I was glad that the plan today was not death for us. The captain said, "No matter how you guys got back, I am glad you're back alive."

The shooting started again, but now, some fire was coming from our own foxholes. We all hit the ground, except for one man. The captain didn't budge. He was standing up with his .45-caliber pistol, cursing at the gooks. Tracer rounds were coming in straight for the captain. He turned slightly when two rounds went through his backpack. Something was running down the captain's leg, but he didn't drop to the ground. *Doesn't he know that he is hit?* I think.

The captain looked at Chuck and I and said, "Dang it, they got my lima beans and ham."

This was a joke, for everyone hated the lima beans and ham C-rations. We were still frozen to the ground. The captain said, "Sergeant Rodgers, there are gooks in our holes and there is a .50-caliber in your hole that is firing hard."

I thought to myself, *So what, Geronimo? Let's call in artillery. You still have a working radio!*

13

He said, "What are you going to do about it?"

When I saw him still standing there, upright and proud, with his chest stuck out, I was embarrassed. He was a true leader. I felt like I could not even be a pimple on the butt of such a brave man. I stood up and looked at my men. "Let's get our holes back!"

Chuck stood up and grabbed everyone. He pulled them to their feet. "You heard the sarge; let's kill some NVA!"

We borrowed the rifles and grenade launchers and started to attack our own foxholes that were now occupied by the enemy. We felt like we could not be denied. We took back our perimeter within fifteen minutes. But be assured, there were no prisoners. When this small battle was over, there were twenty-two dead NVA. We had captured two .50-calibers, one quad-fifty, several LAAWs (lightweight anti-tank weapon), and twenty-two AK-47s. The captain and his group followed behind us. "Is your radio working, sir?" I asked.

"No, but I think if we can dry it out, it might." The captain continued, "Were you scared?"

"I thought it was over for all of us," I said.

The captain goes on to say, "Did you tell your men they were going to die?"

Why did he have to ask me that question? He could have asked me any question but that. I did not want to answer him, because he knew as I did — a leader has to keep his men's spirits up at all times. I hung my head and said, "Yes I did, sir."To my amazement, he just looked at me with a slight grin, with a gleam in his eye, and said, "OK."

"Did you tell your men that they were going to die, sir?" I mumbled.

"Yes I did."

Then he smiled a little larger and said, "If you tell anybody, I'll beat your butt!"

I never knew if he actually told his men that they were going to die, but I did ask a few of his men if the captain was scared. They said that he was, but not as afraid as they were. I felt proud to be a squad leader. The captain had shown his leadership quality in bringing me back up to leadership ability. Then I heard, "Thanks, Sarge."

It was Emerald.

"For what?" I asked.

He came over and shook my hand and said, "For not killing me when I asked you to."

"I don't think that I could have shot you unless you were in pain. God saved us, huh?"

"He sure did! Do you think we can make it through the night with thirteen men, when they have so many?"

Emerald had that worried look again, but I guess we all had that look. Now was the time to reassure the men. "Sure, all that we have to do now is get the radio working again."

We have to make it through this January 9, 1968, day and night. I hope that more men are alive than just the thirteen that we have here. It is going to be a very long night. I tell the men to keep quiet and to pray that the radio will start working. We take our positions in the foxholes.

CHAPTER 2

Mike Rydser

After spending the night listening to the horrifying screams, morning finally came. We had now been without sleep for forty-eight hours, but not one of my men complained. They knew as well as I that the enemy was still in the area. But at least they were not right on top of us as they were during the night. The rain had lightened up. Now, we could work on the radio some more. When we finally got it repaired, the captain came up to my position and we went over the grid coordinates together. We were going to call in for a lot of artillery support. We knew that we had to call it in close. I had been the one in my platoon that generally called in fire strikes. I was hoping for the chance to do it again, but the captain would have the final say on the matter. "Do you want to call it in?" the captain asked.

"Yes, sir," I replied.

I had already figured out how I would call the firepower in, so that it would protect us but not kill us. Although I was reasonably sure of our exact location, it never hurts to be on the safe side. I was going to call in the artillery about 150 meters away from our position, and then start dropping off meters until it was very close to us. This way, we would kill the NVA and protect ourselves. Now my only worry was for the men outside our perimeter. *How many of our own men will I kill if I make a small mistake?* I looked at Chuck. "Here we go."

I started talking on the radio. "Fireball Five-Niner, this is Blackhawk Three, over."

"This is Fireball Five-Niner, we thought that you guys were all dead, over."

If we were in the States, we would be insulted by these remarks. But death was a fact of life in Vietnam. The voice on the other end of the radio was plain and simple. Feelings did not count anymore. He was not being cute or amusing. I could hear in his voice that he was very much concerned, and that he was happy to offer his services to us. "We are not dead yet, over."

I loved to talk to Fireball Five-Niner. I could tell by his voice that he was only nineteen or twenty years old, but he always gave me a feeling that everything was going to be alright. He was like my dad in a way. I used to come in, yelling about some problem like the starting position on the baseball team, asking him what I did wrong, or complaining that I lost a go-kart race. In a calm voice, Dad would settle me down and say, "Everything will be alright son." I loved Dad. Dad would have made a good soldier. However, by the time he was eighteen and old enough to fight, he had two kids, my brother Dwight and me. This kept him out of the previous war.

"We are ready to supply you with all of the firepower you need, all night long, over."

I felt relieved to know that we would be getting the artillery we needed. "We will probably need it all night, over."

"What you got? Over."

"We have gooks in the open. We need VT. We need November Papa, and we need shells." I gave the coordinates and said, "Over."

"It is on the way. Good luck, out."

"Thanks. Roger, out."

Chuck, with his big wide grin, says, "Well, this will be interesting. What is VT again?"

"VT explodes above the ground like millions of small pieces of shrapnel."

"Oh, yeah, I remember. And November Papa is napalm — a gasoline and plastic mixture, a burning, melting plastic used to clear brush, set equipment on fire, light up the sky, and kill the enemy."

"Wow, Chuck, you have been doing your homework. Did you know that when napalm hits the skin, it keeps burning until the oxygen is removed?"

"Yes I did. And did you know that once the enemy is hit by napalm, he can cover it with his hand or rag, but once he removes it, the napalm will continue to burn deep into the skin?"

"Yes I did. You sound like a textbook. What about shells, Chuck?"

"A shell explodes within itself, causing the shell to break apart with high-velocity shrapnel that will travel in all directions above the ground. The concussion of the shell alone can blow limbs off."

"Well, Mister Smarty Pants, why don't *you* just call in the fire support?"

We started to laugh. "Danny, I got my info from Fireball."

"I remember the Army taught us, but I got my info from Fireball too."

Many of us grunts would call in for Willie Peter when, in fact, we wanted napalm. The artillery support always figured it out for us. Willie Peter is white phosphorus, the same material used in tracer rounds. The correct time to call for Willie Peter is at night, when you want to detect the enemy. I would generally call in for a shell at first, so I could judge my position from the blast. My rule was to never call in Willie Peter or napalm on the first few shots. It would be a shame to inflict pain and injury on my men if I misjudged our location.

I saw what looked to be a lot of movement about 200 meters away from our position. "Fireball Five-Niner, this is Blackhawk Three, over."

"This is Fireball Five-Niner. We are ready, Blackhawk Three."

I gave the coordinates to Fireball with the request, "We need shells."

"They are on the way."

The first rounds were approximately 300 meters away from our position. "Fireball Five-Niner, this is Blackhawk Three. From my position, drop 150. That's one-five-zero, and give me three rounds."

When calling in artillery, it's important to always say "From my position" because it's not clear whether fire support is coming from the north, south, east, west, or from a Navy battleship, the Army base camp, artillery support, or even the Marines.

The rounds were closer. "Drop another seventy-five from my position."

By this time, we had developed a dialogue, and we recognized each other's voices. There was no need for formalities any longer. The rounds were getting closer. Now we could hear the shrapnel whizzing over our heads, but it was still not close enough. The NVA were very close to us.

I ran to the captain. "Sir, I think we need to drop another forty meters. This would mean taking a big chance. The rounds would be dropping within thirty-five meters of our position. If the rounds were all in a flat line base trajectory, we would all be blown to bits. I would rather be killed by friendly fire artillery than by these gooks."

"I agree. Do what you got to do, Sarge!"

I got back on the horn. "Fireball, I want you to drop another forty from my position. And no VT and no Willie Peter. You are going to be right on top of us. I say again, no VT, no Willie Peter."

A couple of rounds hit where I wanted them to hit. I jumped on the radio again. "Fire! Fire! Fire! Fire for effect! Fire now! Don't stop! Out!"

The trees started exploding. The branches flew everywhere. The high-pitched, eardrum-pounding sound of metal flying over our heads was deafening. But we knew from experience that if we could hear the sound, then we were not hit. The shrapnel flew much faster than its sound. In many cases, the shrapnel would cut down a tree right next to us and keep going.

"Watch out for falling trees!" I yelled to my guys.

We pounded our perimeter all day and all night with artillery. The voice on the other end of the radio stayed up with us all night long. This was somewhat of a comfort. I trusted the guy at the other end of the radio and did not want a change. After fifteen minutes or so, I would back the shells off and call in the VT and napalm. I would send the artillery all the way to the NVA regiment headquarters in the hills and mountains. We rocketed and shot artillery continually, bringing it from the mountains back to our site. Someone said that we used a million dollars worth of firepower.

The captain came up to me and advised, "Slow down the fire for a little bit; we have choppers coming in fifteen."

"Yes, sir," I replied.

"Fireball, will you give us six more rounds of VT, then hold up for a while? I appreciate all your help."

"Yes I will, Blackhawk. Good luck. I think I'll take a nap."

The choppers started coming in with M-60 machine guns roaring. They were bringing us more ammo. Chuck looks at the cargo on the chopper. "Hey, Danny, why are they bringing ammo and supplies? Aren't we getting out of here?"

"I don't know, Chuck. Something isn't right about this, is it?"

Generally, after a large battle, when a company loses a lot of men, there is a stand down. This is when a company goes to the rear or a safe hill to replenish the troops. The company will stay on the hill for a few days to rest and get re-supplied. Not this time. The Tet Offensive was stronger than ever, even though we had killed a lot of the NVA. Every company needed to be in the field.

I hear the sound of the blades of a Huey helicopter cutting through the thick, humid air — *pop, pop, pop, pop, pop, pop.* There are more choppers coming in. I think that maybe we are getting out of the field after all. No such luck. The choppers are full of soldiers. Then I thought that maybe another company had lost a lot of men as we had, and both companies would be combined as one.

Now my mind was racing. *Would we keep our same captain? Would I keep my squad? Would I even be a squad leader any longer?* I realize that I am thinking too much. This was a no-no in Vietnam. Don't let your mind wander, or you are asking for trouble. The choppers land, and I can see that the men in the choppers are new recruits, fresh from the States. "Hey, Danny, these guys won't last five minutes in this mess," says Chuck.

The medics are coming over to my squad. Some of our guys have shrapnel buried in them. Some are very fatigued. The medics are looking at Chuck. Chuck is raising heck about something. He is shaking his head. I ask, "What is going on now?" as I look at the group.

Chuck looks at me and says, "I am not going anywhere, Danny. Tell these boneheads to go back where they came from."

Both medics look at me. "Sarge, this man needs to get out of the field now. The infection has already set in. If we don't get some antibiotics in him, he will lose his feet. Look at his feet."

I looked Chuck in the eye. "Take off your other boot, Chuck."

When I saw how bad both his feet looked, I realized that the medics were right. His legs had red runners up on all sides. Chuck had that type of skin that would get infected from just scraping up against a back-up bush. This was a heavy, thick, thorny bush that would rip into your skin and hold you there. Some men called them Wait-a-Minute bushes. The only way to get loose was to back up, hence, the name. The thorns were so thick that they would stay attached to the bush. Chuck also had trouble with his feet. During the day, we would be sweating from morning to dark. At night, it would generally rain. Therefore, our feet and our bodies were wet almost all the time. Chuck's feet would get so raw that they would bleed. This would cause him great pain.

Chuck walked over to me and moved in close so no one else could hear. I could see in his eyes that he was in pain now. He had tears in his eyes. "Danny, I can't leave you guys. You need me and every man we can get."

He was right, and besides, we were closer to each other now than ever before. I looked at his other foot. I said, "Take off your other boot again," knowing, of course, that it was no better than when I looked at it a few minutes ago.

He took off his boot again. It looked as if it had been shot. The foot had a lot of dried and fresh blood. "Buddy, why don't you go on in and drag it out as long as you can? When you come back, you will be in good shape again. Don't worry about us. Just look over there."

I am trying to get chuck to take off his boots

There were thirty or so men fresh off the chopper. Chuck and I walked over to look at the new guys. I noticed that Chuck was trying not to limp. They did not look half bad for guys fresh from the States. I walked fast over to the captain, because I wanted to get the best four or five for my squad. "How many can I have, Sir?"

The captain says, "One."

"One? But I only have seven!"

"You only have *six,* because Lewis is being lifted out."

I walked back to the group of men. "How was the trip out here? Did the door gunners scare you half to death just before you landed?"

The door gunners loved to scare new recruits. Just before landing, they would open up with twin M-60 machine guns. The inside of the chopper is nothing but steel, aluminum, and metal. There is nothing to absorb the sound. I wanted to talk to the men so they would speak to me a little. I was probing, so to speak. "Yes, Sergeant, the gunners scared us."

"How was the lift?"

"Not bad, Sergeant."

Another said, "Bumpy."

"Hey, Sergeant Rodgers, we saw a lot of bodies out in the rice paddies. Are any of them ours?"

"How many did you see?" I asked.

"About three to four hundred," says one of the men.

"One hundred and twenty-six of them are our guys."

"What did you say, Sarge? How many?"

"A hundred and twenty-six. They ambushed us. It was real bad."

One of the men swallowed. "Is that very common, Sarge?"

"No, it isn't. Usually, we win every battle."

It was time now to change the subject. "OK, listen up, but don't answer yet. Who wants to be in my squad? I take no lip. I shoot people for falling asleep on guard duty. I take my turn at point. I have been in country for six months. I am no acting jack.

23

I am a real sergeant. I made rank in the 'Nam. You will do what I say, when I tell you to do it, and you will survive."

One of the men said, "Do you bring us donuts and hot chocolate too, before you tuck us in at night?"

He was a red-faced guy, about five feet-eight inches tall, and a little stocky. A lot of squad leaders would have been very upset at these comments. Everyone was laughing and looking straight at me to see what I was going to do. This remark was like something my brothers, Dwight, Duane, Denis, or Doug, would say. I was glad that my brothers were too young for this brutal war. I started laughing very hard. This was the first time in a very long time that I really laughed. All of my worries were gone for an instant.

"OK, does anyone want to be in my squad?"

Every man held up his hand. They all wanted in my squad. This surprised me somewhat after my speech. Maybe it was my laughter; I had shown the human side. I chose the donuts and hot chocolate guy. His name was Mike Rydser. He came from Minnesota, from one of those towns that starts with an *M* that no one has ever heard of. I wanted a little humor in my squad and a little spunk. This decision would later turn out to be one of the best choices I had ever made.

"Here comes another chopper," someone yells.

It looks like Top. Top is a name for Top Sergeant. He has all of the sergeant stripes. A Top has usually been in the service for a long time. We had not seen Top in four months. Top jumps off of the chopper and goes straight for the captain. They are having some sort of a conference. Chuck comes toward me. "How come you picked another red-headed guy, Danny?"

Chuck was red-headed also, but he and I were the only ones he would allow to talk about it. He hated his red hair. I laughed. "I picked him because he is pretty funny, and we need a little humor in the squad."

Chuck laughs. "You don't think I am funny anymore?"

"Yes, you will always be the number one comedian in this squad." Chuck laughed. I said, "Do you see what I mean? The new guy is already making us laugh."

Top is over, close to the wood line, speaking to seven or eight men. He is having each man hand over their wallets to him. It appears as though they are giving him the wallets with no real hesitation. "What's going on, Top?"

Top looks at me with a serious look. "We need volunteers to go out and try to find any of our guys that may be alive. Then we will police up our dead."

"You can count me in, Top."

Top extends his hand. "Give me your wallet."

"For what?" I asked.

"So I can notify the next of kin."

"What?"

Top motioned for me to follow him over to the side, away from the men. Top says, "I don't think that anyone can hear us now."

I look at Top. "What is really going on, Top?"

He looked into my eyes. He has a look of hopelessness. "You should know that no one is going to come back."

He was telling us that we were going on a suicide mission. He did not completely know what we had been going through for the past few days. In my opinion, this little task was nothing. This was a piece of cake. "Top, I am going out there with these guys. I am not giving you my wallet! We are not going to be killed. I am going to call in artillery strikes every five minutes, and they will be so close they will burn our butts! Top, you don't know what we have just been through. A few sniper rounds now ain't jack."

I liked Top a lot, but this time, he was getting on my nerves. Top would probably be mad at me for speaking to him the way I did. However, the worst he could do was court-martial me. That would at least get me to the rear, where it was safe. I thought about it a little more and realized I would never want to leave my men to fend for themselves.

I heard a voice. "Hey buddy, I am lifting off." It was Chuck. He gave me a big hug. "Don't get shot."

Then, he ran the best he could to a waiting chopper. I never was the type to show physical emotions, but Chuck would get excited and give me a hug once in awhile. "Milk it for all you can, Chuck!" I yelled.

Top returned to our group. "Are you ready to go, Sarge?"

"We are," I said.

Top was not mad at me. This made me feel better. I asked the seven men to come to me for a quick meeting. "Men, it may be dangerous in the open rice paddies. Some of you are new, so this is what you can expect. We are going to police up our soldiers' bodies only, the heck with the gooks. Look for live soldiers first. The choppers will come in fast. If they receive any fire, they will unload with both M-60s. Two of you will secure either side of the chopper when it lands, one on each side. Four of you will start loading the bodies in the choppers. I will be in the middle of the choppers to stack the bodies, and the last man there will get into the other chopper."

We head out toward the bodies. The radio goes off, "Blackhawk Three, this is Annihilator Three-Three, over."

I responded, "This is Blackhawk Three, over."

"Blackhawk Three, we have a change of plans. Come to the Charlie Papa." (Charlie Papa is code for Command Post. In 1968, the Army was using the new phonetic alphabet.)

I told my men to start stacking the bodies and that I would be right back. I arrived at the command post and looked at Annihilator Three-Three (the captain). "The change of plan is we are going to rack 'em and stack 'em until tomorrow."

This meant that we would stack the bodies and the stacks would be far enough apart so the chopper could get in between them. I told the volunteers the new plan. Seven men and I started toward the rice paddies. The rice paddies were approximately one mile or more across and many miles long. The smell of the rice paddies, with hot water in them, was like dead, week-old, rotted fish. The sun would heat up the water in the paddies. Sometimes the water was too hot for us to walk through. The smell today was heightened because of the dead bodies and, of course, the crap. Almost every person that I have seen dead in the 'Nam craps his pants just before dying. Today's smell was like walking through a cesspool. It did not take long to see what we were looking for. What a sight. The bodies were so intermingled in some areas that it was hard to tell a gook from an American. I looked up and saw the new guy, Mike Rydser. "Rydser, why did you volunteer for this?"

He said, "Sergeant Rock, I feel safer with you here than back there."

He pointed with his thumb over his shoulder toward where the choppers were landing and taking off. Another chopper takes off. Chuck is on the skid of the doorless chopper, waving at me. I had a tear in my eye as I watched his chopper fly out of sight. I briefly started thinking back to when Chuck and I first met in basic training. We always thought that the same things were funny. We hated the same things. We liked the same things. We always seemed to get into the same trouble together. Now, I really felt lonely.

Then I looked down at the bodies and thought, *How lonely will the parents of these soldiers be?* I felt like a selfish fool. Then I thought, *Was this another time when I had to kill many to save a few? Did the artillery I called in last night kill a lot of these men? Or were they already dead?*

I told my guys to stack the gooks and lay out our guys side by side. This was not exactly what the captain told me to do, but out of respect, I decided not to stack up the bodies of our soldiers. That would have reminded me of the Holocaust.

"Do you want me to take the tags off, Sergeant Rock?"

"No!" I said.

We were taught in basic training and advanced infantry training to remove the dog tags from the necks and shove them between the two front teeth, if there were any teeth left. This

27

seemed to me to be undignified, for I had grown to really like most of these guys. I thought I saw something move. "There is something moving over there. Be careful!"

I looked a little farther and thought I saw a body move. We ran over to the body. It was one of ours. He was lying on his back, just barely breathing. He had leeches stuck to his face. There were two leeches that were eight to nine inches long, and about three-quarters to one inch in diameter. The soldier opened his eyes and looked straight at me and smiled. I nodded my head back at him. "We are here now, so don't worry."

"Is that what leeches look like, Sergeant Rock?" Rydser asked.

Someone said, "Yep."

We took our insect repellent from the bands on our helmets. We started squirting the leeches' heads, being careful not to get any in the eyes of the soldier. The last thing we wanted to do was cause this guy any more pain. The bloody leeches finally released. It was time for more artillery, but this man needed medical attention right now. "Check under his shirt for leeches," I told Rydser.

Rydser opened the soldier's shirt and found another five leeches. We went through the procedure to release the foul, nasty leeches from the soldier's body. We started to clean up the blood on the soldier very carefully. What we found next defies any logic. We could not believe it. This man had been shot *seventeen* times. He was very pale and more dead than alive, but still had enough energy to smile every once in awhile. I found out later that he lived and was sent home.

A blast sounds, a bullet whizzes past, and mortars are what we hear next. "Incoming!" someone yells.

The ground explodes again. I need to call for more artillery, but we have to wait until the choppers get out of range. The choppers are now at a safe distance. I can now call Fireball Five-Niner for support. Our support rounds start coming in again. What a feeling; we are in control again. The radio sounds off, "Blackhawk Three, cut your fire back for a few, over."

I know that choppers are coming in again. "Roger, out," I reply.

Then I again call Fireball to stop the firepower for a while. We continue to look for more American bodies. We find 120, but no more live soldiers. We keep with the every-five-minute artillery plan for another hour. We are exhausted when we return to the perimeter. The injured soldier that we have been carrying is somehow still alive. I walk over to him, grab his hand, and say, "We are all very proud of you. I know that you will make it. If I see you again, I hope it is in the States."

I head back over to the command post. Top is awaiting us with a big smile. He is a Mexican man, five feet and ten inches tall, and weighs about 190 pounds. Top ran everything in the rear. He kept us supplied with ammunition, guns, food, and clothes. He would now have to furnish us with lots of body bags.

Top asks, "Is Lewis dead?"

Chuck and Top had always gotten along well. I told both of them that the reason they liked each other so much was because Chuck came from Tulare, California. There are a lot of Mexicans in Tulare because it is mainly farming. Top would say, "If it weren't for us Mexicans, you gringos would starve to death." We would all have a good time when Top teased Gringo Chuck, lots of laughing. We were not laughing now. We decided that the best way to pick up the bodies in this hot LZ (Landing Zone) would be to land the chopper between the bodies and load the bodies from both sides of every chopper.

Top asks, "What do you think about bagging the bodies first?"

I thought for a minute. This would be more dignified, but it would take us longer. "No, we cannot afford to lose another man from sniper fire, so we better do this as quickly as we can. We can bag them at the base camp."

This was a base camp that we had not seen for six or seven months.

"You got plenty of smoke?" Top asks. (Smoke, or smoke grenade, is just like it sounds. We would throw this smoke out so the aircraft could see where to land.)

"Yes I do, Top."

My squad and I went back out to the rice paddies where the bodies were laid out. I set up my guys on both sides of where the choppers will land. I keep the RTO with me. The radio blasts, "Blackhawk Three, this is Boomerang One-Seven, over."

This was the call sign of a chopper pilot. "This is Blackhawk Three, verify smoke, go."

I threw a blue smoke grenade into the rice paddy. We could not see the choppers yet, but we could hear them. "Blackhawk Three, I see yellow smoke, is that you?" the pilot asked.

"No, no, no!" I replied.

"Blackhawk Three, it is probably gooks with the yellow smoke. We are going to light them up."

We listened. The choppers started firing full force with all machine guns on every chopper. "I guess that will teach them. Throw another smoke, Blackhawk."

I throw green smoke this time, and Boomerang One-Seven acknowledges it. The aircrafts come in a-blazing, both door gunners with their M-60 machine guns firing. I have always thought that this was a pretty sight. Every fifth round was a tracer round. When the choppers land, I run to one and jump inside. My men throw the American soldiers in as fast as they can. We had to stack them now because they had to be placed on the floor. The bodies were water-logged and very cold and heavy. As the bodies would start stacking up on top of each other, I would have to push down on the bodies, trying to free my legs and feet. On several occasions, other men would have to come in and help to free me. When I looked down at my legs, they would be covered with blood. The stink was terrible. The combination of smells — blood, mud from the rice paddies, and the pee and crap — was unbearable. I wore a kerchief over my nose and tied it behind my head. I would have to take a break every ten minutes to throw up, not because I was sick at what I was seeing, but because of the heavy smell locked in my chest cavity. We stacked the bodies six to eight high, and I jumped out and signaled to the pilot and off they would go. At least this was the plan.

The first chopper started to take off, but something was wrong. It would go forward for ten feet or so, at an elevation of one to two feet, then land again. Rydser runs over to me. "What's wrong?" he asks.

I tell him that the chopper is too heavy. I now realize what we had done. The air was so hot here in Vietnam that the choppers could only carry six to seven men at a time. We had loaded eight wet bodies on a six-man chopper. Boomerang One-Seven did not have to call us. He saw that we were running to the choppers. We pulled two men off. The pilot and door gunners gave us thumbs up. I did the same, and off they went, guns roaring. Now we knew that six bodies were plenty.

We continued to load bodies for the next two days. We could have completed this terrible task in one day, but the mortaring and sniping kept us pinned down a lot of the time. We would slow the choppers for landing every so often so that we could call in artillery. We finally made some headway and got all of our American bodies loaded. On the third evening, we returned to the perimeter and called in artillery.

We called in lots of firepower during the night. The foxholes still had four inches of mud and water in them. We were not going to sleep again tonight, but that did not matter, because we were going to go to the rear tomorrow. I leaned back against the foxhole side and thought of the warm shower I would take. I thought about the food, and the sleep, and the clean clothes. Rydser asks, "How long will we be in the rear?"

I shook my head up and down. "I hope for two weeks."

He had a puzzled look on his face. "When was the last time you guys got to go to the rear?"

I said, "Never."

His eyes got larger. "Do you mean that you have been here seven months and have never had a stand down?"

"Yep," I said.

Then I asked him about his life in the States. He told me about his fine mother and father, who were very proud of him. The whole town knew that he was going to Vietnam. Rydser seemed to love his family and his small town deeply. We talked a lot about family. I had always believed in getting close to my family, and I expressed that to him. I had also believed in getting close to my men, because here in Vietnam it was a squad leaders' war, not a company or battalion war. If you really know your men, you will know what to expect from them during battle.

Morning was finally here and not a minute too soon, for I was getting really sleepy. Now, all we had to do was wait on the transportation and fly for about an hour to a base camp somewhere.

Rydser asks, "What are you going to do first, Sergeant Rock?"

I look at him and ask, "Why do you call me Sergeant Rock?"

He says, "Because you are hardcore, as hard as a rock, and you are dependable."

Somehow this statement, coming from the donut and hot chocolate guy, did not seem genuine. I think that he was really referencing the comic strip cartoon, with me as the main character. The name caught on fast. The name Sergeant Rock stuck. I was now Sergeant Rock.

"Well, back to your question. The first thing I was going to do was get a cold Coke, eat some real food, take a shower, and sleep for three days with no guard duty, no shots, no snipers, no leeches, no rice paddies, and no gooks."

I looked at the command post (CP) and saw Top and the captain speaking. *What were they talking about now?* They were in a huddle over the RTO. Top walked over toward me. Something was wrong; I could see it in his dark face. "What the heck is the matter now, Top?"

He says, "We are not going in for a stand down."

"What?" I shout.

He goes on to say, "Another company is already there."

Top told me what company it was, but I was so angry I could not remember the name. I said, "Do you mean to tell me that there is another company blown to bits worse than we are?"

He says, "No, it is just Delta Three's turn."

Delta Three was a good outfit, but they did not deserve a stand down as much as we did. Rydser asks, "What does that mean now, Sergeant Rock?"

"That means we have to be out here while Delta Three is eating our food and sleeping in our beds."

My radio goes off. "Blackhawk Three, this is Annihilator Three-Three, over."

"This is Blackhawk Three, go."

"Get ready to move 'em out, go."

I respond, "Roger, out."

"Annihilator Three-Three, out."

"OK, men, we're moving."

They looked like beaten dogs. Their eyes told the story of no hope and complete discouragement. *How can we go on?* Their clothes were ripped and torn. We did not look like soldiers. We loaded our sacks with C-rations. We placed bandoliers filled with ammunition over our heads and on our shoulders. We filled our canteens with water. I walked over to where the captain was standing, unfolding my map as I walked. "Where are we going, sir?" He pointed to a spot on my map. "There, over the mountain to find caches."

The captain finished loading his sack with C-rations while we talked. "What did your men say about not getting a stand down, Sergeant Rock?"

That was the first time he had called me anything but Sergeant Rodgers. He says, "I think Sergeant Rock is a good name for you. I should be called Captain Rock. You and I have been through a lot together, haven't we?"

"Yes, sir, you could be Big Rock and I could be Little Rock." He laughed. "My men were not happy about no stand down," I added.

"We will get in before too much longer. Let's go. Your squad has point," he said.

"OK, sir, I'll move 'em out."

Both the captain and I knew that we were taking a big chance now. Everything was going against us. The company morale was lower than ever. *We called ourselves a company? We did not even have enough men for a platoon. If we get hit now, what would happen? Could we fight another NVA company and win? Could we fight another NVA platoon? Could we even fight and win against another squad with our low morale?* Maybe we would get lucky and a VC would just shoot at us. Most VC are poor shots. That would be alright.

"Rydser, you are point. Let's get it."

CHAPTER 3

Mike Rydser (Killer)

We didn't find but a few caches. We'd heard of large underground rooms and tunnels, but not this time. We only found a few rifles that had belonged to the American soldiers — an M-16, an M-60 (commonly known as the Pig), and a few grenade launchers. We received the usual sniper round once or twice a day.

According to my map, we were heading to a hill called Baldy. We arrived at about 6 a.m. We could smell the aroma of bacon in the air. The smell was great. It reminded me of my mother's fine cooking. My squad and I headed for the center of the hill. There, we saw bunkers. Not just bunkers, but multi-room bunkers. These guys on Baldy had it made. This was a mortar platoon that I would love to be a member of. We divided our men up around the hill's perimeter, not really pulling guard like we usually were accustomed to doing. We were just sort of laying back and watching. I grabbed Rydser and we walked over to a bunker next to an 81 mm mortar. "Let's see the Holiday Inn," I said to a sergeant, the same rank as myself.

He knew that we were impressed with his bunker, so he invited us in. I could see in his face and big smile that he was happy to show us what they had made inside. Rydser and I walked through the entryway down two feet. What we saw next would amaze a Sea-Bee. First, we looked at one wall and saw bunk beds with clean sheets. "Clean sheets! You've got to be kidding me!"

The sarge laughed and said, "Look at this."

It was a poker table in the center of the room, complete with poker chips and cards. The chips were laid out for six players. Above the table was a hanging light, a real electric light, not a battery pack.

In the corner was a small refrigerator. The sarge opened the door and pulled out a couple of beers and threw them to us. I politely asked him if I could have a root beer in lieu of the ice cold Coors. "Sure enough," he said, and he threw me an ice-cold drink.

On the other wall, there were some Playboy Bunny posters. Rydser says, "How did they get a copy of my girlfriend?"

We all laughed. Below the beautiful women, there were chests of drawers. One per each man, I figured. The sarge says, "Hey Sarge, look in here."

He showed us another room complete with a bed, electric lights, plenty of girl posters, another refrigerator, cabinets, and a place for maps. He said, "This is my room until I DEROS (Date of Expected Return from Over Seas) in a couple."

All I could say was, "Whoa!"

I had a chance, once, to go into a mortar platoon, but I wanted to move around the country, so I refused the offer. What an idiot I was. I wished, now, that I could get a taste of this good life, even if it would be for a short period of time. But I knew that it was never to be.

"How long will you be here?" the sarge asked.

"For two days, I think."

Then he asked, "Do you want to stay here in the Holiday Inn with us tonight? We will take your money at poker." Before I could answer he said, "Wait a minute!" He went to the entrance and yelled, "Do you guys care if the grunt sergeant stays with us tonight?"

The reply came, "Yeah! How much money can he afford to lose?"

I said, "Thanks. This is going to be a good night. I love poker."

Rydser and I strolled out of the bunker toward the perimeter. "Can you believe that these guys get to take a shower every single night?" I said to Rydser.

Rydser replied, "They probably think that we stink. Do you think I can play poker with you guys tonight?"

"I don't see why not. This is going to be fun."

We coasted the rest of the day until about four in the afternoon. The captain sent for me. I said to the guys, "Maybe we are going to stay here a few more days."

Their eyes lit up with excitement. I hurried to the center of the hill toward the CP, anticipating how much I was going to thank the captain for getting us this R&R (rest and relaxation). The captain was there along with the mortar platoon captain and a couple of lieus (lieutenants). The captain shook my hand. "How you doing, Rock? I heard about your new name. Did the chocolate chip kid give it to you?"

I laughed. I knew that he meant Mike Rydser. "Yes, sir. What's up?"

"We need you to take your squad on an LP (listening post). Do not engage the enemy, and keep quiet. There has been a lot of VC activity, and we need to find out how much. I want you and your squad to leave at dark thirty tonight."

If the captain could have read my mind at this time, he would have court-martialed me. I said, "OK, see you in the morning."

"No you won't," he replied. "I want you to go to Village Hill tomorrow before daybreak and set up a daytime LP."

I put my head down and said, "See you when we get back."

Then the captain said, "Sergeant Rock, I know what you are thinking, but you are the only guy left that I can trust. I'll make it up to you."

"No, sir. You don't know what I am thinking, or you would court-martial me!"

"It isn't me; it is this crazy war. I thought that we could all rest for a day or so."

I shook my head to acknowledge his comments. "Yes, sir."

I walked toward my squad. I was thinking all the time I walked. I had made up my mind what we were going to do before I got to my guys. It was not quite what the captain expected us to do. I saw the men. "OK, everyone, listen up! We are not staying."

Needless to say, they were very angry. "What the? What do they want us to do now?"

"Is the whole company going? Or is this just another detail the captain is sending us on?"

I felt the same way. We had been through the toughest days a company could take. I listened to a few more complaints, and then I said, "Now listen up! I feel exactly the same as you guys, but listen to me. We are not going to do precisely what the captain wants us to do. You guys remember the little hooch at the bottom of the mountain?"

"Yes."

"Well, we are going to go to the bottom of the mountain, and we are going in that little hooch with the Mamasan and the kid, and we are going to spend the night there, out of the rain."

Someone said, "Sounds like a plan to me."

I said, "Well, we still have to take care of business. I will have one guy pulling guard, and we will trade off. We won't get wet, and if we are lucky, we will find a bed."

"When are we leaving?"

"Just before dark."

Then I gave them the bad news. "Oh, yeah, and the next morning, we are going on another LP to Village Hill."

The squad started up again, "Will it ever stop?"

Rydser says, "If it weren't for you, Sarge, we would refuse to go. What could they do to us? A court-martial?"

Eckert says, "In prison, we would at least sleep in comfort, no rain, and eat good. Oh, yeah, and get to take a shower once in awhile."

We started packing. We loaded our rucksacks with C-rations, filled our canteens, and grabbed plenty of ammo. I walked over to the Holiday Inn bunker. "Are you ready to lose your money?" the sarge said.

"Well, I have some good news and some bad news. The bad news is my squad has to go on an LP. The good news is you guys will get to keep your money."

Then the sarge pulled me close to him and whispered to me, "Why don't you guys just stay right here with us in the bunker? Pretend that you are leaving at dark, then come back in the perimeter and sleep all night in the bunker out of the rain."

"Man! What a great idea!" I said.

Then I remembered that we had to go to Village Hill the next morning. There was no way that we could get from here to there in time. The captain would be calling, wanting to get a sit-rep (situation report) early the next morning. I explained the problem to the sarge. He says, "Good luck, and remember, you guys are welcome here anytime. Don't get shot!"

We hung around shooting the bull until it was near dark. We moved out. We stopped to tell the Holiday Inn sergeant where we would actually be during the night. I told him just in case of a big firefight. I did not want the mortar platoon dropping 81s on us. Two and a half hours later, we made it to the hooch.

We approached the straw hut with great vigilance and caution, not knowing for sure what we would find. *Would we find the hooch full of VC? Maybe NVA! Maybe we would find just a lady and a couple of kids.* That is what I wanted to find. I motioned and pointed for one of my men to go to the right. I whispered to Eckert, "You go left."

The darkness made it hard for the men to see my commands. The men had been with me during many firefights and lots of scary times like this. They generally knew what I wanted and acted accordingly.

I whispered to two other men, "You guys go to the back of the hooch."

Once the men were in place, I said, "Go, go, go!"

We moved in quickly. We heard a terrifying yell and a scream. The scream came from the younger woman, about twenty-five-years-old. The yell appeared to have come from the old Mamasan. There was a boy, about nine-years-old. They were very scared. *Could there be a VC hiding in a dim lit corner?*

We looked all around the hooch for VC and for weapons. They had two dim lanterns. We grabbed both lanterns and looked closer in every corner and crevice. They also had two makeshift beds made from bamboo. At least we would not have to sleep on the ground tonight. I could speak a little Vietnamese, enough to explain to the Mamasan that we were not there to hurt them. We only wanted to spend the night. She agreed, but what else could she do? Rydser looked at the twenty-five-year-old girl. "Can she keep me company?"

"Of course, if you want a VC bullet," I replied.

"What do you mean?"

"A young girl like that probably has a VC husband, so keep your eyes open. Besides, she may be young, but she is too old for you."

We laughed. I gave the men guard duty assignments and, as usual, I pulled as much guard as my men. We figured out how many hours there would be until just before daylight the next day. Then I would divide the number of men into the total hours. We would come up with a figure such as one hour or one hour and fifteen minutes. Sometimes we would only pull a guard duty time of forty-five minutes. When the period of time was less than an hour, I would have every man pull guard twice. I had found that pulling more than one hour guard at one time was very hard for many of the men. Since we'd had an easy day at Hill Baldy, I decided to let each man pull seventy minutes each. Most men wanted the first guard because they knew it would take them a little to unwind and get to sleep.

"OK, whose turn is it to go first?"

Eckert says, "It's your turn, Sarge."

That was good, because I knew that after my single guard duty, I could sleep on a bamboo bed. "Hand me your M-79 (grenade launcher), Eckert."

Eckert handed me his 79, and I loaded it with a canister round. "All of you guys use the 79; it has a canister round in it."

A canister round is like four 12-gauge shotgun shells going off at the same time. Everyone acknowledged me. I looked at the Vietnamese people in the hooch. They seemed to be very nervous. They were lying on a blanket toward the back of the hooch. We had spent several nights close to Vietnamese people before and had no problems. "You guys keep an eye on the girl and the kid. Don't let even one of them leave this hooch. Do what you have to do. Don't let them out."

I knew that if they were VC-related, they might try to run and convey our position. We did not want any trouble. We just wanted a good night's sleep. I started pulling my shift. My hour and ten minutes were up. My guard was uneventful. I heard next to nothing. I had beaten the system. We were supposed to be miles away from here. We were supposed to be sitting on the ground in the mud, in the water, and in the rain with leeches crawling all over us. We were supposed to see the enemy walk past us and not do a thing. Yes, indeed, this was much better. I woke up Emery for the next shift. Emery says, "This is cool. The roof doesn't leak, and I slept great."

I told him to wake up Eckert next when his time was up. He knew this, of course, but it never hurt for me to be sure things were going to go per plan. I fell asleep fast, but I always woke up at every little noise. I woke up at every guard change. I woke up again to hear Rydser moving to the front of the hooch for his easy hour or so of guard duty. I fell back to sleep and started dreaming of my home.

I was dreaming of playing baseball with my four brothers, my mom and dad, and my beautiful wife who I had married just eight months earlier. I had a great life back in the States, with a good, close-knit family, two contracts — or rather letters of intent to sign a contract — to play professional baseball, a new car, and a devoted wife. I was startled by the sound of Rydser. "What the heck? A gook! A gook!" he yelled.

Something or someone hit my side and almost knocked me out of the bamboo bed. I grabbed my rifle, adjacent to me in the bed, cleared my head, and stood up. I saw a stranger in the hooch. He was disoriented, fumbling over the bed, and stumbling over our rucksacks that were on the floor. We had moved the beds around prior to going to sleep. The gook ran into me and made me trip. I fell almost to the ground, catching my balance by placing my hand on the bed. He ran toward the front of the hooch and outside, passing Rydser again, but this time, he was trying to get away.

I jumped back to my feet, upright again. Before I could recover my balance completely, I heard a loud blast. It was a sound that I had heard hundreds of times. It was the sound of an M-79 grenade launcher firing a canister round. I ran to the blast area. Rydser was leaning over the almost dead VC. "What happened?" I asked.

Rydser replied, "He came running up the path so fast, I did not have time to shoot. He ran straight in the hooch. He ran right by me. He didn't even know that I was here. I could not shoot into the hooch to get him because of you guys. Then he came running out again. Again, he didn't see me. He tripped over me, fell on the ground, got back up, and started to run. His foot was caught in the strap of the grenade launcher. Every time he would try to run, the weapon would trip him. He finally got loose. I shot him in the back while I was still on my knees."

"Man, Rydser, this is going to be a great story."

"Sarge, all of this only took about one minute, but it seemed like an hour. I was almost scared to death, frightened, afraid, and terrified. Did I say petrified?"

"He scared me too," I said. "By the way, thanks for not shooting into the hooch. That was a good idea."

Rydser knew that I was being facetious. Then we heard a loud moan coming from the VC gook. The moans became groans and got louder. We had to shut him up quickly. There may be more VC in the area, and this guy was giving away our position. If he kept making noise, the other VC could zero in on us. By this time, all my squad was on their feet. I looked at them. "Everyone stay alert. We don't know how many more are out there."

My men started watching, very intent on the surroundings. The VC was in agony. I felt sorry for this VC. He was hurting physically. I was hurting for him mentally and physically. My stomach was aching with great pain, but it was nothing compared to pain that this enemy lying on the ground was feeling. I walked cautiously next to the VC. I had to protect my men from other Charlies. This VC must be quiet. "Stand back, Rydser."

I took my M-16 rifle and smashed his face with the butt of it. I heard the face bones cracking. I not only wanted to knock him out, I needed to knock him out. I wanted to knock him out with one blow, but like so many other things in Vietnam, this was not going to be easy. The Victor Charlie was getting louder. His pain must be terrible now. I cannot worry about his pain; I have to protect the men. I strike him again with the butt of the rifle as hard as I can. This stroke was so forceful that it made the bolt of my rifle jump open and close. We hear more bones break and see more bleeding, but he is still moaning. I get tears in my eyes. I don't want to do this, but my men are more important to me than this VC. I have to vilify this enemy for me to have the mental strength to carry on.

I needed an M-14 rifle instead of my M-16. The M-14 was much heavier. I could have knocked him out with one blow with the M-14, but we didn't have one. Rydser says, "We have got to gag him."

I grabbed a dirty towel and Rydser tried to stick it in the VC's mouth. Just as Rydser got a portion of the towel between the VC's teeth, the VC grabbed Rydser's wrist. This scared Rydser and me very much. We had thought that the VC was too weak for resistance, but we were wrong. The VC's hand finally released Rydser's wrist, but he was still moaning. At least it was now being muffled. My heart reached out for this guy. *Why wouldn't he be knocked out? Why wouldn't he just die? What were the VC's wife and child thinking about us brutalizing their husband and dad?* Sometimes I hated myself for the man I was starting to become.

"Why won't this guy shut up, Rydser?"

Rydser says, "I'll take care of him. Give me a machete and I'll cut his head off."

"We don't have one," I said.

We did not have a machete because we are not humping in the jungle. Rydser says, "I'll use my bayonet."

"What?"

"I'll cut off his head, and keep him from yelling, with my bayonet."

"Killer, there is no need for that. He will bleed out soon and die."

"But, Sarge, listen. He is still making too much noise. Even with his mouth muffled, he is giving away our position."

Killer was correct; the gook was still making too much noise. But the sounds of our voices were also going to give away our position. "OK, Killer, but do it fast."

Rydser started cutting, but he soon found out that the bayonet was not sharp. As a matter of fact, all of our bayonets were really dull. We used our bayonets for opening C-rations, cans, bottle caps and much more. We would even use the bayonets for tent pegs. The gook was still groaning. We needed light so we could see what we were doing.

Rydser says, "Sergeant Rock, I cannot perform surgery without any light."

"I'll get a poncho," I said.

I located a poncho and got a flashlight from Eckert. Eckert says, "What's happening, Sarge?"

"Rydser is cutting off the VC's head."

"What?"

"Yes, he is cutting now. He needs more light for surgery."

We set up the poncho over Rydser and me. We also covered the VC's head with the poncho. We turned on the flashlight. Now, I could see the awful mess Rydser was making. I could see where to hold the body so the surgeon could work and not be disturbed by the VC. Rydser was doing it wrong. He was starting from the side of the neck where the muscles are located.

"Rydser, start in the middle and cut the vocal cords first."

I wanted him to do it this way for two reasons. The first reason was so the gook would stop making noise. A person cannot speak without vocal cords. The second reason was that I thought that once Rydser saw all of the front part of the neck separated, he would be satisfied.

Rydser drove the knife hard through the neck and behind the vocal cords. The bayonet was so dull that instead of cutting the vocal cords, he had to pull them. Rydser was trying hard to take the life away from this defiant VC. This was not like you see in the movies where a person dies from a single wound or shot. Rydser did not know this, but I did. I had seen NVA and the VC get shot three times before falling down. I had seen them get shot four times, get back up, and keep firing at us.

Finally, the pointed end of the bayonet penetrated the throat near the vocal cords. Rydser gave another heavy pull and then a jerk. Rydser pulled and tugged some more until the blood started gushing. A couple more gurgles, then silence. During all of this final commotion, I had not noticed that the VC's hands had latched on to my wrists. The gook had the death grip on my wrists, and it was cutting off the blood supply to my arms. Rydser had to break three fingers from both hands to free me. I had never been through anything like this in my life. I was supposed to be tough, but this was making me sick.

"Well, you did it," I said to Rydser.

"What do you mean? I am not finished! I am going to put the head over there." He pointed to the right. "And I am going to put the body over there." He pointed to the left.

"Rydser, are you crazy?" He laughed. I said quickly, "No, I just want you to clean up your mess! I am going back to the hooch."

"OK, but it will take a long time."

"Rydser, you are something else."

Again, he laughs. Rydser had only been in country for a short while. I was in country for two or three weeks before I shot my first VC. It was a simple uneventful kill. The higher ups wanted body counts. Every day, we would hear on the radio, "What's your body count? How many do you have now? How many did you get last night? Dig up the graves. Find out how the VC or the NVA died." Although I would hear this day after day, I did not like the killing. I would kill at the drop of a hat, but I generally felt bad about it. I wondered if I would eventually get so that I wouldn't care. Now, a rookie grunt was taking the head from another human being. *Was he doing it to impress me? Or was he doing it because he liked it?* Maybe he was doing it to show everyone he was hardcore. Time will tell me the answer.

Forty-five minutes later, the head was removed. I wished that I could say it was surgically removed, but it was not. I had seen lots of soldiers with their legs and arms blown off. This head separation was as bad as the legs and arms that I had been accustomed to seeing. Rydser brought the head right up to the hooch. He had blood on him from head to toe. Everyone looked at it, except the Vietnamese family. By this time, they had gone into the underground shelter. The shelter was just a hole in the ground, big enough for three people. The shelters were generally toward the back center of the hooch.

I looked at the head and said, "Get it out of here, you idiot! Go put it back!"

Rydser stands there with the head in his hand, holding it by the hair, and says, "I am going to take it with me. I am going to put it in my rucksack."

"No you are not! I'll kick your butt from here to eternity. Go put it over there!"

I pointed toward the body. Rydser started walking away, then turned toward me and said, "Come on, Sarge."

I think he's joking. Then, he placed the head three feet away from the body. I was so happy that the Mamasan, the young girl, and the little boy were not here to see all of this mess. I said a short prayer, asking God to forgive Killer for what he had done. I also was very remorseful for the family that would see what we had done in the daylight hours. I was realizing that the circumstances of war are never the same. My view of this particular killing was necessary, *but had I allowed one of my men to go overboard?* God will judge me for what I have done.

"Rydser, why did you do all of that?"

He said, "Because it was there."

He then gave the big Mike Rydser laugh. No matter what the true reason was, Mike Rydser would soon show the whole company what a brave man he was in the coming days. The next morning, my squad was to be on an all-day LP. Our objective was to listen and not engage in combat.

CHAPTER 4

LRRP

"We are going to be heading out at zero three-thirty to our LP. I don't want to be anywhere near here when the VC's friends see their buddy like this," I said to my squad.

"Yeah, let's leave right now," Emery said.

"No! We'll wait a little while longer. We want to reach the new LP just before daylight."

Emery was looking scared. "Do you need to throw up?" I asked.

He nodded his head up and down and moved to the outside corner of the hooch. He started vomiting, heaving over and over. This was old hat to us. No one paid attention anymore when Emery started getting sick. Emery returned and said, "My turn for guard duty."

"Yep, your turn, and try not to wake us up, huh?"

I knew that not a single person would sleep. We were all on edge and at arms. We were waiting for the unexpected. Rydser says, "Emery, if you see another gook, blow his head clean off. I am tired."

Rydser laughed. He made us all laugh. Sometimes in the worst of times, Rydser could come up with an adage, a proverb, or just a saying that he had made up. The rest of the night was really dark and quiet.

At zero three-thirty, we headed out. No one could resist one last look at the gook. A head without a body and a body without a head is really something unusual to see. Rydser had something else in mind. He placed his feet against the side of the body. He then took a few sidesteps as if to measure a distance. Then he kicked the head a few more feet away from the body. I just shook my head in distaste.

"Let's go. Keep it quiet."

We started moving very quietly through the jungle, finding a good path to our LP destination. We located the place called Village Hill. We called it VC Village because it was a gathering place for the enemy. The next part of this journey was very intense. We could see the village just a short distance away. We had to climb a small hill without being seen or heard. Our location was perfect for an LP. The small hill was covered with triple canopy jungle. We scratched and smashed our way through the thick brush until we found a large opening where we all would fit. We were at the top of a little rise. We could see the little village through the trees. We were less than fifty meters away. We could also see the next mountain and the hooch where we had been the night before.

We observed by looking through the night vision starlight scope until daylight. The day was bright enough now where we could look through the binos. Not much was happening except for a few VC carrying their rifles and speaking to their families. We did not understand a whole lot of Vietnamese, but from the sound of their voices, there was no reason for us to be alarmed. We could hear a couple of kids playing in the distance. The radio went off at a low volume.

"Blackhawk Three, this is Annihilator Three-Three, over."

I replied, "This is Blackhawk Three, go."

"Blackhawk Three, are you in position, over?"

"Affirmative, over."

"We have a lurp (LRRP) patrol in your area, so be aware. Don't shoot them!"

"Are they on our frequency?"

"Affirmative."

Rydser, now known as Killer, asked, "What the hell is a lurp?"

"LRRP stands for Long Range Reconnaissance Patrol. They are an elite group of Army guys. They scout, inspect, and explore the enemy."

Killer says, "Like we do?"

"Not quite. They run around with soft hats on instead of these helmets. They carry a single bandolier of ammo, a rifle or pistol, and they are usually in small groups. They go out at night or during the day for a few hours, then go back to camp and go to sleep. They think that they are bad butts, if you know what I mean."

Killer says, "Sounds like a good gig to me."

"Yeah, I know it. I am just jealous. They actually do a great job, but they still think that they are better than us grunts."

The main reason that I was so jealous was because we had to pack and carry so much weight on our backs. We carried twenty-eight pounds of C-rations. They carried dried lightweight LRRP rations. We carried multiple pouches of ammo and several bandoliers. They carried bandoliers of ammo and usually only one. We had to help our machine gun guy carry his ammo. The lurps did not take an M-60 with them most of the time. The lurp guys thought that they were bad to the bone. We acted like we hated them, when in reality we were just envious. We would love to hump through the jungle when we felt like it. We would love to wear lightweight gear, kill a few gooks, and run back to a base camp. We had no base camp. They had it made.

"Sergeant Rock! Look, look, look at the bad boys!" Killer said.

He was looking through the binos at the hooch where the dead VC was decapitated. "What are you looking at?"

"Take a look for yourself, Sarge."

The lurp guys were looking at the dead VC. They could not believe their eyes. By this time, the body was starting to swell. It would really be a mess by now. The lurps were walking in circles, staring in amazement. They could not believe what they were seeing. We let them look for about six or seven minutes longer, and then I got on the horn (the radio). "What's wrong? Haven't you guys ever seen a dead body before?"

They did not know that we could see every move they were making. Their leader got on the horn and said, "Who are you?"

"I am Blackhawk Three," I said in a commanding, superior voice.

"Do you know what we found?"

"Yes, we know!"

"Do you think this happened by shrapnel?"

"Nope."

"Was this your ambush spot last night?"

"Affirmative."

"Oh, man! You guys are bad; maybe we will meet up with you sometime."

"I hope so. You guys better get out of there, because there are going to be a bunch of mad gooks coming after you!"

"Why us?"

"Do you think that you guys can explain to a lot of mad Victor Charlies that you found the body like that?"

"We are out of here. See ya."

"Good luck, lurps."

I knew that the captain would be calling soon. He would be asking, "What is going on? How come you and lurp are not using proper call signs?" We sat at our LP just watching and listening for thirty minutes longer, and then we heard from the captain. "Blackhawk Three, this is Annihilator Three-Three, over."

"This is Blackhawk Three, go."

"What is going on, Blackhawk Three? I have been on the horn for half an hour. The other companies are calling and asking if my men not only kill VC and NVA, do they also cut their heads off?"

"Annihilator Three-Three, can we talk about this in person? Over."

"Yes, see me ASAP, out."

Was the word spreading due to Rydser, now known as Killer?
Does Blackhawk Three have the meanest and toughest squad in
Vietnam? If this were so, Killer would eat it up. Killer was very
happy that he had made his mark in Vietnam.

Another hour, and we could head back to Hill Baldy. We
loaded up our gear and headed back toward Baldy. "Hey men,
move as quietly as you can. I heard a dog barking in the distance
a while ago, so move quietly."

We made our way out of the bush and started back down
from the LP. The small dog had found us and started barking.
Killer was not completely finished with his breakfast, so he gave
a small portion of his canned turkey loaf and canned bread to the
dog. The dog stopped barking. "Killer, you have made a friend
for life," Eckert said.

We had a light hump through the jungle, through the valley,
and near the hooch where Killer had cut off the head. Killer says,
"Let's go by and take another look."

I don't know if he was really serious, but I said, "Are you
crazy or are you just an idiot? We are never, ever going to go by
that hooch again! We won't go within a thousand meters of that
place!"

Then I went on to say to all the squad, "Can you guys just
imagine how the wife and son feel about their husband and dad?
What about the Mamasan? If the VC was her son, she will be
extremely vengeful. I can guarantee you that if the VC capture
any of us, they will stand us in front of that hooch, and it will be
the most painful death you could possibly imagine!"

Emery's eyes were as big as saucers. He says, "Let's get out
of here, Sarge!"

He looked so panicky that it made us laugh. We could see the
hooch in the distance. "Pass the word to Eckert. We are getting
too close to the hooch. Swing way right," I said.

Eckert was pulling point as we headed back to Baldy, so
to keep from yelling, I would just pass my commands to the
men in front of me. We humped for a couple more hours, and

then we saw the outskirts of Hill Baldy. I called in to let the hill guards know that we were approaching a secured perimeter. "Annihilator Three-Three, Blackhawk Three, over."

"This is Annihilator Three-Three, go."

The voice that answered back to me was the captain's RTO. "We are approaching the perimeter, over."

"Affirmative. Annihilator wants to see you ASAP, over."

"Affirmatron, out."

We moved on the hill between two guard positions. Everyone was looking at us. We heard an assortment of comments.

"Did you really do it?"

"Which one of you did it?"

"Did you guys bring the head with you?"

Killer had a smile on his face from ear to ear. His chest was upright and sticking out like a proud peacock. He had a swagger when he walked. Then I saw Chuck Lewis. My best friend was back. Chuck came running over to us and gave me a big hug. Chuck asks, "Did you really cut off a head?"

"No, he did," I said as I pointed at Killer.

"You mean the donut man?"

"Yes, he really did it. I'll tell you about it later. You will laugh. But right now, I've got to see Annihilator. I think I am in trouble."

Killer raised his eyebrows. "Do you want me to go with you, Sarge?"

"No, it is my responsibility."

I walked towards the CP. En route, a gunner asked, "Are you Blackhawk Three?"

"Yes," I said with my head moving back slightly and with a dubious look on my face.

He says, "Hang on a minute," as he places another shell in the 81 mm mortar. "When you get finished with your captain, will you stop by and tell us all about it? Nothing exciting ever happens around here."

"OK, I'll do it."

I walked farther and reached the CP. I saw the old man's RTO first, and I approached him inaudibly. I wanted to find out in advance what the company commander had on his mind. "Is he mad?" I asked.

The RTO says, "He was very mad at first. He was worried about the Geneva Convention rules of war. Then, platoon leaders and other company commanders started calling him and giving him accolades. He now acts like he is proud of your squad. Delta Company's commander called and asked me if it was really true that Annihilator Three-Three cuts off heads of complete NVA squads."

"Man, we cut off one head! Now they are saying that our company cuts every gook's head off!"

The captain came out of the CP bunker. "Sergeant Rock, do you know what the Geneva Convention rules of engagement for war are?"

"Yes, sir. Can I explain?"

"It better be good," he said. "First of all, did you guys really cut off a head?"

"Yes, sir, but please let me explain."

I went on for the next ten minutes, explaining my position in the matter. I told the commander that if we did not shut the VC up, he would have given up our position.

"Couldn't you have just knocked him out?"

"No, sir, it didn't work. My M-16 was too light. Sir, I did what I had to do."

"I guess you used a machete?"

"No, we used a bayonet."

"A bayonet? They're not even sharp!"

"That is why it took us more than an hour to cut the head off."

"Oh, man! Don't tell anyone how long it took you. Did you do the cutting?"

"Heck no! Rydser did it."

"Do you mean the new guy?"

"Yep! I mean, yes, sir!"

"Well, Sergeant Rock, our company is getting a reputation, thanks to your squad."

"Is that good or bad, sir?"

"It's good. The other companies, including the lurp guys, say that our company, Company A, is a force to be reckoned with. Delta Company thought that we cut the heads off of a whole VC squad."

"Yes, sir, I heard that as well."

"OK, Rock, that's all for now. Have you met your new platoon leader yet?"

"No, sir. What happened to Fergy?"

Fergy is what we called Lieutenant Ferguson when he was not around. Fergy was our platoon leader.

"He got a little scratch and went home."

I don't think that the captain got along with Fergy very well. "OK, sir, see ya later."

As I walked back to my squad, I started to think, *If Fergy was sent home, it must have been more than a scratch.* I saw Chuck and the squad. They were talking about Killer. Rydser, or rather Killer, as he liked to be addressed now, was eating up the attention. Killer was sitting down with his helmet in his hands. He looked like he was drawing something on the helmet. "What are you doing my man, Killer?" I asked.

"I am going to place a star on my hardhat for every gook I kill."

I simply said, "Don't get too cocky, overconfident, or smug. You have only been here a few days, and you have not seen anything yet."

I looked at Chuck and said, "What's going on, buddy?"

Chuck replied, "How mad was the old man?"

"You know something, Chuck? He was not mad at all. He said that other companies are calling him asking if we are really that bad. Pretty cool, huh?"

"You the man!" Chuck said.

"Chuck, have you heard anything about us getting a stand down?"

"No, we are heading out again. Gibbons wants to see you."

"Who in the heck is Gibbons?"

"He's our new platoon leader."

"What rank is he?"

"He is a second lieutenant."

"Oh, boy, here we go again!"

"What's wrong?" Killer asked.

"Some of the second lieus come over here to Vietnam, fresh out of OCS (Officer Candidate School), thinking that they know everything. They try to command like they would do in the States. It does not work like that over here. The new officers have to listen to the guys that have been here a while. Once they get in a few firefights and get their feet on the ground, they will be alright. Oh, well, we will see. Is he a jerk?"

Chuck replies with a smirk on his face, "Sort of."

I shake my head in disgust. "OK, great."

I walk over to the new platoon leader named Gibbons. "Sir, I am Sergeant Rodgers. What can I do for you?"

I stuck out my hand for the customary handshake. He gave no gesture in return. Under my breath I said to myself, "Yep, he is a jerk."

"So you are the famous Sergeant Rock?"

"I don't know about famous, sir."

"I am told that you can read a map better than anyone, and you can call in artillery within ten feet of our foxholes."

I said, "No one can do that and live."

"Sergeant Rock, did you cut off a VC's head?"

"No, sir, one of my men did."

"The captain likes you."

"The captain and I have been through a lot together, sir. He is OK."

"Will you teach me how to call in artillery?"

"Sure."

Maybe he was not going to be a jerk. Maybe he would listen. Was I too quick to judge? Time will tell.

"Sergeant Rock, the old man, I mean the captain, does not want to hear that you cut off a head. The rules of combat and all that stuff."

"He already knows, sir. I just left him."

"Go get something to eat, Sergeant Rock. We are moving out soon. Remember, I am depending on you to keep me alive. Glad to meet you."

"Same to you, sir."

I turned and started to walk away. We did not salute in Vietnam, because it showed the enemy who was in charge.

"Oh, yeah, Sarge, from now, go directly through me. Don't even speak to the captain unless I tell you to do so."

I gritted my teeth and nodded my head. He *was* a jerk! I returned to my men. I saw that Killer had finished placing a star on his camouflaged helmet cover. Chuck asks, "Well, what do you think about Gibbons?"

"He is a jerk! OK! Load 'em up. We are moving out!"

CHAPTER 5

Lieutenant Gibbons Busts Sergeant Rock

The company and our platoon started moving out, heading north. Our platoon seemed to be disoriented. We had no direction, such as which squad goes first, what order, who is pulling point. I knew immediately what was wrong. The new lieu had not given us any orders. I approached Lieutenant Gibbons, but before I could speak, he started talking. "What is going on, Sarge? The rest of the company is leaving us behind!"

"Sir, you have to give us instructions, information, guidelines, commands."

He replied, "I already did. I said move out."

"No, sir, you have to appoint a squad for point. You have to tell us what order. What squad follows what squad? Do you want me to do it this time, sir?"

"Yes!"

I get on the radio. "Blackhawk One, this is Blackhawk Three, over."

The reply came back, "This is Blackhawk One, go."

"Blackhawk One, I am here with Blackhawk. Your squad has point."

"Affirmatron."

"Blackhawk Two, you follow Blackhawk One. Blackhawk Four, you follow Blackhawk Two."

"Affirmatron," both squads replied.

"Blackhawk Three, this is Annihilator Three-Three, is Blackhawk's radio broken?"

There was nothing wrong with the lieutenant's radio. I looked at Gibbons, and he shrugged his shoulders as if to say, "What do we do now?" I got back on my radio and said, "Blackhawk's radio was down, but it is working now."

"Roger, hurry it up."

"Where are we going, sir?"

He shrugged his shoulders. "I don't know."

"Sir, we have to know where we are and where we are going in case we get hit, so we can call in firepower."

I pulled the lieutenant's RTO off to the side. "You have been in country long enough. Why didn't you tell Gibbons what to do?"

"I tried, Sarge, but he just will not listen. He thinks he knows everything."

I just shook my head in disgust. We started moving, trying to catch up with the rest of the company. Gibbons did not even give me a thank you for the help I had given him. Again, I thought that he was a jerk.

We humped through the jungle and the wet rice paddies for the balance of the day with no real incidents — no sniper rounds, no one getting hurt, and only a little rainfall. We arrived at an area that had a small tree line around it. It was like a small island in the single canopy jungle. We made a perimeter around the island and started digging our foxholes. The firmness of the ground and the enemy activity would determine how deep we would go with the holes. I generally had my guys dig at least two holes, typically two feet deep, three feet wide, and six feet long. This would allow a couple of people, maybe more, to get in the same hole. I would take my turn digging as well. All the sergeants and squad leaders took their turns digging. I felt that if enemy fire hit us, and all of us had to dive into the foxhole, then I had better have helped dig it. The platoon leader, Lieutenant Gibbons and his RTO would dig their foxhole toward the middle of the perimeter and usually behind their platoon. I walked the perimeter from one end of our platoon to the other, as I usually did before we shut down for the night. I was just checking with the other squad leaders on our fire support coverage, making sure that we had a little bit of overlap coverage in case we were attacked.

After our holes were dug, we laid out our position. Each man was responsible for the location of his own grenades, ammo, and weapons. Each man was responsible for knowing where his C-rations and water were located. I hated nothing more than a man pulling his turn at guard, and looking all over the place for his food and canteen. We were now set for the night. Then I saw Gibbons's RTO walking toward me.

"Sergeant Rock, the lieu wants you to send one of your men over to our position."

"For what?"

"To help dig our foxhole. He wants it four feet deep and six by six wide."

"Do what? Is he helping to dig?"

"Not one shovel full."

"OK, watch and listen to this!"

I turned to my guys, who had been listening. "Do any of you guys want to go to the CP and dig a foxhole for Gibbons?"

"Hell no! Why can't he dig it himself?"

"Well there you have it; tell Gibbons that I refuse."

"OK, Sarge, I'll tell him."

As the RTO walked away, I turned to my men. "This guy couldn't find his butt if he had both hands on it."

Not more than three minutes had passed before my RTO tells me that Gibbons called, and he wants me at the CP. As I strolled to Gibbons's location, I thought that this was not going to turn out well. I saw Gibbons, and he looked hotter than a firecracker. "Sergeant Rock!"

"Yes, Lieutenant Gibbons."

"Did you refuse to send a man to dig my foxhole?"

"Yes, Lieutenant Gibbons."

"Do you expect an officer to dig his own foxhole?"

"Yes, Lieutenant Gibbons."

"Are you trying to be funny?"

"No, Lieutenant Gibbons."

"Quit with the yes and no lieutenant crap!"

"Yes, Lieutenant Gibbons."

"Stop the crap!"

"I request permission to speak to the lieutenant freely and off the record, sir."

"Permission granted."

"You are a jerk! Every officer in the 'Nam digs his own foxhole. Go up and look at the Annihilator's position. The only time he does not dig is if we need him to command. Sir, you don't need a hole four feet deep. You don't need a hole six feet wide and six feet long. For Pete's sake, there are only two of you!"

Before the lieutenant could answer, I heard *blup, blup, blup, blup.* I knew that sound; it was incoming mortars. "What's happening, Sarge?"

"We are being mortared!"

Then the lieutenant's RTO handed me his radio and said, "The captain wants to talk to you, Sarge."

"This is Blackhawk Three, over."

"Do you know our position, Sergeant Rock?"

"Yes I do!"

"You know what to do. Blow these guys away! Call it in!"

"Affirmatron. I'll take care of it, out."

I looked at Gibbons. He was as white as a ghost. "Sir, can I use your radio? The captain wants me to call in the firepower."

"Yes! Go, go, go!"

I started calling in the artillery. "Fireball Five-Niner, this is Blackhawk Three, over."

"This is Fireball Five-Niner, what can I do for you?"

I gave Fireball the grid coordinate. Fireball said, "What do you want?"

"I want shells."

"I'll fire a spotter."

A spotter round is a round to make sure that Fireball and I are on the same page, so to speak. We heard the first round go over our head before it went off. Hearing the whiz of the round told us that Fireball was shooting from behind us. The first round hit about 100 meters behind where the enemy was set up. "Fireball Five-Niner, from my position, drop 100."

"On the way."

The next round was closer to our position, but was in front of the enemy. "Fireball, from my position, add fifty."

The round hit, but it was still short of the enemy. Then Fireball called me, saying, "We are going to get help from the Navy; they need the practice."

Fireball was only joking about the Navy needing practice. The Navy battleship's artillery was absolutely perfect. From twenty-five miles out, they could land a round within two meters of a target.

A few more rounds hit, but this time, I heard no whiz over my head before the explosion. This meant that the Navy was in front of our position, shooting toward us. This is why I always had to say "from my position" before calling in the artillery.

"Fireball, from my position, add another fifty, five-zero."

"They are on the way. Tell me when to stop!"

I was trying to be extra calm, composed, and serene, to show the lieutenant how it was done. This was very common for me now, for I had called in artillery at least sixty to seventy times. The rounds were still seventy-five meters short of hitting the enemy's location.

Then I hear, "Let me try."

The lieutenant grabbed the horn from me and started to talk. "Fireball Five-Niner, this is Blackhawk, over."

"This is Fireball, go."

"Fireball, you do exactly as I say, and we will kill these gooks. I am getting tired of fooling around. You add 125 meters and do it now!"

"Blackhawk, are you certain?"

"Yes, do it and do it now!"

"They are on the way. You guys better duck!"

I grabbed the horn from the lieutenant and said, "Cease fire! Cease fire! Fireball Five-Niner, this is Blackhawk Three again. From our position, I say again, from our position, add seventy-five, seven five!"

"On the way."

The rounds hit right on target, but I see more movement to the enemy's right side. "From my position, move left fifty, five-zero, and fire for effect!"

The rounds start hitting perfectly. "Fireball Five-Niner, give me two more rounds. From my position, add fifty, five-zero, and that will be enough for now."

The final rounds hit in the direction of the enemy that, I felt, would be retreating. Gibbons grabbed the horn out of my hand. "Who do you think you are? You will pay for that little move. I guarantee it!"

As calmly as I could, I tried to explain. "Sir, when you are calling in artillery you must always, always say 'From my position'! The Navy was firing from a ship in the ocean twenty miles from us. They were shooting toward us. When you told Fireball to do exactly what you told him, and you said to add 125 meters, you would have killed us all. In this case, when the Navy is told to add 'from our position,' they will drop from their position. If you just say 'add,' they will add from *their* position. That is why Fireball questioned your command."

The radio sounded off, interrupting our conversation. It was the captain. "Blackhawk Three, have you got your act together now?"

"Yes I do!"

"Come see me in person in an hour. Out!"

I did not respond to the captain's command, for I knew from previous experiences that when the captain raises his voice and ends his sentence with "out," he is mad. Gibbons started up again. "I told you not to speak directly with the captain again, didn't I?"

I replied, "You need to speak to the old man about that. You need to tell the old man that I cannot talk to him any longer!"

"You know, Sergeant Rock, we have a lot to talk about."

"Yes we do, sir."

The lieutenant started talking. "First of all, I want my radio call sign to be 'The Boss Man One.'"

"Sir, you cannot change the company's call signs. The call signs were set up long ago. They are Indian names. I asked the captain about this in the past. He said this was our company's policy. Before you got here, the officer of the platoon was known as Blackhawk. When you leave, it will be Blackhawk. When the next guy leaves, it will be Blackhawk. My position of being the squad leader of the third squad is, and will always be, Blackhawk Three."

Then the lieutenant said to me, "Well, I'll fix that right now! You are no longer a squad leader. You are no longer a sergeant. You are busted to a private."

I was so mad by now that I could have shot him on the spot. I knew that his time was coming, so I held my thoughts to myself. "May I be excused, sir?"

"Yes you may, Private Rodgers."

I walked over to my squad. "Anybody hurt?"

"No! What happened up there, Danny?" Chuck asked me.

I started explaining to Chuck what the lieutenant had done. All of the men in my squad were adding to the conversation. I said, "Oh, yeah, I am now a private, and I am not the squad leader any longer. He busted me."

"For what?" Eckert asked.

"For telling him the truth. Did you guys know that if I would have allowed Fireball to bring in the artillery like Gibbons wanted, we would all be dead? We had a little talk about it, and now I am a private."

"We know how to take care of him, Sarge. The next firefight we get into, maybe he will be hit by friendly fire," a few of the men said.

My radio sounded off. "Blackhawk Three, this is Annihilator Three-Three, Romeo Three-Three, over." (Romeo Three-Three was the Captain's RTO.)

"This is Blackhawk Three, go."

"Annihilator wants to see you."

"On my way, out."

I briskly walked to the CP. The captain was waiting for me. I looked at my watch. I was a few minutes late. The captain said, "Sergeant Rock, you are late!"

"I am sorry, sir. By the time I was finished with the new platoon leader, and speaking to my men, the time had gotten away from me. Sorry."

"What happened with the artillery call in? You speak frankly and honestly."

"Sir, I am going to speak candidly and truthfully."

The captain said, "That's what I want, Rock."

"Sir, Fireball and I had a good dialogue going on. He was bringing the rounds in just as I wanted. I brought the rounds behind, then in front of the target. Gibbons thought that I was taking too long, and he grabbed the radio. He grabbed the horn right out of my hand. He then told Fireball to do exactly as he told them."

"Yeah, I heard most of that," the captain mumbled.

"He commanded that Fireball add 125 for the next rounds, and since he did not say 'from my position,' the rounds would have killed us all."

The captain responded, "That is why Fireball questioned the command. I didn't understand why Fireball was acting up, but now I know."

"Sir, Gibbons is a loose cannon. He will get someone killed. By the way, I have been busted. I am now Private Rodgers."

"Come again?"

"Yep, he busted me."

The captain shook his head in revulsion. "I'll talk to him. Maybe *he* will be the one to get busted."

"Sir, if you don't mind, let me handle it."

"OK. What do you have planned?"

"You will see soon, but don't be too alarmed if the artillery is a little late. I don't think the lieutenant can read a map."

"OK, you know what you are doing. See you later."

I returned to the squad. The men and I sat around and talked for a while. Now that I was calmed down, they saw that I was in a better mood. The men took turns making me laugh. They would pretend that they were Gibbons, acting like an idiot. One man said again, "I will shoot him if you want."

"No, don't do that. You don't want to take a chance of ruining your life for this piece of crap."

Then Eckert said, "I got it! Let Killer cut his head off in his sleep."

That brought the house down. We laughed until our sides hurt. Then our laughter stopped, for we saw the lieutenant coming toward us. Lieutenant Gibbons, with a frown on his face, says, "Lewis, you are squad leader now."

"What do you mean, sir?" Chuck asked.

"Rodgers is now a private, and I will not have a private running one of my squads."

"Sir, I think you need to get someone else. How about Eckert?"

"You heard what I said. You are squad leader! Have a good night, and see me in the morning."

Killer started in with his funny remarks. "Hey, Sergeant Lewis, since Sergeant Rock is gone, do you want to be Sergeant Boulder or Sergeant Pebble?"

Again, the laughter broke out. Then Emery came up with a good one. "Let's go between Boulder and Pebble. How about Sergeant Stone?"

"Yeah," everyone agreed, except for the one that counted.

Chuck said, "No, Sergeant Lewis is just fine. Call me Sergeant Lewis."

I said to Chuck, "You will be in charge tomorrow. Just watch out what Gibbons tells you, because he can get us into trouble really fast."

We pulled our guard and had an uneventful night. I enjoyed a night without incident. The next morning arrived, and, like almost every morning now, it was pouring down rain. The lieutenant, as he had promised, came over to see Chuck. "Are you ready to go, Sergeant Lewis?"

"I guess so, sir."

"Your squad has point! Who is your point man?"

"Eckert. It is his turn."

The lieutenant looked at me and said, "No, I want Private Rodgers at point."

Chuck said, "No, sir. It isn't his turn."

"Are you going to give me trouble too, Lewis?"

"I guess so, sir. It is not Danny's turn."

I stood up. "Don't worry about it, Chuck. I'll walk point."

The lieutenant said, "Let's go!"

He was all upset again. We started out. I told Chuck to find out where we were going. Chuck walked back to the rear of the platoon and found out that the lieu did not know again where we were going. Gibbons said, "I'll call the captain and ask where we are going."

Chuck responded, "Don't do that, sir. He will not tell you over the airway. If he did, every VC listening to our channel would know exactly where we are going and set ambushes for us."

"Man, Lewis, I have a lot to learn, don't I?"

"Yes you do, sir, and Sergeant Rock is trying to teach you. Just give him a chance to teach you. Did you know that the captain taught him?"

"No wonder they are so tight with each other," Gibbons said.

"They get along so well because Sergeant Rock listened and did everything the way he was told. Rock was not afraid to ask for help if he did not understand something. The captain can do anything that Sergeant Rock can do, but he wants to keep training him because he will be leaving in a few months. Did you know that the captain is good friends with General Westmoreland? The last time the general was here, the captain called Sergeant Rock to the CP and introduced him to the general. The whole company was jealous."

"Do you mean to tell me that Sergeant Rock is friends with General Westmoreland?"

"I don't know for sure, but I'll guarantee you that the next time the general comes in, he will ask for Sergeant Rock. He only knows him as Sergeant Rodgers. I had better get back up there with the squad. Let me know where we are going when you get a chance."

Chuck came back to the front. "Hey, Danny, he didn't know anything."

"That's OK. While you were gone, I went over to the captain. He told me where we were going and gave me the new map." I pointed to the map. "Here is where we are, and here is where we are going. You see this big mountain here? The company will split up at the base. The captain expects an ambush. We are going to take the lower area. Keep it to yourself. Don't tell Gibbons, because I have a plan."

"I knew that you would have a plan," Chuck said with a wide grin.

We started to cut through the double canopy jungle on the way to our destination. We were heading to Hill 881. It was only ten miles away, but it was rough going. We had been there before. There was a mountain that we would be climbing. There were also two other ways to get to Hill 881. One of the ways was to go around the mountain on the left. Going this way there was triple canopy jungle. However, after 1,500 meters, there were trails the rest of the way. The second alternate was to the right of the mountain. Going this way was single canopy jungle, but it was 2,000 meters farther. Going around either way was dangerous. There were areas that were perfect for an enemy ambush. Traveling up the mountain was the safest, but it was the hardest for traveling. Each time we had come this direction in the past, snipers shot at us.

After cutting through the bush for four hours, we had made it to the clearings just before the mountain. The captain called for a take ten. We spread out and watched. The captain was most likely going to split the company now. My radio sounded off. "All platoon leaders, come to Annihilator Three-Three."

Gibbons and his RTO took off. Chuck came to where I was standing.

"Hey Rock, do you think this is where we will split? I hope Gibbons gets it right."

"Yeah, this is where we always get the sniper rounds. I hope Gibbons gets it right too."

"Which way would you want to go, Danny?"

"Heck, I want to go up the middle, over the mountain. Halfway up, we can see the valley on both sides, and it would be easier to call in fire support."

Gibbons was back. "Sergeant Lewis, we are going to the left. Expect a few snipers."

Gibbons walked away. I told Chuck to get the guys to sharpen the two machetes. We were going to need them.

Chuck said, "Rock, you are still the leader of this squad, no matter what Gibbons says. OK, men, whatever Sergeant Rock says, do it! We are not going to have an OCS cupcake getting us killed!"

I started telling the men what to do. "Guys, take care of the machetes. It is going to be hard going for three hours, but then we will be in the open. Once we are in the open, watch out for snipers. I'll start out at point cutting. The second man will hold the point's weapon. Point will be for fifteen minutes each."

Going through this jungle was tough, to say the least. Leeches constantly dropped on us from the big wet plants in the jungle. We worked the plan, making changes every fifteen minutes. Finally, we had made it through the jungle and into a clearing with a few trails. Eckert was on point now. I went to the front so I could regain point. "Eckert, let me take over. Be ready. If we can make it another 2,000 meters, we will be OK."

I was on point, feeling a little more comfortable now that I was in front. I watched everything — the trees above, the tops of the mountains, the sides of the trails, and especially the path for trip wires. I motioned for Chuck and our RTO to come forward just behind me. Chuck said, "You see something?"

"Not yet, but it is awfully quiet."

We walked on another 500 meters. Chuck whispered, "Hey Rock, did you see that?"

"Roger, there are four more just around the bend."

We have now seen at least six VC. They are heading in the same direction that we are, but we are on a higher level. They had not seen us yet. *Or had they?*

Chuck said, "Should we tell Gibbons?"

"No! He will scream like a little girl and give us away."

My men started snickering, almost laughing out loud. I said "Shut up" as softly as I could, but still loud enough for them to hear me. I turned toward Chuck. "You remember the other day when the five VC set the trap for us?"

"Yes, January ninth, at ten in the morning. I'll never forget that date."

"Well, I think that the gooks have seen us, and they want us to get out in the rice paddies and chase them."

"I think you are right, Rock. Should I tell the lieutenant now?"

"No! Wait a few hundred more meters, and we will be right on top of them. I want to reverse the ambush and put it on them. Chuck, listen up! In just a few minutes, we will hear mortars. Watch and listen. We can wipe them out."

The mortars started. The firing began, but they had sprung their ambush too soon. Just when I thought we were in control of the situation, the shells started coming in. This was not a typical VC ambush. This was an NVA ambush with lots of firepower. The shells were exploding in the valleys and behind us, between our location and the mountaintop. At this time, the rounds were not too close to us. Evidently, the NVA did not know our exact location. However, the shell explosions were deafening. Chuck came running up to me. "Gibbons wants you to call in artillery!"

"Tell Gibbons that a private does not have the experience to call in firepower!"

"Blackhawk, this is Blackhawk Three. Rock says he can't call it in, because he is a private."

Gibbons said, "I am coming up there!"

Before Gibbons could get to our location, the radio went off again. "Blackhawk Three, this is Annihilator Three-Three, over."

Chuck shrugged his shoulders because he knew that the captain really wanted me. Chuck answered, "This is Blackhawk Three, over."

"Is this Lewis or Rodgers?"

"It is Lewis."

"Give me Rodgers, and now!"

I picked up the horn. The radio was still attached to the RTO. The RTO was handing the horn back and forth between Chuck and I. "This is Rodgers, but I have been instructed not to talk to you by our platoon leader. He told me never to speak to you directly again."

The shells were pounding. They were being walked toward us. Now I was getting worried, but I had to teach this Boy Scout, Gibbons, a lesson. By this time, Gibbons was right next to me. He had been listening to the whole conversation between the captain and me. I looked up at Gibbons. "Do you want me to speak to the captain?"

"Yes!"

Now I knew I had Gibbons on the run, but I had another ace up my sleeve. "Annihilator Three-Three, this is Blackhawk

Three. I have Blackhawk in my position, and he can call in the artillery, out."

Gibbons said, "I don't even know where we are! You do it!"

I said, "No! A private cannot call in artillery!"

"You had better get on the horn and call it in, Sergeant Rock!"

In an extremely calm voice and manner, I said, "Just get out your map and call in the coordinates." I pulled out my map and pointed to a spot. "We are right here. Call it in and make the CO proud."

I am really getting worried now. I think that I have pushed the issue far enough. *What sense would it make to prove a point, but get someone hurt or even killed?* Then Gibbons humbly said, "Please, Sergeant Rock, call it in. You have your stripes back. I'll even put in for a promotion. Please! You are a sergeant again."

I grabbed the horn and started what I had done so many times before. I loved it! "Fireball Five-Niner, this is Blackhawk Three. We need your help fast!" I gave Fireball our grid coordinates and where I wanted the first rounds to hit. "Send me a spotter."

"Roger, it is on the way."

The first round was 100 meters behind the enemy. "From my position, drop fifty, five-zero."

The next round comes, but it is fifty meters too far to the right of the enemy, and it is still fifty meters short. "Fireball Five-Niner, from my position, drop another fifty, five-zero, and from my position, move left fifty, five-zero meters."

The round comes in near perfect. "That's it, Fireball! Looks good."

"OK, Blackhawk, what can I give you?"

I wanted to have the lieutenant see an abundance of the rounds we could get, so I decided to show him some of my favorites. "Fireball, send me two shells (HEI) followed by four VT, and top it off with two napalms."

What a sight to see! The NVA were on the run. "Fireball Five-Niner, I want VT and fire for effect!"

The VT would get them on the run. We could see bodies flying through the air. We could see the NVA trying to retreat, but as soon as the VT hit, it was all over for them. Tomorrow, or maybe this afternoon, we would go into this field of death and try to find information.

I started to think, even with the explosions going off, that this whole battle is ironic. We will find the enemy. We will kill the enemy. We will find out where the enemy came from. We will turn in the body count of the enemy. We will eat and sleep. Then we will try to locate more of the enemy to kill again.

This was getting routine to me. These routines were much more than I could have ever anticipated. I loved the action. I loved the adrenaline rush. I wanted more and more of the action. But somehow, I did not like the end result — the deaths. Then I remembered what I have been taught. *Don't think too much, or you will get into trouble.*

Five more minutes, and I called for a cease-fire. The rocketing that the NVA were giving us had been severe. If they had known of our exact position, they would have been relentless with their firepower.

The following is something that I placed in my mind to never forget: *Don't chase gooks that are running in the open. When going around a blind bend and we see gooks, call in for fire support; don't try to kill them one on one.*

I looked around for Gibbons. The lieutenant was still hiding near us, in the bush just off the trail. He rolls his eyes. "Sergeant, that was intense. You scared me half to death, you A-hole!" He shook his head and laughed. "What a day!"

"Yes, sir, and we will have a lot more situations like this, even worse," I said, looking straight at Gibbons.

He had a serious look on his face. "Will you teach me?"

"Sir, there is more than calling in fire support to be a good leader over here."

"I want to learn it all," he said as he nodded his head.

"Now you've said the magic word — learn! None of us can do it alone. Do you know what it takes to call in artillery and really be good at it, sir?"

"I guess knowing the enemy's location."

"No! You have to be a good, no, a *great* map-reader! Do you know who the best map reader in the company is?"

With a smile on his face, he said, "Yes. You are, Rock."

"Wrong again! It is the captain," I continued to explain. "Many men think that reading a map is just north, south, east, and west. The captain taught me elevations. If the enemy is in a valley surrounded by mountains, how are you going to get them without hitting the mountain first? The most important thing is to know exactly where you are. That is even more important than where the enemy is located. Knowing both is key."

The RTO's radio sounded off. "Blackhawk and Blackhawk Three, this is Annihilator Three- Three. When we get to our destination, both of you come see me, out!"

Gibbons and I rolled our eyes and looked at each other. He opened his eyes wide and asked, "What is he going to say, Rock?"

"Oh, he will just jump on me for not calling in the artillery earlier."

The lieutenant said, "Let's go! Get on point!" He looked at me.

This made my blood boil. We had just talked about how to be a good leader here in Vietnam. "Sir, there you go again! Here in the bush, when we depend on each other to survive we are supposed to work together. Do not give any hard-pointed demands!"

"What am I supposed to do, beg someone to take point?"

"No! You actually look around and think about who you want on point. Sometimes you do not want a particular guy in a certain area to pull point. Some guys are really good at finding trip wires. Others are good at locating gooks. Some pull point and they end up being nothing but a target for a VC. If you keep on treating your men like you treat them in the States, you will trip on a trip wire yourself and not even be pulling point."

"How could that happen, Rock?"

"Just like this — the point guy sees a wire. He does not call it in. He tells the second man. The third tells the fourth and so on and so on. No one would tell you. In this scenario you would be the only man that did not know about the trip wire."

"What about the men around me? Wouldn't they be blown up too?"

"They would hit the ground. Sir, this is Vietnam. Stuff happens. I have always thought that it would be much easier just to shoot the guy you don't like in a firefight."

"Then how should I ask a man to pull point?"

I respond, "In this case you would say, 'Sergeant Rock, how about pulling point again?' And I would say, 'Of course! It would be my pleasure.'"

"Yeah, right," the lieutenant said as he made his lips tight.

"Sir, it is not really that polite, but you get my drift, right?"

Then the lieutenant said something that made us all laugh, and maybe we were going to start getting along better. "Sergeant Rock, if you are not doing anything at the moment, and you can find an hour to spare, would you mind pulling point? Of course, at your convenience."

We all laughed very hard. The lieutenant looked at the men, his eyes widening in amazement. He clearly couldn't believe that he'd made us laugh so hard. For the first time since he had been in country, he was one of us. He was still like a scared bunny rabbit, but everyone is afraid when they first arrive in the 'Nam.

I said, "Yes, sir! I am on point."

We took off again in the direction of Hill 881.

On our way to the hill, walking around the bend, we could see plenty of bodies (or parts of bodies). My quick estimate was thirty-two, but it was hard to tell because of the body parts. *What arm went with what body? What leg went with what body?* We were at a distance. We will get a true count in the morning when we are among the dead. Again I thought, *It is another good day when we don't lose any men.*

We arrived at the hill. We were glad that our last hump had no more incidences. Sometimes it was nice just to have a simple portion of the day with no worries. We did not get many of these days, and I knew that more bad days were yet to come. We had not been on the hill ten minutes when the captain called for us. The lieutenant came to me and said, "Are we in trouble?"

"Probably. Just tell him that we are getting along just fine. He does not like to hear squabbles."

Then he said, "I still want my call sign changed!"

"Don't say anything about it now! We have enough to worry about. Besides, he will never let you change your call sign to 'The Big Boss Man' or whatever you said you wanted. Think of an Indian name."

We started walking toward the CP. Gibbons said, "How about Hatchet Man?"

I say, "No!"

"How about Chief?"

"No! But you are getting closer."

"How about Apache?"

"No! That's the name of some of our chopper guys."

"How about Cherokee?"

"That may work, but don't ask him now!"

We were talking finally. The lieutenant and I finally had some thoughts in unison. *Was this a breakthrough for Gibbons and me?*

The captain saw us and said, "I need to speak to both of you! Come over here." We both walked toward him sheepishly. "Lieutenant, what happened during the firefight this morning? What was the mix up? What is going on between you two? Let me hear it!"

The lieutenant explained, "The NVA were going to spring an ambush on our platoon. I spoke to Sergeant Rock about fire support. He had a suggestion to spring the ambush on them with artillery. I agreed, and he called it in right on top of them."

The captain was not buying it. "OK, Lieutenant, you go back to your platoon. Sergeant Rock, you stay here. I want to talk to you."

Gibbons walked away. The captain said, "I do not believe any of that crap. Rock, when you told me this morning that you would take care of Gibbons yourself, I did not realize that you would make me crap my pants. I couldn't tell where their artillery ended and ours began. Did you have it under control?"

"Well, sort of. Their artillery was a little closer than I wanted."

"Rock, I bet Gibbons crapped his shorts."

"Yes, sir, he was scared."

"How did you know that we were going to be ambushed?"

I explained, "Do you remember the five gooks that led us into our ambush on January ninth?"

"How could I forget? We lost over 100 men. I'll never forget."

"Sir, here is how I knew about the ambush. We saw a few gooks moving through the valley on our left. Then there were a few more just ahead. It seemed like they wanted us to see them. I think that they wanted us to get on line down in the valley and start shooting, just like we did on January ninth. So I turned the table on them, and we ambushed the NVA with firepower."

"Alright, but next time, keep me informed a little better, please! So you and Gibbons are going to make it together without killing each other?"

"I guess we will see. He is really worried."

"Yeah, aren't we all?"

"Sir, how long will we be here?"

The captain replied, "Sorry, but it will just be until tomorrow. We will get resupplied and move out in the morning."

"Sir, the men are tired, and we don't have but a few men left."

"I know. Someday we'll get a stand down. Enjoy the night with no guard duty."

"Yes, sir."

I walked back to my squad. I divided my men near bunkers at the perimeter. They were really happy to know that others would be protecting them for the night.

CHAPTER 6

Agony and Thirst

It's early morning, and we are preparing for another journey. All we know is that we are heading north again, looking for regiments of NVA. Mentally and physically, we are all feeling the strain of war. However, on an up note, we have a new lieutenant, with a better attitude, for our platoon leader. Chuck was back, and for the moment, my spirits were lifted. The radio sounded, "Blackhawk Three, come to Cherokee!"

It appeared that Gibbons got his call sign name changed. At least Cherokee was much better than "The Big Boss Man." When I arrive at the lieutenant's bunker, I see something that would make any soldier in Vietnam laugh out loud. The lieutenant's RTO looked at me, and with every fiber of his being, he tried not to laugh. Lieutenant Gibbons was wearing a flak jacket, eight bandoliers of ammo, eight canteens of water, a bayonet, an M-16 rifle, a loaded rucksack, and a .45 pistol strapped to his side. No one on earth could hump through the jungle with all of that equipment on. There were times in Vietnam when the temperatures were as high as 135 degrees under the jungle canopy. When temperatures were that hot, we could not even touch the metal on our rifles. The humidity felt like 100 percent. Our lungs starved for some kind of fresh air. The water in our canteens would burn our already-parched lips.

For a moment, I remembered the letters that my dad would write to me. Dad would always close his letters with, *"Keep your bulletproof vest on at all times, and keep that long neck of yours down!*" I was six feet, two inches tall and weighed 165 pounds. I guess that I did have a long neck. In my dad's later letters, he started requesting that I wear two flak jackets. He called them bulletproof vests. I never had the heart to tell him that it was too unbearably hot over here to wear a flak jacket. I would let him believe that I was wearing the jacket because it would allow him to be less worried about me. One time, the choppers brought us a supply of extra-lightweight flak jackets to wear. They were really nice. All of us gave them a try, but the extra weight and the air that they cut off to our bodies was still too much to take. We turned them back in. It only took us about a week to figure out that trying to hump through the jungle with even a small amount of extra weight was too much.

Our platoon was ready, but the rest of the company was not. The lieutenant walked over to my position. "Sergeant Rock, before we head north again, our platoon has to get a body count from yesterday. The rest of the company will stay here until we get the count."

"Sir, I guess since we killed them, we have to count them. Do you want your squad on point?"

"OK."

I was still amused at the look of the drugstore, cowboy-looking soldier. We started in the direction of the ambush. We arrived at the site when Gibbons summoned me.

"How should we do this?"

"Sir, we need to spread out our men all the way around where the NVA were planted. Then we should get five to eight men in the middle to locate and count the bodies. My squad has done this many times before. We will go out there and count."

"Rock, I want to go also. I need to get a taste of what this body count stuff is all about."

"No problem, sir."

We set the perimeter and started searching. We had done a good job on this group of enemies. We found part of a body here and another part over there. I told the men to start locating as much of the body as possible and to count that main portion as one body.

Gibbons asks, "Do we need to put the arms and legs near the bodies?"

"No sir, just count them."

Emery says, "Sergeant, we have seven."

"Emery, start counting limbs."

"Yes, Sergeant."

Chuck had a body count of twelve. Eckert and I had located six bodies. White and Emerald had a body count of two, and Warmont found one.

"Men, our count is twenty-eight. Now we need to count the limbs that are not attached!"

"Sergeant Rock, I found three that were almost complete with legs and arms," the lieutenant said. He went on to say, "Why can't we just give them an estimate?"

"That is what we will do once we count the arms and legs. Hey men, bring all of the weapons over to where I am now, even if they are broken."

Our final count was twelve more legs and eight more arms. Sometimes we could not tell the difference between an arm and a leg. It was time for an estimate. Some of the bodies that we had already found were missing a leg or an arm. Therefore, I figured thirty-one total. I informed the lieutenant, and he confirmed my count. The lieutenant called the captain. "Annihilator Three-Three, this is Cherokee Three, over."

"This is Annihilator Three-Three. Do you have a count yet?"

"Yes we do, Annihilator Three-Three. We have thirty-one."

"That is great, Blackhawk, I mean Cherokee Three. Way to go. Come on in."

The captain, due to what Killer had done, had a reputation to uphold. He wanted the body counts. The squad brought me what was left of a few broken rifles. "Destroy any good parts of the rifles. Good job, men. Let's get out of here."

Every time I heard about going to the DMZ, I would cringe. Not many infantry companies came back alive from the DMZ.

"Yes, sir, we will be ready."

As we were walking away, Roberts followed the captain, leaving his rucksack open. I saw the transistor radio that I had given to Johnson. I took the radio. The lieutenant said, "What are you doing?"

"It belongs to me. I gave it to Johnson."

We both laughed. I tucked it under my shirt. We walked to our platoon. I gathered up my men. "Hey Chuck, you said that your transistor was acting up. Take this one."

I tossed the radio to Chuck. "Compliments of Johnson. He got shot this morning. Not dead, only wounded, I think."

Chuck is on the left I am on the right

Then Chuck said, "Here Emery, you take my old one."

"Men, we will be pulling out at six-thirty, going north again. Sleep well tonight. I think it will be a hard drive for a long time."

The next morning, we were ready to pull out when Gibbons came to me and said, "Your squad has point."

The lieutenant was still overdressed for this hot, humid climate. I could hardly keep from laughing. "Sir?"

"Your squad has point."

My squad had pulled point a lot since Gibbons had arrived. "Yes, sir, but again, you are too demanding."

He made a slight grunt as he walked away. "OK, men, we have point. Who wants it?"

Chuck said, "I'll do it."

Chuck was always ready to help out. I showed Chuck the mountain to head for on the map. We were starting to move. The choppers had brought a few more new recruits while we were doing the body count. The company now had almost 100 men. The company was building back up again, which made me feel much better about our battling situations. I was always worried about the strength of the company, but lately it made me worry even more. Just a few days ago we had seventeen men, and now we were almost up to 100. Maybe we would have full strength before long.

We humped for the next eighteen hours before digging in for the night. We were exhausted, as usual, but at least no one was shooting at us. I set out the guard duty while we ate and talked. Chuck said, "Danny, do you think Gibbons will make it?"

I answered, "I think he may be an idiot!"

He shook his head from side to side. I took another spoonful of pressed ham. "Did you see his outfit?"

"Yes, I did! If he makes it through tomorrow, he will be a better man than me," Chuck said.

"Me too."

Killer joined the conversation. "Hey, Sergeant Rock, why do you think that some people will ask questions and listen, and some will not?"

He took a big drink of water from an almost dry canteen. Chuck replied, "Why do some guys cut a guy's head off, and another guy would not?"

All of us laughed. Killer responded, "That is right. Everybody is different."

And we laughed again. I started thinking that we were going to be a very good squad again. We need to be together and laugh every once in a while. It takes our mind off of the death that surrounds us.

"Killer, can you name everyone in our squad?"

"Yes, I think so. Let's see. We have Chuck Lewis, Sergeant Rock."

Chuck said, "That's right, name me first, and don't forget it!"

Once more we all laughed. "Then we have Emery, Emerald, White, Eckert, Brant, and what is the name of the guy that sleeps on guard duty every night?"

"Warmont," a few of the guys articulate.

Chuck says, "That guy is going to get us all killed. Can't you get him transferred before Killer cuts his head off?"

"I would like to get him transferred, but who would want him? Anyhow, he can shoot a rifle, and we only have eight men."

We start smelling something good. "Hey Emery! What are you making?" Killer asked.

"Chocolate pudding," answers Emery.

"Where did you learn that?"

"Sergeant Rock taught me, but you will have to be in country for six months before he teaches you. Do you want a bite?"

"Sure." Killer takes a bite. "That is great!"

No one taught me how to make it. I did a lot of trial and error to finally come up with my recipe. Everything that I used came from C-rations. I don't mind saying that it was really good. Here is how I made it: I took the Oreo cookies and mixed them with water and let the mixture set for ten minutes. I took the hot chocolate mix, added water, and brought it to a boil by burning C-4 under it. Don't worry; C-4 is not dangerous unless there is an electric charge hooked to it. Almost all of us carried C-4 in our backpacks. Here is my secret ingredient: I would open a can of pound cake and chop it up in small pieces. I would then mix all of the ingredients together.

I would let it all cool slightly, then cook it all again, bringing it almost to a boil. Now I had the best tasting pudding in Vietnam. Many men try to match my pudding, but they all fall short.

Killer came over to where Chuck and I were resting. "Sergeant Rock, I want you to teach me how to make that chocolate pudding!"

"Where did you taste my chocolate pudding?"

"Emery is making it. My mom is a great cook, but I think your pudding beats hers."

"What did Emery tell you?"

"He said that I would have to be in country for six months before you would teach me."

Chuck said, "Killer, you have been here less than a month, actually less than two weeks. Sergeant Rock is teaching you nuttin' for six months. In six months, I'll even show you how to make cupcakes."

Chuck could make some killer cupcakes. We would trade with one another whenever we had the chance. Most of the time, we were so exhausted that we did not feel like making dessert after our lima beans and ham entrée.

Killer went on to say, "But, Sarge, what if I get killed within six months? Or worse yet, what if you get killed and you have not given us the recipe? That would be terrible, Sergeant Rock. Come on, give it up."

Sarcastically, I said to Killer, "Yes, you are right, Killer. I apologize for being so inconsiderate. I will make out a will tonight and place the recipe in my rucksack. I am so sorry for not thinking of you. Now get your butt over there and start pulling guard before I make your stay in Vietnam shorter than you think!"

We had another good laugh. Killer was laughing harder than any of us. Killer started toward the foxhole. Chuck said, "You really do like that guy, don't you?"

"You know what, Chuck? I do like Killer. He is going to be a good man. I know that during a firefight, I want him right next to me. I like every man in the squad with the exception of Warmont.

I actually like Warmont himself, but he is useless on guard duty. Other than Warmont sleeping half the time, we have a great squad." I paused before I added, "OK, Chuck, I am turning in."

"Goodnight, Rock."

"Night, Chuck. Don't let the leeches bite."

Morning came, and we moved out. We started going up a mountain with triple canopy jungle. We were only moving forward about fifteen feet every ten minutes. Every squad started taking their turn at point. The machete man was the first man, and the second man held the machete man's weapon. One man could not make any headway through this bush. We started using two men up front with machetes. We were in the worst bush that I had ever seen. The temperature was nearing 135 degrees. We had triple canopy over our heads. We had triple canopy-looking bush to the right, to the left, and in front of us. *When would it ever end?* The heat was unbearable. We could not get any fresh air. Our lungs were pumping. No one was speaking because it took too much energy. I thought to myself, *Someone is going to pass out. I hope it's not me. The squad leader cannot show weakness.* However, I was getting worried. *What about Gibbons with all of that garb that he was wearing?* We have two men cutting, and we are still not making any headway. This was like being in a long, five-foot-tall by eighteen-inch-wide hallway with no air coming in or out.

My radio sounded off, "Blackhawk Three, this is Cherokee Romeo Three, over."

I struggled to answer, "This is Blackhawk Three, go."

"You need to come back here to see Cherokee, over!"

"On my way, out."

I arrived to see Lieutenant Gibbons very, very pale. Then he started to vomit. "What is wrong with me, Sergeant Rock?"

He heaved again. Snot was running from his nose, tears coming from both eyes, and he still had vomit all over his chin. "You are overheated, sir."

"You need to take the platoon."

He sniffed like he was through throwing up. "OK, no problem, sir. Sir, you need to get rid of your flak jacket and half of your ammo. We get a lot of days like this."

"Maybe you're right."

"No *maybe* about it."

I saw Roberts. "What are you doing over here with the lieutenant?"

"The captain made me trade with his X-ray!"

"Roberts, you take the lieutenant's ammo and divide it up among the squads. Give me a bandolier. Roberts, do you remember the battery deal? I should make you carry two of his bandoliers because of that little episode. You are a useless pile of garbage!"

I turned, but before I could get three steps, Roberts said, "I am your RTO now! I will go with you."

"Get lost, Roberts. You wouldn't make a pimple on my RTO's butt! You get over there and babysit the lieutenant."

I returned to my squad. Chuck looked at me. "Was Gibbons sick?"

"Yes he is. He has got to get rid of all that crap he's wearing!"

Killer said, "Yep, he is real sick alright!"

"Are you in charge again now?" Emery asked.

"Looks like it, and you are the RTO for me and the lieutenant."

"What about Roberts?"

"The heck with Roberts. He can eat crap and die for all I care. He's a jerk... No, guys, I am sorry for saying that. He just makes me mad sometimes. When he was my X-ray, he was a good guy. I don't want anyone to die. Alright, men, listen up. We are going to start moving through this jungle crap! We are going to have two men cutting as hard as they can for five minutes, then switch off."

This worked. All of the men, even though they were dead tired, were in competition with each other. We started making progress. Chuck is now on point. We are stopped again. We are into back-up or Wait-a-Minute bushes. Chuck had his whole arm jammed in the bush. I took my M-16 rifle strap and hooked it over the bush. Chuck and I pulled in the opposite direction. He was freed from the bush. My buddy's arm started to swell up very quickly. There was something in these bushes that would poison your skin. The back-up bush would bother me by making my limbs swell up a little, but not half as bad as it affected Chuck and some others. Chuck was allergic to the back-up bush's secretion. Chuck and I had been through this before. My skin would be back to normal in a few days. Chuck's skin would take four to five days.

Progress was going extremely slow again. Every man, by now, knew about the back-up bushes. Well, maybe not everyone knew. I needed to check on Gibbons. I approached the lieutenant. He was looking a little better now. "Sir, I am going to take us downhill slightly toward this clearing."

I pointed to a spot on the map. It took a lot of energy to speak these few words. My chest cavity felt like it was burning up with hot water. I would have to pause after four to five words. I felt no different than my men. I was squad leader, so I had to suck it up. I was glad when the lieutenant simply said, "You're in charge. Go for it."

He also could barely get the words out. *How much more could our bodies take?* I told Romeo (the name for an RTO) to have Gibbons watch out for the back-up bush. I turned and went back to the squad. Soon, we started to get out of the back-up bushes, and we were making progress through the jungle again. The heat was getting to us even more, if that could be possible. Our eyes were burning from the salt that came from our sweat. Our eyelids were blistered from rubbing the perspiration from them. We were getting blisters between our legs. If I found this painful, Chuck must be in real pain. Killer must be in pain also, for he said, "I would give $100 for a bottle of baby powder." He fell to his knees.

"Me too!" someone said.

I was too tired to see who said it. "Sergeant Rock, come here, come here, look, look!"

I walked to where Emerald was standing. He started grabbing at my rifle sling. I looked at where he was pointing and saw nothing but a log laying next to a boulder. In agitation, I said, "I only see a log."

Was Emerald so worn out that he was seeing things that were not there? I was too tired for this nonsense. "Sarge, it ain't a log; it's a snake. Look at the head!"

Emerald ran back down to the line of men and told them all. I have heard of an old saying, "You can't see the forest for the trees." The head of the snake was as large as both of my fists side by side. Five of my men had walked past the creature and never even noticed it.

The captain radioed, "What is the hold up?"

"We have found a gigantic snake!"

"Take a .45 and kill it!"

I got Gibbons's pistol and handed it to Killer. Killer pointed the pistol at the snake's head, but his hands were so shaky, he missed by two feet.

I said, "Get out of the way before you shoot all of us, Killer!"

Killer stepped back. I leaned in toward the snake with my rifle. I took careful aim right at the reptile's head and pulled the trigger. Nothing happened because I had forgotten to release my safety. Killer was leaning over my shoulder and Chuck was leaning over his. I was really getting nervous now. But maybe the snake was dead. I took off my safety. I shot and missed from two feet away.

The snake started moving quickly toward us. We took off running with the snake chasing at our heels, toward the front of the squad. Killer was first, Chuck was second, and I followed just as close to Chuck as humanly possible. We looked like the Three Stooges. We made it to the guys that were on point and had been cutting through the jungle. The jungle was still so thick that the snake, of course, took the path of least resistance, and this was the path we had just cut. We were jammed up against each other, yelling and hollering. Our adrenaline was building. By this time, every man was looking back at the ground in hopes that the snake may choose a different direction. The snake kept coming. One more look back, and the men and myself shoved the point men as hard as we could.

All of a sudden, we broke through the jungle, but something was wrong. We were free-falling in mid-air. Then we hit the ground. Our bodies bumped and fell over one another. We were in pain. Now we looked like twelve of the Stooges. Our bodies are mingled. We are in a pile, trying to get free, but we are so tired that some men just lay there. We have fallen off a cliff. Luckily, it was only a twelve-foot drop. The snake comes off the cliff and is also airborne. The snake hits the ground and keeps on going.

"I guess the snake was as scared as we were," Killer said, pulling himself off of Chuck.

"I don't think so," Chuck said as he tried to locate his rifle.

"How big was that sucker?" Killer asked.

I said, "He had to be twenty foot long, at least."

"That has got to be a record," Emerald says. "Let's go to where the snake was and measure."

"Man, Emerald, are you not as tired as I am?" Then I added, "Well, it would be a record and something to tell our grandkids someday. Let's do it. No one will believe it if we don't get proof. Emerald, do you know where the beginning and the end of the snake was?"

"Yes, and my foot is about twelve inches long. I will step it off."

To this day, I don't know how we got the strength to climb back up the cliff and to the boulder where the snake had been laying. The snake was twenty-two feet long. Someone said it was a python.

We dug in for the night in the clearing that we had just fallen into. Gibbons was glad for the rest. We did our usual guard duty, posting coordinates, and ammo checking. I was so tired that I felt like I couldn't eat, but I knew that I had to eat something. "How much water you got, Danny?" Chuck said.

"I've got two left."

I only carried four canteens because I only seemed to need half of the water that everyone else needed. Chuck carried six canteens. "I only have two left with water in them. Man, it is still hot!" Chuck says as he takes a light swig of the hot water.

"I am going to take another look at the map. I don't remember seeing any rivers or streams. We may be in trouble; there is no water for at least forty miles. I think that is about sixty-four klicks!" I said to Chuck and Killer.

Chuck looked up at me. "I need a bath. My arms are killing me, and I stink."

"Don't blame the stink on Vietnam," the donut man said with that distinctive laugh of his.

Killer gave a sigh as he dropped to the ground from exhaustion. I looked at him. "Mister Rydser, Sergeant Lewis is your superior, and you should treat him as such."

Killer responded, "I am sorry, Sergeant Lewis. It just seems like I am one of the boys."

"You are one of the men, just hold it back a little," Chuck said.

"Yes, sir!" Killer concurred.

I glanced at my men. "Are you guys ready for some firepower?"

The captain called the fire support base for a little heat. He set up firepower for all of our surrounding areas. We called in our location and had Fireball Five-Niner fire a few spotter rounds, in case we needed artillery help during the night. I always enjoyed calling in the heat, but to tell the truth, on this night I was dead tired.

We made out our guard duty assignments. Other than a few sniper rounds and a few misplaced mortar rounds, it was an uneventful night. I loved quiet nights. Morning came too soon.

93

Our bodies were not ready to move out at zero-four-thirty, but we had to keep moving, trying to find those NVA regiments.

We started right away, cutting through the triple canopy jungle. We were heading up a mountain, struggling, and moving very slowly. Again, we were cutting with the machetes, taking turns at five-minute intervals. The jungle was just too thick to make a good path. It seemed that our rifle slings were catching on every limb and branch of bamboo. Our grenade belts were constantly being pulled. This could be very dangerous because if a grenade pin was accidentally pulled, it could kill three or four of us in these tight quarters.

The path that we were cutting was getting down to about fourteen inches wide. Our rucksacks were getting torn and ripped. Again, we were in the back-up bushes. Our shirts and pants were getting long tears in them. Suddenly, we heard a loud boom. We hit the ground. The radio sounded off, "Blackhawk Three, this is Cherokee."

"This is Blackhawk Three, go."

"What is going on? Are we being rocketed?"

"No! Rockets don't sound like that! I'll find out."

Again, my radio sounds off. "Blackhawk Three, this is Annihilator Three-Three. What the Sierra is going on?"

We were not supposed to curse on the radio, so we used other words in lieu of the cuss word. "I don't know what that was, but it was real close to my position. It sounded like a mortar round. I'll find out! Chuck, go see if anyone is hurt!"

"I'm on it."

Chuck was gone for about three minutes and came back with a soldier. The soldier was from another squad. His name was Hunt. Hunt was a big, burly kind of a guy, six-foot, three inches tall and about 220 pounds. Hunt was as white as a sheet, and he was trembling profusely. "Are you hurt, man?"

"No! I... I just burnt the heck out of my chest."

I did not know what he meant. I thought, *How could a mortar explosion only burn your chest without killing you?* Then I saw his

M-79 grenade launcher. I immediately knew what had happened. "Your 79 got caught in the bush and went off, didn't it?"

I knew that because it had happened to me when I was carrying the M-79, but I was lucky it didn't fire. This time, it had fired. However, the ammo for the launcher has to turn three revolutions before it explodes. Hunt was very lucky, because his chest had slowed the projectile's revolutions. He could have put the ammo (grenade) through his throat. Even without the explosion, the projectile has enough force to kill a person.

"How bad are you burnt?"

Hunt looked down at his torn and burnt shirt. "Pretty bad, Sarge. I am really, really sorry. I tripped and caught the trigger on a limb."

"You are lucky the 79 wasn't pointing straight up, because you may have killed three or four good men, including yourself!"

Hunt replies, "I know, Sarge. Again, I am sorry."

I saw in his face how sorry he was. "Don't worry, Hunt. Just try to keep your finger on the safety."

Chuck looked at Hunt and me. "Go ahead and tell him, Sarge."

I knew what he wanted me to tell Hunt, but I pretended not to know. "Tell him what, smart-butt?"

"Tell Hunt about the time it happened to you."

I begin telling Hunt the story about my episode when I carried the 79.

"We were in a firefight when I decided to change positions. I leaped over Sergeant Lewis. My body hit the ground so hard that I thought I had broken three ribs. The ground knocked the breath out of me. My helmet fell off in front of me. I reached for it just as fast as I could. My finger was still on the trigger of the grenade launcher. It went off. The projectile hit the helmet and went to the left, landing about twenty meters from our position. I was so happy that the grenade had to make a few revolutions before it would set itself and explode. You see, Hunt, you were

95

lucky. On *your* mistake, you could have only killed yourself; on *my* mistake I could have killed many."

Hunt felt more at ease knowing that he was not the only soldier to do a stupid thing. "Another thing, Hunt. Remember to watch out for that safety on top of the weapon, it catches on every vine and limb. Keep your thumb on the safety."

I summoned the captain and the lieutenant. "Annihilator Three-Three, Cherokee, this is Blackhawk Three, over."

"This is Annihilator. What happened?"

"A 79 friendly fire went off."

"Did you take care of it?"

"That's affirmative, over."

"Good. Roger, out."

At least we got a little rest during this five-minute ordeal. We started humping again. Another four hours of brutally exhausting toil and we cut through the jungle to some rice paddies. The water that was trapped between the dikes was very hot, muddy, and smelled like cow crap. The mucky water was about four inches high, and the mud below was four to six inches thick. Just right for growing rice, but horrible for us to cross through. This crap we were in made for an almost impassible situation. We placed a few men to pull guard, for it looked like we would be here for a few minutes to check out the water.

Now the sun was beating directly down on us, but somehow it was better than being trapped in that hot triple canopy jungle. Even though the humidity was draining energy from our already tired bodies, we could breathe again, being in the open. The odor of the water was breathtaking, but not in a good way. Some men were completely out of drinking water; others had only half a canteen left. I still had an almost full canteen, but now I was getting thirsty. I could never figure it out. *Why did I need so much less water than the other men?* Most of the time, drinking water was not even on my mind, but now I too was thinking of water. Even with our purification tablets, we don't dare drink the water from this rice paddy.

I see Killer approaching. "Hey, Rock, Emery has been out of water for three hours."

I replied, "Three hours is a long time when you are humping in this mess. What's he doing?"

Killer knew that I was asking if he was in convulsions or just throwing up. "Nothing yet."

"Send him to me!"

Emery came to my location. He had the usual pale-looking face that always accompanied the dehydration. I gave Emery a little of my water. He was very appreciative. Emery said, "Tank thu, Tharg."

His tongue was so thick from the lack of water, I could hardly understand him. "Try to take it easy, Emery."

He shook his head to say yes. We started going uphill again. We humped another hour and took a small break, then humped two more hours. *Are we ever going to stop?* I thought. Again, I was wondering how much more my men could take.

Chuck looked at me. "Hey Rock, Emery has stopped sweating."

When a person stops sweating his body will stop working soon after. "Go tell the point to hold up!"

I walked toward Emery and found him ready to pass out. "Lay down, Emery. We are going to stop for a while."

I headed toward Lieutenant Gibbons. He looked like death warmed over. "Sir, we need water to keep going."

He replied, "I know."

"Sir, we need to rest here for the night! This looks like a good area to get some rest."

The radio sounded off, "Cherokee, dig in for the night, over."

The captain noticed the good area for a bivouac. "Affirmative, Annihilator."

We dug very shallow foxholes, too tired to dig deep like we were supposed to. I looked over our situation. The men had blisters that were now broken and festered. The men had bleeding lips, scorched bodies, bleeding arms, peeled red feet from all of the rice paddy crap water, ripped and torn clothes, and shattered spirits. I looked at these men and decided to go ahead and confront my superiors.

I went to the middle of our perimeter to the CP to the captain. "Sir, why can't we get a chopper and water?"

He replied, "There is no water."

"What do you mean?"

"Well, Rock, I have good news and bad news. We are going to get a chopper tomorrow at 10 a.m., but it won't have water."

I respond with a smirk, "Oh, yeah?"

"It will have soda and beer."

"You mean to tell me that they can load Cokes and Budweiser, but they can't send us water? We need water, not alcohol!"

"Just calm down, Sarge! All of the water at Baldy has been destroyed by rockets."

"Are we going to get rations?"

"Maybe."

"I'll tell my men."

I told my men what I found out. They wanted water, but any form of liquid would do. Emerald said, "I would give fifty bucks for a Coke with ice in it. Make it $100."

Emerald was a good friend of Emery. They both came to the 'Nam at the same time. Emerald was a good soldier, but he constantly needed to be reassured that he could kill someone. It was not the actual killing that bothered him. He was just afraid of being killed himself. We were all afraid of being killed, but in Vietnam, a soldier had to suck it up. I could see more and more that he was a weak link in the chain. Even Warmont was a better soldier than Emerald; however, Warmont would fall asleep on guard duty. In general, Emerald would take orders from me better, but he was completely lost in a firefight.

"OK, guys, let's do guard duty. Emery, can you pull guard?"

"Yes I can, Sarge!"

"Alright, Emery, you rest for a while and you pull second."

"Hey, Chuck, you want to assign the rotation?"

"Sure do."

"Emerald first, Emery second, Warmont third. Then Killer, myself, Sergeant Rock, White, Brant, Eckert. How long, Sarge?"

"One hour."

Chuck spoke to the men. "One hour each, and no sleeping."

Chuck looks at Warmont. We started pulling guard. Emerald went to the shallow foxhole and the rest of us found a place to sleep. We were very tired. Some of the men fell asleep fast. I, however, would take much longer to fall asleep. On this night, I was worrying about our shallow foxholes. *What if we were attacked? How was Emery? How were Chuck's infected sores? How was the morale of my men? Would Warmont fall asleep again tonight? Where would we go tomorrow?* I started setting up the area where I was going to sleep.

I laid out my thin sheet of acetate (thin plastic sheet about as thick as a dollar bill) and placed my poncho liner on it. For a pillow, I took my canteens and hand grenades and slid them apart on my ammo belt. This made a cradle for my head to lie in. I placed another sheet of acetate to the side in case of rain. I positioned my rifle just as close to me as possible. I placed all of my ammo bandoliers next to my head, along with a few more grenades. Many of the men made up their place to sleep a little differently, but in general, they knew where their weapon and ammo were located. I finally fell asleep.

I was awakened three hours after I had fallen asleep by a commotion in the foxhole. I got up quickly, grabbing my rifle, ammo, grenades, and, of course, my helmet. I ran to the foxhole as quickly as possible in the dark. I found Killer smacking Warmont alongside his head with his ammo bandolier. Killer hit Warmont in the face three more times and again on the side of his head. It did not take a rocket scientist to figure out that Warmont had fallen asleep again on guard duty.

"OK, Killer, stop hitting him!"

"We are going to die because of him!"

"Killer, what's wrong? Did he fall asleep again?"

Killer stared at Warmont. "He is the stupidest piece of crap I have ever seen. I am going to kill him!"

Killer took his rifle butt and rammed it into Warmont's belly. Warmont folded over. Chuck reached in the foxhole, grabbed Warmont, and threw him out of the hole. "You are an idiot, Warmont!"

Killer started speaking to Warmont. "You listen to me, Warmont. If you fall asleep again tomorrow night, you are dead!"

I was almost feeling sorry for Warmont, but when I thought about it a little longer, I was not sorry for him at all. He had fallen asleep on guard duty too many times before. Killer jumped in the foxhole with an M-79 grenade launcher to take his turn at guard duty. By this time, Killer only had about twenty minutes left of his duty. Warmont had fallen asleep, and his guard time had run over, extending into Killer's time.

"Killer, I am going back to sleep. You take care."

I went back to my poncho liner to get some sleep. I started to lie down when Chuck came over to me. "He is going to get us all killed!"

"I know. He is dumb."

"Danny, someone is going to kill him if he falls asleep again!"

"You really think so, Chuck?"

"Yes. See ya in the morning."

Chuck walked away. If anyone needed to be shot, it was Warmont. He was generally useless. He had no sense of responsibility. He was not a stable individual. I finally drifted back to sleep. An hour later, Chuck woke me up for my guard.

"Anything happening, Chuck?"

"No, nothing. All is calm."

I pulled my shift and then went back to sleep. Morning finally came after another restless night. We opened up cans of C-rations and ate breakfast. Many guys complained about the rations, but I never found them that bad. Lima beans and ham, together in one can, was the only item that I did not care for. Besides, the can was too heavy to carry.

We now had to find an opening for the chopper to land. We could not find a proper LZ (landing zone). We found a very small clearing. We heard the chopper pilot requesting for our exact location. I would always listen to the pilots' voices in hopes of finding another of my best friends, Terry Waggoner. It didn't sound like him. The pilot said, "Let's see smoke, over."

Chuck threw a red smoke grenade to mark the spot. "Smoke out," Chuck said.

"I see red, do you confirm?"

"Red is confirmed. Bring it in."

The first chopper came in quickly at about sixty-five miles per hour. Since there was no place to land, and the worry of being fired upon, they needed to get in and out quickly. The first chopper kicked off eight cases of soda and took off. Another chopper came in and did the same. Many cases were breaking apart, and the sodas were spewing. The choppers made a circle and came back from another direction. The door gunner in each chopper was in the bay, kicking more sodas off. I thought for a quick instance, *Why didn't they kick off all of the sodas on the first pass?*

Then I realized that the door gunners, with two on each side, had very important jobs. In this case, one gunner would unload the cargo from one side while the other gunner stayed behind his mounted or bungee-corded M-60 machine gun, shooting if need be. The choppers would change directions and the gunners would switch places. I would love to be a gunner. But for now, I would be a grunt.

We started picking up the sodas. We split up the sodas. We received six sodas each. Some of my men drank one right away. Warmont, being his stupid self, drank two, never thinking about how thirsty he would be tomorrow. After he drank his two sodas, he started in on a canteen. I motioned for Chuck. "Hey, Chuck, how come Warmont has water left in his canteen? I thought that he was out of water yesterday."

"Emerald was saying that someone stole some of his water last night."

I shook my head. "I think Emerald was right. Well, it is time to move out, Chuck."

Chuck said, "OK, pilgrims, head 'em up and move 'em out." He pointed with his thumb over his shoulder.

"You've been watching too many John Wayne movies, Chuck."

I slapped him on his back. We started moving out, cutting through the bush as we had done for many, many days. Now we had even more problems. I looked around at the men with their rotted clothes. Most of the men's pants had the inseams ripped out. It looked as if they were wearing dresses in lieu of fatigue pants. All of us had cuts and rips in our skin. Everyone had infected areas. I was especially worried about Chuck getting gangrene. More than anything, we needed a river, a stream, or some way of catching water if it would rain. We needed fresh water to drink. We needed to wash out our wounds. And we needed baths really bad.

We traveled again, but no water was in sight. Sodas did not quench our thirst for long. The radio sounded off, "Blackhawk Three, this is Cherokee, over."

"This is Blackhawk Three, go."

"Choppers coming in fast. This is going to be a hot LZ we think."

"OK, we will watch it."

"They have two containers of water and Cokes."

I replied, "Cool. Roger, out."

As I have seen in the past, the water would be in large plastic bladders. Not enough to take a bath, but enough to fill a canteen for each of us. I told my men to get ready to shoot anything that moves. I said, "Watch for the choppers. Don't shoot one down!" I added, "Chuck, Killer, the water is coming, but they say it will be a hot LZ."

Chuck replied, "I haven't even seen a gook today! But we will be ready."

We hear the best sound in the world in the distance — *pop, pop, pop, pop,* as the blades cut through the air. The first ship (chopper) is a gunship. It comes in low with guns and rockets a-blazing. It lights up the tree line like an exploding dynamite factory. The sound is louder than the most extreme rock concert a person could hear. The gunship makes its scrape and makes a sharp left turn. This time the ship is seven to eight feet off of the ground. It starts firing again. This time it opens up with the cannons, the rockets, and what sounds like a .50-caliber. The trees start exploding. I get cold. Cold chills almost overcome me with excitement. There is so much fire and smoke and noise that we cannot see if the ship is being fired upon.

"Here come our choppers, men."

This is the part that I also loved. The two choppers were approximately twenty feet apart and staggered by thirty feet. Each chopper had two door gunners. The gunners opened up with so much firepower and noise, we had to cover our ears. All four gunners were shooting toward the tree line with their M-60s.

As expected, the VC starting firing at the door gunners. The gunners started pounding the bush even more. The shots firing up toward the gunners and the gunners firing down made for lots of excitement. But we could not let the choppers get shot down. I summoned my men with hand signals. Yelling would be useless. I motioned for the men to spread out and start firing. The men were on the ground, lying in the prone position. I ran to each man telling him to keep firing into the tree line but below the choppers.

We wanted that water bad! The choppers seemed to be moving at full speed. It seemed as though they were moving at 100 miles per hour. The gunners kicked off the water and the sodas, but the chopper was too high. We watched as all of the water containers busted and half of the sodas. The gunners and the gunship came back to our position and started more firepower. They did this so we could get to the open field and bring in the cargo that they had just delivered.

The choppers took off for home after we had policed up the sodas and the broken bags of water. Now we were upset. The gooks had caused us not to get our water delivery. We called in artillery in an attempt to kill as many VC or NVA as possible. We blew up the tree line for a solid twenty minutes straight.

Now it was time to divide up the cargo. We divided up what we could find with all the men of the company. It was time now for another hard night. Chuck came over to me with tears in his eyes. "How much can we take? I really mean it, Danny. How much can our men take before they crack?"

"I don't know, Chuck. How is Emerald holding up?"

"I think he is going to crack."

"Well, Sergeant Lewis. It is time to assign guard duty."

"OK, Rock. I'll take care of it."

Chuck walked away downtrodden and discouraged. Guard duty was a necessary evil. Night after night after night, we pulled it. It was a commitment, an obligation, and a liability on our bodies and our minds. We all hated guard duty. I looked over at my men. Something was up. The men were whispering and talking among themselves. I was not included. This certainly puzzled me. *What were they up to?*

I walked over to Chuck. "Hey, Chuck, what's going on?"

Chuck got a big wide grin on his face. "Nothing, Sergeant Rock, nothing."

Now I knew that something was up for sure. Chuck only called me Sergeant Rock in front of the men. When he called me Sergeant Rock away from the men, typically a joke or prank was coming soon. I grinned because I thought that they were going to play a joke on one of the guys. Chuck motioned for me to come closer. "Hey, Rock, if you hear a loud sound tonight, do not pay any attention to it, for it will be friendly."

"Oh, OK. Are you going to scare someone?"

Chuck replied, "Yeah, something like that."

"Time for guard, Chuck."

My guard duty was first. I liked being first for a couple of reasons. One reason is that the men would just be going to sleep and they could wake up more readily in case we were attacked. The second reason was the fact that I could sleep the rest of the night as long as we did not get any incoming rounds.

My guard was up. I took a last scan of the area in front of me to be sure all is well, and then quietly walked over to where Chuck was sleeping. I placed my hand on his shoulder and said, "Your turn, buddy."

Chuck jumped right up like he was going to receive an ice-cold soft drink, or in his case, a cold beer. *What was he up to?* Chuck was like the rest of us; he hated to get up. I gave it a little more thought, then I started setting up my place to sleep. I set up my ammo belt with grenades and canteens spread apart to make a place to lay my head. I did the typical preparation for the sleep I hoped to get.

At three-thirty a big blast sounded off. I grabbed my rifle, ammo, and hardhat, keeping low to the ground so I would not get shot. I headed for the foxhole. Emery was running toward the foxhole. Eckert was moving quickly toward some cover. Something was wrong. Chuck, White, Emerald, Brant, and Killer were not scrambling for their rifles. My heart sank. They were dead; all of my good friends had been killed.

I jumped in the hole with the others and noticed that Warmont was slumped over, lying on his face. He was bleeding badly. Half of his back was ripped off, and it looked as though his arm was going to fall off. I took his poncho liner, what was left of it, and covered his back. I was getting prepared for more incoming grenades to be thrown or incoming mortars, but nothing more happened. It was quiet — no more booms, no more explosions. I climbed out of the foxhole and went over to see what I could do for Chuck and the other men. They, to my surprise, were sitting up with smiles on their faces. They were not even alarmed. "You guys aren't shot or fragged?" I asked.

"No, we are just fine. How is Warmont, the guard duty sleeper?" one of them asked.

It now dawned on me. One of my men had thrown a grenade in the foxhole where Warmont was probably sleeping. I had mixed feelings of the actions of my men. Warmont would surely get us killed if something was not done about his sleeping. I did not accept the actions of my men. However, in wartimes, atrocities happen. In Vietnam, we had to adapt to this different kind of reality. I must keep my men in check.

"Eckert, go get Doc!" I yelled.

Eckert hustled to find Doc.

Eckert showed up with Doc. "Who is hurt, Sarge?"

"It's Warmont. He is in the hole."

Doc runs to the foxhole. I looked at Chuck and the men. "OK, men, let's talk."

At that moment, the radio sounded, "Blackhawk Three, this is Annihilator Three-Three, over."

"This is Blackhawk Three, we received one incoming round, over."

The captain replied, "I didn't hear the mortar sound that goes along with a mortar round. Was it a grenade?"

"Affirmative."

"Was anyone hurt?"

"Affirmative. I have the Doc here now."

"Keep me informed. We are going to pepper the perimeter, out!"

If the captain finds out what my guys have done, I will be in trouble. The captain called in the artillery to pepper the surrounding area. After fifteen minutes, the pounding stops. I look at my men. "Now let's talk!"

Killer is the first to speak. "Did Warmont fall asleep on guard duty again and a VC got him?"

Chuck looks at the men. "That is what happens to you when you fall asleep in Sergeant Rock's squad!"

The men all laughed. White said, "Maybe we will get a good replacement for him."

After hearing these comments, I knew deep inside that Warmont was wounded by friendly fire. We sure wasted a bunch of artillery peppering the area, shooting at nothing. "Men, I want you to listen up. Do you guys know what a moral compass is?"

"Yes," the men said.

"Before you guys do anything like that again, and don't deny it, just look at your moral compass."

Doc returned with Warmont. Doc had wrapped his back and ribs with white wraps and taped his arm to his body. "I am going to take him to the CP. We will have to lift him out tomorrow. I'll be back in a minute. Will you get someone to help me carry him?"

"Sure, who wants to help?"

There was some hesitation, and then Killer stood. "I'll help him."

He grabbed one side of Warmont and guided him to the CP. Doc said, "Be back in a minute, Rock."

Doc was a medic. He was not a real doctor. Sometimes we would call out for a medic in time of need, but when we were face to face, we called the medics "Doc." Doc was a really big guy — 250 pounds and six feet, four inches tall. He was from Mississippi. Every chance he would get, he would come to my squad and we would talk. I knew the names of his brothers and sisters, the names of his nieces and nephews, his mom's name, the food he liked and disliked. He liked the things I liked. We both loved cars and engines. He was more than a friend; he was like a brother to me. A captain told me one time, "Don't get too close to your men." I could not help it; I loved these guys like brothers. I did not consider all of my men my brothers. Warmont was one that I did not like much. I was actually glad to see Warmont leave the squad. Sooner or later, he would have gotten all of us killed.

Emery motioned for me to move away from the men. "Sergeant Rock, did our guys do that to Warmont, or do you think it was a VC?"

"I don't think it was a gook. I don't know for sure."

"He deserved it, didn't he?"

"Sure he did. He was a joke. I hope he never comes back to the field."

Vietnam was making us hard. In normal circumstances, a person would feel a little sorry for Warmont, but we didn't. I hope that the way I feel now is just an isolated case. I had to be tough, but I wanted to have feelings. I will never know if Killer or someone else threw a grenade in the hole. When people asked me what happened, I could only give my standard answer. I could only state the facts. "I was asleep. A hand grenade landed in the foxhole where Warmont was pulling guard."

"Was he asleep?" most people would ask.

"Most likely, he was asleep," I would answer.

The rain started to fall. We grabbed what we could and tried to catch the falling water. I had placed my helmet upside down just below a tree with big leaves. While the water dropped in our hardhats, we looked to the sky with our mouths opened, getting as much water as possible. Fifteen minutes, and the rain stopped. I looked in my hardhat and had enough water for a third of a canteen. Daybreak came, and we were getting ready to move out again.

Lieutenant Gibbons came to our location. He saw Chuck's pants that had no inseam. The pants look like a skirt. "Sergeant Lewis, I have an extra pair of pants. Do you want them?"

"Yes, sir!" Chuck said with excitement, "Thank you, sir."

Gibbons nodded as if to say, "You're welcome." Chuck simply pulled the waistband of his pants and the pants fell to the ground, ripping apart. Chuck, like most of us, did not wear underwear beneath his fatigue pants. The underwear would bunch up and, in general, it made it too hot. Modesty was not in abundance in the 'Nam. Chuck was exposing it all.

Brant said, "Sergeant Lewis, go ahead and wear your birthday suit."

Killer said, "No way! That white butt would be like a beacon. Every VC in Vietnam would be shooting at us."

Chuck laughed as he slipped on his new pants. It had now been forty-four days since we'd had a bath or any real amount of water to drink. We are losing even more weight. Our skin is getting worse as infection sets in. The stink of our bodies is getting terrible. We cannot take time to nurse our wounds. We have to find an LZ to lift off Warmont.

My men take turns helping Warmont through the jungle. The map shows a large opening that would be just right for an LZ. We humped for a few hours and found the area. It was a very large rice paddy. The water was very hot and had a strong smell to it. Brant asked me, "Do you think the water is safe to drink?"

"I don't know for sure, but look to see if anything is swimming in it."

In general, if there is life in the water, it may be safe to drink. I told the men to be certain to put a purification tablet in the canteen and wait fifteen to thirty minutes before drinking the water. White and Emery started filling their canteens and drinking the water without the tablets. I filled two canteens and added some Kool-Aid that my family had sent me. I added the purification tablets next. The Kool-Aid would lessen the bad taste of the water. We set up our perimeter, waiting for the lift off. We started hearing the chopper in the distance. The lieutenant started a conversation with the chopper pilot. "Boomerang One-Two, this is Cherokee Three, over."

"Cherokee Three, how about smoke?"

Cherokee's RTO threw out a grenade of blue smoke.

"I see blue, over."

"Affirmative."

The chopper started to come in, but I noticed that it was not marked as a med-vac or hospital ship. In war, the soldiers are not supposed to shoot at a hospital ship. However, many times the NVA and the VC have tried to shoot them down. The chopper got closer to the lift off point and started receiving fire. The door gunners start firing back ten-fold of what they were receiving. The chopper cannot land until we secure the LZ.

We got on line and started firing furiously. For three minutes we fire our weapons. "Cease fire! Cease fire!" we hear.

The captain believes the gooks are on the run. I yell to my men, "Cease fire! Cease fire!"

A few more rounds, and the shooting stops. The area seems to be secure. The chopper comes in again. The door gunners are not shooting, but they are on high alert. The chopper is moving at five miles an hour and two feet above the wet rice paddy. Warmont is thrown on the chopper. It takes off, and the door gunners start firing with a vengeance. The tracers are flying toward the ground into the tree line. We see a tracer round from the tree line go up and hit the chopper. We open up on the tree line and the jungle with our weapons, firing full force. The incoming fire on the chopper has stopped. The chopper is heading back to a base camp somewhere in the 'Nam.

Brant asks, "If the dust-off was marked, do you think it would have received incoming fire?"

"Yes! These gooks don't care about the rules of war."

"Good riddance to one piece of trash," someone says.

I knew that they were speaking of Warmont. Killer says, "He will probably fall asleep and fall out of the chopper."

All of us laughed. "OK, men, enough about Warmont. It is time to start moving again."

We started humping through the jungle. White and Emery start throwing up. They have diarrhea and they are grabbing at their stomachs. I realize that they are sick as a result of drinking the bad water before they put a purification tablet in it. I walked over to them. "You two suck it up. We are moving out."

During the day, I drank one of my sodas and some of my water. I started feeling a little sick from the water but not near as much as some of the other men. We arrived at the top of a mountain just before dark. We set up our perimeter in a very large circle. We could see the valley below. It would be hard for the enemy to attack us. I felt comfortable with our location.

"Sergeant Lewis, will you set up guard?"

Chuck and I would goof around with formalities with one another just to keep our spirits up. "Sure, Sergeant Rock."

Chuck continued to set up guard as he had done so many times before. We ate our delicious C-ration meal, and after that, we sat around and simply talked to one another. After shooting the bull with the men for a while, I decided to try to get some needed sleep. During the night, we are awakened by artillery fire. The artillery was not being shot at us. There is an intense firefight in the valley below. It was hard to tell our men from the enemy. Chuck is eating a can of pound cake from his C-rations. "Who is winning, Danny?"

"I think we are, based on where the shells are hitting. We will find out in the morning. That's where we will be heading."

Chuck replies sarcastically, "Oh, great!"

The firefight lasted most of the night. Daybreak came, and we started moving out. We were cautiously moving in the direction of the battle. I hoped to see a lot of dead VC. While heading down the hill, Chuck comes close to me. "Hey, Rock, what about water?"

"Do you mean rivers or choppers?"

"Yeah, both."

"Well, there are no rivers or streams on the map. Maybe a chopper today."

Killer overheard the conversation. "I never thought that I would say it, but I am getting tired of this hot beer. This hot beer is hurting my gut."

We finally got closer to the battleground. We saw a body in the distance, then another. We walked closer. They were

American soldiers. I could count thirty, but there were more. There were fifty or more NVA and ten or more VC. We checked all of the bodies, including the enemy, to be certain they were dead. We hoped for American survivors, but there were none. We checked the gooks and found all were dead. After gathering up the weapons, we did something that I never dreamed we would do. We took the canteens from our American soldiers and drank their water. The water tasted much fresher than the water from the rice paddies. Chuck came over to me. "Danny, do you think it would be OK to take their clothes?"

"Man, Chuck, it would be sort of morbid! But all of us need fatigues. I guess it would be alright."

My pants and shirt were ripped to pieces. My pants had almost rotted off. My pants had no insides between my legs. I was wearing a skirt like so many others. I started looking for a dead soldier that was my size. I also needed clothes that did not have a lot of blood on them. I wanted a shirt and pants with no holes. I was picky because I only wanted to remove the clothes from a dead body one time and one time only.

I found a shirt that only had a few shrapnel holes in it. I could not use the pants because they had too much blood on them, and there was a leg missing. I took the shirt. I found a body with chest wounds. The pants had a small amount of blood on them but very few rips. Removing the trousers was much harder than the shirt. I had to try to get the pants over the boots and pull them off. I had to turn the body over several times to free the pants. Each time that I turned the body, I turned it with respect. I hated what I was doing.

I finally had a shirt and a pair of pants in my hand. I changed my clothes and felt much better. I also took a few more canteens of water. Most of the guys could not find a clean pair of pants. When most men are killed, they crap their pants because their bowel muscles relax. The lieutenant approached. His pants were split out in the rear. His bare butt was sticking out.

"Hey, Sergeant Lewis, I want my pants back!"

"No way, sir! No way! You are going to have to borrow a pair from these bodies!"

"I can't do that. It will make me sick. OK, Lewis, I will remember you."

Gibbons left us and started looking at the bodies as he walked. Vietnam is taking a toll on us. We are doing, in my opinion, unspeakable things.

My radio sounds off. "Blackhawk Three, we are going to take a break until we get word on what to do with the bodies, out."

I sat back and relaxed. I found myself trying to figure out the time difference between the 'Nam and Houston, Texas. I wanted to know when it was nine o'clock in Houston, because my family prayed for me every single night at that time. While they prayed for me, I prayed for them. Many times, I would feel a strong impulse to just thank God for my great family. I drifted back to times when each of my four brothers would make me laugh. I thought of my mother and her sharp wit. My brothers and I would wonder what my mom would do next for a laugh. She was always playing a joke on us boys. My dad would fall out of his chair with laughter from my mom's shenanigans. He was always up for a good prank. Dad would play jokes on my mom for payback. What a great family I have. I came out of my daydream and said a little prayer. I thanked God for allowing us to make it through another day.

Chuck saw me thinking. "What are you thinking about, Danny?"

"The usual, Chuck."

"What is that? When we are going to get a bath?"

I grinned. "No, home."

Chuck looked at me. "Don't you wish that you had a big glass of iced tea? And you know how sometimes you take that big glass and tilt it up too high and all of that tea runs down your chin and all over your chest? Man, that would be nice!"

"Yes, and my mom puts a lemon mix in ours. What a taste."

Chuck is going through the rucksacks of a few of the dead soldiers. "Hey, this guy has Kool-Aid."

He throws me a pack. "This Kool-Aid has sugar in it. It will make that water taste better."

Any kind of flavoring helps the taste of rice paddy water. The radio sounds, "Blackhawk Three, choppers will be coming in with supplies, and then we will load the dead."

"Affirmative, we will be ready."

We started hearing *pop, pop, pop, pop* — the sounds of the choppers getting louder. The choppers started coming in. As the choppers landed, we would unload C-rations, sodas, and a little water. After we unloaded the small amount of water and supplies, we would start loading the American soldiers. We made sure that no more than six bodies per chopper were loaded. Loading bodies was becoming routine. I was getting accustomed to the way that we did it, but I hated every minute of it. It was always a rotten feeling to see your fellow Americans being loaded like that. We were supposed to place the soldiers' dog tags in his mouth, but this was hard to do in many cases. Sometimes the mouth would be shut. It would be hard to open. I did not even try to force the mouth open.

Before loading the soldiers, we were supposed to find the missing arm or leg and place it with the body. I would simply grab the closest limb and place it with the body. Most of the time, I felt that I was correct. Again, this was an eerie, creepy, and weird feeling. I wanted to finish this job as fast as I could. Sometimes, while performing this activity, my stomach would start hurting, and many times, I would vomit.

The bodies were loaded. Now it is time to start looking over the gooks. The VC had already policed (searched) the bodies. The only things that we found were canteens and a few bandoliers of ammo.

Brant approaches. "Hey, Sarge, here is some more water."

He was holding up two canteens. "Did you pull that off of a gook?"

"Yes!"

"No! Pour that out. The VC probably poisoned them. Never drink gook water!"

Brant poured the water out. My radio sounds, "Blackhawk Three, we will be moving out in ten, over."

"Affirmatron," I replied.

Although I gave an affirmative answer, I had some questions on my mind. *Why did we have to load another company's bodies? Why can't we get some clean clothes? Why can't we get fresh water?* I was fed up with this crap. I told my guys, "I am fed up! This has got to stop. I am going to see Gibbons."

I walked briskly to the lieutenant. Gibbons could see that I was mad. "What's on your mind, Sarge?"

"Sir, do I have your permission to talk freely?"

"Yes you do."

"Sir, why can't these bodies be policed by their own company? Why can't we get any clothes? Why can't we get fresh water?"

"OK, Sergeant Rock, one at a time. These dead soldiers are from Bravo Company. They have been nearly wiped out. They don't have enough men to secure the area. Many are wounded. We can't get fresh clothes because every base camp has been hit hard. We can't get fresh water for the same reason."

"That is stupid, sir. I am not buying it! I don't think the captain is telling the rear what is going on here. Somebody just doesn't give a flying flip about us!"

"Well, Rock, that is what the captain is telling us. I agree with you. How often did you get a change of clothes before I got here?"

"Once a week," I answered.

"How about water?"

"We would usually run across a river or stream, but if we didn't, we would get water the next day."

"I'll tell you if I hear more."

"Thanks, sir."

I turned and headed back to my men. We started moving. We humped and pulled guard another day, another night, then another, and more. We were getting very weary and exhausted. I am glad that we have had only few skirmishes with the enemy. It was getting almost dark, so we stopped for the night. We would simply fall to the ground, leaning back on our rucksacks, resting for a while before digging in for the night.

Emery asked, "Sergeant Rock, do you know how long it's been since we had Gibbons take over?"

"Who gives a flying flip?" Killer says.

I responded, "Too long, why?"

Emery looks at all of us. "It has been fifty-six days."

"Who cares?" Killer responds.

Emery looks at Killer. "That is how long it has been since we have had a bath or seen a stream or river. It was when Gibbons took over."

I respond, "Oh, you can't blame this on Gibbons; he is hurting just like us."

Suddenly a round rips through the bushes. We are tired, but not so tired that we can't grab our hardhats and weapons and hit the ground. Killer says, "Here we go again. Why couldn't we have Warmont for a scarecrow? Maybe we would not get shot at!"

We all laughed. Another shot rips. We open up our weapons, firing on full automatic in the direction of the snipers. I start commanding, "Killer, get over to the right flank. Chuck, go to the left. Emery, go to the back. White, you and the radio come with me."

I moved closer to where I thought the rifle sound had come from. I hear from the radio the captain calling in artillery. The shells hit all the way around our perimeter for five minutes. We know that the bullets came from a sniper. I turned toward my men. "The little coward probably shot at us then jumped back in his VC tunnel! Our artillery probably never even touched him."

I look over at the men and I see that Brant is bleeding. "Brant, you are hit! Your cheek is bleeding bad!"

"I feel alright, Sarge."

"I am going to get the doc anyway."

"I'll get him!" White says as he sprints away.

Doc shows up. "Rock, what's up?"

"It's Brant!"

Doc looks at Brant. "What happened?"

"The second sniper round hit me."

Doc looks puzzled. "Open your mouth! Does it hurt?"

"Not really."

Doc gets his surgical tool that looks like a long and skinny pair of pliers. "Hold still, Brant! There is something lodged in your cheek. It's a bullet! It is actually a bullet in your mouth! Now open wide."

Doc pulls the round out of Brant's mouth with the pliers. Doc hands it to Brant. "You are a lucky son-of-a-gun, Brant."

I look at Doc and Brant. "How could that have happened, Doc?"

"I don't know, Rock, maybe a ricochet."

"Yeah, it had to be, because a straight shot would have blown his jaw off."

Doc turns to Brant. "I'll get you out of here tomorrow."

"No way, Doc. Rock needs me!"

Brant was just saying what he thought I wanted to hear. He was worn out like the rest of us. I looked at Brant's now-taped up cheek. "You get to the rear and get that taken care of. That will get infected out here."

Brant said, "OK, Sarge, I'll do that."

"And another thing, Brant. Save that bullet. It will be something to tell your kids one day. Someday, I will write a book, and you and the bullet will be in it."

"That will be cool, Sarge."

We set up the perimeter for the night. My radio went off, "Blackhawk Three, this is Cherokee Three, over."

"This is Blackhawk Three, go."

"Blackhawk, come to the CP, out!"

I walked to the CP, wondering what was going on as I walked. Lieutenant Gibbons had a grin on his face. "What's happening, sir?"

Gibbons placed his hands on my shoulders. "Finally, finally, we are going to get water and clothes tomorrow."

"That is great, sir."

"You are also going to get a replacement for Warmont, and Brant will be lifted out. Go tell your men."

"Yes, sir."

I moved quickly back to my squad. I told the men about the good news. They were relieved. I could see it in their faces. White said, "Let's set up guard duty."

This was unusual for White to sort of take command. Chuck, who usually set guard, said, "OK, White, what do you suggest?"

White assigned the duty. His assignments were fine. We started taking turns. No excitement during the night. Morning came, and we were getting ready for the choppers. We could hear the choppers' distinguished sounds. The best sound in the world, as far as we were concerned. The choppers came in, but they were getting fired upon. This was now a hot LZ. The door gunners started clearing out the tree line. They made a pass and got out of harm's way. We then started our typical firing and calling in artillery. The artillery dropped shells for ten minutes. I don't know how anyone could live through the bombardment. I think the shells hit every square inch for a half mile. The choppers returned with the gunners firing fast and furious. They had no retaliation this time around.

The choppers would make another circle, keeping very low to the trees, and land in the LZ. We unloaded the water, the fatigues, and the C-rations, beer, and sodas. It was a good day, we thought. Fifty-seven days in the same clothes, and now we can change into clean fatigues. I had made a change of clothes with one of our dead soldiers, but I felt creepy in them, and besides, they were starting to stink. Two men jumped off the chopper and ran to our tree line, keeping their heads low. The incoming firing started again. The gunners opened up. We started firing as fast as we could. We had plenty of ammo now. The choppers had dropped it off with the rest of the supplies. Something was wrong. One of the choppers was smoking and spinning out of control. The chopper crashed on its side in the enemy's tree line. My radio sounds, "Cherokee Three, this is Annihilator Three-Three. Take your men to the chopper and see what you can do!"

"Affirmative, out."

The lieutenant calls me. "Blackhawk Three, did you hear?"

"Yes, we are ready for your go."

"Take squad two and bring the men back."

"We are on our way."

We had renewed strength, just knowing that we had water and food waiting for us when we returned. We ran across the rice paddies to the chopper. We located the men. The chopper pilot and one of the door gunners were hurt. The co-pilot and the other gunner were not harmed. We helped the men from the chopper. The two men that were hurt could walk, with help from my men. The helicopter was totaled. "We need to get to our perimeter," I told the chopper crew.

The pilot said, "We need to dismantle the guns and blow up the bird."

I looked at the guns. "Gunner, can you take them off?"

"Sure, we are using only bungee cords to hold the Pigs in place!"

He hopped inside. We carried the guns and ammo to safety. We helped the pilots and gunners to safety. It was time to call in artillery. A few rounds hit, and then we walked them in on the chopper. The chopper was hit by two rounds and was destroyed.

"Blackhawk Three, this is Cherokee Three. We have choppers coming in to pick up their men."

"I'll get them ready."

I started speaking to the chopper crew. "Hey, guys, do any of you know a warrant officer named Waggoner? His first name is Terry. He is my wife's cousin and one of my best friends."

"Yes we do. He was shot down south of Saigon."

"Was he killed?"

"No, I don't think so."

"I think his base is called Bearcat or something like that. His call sign is Boomerang something, I think. Here comes your ride."

The choppers start coming in. There are three of them. We escort the men to the choppers. They load in, along with the guns and ammo. I tap them all on the helmets to say goodbye and good luck. We ran back to safety.

It was a good day; no one killed. We had food, water, and clothes. We saved the lives of two chopper pilots and two door gunners. I had a new man named Raymond. Maybe things were looking up.

CHAPTER 7

Proud Mary

It was a very hard fifty-seven days. When I was home in the USA, I took a shower every day and changed clothes every day. I even wore underwear. Over here in the 'Nam, it was a different life.

White walked over to me. "Sergeant Rock, Cherokee wants to talk to you."

He handed me the radio handset. "This is Blackhawk Three, over."

"I am sending you your new man."

"Affirmative," I replied.

We were still short a man because Brant had been taken to the hospital. I sure hoped that Brant would return soon. He was a great fighter and a good shot. He was our company sniper, and now we had to find a new sniper. He never complained about carrying the M-14 rifle. The M-14 was much heavier than the M-16 rifle, which most of us carried. The ammo was heavier. The M-14 would get caught in the bush because it was also longer than the M-16 weapon.

"Blackhawk Three, this is Cherokee Three, over."

"This is Blackhawk Three, go."

"I have the sniper rifle; find a man to carry it!"

"Affirmative, I'll send a man to pick it up."

I turned to Eckert. "Go to the CP and grab the M-14!"

He took off. Eckert brought the M-14 back with him within a few minutes. "OK, men, now we have to find a sniper!"

A few of the men could shoot very well, but I received no volunteers because of the extra weight of the rifle and ammo. I did not blame them, for I didn't want to carry the gun either.

"Alright, men, I will carry it. I hope that I shoot six VC today, and then all of you will want to be a sniper!"

For the time being, I had to carry both my M-16 and the sniper rifle. The new guy walked up. Chuck said, "Here we go, Sergeant Rock. Let the new guy carry the M-14."

"No, I am not going to put that load on a new guy."

I looked at the new guy. He was a black guy about five feet, eight inches tall. He was from Nigeria or someplace like that. His speech did not have the typical American accent. He had a thick accent. He looked at the M-14. "I have no problem in carrying the rifle. I will do it if you want."

"No, but thanks anyhow. What's your last name?"

"Raymond."

"Glad to meet you, Raymond. I am Sergeant Rock. This is Sergeant Lewis. You have already met Eckert. White is over there sitting by Emery. You will meet the other guys later."

Killer walked up to us. "Hey, Killer, this is Raymond."

They shook hands. Killer says, "Hey, Sergeant Rock, since I have been here, all that I have seen is killing and misery. Does anything happen in the field that is funny?"

Chuck says, "Tell him about Proud Mary, Rock. We have a little bit of time before we move out."

I laughed. "You might have thought it was funny, but I didn't."

White says, "Go ahead, Sarge, tell him about it; I don't mind."

I began to tell the story.

"We were North of Da Nang, about twenty miles. We had previously been in a firefight for two days straight. After we had annihilated the VC, my squad had to search for VC bodies. We had orders to find out where and how they were killed. Our platoon leader was called Blackhawk at this time. We ran across a fresh mound of dirt like a grave.

"I asked White to hand me the horn, and I started speaking. 'Blackhawk, this is Blackhawk Three, over.'

"'This is Blackhawk, go.'

"'We found what looks like a grave. It has been freshly dug and covered over.'

"'Stand by, Blackhawk Three!'

"I knew that the lieutenant was going to check with the captain about digging up the grave. I was sure hoping that we would not have to do any digging.

"'Blackhawk Three, dig it up!'

"Reluctantly, I said, 'Affirmative, we are on it.'

"White, Lewis, and I took off our equipment, ammo, and rifles and laid them on the ground near the head of the grave. We started digging in the dirt and placing it to either side. I placed the rest of my squad in the tree line about 100 feet away. The grave was in the open with no protection. If we were hit by enemy fire while in the open, we would be in real trouble. As we dug, the ground started to get harder. This made me think that the grave was not as fresh as I had told the lieutenant. After an hour or so, we reached the body.

"Normally, White did not like digging. I remembered a few times when he had been humping through the jungle all day with twenty-eight pounds of C-rations, five pounds of ammo, a rifle, canteens and more. After cutting with a machete, and he would not dig a foxhole. I would tell him that if he didn't dig a foxhole, he would be left out in a firefight. Sure enough, when we would get a few rounds, he would be the first to jump in the hole that others had dug.

"But this digging was different to him. Digging this grave was enticing to White. He was digging like there was a pot of gold a few feet down. We found the body. As we dug, exposing more of the body, White reached down and pulled the soiled rags from the body. The rags, at one time, were the gook's clothing. White had no problem, mentally, with pulling the terrible smelling, disgusting rags from around and off the top of the body. He was trying to find out what had killed the thing in the grave.

"It looked like a large bloated whale, but it was a human. We started looking for holes in the body. I started examining the head, being careful to only move it with my rifle. The clothes that were left on the body were stretched tight. They were a lot tighter than the usual bodies we found. I am starting to gag, but I cannot show weakness to my guys. Hopefully, the men are pulling guard and not watching me get sick.

"The smell was getting worse. Worse than any corpse we had ever found. The odor was even worse than the smell that came after we had cooked a VC with napalm. I took the dull bayonet and started cutting the clothing from the body. I started cutting at the stomach and the chest area. The stomach and the chest were the two areas that would generally show a wound. I made just a small cut in the cloth and it started ripping apart by itself. Every time a section of cloth would be removed, the stink would get even worse.

"The body started to move. It was starting to grow, like a balloon being filled with helium coming from a compressed air tank. Now my legs were trapped between the side of the grave and the ever-pressing body. White saw what was happening to the body. He tried to jump from the grave in an attempt to get free of the creature, when he slipped and fell backwards. White's right arm and shoulder were now between the legs of the expanding body. His head was against the side of the grave and being covered by the growing stomach. His legs were above the grave, keeping him from getting leverage to get free. I started to laugh at White. I was in a strange predicament myself, but his was even worse.

"With some pushing and shoving, I freed myself and started to help White. White took a little longer to get free. I had to grab his left arm and pull it, while pushing his legs back in the grave.

Now he had the leverage to completely free himself. White laughs. 'What a bad deal! It is time for lunch.'

"We had not found the cause of the creature's death yet, but it could wait for a few more minutes. Our rucksacks were close to the grave; therefore, White, Chuck, and I would be eating lunch at the gravesite. I wanted to get away from the grave for lunch, but I had to stay so I did not look like a sissy. We sat with our feet dangling in the hole. White would let his feet kick the body every couple of strokes. I was eating a can of pork and beans. We were looking at the body and laughing at our ordeal. White says, 'What a story we can tell our children someday!'

"Of course none of us had any children yet. I looked at Chuck, 'Hey, Chuck, where were you when me and White were trapped?'

"'I was throwing up.'

"We laughed. 'Chuck, go tell the men that we will be moving out in thirty minutes or less!'

"Chuck replies, 'I'll be happy to get away from this smell.'

"He ran to the tree line. We were not quite finished with lunch when I decided to investigate the body further. I thought, 'What had killed this person?'

"I pulled the cloth from the head and face. I found that part of the skull, just behind the ear, was missing. A large piece of metal, the size of a sliced grapefruit, was lodged in the skull. It was apparent that this was shrapnel. This was great. All we had to do now was call the lieutenant and let him know. 'Blackhawk, this is Blackhawk Three, over.'

"The lieutenant's RTO answered, 'This is Blackhawk X-ray, go.'

"'We found the cause of the Victor Charlie's death. It is shrapnel, go.'

"The RTO replied, 'Annihilator wants to talk to you directly. He will be calling you in five, out.'

"From my previous experiences with the captain, I know he will want details. 'Blackhawk Three, this is Annihilator Three-Three, over.'

"'This is Blackhawk Three, over.'

"'What caused the death?'

"'It was shrapnel.'

"'Can you see it? Bring it to me!'

"I paused. 'I will check it out further, over.'

"'Keep me informed. We need all of the intelligence we can get.'

"I liked the captain, but I was not going to fumble around with this body any longer.

"I turned to White. 'The old man wants us to pull the shrapnel from the body. Do you want to do it?'

"'No way, Sarge! That would be a lot of work. No thanks!'

"I called the old man. 'Annihilator Three-Three, this is Blackhawk Three, over.'

"'This is Annihilator Three-Three, over.'

"'There was no metal to be found in the body, but it was obvious that shrapnel had blown away part of the head.'

"'Affirmative. Is it male or female?'

"'The body is so bloated that we cannot tell.'

"'Find out and get back to me.'

"White looked at me. 'What does he want now?'

"'He wants to know if it is male or female. Man, White, the body is too bloated to tell us the sex.'

"'Just tell him anything, Sarge.'

"'No, not yet.'

"I climbed back in the hole to make another feeble attempt, because the captain was a very tough guy. I had all of the respect in the world for him. I took off the rest of the rags from the chest to see breasts, or maybe none. Once the chest clothes were removed, we still could not tell the sex, for the body was too swollen in that area also. What was left to do was the obvious. We needed to look between the legs. The belly was lapped over the private parts. I placed the bayonet on my rifle and started cutting away the soiled rags from between the legs. I could only see a small amount of cloth on either side of the private part. The bayonet was dull and made it difficult to free the cloth from the body. The body was very tight and filled with gasses in this area. I freed the cloth, and the body moved again. The gasses were shifting inside the creature. I started poking gently with my rifle, trying to discover more. White was growing impatient. With his annoying, smart-mouth laugh, he jumped into the grave beside me with his bayonet in hand. 'There is only one way to find out the sex!'

"White jammed his bayonet hard between the legs of the body. White yelled, 'Oh heck!'

"He quickly pulled the bayonet out. We were both scrambling to get out of the grave. The body was releasing all of the gases that it had been holding. It was as big as a small cow and was now deflating. We were choking. Our eyes were watering. White started throwing up. I looked at him. 'Serves you right, you idiot.'

"Now I knew that there was a stink in life or death worse than the stink I had encountered just ten minutes ago. White was still throwing up his guts. I decided to finish my lunch just to make White even sicker. I sat on the side of the grave, eating my pork and beans lunch. Every time he looked at me, he would vomit. I, myself, could hardly keep my lunch down. I did not finish my food because the gases from the body had now mixed with the pork and beans mixture, or maybe it just seemed like it. I looked at White as I threw my food away. 'You are stupid, White!'

"White replied, 'At least we now know that it is a girl.'

"'It is not a girl. It is an older woman.'

"'What should we name her, Sarge?'

"'What?'

"'She needs a name. Let's call her Mary. Let's call her Proud Mary, like the song!'

"I shook my head in disbelief. 'You are an idiot, White, an idiot!'

"I looked in the grave, wondering what we were doing. When I signed up for Vietnam, I never thought I would be digging up bodies. I started to speak to White again when we start getting shot at.

"The shots were coming from three different directions. My men started firing back. White has his rucksack and his rifle strapped to his back. He reaches down, grabs my rifle, and runs 100 feet away to the tree line perimeter. White has left me in the open without a way to defend myself. The bullets are hitting the fresh dirt that we had just dug up. Rounds are hitting the sides of the grave. I yelled to White, 'White, you bring back my rifle, and I mean now!'

"He says in his usual manor, 'Are you crazy? Jump in with Proud Mary.'

"I wanted to kill White on the spot. I jumped back in the grave with the body. I wedged myself between the bloated body and the side of the grave. The body, now, had meaning to me. Proud Mary could protect me from death. Proud Mary's skin was cold. Most of the skin was still tight, but it was starting to loosen. The skin was loose around the arms and wrists. As the gas was running out of her body, she was getting smaller. I could feel every inch of my own skin tighten up as I lay there beside the body. This was a horrible feeling. I yelled to White over and over again, 'I am going to kill you!'

"Now, I heard the big bass drum sounds. The booming sounds, like large elephants stomping on the ground. I had heard this sound many times before in the 'Nam. It was mortars. Now I began to worry. The snipers were generally just bothersome. They had poor weapons, and they were bad shots. Usually, they were nothing to worry about. But these guys were serious. They had mortars. The mortars were getting closer and closer. They were walking the mortars in toward our position. Before long, they would be right on top of us. I did not want to die in a grave with a fat gook lying next to me. I wanted to strangle White with my bare hands. I yelled to him, 'White! Don't get killed because I am going to kill you myself!'

"I heard a slight laugh from Chuck. Chuck tells White, 'Watch out! He means what he says!'

"We heard artillery hitting in the direction that the mortars were coming from. Another company had called in the fire strike on the gooks. After thirty-five minutes of being in the grave, which felt like an eternity, the firefight was over. I jumped out of the grave. I took after White with the vengeance and rage of a mad dog. White saw me and started running. He held my rifle behind him as if to hand it to me. I caught him and like the song goes, 'Then from a blow of a big right hand, he sent a fellow to the promised land.' These were not the exact words of the song, but they were the words that I was thinking.

"I popped White in the mouth with such a hard blow that it knocked him over Chuck. I pulled him to his feet and hit him again. He fell to the ground. Chuck grabbed me as White was getting to his feet. I broke loose from Chuck's grasp and went after him again. I made another attempt to knock him out. He fell to the ground, and I jumped on top of him. Chuck and another one of my men were pulling me off. I finally stopped trying to rearrange his face. I looked around and found my M-16 rifle. As I was checking out my rifle for damage, White started pulling himself from the thorn bushes. He started talking while wiping the blood from his face. 'Sergeant Rodgers, I did not realize that I had my rifle strapped to my back. I grabbed yours by mistake. I thought it was mine. I am truly sorry.'

"I turned to White. 'What have you learned today, White? And don't be cute or I'll kick your butt again.'

"My blood was starting to boil again as I looked at him. I knew that he was going to come up with some smart-butt remark. I was ready to jump him again. Today, in my opinion, he was a big-mouthed piece of crap. 'This is what I have learned — never take another guy's weapon, especially yours. Make sure

I always know where my weapon is located. And I learned that your fist hitting my face felt like I was being kicked by a mule.'

"I never apologized to White for that day, but somehow, we started getting closer toward one another. He stopped being so much of a big jerk.

"My radio sounded, 'Blackhawk Three, this is Annihilator Three-Three. Are you guys OK?'

"'Affirmative, just snipers and mortars.'

"'What sex was the Victor Charlie?'

"'No Victor Charlie. It was female!'

"'See me when you return!'

"'Affirmative.'

"We started moving to the location of the rest of the company. I say to the men, 'Men, be real careful, because there will probably be VC between the CP and us. Watch out for an ambush. Eckert, take point!'

"We move out, being very careful and quiet. Eckert was at point, White next, then Chuck, Jacop, me, and Johns. I did not know Jacop and Johns all that well. Jacop had just come to me by way of another squad from a company that had been wiped out. He had only been in my squad for two weeks. Johns had just arrived five weeks ago from the USA. They both seemed to be very good soldiers. Johns, like many of us, had just gotten married before he was sent to Vietnam. We would joke with each other about how stupid we were for getting married before getting drafted. He was dumber than I, for he had a child on the way. Johns and the squad had been in a few firefights together against the VC. He would listen to me speak on the radio during a firefight, calling in artillery. He watched as I commanded my men in times of battle. This made me feel very good, for he was trying to learn. I would try even harder when he was watching not to make mistakes. We would talk every night about grid coordinates, call signs, and what type of artillery to call in. Johns was going to make a good squad leader. We would also talk about home and family.

"He told me that he was going to name his little boy, when it was born, Rodger with a *d,* after me. I thought that he was joking. I would say, 'Just call him, Sarge, or maybe Sergeant Dan.'

"Johns would say, 'No, I will stay with Rodger. I have already spoken to my wife about it.'

"We were now halfway back to our command post when I heard the sound of mortars. We were walking on a path with mud and water on each side of it. A mortar hit ten to twelve feet to the right of me. I am blown off of my feet. I land in the mud to the left of the path. My helmet is five feet away from me. My face was in the mud. I can feel the sandy texture of the mud in my mouth. I start to spit out the water and mud, but I cannot. I am gasping for air. I am thinking that my life has ended. But I am still alive. The concussion from the mortar or rocket shell had knocked the breath out of me. My legs are numb. I try to move my legs. I realize that I was able to move.

"I look for wounds on my body and find nothing but a few cuts. I started gaining my breath and my composure back. Now it is time to find out how everyone else is doing. I looked in front of me, and Jacop was dead. Chuck came to our location. 'Are you OK, Danny?'

"'Yeah, what about you?'

"'I am fine. Only one round hit. It must have hit close to you. Can you stand up?'

"'Yes, I don't think I am hurt.'

"'Man, Danny, Jacop is dead!'

"'Yeah, I saw him. Where is Johns? He was right behind me.'

"We started looking for Johns. We found him face down in the water with his guts blown away. He was also dead. Chuck says, 'Someone is watching over you. Weren't Jacop and Johns in front and in back of you?'

"'Yes, Jacop in front and Johns in the rear. Man, Chuck, they both got killed and I only have a scratch.'

"I should have gotten Johns's wife's address so I could write to her. The captain calls, 'Blackhawk Three, this is Annihilator Three-Three. Give me a sit-rep!'

"I reply, 'We have two dead.'

"'Can you bring them in?'

"'I think we can, over.'

"'Bring them in, out.'

"We started looking for something to load the bodies in. I did not want to spend the time to make stretchers. I told the men to tie a few ponchos together and load a body in each. White and Eckert loaded Jacop into the ponchos. Chuck and I loaded Johns.

"Chuck says, 'Danny, you are getting too close to the men. Don't you remember what we were taught? Don't get close to your guys, or it will tear you up when they die! You and Johns were getting too close.'

"'No we weren't, Chuck. I don't even know his wife's name.'

"'That is what I mean. Why should you even care what his wife's name is? Are you going to boo-hoo when I get killed?'

"Jokingly I said, 'Probably not. I don't even know your last name.'

"Eckert says, 'You don't even know his last name? Isn't his last name Lewis, as in Sergeant Lewis?'

"I answer, 'We are only joking. Chuck and I go back a long way. We were drafted at the same time, and we went through basic and AIT (Advanced Infantry Training) together. OK, men, let's get started.'

"It was very hard carrying the bodies back to the CP. It took us two hours. Once we arrived, I went to the captain for my debriefing. The captain asked, 'What are your dead guys' names? Was it a mortar?'

"'Their names are Jacop and Johns, and, yes, for sure it was a mortar.'

"The captain hangs his head. 'They were only here for a few weeks. Your clothes are ripped up. Are you alright?'

"'Yes, sir, I am just fine. I am just shaken up a little bit. The mortar knocked me off my feet.'

"'You are lucky. Now tell me about the gook in the grave. How come it was so hard for you to tell the sex?'

"I explained to him about how bloated the body was, and he laughed. I did not tell him about my ordeal with White. The captain went on to say, 'Now let's talk about all of the firing that was going on.'

"'OK, sir.'

"'There were firefights going on in three locations. Were you guys in one?'

"'Yes, sir! While we were digging up the grave, we started getting hit by three snipers, and then we got mortared. Some company called in artillery, and the mortaring stopped.'

"The captain replies, 'I did not call for support because I did not know where all of the players were located. There was a firefight going on to the west, the east, and I guess you guys to the north. I am glad you are OK. Sorry for your men.'

"'Thank you, sir, I appreciate it.'

"I walked over to where the Doc was looking at Jacop and Johns. 'Hey, Doc, how ya doing?'

"'Better than you or these guys. Was it grenades?'

"'No, it was a mortar.'

"'It must have been an 81 or 82.'

"'Yeah, Doc, I think you're right.'

"I started to walk away when Doc said, 'Hey, Sarge, I will get them to the rear tomorrow. Sorry.'

"'Thanks, Doc.'"

I paused before ending, "Well, Killer, that is the story about Proud Mary."

CHAPTER 8

Culture Shock

Killer is looking at me with his mouth open. "With all of that Proud Mary stuff, how is it that you and White are still friends?"

Eckert says, "I don't think that you could call Rock and White friends. Sergeant Rock just tolerates White."

White is listening to everything that is said about him. White, in his usual smart-butt way, says, "What are ya talking about? Rock and I are tight. He loves me, don't ya, Sarge?"

"Yeah, I love you about as much as I love the Black Plague!"

"Hey, Sarge, you never did tell me that you forgave me for taking your rifle."

"Don't push it, White. I'll never forgive you for that one. But you have been doing better. Your mouth has toned down a little."

"I actually *have* been trying harder!"

"OK, White, quit yelling."

I look at the new guy. He has been listening to every word of every story. "Your name is Raymond, huh?"

"Yes, Sergeant."

"What did you excel in at AIT?"

"Do you mean what was I good at?"

"Yeah! What were you good at?"

"I was an expert at the M-16 and the M-60 machine gun."

"How would you like to carry the Pig?"

"The Pig?"

"Yeah, the M-60."

"I would like it, Sarge."

"You know that you will have to carry a lot of ammo belts and not always will you have an AG (assistant gunner)."

"No problem, Sarge."

"Come with me, Raymond. The guy carrying the Pig wants a change."

We walked over to the second squad. "I have some good news for you, Dodson."

"What's that, Sarge?"

"The new guy is going to start carrying the M-60."

Dodson jumped to his feet. "Hallelujah!"

He started getting all the metal ammo belts (pre-link rounds, 100 bullets each) ready. While I am looking at the stack of arsenal he is getting together, I ask, "How many rounds do you carry?"

"I carry 300."

"How many does your AG carry?"

"Usually 400."

"Do you have a spare barrel and bipod?"

"I only have a bipod. This thing is heavy enough without a spare barrel."

Dodson looks at Raymond. "I guess that I will get his M-16, huh?"

"Yes, I will go to the CP and get the weapon's serial numbers straightened out."

Dodson looks at my M-14 and my M-16. "Are you going to be our new sniper?"

"Yeah, unless you want the M-14."

"No thanks. I just got rid of a lot of weight I don't want anymore."

Every man liked shooting the M-60 during a battle, but they did not like carrying it. They did not want the extra weight. I was the same way. I enjoyed shooting the gun but hated humping with it. Raymond and I picked up the gun, ammo, and bipod and went back to the rest of my squad. When we approached the squad, the guys were looking at all of the gear that a machine gunner must carry. White sees the M-60 cartridges. "Hey, Sarge, at least you will never run out of ammo for your sniper rifle."

All of us knew that the 7.62 round of the M-60 machine gun was the same as the M-14 sniper rifle. "Yes, you are correct. Grab two ammo belts and carry them for our gunner."

Eckert grabbed two more without being told to do so. The company started moving out. Raymond did a good job humping with the Pig. I was humping with the sniper rifle and my M-16. I did not like it very much, but someone had to do it. We were humping for two more hours in and out of tree lines. We were heading for a large river. We heard the mortar sound, then a barrage of incoming fire. We hit the ground and started firing back. Raymond yelled, "Give me the bipod! Ammo carriers, get next to me!"

Raymond was raising his voice because of the noise the incoming firing was making. He was not yelling from being out of control. He yelled to be heard. I was very impressed. The NVA were starting to charge. Raymond started to fire the Pig. Raymond started making the Pig work like a well-oiled sewing machine. He was firing short, seven round bursts in order not to get the barrel too hot. The Pig would jam up if the barrel got too hot. The Pig's barrel would have to cool before more rounds were shot. Raymond was doing everything perfectly. He was hitting what he was shooting at without wasting bullets.

White was lying next to Raymond, holding the ammo chain up level as to keep the shells running through the gun straight and smooth. Eckert was lying next to White. Eckert was hooking up his ammo chain to the chain that White was feeding to Raymond. White would tap Raymond on the helmet to direct him of an approaching NVA. I watched them when I didn't have a clear shot. I was really proud of how well they worked together. It was as though they had been working together for years. A simple tap on the hardhat and a finger point, and Raymond would kill a gook. I had already counted four kills for Raymond. A few more minutes, and the firing stopped. It was time to see how many kills we had made.

I had killed one and shot another which someone else had finished off. Raymond had killed six. Killing six men on the first outing is a great feat by any soldier. My men were all jumping around and dancing. Chuck had shot one. Emery and Killer had shot a couple. We had killed ten hardcore NVA. This was good for the company's total body count. No telling how good the rest of the company had done. Raymond looked at the men dancing and shaking hands. "Why is everyone so happy?"

Eckert explained, "Sergeant Rock's squad has a reputation to uphold."

Raymond looked surprised. "What do you mean, Eckert?"

"Killer cut the head of a VC off a while back. Rumors got started about Sergeant Rock's squad, and before long, we were known as the hardest, toughest squad in the 'Nam."

I added, "A lot of what people say we did is not true."

"Did Killer really cut off a VC's head, Sergeant?"

"Yes, he really did do that! The guys are happy because the body count is so important here in the 'Nam."

Raymond started gathering up his ammo and M-60. "Why didn't we call in any artillery, Sarge?"

"Because the NVA were too close. I think that they were setting up an ambush for us. OK, men, we are moving out!"

Raymond took his Pig and four ammo belts and wrapped them around his shoulder and chest.

"Blackhawk Three, this is Annihilator Three-Three, over."

"This is Blackhawk Three, go."

"Come see me!"

"Affirmative. I am on the way!"

I arrived to the CP squad. "Hey, Rock, how many kills did your squad get?"

"Ten, sir. The new man, Raymond, killed six with the Pig."

Just then, the lieutenant walked up. The captain asked, "Lieutenant, how's your body count?"

The lieutenant looked at a small piece of paper in his hand. "Let's see, Rock, you guys got ten, didn't you?"

"Affirmative."

"Sir, with Rock's and twelve more, we killed twenty-two."

"Man! Men, that is cool. We as a company killed forty-two." He looked at me. "You know, Rock, we have a reputation to uphold." I laughed because I had just had the same conversation with my squad. "Rock, I want you to call in artillery here." He points at the map to a location northwest of our position.

"Is that where we are going, sir?"

"Yes, affirmative, and I want to clean it out before we get there."

"I'll make it happen."

I turned and walked away, leaving the old man and the lieutenant to talk over the day's events. I arrived to see the men being jubilant. I started calling in the fire support. "Fireball Five-Niner, this is Blackhawk Three, over."

"This is Fireball Five-Niner, go."

"I need some shells and VT, over."

"Are you in a bind?"

"No, this is for immediate future."

Fireball knew from my comment that the fire support was just for clearing out the enemy from that location. I gave Fireball the coordinates. The rounds started hitting. We could only hear them, for they were too far away to be seen.

"Fireball Five-Niner, now spread the rounds in a 150-meter radius from the coordinate that I gave you."

Five more minutes, and the rounds stop. "Blackhawk Three, are we done?"

"Did you fire VT also?"

"That's affirmative."

"We are complete. Thanks, Fireball, out."

Raymond said, "That was pretty good, Sergeant Rock. How did you learn to do that?"

I grinned at him. "Practice, practice, practice! I will tell you about it sometime when we have time."

"By the way, Sarge, where did you get that nice wristwatch?"

"I got it in Cam Ranh Bay or Da Nang. I cannot remember which one. Hey, Chuck, where did I get my watch? Do you remember?"

"Yep, you bought it in Da Nang at the PX (post exchange)."

Raymond looked at the watch again. "I didn't have time to do anything in Da Nang. I landed with a whole lot of guys, and then I received orders to go to C Company. C Company was wiped out, so I was sent here. How was your entry into Vietnam?"

Chuck says, "Tell him about our adventure in Da Nang, Sergeant Rock!"

"Alright, Raymond, I'll give you the short version. Chuck Lewis and I had arrived in country at Cam Ranh Bay, the inlet of the South China Sea. We landed in a very large jet airplane that had hundreds of men on it. It was the largest plane that I had ever seen. As we got off of the plane, a sergeant was calling out names and handing out pieces of paper to each of us. We assumed that the paper was our orders. I looked at my paper and saw that it was orders for me to go to Da Nang.

"'Chuck, what do your orders say?'

"'They say to go to Da Nang.'

"I say, 'Well, that's a relief. At least we were going to the same place.'

"Chuck looks around and says, 'Do you mean that we are all not going to the same place?'

"'No, the men are being divided up in small groups and sent all over Vietnam.'

"We started walking in the direction that most of the soldiers were going. This place was not an airport with buildings for people to wait for their departure or arrival. This was an airport with a runway and a few metal buildings for cargo. If a sign were to be posted at this airport, it would say, 'Get your butt off this runway. Just leave!' In other words, it was not traveler-friendly. We walked over to a dirt road in front of the landing strip. Some of the men were jumping into the backs of trucks. Chuck said, 'Did you notice something about our orders?'

"'No, what?'

"'There is no time on them.'

"'What?'

"'There is no time or date telling us when to be in Da Nang.'

"I looked at my orders to be sure. 'You are right. Let's look around.'

"There were beautiful beaches and great views of the ocean. The water was crystal clear. The only concerns we had at this time were the people cleaning windows and working at the airport. They were wearing black pajamas, and they had large black hats. They were exactly what we were taught VCs looked like. I looked at Chuck. 'Do you see all of these people?'

"'Yeah, but they couldn't be all VC. This is weird, isn't it, Danny?'

"'Yes, but it has to be safe. What do ya wanna do now, Chuck?'

"'Let's go swimming!'

"'What?'

"'Yeah, let's go swimming!'

"'OK, let's go.'

"We headed for the water. We took off everything but our underwear. We got in the water. I was constantly looking over my shoulder at the people in the pajamas. Chuck was diving in and out of the water like a fish. Two more soldiers saw us and decided to jump in with us.

"One of the soldiers says, 'Hey, Vietnam does not seem so bad, huh?'

"I told him, 'We are in the south. All of the action is in the north. Where are you guys going?'

"'We have orders to go to Da Nang, and then we will be deployed to a company.'

"'Yeah, that is where my buddy and I are going. Aren't you surprised that we don't have any transportation to get to Da Nang?'

"'Yeah, this is crazy.'

"I thought that once we arrived in Vietnam, there would be planes or choppers or trucks waiting to take us to our next location, but there were none.

"'Chuck, are you getting hungry yet?'

"'Yes, let's find a chow hall.'

"We knew that a base was nearby with a mess hall, because we saw a lot of deuce-and-a-halfs (two and a half ton Army trucks) running around. We stopped a truck and asked the driver where to eat. He told us to hop in the back, and he would drop us off. Chuck and I went in the mess hall. There were thirty to forty men in the hall. We jumped into the chow line. Gooks were serving the food to us. We were surprised, again, to see the black pajama people. My mind ran wild. They could poison all of us. They could put glass in our food. They could pull out a gun and kill us all. I was overthinking the situation. We sat down beside a group of soldiers that looked like they belonged at this base camp.

"They looked at us and said, 'Do you have orders, and to where?'

"'Our orders say to go to Da Nang, but how do we get there?'

"'There are two ways. You can go by truck or hop a cargo plane.'

"'How do we get on the plane?'

"One of the men answered, 'You guys just hop a truck to the airport, and once you get there, go up to a plane that is loading cargo. Ask the guys or the pilot where they are going. Once you find one going to Da Nang, jump on it.'

"Another man said, 'I hope you have earplugs.'

"Then they all laughed. Chuck said, 'I noticed that not many guys have rifles. Is it that safe here?'

"One of the men answered, 'Yes, there are so many companies guarding this airport, you wouldn't believe it.'

"'What about the gooks just walking around? Aren't we supposed to be shooting those kinds of people?'

"The men laughed again. 'They are South Vietnam residents. They are safe. They have all been screened.'

"I lean back on the bench that I am sitting on. 'How can we tell who is bad and who is good?'

"One of the men explained, 'In general, but this is not a hard fact, if a gook is between the ages of fourteen and let's say fifty years old, he has to be in the South Vietnam Army or a VC.'

"Then another man said, 'I just do it this way; if a gook shoots at me, he is the right age to be killed. I don't care if he is five years old or seventy-five years old. He is going to die!'

"Chuck and I finish our food. 'Hey, Danny, do you want to hang around here for another day?'

"I was a little worried because we did not have weapons. We would not get a weapon until we were sent to our company. 'I guess so, Chuck. Hey, guys, where can we find a bunk?'

"They directed us to a large tent where we found twenty to thirty cots. We found beds and placed our duffel bags under them. 'Hey, Danny, let's go sight-seeing!'

"'Alright, let's go.'

"We walked to the front of the tents and hopped on a deuce-and-a-half. We just started to laugh because we did not even know where the truck was going. Chuck said, 'You know this is great, but I would still feel better with a gun.'

"'Yeah, me too.'

"We found a little bar on the beach. Chuck ordered a beer, and I ordered a root beer. There were a lot of guys swimming and fishing. 'Man, Chuck, something is wrong. This is like a big country club.'

"Chuck took a drink from his cold beer. 'I know it. Maybe we can get orders for here.'

"'Chuck, when we get to Da Nang, maybe they will send us here.'

"'That would be cool, Danny. Let's go get some sleep.'

"We started walking for a while, then found a truck going in the direction of the tents. We asked the driver if he would drop us off at the tent motel. He told us to hop in the back.

"'Chuck, what do you want to do tomorrow?'

"'I would like to go swimming again at that beautiful beach.'

"'Yeah, me too. Maybe we can find a couple of surfboards.'

"Chuck replied, 'I don't know how to surf.'

"I tilted my head back. 'Do you mean that we both came from California and you don't know how to surf, Chuck? That is disgusting!'

"'When did you learn to surf, Danny?'

"'I don't know how either.' I laughed.

"Chuck said, 'You idiot.' Then he laughed.

"The truck stopped and we heard, 'Here we are, guys.'

"We jumped out of the back of the truck and thanked the driver. The truck drove away. We went in the tent. We located our cots and closed up the mosquito net. During the night, other soldiers came in. I woke up the next morning and noticed that there are twenty men in the tent. 'Chuck, wake up. Let's go eat breakfast.'

"'OK. I hate the Army.' Chuck said this every morning. I cannot remember a morning when he did not say it. We walked to the mess hall. After breakfast, we hopped a truck and went to the beach. We swam and relaxed for three hours. 'Chuck, we better get moving so we can be in Da Nang before dark.'

"'Alright, party time is over. Man, I wish we could be stationed here.'

"We hopped a truck back to the tents. We grabbed our duffel bags and hopped a truck to the airport. There were a lot of cargo planes loading cargo. We walked up to the first plane. 'Where are you guys going?'

"'Near An Khe.'

"'Is that near Da Nang?'

"'No! Go and ask the next ship.'

"We walked to the next plane. The pilot was starting up the ramp. 'Sir, are you guys heading to Da Nang?'

"'No, but two more ships down the line — they are heading to Da Nang.'

"'Thank you, sir.'

"'Good luck, men. Do you have earplugs?'

"That is the second time that earplugs had been mentioned. Chuck said, 'No, sir, we don't!'

"The pilot reached in his pocket and handed us a package with four earplugs in it. 'Here, take these. You will thank me later.'

"We walked to the specified cargo plane. There were four men and a forklift loading the plane. 'You guys are going to Da Nang, aren't you?'

"'Affirmative. Do you need a lift?'

"We have to yell now, for the plane is increasing the engine speed. I yelled and nodded my head up and down. 'Yes!'

"The cargo loader said, or should I say yelled, 'OK, but help us load. Throw your duffels onboard!'

"We started loading. The heat of the metal and wood boxes of ammo was almost unbearable. My sweat was dropping on the metal bands that held the wood boxes together, and it would sizzle like frying bacon. The ammo boxes were getting so hot from the plane's exhaust and the sun, I thought the ammo would explode. We finished loading, and one of the men motioned for us to get in the plane.

"We ran up the ramp and a cargo loader pushed a button. The ramp lifted up to the closed position. The loader made a motion for us to insert our seatbelts. These were seatbelts like a racecar driver would wear. The belts came over both shoulders and around the waist. The seat was nothing more than a woven net, similar to that of a racecar. The plane taxied out to the runway. The plane started increasing the power more and more. It was at a feverous pitch. The loader man motioned for us to put in our earplugs. We took out the package and inserted the earplugs. The plane's engines roared even louder. It sounded like the plane was going to blow up. Our eyes were very big from the excitement.

With a big and mighty thrust, we took off down the runway. We could just feel the torque as the motors shot up to full speed. This was exhilarating, mind-blowing, and rip-roaring fun.

"We traveled for quite some time before we landed in Da Nang. The plane taxied to an area where a lot of planes were unloading. The ramp came down, and we unbuckled our seatbelts. I motioned to the pilot to thank him. We shook hands with the cargo loaders and ran down the ramp. We walked a little farther when Chuck looked at me. 'Man, that was loud!'

"I answered, 'Yep, it was. Can we do it again?'

"'Not until I get my hearing back!'

"We laughed and started to talk about drag racing. Chuck said, 'You know, that was louder than a top fueler.'

"'I know. It was great. I was in the pits one time at a drag race when a fueler started. The noise made my chest move. I could feel the vibrations in my body.'

"'Yeah, that is cool, isn't it?'

"'We better find out where we are supposed to go.'

"We started asking around, and finally we saw a sign that read, *'Grunts, get your orders here. See Sgt. Cooper.'* We walked into the little office and asked for Sergeant Cooper. 'He is over there,' a private pointed.

"We walked toward the sarge. 'Sergeant Cooper, I am Rodgers and this is Lewis.'

"'Are you both 11-B10 grunts?'

"'Yes.'

"'Give me your papers.'

"He looked at the papers. 'What took you guys so long to get here?'

"'We had a hard time getting a ride.'

"Chuck and I looked at each other and grinned, for we could have been here a day or even two earlier. 'OK, wait for me outside.'

"We waited outside the office along with six other soldiers. The sergeant finally came outside. It had only been twenty minutes, but we were getting impatient. Sergeant Cooper started reading from a list. 'Dickerson you are going to the 196th, Company C. MacDougle and Hanks, you two are going to Company D. All of you will be going to the 196th, just different companies. Richards, you are going to Company C. Rodgers, you are going to Company A. Lewis, you are going to Company D.'

"Chuck and I looked at each other and said, 'No way.'

"We had to go to the same company. 'Sarge, we need to go to the same place.'

"The sarge said, 'I have my orders. Each company needs men. I have to divide you guys up the way that I see fit.'

"Chuck said, 'Sarge, Rodgers and I came from the same place in California. We went through basic together. We went through AIT together. We have never been separated.'

"The sarge replied, 'Where did you guys go to AIT?'

"I answered, 'Fort Polk.'

"The sergeant laughs. 'Me too! Wasn't that a swamp hole?'

"He was getting much friendlier now. I asked, 'Did you have to go through the compass course at night?'

"'Heck yeah, through the swamp all night with mosquitoes and gators.'

"I replied, 'I know! I hated that more than anything, but at least I stayed on course.'

"'You were lucky. Do you know the reason why the Army does not want brothers or friends in the same area?'

"'Yes, we do, because a family could lose two members instead of one.'

"'But, Sarge, we are not brothers — almost brothers, but we aren't.'

"The sarge says, 'Just a minute.'

"He goes in the office. He comes back out with a new piece of paper. 'OK, men, you are both going to Company A. Now don't ever tell anyone that I did this for you.'

"He handed Chuck the new orders. We both thanked Sergeant Cooper. 'Sergeant Cooper, how do we get to Company A?'

"He answered, 'You'll take a chopper. It is on the orders.'

"We read the orders. We were to be in a place called Chu Lai in a few days. 'Hey, Chuck, do you want to stick around here for a few days longer?'

"'Yeah, why not?'

"We started asking around for a place to sleep and a place to eat. We saw the mess hall. We walked in and got in line. We still had our duffel bags with us, which made it hard to carry our metal trays. We received our food. 'Chuck, let's sit by those guys over there. They don't have duffels. We can ask questions.'

"'Cool.'

"We sat next to the guys with no duffel bags. I looked at the group of six men. 'Are you guys stationed here?'

"They could see by our bags that we were going to keep moving. 'Yes. Where are you guys going?'

"I looked at our orders. 'We are going to a place called July, spelled C-H-U-L-A-I.'

"'No, that's *chu*, like you sneeze. *Ah chuuu. Chu*, then *lie*. Like Peterson over there, he lies all of the time.'

"We all started to laugh. 'OK, we get it — Chuuu Lie.'

"'Now you got it. You guys are lucky.'

"Chuck tips his head back. 'Why do you say that?'

"'Because although there is a lot of fighting down there, it is mostly guerrillas, you know, VC.'

"'What do you mean, *down there*?' I asked.

"One soldier replied, 'Chu Lai is south of here. We are in Da Nang. You never want to be sent north of Da Nang, especially near Way.'

"'Do you mean way like W-A-Y?'

"'No, it is spelled H-U-E, but pronounced *way*. You never want to go there because the next stop is the DMZ. Most companies don't return from Hue. The DMZ, or demilitarized zone, is even worse!'

"I ask, 'I thought the DMZ was a place that war was not allowed?'

"'The NVA in the north come across the DMZ every night. If you ever have to go, just take out your starlight night scope and watch them come over to the south of the DMZ, hundreds at a time.'

"'Maybe we will stay in Chu Lai. Where can we grab a cot for the night?'

"They told us where to find the sleeping quarters. We stood up and thanked them. They said, 'Good luck, and stay in the south.'

"On our way out, Chuck says, 'Do ya wanna stay here in Da Nang for a day or so?'

"I replied, 'I guess so, but I sure would feel safer with a weapon, Chuck.'

"'You big sissy. Let's stay here a few more days, alright?'

"'Alright, Charles, but just a few more days. I guess we can tell the company that we had trouble getting transportation again.'

"Chuck says, 'Let's go to the beach after we find a place to put our bags.'

"We jumped in a truck that was going our way. We located the place called Tent City. It had ten to twelve tents with twenty cots in each. We found a couple of cots near the front entrance and placed our bags underneath before heading for the beach. Chuck looks at me. 'Hey, Danny, can you believe how much fun we are having in Vietnam? I cannot believe all of the bad stories we have heard about this place.'

"I knew that he was partially joking, but I was surprised, myself, about our last four days' adventure. We arrived at the beach, but this was different than Cam Ranh Bay. There were soldiers carrying rifles and ammo. There were bunkers with soldiers behind M-60 machine guns. In this area, we didn't see anyone swimming. I walked up to a soldier. 'I guess it is not safe to swim here?'

"'No, you need to go a few miles down the road for that.'

"'Is there always someone on guard here?'

"'Yes, we are guarding the base. This is one of the most important bases in the 'Nam!'

"'Thanks!'

"Chuck was listening to everything that was said. 'Let's go back to the Tent City. Let's check out the PX.'

"'Sounds like a plan.'

"We hopped a truck to Tent City. We located the PX and started looking around. They had very good prices on the merchandise. I don't remember what Chuck bought, but I bought a real nice watch. The watch cost over $100 in the States. I think I paid only $23. We headed back to the tents. We lay around for a few hours, talking to other guys about where they were being deployed. 'Let's go eat supper, Chuck.'

"'Let's do it, and tomorrow we will go down to the beach swimming area.'

"I replied, 'Do you still want to go?'

"'Sure, what could happen?'

"'Alright, we will go.'

"We finished our supper and came back to the tents. We sat around talking to everyone about what they thought about Vietnam. Some were scared, some were not, but all were concerned about what was to come in the year ahead. It was after dark now. 'Chuck, I am going to bed. I hope that I can sleep with all of these mosquitoes biting me. Have you noticed that the mosquitoes are worse here than in other places that we have been?'

"'Yes, but that is because of all of the shallow drainage ditches around the tents. All of them have six inches of water in them.'

"The ditches were about a foot deep and eighteen inches wide. I got on the cot and pulled the torn mosquito net around me the best that I could. I fell asleep, waking every so often to kill a bug. We were awakened with a loud boom. The booms were getting louder and louder. By this time, Chuck and I and all of the men in the tent were on our feet. Explosions are hitting closer and closer to us. We didn't know what to do! We had no weapons! The noise was now too much for our eardrums. We held our hands over our ears. An explosion hit one of the tents behind us. Shrapnel was now flying through our tent, knocking over cots and ripping the tent to shreds. We started running out of the tent.

"We did not know where we were going, but we knew for sure that we had to get out of the tent. Chuck and I ran out of the tent and jumped in the drainage ditch. The rockets were still coming in. Everything was exploding. We were lying in six inches of mud, but that did not matter. Large, large explosions were now shooting toward the sky. The rockets were increasing. We could hear the whizzing as the shrapnel ripped over us. Two more explosions went off really close to us. We were in the ditches with no shirts on. Some men were only in their underwear. Chuck and I had our fatigue pants on, but no shirts or shoes. The explosions made a fiery boom.

"The fire came over our backs, burning the hair off. All of the tents were on fire. The small wood bridges over the ditches were on fire. The firing stopped, *but was it over or was it a pause?* Chuck says, 'Danny, we are never going to make it out of Vietnam alive! I am scared!'

"I did not say it, but I thought that it was over for us. I thought that we were going to die here in Vietnam. The firing was still quiet. 'Chuck, let's see if our duffel bags are OK. I want my hardhat.'

"Chuck looks at me in dismay. 'The tent is still burning!'

"'No problem. Let's go!'

"We jumped out of the ditch and ran to the burning tent. The tents were not like a house on fire. The tents burned quickly. We ran into the burning tent and located our duffel bags. To my surprise, they were in pretty good shape. The firing started again. We grabbed our bags and jumped into the ditch. I opened my duffel and placed my helmet on my head as fast as I could. I looked at Chuck, and he had already put his hardhat on. He must have been quick. Maybe he put it on while he was on the run. The firing was now moving away from us and going in the direction of the airport storage areas. The rockets were pounding the airports. We did not hear the shrapnel flying over our heads any longer.

"We sat up from the ditch, stood up, and watched the explosions. The fuel depot was being hit, and the ammo storage was exploding. We could see the big fiery clouds, and we could feel the heat as each one exploded. *Were the explosions coming from gasoline, diesel fuel, or napalm?* Needless to say, we did not even try to sleep any more for the rest of the night. Even if we wanted to sleep, most of the cots were broken. The firing stopped. The place was a mess. I looked at Chuck. 'Do you still want to stay here a few more days?'

"'No! Let's get out of Dodge, and I mean right now!'

"We headed toward the airport, seeing blown-up cargo planes, holes in the runways, and buildings still smoldering. I didn't even know if we could get out. We located a sergeant who looked like he was in charge of a clean-up area. 'Sarge, we are supposed to get a lift to Chu Lai.'

"'Were you guys in Tent City last night?'

"'Affirmative!'

"'How many men got killed?'

"'We don't know. We were in the tents in front. The back tents got hit. We left straight from our tent area.'

"The sarge pointed over his shoulder. 'Go over to the CP and see the sarge there.'

"We hustled to the CP, looking at the damage as we moved quickly. I wanted to get to my assigned company fast. I wanted to have a gun and ammo in my hands before nightfall. The sergeant at the CP saw us coming. 'Where are you guys trying to get to?'

"I answered, 'Chu Lai!'

"'You men are lucky. We have a chopper leaving in thirty minutes.'

"'Great, where do we wait?'

"'You wait over there, near what used to be the circle with an X in it.' He pointed. 'Have you guys eaten?'

"'Not yet!'

"'Go over there to where that line of men is waiting. You have time before your chopper comes in.'

"We ate breakfast, and choppers started coming in. We did not know which one to get on. We ran to the chopper and yelled to the door gunner. 'Are you going to Chu Lai?'

"He nods his head *yes*. He yells back as he lifts up one side of his helmet, 'What outfit are you going to?'

"I yelled back, 'Company A! The one 196th!'

"'OK, hop in!'

"Men started to load the chopper with supplies. We took off. We could see rivers, creeks, and lots of rice paddies. Every once in a while, the chopper would drop down from the sky and fly really close to the trees. On the third drop toward the ground or tree line, the door gunners grabbed us and shoved us to the middle of the chopper. Just then, we heard a metal hitting metal sound. I looked to the tree line and saw a flash and a tracer round coming toward the chopper.

"The gunners started opening up with their M-60s. This sound scared the you know what out of us. It was very, very loud. Our ears were ringing. The door gunners were firing heavily at the gooks that were trying to shoot us down. The chopper lifted back up toward the sky and the firing stopped. The gunners and the pilots acted like this happened every day. I guessed that maybe it did happen every day. We saw an area that was like a big, bald hill. Surrounding the hill were bunkers and coiled barbed wire.

"The chopper dropped swiftly and quickly to the LZ. The chopper landed and the gunners motioned for us to get off. We jumped out of the chopper, and the gunners nodded their heads to say goodbye. We tipped our hardhats to them in an effort to say thank you. The chopper took off. One more friendly wave by a door gunner, and they were gone. *Were we in Chu Lai?* Chuck and I walked to the closest bunker near the LZ. The supply sergeant met us. 'What're your names, soldiers? Did you come from Da Nang? How many men were killed?'

"'Our names are Rodgers and Lewis. He is Lewis. Yes, we came from Da Nang, and we don't know how many are dead. Is this Chu Lai, Sarge?'

"'Yes. Follow me, and I will get your rifles and the rest of your gear.'

"I was relieved, for we were finally getting a rifle and ammo. After receiving our brand new M-16 rifles, the supply sergeant assigned us to our barracks and our bunks. He pointed to the location of the mess hall. 'Chow is served at zero-six-thirty, twelve-thirty, and seventeen hundred hours. You men better get to the chow hall ASAP. It is almost done until tonight.'

"'OK, thanks, Sarge.'

"'By the way, men, this is not your base camp. This is just a place to store your crap. We supply you from here, but once you guys leave, you won't come back here until you go home in a year.'

"I asked, 'Where will our base camp be located?'

"'Your company will stay in the field for the entire year. You may get a stand down for a few days, but there is no going to the rear! This war is not like other wars where you fight for a while on the front lines, then go to the rear for resupply. This is called a squad leaders' war. No front lines. The squads go in and out of the jungle, tracking the VC and fighting the NVA.'

"'Thanks for the bad news, Sarge.'

"Chuck and I put our gear away and walked to the mess hall. We pulled out the typical steel trays and went up to the food counter. The food handlers slopped the food on our tray. We looked around, and every eye was upon us. We were the new guys. We found a place to sit across from a black soldier. He said nothing to us. He just stared at us. Chuck asked, 'Have you guys seen any action?'

"The black guy stands up. 'Have we seen any action?'

"Then he yells out so all of the men could hear, 'These guys want to know if we have seen any action!'

"He is the only one laughing. This comment made Chuck and I very mad. He was trying to belittle us in front of everyone. He was a jerk. I said, 'I guess you haven't seen any action, or you wouldn't act like a jerk!'

"He walked away without saying another word. Another soldier came up to our table and sat down beside us. 'My name is Craig. Don't pay any attention to the guy you were just talking to, he is an idiot.'

"'My name is Rodgers, and this is Lewis.'

"We shook hands. 'Yes, we have seen a little action, but it is all VC action. Once the company gets built up, we will move to the field. Right now, we mine, sweep, and go on daily patrols. I am the RTO for Sergeant Brock. You better hope that you don't get in his squad!'

"Chuck replied, 'Why, is he another jerk?'

"'You got it. He thinks that he knows everything, but he knows nothing. He tries to treat us like we are in basic training. When he calls in artillery, it may hit two miles away from our location. He pretends that he has seen a lot of action, but he hasn't.'

"I look at Craig. 'Then how did he become a sergeant?'

"'He's not. He is just an acting jack. You know, a sarge that does not have his official papers yet.'

"We knew what an acting jack was, but we didn't say anything to Craig. We left the mess hall and went to our bunks. A staff sergeant met us. He had all of the stripes a sergeant could possibly obtain. We called him Top, as in Top Sergeant. Top was a really nice guy that had a couple of tours already in Vietnam. 'You two will be in squad three!'

"We both replied 'Yes, Sergeant!'

"'Just call me Top! Good luck!'

"Top walked away. We hoped that we were not going to be in the jerk's squad, Sergeant Brock's. We looked over to where Top was heading, and a soldier stopped him and started carrying on a conversation. The soldier walked briskly toward us. I looked at his nametag and saw in big letters, *BROCK.* We knew that we were in the jerk's squad, but maybe Craig was exaggerating. Before we could introduce ourselves, Brock says, 'I am Sergeant Brock. You grunts are in my squad!'

I held out my hand to shake his hand, but he did not acknowledge it. He says, 'I am giving you guys guard duty. Go to Bunker Three!'

"I reply, 'Where is that, Sarge?'

"He says, 'Just ask someone. Don't bother me!'

"We grab our rifles and ammo from our cots and start walking toward the bunkers. On our way to the bunkers, we start talking. 'Danny, Brock is a jerk. I want to smash his face in!'

"'Wait in line behind me!'

"We stopped at a bunker and asked where Bunker Three was located. The bunker was only four away. We approached the bunker. The two men in the bunker started to move around when they saw us coming. They looked at us. 'You guys are newbies, huh?'

"'Affirmative,' we both answered.

"One of them went on to say, 'I guess that you guys are in Brock's squad. That is too bad. You guys will be relieved in four hours if Brock has his head out of his butt!'

"I ask, 'How did you know that we were in Brock's squad?'

"One of them answered, 'Brock is in charge of these four bunkers on this side. We knew that you were new because we never saw you before.'

"They grabbed their rifles, ammo, and water. *Uh-oh,* I thought, *we did not bring any water with us.* The men left, and we started watching intently. We saw nothing. It was very hot. 'You know, Chuck, I am going to take a canteen of water with me every place that I go from now on!'

"'Me too! I am going to take two or three with me from now on!'

"I started studying the map. When we received our orders, there was a map of Vietnam enclosed. Every chance that I got, I would study it. I knew exactly where we were. I had the coordinates down pat. I showed Chuck where we were on the map. He was impressed. A few more hours passed, and our relief showed up. One of them says, 'New guys, we are here to relieve you. You didn't see anything did you?'

"'No, everything's quiet.'

"Chuck and I started heading for the chow hall. We arrived at the chow hall, but it was closed. We were too late. 'You know what, Chuck?'

"'No, what?'

"'I am going to start carrying C-rations and water with me from now on!'

"Chuck laughed. 'Me too.'

"We start walking toward the large twenty-man tents. We see Brock. 'Oh no, here he comes!' Chuck said.

"Brock walks toward us. 'We are going on patrol after we mine sweep the road tomorrow. Rodgers, you have point!'

"I said nothing. I just shook my head. Then he says, 'Don't forget to pay attention!'

"Now, I am puzzled. *Am I going to hold the minesweeper? Am I going to pull point during the patrol?* We saw Craig as we walked to our cots. We told Craig of our stupid ordeal of no water in the bunker and missing chow. We all laughed. Craig reached in his rucksack and asks, 'Who wants ham, and who wants beans?'

"We flipped a coin, and I got the ham and a can of bread. 'Thanks, Craig!'

"'No problem.'

"We spoke for a while, then we went to sleep. We woke up from time to time when we heard bombing in the distance. Craig says, 'Don't worry. The bombing is our planes bombing the gooks.'"

I looked at Raymond. He had been listening intently.

"Raymond, that is the story of Sergeant Lewis's and my entry into Vietnam. Man, did we have a *culture shock*!"

Raymond says, "That's a great story. Is it true?"

Chuck says, "It is true, and there is a lot more! Tell him how you became a sergeant! That is a real good story."

I say, "Maybe tonight. We are going to be moving out soon."

CHAPTER 9

How I Became a Sergeant

My radio sounds, "Blackhawk Three, this is Cherokee Three, over."

I reach for the horn. "This is Blackhawk Three, go."

"We will be here for an hour. Annihilator is trying to get intelligent."

I laugh along with my guys. "Do you mean that Annihilator is gathering intelligence?"

I was laughing so hard that I wondered if he could understand me. Cherokee answers, "Yes, yes gathering intelligence. If you are listening, Annihilator, I am sorry."

Annihilator was a no-nonsense kind of a guy. I just wondered what he was going to say. Maybe he was not monitoring his radio. I hear my radio. "Gibbons and Rock, now I know what you two really think about me, out!"

He was in a good mood, lucky for Gibbons. I hear Chuck say, "Now we have time. Tell Raymond how you became a sergeant!"

I nodded my head. "OK, I'll try for the short version. I have already told you a little about how Sergeant Brock had acted and his RTO named Craig. Listen up. I only want to tell the story once!"

"We are listening, Sarge!"

"Morning came, and it was time to eat. Chuck and I were ready for breakfast. On the way to the mess hall, I asked Craig, 'How much longer does Brock have in country?'

"'He has four more months!'

"I reply, 'That is too bad.'

"We finished eating, then we went back to the barracks. Brock says, 'Everyone get your crap and get outside!'

"We all move to the front of the barracks. I am ready to accept the minesweeper when Brock tells another man to take it. Maybe I am not pulling point. Brock looks at me, 'Rodgers you have point!'

"Now I am really thinking that this is stupid. *Shouldn't the guy with the sweeper go first?* Chuck leans over and says, 'If he expects the road to have explosive mines in it, then why doesn't the mine detector go first?'

"'I don't know, Chuck. He is an idiot.'

"I started out first with the sweeper and the rest of the squad behind me. I watched and looked at the road very carefully. I spotted an area that looked like there was fresh digging. I held up my hand to hold up the patrol. I showed the sweeper the spot, and the machine sounded. We probed with our bayonets like we had been taught, but found it to be just a tin of C-rations. We swept the balance of the road. When we reached the top of the hill, there were trucks and Jeeps waiting for the go ahead.

"The sweeper placed the machine in a Jeep, and we were on our way to our patrol. The way that the soldier placed the machine in the Jeep led me to believe that they had done this many times before. The Jeep driver just nodded his head and drove off. Brock came to me from the rear of the column. He pointed toward a mountain. 'Just head that way!'

"He walked back to the rear. I looked at my map and figured out the coordinates. We traveled through a village, then another. We traveled for three hours more. We were just outside of another village when we started being fired upon. We hit the ground and started firing back. The firing was coming from 200 meters away. We started to hear the mortars as they were dropped and shot from the tubes. Sergeant Brock came to my position. 'Where are they?'

"I pointed in the direction of the noise I was hearing, 'They are 200 meters away.'

"He started calling in artillery. I listened, but it made no sense to me. He was giving coordinates that were a mile farther than we were located. Maybe I was wrong. The first rounds hit so far behind the enemy that we could not even see the blast. He called in more artillery. I listened again to the coordinates he was giving. This time, they were going to hit a half-mile behind us. This guy was crazy. The enemy's mortars started to hit very close to us. I yelled to Brock, 'Try this!'

"I gave him the coordinates. He says, 'What do you know, rookie?'

"'I know that we are here and they are there! Use this coordinate!'

"He finally called in the fire support using my coordinates, and within a few rounds, the enemy had been wiped out. I thought that I would get a *thank you* from him, but I did not. Brock said, 'Rodgers, if you ever interfere with me calling in artillery again, I will have you court-martialed.'

"I saluted and said, 'Yes, sir, General Brock. Yes, sir!'

"I knew that I was going to be in trouble, but I'd had enough of this guy. He says, 'Rodgers, you don't know who you are dealing with!'

"I respond in my smart-aleck way, 'Don't you mean *whom* you are dealing with?'

"He says, 'What?'

"I look at him and say, 'In your sentence, "Rodgers, you don't know who you are dealing with," the word should be *whom* not *who*!'

"'Rodgers, you are going to pull point in this squad for the rest of the year! Let's go and get a body count. Rodgers, you have point!'

"We went to the VC location. We counted ten VC dead. We also found parts of mortar weapons. I started turning over the VC one at a time while Chuck would point his weapon at them.

We did this as a team just in case the gook was playing dead. Brock came up to Chuck and I and asked, 'What are you two idiots doing?'

"Chuck answered, 'We are making sure they are not playing possum.'

"He shook his head and walked away. 'Man, Chuck, we know more than he does, and we have only been here a week!'

"'He is awfully stupid for a sergeant, huh, Danny?'

"We moved out and started toward the camp. I, of course, was pulling point again. We arrived at the base camp four hours later. It was too late for eating in the mess hall. We sat on our cots and started in on our C-rations. The chow hall had open boxes of C-rations behind the tent for anyone to take on their way out or in from the field. Craig came over to my bunk. 'Rodgers, way to go! You are the only guy to ever speak up against Brock!'

"'How much longer does he have in country?'

"Craig laughs, 'Four more long months! Be quiet. Here he comes!'

"Brock is carrying something in both hands. He makes it to our location, and we see that he is carrying boxing gloves. The men get excited. I look at Craig. 'What's going on?'

"'Oh, we box every so often. It's a lot of fun!'

"I was ready for Brock. When I was a kid living in California, I was taught to box. A friend's brother, named Jimmy, trained me. Jimmy had won almost every Golden Gloves championship there was to win. He could go pro at anytime. Jimmy trained me for a few months. Then he set up local fights for me against other Golden Glove opponents. I had no time to join Golden Gloves, because I raced go-karts and played baseball. But I loved to fight, and Jimmy could see it. I never lost a fight, and I didn't expect to lose one now. I was ready for Brock, and I was ready now. Bring it on!

"A couple of men started to box. One man went down quickly, but when it was all over, they shook hands and started telling each other what each had done wrong. This was good.

The men were just boxing for the fun of it. It was fun to watch. The next bout was over when Brock brought the gloves to me.

"'Now, you and Lewis fight!'

"'I am not going to fight Lewis, but I will fight you!'

"'Are you afraid of Lewis, Rodgers?'

"I thought for a minute. I was not afraid of Chuck, but I was not going to fight a friend. I said, 'Yes, Chuck is real tough. He can kick my butt!'

"To my surprise, Brock says, 'OK, then, me and Lewis will fight!'

"Chuck jumps to his feet with a big smile on his face. 'Danny, you be my corner man!'

"I jump off of the sand bags to my feet. 'OK, let's go!'

"The fight was on. Chuck was sort of dancing around like a real prizefighter. Brock takes a haymaker swing and misses. Brock comes in again head on, and Chuck releases a fury of intense rage right to Brock's face. Brock is falling backwards. Chuck hits him with one last uppercut, and Brock is lying on the ground. Chuck is standing over him and moving his gloves in small circles as if to say, 'Get up and I'll do it again.' Brock takes off his gloves and throws them.

"Brock stands up and says, 'This was supposed to be fun!'

"I say, 'It was for Chuck! We both had a real good time, Sarge!'

"Brock looks at me and says, 'Alright, Rodgers, it is your turn!'

"'OK, whom do you want me to fight?'

"I stressed the word *whom*. I really did not know if the correct word was who or whom, but I did know that this pushed his angry button. He shakes his head. 'There you go with that *whom* crap again. Roka, get over here and box Rodgers!'

"Roka was the black guy that had made fun of us in the mess hall. I had my gloves on and laced up before Roka even got one hand in his gloves. I was going to enjoy this. I moved around, letting him land a few light punches. Then I threw a punch to his chest and hit him square in the nose. He went down. He was knocked out for twenty to thirty seconds. Boxing time was over. I think Chuck and I had the most fun!

"We go back into our tent and start drinking water. Brock walks in the tent and looks at me. 'Rodgers, you and Lewis have guard duty. Go to Bunker Four!'

"Brock was still mad at me for the artillery thing. 'Lewis didn't have anything to do with the artillery call-in, why does he have to go?'

"He looks at Chuck. 'You two get on guard duty, and I mean now!'

"We picked up our rifles, ammo, water, and some cans of C-rations. On our way to Bunker Four, we stopped by the mess hall and went to the rear where the C-rations were stacked. I found a can of peaches and a can of pound cake. Chuck did the same. It was very dark now, so we made a little noise as we approached the bunker as to not startle the men on guard. We asked the men on the bunker, 'How long is each shift?'

"They started picking up their gear. 'About four hours.'

"We took our position in the bunker. We squirted mosquito repellent on our hands and face. We sat on two sand bags stacked on top of each other. The bunker had four walls made of sand bags. The walls were five feet tall on three sides and four feet tall on the front side. There was an opening on the left for in-and-out egress. The egress opening was made up in a zigzag so shrapnel could not penetrate the opening. The lower wall in front was to place your weapon upon, and it was made low enough to see the enemy approaching. The size of the bunker on the inside of the sand bags was five feet wide and six feet long. Chuck and I watched for any enemy activity while we talked and enjoyed our C-rations, namely peaches and pound cake.

"We watched and listened to the distant bombing and rocketing. Some of the explosions were beautiful. We tried to take turns sleeping, but it was very hard to sleep while sitting up on sand bags. Our four hours were up, and our relief had come. We walked back to the barracks.

"We would only be getting a few hours sleep, so we just lay on our cots without removing our boots or fatigues. Morning came quickly, and we started moving around. I heard, 'Man, I hate the Army.'

"It was Chuck. 'Hey, Chuck, I think you ought to change it to *I hate Vietnam.*'

"He laughed. 'Look, Danny, here comes the bimbo!'

"Sergeant Brock walks in. 'We are going on patrol, but we are not sweeping today. Get your crap together and eat!'

"We ate breakfast and went back to the barracks. Brock came in and said, 'We are going past where we were yesterday! Rodgers, you know your position!'

"'Of course, Sarge. I am on point!'

"We headed out. Brock took his usual spot to the rear. I took out my map and glanced at it. My map was covered with a plastic see-through bag, like a heavy-duty sandwich bag, but much larger. I took out my grease pen and marked a line in the direction we were heading. I had already marked yesterday's coordinates for reference. We humped for four hours. We finally reached the area where we'd had the firefight yesterday. We walked through the area where the VC bodies had been. The bodies had all been removed. This gave me an eerie, fearful, and strange feeling. I felt like we were being watched. I was glad that I was on point. I was alert to the utmost high. I watched every movement of every tree and bush. I could feel mosquitoes biting me, but I did not even swat at them. I could see a small section of hooches just ahead.

"We walked to the small village, but something was different. No one was in the village. I'd heard, 'If a village has no people in it, beware.' Be ready for an attack by the VC. The village did not have very much protection in case we were attacked. I heard the VC mortars leaving the tubes. I yelled, 'Incoming! Incoming!'

"Just as I yelled, the VC started firing at us. The mortars were off target, for now. I knew that it was only a matter of time before the mortars would be right on top of us. I could see the rifle flashes from 200 meters away. We found a small berm and jumped behind it. I took out my map and found our coordinates. Chuck was next to me. I looked at Chuck. 'What is Brock doing? We need artillery!'

"We hear the first rounds of our artillery start coming in. They hit 200 meters behind us. The next round hits 200 meters to the right of us. 'I have got to go and help him, Chuck! The mortars are getting too close!'

"I ran to Brock and the RTO's location. Brock was calling in a coordinate that was not even close to the enemy. The round hit behind us again. Brock started calling in the next coordinate. I looked at my marked map. The coordinate was exactly where we were located. We were all going to die because of a hard-headed acting jack squad leader named Brock that didn't know his butt from a hole in the ground!

"I grabbed the horn. 'Cease fire! Cease fire! Cease fire! Here is our coordinate.'

"I gave the new coordinate. Brock was reaching for the horn. I jerked it away from him. 'You were going to get us killed, Brock!'

"The round hit twenty-five meters behind the VC. I get back on the radio. 'From my position, drop two five!'

"The round came in right on target. I started speaking again, or should I say yelling, 'Fire for effect! Fire for effect!'

"Ten more rounds, and the VC were wiped out. Brock grabbed the horn from my hand. 'You have done it now, Rodgers. I am going to have you court-martialed!'

"'For what? I saved your life! I don't care about you, but I do care about these other guys and myself!'

"Brock says, 'You never interfere with me calling in fire support!'

"I was very angry, but I kept my cool. I knew that if I hit him, I would really be in trouble. We traveled to the location of the VC to get a body count. The body count was fifteen to seventeen. Many bodies were broken and torn apart. I counted fifteen heads, but it looked like there were more than fifteen bodies. We started heading back to camp.

"We had nine men in the squad, and not even one of them was hurt. On our way back to camp, many men came up to me and told me *thank you*. The squad arrived in camp at five in the afternoon, or in Army time, 1700 hours. Brock walks up to me and gets in my face. 'Rodgers! Follow me to the CP! Let's go!'

"He was going to try to get me court-martialed. I was worried, but I would rather be in jail than be dead. All that I could do was tell my side of the story. We arrived at the CP. Top was sitting at his desk doing paperwork. Brock yells out, 'Top, I want this man court-martialed!'

"Top stood up. 'For what?'

"'He interfered with my artillery calling!'

"Top answered, 'Do you know that I was monitoring the radio? Before we court-martial anyone, we need to bring the platoon leader in on this.'

"Top, very calmly, called the lieutenant on the radio and asked him to come to the CP. The lieutenant came into the CP. Top started speaking to the lieutenant. 'Sir, this is Private Rodgers, and you already know Sergeant Brock.'

"The lieutenant reaches out to shake my hand. I acknowledge it with a firm hand and say, 'Pleased to meet you, sir.'

"The lieutenant says, 'What's going on, Top?'

"'Well, Brock wants to court-martial Private Rodgers.'

"The lieutenant looks at Brock and says, 'For what, Brock?'

"'He interfered with my radio transmissions to the fire support! I want him court-martialed!'

"'I will tell you what, Brock; Top and I listened to the complete radio transmission, every word of it. Now let's hear what you have to say.'

"'I gave the coordinates to the fire support base, and it was off target.'

"The lieutenant replies, 'So you think that the fire support base was off target?'

"'Yes, sir! Then I gave another coordinate, and it was also off target.'

"Top says, 'Give me the correct coordinates for where you guys were located!'

"Brock says, 'Well, I don't know exactly, but let me finish! I called in the next coordinate and Rodgers grabbed the horn out of my hand!'

"I said, 'That's right, because he was calling it in on top of us. We would have all been killed.'

"Top says, 'OK, Rodgers, let's hear your version!'

"'OK, sir and Top, here we go. First of all, when you call in artillery, you give the grid coordinates once. Then you give commands of *drop*, *add*, *left*, or *right*. And you always, always say *from my position* before you say *drop* or *add* or any other command! I pulled out my map. You see, look here! This is where we were, and here is the coordinate. I already had it written in just in case we were attacked.'

"They looked at my map, and they nodded their heads. I could see that they were impressed. Top says, 'Go on. What happened next?'

"'I saw that the artillery was hitting way off target. The mortars were hitting very close to us by now. I ran to Brock to show him the coordinate just to help out. I listened for his next command. His next coordinate called in was going to be right on top of us. I looked again at my map and marked location to be sure that I was correct. Then I grabbed the horn and said, "Cease fire! Cease fire!" Brock was grabbing for the microphone, and I jerked it back. By this time, the mortars were very close to us. I knew the coordinate where the VC were, so I stayed on the radio until we wiped them out. That is the truth and the whole story, sir and Top.'

"Brock yells out, 'It doesn't matter! I want him court-martialed!'

"The lieutenant says, 'It *does* matter, Brock, and guess what? If Rodgers had not been there, you would have killed everyone. You don't know jack about artillery calling. Why would you keep giving coordinates? You give them once! You didn't even know where you were!'

"Brock says, 'Alright, if you won't court-martial him, then move him to another squad!'

"The lieutenant responds, 'Sit down, Brock! Not only is Rodgers not going to be court-martialed or moved to another squad, he is now an acting jack. Brock, you are busted to private, starting immediately.'

"'Sergeant Rodgers, you are now the squad leader of Brock's squad, starting immediately. Brock, you are dismissed. Sergeant Rodgers, you stay here!'

"Brock stood up and stormed out the door. He was very, very mad. Top began to speak. 'Sergeant Rodgers, let's talk about tomorrow. First of all, can you handle the job?'

"'Yes, Top, I can!'

"The lieutenant started giving me the location for tomorrow's patrol. After he showed me, he said, 'This will probably be the last patrol here. We are going to move out in a few days to the north, and we probably won't be back here until we leave the 'Nam. OK, Rodgers, go back to your new squad. Do you want Brock out of your squad?'

"'Not for a few days, Top. Not for a few days!'

"Top takes a paper from his desk. 'Here is the bunker guard duty for the night. It is self-explanatory.'

"I left the CP and went to the barracks. All of the men were looking at me. Craig was first to see me. 'What happened, Rodgers?'

"'I am the new squad leader!'

"'Way to go! I was wondering why Brock came back in such a huff!'

"Chuck comes over to me. 'You better tell the men.'

"I stood up. 'OK, men, listen up! I am the new acting jack sergeant. I am the new squad leader. If you have any complaints, let me know now!'

"No one had a complaint. They actually looked happy. I looked at the piece of paper that Top had given me. It said that the next guard was going to start in ten minutes. It was time for a little payback. I yelled out, loud enough for everyone to hear, 'Brock, you have bunker guard duty at number three. Get on it, and I mean now!'

"I heard a few muffled laughs, then a few whispers. Brock grabs his rifle and ammo and heads out of the barracks. He looks back at me. 'Who is going with me, Rodgers?'

"'Don't you worry about it! And the name to you is Sergeant Rodgers!'

"After Brock was out of sight, I turned to Craig. 'How about getting another man to go with Brock?'

"'Affirmative, Sergeant Rodgers, we usually have a rotation. I'll find the right guy.'

"It was time for chow. We made it to the chow hall and found a table. Chuck came up to me. 'Did you see how mad Brock was?'

"'Yeah, and listen to this! He didn't take any water or food with him!'

"We laughed. After dinner, we went back to the barracks. We spoke for a while, and then we went to sleep. Brock came in four hours later. We slept the balance of the night until morning. Soon, we would be going on our final patrol in Chu Lai. I was not done with Brock yet. 'Brock, we are going on patrol, and guess who has point? Eat and get your crap together!'

"I kept Brock in my squad for another week. The company was moving north. I made Brock pull point every day. I could not stand the guy. Top was not around, so I couldn't ask him to transfer Brock to another squad. I started visiting squads in hopes of trading Brock for one of their men. Finally, I found a sucker that agreed to take Brock off my hands."

"Raymond, that is how I became a sergeant, or at least an acting jack. Over here, you become an acting jack while you are waiting on your real orders."

CHAPTER 10

RTO Roberts Goes to Delta Company

Raymond asks, "Do you have any more stories, Sarge?"

"Yes, there are plenty more, but we need to get ready to move out! You know what, Raymond? You already have a story."

"How is that, Sarge?"

"The way that you handle the Pig. You are really good!"

"Thank you, Sarge. That means a lot to me."

The company started moving in the direction of the area I had just cleared out with artillery. It looked like it would be a six-hour hump. I was carrying the M-14 sniper rifle and the M-16.

I could tell right away that this was a mistake. Carrying two weapons at the same time in the jungle is a stupid thing to do. If the M-14 was not getting caught in the bush, the M-16 was. The ammo bandoliers of both weapons were heavy, and both were getting caught in the thorns.

I am carrying M-60 Ammo along with my typical gear

Chuck asks, "How are you doing, Rock?"

He could see that I was struggling. "Fine, Chuck, thanks for asking. I'll bet that my load is lighter than Raymond's load, carrying that Pig, don't you?"

"Yeah, you are probably right. I wouldn't want to carry that gun. Are we going to hit water before long? I'm getting sick of rice paddy water!"

I pulled out my map. I had already looked over the map, but I wanted to show Chuck. "That is where we are going, and we are here." I pointed at the map. "The river is here, about an hour ahead."

Chuck looks at the river location on the map. "Man, Danny, that is a big river. It looks really wide. At least we can take a bath and get plenty of water!"

We hear a chopper coming in. I turn to Craig, my RTO. "What's happening, Craig?"

Craig's job was to not only carry the heavy radio, but he was supposed to tell me what was being said when I was not monitoring. "The chopper is dropping off a rope."

I lean my head back. "A rope?"

"Yeah, a rope," Craig said.

I take off my hardhat and scratch my head. White says, "Maybe, instead of shooting the VC, we are going to hang them."

We laughed. The chopper comes in fast in a small LZ. The chopper does not land. The door gunner simply throws out a large rope. The rope was at least one inch in diameter and 300 feet long. The lieutenant called for Chuck and I to come to the CP. Chuck and I strolled over to the CP. The lieutenant looks at us. "The captain and I cannot find a strong enough swimmer to get across the river."

I said, "Aren't we all going to have to cross the river?"

Then it dawned on me. The rope — I now knew what the rope was going to be used for. Lieutenant Gibbons says, "Someone needs to take that rope and swim the river. Once the rope gets to the other side, it needs to be secured to something. Then this side will be tied off. Each man will cross holding on to the rope."

I looked at the river. It was moderately swift. I could see why the captain was concerned about the river crossing. Gibbons looks at us. "Find a guy to take the end of the rope and swim to the other side!"

With no hesitation, Chuck says, "I'll do it!"

The lieutenant says, "Great, we have a volunteer swimmer!"

I looked at Chuck. "Don't you remember the first rule of being in the Army?"

Then in unison we say, "Don't volunteer for anything!"

"I remember, but someone's got to do it!"

Chuck started taking off his boots. "Chuck, do you think that you need to take your rifle?"

"What do you think, Rock?"

"I think that you should. All of our 16s will get wet. Yours will just get drowned even worse. Besides, you will have it when you get to the other side."

He takes the rope. "Yeah, *if* I get to the other side!"

He jumped into the river with his rifle strapped to his back. I was proud of my buddy, Chuck. I sure did not want to swim, being restricted by a rifle on my back and an ammo bandolier getting filled with water while holding a large rope. Chuck was quite the man. The river was deep. He started swimming straight, heading toward the other side, and two other men started letting the rope out to give Chuck the slack that he needed. Chuck was almost to the middle, but the rope was getting soaked and it was getting heavier.

Chuck had tied the rope around his waist. There were 100 feet of rope in the water behind him. The rope behind him was getting heavier and heavier as it soaked up the river water. Chuck was struggling. Instead of swimming straight, he was going downstream. I dropped my rifle and my rucksack in case I had to jump in. Chuck was now swimming for all he was worth, trying desperately to get to the other side. He was spending more time under the water now than on top. I yelled out, "He isn't going to make it!"

I slid off of the muddy embankment and into the water. I started running on the rocks, trying to get to the deeper water. Before I got to the deeper water, I started hearing, "He made it! He made it! Sergeant Rock, come back! He made it!"

I was in two feet of water, lying on my side, because in my haste I had tripped. I stood up and saw Chuck holding the rope and sitting in two feet of water. He was resting. He was completely worn out. No one said anything to Chuck, for all could see how exhausted he was. I climbed back up the small, muddy cliff and the men started patting me on my back. "That was close!"

"He is really a hero for doing that!"

I get to the top of the embankment and look at Chuck. He is tying off his end of the rope to a tree. Two men on our side of the river start to tie off the rope. They dropped the rope. The end of the rope drops in the water. Twenty men yell out, "Get it! Get it!"

Two men jump in the water and grab the rope. Lieutenant Gibbons says, "If you lose that rope, I'll shoot you myself!"

I reply to Gibbons, "Sir, don't worry about shooting them. If they lose that rope, Chuck will kill them himself."

The lieutenant laughs. "I bet he would for sure!"

The men secured the rope to a tree on our side of the river. The company starts to move across the river. Each man was holding on to the rope, and trying to hold their weapons above their heads. We started off in the usual manner — first platoon, first squad, second, third, and fourth squad. Next was the second platoon, first, second, third and fourth squad. We kept this up until all four platoons were across the river.

As we were crossing the river, I couldn't help but wonder, *What if we were attacked while we were in the water? What if we were attacked before we could get set up on the other side? What if Chuck had drowned?* There I go thinking too much again. My squad reached the other side. Chuck was waiting for us. "Man, Chuck, that looked terrible. I thought that you were a goner!"

Chuck smiles. "I was just pretending it was bad so I could get a medal!"

I replied, "Yeah, right!" and slapped him on the back.

"Hey, Danny, what were you doing in the water anyhow?"

"I was coming to save you."

Chuck says, "Save me? I thought that I was going to have to drop the rope and go back and save you! You know that I can outswim you any day!"

We laughed. "I know it, but you still had me worried."

"Yeah, I know it. We try to take care of each other. I know that you always have my back."

My radio sounds off, "Blackhawk Three, this is Annihilator Three-Three, over."

"This is Blackhawk Three, go."

"Tell your man Lewis that he did a good job. We need more men like him."

"Affirmative. I will tell him, over."

"That's all, just tell him, out!"

I walked over to Chuck. "Hey, Chuck, you impressed the old man!"

"How is that?"

"By your little swim across the river."

"For sure, did the old man really say something?"

"Yep, you made him proud!"

My radio sounds, "Move out!"

We had filled up our canteens. We did not take a bath because we were soaked anyhow. Besides, this river was just too deep and swift. We started moving. A few hours later, we reached our destination. We did the usual, setting up a perimeter, assigning guard duty, and digging foxholes. Chuck comes to me with a request. "Hey, Rock, my transistor radio is dead. Does your RTO have any extra batteries?"

"No, but I will go to the CP. The captain's RTO always carries extra batteries."

I walked to the center of the perimeter to where the RTO would be. Then I saw Roberts. He would not let us have any part of his batteries in the past. He would burn them. Maybe after we had had our little confrontation a while back, he has changed his mind.

"Roberts, I want a section of your old battery from your radio. Do you have one?"

"Yes, I am going to burn it tonight."

"No you are not! We want to listen to the Armed Forces Network."

He says, "I can't do it! I am supposed to burn it!"

I got in his face. "Don't you remember our last conversation?"

He backs up. "I remember, but you are not getting the battery!"

"You know something, Roberts? I have quite a few men over there that want to listen to their transistor radios!"

He answers, "So what?"

I get back in his face. I start to whisper, "Now let me finish what I was telling you. The next time we are in a firefight, don't be surprised if you were to get shot by a friendly. The shot could come from a guy that has a transistor radio that does not work."

"Is that a threat?"

I smiled and said, "Oh, of course not, Roberts. It is just that guys, without transistor radios to listen to, get nervous. Sometimes they shake a little when they start to shoot. You know what I mean? Their aim is completely off!"

"Well, Sergeant Rodgers, you won't have to worry about it very much longer!"

Everyone else called me Sergeant Rock, but not Roberts. This also made me angry with him. "What do you mean, 'I won't have to worry about it much longer?'"

"I am being transferred to Delta Company in a few days. Maybe the captain's next RTO will break the rules, and maybe he will give you his batteries."

I started to walk away. I turned back toward Roberts again, getting very close to him. "You are a piece of crap. I hope that you get shot."

I turned and headed back toward the squad. On my way back, I started to think about what I had said. I really did not want him dead. I actually wanted to just beat him half to death. Yeah, that is what I wanted. I just wanted him in a lot of pain. I arrived at the location of my squad. Vietnam was changing me.

"Hey, Danny, did you get the batteries?"

"No, the crap-face wouldn't let me have them!"

Killer says, "You mean Roberts?"

"Yes."

White says, "Hey, Killer, the next time we get into a firefight, let's shoot him!"

Killer replies, "OK with me. Sounds good."

I start to speak. "You men listen to me. We are not going to kill any of our own people! You guys listen to me!"

Killer looks at White. "White, the sarge is right! We shouldn't kill any of our own men. Don't you agree?"

White tilts his head to the side. "What?"

Killer continues, "Yeah, we won't kill him. We will just shoot him."

White responds, "Yes, that's the ticket. Target practice!"

I shake my head. "I am your sergeant. If you shoot him, I will be in trouble! Remember your moral compass."

"Would you tell on us, Sarge, if we did shoot him?"

"No, I wouldn't, but don't place me in that position!"

Killer says, "Do you guys remember when Warmont was asleep on guard duty and someone threw a grenade in the foxhole with him? Sergeant Rock did not tell on us then, so he won't tell on us now!"

I answered, "No! No! No! I never knew if the grenade was friendly or incoming. I had my suspicions, but I had no facts!"

Chuck says, "Sergeant Rock knows that we have to have each other's back over here in the 'Nam, but he wants you guys to just think before you act."

I look at Chuck. "Thanks, man! How about assigning guard?"

"I already did it, Sarge!"

"Cool, where am I?"

"You are fourth, after Raymond."

We sat around for an hour or so, just shooting the breeze. I was very lucky to have a group of guys like these in the 'Nam. We started pulling guard and listening to the sounds of Vietnam in the distance. I remember times in the States while camping, listening to the sounds of the woods at night. I would hear birds chirping. I would hear a couple of woodpeckers. I would hear crickets. I would hear the crackling of the fire as it burnt down to just an ember. I would always hear an owl. I sometimes would hear a coyote in the distance.

Here in Vietnam, I also heard the sounds of night. I heard the rockets exploding in the distance. I heard the mortars going off. I could hear the firefight as the M-16s and the enemy's AK-47s were firing. I could hear the helicopter blades hitting the damp, heavy Vietnam air. I could hear the tanks firing their big guns.

There is one thing that Vietnam had that was better than the States. On a clear night, and when we were on top of a hill or mountain, we could see all of the firefights going on in the surrounding areas. It was beautiful. The view was better than the Fourth of July fireworks display. The night was now over, and it was time to get ready for the day.

We ate our C-ration breakfast and started to get our equipment ready for the day's hump. The lieutenant called me to his location and pointed on his map where we were heading. I pulled my map out and marked it. The lieutenant grabs the sling of my M-14. "I see that you are still carrying the sniper rifle and the M-16. Is it getting heavy yet?"

"Affirmative. I am just glad we are not in triple canopy jungle!"

I went back to my squad. White asks, "Do we have point, Sarge?"

"No, squad two has it. I'll pull point for our squad. Let's go! Raymond, you follow me, then White!"

We started moving. It was another very hot day. We kept hearing that the temperature was between 120 and 135 degrees. I did not know if that was factual. All that I knew was that it was really, really hot. We humped for an hour, and White starts complaining that he cannot carry ammo for the M-60 machine gun any longer.

Raymond says, "Give them to me, White!"

Raymond is already carrying two more ammo belts than he should. Raymond grabs the two belts from White and slings them over his shoulder. I look at Raymond and hold out my hand. "Here, give me an ammo belt!"

He says, "No, Sarge, I can handle it. Let me hump for a while with them. If they are too much, I will tell you."

"OK, but let me know if it gets too much on you."

We start to travel in and out of rice paddies. This is dangerous because when the company is in the open, in a rice paddy, the enemy can wipe us out. Our captain was very smart about situations like this. He would have us get extra space between us, like the old Army saying, "Spread out. One round will get you all!"

The captain, as I did, took this to heart! The captain would also keep one platoon in the tree line while another platoon crossed the flats to get to another tree line. The first platoon crossed the flat rice paddies and got into the tree line. The captain was in the second platoon, along with Roberts. The second platoon started crossing while the rest of the platoons watched for any enemy movement.

The second platoon was halfway across when all heck broke loose. The enemy had the captain and his men pinned down behind a rice paddy dike. I could tell by the excessive amount of firepower that these guys were NVA. They were not VC. Raymond hit the ground, firing the Pig as he hit the earth with his knees. My men knew what to do. They all started spreading out and firing their weapons. Raymond started firing rounds over the second platoon's heads and into the tree line opposite our first platoon.

Again, Raymond was dead on. I started firing, shooting five round bursts and then taking careful aim, trying to kill without wasting ammo. The second platoon was pinned so tight against the dike that they could not fire back. I saw the captain's RTO, Roberts, in the open.

Roberts was protected from the enemy by the dike, but he was in the open from our view. I looked over at Killer and White. They were huddled together, pointing in the direction of Roberts. Now I not only have to worry about the second platoon getting killed by the enemy, I have to worry that White and Killer are going to shoot Roberts. I roll and dive and run and lunge until I reach them.

"Don't shoot Roberts!"

They laugh. I think to myself, *How can anyone laugh at a time like this?* "What are you guys laughing at?"

"Sarge, we aren't shooting at Roberts. Just look at him!"

I looked at Roberts and started laughing myself. He had a clear view of us. Roberts was watching every move that we were making. He would look forward, then he would look back really fast. He spent more time looking at White, Killer, and myself than the enemy. He was so afraid of being shot by us that he probably crapped his pants.

Killer says, "Now look at this, Sarge! I am not going to shoot him, but watch him!"

Killer held his sights right on Roberts. Roberts sees the rifle being aimed at him. He covers his head with his hands and arms and puts his head between his legs. We laugh again.

"OK, guys, keep firing into the tree line. Artillery will be here soon."

I took off toward Raymond, acting like a scared rabbit as I ran, trying to get back to my position. I hit the ground hard next to Raymond. I asked my RTO if anyone wanted me to call in firepower. He says, "No, it sounds like the captain is going to call it in!"

I look at Raymond. "How are you doing, Raymond?"

"Great! Do you wanna shoot the Pig?"

"Heck yeah!"

I jumped over him and started shooting. I was shooting over the captain's and Roberts's heads, but I needed to be more accurate. I had to lower my bullet trajectory so I could hit my targets. I was shooting one foot over their heads, trying to make my rounds hit the tree line targets. This was not close enough. I had to get lower. I started shooting six inches above the heads of the captain and Roberts. I started hitting my targets. Our artillery started coming in.

Roberts looks back at me. He notices that I am firing the Pig. Raymond, White, Killer, and I look at each other and grin. I say, "Watch this, men."

I started firing the M-60 rounds, hitting three feet away from Roberts. The rounds were hitting the dike and making mud fly on him. I wanted to scare him even further, so I brought the rounds closer to his frightened, scared, sissy girl body.

"I bet he has crapped his pants now for sure," I said.

The rockets were hitting hard and fast. The captain was doing a great job. I didn't know how he could see his targets, being pinned down like he was, but he made it happen. The enemy's rounds had stopped coming in our direction. The second platoon started moving. They moved to the tree line and took their position to cover our platoon.

Our platoon moved quickly to the tree line, followed by the fourth. Chuck moves close to me. "I see that Roberts made it! I saw you going over to White and Killer. Were they going to shoot him?"

I proceeded to tell Chuck the story about Roberts and how he acted. He laughed so hard that I thought he would split a gut. I walked over to the captain. Roberts sheepishly looks at me. I get a big grin on my face. "How are you doing, Roberts?"

He frowns. "Don't talk to me!"

The captain hears him. "Don't you ever speak to a superior like that again, Private Roberts! You speak to Sergeant Rock with respect!"

Roberts shakes his head. "Yes, sir."

The captain asks, "Hey, Rock, how did you like that fire support call in?"

I answered, "It was really, really good. I couldn't have done it better myself!"

The captain looks around as if looking for something. "Hey, Rock, who taught you to call in fire support?" I grinned because he was the one that made me a specialist at it. Before I could answer, he looked at Roberts. "Oh, yeah, it was me that taught you fire support."

We both laughed. The captain started to walk away and with a grin on his face he says, "See ya, Rock."

"See ya, sir."

I looked at Roberts. "When did you say you were leaving?"

He answers, "The sooner I can get away from you guys, the better!"

"Don't let the door knob hit you in the butt on your way out! You know something, Roberts? You could be a good soldier if you would try to get along with people. Good luck."

CHAPTER 11

Roberts Dies a Horrifying Death

I left Roberts and walked back to the squad. While I was walking, I was aware that we could be hit again at anytime. I reached the squad, and immediately Lieutenant Gibbons came to our location.

"Man, Rock, that was sort of hairy! I thought that the captain was going to eat it!"

"Yeah, he could have, but did you notice how he kept the platoons all spread out? If we would have been all bunched up, we would have been caught in the open in the rice paddies."

"Do you think the captain is a good leader?"

"Yep, he is one of the best!"

Gibbons looked at me. "Do you think that you would be as good as he is, if you commanded the company?"

I thought for a moment. "No, he is the best. I still have a lot to learn, but I think that I could handle the job. It would just take a little time for me to be of his caliber. We have already told you about January ninth at Khe Sanh, right?"

"Yeah, you guys have told me a lot."

I pointed at my rucksack. "Sir, this is worth telling you again."

"What's that, Sarge?"

"When the captain stood up — actually, he was already standing up — he had his .45 pistol out. Rounds were coming in, along with tracers. He had his rucksack on when an NVA round hit it. He just said, 'Dang it, they got my lima beans and ham!' He also had another round hit his rucksack. What a man!"

"Rock, you said something about letters?"

"Oh, yeah, he is a little strange in that regard. When he gets his letters from home, he says that he does not have time for them, and he burns the letters. *Them* being his family from home."

Gibbons says, "Man, I love my letters from home!"

"Yeah, me too, sir. I also love the care packages. You know, the cookies, Kool-Aid, and other things."

"Oh, yeah, Rock? When is your mom going to send some more of those delicious cookies? What kind are they?"

"They are persimmon cookies! Yeah, my mom is the very best cook in the world!"

The lieutenant's radio sounds, "Move 'em out!"

"Roger, out," the lieutenant's X-ray said.

Normally, the lieutenant would call me to forward the message, but since he was right in front of me, he said, "You heard him, Sergeant Rock, move 'em out!"

My men were listening to our conversation. My squad was getting ready. Chuck had already assigned point to Eckert. We were heading, once more, to the clearing. We called it the clearing because it was the area where I had called in the artillery to clear out the enemy. We started to travel. I received a call from the lieutenant. "We are holding up for Platoon One to count bodies."

I answer, "Roger, out."

We are in limbo for fifteen minutes. Annihilator gets on the radio. "Forty-four. The body count is forty-four. Very good, men. Out!"

The captain is very happy. Body count, body count, body count is all that we ever hear. But just like the captain, the men and I would get all excited about how many gooks we had killed. The excitement of the killing was getting in our blood. Killing forty-four was good, but when we kill them with bullets and artillery, it is not as exciting as bullets alone. The company, of course, would get the credit for the kills. We could not say that my squad got four, or another squad got ten, or a platoon got twenty. We could only say that the company, as a whole, killed another forty-four. Our company was keeping up with our reputation, and the captain loved it. I have to admit that I loved the reputation also. The company started moving again.

We humped for another couple of hours to the clearing. It was still daylight when we arrived. We set up the perimeter and assigned guard duty. My RTO, Craig, is on the radio. He listens, then he walks toward me. "Hey, Sarge, Annihilator says that a chopper is coming in to give the company ammo."

"Yeah, we could use a little more! I hope they have 7.62 for the Pig!"

We start to hear the distinctive sound of the Huey chopper. The sound is in the distance, but we know it is coming. It is now in sight. We hear shots being fired at the chopper. It is now a hot LZ. I know what is going to happen next. We didn't need any orders. The whole company starts firing as furiously and as fast as possible. The door gunners start firing continually with only a pause after twenty rounds or so. This was great. This part of Vietnam I loved. My heart was beating very fast with excitement. My men were yelling as they were shooting. "Yeah, yeah, yeah, kill them all!"

This made me laugh, because we could not see a gook anywhere in sight. My men were just like me; they loved to shoot their guns. The chopper started to slow and drop down closer to the rice paddies. The helicopter was hovering. The captain had already assigned men to grab the ammo. I looked at the chopper and noticed that it was staying in the same spot longer than it usually did, especially since it had just received enemy fire.

I saw someone running to the chopper. It was Roberts. Killer and Chuck are watching. Chuck says, "Good, good, good, he is finally gone!"

Killer says, "They will hate him if he acts the same there as he did here. By the way, where is he going?"

"He is going to Delta Company. He is going to be their captain's RTO."

"He actually is a good RTO; he is just a bad person!"

The chopper takes off, hauling the trash, or should I say Roberts, out with it. My men are giving Roberts the finger. Everyone is flipping Roberts off, except for Emerald and me. I look at them and shake my head. "What are you guys doing?"

Killer says, "We are giving him the one finger salute. Aren't you really actually glad that he is gone, Sarge?"

"Yes, I am."

Night was almost upon us. I heard my radio. "Blackhawk Three, we are going to have a mad minute in zero-five."

I loved the mad minutes. They were exciting, heart-throbbing, blood pumping, mental stimulation minutes. Although I hated everything about Vietnam, I loved these minutes. I tell my men, "We are going to have a mad minute in five minutes!"

My men could tell by the excitement in my voice, the look in my eye, and my big smile that this is my moment. My men all jump to the ground with their rifles in the prone position, except for Raymond. Raymond asks, "Sarge, what in the heck is a mad minute?"

"Oh, man, Raymond, you will love it! The whole company fires as many rounds as possible in one minute. We fire away from our perimeter, you know, sort of like the circled wagon trains fighting the Indians. We fire as fast as we can, and sometimes we call in artillery. If an enemy is out there, they will be gone in one minute!"

Raymond responds, "That is the reason we received all of this extra ammo?"

I answered, "Yep, the captain plans ahead."

Raymond starts to get in his firing position. I move in his direction. "Oh, yeah, Raymond, I forgot to tell you, it is a law that the squad leader gets to shoot the machine gun during the mad minute!"

"Is that for real, Sarge?"

"No, I am just messing with you, Raymond."

I pretended to be sad. Raymond looks at my fake sad face and laughs. "OK, Sarge, take it. I'll feed the ammo to you."

"Thanks, Raymond."

I am standing up when Raymond says, "Aren't you going to lay down in the prone position?"

My sad face was gone and I was smiling from ear to ear. "No, I ain't no sissy!"

I hear the radio. It is the captain's voice. "Men, listen up! In five, four, three, two, one. *Fire! Fire! Fire!*"

The whole company opened up at the same time. The sound was as loud as a top fueler drag car at the drag strip. I was opening up on full automatic, moving the Pig from side to side. I was chopping up the jungle. Tree limbs were flying. I was not taking my finger off of the trigger, like we were supposed to do. Seven round bursts were not something that I wanted to do during this mad minute. The barrel was getting hot, hot, hot. The barrel was turning white from the heat. I was in the zone. I could do this all night long. With ten seconds left in our mad minute, the Pig jammed. This was not going to stop me. I grabbed my M-16 and my M-14 rifles. I started firing both weapons at the same time. It was hard to do, but my adrenaline was at its peak. I was John Wayne; nothing was going to stop me now. Then I heard those discouraging words. "Cease fire! Cease fire! Cease fire!"

I wasn't ready to quit. I jammed another magazine in my M-16 and ripped off the whole magazine. The mad minute was over. My men were all in jubilation. "Thanks, Raymond. That was fun!"

Raymond says, "If I had another barrel, I could have changed it out for you, Sarge!"

"Yeah, that would have been cool, but carrying another barrel is just too much weight!"

Artillery starts coming in. We all hit the ground. *Is it our firepower or the NVA?* It is not long before we realize that it is friendly fire. The captain is dropping shells all around our perimeter. He is doing another good job. The men and I pull out our C-rations and start eating. We are just sitting around talking. Killer says, "You know, that mad minute is really fun!"

The men start saying, "It is, isn't it?"

"There is not a living thing alive after that!"

"Hey, Sarge, do we ever find dead people after the mad minute?"

"No, not usually, but we have a few times. Generally, they are VC."

Eckert looks at me. "Man, Sarge, you still love the mad minutes, don't you?"

"Yes I do, Eckert. Don't you?"

"Oh, yeah, I do too!"

Chuck is going through his C-rations. "Anybody want to trade canned cookies for pound cake?"

Emery says, "Do you have the cookies?"

"Yes, I want your pound cake for my cookies."

They swap the food. I say to Chuck, "Do you remember when Warmont gave thirty-five dollars for a can of fruit cocktail?"

"Yeah, but it was peaches."

"Oh, yeah, peaches."

"Yes, he was a piece of work."

Raymond says, "Was he the guy that I took the place of?"

"Yes he was."

"He got wounded, didn't he?"

Killer says, "Yeah, he got wounded alright."

Raymond says, "I guess that he got a Purple Heart?"

There was a dead silence among my men, then Killer says, "Man, *we* gave that idiot a medal, didn't we, Sergeant Lewis?"

Chuck says, "You mean *you* gave the idiot a medal. I had nothing to do with it!"

I look at Killer. "Are you telling me for sure that you threw the grenade on Warmont?"

Killer, with a big grin on his face answers, "Oh, no, Sarge, I just meant that if we would have given Warmont more protection, then he wouldn't have been wounded. The grenade must have been from a VC."

"What do you mean *more protection*?"

Killer, again with a big grin, says, "I just think that we should have protected him by way of not letting him pull guard duty, because he always fell asleep on guard duty."

I rolled my eyes and tilted my head back. "Yeah, right."

I was 99.9 percent sure that he threw the grenade that wounded Warmont, but I had no proof. I tried to forget about it, because I knew that over here in the 'Nam, surviving is the name of the game. To stay alive, we would need every good man we could get. Killer was one of the best when it came to fighting. Raymond asks, "Do any of you men have a Purple Heart?"

I answer quickly, "Yes, Sergeant Lewis at Khe Sanh Valley."

"Is that the place that you guys call Death Valley? Where did you get shot, Sergeant Lewis? Why do you call it Death Valley?"

Chuck answers as he points at the back of his leg. "It wasn't a bullet; it was shrapnel. We call it Death Valley because there are so many deaths."

"How long were you out, Sergeant Lewis?"

"About two weeks."

"Why did you come back to the field so quick?"

"Sergeant Rock needed me. Our company needs leadership people because we lose men so fast. Besides, I protect Rock and he protects me."

I tell the men, "OK, men, get some sleep."

Chuck immediately sets up guard duty assignments. The balance of the night was quiet.

Morning came, and it was time for breakfast. Craig, my RTO, speaks to me. "Cherokee and Annihilator want you at the CP."

I arrived at the CP. I saw all of the platoon leaders and the platoon sergeants standing around talking. I see squad leaders, Mack and Windel, from another platoon. "Hey Mack, hey Windel, what's happening?"

Mack says, "Don't know, but something big is going on!"

The captain says, "Is everybody here?"

We start looking around. Gibbons says, "Looks like it, sir."

"OK, listen up. There is a lot of enemy activity where we are going. Both NVA and VC. You guys see that mountain behind me? That is where we are going, but here is the bad thing — it is mined on the other side. We will bivouac for the night on top of the mountain, and then we will have to go down the other side tomorrow. I believe that we will be engaging the NVA. Put your best men on point. OK, men, dismissed."

There was not much said as we walked away. We knew that this was serious. I arrived at my squad and proceeded to tell them the plan when my radio sounded, "Blackhawk Three, this is Cherokee Three, over."

"This is Blackhawk Three, over."

"We have point, and I think that your squad should pull point!"

"Affirmative. I'll set it up!"

Raymond says, "I'll pull point!"

I say with a slight grin, "No, but thanks anyhow. I think that we need a real experienced guy."

Chuck says, "Rock, I know that I am your team leader, but I want to do it!"

"OK, Chuck, but when you get tired, I'll relieve you."

Pulling point today was going to be a mental challenge. "Men, Sergeant Lewis, our team leader, is going to pull point! How is your water supply?"

Every squad had two teams. The squad leader is in charge of the whole squad and half the team. The team leader is in charge of the other half of the squad. Chuck and I worked very well together. He could take over as squad leader at any time, and I would have complete confidence in him. The men start telling me how much water they have in their canteens.

Over here in the 'Nam, little things like water are important. I sure wish that I had a glass of Mom's iced tea. I was sure that everyone wanted something cold to drink. The water in our canteens was hot; not warm, but hot! We started moving out.

Chuck is at point and I am second in line. I look at Craig, my RTO. "Be sure and have the antenna turned down."

Craig unscrewed the swivel and placed the antenna in the down position. If the antenna is in the up position, above the radio, the enemy could see it. It could also get caught in the bush. However, the main purpose for turning the antenna down is to protect the man in front of the radio. The enemy knew that there was always an important man near the radio. Many times, a sniper would kill the man standing nearest the radio.

"Craig, it is starting to rain. Be sure your plastic sheet is on the radio!"

"Will do, Sarge!"

We were humping toward the mountain. My squad was pulling point for the whole company. The captain decided to have each squad and each platoon follow one after another in single file. Emery gets close to me. "How come everyone is in single file? The whole company?"

"The old man is worried about landmines."

"Are you, Sarge?"

"Very much so. I am worried."

It was raining harder now. I slow up to wait for Emery. "Emery, be sure and turn your rifle upside down and try to keep it dry. Pass it on."

Emery waited for the next man and passed the message. I really did not know if turning the rifle upside down would help keep the water out. It was raining so hard now that it didn't matter which way we held our weapons. We were getting soaked. The rifles had water running down them. The rain was falling so hard on our helmets that it sounded like little hammers hitting them.

The water was running over the lip of our helmets and into our faces. It was hard to speak with the rain running so fast over our faces. I hoped that we didn't get shot at now because we had to keep our faces looking down to keep the water away from our eyes. Emery came closer to me. He held his hand above his top lip so he could speak. "Sarge, a guy could really drown in this mess! How long will this last?"

"I don't know. It is hard to say, and you are right, a guy could actually drown with all the rain that is falling."

I could just picture the gooks sitting back in their hooches laughing, keeping dry while we are humping through the monsoon. We were starting to slip and fall. I watched Chuck trying to get up a small ledge. He fell three times before he made it. Normally we would laugh, but not in this mess. Moving was like being in ice. It was not quite that slippery, but slippery enough for someone to break a leg or an arm. I looked around and saw that everyone was muddy.

I looked back at the men and saw that the pounding rain was washing off the mud. As we fell and took our spills, the mud would get under our fatigues. This feeling was terrible, but we had to keep moving. After another four hours, we reached the top of the mountain. Our destination took one and a half hours longer than it should have. The rain starts to slow. We start to set up our guard assignments. Chuck is telling the men who is first, second, third, etc. Craig says, "Sarge, Cherokee wants to see you!"

"OK, thanks, Craig. How is your radio?"

"Seems to be working fine."

I walked toward Lieutenant Gibbons's location. As I walked, I thought about what Craig said about his radio — "Working fine."

I remembered January ninth, when none of our radios were working. But in that case, the radios were under water in the river. I guess I will never forget about that battle and all the men that died. I arrived at Gibbons's location. "Hey, Rock!"

"Hey, sir!"

"Tell your guys when they dig in tonight to watch out for mines. This whole area is supposed to be mined."

"OK, sir, we will watch it."

I turned and walked to the squad. "Hey, men, stop digging and come over here! Watch out for mines when you are digging the foxholes!"

The men acknowledged what I had told them. Chuck says, "Do you really think that this area is mined?"

"Yes, but I think that the mines are going to be planted in the path on our way down the other side."

The men and I were searching and digging very slowly. We finally dug a few holes half the size that they should have been. We also probed the ground before we placed our ponchos for sleeping. The rain has now stopped, and the stars are out. We can see the valley below. We start guard duty and try to get some sleep.

At 3:30 in the morning, the sound of weapons firing awakens us. I look in the distance and I can see where the battle was happening. I run over to the lieutenant's location. "Do you know what is happening, sir?"

"Not yet. The captain is finding out right now."

The radio sounds. "It is Delta Company, and they are in an ambush! We cannot call in fire support because we don't know who is who; they are too close to one another!"

"I am going back to my squad, sir!"

"OK."

I arrive and see that all of the men are awake and alert. I tell them it is Delta Company in an ambush. White says, "Isn't that where Roberts was transferred?"

Killer says, "Yeah!"

There was a dead silence with the men. We could see from the firefight that this was serious. We sat watching the firefight like it was a drive-in movie. As we watched the rifle flashes and the tracer rounds, we could see that the enemy was in a half circle on the right. The men from Delta Company charged the enemy while firing their weapons at the half circle. The enemy in the half circle on the right stopped firing. As soon as the firing stopped on one side of the circle, the other side of the circle started firing.

More of the Delta Company's soldiers started charging the circle on the left. The enemy stopped firing from the left circle and started firing again from the right. Eckert says, "What do you think, Sarge?"

"I think that they are surrounded."

"But how do the gooks keep from shooting each other?"

"I am not sure, but they sure have it down pat. They know what they are doing!"

I now see long blasts of fire coming from the enemy. White runs toward me. "Sarge, they are using flamethrowers!"

I answer, "Man, this is going to be bad!"

We can see large things burning like trees, bushes, and hooches, and we can see small things burning. The small things that are burning are moving. Sometimes moving a lot, sometimes moving a little. Delta Company has only four men firing at the enemy, then three, then two, then one, then none. Delta Company is wiped out. But we see that more is happening.

The NVA or VC are walking around, or so it appears, because we hear a shot and then a body is burnt with the flamethrower. I say to White, "Go get the starlight night scope!"

White takes off in a hurry. He returns and gives me the scope. I look through the scope, and what I see makes my stomach start to ache. The NVA are standing our men up and setting them on fire with the flamethrower. It looks as though the gooks are finding the soldiers that are just wounded. The gooks are making them take off running and then setting them on fire. It appears that once our soldiers fall to the ground, the gooks hold the flamethrower on them until their insides are burnt out.

The gooks are now going around to the rest of the bodies and scorching them. My blood is boiling. I want to kill every gook that I see. Killer comes up to me. "You see why I want to kill every man, woman, and child that lives in this country?"

"Not the kids and the old ladies, Killer, not them!"

Killer answers, "All of them! Every one!"

My radio sounds, "All leaders come to Annihilator!"

I walked to the CP. The captain says, "Men, this is going to be dangerous. We are going to move out now!"

I hear grumbling. I say, "Sir, it is only two hours before daylight. Can't we wait until then?"

"No, we can't, Rock! Command says Delta Company needs us now! I know that it looks like they are wiped out. Command cannot see what we just saw. I know that the trail may be mined. We are moving out. No more questions!"

I walked toward the squad. "Men, we are moving out!"

Emerald says, "To where? Delta Company just got wiped out! We will get wiped out too!"

Killer says, "Don't worry about the NVA or VC wiping us out, because a mine is going to kill us all anyhow. In the dark, we don't stand a chance!"

Eckert says, "What platoon has point, Sarge?"

"It shouldn't be us, Eckert. We pulled point all day!"

My radio sounds, "Blackhawk Three, it will be platoons one, four, two, then us."

What a relief. Our platoon did not have to pull point. I also knew that if my platoon were assigned point, then most likely my squad would have to be first. I motioned to my men to come to me. "Men, it is going to be dangerous. Stay in the footprint of the guy in front of you. Walk where they walk! Now, this part is very important. If you hear a boom, don't jump to the side; just squat down!"

I hear my men say, "OK, Sarge!"

This was ignorant. I was scared just as bad as everyone else. There was no earthly reason why we couldn't wait two more hours before traveling down this mine-infested mountain. This is one time the captain may be wrong. But maybe I was over thinking the situation. In my opinion, it looked like it would take four to five hours to get to Delta Company.

We moved very slowly, watching where the guy was stepping in front of us, and then placing our foot in their footprint. I hoped that the point guys were doing the same. It was so dark that it was hard to see exactly where to step. For an hour, we moved down the mountain with no incidents. Some of the men were starting to whisper things like, "I am hungry. I need a drink."

I turn and say, "Man, you guys shut up!"

We see, hear, and feel a big blast, then another, then another! My men and I squat, except for White; he is in the bushes, covering his head with his hands and arms. We hear screams, and then it is silent. Emery says, "What do you think happened, Sarge?"

"The first platoon has stepped on three mines."

Emery says, "Do you think it happened like you said? Instead of squatting, they jumped to the side?"

"No! When the first one went off, it blew a few men on top of another mine. The sound was located in the same area."

"How many men do you think it got?"

"I don't know, but this was a stupid, air-headed, birdbrain, bone-headed idea. We should have waited until daylight."

My radio makes noise. "We are going to wait here until daylight!"

I wanted to scream out as loud as I could, "That is what I said! Wait for daylight!" I am really hot. This made no sense to me. Delta Company was already wiped out and now we have dead men. With explosions that large, no man is going to live.

My radio goes off again, "Men, it appears as though we have five dead and two wounded!"

Emery says, "It *appears* though. It *appears* though. What does that mean, Sarge?"

"It means that they are so blown to bits that they can't find the bodies! This was a stupid maneuver."

"What will we do now about the body parts?"

"We can't police them up now. It is too dangerous. Later, we will send up a group of minesweepers to find the body parts."

Emery says, "Isn't this strange, how we talk about body parts as if it were just merchandise that was misplaced?"

"You know something, Emery, you are right. But the thing is, most of us have seen so much that I think we get a hard heart when it comes to death. I hope that when I get out of here, I will be normal."

We waited another hour and a half before we started moving slowly down the mountain. The point man would locate the mines and try to mark them. We didn't blow them up. We would do that later with artillery. We were finally on the outskirts of the Delta Company's demise.

Our company completely spread out in case the NVA were in the waiting. We approached closer to where the fighting had taken place. Now I understood how the enemy could crossfire on each other without shooting one another. The NVA had dug a ditch that was four feet deep and in an almost complete circle. It was approximately 270 degrees round. Therefore, they had left ninety degrees of the circle open for a trap. I could see the path between the tree line that led straight to the ambush circle.

The NVA had hidden in the ditches as the Delta Company came through the opening. Delta Company started firing in the direction of the enemy fire. The enemy on one side of the circle would drop down in the ditch, then the enemy on the other side would open up. Delta Company had been caught in crossfire. The captain assigned our platoon to check for the wounded.

The balance of the company pulled guard while we started examining the bodies. The men were angry. We first walked around the ditches, checking for bodies. Killer was on a rampage. Killer shot every gook he saw, wounded or not. The captain was also checking out the bodies. "Sergeant Rock, is Killer having enemy problems?"

"No, I think that he is just having a *no-prisoner* moment."

Finally, we found a live American soldier in the ditch, with two dead NVA.

The soldier's leg was missing, and he was burnt very badly. He had enough strength to say, "Am I going to make it?"

I answered, "Yes, no problem. You will make it!"

We all knew that he was going to die very quickly, but there was no way that we were going to tell him the truth. The soldier died within ten minutes. Now it was time to look inside the perimeter of the circle for wounded soldiers.

Eckert is checking a body. "Sarge, this guy is not burnt, and there are some more over there. Maybe they ran out of fuel!"

"You are probably right."

"Sarge, isn't burning bodies like this against the rules of war?"

"Yep, but according to the newspapers back home, the NVA are not even south of the DMZ. North Vietnam keeps telling America that they don't even come in the south."

"Well, we sure know that that is a lie!"

"These gooks don't care about the rules of war. I am starting to feel like Killer. *Kill them all!*"

"Sarge, did you notice that the gooks took all of the weapons?"

"Yep. I am going to the burnt hooch. Keep looking!"

Before I could get to the hooch, Killer yells out, "Here is a live one!"

"A live what, Killer?"

"One of ours!"

I looked at the soldier. He was not wounded badly, and he even had his M-16. He looked up at four of us standing over him. "Man, am I glad to see you guys. Is everyone dead?"

I said, "It looks like it, but we are still checking. How did you survive?"

"It was all a bunch of dumb luck. Help me out of this ditch, and I will tell you."

We pulled him away from the dead gooks that surrounded him. The soldier began to tell his story.

"My squad was pulling point when we saw three VC running away from us."

I interrupted, "Do you mean NVA?"

"No, they were VC. I know that all you see in the ditch are NVA, but we were chasing VC. We chased them right into an ambush. I was the fourth guy in line. When the NVA opened up on us, I started shooting on full automatic and ran for cover any place I could find. It was so dark that I could not see where I was going. I fell into the ditch right on top of the NVA. I think that I scared them. I just kept shooting and reloading, shooting at point blank range. I killed two or three. Then I pulled the dead men on top of me to hide. I feel a little like a coward, but it looked like there was just no hope for us."

I had a slight grin. "No, you are not a coward. You are just lucky! You know I may write a book someday about all of this? What is your name?"

"My men just call me Dutch."

"My men call me Rock, Sergeant Rock. Where were your captain and his RTO during all of this?"

"The RTO's name is Roberts and he is an idiot. They were both over there by that…well, it used to be a hooch."

"Thanks, Sergeant Dutch."

"No, just Dutch. I am a real sergeant, not an acting jack, but I like Dutch."

"OK, good luck, Dutch! You men keep looking! I'm going to the hooch."

I walked over to examine an area near what used to be a hooch. The hooch was burnt, except for a partial amount of a back wall. There were two bodies. One body had the remains of a radio on its back. This had to be Roberts. The only things left on the body were the soles of his shoes and a couple of small canvas areas of boots. He had some bamboo covering his head and upper chest.

Roberts was too close to his captain for me to walk between the bodies. I decided to pull Roberts out and away from the other body. I placed my hands on what was left of his feet and shoes and pulled as gently as I could. There was a little portion of burnt flesh on each leg, but what I could see mainly was a skeleton. I pulled the body along the ground for about twelve inches when something happened that I thought I would never have to deal with.

Both legs pulled away from the body. Emery and Emerald started vomiting at the sight. I was getting woozy also, but now

I had to look at the rest of the body. I knew that it had to be Roberts, but maybe it wasn't. No, it had to be him, because Dutch had given me the correct information. Maybe I could see his face for a positive identification.

I got closer to the head of the body and started pulling the bamboo and hooch material away. What I saw next made me sick. Roberts had no face. He had no skin or hair whatsoever. I looked at his eye sockets and I could see clean through the sockets to the inside of the back of his head. His brain had been completely burned and boiled from his head. I did not know that this was even possible. I also examined the rest of the body. The radio was melted into Roberts's back. Killer comes up to me. "Is that Roberts?"

"Yes. This will be a day I will remember forever."

Killer places his rifle near Roberts head. "Did you see this, Sarge? You can see the inside of the back of his head."

"Yes, I saw it."

Killer says, "I knew that I was right. I just knew it."

"What do you mean, Killer?"

"I told Roberts lots of times that he was stupid and brainless. This proves it. He didn't have a brain."

"Man, Killer, even Roberts didn't need to die that way!"

"Yeah, I guess you are right, Sarge, but he did mess with you and Sergeant Lewis too much."

CHAPTER 12

Don't Mess with Rock and Lewis

We spent a few more hours checking out bodies. Many of the soldiers were not burnt. I had originally thought that all of our soldiers would be blackened from the flamethrower. I was happy to see dead bodies that were not charred. Eckert approaches me. "Isn't this terrible, Sarge?"

"It sure is."

"Sarge, do you think that other companies have seen as much action as we have?"

"Yes I do, but I don't think that they have seen the horror like we have seen. We lose men every week now. That is bad enough, but the way we see men killed is what gets to me. Some of our guys die horrible deaths. Like Roberts. He was a jerk, but I really didn't want him to die!"

Eckert replies, "Maybe his death will be a lesson to the men. Don't mess with Sergeant Rock or Sergeant Lewis or something may happen to them!"

He laughs and slaps me on the back. My radio sounds, "Blackhawks, all of you, come to Cherokee's location."

I turned and looked around. *Where was Cherokee?* I saw him at the opening of the gooks' circle. I walked toward the lieutenant's CP.

While I was walking I saw all three of the other squad leaders. "Man, Rock, this is bad. How do you think we will load them on a chopper? Or will we?"

"Yeah, I think we will probably glad-bag 'em, you know, body bag 'em."

"That will be better than trying to carry them in pieces."

I arrived at Gibbons's location. The lieutenant started speaking. "Men, this is the worst that I have ever seen. Sergeant Rock, is this worse than your battle of January ninth?"

"Yes, sir, it is worse. These men were individually destroyed. On January ninth, our guys were just shot over and over again until they died. Then they were robbed of their belongings. Yep, this is bad!"

The lieutenant says, "Here is what is going to happen. The choppers are going to bring in the body bags, then take off. Once we have them bagged up, we will rack 'em and stack 'em. Place the stacks where they will be on each side of the choppers when they come in. How many can we get on a chopper, Rock?"

"Six. No more or the chopper can't lift!"

"OK, men, load six! Go back to your squads and wait."

All four of us head back to our squads, talking as we walk.

Wyman says, "Rock, you know how you hear the saying, 'I am too old for this'?"

"Yeah, I have heard that saying."

"Well, Rock, here is my saying. 'I am too young for this'!"

"Yep, I know what you mean. How old are you, Wyman?"

"I am nineteen, almost twenty. Do you think we will make our whole tour of Vietnam without being killed?"

I say to him, "What is a squad leader supposed to tell his men about that?"

Wyman rolls his eyes. "I know. I know we are supposed to tell them that we are winning every battle and no one is going to die. But, just between you and me, what do you think?"

"Alright, Wyman, here is my true belief! If things don't start getting better soon, we are all going to die. But don't tell your men a thing."

"I won't. See you, Rock."

He walked away, heading back to his squad. Artillery starts coming in. I hurry over to my RTO.

"Craig, is that ours?"

"Affirmative!"

The artillery shells were coming in, hitting all around our perimeter. The captain was calling in the artillery. He kept the firepower coming in for ten minutes. Five minutes later, the choppers start coming in. The first three choppers drop off the glad bags and fly away. Our platoon was in charge of loading the bags with bodies. The bags were really heavy-duty bags, much, much thicker than heavy-duty garbage bags. Each bag had a zipper. My men were picking and choosing which bodies they wanted to place in the bag.

The men were going first for the bodies that were not burnt. I was doing the same thing. I found a body that had been shot four or five times, maybe more. I pulled opened his shirt to locate his dog tags, being as careful as I could not to touch the skin. Touching the skin of a cold body gave me the creeps. I placed one of the dog tags in his mouth between his front teeth.

After I had placed the dog tag between the teeth, it was time to get the body into the bag. I looked around for Chuck, but he was helping someone else. "White, come and be my partner!"

"Sure, Sarge."

We loaded the body in the bag and dragged it to the middle of the circle. "White, let's go get another one!"

We started looking for a non-burnt body, but they were all in bags. "Let's load this one, White!"

"Man, Sarge, this one is burnt too bad. I will find a better body."

"White, I thought nothing like this bothered you. Don't you remember Proud Mary?"

"Yeah, but this is much worse than her."

"I agree."

I stayed next to the body that I had picked out while White looked for another. I started to look for the dog tags, but I was getting grossed out. I decided to not place the tags in between the teeth like we were supposed to do.

White comes back. "We had better stick with this one."

"The others are even worse, huh?"

"Yep."

"How are we going to do this, White?"

I hoped White would have a better idea than I.

"You are the boss, Sarge!"

We placed the glad bag along the side of the body and unzipped it. We unfolded the topside of the bag. We proceeded to pull the bag as close as possible to the body. "White, we are going to have to suck it up, bite the bullet, take the pain, and push the body in the bag!"

White is shaking his head. "Man, oh man, Sarge! OK, let's do it!"

White and I quickly reached down and grabbed the legs and arms, shoving them in the bag. The back of the body was not in the bag completely. I looked at White.

We were both on our knees. "On three, White. One, two, now!"

We both pushed the burnt back of the soldier into the bag. We placed the body on the stack. "Sarge, do you know what we forgot to do?"

"No, what?"

"The tags!"

"No, I didn't forget. They were probably melted anyhow. I just didn't want to do it. Besides, if the body is in a bag, they will just have to look for the tags when they take the body out. I really think that the dog tags being placed between the teeth or on the big toe is for bodies that we have to leave behind. Now for the hard one, White! We are going to load Roberts."

White says, "I thought I heard he had been killed."

"Follow me, White."

We walked to the body of Roberts and his captain. White stops in his tracks. "My, oh my, these guys are bad! How do you know which one is Roberts?"

"He has a radio melted to his back. Also, the guy named Dutch told me it was him."

White is looking at the hardhat of the other man. "Look, Sarge, doesn't that look like captain bars on his camouflage cover?"

The ranking bars in Vietnam are not bright and shiny; they are black, or they may be marked on the camouflage cover with an ink pen or a felt-tip pen.

"Yeah it is. OK, this proves it. This is Roberts."

We start to spread the body bag next to Roberts's cold, black, burnt body. Roberts looks more like a skeleton than a dead body. Together we push and shove Roberts until we get him in the bag. I see no dog tags, but it does look like something is melted to his chest bones. Emery and Emerald come up to us. "We'll drag the body to the pile, OK?"

White grabs the bag. "Heck no, we loaded it and we will drag it. You two put the captain in a bag, not us!"

White thought that they wanted to drag a glad bag rather than touch a burnt body. I knew that White was correct in his assessment. I looked at Emery. "How many have you two put in a bag?"

"None, Sarge."

"Well, it is time that you did. I don't like this any better than you two birds, so get after it!"

White and I drag Roberts over to the stack of bodies. I looked at White. "White, go over and see Doc. Ask him for one of those information cards and fill it out for Roberts. Stick it in the bag."

"OK, Sarge. What should I fill in for his job? *Jerk?*"

"Yeah, right."

I looked over at Emery and Emerald. They were having a hard time loading the Delta Company's captain into the body bag. I walked up to them. "What's happening, men?"

"Sarge, this is gross. I hope this never happens to us!"

"Yeah, me too! But you can see what happens if the whole company chases a few gooks right into an ambush!"

"Sarge, isn't that exactly what happened to us on January ninth?"

"Yes, man. We will never forget that one, will we?"

"Never, Sarge, never!"

"OK, I'll help you guys put the captain in the bag."

"Thanks, Sarge!"

I tied my stinky towel around my head, covering my nose. The men did the same. The towel that each man carried around his neck was only dry once, and that was when it was supplied to us. We kept the towels around our necks, wiping the sweat off our faces all day and during the night. For some reason, we could only get a clean towel every two or three weeks. Our towels were soured and smelled like vomit. Together, all three of us finished loading the body.

"Emery, hold my canteen and pour the water over my hands!"

I had to wash my hands. My hands had dried blood, charcoal, and other foreign matter on them. I finished washing. "Emery, hold your hands out! Emerald, hold your hands out!"

I poured the water on their hands. They both washed briskly. Emerald looks at Emery. "Hey, Emery, the sarge is using his own water to wash our hands."

Emery laughs. "Maybe he will loan us his water for a bath tonight!"

"You two guys don't get cocky!"

They knew how important water was to us. "You two, drag the body to the stack!"

They are both grinning. "OK. Thanks for the water!"

"Get moving, you two clowns. Get moving!"

They saw the grin on my face and they knew that I was joking. The choppers started to come in. We had stacked the bodies in groups of six, with three on either side, leaving enough room between the stacks for a chopper to land. My men were standing by, ready to do what we had done so many times before — load Americans into helicopters.

I was surprised that the choppers were not being shot at, because there were so many enemies in the area. Maybe the artillery had scared them off. But I knew better. They would be back, and it would probably be tonight.

We continued to load the bodies in the usual manner, one man inside the chopper arranging and two men on each side of the chopper loading the bodies. We loaded for another thirty minutes. My men and I finished this horrible task. The men come to me for further directions. "What's next, Sarge?"

"I hope that we are getting out of here. It is starting to stink real bad now!"

Raymond says, "Sarge, other than January ninth at Khe Sanh, is this the worst that you have seen? And how come everyone hated Roberts?"

My men start talking all at the same time. I say, "OK, men, one at a time, and I'll go first!" I proceeded to speak. "Roberts would not let us have his used RTO batteries for our transistors. When Emery had twisted his ankle, he wouldn't help carry his ammo. He mouthed off to Sergeant Lewis, and Lewis almost popped him in the mouth. One time, we were pulling an ambush in a place that we were not supposed to be, and he told the captain on us. As far as Sergeant Lewis and I are concerned, he is an a-hole. OK, men, it is your turn!"

White says, "I asked him where we were going next, and he told me to take a hike!"

Eckert says, "I asked him to request an eye medicine when he called in for supply. He told me that he was too busy!"

White says, "Emerald and me were having a slight disagreement over something, and he told the captain that we were having a big fight. The captain called Sergeant Rock and jumped all over him for not being able to control his men. Yep, he is...or he *was* an a-hole."

Craig, my RTO, approaches. "Sarge, the lieutenant wants you to go and talk to him."

I reached for the horn. "No, Sarge, he wants you in person!"

"OK, thanks!"

I walked to Gibbons's location on the outside of the perimeter. I tip my head up. "Sir, you asked for me?"

He pulled his map out and pointed to a spot farther north. "We want to make it here before dark. It is probably going to get hairy!"

"I've got it!"

"What do you think, Rock?"

"I think that you are right. We will get into a battle before the day is over. What platoon has point? Not us again, I hope."

"No, not us. The First Platoon has point."

"Cool, sir. That is cool."

I walked back to the squad. "Craig, I forgot to ask Gibbons when we were moving out. Call his RTO and ask, please." To the rest of the men, I say, "OK, men, we are heading north again!"

I hear grumbles. Craig says, "Thirty minutes!"

"Men, we will move out in thirty. Let's get out of the middle of this death trap. Eat something now. We may be too busy to eat later!"

Emerald, in a shaking voice, says, "We are going to do battle today. Is that what you are saying?"

"That is what I am saying, but maybe not."

I still had to constantly reassure Emerald. We started opening our C-rations and talking. White is listening to the Armed Forces Network on his transistor. "Hey, guys, have you heard about this Jane Fonda chick leading the draft dodgers in a rebellion against us at Berkeley or a preppy college like Berkeley?"

Emerald says, "Who is Jane Fonda?"

I say, "You have heard of Henry Fonda, right?"

"You mean the actor?"

"Yes. Jane is his daughter, and Henry has another kid named Peter. Jane is real cute, but she doesn't know her butt from Shinola, or about what is going on over here."

White says, "If she could only see what these gooks did to our men, she would change her tune!"

I reply, "I agree with you, White! The college draft dodgers and her all sit around with nothing to do but bad-mouth us. She loves the Viet Cong and hates you, White, and you, Emery, and you, Emerald, and all of us. It seems like she wants us to all get killed and our enemy to live. If she could see these guys that we just placed in the body bags, maybe she would change her mind."

Chuck says, "Rock, tell them about us being here and the Geneva Convention."

"OK, Chuck, I will tell them what I know, or what I think that I know."

The men laugh. "This may not be exactly correct, but I have most of the info right! In 1859, a guy named Henry Dunant, a Swiss citizen, saw how bad people were being treated. He set up the first convention for the humane treatment of soldiers during war. There were two more conventions, basically adding to the first. Now we have the fourth convention. A lot of the most powerful countries have signed the Geneva Convention agreement. Basically, if a country or state is mistreating their citizens, other countries can move in and help out the people that are being mistreated."

Chuck says, "Like Vietnam."

I reply, "Yes, North Vietnam is trying to take over South Vietnam. Until we got here, the North Vietnamese were killing and torturing a lot of the South Vietnamese people, including women and children. Now back to this creep, Jane Fonda. Let's say that America lets every country do an unprovoked attack on another country, and America does nothing about it. Before long, the attacking country would be on American shores attacking us. Jane Fonda just does not get it."

Killer says, "I wish that she was over here. I would shove her head in a few body bags just to show her what her good friends have done. Then I would kill her!"

"OK, enough about that slut! I have to do something personal."

Killer says, "Do you have to take a crap, Sarge?"

"No, I have to write a letter."

I took out a letter that I had been previously writing. The letter was to my wife and family back home. Generally, it would take me three days to complete a two-page letter because I did not have enough time during the daylight to complete it. I started writing again, making sure that I did not tell my family what was actually happening over here.

Raymond opened his rucksack and pulled out a piece of paper. "Sarge, do you notice how the paper sounds? It is quiet."

"Yes, I know."

In the United States, when a person picks up a piece of paper and shakes it, a sound is heard. It is a sound that I missed. It is a sound sort of like crackling. Over here, in the 'Nam, a person could shake the paper next to his ear and not even hear it. There was just too much moisture in the air.

Emerald and Killer are playing around and spill water on the second page of my letter. I jump up. "You idiots!"

"Sorry, Sarge! We are sorry!"

"Man, guys, I was almost done! Do any of you have any more paper?"

Each one started to look, but no one had any paper. "I am going over to Mac's squad. I'll be back in a minute."

While I was walking, for some reason I remembered that I had forgotten to get rid of one of my weapons. I had told Chuck, White, and Emery to remind me, but it was not their responsibility. Maybe I would remember the next time a chopper came in. I arrived to see Sergeant MacDaniels speaking to one of his men.

"Hi, Mac, how are you?"

He stuck out his hand, and I shook it. "Hi, Rock. You are not here to trade a man, are you?"

"No. Why? Do you have one that you want to get rid of?"

"Yes, it is Brock!"

I laugh and say, "I traded him with another squad leader. What are you doing with him?"

"I traded a can of pork and beans for him. I got took!"

"What?"

"No, not really. He was sent to me when we lost the five guys by the mine explosions."

"How is he working out?"

Mac shakes his head. "He is an egotistical, worthless piece of crap. He thinks that he knows everything."

"You know that he was a sergeant?"

"Yes, but I don't know how he ever made it. What did ya need, Rock?"

"I need some paper so I can finish a letter. Two of my men were playing grab-butt and spilled water on my letter."

"I don't have any, but Byron has half a notebook full."

"Cool, where is he?"

"Over there by Brock."

"Oh, boy, I don't want to see that idiot again!"

I walk over to Byron. "Hi, Byron. How is it going?"

"Fine, Sarge, how are you?"

"I am good, but I want us to move away from here, it is too dangerous. Mac says that you have some writing paper. Can I have a piece?"

"No, I only have enough for me and Brock."

"Mac says that you have half of a notebook."

"I do, but I cannot share. Brock told me how you got him busted!"

"I didn't get him busted. He got himself busted! Are you going to be like Roberts? You know, bad things happen to bad people?"

I look around and Killer is standing behind me. "Are you having a problem, Sarge?"

"Yes, this idiot doesn't want to give me a piece of writing paper!"

"Which one, Sarge?"

211

"That piece of crap there, Byron."

Killer has borrowed a grenade launcher. He points it at both of them and takes the safety off. "You see, men, I am the one that ruined Sergeant Rock's letter. I am real calm now, but do you two know why they call me Killer? Some say that I am crazy! What do you think, Sergeant Rock?"

I look at the two scared rabbits and I decide to play along with Killer. "Killer, you are a little crazy. Watch out, that thing may go off!"

Killer yells at the top of his lungs, "I am not crazy! I just love the body counts! Now give Sergeant Rock the paper, *now!*"

Brock and Byron jump. Byron scrambles to get the notebook from his rucksack, and he throws it to me. Killer still has the M-79 grenade launcher pointed at them. I look at Byron. "Now, Byron, before I take a piece of paper from your notebook, are you giving it to me of your own free will?"

Killer shoves the M-79 against his ribs. Byron answers, "Yes, sir! Yes, Sarge. Yes!"

Killer says, "It is Sergeant Rock to you, you piece of Siberian sheep guts!"

Killer pokes him again. Byron says, "Yes, Sergeant Rock! Yes!"

Killer pulls the trigger — *click* — and they both jump. The grenade launcher was empty. Killer looks at me. "Man, Sarge, I hate it when I forget to load my weapon!"

Killer leans in toward Byron and Brock and with a pleasant voice says, "Man, guys, was that fun or what? We sure have a good time in Vietnam, don't we?"

Byron says, "You are crazy, Killer! I am going to tell Sergeant Mac!"

Killer responds, "I wouldn't do that if I were you. Friendly fire can kill as much as enemy fire."

I took one page from the notebook and threw the notebook back to him. We turned and walked toward Mac. "Mac, you may get a report about how I got my writing paper from Byron or Brock!"

"What do you mean?"

"Killer was having a little fun with them and they got mad."

"OK. See ya, Rock!"

"See ya, Mac!"

"Take care, Killer!"

"You too, Sarge!"

"Killer, that may bite us in the butt later!"

Killer laughs. "You got your paper, didn't you?"

"Yep."

We arrive back to the squad. "Men, we are moving out! You take point, Killer!"

"On it, Sarge."

We did not actually have point for the whole company, but my men knew that point simply meant the first man in line. We started moving, being very careful, and always watching our surroundings.

We moved north for about three miles before we started getting fired upon. We did the usual jump to the prone position and fired in the direction of the flashes coming from the enemy's weapons. Fifteen minutes and it was over. My radio sounds, "One man hit! A man is hit!"

I wondered who it could be. The captain started calling in artillery in the direction of the enemy. The artillery support started hitting behind the enemy. I listened on the radio to the captain orchestrating the firepower. "Fireball Five-Niner, from my position, drop five-zero."

The captain was really cool when he called in fire support. The rounds started hitting closer and closer to the enemy. We started seeing enemy movement again. The rounds kept coming, driving the NVA from their position. As the enemy started moving toward us, we shot them. The NVA were too busy trying to stay away from the artillery to worry about us.

The NVA would move closer and closer to us as the artillery hit behind them. The captain started moving the artillery even closer to our position. Now a lot of the gooks were between the firepower and us. They were shooting at us as we shot back. Five more minutes, and the short battle ceased. I looked at Chuck. "Someone got hit!"

"Who, Rock?"

"Don't know!"

Craig, my RTO, is on the horn. "Sarge, the first platoon is checking the body count and the rest of us are on guard. Someone from Mac's squad got shot!"

"Is he dead? It isn't Mac, is it?"

"No!"

"I am going to Mac's location. Be back in a minute."

Killer says, "Can I go with you?"

"Yeah, let's go!"

Killer and I start walking. Killer says, "Wouldn't it be a kick if your old buddy Brock got it, or even Byron?"

"Killer, if everyone got killed that has made me mad, there would be a lot less of us to fight the enemy!"

"OK, Rock, but I'll bet you my pound cake and peaches that the guy shot was either Byron or Brock!"

"OK, you are on!"

We arrive to see Mac talking to Doc. "Hey, Doc, who got it? Is he dead?"

"Hey, Rock! He is dead, and it is Byron."

Killer shoves me with his shoulder as if to say, *I told you so.*

I look at Mac. "Sorry, Mac. I just wanted to be sure that it wasn't you that got hit. We had better get back to our squad. See ya!"

"Thanks. See ya, Rock. See ya, Killer."

We head in the direction of the squad. Killer says, "When do I get it?"

"Get what?"

"My pound cake and peaches?"

"I'll give it to you tonight. I won't forget!"

We arrive to see the squad ready to move out. Chuck says, "Who got shot, Danny?"

"Byron."

"Did you say Byron?"

"Yes, it was Byron."

"Is he dead?"

"He is dead."

Chuck shakes his head. "I guess that he should not have messed with us!"

Killer says, "Don't mess with Lewis and the Rock or you will have to pay the consequences!" Killer laughs.

Craig says, "Annihilator says to stand by!"

Craig hands me the horn. "Men, this is Annihilator Three-Three. We have a body count of twelve, maybe more. Good work."

We start moving, but I don't know where we are going. "Craig, have you heard where we are going?"

"No, Sarge!"

"I'm waiting for Gibbons. I'll catch up."

The lieutenant reaches me. "Hi, Rock."

"Hello, sir, Where are we going?"

He pulls out his map and points. "Right there, Rock. We are still going north."

"OK, but what about the guy that was shot?"

"Speak to Sergeant Erickson about that."

I waited for Sergeant Erickson, who was always in the back of the platoon. "Hey, Sarge, what about Byron?"

"Hey, Rock, how are ya? Byron will be carried to an LZ by Mac's squad."

"I saw an opening on the map. Is that where we are planning the LZ?"

"Yes. Hey, Rock, how come you are still carrying two weapons?"

"Oh, I just keep messing up. Every time a chopper came in, I was so busy that I forgot to turn one of them in. When this chopper comes in to pick up Byron, I am getting rid of this M-14. I have not shot even one gook with it!"

"OK, Rock, give me the serial number. I'll call it in myself. Now, when the chopper gets here, be sure and load it with the body!"

"Sounds good, Sarge. Thanks."

I moved quickly to catch back up to my squad. We were humping through moderate jungle, staying on the paths. We humped for five hours before getting to the LZ. We were also going to spend the night in the tree line next to the rice paddies. We did the usual digging of foxholes, setting up guard duty, and discussing the day's events. My radio sounds, "Blackhawk Three, this is Cherokee Three. Come to the CP, over!"

I answer, "On my way, out!"

I started in the direction of Lieutenant Gibbons and the CP. I saw Chuck speaking to Marsh. Marsh was an RTO from another platoon. Chuck and I had a few problems with him before. The problems he gave us would have been easily handled in the United States, but here in Vietnam, it was a different story.

"Chuck, what's happening?"

"Rock, this guy says that he still doesn't have our pound cake and our ham! We gave our C-rations to him over two weeks ago. Now hand it over, Marsh!"

A few weeks ago, Marsh had run out of C-rations, or so he said. I gave Marsh my last can of ham, and Chuck gave him a can of pound cake. Marsh continues to deny. "I don't have but three cans of C-rations!"

Chuck says, "You are also the guy that turned Sergeant Rock's squad in for not going to the correct ambush site!"

I felt like the offense of the rations was very minor compared to him telling the lieutenant and the captain that my squad was pulling an ambush in the wrong place.

Marsh answers, "Well, you guys didn't!"

I spoke up. "Marsh, you know I try to protect my men. If I would have taken my squad into the jungle like I was told, we would have been ambushed ourselves."

He says, "Yeah, right."

I sternly looked at Marsh. "You piece of crap. I have already talked to the captain about that! But I will tell you one more time! My squad was going to the ambush site when we saw gooks in the near distance. There was no reason to go farther and get caught up in an ambush. We set up our ambush in the location that I felt was safe for my men!"

Chuck grabbed Marsh's rucksack and dumped it out. The C-rations came tumbling out. There were three cans of pound cake and three cans of ham, along with plenty more cans of C-rations. Chuck gives Marsh a chest bump. "What do you call that, Marsh? Here, Rock, here is your ham!"

Chuck tosses me the can. Chuck reaches for the pound cake. "I am taking this, Marsh! You are just a sorry human being."

I look at the pile of C-rations. "Chuck, look and see if he has any peaches!"

"He has four cans."

"Four cans? No one has four cans of peaches! Marsh, I am taking one for the interest. You told us that you would pay us back in two days. You lied. So this is interest that you owe us."

Killer walks up to our location. "Are we having trouble with Marsh?"

Chuck says, "Yes, we are Killer. He owes us C-rations."

Killer looks at Marsh. "You owe me peaches, Marsh!"

Chuck points at the C-rations. "There it is, Killer. Take it!"

Killer reaches for the C-rations when Marsh says, "You can't do this!"

Killer stands straight up and gets in the face of Marsh. "Marsh, you remember Roberts and Byron, don't you?"

"Yeah, they both got killed."

"Yes, and did you know that they both crossed Sergeant Rock and Sergeant Lewis just before they died?"

Marsh responds, "I am going straight to the captain about this."

I look at Marsh and shake my head. "If I were you, I would go through the chain of command. The captain would eat you alive for nonsense like this. Do you remember your chain of command? Go to your team leader, then your squad leader, then your platoon sergeant, then your platoon leader (lieutenant), then the captain."

Marsh looks puzzled. "Well, how do you and Lewis get to go straight to the captain for problems?"

"We don't take problems to the captain, and besides, we have proven ourselves to him. Chuck and I are always part of the solution, not the problem! We have been in country longer than you. So if you want, go ahead and tell the captain. Get after it!"

Marsh's radio sounds, and we listen to the conversation. Marsh and the squad that he is in, Smitty's squad, are ordered to go on an ambush. Killer says, "Marsh, you have crossed Rock and Lewis, so be very, very careful tonight!"

Marsh answers, "You guys are crazy!" I continue towards the lieutenant's location.

"Sir, did you request my presence?"

"Yes. First Platoon is going out on ambush tonight."

"No, not the whole platoon. I just spoke to the X-ray, Marsh, and I heard that only Smitty's squad is going on ambush."

Sergeant Erickson is listening to our conversation. "That's right, sir. The captain changed it."

"Regardless, Rock, if they get in trouble, we are moving in to help them!"

"OK, sir, I'll tell my guys to be on alert. See ya, sir. See ya, Sergeant Erickson."

I turn around and start to leave the platoon CP, heading for my squad.

Sergeant Erickson says, "Wait, Sergeant Rock, the chopper is coming in for Byron. Do you still want to turn in your M-14?"

"Yes, sir, Sarge! Yes, sir!"

Erickson answers, "Don't call me sir. I work for a living!"

"Yes, sir. I mean, yes, Sergeant."

Sergeant Erickson was joking, but it was true. Only officers are addressed with sir. I liked Sergeant Erickson as a person, but in a firefight, he was worthless.

The chopper came in and three men placed the body of Byron inside. I ran up to the chopper and slid the M-14 under the body. I headed back to my squad.

Killer was telling my men about Marsh. I noticed that the men had dug some pretty good foxholes. They were nice and deep and wide. "Sorry that I couldn't help you guys dig."

Killer says, "No problem, Sarge. What did the lieutenant want?"

Chuck jumped right in on the conversation. "Killer, don't you remember the chain of command? You are not supposed to ask Sergeant Rock questions. You ask me, and I will ask the sarge."

Killer replies, "OK, Sergeant Lewis, what did the lieutenant want with Sergeant Rock?"

Chuck turns to me. "Sergeant Rock, what did the lieutenant want?"

White is standing near us. "Yeah, Sergeant Lewis, what did the lieutenant want with Sergeant Rock?"

This was getting comical because all five of us were within five feet of each other. I start laughing. "You guys are all crazy!"

White answers, "Yeah, you are right. We are all crazy, but don't we have a great squad?"

Killer says, "I would put our squad up against any squad in the 'Nam!"

"Me too," Chuck said.

I proceeded to tell the men what the lieutenant had told me about the ambush set up and for us to be on alert to help out if needed. It was just before dark when the squad from the first platoon moved out for their ambush location. We took our turns at guard duty. It was a peaceful night until just before daylight. We heard lots of gunfire in the distance. We could hear AK-47s and M-16s. I listened to my radio.

Our men from the first platoon were in a firefight. They had sprung their ambush, but the gooks had more men than they had anticipated. The sounds of the AK-47s told me that the gooks were probably NVA. I told my men to get ready, for we were going to move out.

Our platoon, as planned, moved out to help our men being fired upon. My squad had point. "Eckert, get on point! Craig and I will be next. Killer, you go behind Craig! Where do you want to be, Chuck? This may get hairy."

"I want point, Rock, let me have point!"

"No, you keep the rest of the guys in line!"

We moved very quickly through the dark in the direction of the firefight. It was getting a little lighter but still too dark to see the enemy. We arrive at the firefight and start shooting at the flashes of fire coming from the AK-47 rifles. We move closer and closer to the enemy, jumping to the ground then charging forward. Craig yells at me, "I just heard that someone is hit from the first platoon!"

I say nothing. I just nod my head. My first objective is to keep my men safe and organized. My second objective is to kill the gooks. I will worry about the first platoon's casualties in a little while.

My radio sounds. "Blackhawk Three, do you need any help?"

I tell Craig, "Tell them no, we have it under control!"

Craig gets on the horn. "Negatron, negative, we have it under control!"

The radio goes off again, "Blackhawk Three, this is Cherokee Three, who got wounded?"

I am on the ground firing as fast as I can at the AK-47s flashes. Craig says, "Gibbons wants to know who got shot."

I fire off another couple of rounds. "Man! Tell them to quit bugging us. I'll give them info later. Leave me alone!"

Craig gets back on the horn. "Blackhawk is busy trying to keep us alive. When he is complete, he will give you the info, out!"

The firefight starts to increase. I hear, "Man down! Man down!"

I turn to Craig. "Is it one of ours?"

"Yes!"

"Killer, are you OK?"

"Yes, Sarge. It is Sergeant Lewis!"

I take off running to the middle of the squad. Chuck is lying on his side, clenching his leg. Blood is all over his pants. I kneel beside him and lift up his head. "Is it a bullet or shrapnel? How bad is it?"

Chuck is in real pain. "I don't know if it was a round, but it hurts real bad, Danny!"

"Chuck, I am going to turn you on your stomach so I can see it."

I rolled Chuck over and I could see the wound, but I could not tell if it was a bullet or shrapnel. I took his towel and tied it above the wound. "OK, Chuck, the bleeding has stopped! My tourniquet worked perfectly. Just hang on until we get these gooks. Emerald, you help Chuck!"

Now was the time to do as I preached. I have always taught my men to fight not in anger, but with skill. I had anger in my heart, but I was learning to control it. We moved in even closer toward the enemy, opening up our weapons at a fiery pace. The incoming firing stopped. I could see ten to twelve dead NVA. I assumed that the rest of the NVA had retreated. We could now see the squad from the first platoon.

I turned to Killer. "You guys bring Lewis up here and check out the gooks! I am going to see who got shot!"

I walked over to the squad leader. "Hey, Smitty, that was hairy, huh?"

"Man, was it! I thought that we bought the farm! Our ambush worked perfectly, but there must have been fifty NVA. We couldn't hold them all off. There were just too many!"

"Who got shot, Smitty?"

"It was Marsh."

"Is he dead or wounded?"

"He is dead. He got shot right in the stomach! Didn't you and Lewis have trouble with him?"

"Yes, a little bit! I am going back to my squad. See ya, Smitty."

I started hearing single shots from an M-16. The shots were happening every ten seconds or so. I saw Killer shooting each NVA in the head one at a time. I did not stop him. I was getting pretty fed up with these gooks over here in the 'Nam myself.

Killer saw me. "Who got shot in Smitty's squad?"

"It was Marsh."

"Is he dead?"

"Yep, he ate it!"

Killer says, "Good. Like I have always said, don't mess with Rock and Lewis!"

"Killer, isn't it strange how we now feel about the death of our comrades? Marsh was an a-hole, but he didn't need to die. You seem to celebrate his death. This war is changing us. We are getting so tired and worn out that we are getting caught up in the events. We no longer think clearly."

"I know that you are right, Sarge, but sometimes it is hard to separate who or whom should die. Should it be the enemy or someone that did us wrong?"

"Killer, we all need to remember this: every time we kill a gook, VC, NVA, or when one of our guys gets killed, it has repercussions. Every man we kill is somebody's son, brother, or father."

CHAPTER 13

A Night Roving Patrol (LRRP)

Our platoon and Smitty's squad were waiting on the rest of the company to come to our position. The company arrived, and we set up a large security perimeter for the choppers to come in and lift out Chuck and Marsh.

I walked over to Chuck. "How bad is it, Chuck?"

"It is feeling a lot better."

"Turn over and let me see!"

Chuck turned over. I saw that his leg and buttocks were really swollen. "Here comes Doc!"

Chuck says, "Hi, Doc. It's only a scratch. It feels much better now. Is it a bullet or is it shrapnel? I can't leave the field, so pull it out!"

Doc examines the wound. "It is shrapnel, Sergeant Lewis."

"Can you pull it out?"

"No. You will have to go to the rear. You will be lifted in a few minutes!"

"No way, Doc! They need me out here!"

Doc shakes his head. "If you stay in the field, it will get infected."

"Man, Danny, you guys need me. Buddy, I can't go to the rear!"

I give Chuck a hug. "Hey, buddy, you go to the rear and coast as long as you can. By the way, when you come back, bring me a new towel."

"You got it. I'll be back ASAP!"

"No, Chuck, drag it out!"

The chopper sound is in the distance. The Huey chopper lands and three men place Marsh on the floor of the chopper. I help Chuck to the chopper and help him get into the seat. "Hey, Chuck, check to see if those AK-47s of mine are still there!"

"You got it!"

Chuck has tears in his eyes. I see the tears. "Get out of here, you big cry baby. Soldiers don't cry!"

The chopper takes off. Chuck gives the thumbs up. I hustle to the perimeter. The lieutenant is waiting for me. "Sorry about Lewis. We are moving to here." He is pointing at his map. We are heading farther north. "Rock, I have good news and bad news."

"Good news?"

"Yes, we are going by chopper."

"Alright, sir, now what is the bad news?"

"As you can see, we are still heading north."

"Yeah, but we always head north. So what's the big deal about that?"

"Rock, it is going to be another hot LZ and lots and lots of NVA! We are going for support!"

"OK. When are we moving out, sir?"

"Forty-five minutes!"

"We'll be ready."

I turned to head back to the squad. Gibbons stops me. "Hey, Rock, how bad was Lewis hurt?"

"Pretty bad. I couldn't tell if it was a bullet or a piece of shrapnel; lots of blood! See ya, sir."

"Later, Rock."

As I walked toward my squad, I started to think about other chopper combat assaults that we had done. In the southern portion of Vietnam, we would have quite a few chopper assaults with no one shooting at the chopper. Even when we were shot at, it would generally be a few VC. This type of attack on the choppers, with the VC shooting at us, did not bother us a great deal. However, the NVA shooting at us was a different story.

I told my men about the choppers picking us up. The men were excited and happy. I told the men to settle down and listen up. "It is great that we don't have to hump, but we are going north, and it most likely will be a hot LZ."

The men got quiet. Killer says, "How does the captain know that it will be a hot LZ with the NVA trying to kill us?"

I look at all of my worried men. "There is probably another company in a firefight, and we will be landing very close to the fight."

Emerald is shaking. "I hate combat assaults from choppers!"

I place my right hand on Emerald's shoulder. "Don't worry. Maybe we won't even be shot at."

I knew better, but I had to pretend that all might be well to keep Emerald calm. I was very worried myself. If this was going to be a really hot LZ, then we would lose some men.

Killer walked up to me. "Sarge, since Sergeant Lewis is gone, who do you want to be team leader?"

I grin. "Don't you mean '*Whom* do you want to be team leader?'"

"Yes, Sarge, *whom!*"

We both laughed. I motioned for Killer to walk with me away from the men. "Killer, you would be the perfect guy for a team leader, but Eckert has been with me longer and he expects for me to make him an acting jack."

Killer smiles. "That's fine, Sarge. My time will come!"

"Yes it will. Killer, you may take my position when I leave this place."

"Yeah, that would be cool, Sarge!"

I could hear the birds coming toward us in the distance. I loved the sound of the Huey helicopters. I walked toward Eckert.

"Eckert, you are team leader. Take charge of White and Emery; I'll take the rest. When the choppers come in, you guys get on the chopper behind the one that I get on!"

"Rock, do you think that I should take Raymond and the Pig with me because of the weight that you will have on your bird?"

"Good idea. Keep him on your team."

I started to yell at Raymond, and then I turned to Eckert. "Eckert, you command Raymond to go with you!"

Eckert turned to Raymond. "Raymond, you and the Pig come with me!"

Raymond looks directly at me. I nod my head in agreement. Eckert would not be as good of a team leader as Chuck was, but he would be great. Chuck was more than great, and I was missing him already.

My radio sounds. "Blackhawk Three, you take choppers three and four, over!"

I motion for Craig, my RTO, to acknowledge the transmission. Craig responds, "Cherokee Three, this is Blackhawk Three X-ray (RTO), affirmative, birds three and four!"

The choppers started to land. We saw our choppers. I motioned for Eckert to take his men to the fourth chopper. I motioned for my group and pointed toward the third chopper. We ran and jumped aboard. The door gunners acknowledged us with a head motion. The choppers took off before we could get completely aboard. This was common, leaving as fast as they could, because every gook in Vietnam wanted to shoot down a chopper.

I looked behind at the fourth chopper and saw Raymond and Eckert pulling in Emery. I looked at the door gunners and I noticed that these gunners did not have a bipod or a tripod holding their M-60 machine gun. They had bungee cords that attached the gun to the chopper. This seemed to give them more maneuverability than the semi-fixed position of the bipod or tripod. The gunner helped Emery into the bird.

We had been traveling for thirty minutes when I started to get sleepy. I fell asleep listening to the rotor blades and the wind blowing past the openings that used to be doors. My wife had told me that I could sleep anywhere. I guess that this was true, because I had fallen asleep while riding on the topside of a tank once or twice. All of a sudden I was awakened. I jumped and almost fell out of the chopper. Both door gunners were firing. My men saw me and started laughing. The door gunners were looking at me and they were also laughing. Killer had set me up.

The gunners were shooting at nothing. Killer had told the gunners to look at me while I was sleeping. The gunners looked at each other and counted with their fingers, one, two, and they opened up with the M-60s. My heart almost stopped beating. The sound was as if your head was in a steel bucket and a few men started hitting the bucket with sledgehammers. I was mad at first, but then I started laughing myself. I yelled at Killer, "I am going to pay you back, buddy!"

"Sure, Sarge. I know that you will!"

We traveled in the choppers for another fifteen minutes. One of the gunners grabbed my shoulder and motioned for me to look ahead. I saw lots of tracer bullets firing in different directions. We were headed for the middle of the firefight. My heart started pounding, but this time it was not because of one of Killer's jokes. This was going to be bad.

The door gunners started firing. Every door gunner in our group of twenty-four choppers was firing. The choppers were moving very fast. My men and I moved to the edge of the opening of the bird. As we got closer and closer to the ground, we moved farther out of the chopper. The choppers were coming in fast. We were twenty feet off of the ground, then fifteen, then ten. The door gunners were motioning for us to jump. The NVA were shooting at the gunners. The gunners wanted to get out of the hot LZ. They wanted us to jump. Our elevation was now five feet above the ground.

Frantically, the gunners were pushing for us to get off the chopper. They were yelling, "Jump! Jump! Jump!"

My men were waiting for my signal. I gave them the signal to jump. The choppers were still moving at approximately twenty miles per hour. We jumped.

Killer's helmet flew off as he did a body roll. Emerald lost his rifle and his helmet in the rice paddy water and mud. He found them quickly. I had done this many times before, so I knew to keep one hand on my helmet and to hold on to my rifle as tight as possible. I did my involuntary roll, as did the rest of my men. We started shooting, trying to get out of the rice paddy.

The mortars were coming in all around us. The NVA were firing more at the choppers than at us. I looked over at Eckert's men and I notice that they were all firing into the tree line. No one seemed to be hurt. We fight our way to the tree line. I hear a loud explosion. This explosion sounds worse than a mortar round. I look back toward the twentieth and twenty-first chopper. They are down. Men are running back and forth between the tree line and the choppers. The choppers are burning. The flames are very high. I cannot tell if anyone is hurt. There is just too much going on for me to get a clear look. Artillery starts coming in.

I can tell that it is our friendly firepower by the placement. This was one time that I was glad I was not in charge of calling in for fire support. I knew our exact location, but I didn't know where the other company was located. I was not even sure of where the enemy was located. I only knew that there were gooks directly in front of us, trying to kill us. We fought for another thirty minutes, and the firing stopped.

We advanced forward and slightly to our right, making sure that the NVA we had shot were dead. White approached me. "Sarge, isn't it strange that right after a firefight, we can never find many of their AK-47s?"

"I think that the live ones shove them in their tunnels before we get to the bodies."

White replies, "Well, I am your tunnel rat if you need one! Two choppers went down. How many killed, Sarge?"

"Don't know yet!"

Craig is moving toward me. "Craig, did the radio get very wet when you jumped out of the chopper?"

"Man, Sarge, I don't mind jumping four or five feet out of a helicopter, but I hate jumping out at fifty miles per hour! No, Sarge, the radio just got a little wet."

"What have you heard, Craig?"

"I have heard that two choppers went down. Two door gunners killed and three of our men dead."

My radio sounds, "Blackhawk Three, come to Cherokee Three, over!"

"Take the call, Craig!"

"This is Blackhawk Three X-ray. Blackhawk Three is on his way!"

I arrived at the CP. The lieutenant and the captain were talking. I walked up to them. "Hi, sir. Hi, Lieutenant."

The captain says, "Rock, we have a situation. We need a roving patrol tonight at 2100 hours. The patrol will stay out until 0700 hour."

He pointed at his map. "The patrol will go to this point then return back here."

I looked at both of them with a *"do what?"* look! I scratch my head. "So you want me to take a squad at night through enemy territory. You want us to leave at nine o'clock at night and arrive back here at seven in the morning. Is that the gist of it?"

The captain responded, "I did not say that you and Lewis had to go, but you guys are my killer squad. I would appreciate it if you and Lewis went!"

"Sir, Lewis got wounded. He is not here!"

"Sorry. With everything that has been going on, I forgot about Sergeant Lewis. Sorry, Rock, I know you two are like brothers."

"I will do the patrol on one condition!"

"What's that, Rock?"

"We will do it if we don't have to wear our hardhats. We want to wear our soft hats, our baseball caps, like the lurps."

"OK, Rock, whatever you want. We will rotate RTOs all night long. I know you have to be quiet, so if your sit-rep is negative, just break squelch (squeeze the button on the mike) twice, just like we learned in AIT. Also, your squad doesn't have to pull guard on the perimeter."

"OK, sir, I'll go and tell my men." I walked away.

The captain did not realize it, but my squad loved night roving. I loved it too. We did not have to wear that heavy helmet. We did not have to carry as much ammo as we normally carried. We did not have to pull guard on the perimeter.

I told the men and, as I expected, they were excited. The worrywart, Emerald, was the only guy not showing enthusiasm. I spoke to Emerald. "All that we are going to do is walk from here to there and come back at seven in the morning!" I knew that it would be much more dangerous than that, but why worry the wart even more? "We don't have to pull guard, so get a couple hours of sleep. Get up at 8:30, or Army time, 2030 hours, and be ready to go before nine!"

I started to get ready for a few hours sleep. I spread out my poncho and laid my poncho liner on top of it. As usual, I spread the canteens and grenades on my belt apart so I would have a place to lay my head. I placed the belt at the head of the poncho and the liner. I crawled in the bed I had made and started to lie down on my left side. Something was wrong. I felt a sharp stabbing in my shoulder. I thought, *Could this be a bouncing-betty mine?*

"White, come over here!"

White came to my position. "What's up, Sarge?"

"White, I am not sure, but I think that I am lying on a mine. I can feel a prong pressing on my shoulder. I hope that it is a sharp rock or something like that."

White is worried. "Could you hear the click as you set the mine?"

"No, it feels like I just bent one prong!"

Killer walks up. "Are you guys trying to get up a poker game or what? Sarge, you will have to sit up if we are going to play poker!"

I didn't move.

White says to Killer, "The sarge is lying on a mine, he thinks! What do you want us to do, Sarge?"

"I want one of you to very, very gently put your hands under my poncho and gently feel for the other prongs. I hope that I am wrong, but move slowly. I won't move a muscle."

Killer says, "I will do it!"

Killer moves my pillow (ammo belt, grenades, and canteens) away from the poncho. He gently places his hands under the poncho, just barely touching the ground with his fingertips. I can feel the backs of his hands coming closer to my side and shoulder. He moves his right hand closer to where my shoulder is resting on the pin. He stops!

Killer speaks quietly. "Sarge, I can feel at least two more prongs. They are like cat whiskers, but thick, like a nail or heavy wire! Does a bouncing-betty mine have three or four prongs?"

"I think they have three, but either way, I am on a mine."

Killer starts to move his hands from under the poncho. "Give us directions, Sarge. Tell us what to do. You can't die because you have not given me the recipe for your chocolate pudding."

"Don't make me laugh now, Killer! OK, here is what we are going to do."

White says, "Tell us anything, Sarge. We'll do it."

"White, you go to the CP and tell the captain to come over here quick! Killer, you go and get a large rock or stone!"

The men take off running. I wait for three minutes, which seemed like three hours. The captain and the lieutenant are now standing over me.

The captain says, "Is it really a mine, Rock?"

"Yes, sir, but I have a plan!"

"Let's hear it, Rock." I have my back to the people that I am speaking to. They seem to be keeping their distance. I can't blame them. I know that this could be bad.

"Killer, do you have the rock?"

"Yes I do, Sarge!"

231

"OK, sir, Killer is going to place the rock on the prong that I am on. White is going to place pressure on the prong as I lift up. Then Killer will place the Rock on the prong as White moves his hand. If this works, we will set up one of our claymore mines next to it and blow it up in the morning. Sir, I think that you need to get everybody away from here. If this doesn't work there is no need to kill anyone else."

The captain walks over to me and bends down next to me. "Rock, let me tell you this. If your plan doesn't work, it has been a pleasure knowing you! We have been through a lot together, haven't we?"

"Yes we have, sir. Is that a tear in your eye?"

"No, it is sweat! I'll get the guys away from here. If I don't hear an explosion I want you to come to the CP!"

"Yes, sir!"

I say, "Killer and White, come over here please!"

They both come over to where I could see them. "You know, guys, I didn't even ask if you two wanted to be in my plan. Do you want to help me out?"

Killer is grinning. "Can it wait until morning? You are already lying down. I am only joking, Sarge. We are ready!"

White says, "Me too. Let's do it."

White slipped his hand under my shoulder, next to the prong. "Sarge, I am going to move slowly until I feel the prong."

I say, "I think that you are there."

"OK, Sarge, as I put equal pressure on the prong, you roll over." White is on the prong, applying pressure. "OK, Sarge, roll over *slowly*."

My heart was pounding and I was perfectly still. I rolled over, waiting to be killed. Nothing happened. There was no explosion. The first part of the plan worked. "OK, guys, I am going to move the poncho!"

I moved the poncho and the poncho liner away from the mine. "White, keep the pressure on the prong."

Killer was moving in slowly with the rock. The rock or stone looked like it was around ten pounds. "Killer, be certain that you don't put the rock on all three prongs."

"I won't. I know where the others are."

Killer slides the rock up against White's hand. "White, I am going to set the rock on your finger that is on the prong. As the pressure goes on your finger try to slide your hand out, letting the rock take its place."

"OK, Killer."

I watched intensely as they did the maneuver. It worked! Both men, or should I say *real men*, stood up and walked slowly away from the mine. I did the same. We walked about forty feet away from the bomb and started jumping up and down hugging one another like a bunch of schoolgirls. These guys had saved my life and probably my whole squad. Man, I have some great guys in my squad.

Killer gives me one more hug. "You better go to the captain as he requested!"

"I am on my way! Thanks again, guys."

"Anytime, Sarge!"

I could hear Killer and White talking as I walked toward the CP. "Next time it will be Emerald and Emery's turn."

I heard laughter.

"Hey, captain, I made it!"

The captain stands up quickly. "Rock, Rock, Rock, you made it! We'll get out of the 'Nam alive yet, huh, Rock?"

"Yes, sir, maybe we will! What did you want, sir?"

"I have five R&Rs here. These were for the guys that got killed, but they can't use them now!"

"What's the R&R destination, sir?"

"Three to Hawaii and two to Bangkok."

"Are you offering them to me? I mean my choice?"

I knew that the company was in too bad of a shape for me to take an R&R. The captain was just being nice.

The captain looked at me. "Yes, Rock, if you want it, take it."

"Why don't you take one, sir?"

"Oh, Rock, with us losing so many men, I could not go. I would worry every minute that I was away!"

"I feel the same way, sir. So I'll pass on the R&Rs also."

"You know what, Rock?"

"What, sir?"

The captain placed his hand on my shoulder. "I knew that you would turn it down. You are just like me!"

"How is that, sir?"

"You want things in order and running smooth before you leave for an R&R."

"I guess that you are right, sir, but try me next month on another R&R."

"Rock, you just let me know when you want to go and I'll bump anyone for you!"

"Thanks, sir. See you tomorrow."

"Rock, are you still going on the night-roving patrol?"

"Of course, sir, why not?"

The captain gets that big grin on his face. "That's my boy. I mean, that's my man! You guys be careful, Rock. We'll take care of the bouncing-betty in the morning!"

"See ya, sir."

All of my men were far away from the bomb. "Alright, men, grab an hour of sleep, but be ready!" Most of the men just lie on their equipment and fall asleep. After I put away my poncho and liner, I did the same.

We woke up after an hour or so. We had our equipment ready to go. I had a rifle, a bandolier of ammo, a soft hat, one canteen, and only two grenades. The rest of the men had about the same equipment. Raymond is carrying his Pig. I look at all of the mens' weapons. "Raymond, go and trade the Pig for a 16. Killer, you go and get a 79. I know that we already have one, but I want another one. Eckert, be sure to have plenty of canister rounds (shotgun shell type) for your 79!"

We started to move out. We passed by the captain. "See ya, sir."

"Rock, remember: if your sit-rep is negative, break squelch twice. We don't want you to do much talking because it would give away your position."

"Affirmatron, sir."

The captain shakes his head. "You squad leaders with your *affirmatron* and *negatron*. Come back alive, Rock!"

"We'll try!"

We kept walking until we reached the guys on guard at the perimeter. Mac sees us in our soft hats and our lightweight ammo belts. "Well, isn't it the lurp guys? How ya doing, Rock?"

"Great, Mac, how about you?"

"I am cool. Are ya going on an ambush? Are you going where you are supposed to go?"

Mac knew that in Vietnam, sometimes, depending on how dangerous, we would alter our course a little for an ambush. No matter what I was told, as a squad leader, I would try to get the upper hand on the enemy and keep my men safe. This goes back to what the higher ups have said. Vietnam is a squad leader's war. There are no front lines.

"Mac, it ain't an ambush. It is a roving night patrol. And yes, we are going where we are supposed to go!"

"When will you be back, so I can let the men know not to shoot ya?"

"Seven, unless something happens."

"Hey, Rock, I heard that you laid on a mine! Did you?"

"Yeah, that was hairy. I'll tell ya about it tomorrow."

"Good luck, guys."

We walked through the perimeter. Now we were on a path heading northwest. We were sneaking down the path with our weapons in the ready position, making sure that we made no noise. It was much easier for us to be quiet because we had left the rucksacks and all of our C-rations behind. We also carried only one bandolier of ammo, because two or more bandoliers hit together, making noise. This was fun, giving the guys commands by hand signals. It was exciting.

235

One man would move up, then motion for another to cover him as he moved forward. The moon was full and bright. The full moon was good and bad for us. The good thing was that we could see each other's signals. The bad thing was the gooks could see us. But then again, we could see the gooks better.

Each man on these night maneuvers wanted to pull point, with the exception of Emerald. The men felt like pulling point during the day maneuvers was much more dangerous. In other words, they felt like they may be killed pulling point duty during the daylight. I watched closely at my men moving and pointing. They were having a great time. Eckert motioned that he was moving right and motioned for White to go to point. White moved quietly but quickly to the front. White motioned for Killer to follow him. Killer responded with a hand gesture. He was holding up his middle finger on his left hand. I looked closer and realized that Killer was giving White the bird. Killer moves where White wants him to go. Killer looks at me with that Killer grin that I have seen so many times before. I motioned to him with my hands and fingers: *I have my eyes on you!* He gives me a thumbs up.

We travel a few miles when I hear my radio. The radio's volume is turned down really low. I get close to Craig so I can hear. "Blackhawk Three, if sit-rep is negative, break squelch twice."

I look at Craig. "Craig, squeeze your push to talk button twice."

Craig squeezes his mic twice. I hear the reply from the captain's RTO. It is also a squelch twice reply. He has acknowledged that he understands that we are not in danger. I understand that other companies do this sit-rep thing differently. I can't say that I agree with the protocol that our company uses, but it is the only one that I have been taught. We move on toward our destination. Three more miles, and we hear the radio. "Blackhawk Three, if sit-rep is negative, break squelch twice."

I motion for Craig to affirm the request. We have been away from the company for three hours now. We continue our patrol.

Another hour and we arrive at our destination. I gather my men. "We will stay here just listening and watching for two hours. Then we will head back."

Killer says, "Can we take a nap?"

"No, and don't flip me the bird or I'll kick your butt tomorrow!"

We watched and listened for two hours. We saw nothing, nor did we hear anything during this time.

"OK, men, let's head back. Craig, break squelch twice to alert Cherokee."

Craig squeezes his mic twice. My radio sounds with the sit-rep request, and Craig acknowledges with the two-squelch push. We move out.

As we move, I notice that the men are getting tired. They're not as alert as when we left at 2100 hours. We had not seen anything tonight. Therefore, the men were getting complacent. This could be bad. "Men, stay alert!"

Another hour went by, and we were asked if our sit-rep was negative. We responded and kept moving. I noticed that the point was just walking, not listening or watching. I motion for the squad to halt. "Come over here, men! Who wants to die tonight?"

"What do you mean, Sarge?"

"No one is pulling point! They are just walking! You guys are just walking in single file, like little bitty ants! You guys shape up! I am not joking. Killer, get on point, and I mean pull point, don't just walk!"

"Yes, Sarge."

The patrol was starting to come together again. Sometimes I had to kick a little butt to get the results I wanted. I had been through this night patrol before and it can get bad. I wished Chuck could be here to help me out. My radio sounds, "Blackhawk Three, if sit-rep is negative, break squelch twice."

I acknowledge yes to Craig, and he broke squelch twice. It was my turn to pull point. I moved slowly and quietly down the path toward the company. We were a mile away from the company when I heard gook voices. I held up my hand to stop all movement. I proceeded to slowly crawl up and over a berm. I saw six to seven NVA sitting on the other side of the berm. I pulled away from the berm and crawled slowly back to my squad.

I whispered to the men, "There are six or more NVA on the other side of the berm. Get ready!"

I grab the radio and push the PTT (push to talk button) six times to break the squelch.

Someone came back on the radio. "Blackhawk Three, if sit-rep is negative, break squelch twice." I broke squelch once. The radio sounded again, "If sit-rep is negative, break squelch twice."

I did nothing in hopes that the RTO would understand that our situation was not negative. My radio got quiet. The idiot on the RTO did not know what to do if our sit-rep was positive.

I broke squelch ten to twelve times to get his attention.

"If sit-rep is negative, break squelch twice."

Once again, I broke squelch once! The idiot responds, "I hear your squelch, but it is only one squelch. Your radio must be broken!"

I again gave twelve squelches! He comes back on the radio. "I can hear your squelch, but I cannot hear you speaking!"

If I spoke the gooks would hear me! I was getting fed up with this stupid, redundant idiot. I whispered in the microphone as loud as I could, but hopefully not loud enough for the gooks to hear, "You stupid piece of crap, we are going to be ambushed!"

"Did you say that you are going to spring an ambush?"

"No, no, no, you idiot! We are being ambushed! Oh, shut up! We will take care of it ourselves. You don't know anything about sit-reps. You are useless. Out!"

We started to hear the gooks talk. *Did they hear me? Were they moving out?* "Eckert, have you got a canister round in your 79?"

"Yes!"

"OK, men, if Eckert and I start to fire, you guys get on top of the berm and keep them pinned down! Let's go, Eckert!"

Eckert and I crawled toward the berm where I had seen the gooks. We heard the gooks whispering in Vietnamese. By the sounds of their dialect, they did not know that we were near them. They had not heard me speaking to the dumb cluck on the radio. We crawled to the top of the berm.

The NVA were ready for an ambush. There was another path on their side of the berm that was running straight to where they were set up. If we had chosen that path to travel, in lieu of the one we were on, it could have been death for all of us. The gooks were set up for a killer ambush. This was going to be cool.

We were about to spring an ambush on an ambush. I had never done that before. I looked at Eckert and smiled. He smiled back. We knew that we were in command of this operation. My heart was beating hard and fast. My body was filled with adrenaline, running clear to my fingertip that was on the trigger of my rifle. I motioned to Eckert with three fingers. This would be the count that we would go on.

I showed him my left hand while I had my right hand on my rifle. I held out one finger, then two fingers, then motioned toward the gooks. We exploded with a vengeance, jumping to the top of the berm. I opened up my rifle on full automatic. Eckert opened up with his shotgun rounds. We saw three men go down. The others were starting to retreat in the direction that we wanted them to go.

Killer and the rest of the men did as I had told them. They jumped over the berm and started firing. I heard Killer say, "No prisoners! Kill them all! Kill them all! Don't take prisoners! Kill, kill, kill!"

I was in agreement to kill them all. Prior to now they had torched some of our men. I yelled, "Kill them!"

Eckert and I jumped over the berm and started firing more and more, hitting every blade of grass and bush that moved. The firing stopped after another five or six minutes.

My radio sounds off, "Blackhawk Three, is that you guys I hear?"

I am fed up with this RTO. I don't have to be quiet now. I get on the horn. "Shut up! Shut up! Don't talk to me! You are a stupid, insignificant piece of crap that I want to kill! Don't call me again! Out!"

My men are jubilant. Killer comes running to me. "Sarge, all of them are dead!"

"Great. How many?"

"Eight, Sarge. We killed eight!"

I answered, "Man, that is great!"

White comes up to us. "Sergeant Rock's squad did it again. Man, oh man, Rock, we have twice as many kills as any other squad in the company!"

Eckert comes up to us. "I have been keeping count! If we don't count artillery kills, we have more kills than the company as a whole has!"

I look at Eckert. "Is that a fact, Eckert?"

"Yep, or I mean, yes, Sarge, it is!"

"That's cool. Maybe we will get a raise."

Emerald says, "Yeah, right. We will probably just get more ammo and C-rations!"

Emery says, "Well anyhow, we are keeping our reputation. Sergeant Rock has the meanest, toughest squad in the 'Nam!"

I was very proud to have this reputation. Chuck had told me many times about guys that wanted to be transferred to my squad. I had stringent criteria for the men in the squad. They had to be willing to kill at a moment's notice. They had to put their life on the line to protect others. They had to be willing to give back-up, such as bringing ammo to the men that are running short. Above all, they had to execute my orders without question. I was very proud of these men. I just hoped that all of us could make it home alive, but I really knew that this wish would never happen.

My radio sounds, "Blackhawk Three, this is Annihilator Three-Three, what's going on?"

"We sprang an ambush on an ambush."

"That's great, Rock! I mean Blackhawk. How is the body count, and did you lose any men?"

"The Bravo Charlie (body count) is eight, and we had no casualties!"

"Good, good, good! Eight, huh?"

"Yes, eight. I will talk to you about it when we get in. We are policing up the area now."

I turned toward the men. "OK, men, you did an excellent job. Pick up all the ammo and weapons. Be careful!"

Killer says, "Hey, Sarge, this AK is messed up, do ya want it anyhow?"

"Yes, everything of firepower."

We found eight AK-47s and three .45 pistols.

White has a very nice looking AK-47. "Sarge, can we keep them?"

"Yes, you'll have to send them to the rear. Be sure and tag 'em! You guys take one each."

"What about you, Sarge? Don't you want one?"

"No, I have five that I sent to the rear or Chu Lai. OK, men, let's go!"

Killer says, "Wait a minute, Sarge. I want to make sure that my AK is firing right. I'll be right back!"

Killer crosses over the berm. We hear a shot, then another, then another. He shot a total of eight shots, then returned. "OK, Sarge, my AK works fine. I also checked out each gook., They seem to be all dead."

He laughs along with all of my men. I knew that Killer had shot each gook in the head.

I am taking a crap while on a roving ambush

"Let's move out! White, pull point!"

"I'm there, Sarge."

White moves to the front of the squad.

I look at Killer. "You know that you cannot place eight more stars on your helmet, because you didn't kill all of them by yourself."

"I know. I just shot two and a half!"

"A half? What do you mean?"

"I shot two by myself and helped Emery kill one. I will draw two full stars and a half star on my helmet liner."

"That's my boy, Killer! That-a-boy, do it right!"

We arrived back at company. "Men, you guys get some rest. I'm going to the CP."

I walked to the CP. The captain was waiting for my report. "Hi, Rock. Tell me about it!"

"Wait a minute, sir. I want to talk to your RTO!"

The RTO was sitting down, eating his C-ration breakfast. "Are you the guy that took my sit-rep?"

"Yeah, it was me."

Sternly I said, "Get up! Get up, you piece of crap!"

The captain watched but said nothing. The RTO started standing very slowly. I knocked his C-rations from his hands and got in his face. "Don't you know how to handle a sit-rep that is not *negative*? You ask if we need *help*! You don't say that you think my radio is *broken*! Now get out of my face!"

The captain looks at me with his eyes wide open. "Sarge, what was that all about?"

I gave him the story. He said, "I'll handle him, Rock. It won't happen again! Now give me the story on the body count. I noticed that you sent back the correct protocol."

"What was that, sir?"

"You said Bravo Charlie for body count and that is correct. I should start doing the radio protocol a little better."

"Yeah, I know, but we all get so excited over body counts, we forget about protocol."

"OK, Rock, tell me about it. I have already turned it in. We are doing well as a company."

"OK, sir, I will give you the short version. We were heading back when I heard voices. I was on point. I looked over a berm and saw the NVA. They had an ambush set up on an adjacent path to ours. Eckert and I climbed the berm and started shooting. We drove the gooks back to where the rest of my men were waiting. It worked perfectly."

The captain says, "I can't remember anyone springing an ambush on an ambush! That is great. I have some good news for you!"

"What's that, sir?"

"We are moving by chopper in a few hours. It is a combat assault, but I don't think we will be shot at."

"Don't you mean that we won't be shot at *much*, sir?"

"Yeah, Rock, shot at *much*!"

CHAPTER 14

They Won't Develop Our Pictures

I walked from the CP to my squad. The men were all standing up even though I thought that they would be tired from our roving ambush. The men started talking. "What did the old man say?"

"Was the captain happy?"

"How did he act?"

I looked at them. "He was very, very happy. He had already called in the body count before he even verified the count with me. He said good job to all of you guys."

Killer says, "That's good, Rock. I mean, Sergeant Rock!"

"Alright, men, I have good news."

The men were waiting for the catch. "Let's hear it, Sarge!"

"We are going to travel today by helicopter!"

Killer says, "I get the window seat. The last time I had the aisle seat, the stewardess spilled a glass of wine on me!"

All of us laughed. "I swear, Killer. You can be a comedian when you get home."

Emerald says, "Hey, Sarge, why don't they have doors on the choppers?"

"They are just too heavy, but I have seen a few with doors, Emerald. Listen up, guys, the LZ is supposed to be calm, not hot, but watch out anyhow!"

We hear the choppers coming. Twenty-four start to come into our laid-out LZ. My radio sounds, "Blackhawk Three, you take care of the landing smoke!"

"Affirmative, I'll take care of it!"

White runs up to me. "Sergeant Rock, what about the bouncing-betty?"

"What?"

"The mine that you laid on!"

"All heck! I forgot all about it! White, take your claymore to the mine and blow it up!"

"OK. Can I take Killer with me?"

"Yes, but be careful!"

I got on the radio. "Annihilator Three-Three, in a minute or two, you are going to hear two large blasts. We are going to blow the bouncing-betty mine!"

"Blackhawk Three, you better get on it fast. Out!"

Killer and White take off running toward the mine. They reach the rock that is sitting on the mine prong. White takes his claymore mine out. He places the blasting cap into the claymore. "Killer, take the wire and the triggering device over there behind the berm! I'll stay here and hold the wire so it doesn't pull out. *Don't* hook up the triggering device!"

Killer takes off quickly. He runs out fifty to sixty feet of cord and jumps over the berm. "OK, White, I am protected. Come on over here!"

White runs to the berm. He jumps the berm and quickly hooks the wires to the trigger mechanism. "Are you ready, Killer? This is going to be righteous!"

"I am ready. Let's do it!"

White squeezes the trigger. The explosion is tremendous. I am now at the edge of the rice paddy where the choppers will land. I hear the first explosion, then the second.

Craig says, "Sarge, the second explosion was worse than the first! Man, that bouncing-betty would have killed the whole squad!"

"Yep, they were both pretty loud and powerful!"

I pulled out my smoke grenade and threw it in the rice paddy.

"Boomerang, this is Blackhawk Three. I have smoke, over!"

"Blackhawk Three, I see yellow smoke, over."

"Affirmative on the yellow, Boomerang!"

"We are coming in. How is your LZ?"

"It is cold, Boomerang! It is cold!"

The choppers came in and landed. I see movement toward the last chopper.

Emery says, "What are you looking at, Sarge?"

"Look at the last chopper. What's going on?" We see men carrying men to the choppers. "Oh, yeah, Emery. They are loading the dead door gunners and our guys that got shot down yesterday!"

"You are right, Sarge!"

I started thinking to myself, *How could I have forgotten about the guys that got killed yesterday?*

"Emery, did you forget about those guys that got killed yesterday?"

"Yes I did, Sarge!"

"Man, oh man, Emery, we are sorry individuals! How can we forget about death so quickly?"

"Sarge, we just have so much going on. We are worried about our own deaths all of the time. We can't be expected to remember everything that happened yesterday!"

"Very well put, Emery. Let's move out!"

We headed for the choppers. The door gunners were ready for any movement. The gunners always looked cool, unshakable, self-confident, and composed. I would love to be a door gunner. We jumped on the choppers which we were assigned to.

In general, we would be assigned to the same order of the chopper line-up. My squad usually got the third and fourth choppers. I never asked why, but I was glad to know the general area for climbing aboard. I looked out and saw Killer and White running toward the choppers.

I motioned for the gunner to hold up our take-off. He spoke to the pilot through his helmet radio. I motioned for Killer to come with us in the third chopper and for White to go to the fourth chopper. The choppers started to take off. Both men jumped on the runners of the choppers. I motioned for Killer to hold his position until the pilot got the chopper stabilized.

We were now stabilized, moving at about sixty-five miles per hour. Killer was still standing outside the bird on the runners. I motioned for Killer to come inside. We made room for Killer. We traveled north for another hour.

The door gunners would see something strange on the ground and start firing their M-60 machine guns. They would just start firing, giving us no warning. This would make us all jump. Then we would laugh. We traveled another thirty minutes or so.

The door gunners tapped us on the shoulder. "Get ready!"

The choppers were getting lower. We heard a *ping* as a bullet hit the inside of the chopper. The gunners started firing back. I thought that this was supposed to be a cold LZ.

Here we go again, I thought.

I motion for my men to get ready. We are on the edge of the chopper. Bullets are flying. This has now turned into a combat assault. We start firing our weapons, along with the door gunners, before we leave the choppers. We are now at an elevation four feet from the earth.

I motion for my guys to jump and spread out. We spread out and start firing back at the tree line. Most of the enemy fire is directed toward the choppers, but now the choppers are pulling away.

The firing is now coming in our direction. Raymond has the Pig and is doing well. I can see the bushes and trees flying apart in pieces as his 7.62-caliber bullets fly toward the enemy. Raymond is relentless. Again, he has the M-60 Pig working like a sewing machine. Just watching him work the gun makes my heart beat faster. I want to yell "Attack," but it is not time yet.

We start to advance, but there is a small creek between the tree line and us. The creek is three feet deep with steep sides. We advanced to the creek. In front of me, I see a tree-like bush. I grab it to help pull me from the creek.

I did not see the wasps that were nested in the bush. I was stung in the face, the neck, the back, the shoulders, and all over both hands and arms. This was painful, to say the least. I fell back into the water, releasing the bush. My men were already into the tree line, taking charge of the situation.

I started to feel my hands and arms swelling up. I had to get out of this water. I went downstream, away from the bush, and pulled myself above and out of the creek. I tried to shoot my rifle but my finger was too swollen to bend at the joint. I started running toward the tree line in hopes that my men would take up my slack. I was not worth much to them at this time.

I reach the men. Craig says, "Are you wounded, Sarge?"

I shake my head no. I can hardly talk. My throat is swelling up and my eyelids are closing over my eyes. I am feeling sick.

My radio goes off, "Blackhawk Three, call in artillery!"

Craig looks at me. "Are you sure that you are not shot?"

I try to speak, but the words won't come out. I am trying to say that I can't call in for fire support. Craig gets on the radio. "Annihilator Three-Three, this is Blackhawk Three X-ray. Blackhawk cannot call in artillery. He is out-of-order at the moment!"

The captain responds, "Roger, I'll do it!"

The fire support started coming in. We dove to the ground because it was coming in close. The bombardment kept coming for another ten minutes. I heard my radio. "Set up the perimeter. We are here for the night!"

I was very happy that we did not have to hump through the jungle. My teeth felt like they were going to fall out. I had to sit down.

"Eckert, you take over!"

"I will, but I am going to get Doc first!"

Eckert takes off running toward the CP. He returns with Doc. Eckert says, "By the way, Sarge, our squad shot three. The company killed twenty total."

This was good. I nodded my head; I did not feel like talking.

Doc says, "What the heck did you get into, Rock?"

I tried to explain to him that it was wasps, but he could not understand me. I showed him with my hands. I moved my hand like a bird or an airplane. Then I took my fingers and grabbed his arm and pinched it. He says, "Oh, wasps!"

I nod my head to confirm. He says, "Take off your shirt."

I remove my sweaty shirt. Doc says, "Oh, my! You have over a hundred stings on your back! How do you feel?"

I shake my head side to side to say *no, I don't feel good*. The other guys are now looking at me.

Emerald says, "Look at his face! Look at all of those stings! Are you alright, Sarge?"

I just sat there doing nothing, moving nothing.

Doc says, "I'm going to get you something. I'll be right back!" He returns with the captain. Doc says, "Here, take this!"

He hands me a few pills and a small bottle of something. "Take the pills and drink the entire bottle!"

Doc turns to the captain. "Sir, we definitely need to lift him out. He is bad!"

The captain looks at me. He gets closer. "Yep. Rock, you are getting out of here!"

I know that I would be killing my men if I left the field. I stand up and shake my head no. I say, "No, no, no! You need me, sir, don't you? I am staying!"

"Rock, I do need you. We are the greatest team in Vietnam, but I would rather send you to the rear for a few days so you can come back healthy."

I answered, "Nope, I am staying, sir. I am staying!"

The captain looks at Doc. "Look at him in the morning, Doc!"

The captain looks back at me. "How are you feeling now, Rock?"

I am feeling terrible, but I give him the thumbs up and say, "Great! Much better, sir!"

I felt horrible, but I could not leave the company. I was not trying to be a martyr. I was just worried about my men and the company as a whole. If the captain got killed, there was not another person I would trust, other than myself, to lead the company. If I was to go to the rear and any of my men were to get killed, I could not live with myself. I would be letting everyone down if I went to the rear. I was now getting really sleepy.

The Doc says, "Don't go to sleep yet, Danny. I have some alcohol for your back. Lie down and roll over!"

The alcohol stung as he sprayed it on my back. "Rock, you were stung a lot! I mean it! You are going to be lifted out in the morning if you are not better!"

"Thanks, Doc, but no thanks!"

Doc stood up and started walking toward the CP. "See ya, Danny."

I lean back on my rucksack. Eckert walks up to me. "Sarge, I have already assigned guard duty, and you ain't doing one!"

"Yes I am, Eckert! I didn't help with digging the foxhole, so I am pulling guard!"

"We can handle it, Sarge!"

"Eckert, haven't you ever heard the phrase 'If you talk the talk, you better be able to walk the walk'?"

"Yeah, but this is different. You are sick."

"No I'm not. I feel better already! If I don't pull my weight, then how can I expect the men to act on my commands when they are wounded or a little sick?"

"OK, Rock, what guard do you want?"

"Give me the last one so I can get a little sleep!"

"Alright, just let me know if you change your mind and I will pull it for you!"

"Thanks, Eckert."

I dumped my poncho out on the ground. I spread the poncho out just enough so my body would not be lying directly on the ground. I felt too bad to make my bed any further, so I just laid my head on the rucksack. Emerald walked up. "Sarge, I hate to bother you, but how are you feeling?"

I felt really bad but I had to put up a front for the men. "I feel pretty good now!"

"You don't sound or look good! By the way, when do you DEROS?"

I did not feel like talking. I wanted to sleep. "Not until July."

"Sergeant Rock, one more question, then I'll leave. I know that DEROS means going home and leaving the 'Nam, but what does D-E-R-O-S stand for?"

I answered, "Date of Expected Return from Over Seas."

"Thanks, Sarge. I asked five other guys and none of them knew the answer. Thanks."

All through my life, I would just have to know what an acronym stood for. It would bother me until I found out. For instance, when the news reporters would talk about oil they would always mention OPEC. I would ask people, but they would say, "I don't know what OPEC means, but it has something to do with oil!" This answer was never good enough for me. I would keep searching. I found out that OPEC was Organization of Petroleum Exporting Countries. I have to admit that I was in Vietnam before I found out what DEROS meant.

I laid my head back down on the rucksack, hoping that no one else would bother me until it was time for my guard duty. I fell asleep fast. I think that I stayed in the same position until Emery woke me up for guard duty. "Sarge, if you don't feel like it, I'll pull your shift."

"No, but thanks, Emery. You are a good man. I feel better."

I actually did feel better. My teeth still felt like they were going to fall out. My gums were still swollen. I grabbed my rifle and ammo and climbed into the foxhole. Nothing happened while I was on duty and that was the way I liked it. Morning came and I woke up the men. We started eating breakfast when my radio sounded, "Blackhawk Three, supply choppers will be here in thirty, out!"

This is great because we are getting low on water, C-rations, and ammo. The choppers come in and Platoon Four runs to the choppers to start unloading the goods. I see someone jumping off of the chopper and running with a limp toward us. It's Chuck. He hobbles up to me. "Hey, Sergeant Rock, how are you?"

He gives me a man hug. "Man, what the heck happened to you? They told me that I may be bringing back a casualty with me. Is that you?"

"Yep, but I can't go yet. We don't have enough leaders... What did you mean when you said you were going to *bring a casualty back with you*? Are you not staying with us?"

"No, Danny, I am not staying. I landed the gig of all gigs. I am the new supply sergeant until we get another one. By the way, Top says to tell you 'Hi!' Here is your fresh towel. I brought everybody fresh clothes on the chopper."

"That is cool, Chuck. You are already better than the last supply sergeant. Are my AKs still back there?"

"No, they somehow disappeared. Top thinks that the officers grabbed them when they were being DEROSed."

"Those stupid jerks! Why can't they keep their hands of the non-commissioned officers' stuff?"

Chuck says, "If I would have been the supply sergeant earlier, they would not have been able to steal your guns. I would have hid them."

"Chuck, my guys have AKs that they want to send back with you. Will you hide them?"

"You bet I will!"

Chuck puts his hand on my shoulder. "Come on, Danny. Come back with me. We will go swimming at the beach and all of that stuff. We will take a hot shower every night. You can rest for a few days then come back out to the field!"

"It sounds good, Chuck, but let's say that I did leave the field and the company got wiped out. I could not live with myself."

Chuck shakes his head. "Yeah, I understand. I feel bad knowing that I am in the rear and you guys are fighting every day! I will try to get back here ASAP!"

"Chuck, are you coming back out tomorrow?"

"Yep, I think so. Why?"

"I want to start carrying an M-79. Will you bring one for me, and plenty of ammo?"

"You got it, Danny! Well, I better get back to the choppers before they leave me! See ya, Danny. See all of you guys tomorrow."

Doc runs up to me. "You are not leaving the field?"

"No, I feel better. For real, I actually do feel a little better, Doc!"

"OK, Danny, you win!"

Doc walks away. My radio sounds, "Blackhawk Three, come to Cherokee, out!"

I start walking toward the CP. I arrive to see the lieutenant talking to the other squad leaders. "Hey guys. What's up, sir?"

"How you doing, Rock? You are still swollen up. Where do you hurt the worst?"

"I think it's my gums and teeth, but other than that, I feel better."

The lieutenant looks at us. "OK, squad leaders, all of you will take your squads and roam all day. Each squad will go in a different direction and come back here tonight. Are you up to it, Rock?"

"Yes, sir, I am up for it! Show us where to go!"

Gibbons pulls out his map and shows each of us the direction we will be going. I ask, "Are we supposed to engage the enemy, sir?"

"Yep, engage if you have to!"

"When do we leave?"

"As soon as your squads are ready!"

I turned and walked away, looking at Mac on the way. "Hey, Mac, is everything going OK?"

"Yep, everything is fine, Rock."

"Mac, how come you look so worried?"

"I am just worried about today."

"You mean our patrols?"

"Yeah, with all the NVA soldiers around here," he said, scanning the area, "I'm worried."

"Man, Mac, you can't let your squad know that you're afraid."

"Aren't you afraid, Rock?"

"Heck yeah I am, but we cannot show our fear. Fear spreads like wildfire!"

"How do you cope, Rock?"

"I pray every time that I get scared, and I pray a lot! Sometimes I pray and thank God for just giving us another day of life. Mainly, every day I pray for courage!"

"You pray for courage? You don't act like you need help in courage!"

"Believe it or not, I am afraid every day, but having God with me keeps me centered mentally. God gives me strength."

"I'll try it. See ya, Rock!"

"Later, gator."

I arrive to see the squad getting ready for the move out. I am still not up to par, but I have to pretend everything is peachy. "Men, we are patrolling northwest. Let's go!"

My radio sounds, "Blackhawk Three, this is Cherokee. Annihilator Three-Three wants us to hold up. Come to the CP!"

"On my way."

I took off for the CP. The captain and all of the squad leaders and the lieutenants were there. The captain speaks. "Men, we have orders to find two volunteers."

I say, "Volunteers for what, sir?"

"For door gunners."

I respond, "I am there, sir! I want to go right now! Send me on the chopper!"

I wouldn't have actually gone at the present time. "No, you are not going. This is not for squad leaders. I want you guys to go back to your squads and see if you can find at least two men."

I turned and started toward the squad. I knew that the captain would not let me go at the present time, but at least I let him know that when the time came again, I would be ready.

Being a door gunner is very dangerous; however, being shot at a few times a day is much better than being shot at all day long. We were in many battles that lasted all day long. Some of our battles lasted for two weeks. The door gunners, after a hot LZ, would get to go back to a secured location, eat a hot meal, and sleep on a cot or in a bed. Compared to what us grunts had to go through every day, this volunteering for a door gunner was a no-brainer!

I arrived to see the men still standing, ready to go. Killer says, "What's up, Sarge?"

"Men, the captain wants two volunteers for door gunners. Who wants to volunteer?"

Killer, Emery, White, and Eckert all said, "I do!"

"I do. Let me go, Sarge!"

"No, let me!"

Every man, as I expected, with the exception of Emerald, wanted to go.

Raymond says, "Sarge, I already carry a 60. I should be the one!"

Killer says, "Rock, I hate to leave you, but just think about it! The door gunners don't have to hump. They get shot at a few times a week and get hot showers and food from a mess hall! Count me in!"

"OK, I'll go and tell the captain."

I turned and walked away. I saw the captain speaking to Mac. "Sir, everyone in my squad but one wants to be a door gunner!"

Mac says, "Every man in my squad volunteered too!"

Mac and I laugh. The captain is not laughing.

Here comes Smitty and a few others. "Sir, all of our men want to be a gunner!"

The captain replies, "What? Do you mean to tell me that every man in this company is going to volunteer for a door gunner position?"

I answer, "Looks that way, sir!"

The captain shakes his head. "Forget it! No one is going. You guys get out of here. Just get back to your squads! Rock, stay here!"

A few more squad leaders are heading toward the captain. The captain holds up his hand. "Stop, stop, stop. I know everyone in your squad wants to be a door gunner! I am rescinding the order. No one is going! Get back to your squads! Man, oh man, Rock, what's going on? Don't they know that very few door gunners get out of Vietnam alive?" The captain looks at me. "Just tell me what is going on? Even you want to be a door gunner!"

"Sir, it is simple. They have better living conditions than we have! We struggle every day of the week. They don't!"

"I guess that you're right, Rock. If we had more qualified men, I would let you go!"

"Thanks, sir. Is that all? Are we done?"

"Yep. Head out and tell your men thanks, but no thanks!"

"See ya, sir."

"See ya, Sarge."

I strolled back to the squad and gave them the news. They all had comments such as, "I knew it was too good to be true!"

"Did everyone want to volunteer, Sarge?"

"Yep, almost the whole company! Let's get out of here!"

We walked out of the perimeter toward our patrol destination. We patrolled until noon. Killer was on point. "Rock, there is a village up ahead!"

"Look out for VC, Killer! Head for the last hooch on the left!"

We arrived at the hooch. "Let's eat lunch. You pull first guard, Killer! Get the M-79 with a canister round!"

"Got it, Sarge!"

Killer started pulling guard at the same time he was opening C-rations. The rest of us sort of relaxed, but our peacefulness was cut short.

Two VC came down the path near a small river. They were heading straight for the hooch that we were in. "Rock, do you see them?"

"Yes. Hold your fire until they get closer!"

They both had rifles. They were just speaking and walking. The VC were 100 feet away.

"Now, Rock?"

"No, not yet! Get ready, guys."

The gooks walked straight toward us. They were within fifty feet of our position.

The gooks stopped. They were within forty feet of us. They saw us and turned. I yelled, "Fire, fire, fire!"

Killer shot them in the back of their heads with the grenade launcher. Everyone opened fire.

Killer says, "Well, that was simple! How come you waited so long on the command to fire, Sarge?"

"I wanted to see if there were any more. You need to learn that too, Killer. We had the drop on two, but if there had been a dozen or more, then maybe they would have had the drop on us!"

"OK, Sarge, you're right."

"Men, let's go and check out the damage!"

The two gooks were a mess. Both had the backs of their heads blown away. Emerald started getting sick.

Killer says, "Emery, do you still have your camera?"

Emery replies as he reaches in his rucksack, "Yeah, let's take pictures!"

Eckert says, "Rock's squad does it again!"

I looked at Killer. "Deja vu. Killer, you remember the last time that you blew a gooks head apart, don't ya? You cut his head off. You are not doing that today!"

"Aw, come on, Sarge. Don't you like being the leader of the most treacherous, unfaltering, devoted-to-the-body-count squad in the 'Nam?'"

"Yeah, we are cool, Killer, but the heads stay on the bodies this time!"

"OK. Let's just take pictures!"

Killer and White held the gooks' heads up by the hair and posed for the camera. Emery takes the picture. Eckert and Raymond did the same. Killer says, "Come on, Emery. Let's take a picture of the backs of the heads!"

Emery says, "Man, Killer. You can only see brain matter and blood. I don't know about that!"

"Aw, come on, you wimp!"

"OK, Killer, let's do it. Eckert, take the picture!"

Killer says, "OK, Rock, I mean Sergeant Rock. It is your turn!"

I look at the guys. They are all smiling. "I don't know, guys. I hate to touch dead bodies!"

White says, "Come on, Sarge. The bodies are not even cold yet. Besides, if Sergeant Lewis was here, don't you think that he would do it?"

I remembered what I had always told the men: "We are a team. We do things together." I decided to take the picture to show the men that I was one of them. I was also wrapped up in the body count, and my squad had just bagged two more.

I knelt down between the two gooks. I placed my right hand on the head of one and my left hand on the head of the other. I grabbed a hold of the hair and lifted them up near my head so all three of us could get into the frame of the picture.

As I was lifting the heads, the skin and the scalp from both gooks started to come off of the skulls. The scalps were now pulling the forehead away from the skulls. The eyebrow skin was pulling forward. I yelled, "Take the picture! Take the picture!"

Killer takes the picture. I drop the heads. Pieces of the skull fall out on the ground. I grabbed a piece of the skull.

Killer says, "What are you going to do with the piece of skull, Sarge?"

I tell him, "My brother Duane is always asking me for an ear or something, so I am going to send him this!"

"That's cool, Sarge. I am going to do the same!"

Killer had to stick his hands into the back of the head of one of the gooks to break a piece of skull off. "I have a drinking buddy in the States. He will love it! Now I can throw this eyeball away that I have been carrying for two weeks!"

"An *eyeball?*"

"Yep, an eyeball!"

Killer digs into his rucksack and locates a small box about the size of a ring or bracelet box. Inside the box, he had the eyeball wrapped in tissue paper. Killer opened up the tissue paper to show me that he actually had an eyeball. I could smell the eyeball before he unwrapped it.

"That thing stinks! You are gross, Killer! You are gross!"

Killer tosses the eyeball to the side and places the newly-acquired piece of skull in the box. It was time to call in the body count.

The men gathered around to listen to my report. "Cherokee Three, this is Blackhawk Three, over."

"This is Cherokee Three X-ray, go!"

"We have two Bravo Charlie, over!"

"That's good, Blackhawk Three. No one else has a kill!"

My men yell out with excitement, "Cool!"

"Alright!"

"We are the Vietnam champions for kills!"

White says, "Maybe we will run across a few more VC before we get back and bag a few more!"

Killer says, "Yeah, and I get point!"

White says, "Nope, it is my turn, and I am taking it if it is OK with Sarge. What about it, Sarge?"

"Go ahead. It is your turn at point!"

I have to admit that this body count thing was getting to me. Like my men, I also wanted kills. I knew that deep down inside of me I would never be the same guy that I was before I came to Vietnam. I recognize that my thought process, while necessary in fighting a war, is also disturbing to me on some levels. Before Vietnam, my thought process was based on *what would be next?* For instance, I would have to race my car on weekends to make extra money. I worked in a grocery store while going to college. Therefore, I would make a weekly plan. First, I would go to my classes. Next, I would go to baseball practice. Next, I would go to work. Then on weekends, I would race my car. I had a simple thought process with little conflict. There were no killings in my thoughts at home.

"Craig, call and find out when we can return!"

Craig lifts the horn. "Cherokee Three, this is Blackhawk Three X-ray. We want permission to return, over."

"Blackhawk Three X-ray, come on back. Cherokee says to kill some more Victor Charlies on your way back!"

"Affirmatron, we are on the way. We'll try for a few more gooks, out!"

"Good job, Craig! Let's move out, men! White, you are on point. I'll go second. Killer, you bring up the rear. The rest of you fill up the middle!"

I knew these men well. They would fall in line without me having to tell them what to do. In general, each man would be in the same place day after day. This made my job easier because when I needed a man I would know where to look. However, there was one man that always wanted to be toward the front, and that was Killer.

Killer says, "Sarge, how can I kill anyone being in the rear of the squad?"

"Killer, if we are attacked from the rear, you had better get lots of kills, or we all are in a crap load of trouble!"

Killer walks to the rear with his head hanging down. I look at Craig and White and we all laugh.

We started patrolling back toward the company CP, looking for VC as we watched, walked, and listened. We walk two miles and White sees a gook on the trail. He makes him stop by saying, "*Dung lai, dung lai!*" I knew that the gook was not a threat or White would have already shot him. White motions to me to come to the point. "Sarge, this guy looks pretty old. Do you think he is a VC?"

I look closely at the gook and ask for his ID (identification card). In my very little knowledge of Vietnamese, I say, "*Can-cuoc, can-couc.*"

He shows me his ID card. He is eighty-three years old. He is using a stick for a cane and he can hardly walk. He grabs my hand and places it to his heart and bows to both White and myself. He tells us something in Vietnamese. We cannot understand what he is saying. I see a couple of children. One child is about twelve and the other is around eight.

I ask them to come to me. "Do you speak American?"

The older one holds up his hand showing me his finger and thumb, to say a small amount. He says, "*te te.*"

"What is the Papa saying?"

The boy turns to the old guy and says something. The old man replies to the kids. He says a few sentences and bows to us again.

The boy turns back toward us and says, "He says that he appreciates you American soldiers being here. He says that the VC killed his son and his family for not joining the VC! He wishes you well."

I reach out my hand and shake his hand. "Thank you, sir, and good luck."

I tell the kids, "Thanks, kids. See ya!"

"Goodbye, GI."

The kids went one way, and the old man walked down the path toward Killer.

"No, White, he wasn't a VC. He was just an old guy that hates VC as much as we do!"

"Yep, I think you're right, Sarge!"

White went to the front again to pull point. We started moving again when suddenly we were startled by the sound of two shots. Then we heard a full automatic fire burst from an M-16 rifle. We hit the ground! The firing was coming from the rear of our squad. I jumped over Craig and ran up to Emery. "What's going on?"

"Don't know! It came from the back!"

I slowly walked from one man to the other, heading to the rear of the squad.

I reached Raymond. "What's all of the firing about, Raymond?"

"It's Killer. He just shot a VC!"

"Are there any more?"

"I don't think so, just one!"

I walked up to Killer. He was placing another star on his helmet. "What happened, Killer?"

He motions with his head toward a body lying in the bushes. "The VC tried to attack us from the rear!"

I look at the body and notice two bullet holes in the bottom of his foot. There were more bullet holes in the back of his legs and about fifteen holes in his back. I looked closer and found that he had no weapon, but he was carrying a large stick.

"How could he have been attacking us when he was shot in the back, Killer?"

"Well, Sarge, I told him to stop, and he mumbled a few words and kept walking. He turned and pointed the stick at me. I thought it was a rifle!"

I immediately started thinking about the old man I had just met. I ran to the body and turned the body over. It was the old man.

I yelled at the top of my lungs, "Why, Killer? Why? This old guy was eighty-three years old! He wasn't a threat to anyone! His whole family was killed by the VCs!"

"But, Sarge, he was a gook! I thought he had a weapon!"

"Killer, you are wrong on this kill! And if you put a star on
your helmet, I'll rip your heart right out of your chest!"

"But, Sarge!"

"Don't talk to me, Killer! Just keep your butt back here. I
don't even want to look at you!"

I turned and went back toward the point. White was waiting.
"What happened, Sarge?"

"You know that old guy that was thanking us?"

White says, "Oh, no, Sarge, he didn't, did he?"

"Yep! He unloaded a full magazine into him. He is dead,
dead, dead!"

"Man, Rock, he can't kill innocent people!"

"Yep, I know. I will talk to him, but right now I am mad
enough to kill him myself! He says that he thought the stick was
a weapon! Let's get moving!"

We arrived at the company CP. The lieutenant and the captain
were talking. "How many did you get, Rock?"

I had to think for a moment. We had killed three but one was
just a little, old, harmless gentleman. I answered, "Two, sir, only
two!"

"What's wrong, Rock? You look down!"

"Nothing, sir, nothing!"

I was thinking about how I was going to handle Killer, but I
couldn't let the captain know it.

"The supply chopper will be here in a little bit."

"Thanks, sir."

I walked back to the squad. At least seeing Chuck again
would make me feel better.

Killer was waiting for me. "Sergeant Rock, will you speak
to me now?"

"What do ya want, Killer?"

"Sergeant Rock, I am sorry and it will never, never happen
again. I promise to only shoot people that are trying to shoot me
or us. I promise!"

"Killer, I just want to calm down. I'll talk to you later!"

"Sarge, what did the captain say about our three body counts?"

"You idiot! Two! Two! The old man doesn't count. We killed two! You are not in remorse! Get away from me!"

Killer hangs his head and walks away. I hear the chopper coming in. The chopper lands and Chuck jumps off. He is carrying an M-79 handheld grenade launcher. I meet Chuck halfway. "Hey, Supply Sergeant, how are ya?"

"Good, Danny. You sure look better. How do ya feel?"

"Actually a lot better. My gums are still sore, but I feel much, much better now! Is my face still swollen?"

"Yep, it is, but not like it was. Here is your 79. Be sure to send your M-16 back with me. I heard that you guys went on a patrol and you got two body counts."

"Not me. The squad got the count. You should have seen the gooks! The skin was coming clean off of the skull and facial bones. It was gross!"

"How do ya mean, gross?"

"Well, you know how Killer and White are after a kill! They grabbed the gooks by the hair and lifted them up to take a picture. They took the pictures of both the fronts and the backs of the heads. It was gross! Then they made me do it!"

"Wait a minute, Rock. No one makes you do anything you don't want to do!"

"Yeah, I know, but this time I did. When I lifted the heads, the skin pulled off the scalps. I wanted to drop them right then and there, but I didn't. White or Eckert took the picture. I think it was Eckert."

"You guys took pictures? Show me!"

"No, they have to be developed. You'll have to wait."

Chuck says, "That's too bad. Wait, wait. I know I have to fly to Da Nang tomorrow. They have a place in a PX that develops pictures. Where is the camera?"

I yell at Emery, "Emery, come over here!"

Emery walks to our position. "What can I do for you two sergeants?"

Chuck says, "How is it going, Emery?"

"Great, Sarge. How have you been?"

"I have been great. I hear that you have some pictures to be developed!"

Emery starts fumbling through his rucksack. "Here it is. Can you get them developed?"

"Yes, in Da Nang. How many copies do ya want?"

Emery thinks, "What do ya think, Sergeant Rock?"

"Heck, let's get ten copies. I'll pay for them."

Emery hands the camera to Chuck. "Make it twelve copies. I'll send two home."

Killer hears us talking. "Why don't you make it fifteen, and I'll pay for all of them!"

Chuck responds, "OK, I'll make it fifteen!"

I hear the chopper's motor start revving up.

"Chuck, you better get moving. Here is my rifle, and thanks!"

"Yeah, buddy, I'll see you in a few days. You guys are moving out again by choppers. Did ya know that?"

"No, that is great! Where are we going?"

"I only know that it is north again!"

Chuck heads for the chopper. I hear more choppers coming in. My radio sounds and Craig answers, "This is Blackhawk Three X-ray, go."

"Tell Blackhawk to come to the CP, out!"

I arrive at the CP. Lieutenant Gibbons tells me where we are going and which choppers we will be on. I return to the squad.

"Men, we are getting a lift again!"

Emerald says, "I bet that you are happy about that, huh, Sarge? You probably don't feel like humping yet, do ya?"

"You are right. I don't feel like humping!"

The choppers come in and land. This will not be considered a combat assault because we don't expect to run into a hot LZ.

We run to get on the third and fourth helicopters. The birds take off.

Killer starts to sing the tune "Wild Blue Yonder," but he changes the words:

"Here we fly into the wild blue yonder, with my buddy, Sergeant Rock, and our killer squad. Even though he hates me for all of my sins, I think that someday he will love me again!"

Killer looks at me and I start to laugh. How could I stay mad at a clown? We travel for over an hour, and then we land in a big rice paddy. All of us grunts jump out of the choppers and run to the tree line. Craig walks toward me. "Annihilator says to set up for the night!"

"Got it!"

I tell the men to dig their foxholes. The company sets up a large perimeter, with the foxholes about twenty-five feet apart. I am just finishing up my turn at digging when Craig walks over to the foxhole. "Annihilator wants you at the CP."

I head to the CP to see all of the platoon leaders, platoon sergeants, and Mac. "Hey, Mac, are we the only squad leaders here?"

"Looks like it!"

The captain starts to speak. "Men, we will be here two days. We will not patrol. We are waiting on another company to get in position for an NVA fight. Remember that we are in NVA territory, so stay alert day and night. I am proud of all of you. We have a very large amount of kills and you know as well as I do that the body count is the name of the game over here in Vietnam. You platoon leaders all know Sergeant Mac and Sergeant Rock, don't you?"

I could feel the tension as all of the officers looked at us sergeants! "Rock's squad has more kills than all of the other platoons put together, and Mac's squad is second. Find out how they do it! OK, dismissed. Rock, you and Mac wait!"

I see that the captain is smiling. "The platoon leaders are jealous. They think that you two are my favorites."

I say, "Well, aren't we, sir?"

He laughs. "Yes, but keep up the good work! They also wonder why I let you, Rock, call in so much artillery!"

Mac says, "Let some of them try it, but be sure that you or Rock are monitoring!"

The captain replies, "Yeah, I'll let them have a chance, but it won't be today. It will be later. Rock, I am calling it in tonight. You guys take it easy."

Mac and I replied, "Yes, sir!"

We took off in the direction of our squads.

On our way back, Mac says, "Rock, that was pretty good what the old man said about us in front of the officers, huh?"

"Yep, it is always nice to get accolades, but especially in front of officers!"

"Why do you think you guys get so many kills? Will you teach me?"

"No!"

"Why not, Rock?"

"I don't mean that I won't teach you. I just mean that I cannot teach you!"

"What are you talking about, Rock?"

I stop. "We get all of these kills by being in the right place at the right time. The only thing that I can see that my squad does different is that they love to kill. My men fight for point! Ever since Killer cut the head off of the gook, my guys want more and more body count. Now can you see why I cannot teach you? My guys are just animals!"

Mac says, "Wow, my guys never want point! We get a lot of body count, like your squad does, by being in the right place at the right time also."

"See ya, Mac."

I told the squad that we were going to have a mini stand down for two days. They were excited, to say the least. "Men, I want you to be on alert. We are in NVA territory. We are going to have artillery coming in soon. Don't let it scare you!"

Killer says, "Don't you mean *startle* us, Sarge?"

"Yeah, right, Killer. Don't let the big bomb noise *startle* you!" We laughed. I asked, "Eckert, have you got guard set up?"

"Yes I do, Sarge! Is third OK for you?"

"Yes. Who is fourth?"

"Emerald."

"OK."

We sat around for a few hours then went to sleep. That night and the next day were uneventful. All we did was eat and sleep. This was very unusual for us. It was nice that we had not lost a man to the enemy in a day and a half.

The next morning came and two choppers come in with more supplies. Chuck is on one of the choppers. He jumps off and runs over to our perimeter. He walks up. "Hey, Danny, I have good news and bad news."

"Give us the good news first."

"I will be coming back out in a week. There is a new supply sergeant coming in!"

"Great, Chuck! That's cool!"

All of the guys respected Chuck. They knew that they could depend on him if anything was to happen to me. Chuck pulls me to the side. "There are two R&Rs to Hawaii coming next week. Top says to tell you to take one. Since I will be back, it will be a good time for you to go."

"OK, so what is the bad news?"

Chuck hands me an envelope. I open the envelope and I find the negatives of the pictures, but there are no developed pictures.

Along with the negatives, I found a letter that read, *"We are sorry that we could not develop your pictures. The pictures are just too inhumane for us to develop. The rules of war, such as the Geneva Convention, will not allow us to develop your works."*

Killer and the rest of my men are now standing in front of Chuck and me.

Killer says, "Emery, send the negatives to the States. Maybe they will develop them!"

Emery responds, "Give them to me, I'll send them back with Sergeant Lewis!"

Killer says, "I will take care of this problem quick!"

White looks puzzled. "How is that, Killer?"

Killer replies, "I am going to get a Polaroid camera from home, then we can take all of the horrifying pictures we want. Will you take a letter back with you for me, Sergeant Lewis?"

"Sure, bring it on!"

Chuck looks at the men. "Man, with all the crap that we have to put up with, it is a shame that they won't develop our pictures!"

"Well, guys, see ya in a week. Don't get killed until I get back!"

CHAPTER 15

My R&R in Hawaii

Chuck says, "See ya, Danny. I'll be back in a week. You take that R&R, you hear me?"

"I'll think about it. See ya, Chuck."

Chuck runs to get on the chopper with his M-16 rifle in hand. The chopper takes off and Chuck gives us a wave.

Craig walks over to me. "Cherokee wants you at the CP!"

"Thanks, Craig!"

I walk to the CP. The lieutenant has his map opened. "Hey, Rock, I've got good news and bad news!"

"You know what, sir? It is always good and bad news, so let's hear it!"

He moved closer and pointed at the map. "Pull your map out!" I opened up my map. "We are heading northwest right here."

"That is more NVA occupied territory, sir."

"Right again, Sarge."

"OK, sir, that is the bad news, so what is the good stuff?"

"We will get five more new men in a few days, and Sergeant Lewis will be back!"

"That's cool, but I guess the other platoons will get the new men, huh?"

"Yep. Right again, Rock."

"Sir, if we can just keep the men in our company alive for a few more weeks, we will be in good shape."

"Yes, I like it when we have a lot of warm bodies around. I need to talk to the old man. See ya, Rock."

We both laughed. Sergeant Erickson, our platoon sergeant, was listening to our conversation. Erickson was not much of a platoon sergeant. He was never in on our conversations when it came to viewing a map. I don't think he could even read a map. He would probably get lost in his own bathtub. He was a tall black guy that gave black people a bad name. He was always, always in the rear during a firefight. When compared to Raymond and Doc, both black men, he was a speck of sand, and they were both California beaches.

Sergeant Erickson motioned for me to come to him. "Sergeant Rodgers, why don't you go through me when you want to speak to the platoon leader?"

This actually made me mad. In my opinion, he was nothing but a coward. However, I kept my cool and answered, "I did not ask to speak to the lieutenant. He wanted to speak to me."

"Well, from now on, I want you to go through me first."

I said, "Sure, Sergeant, I will call you to come up to my squad during a firefight to help the wounded. I'll call you up front for target detection. I'll call you when we run out of ammo. But when I do, I want answers immediately! As a matter of fact, let's start now. Tell the lieutenant that I want to call in fire support at the following grids!"

I gave him the grid coordinate knowing that he did not know what the heck I was talking about. Erickson looked puzzled. "Rock, you know that I cannot read a map that good. I don't even know where we are right now."

"You see, Sergeant Erickson, that is why the lieutenant calls on me. I know exactly where we are all of the time. What are you going to do if the lieutenant and I get killed today? You are supposed to take over. Can you handle it?"

I knew that he did not really want to do anything but sit in the rear until his time in Vietnam was complete. He was a coward.

"OK, Sergeant Rodgers, I get your point."

I started to walk away. Erickson grabs my arm. "Tell me again why they call you Sergeant Rock?"

"Because I don't take any crap!"

"I thought that Rydser gave you the name."

"He did, because I don't take any crap. I just want to keep my men alive. That is why I got the name Rock; solid as a rock."

"Well, Sergeant Rock, you just keep on doing like you want. I'll leave you alone."

"Erickson, you need to man up. If you don't, you will get in a lot of hurt!"

"What do you mean?"

"You need to be on offense, not defense. Try to kill a few gooks instead of protecting your butt all of the time!"

"Don't you ever curse, Rock?"

"Not unless I have to make a point, or I get real, real mad."

"Are you that mad at me now? Where you want to curse at me?"

"I am very close, Sarge, very close. See ya later."

I walked back to my squad. The men are ready to go. "Where are we going today, Sarge?"

"Men, gather around."

I pulled out my map. "We are heading north again, right into NVA territory."

Killer and Emerald look at each other. "So what else is new?"

"Nothing new, men."

White says, "At least we will get a chance for more body counts."

"Yep, but you guys be careful! Eckert, assign point!"

Eckert looks at White and Killer. "I know that both of you guys want point, so we will flip a coin."

Eckert flips a coin. "Call it, Killer!"

"Tails."

White, Killer, Emerald, and Emery look at the coin lying on the jungle floor. White says, "Killer, I want point. I will give you pound cake and peaches if you will let me pull it today."

"Not today, White. I think we will hit something today."

I looked at Killer and White. "Hey, men, I want to change it up a little today. I want Emerald to pull point for four hours."

Killer looks at White, then turns toward me. "Sarge, he is too afraid to pull point. Please reconsider."

"Men, I just spoke to Erickson about manning up. If we don't give Emerald a chance to man up, we may all be in trouble. Agreed?"

They both nodded their heads in agreement. I motioned for Emerald to come to me. "You have point today! I'll relieve you in four hours."

Emerald looked around at the other men. "Point?"

"Yep! Point. Can you handle it?"

He started to shake. "I guess so, Sarge."

"I'll tell ya what, Emerald, I will go second, right behind you."

"Thanks, Sarge."

"Alright, men, move out!"

My radio sounds. "Blackhawk One, Two, Three, and Four, we will be in third after the First Platoon."

All of the squad leaders answered but me. Craig looks at me and I give him the OK signal with a nod.

Craig responds, "This is Blackhawk Three X-ray. Affirmatron. We have the info, out!"

Emerald is relieved that we will not be pulling point duty for the whole company. We started moving out, cutting in and out of the jungle canopy, back and forth from a path to the jungle and back to a path. We traveled for four hours when Killer came up to me. "My turn for point, Sarge!"

"OK. Emerald, trade off with Killer."

Emerald didn't say as much, but I could see it in his face. He was relieved to get off point.

We moved on through the thicket for another hour when the point platoon started firing. I hear my radio. The captain is sounding off, "We have NVA on our right flank. They are heading to our rear!"

We are now getting heavy fire coming from our right. We cannot fire back yet, because we are in the jungle and it is too thick. My radio sounds again; it is the captain. "Blackhawk Three, can you call in support?"

"Not yet. I have to get to a clearing!"

"Cherokee, can you call in support?"

Gibbons answers, "No! I can't see anything!"

The trees and the jungle are starting to explode. We are being rocketed. My ears are hurting from the concussions. Emerald is turning white with fear. I yell, "Killer, come with me!"

Killer comes to me. "What are we going to do?"

"You and me and Craig are going toward the right flank to find a clearing so we can call in artillery!"

Killer and Craig respond, "Let's get it!"

We start moving through the bush, heading straight toward the enemy fire. The radio sounds, "Blackhawk Three, where in the hell are you? Are you going to do something about this mess, or what?"

"I am on my way to a clearing, I hope!"

"Sergeant Rock, do you think it will be this year sometime?"

"Yes, sir!"

I could tell by the tone in his voice the captain was getting worried. In the past, he had never yelled at me. I had to move quickly or we would all be killed. I said a prayer for Killer, Craig, and I to get to an open area so we could call in fire support. We finally got to the edge of the tree line.

The earth was shaking. The trees and the jungle were falling on us. Every step we made forward was being blocked by another falling limb. I looked for Craig so I could call in the firepower. He was trapped below a tree. The radio was caught in the vines. Killer ran to help Craig up.

I yelled to Craig, "Are you hurt? How is the radio?"

"I'm OK, and the radio is still working!"

Craig hands me the horn. I start calling for support. "Fireball Five-Niner, this is Blackhawk Three, we need some help right now!"

"Give me the coordinates!"

I gave the coordinates.

"What do you want?"

"One shell to mark our location!"

"On the way!"

The shell hit 100 meters to the left and in the clearing. I was concerned about the artillery. Was it theirs or ours that I just saw?

I got back on the horn. "From my position, add fifty and move right 100!"

"On the way!"

The shells were hitting exactly where I wanted. I knew that the Navy was shooting. I did not know how a Navy battleship twenty-five to thirty miles away could be so accurate.

"Fireball Five-Niner, keep it up. From my position, keep moving right, firing VT every third round, twenty-five meters apart!"

I now have to contact the captain.

"Annihilator, I am right on target. You heard the grids. Do you think it would be a good idea for you to call in other support in front of your position using my grids? You start calling in left and I'll keep moving right!"

"Got it, Rock! Got it!"

The captain started calling in his firepower right on target and moving left with his shells. I hear more and more action from the last platoon.

The noise is getting extremely loud again. The NVA are attacking from the rear. I call Fireball for more support to the rear.

My radio blasts, "We need help in the rear!"

I get back on the horn. "Fire support is on the way, but you need to guide me because I cannot see your position!"

Someone from the last platoon is on the radio. "The rounds are too close! Move them away from us!"

I get back on the radio. "Are you sure that the rounds are my rounds?"

"Yes! Yes!"

Now I am in a bad spot. I am under pressure. I can't see the last platoon. I have to be very, very careful in the way that I call in the support. One wrong word, like *add*, *drop*, *right*, or *left*, could kill a lot of men.

I cannot see where the rounds are hitting. I have to draw a picture in the dirt so I can visualize where everyone is located. My picture looks like a capital *L*. This is going to be tough. I figure it out. "Fireball, from my position add 100, and from my position move right five-zero, fifty!"

"On the way, Blackhawk Three, on the way!"

My radio sounds, "That's perfect, Blackhawk Three, keep it up!"

I get back on the horn. "Fireball, that is perfect, fire for effect!"

"You got it. On the way!"

I hear someone yelling, "Medic! Medic!"

The incoming rounds are now few and far between. I can hear in the background, "Doc, Doc, we need you!"

Killer looks at Craig. "Who got shot, Craig?"

Craig is holding the horn, waiting for information. "I have not heard yet!"

The radio goes off. It is Fireball Five-Niner. "How are we doing, Blackhawk Three?"

"You did a great job, Fireball Five-Niner. Keep firing for five minutes."

"Will do. Good luck out there!"

Craig looks at me. "Are we going back? We are almost in the open!"

"No, not yet; in about ten minutes. Find out who got shot!"

Killer is lying very still. I walk over to him. "Are you shot?"

"No, not a scratch. I am just tired."

We see Craig talking on the horn. He stands up. "It's Erickson."

I looked at Craig. "Is he wounded?"

"Nope, he is dead!"

Killer responds, "So Erickson is dead, huh? I don't know what he did in the first place. He was a loser. No one will miss him."

We waited another ten minutes, then headed back to our squad.

Before we reached the company, I looked at these two brave guys. "Craig and Killer, thanks for going out there with me. That was dangerous for all of us."

Killer says, "It would have been a lot more dangerous if we had been overrun! If we had not gone to that clearing, we would have been overrun for sure!"

"I'll see you two later. I am going to see Gibbons."

The lieutenant was speaking to the captain when I arrived at the CP. The captain looked at me. "Some firefight, huh, Rock? We won another one. I guess Erickson ate it. Good job, Rock. What took you so long?"

"Heck, sir, we had to cut through the bush to get to where I could see!"

"I know. I'm only messing with you, Rock! By the way, I have the choppers coming in the morning. We will have some more men on them. You guys put Erickson on a chopper!"

"We will do it, sir! What about the body count?"

"We will look at that tomorrow. It is too dangerous today."

"Are we staying here for the night?"

"Yes. We will move to the edge of the clearing and set up a perimeter. Once we get set up, I'll call in artillery."

"OK, sir. You did good today!"

We set up our perimeter for the night. I was very surprised and very happy that it was a peaceful night. Morning came and the choppers started to come in.

Five new grunts are on the chopper. The men jump off while the chopper is still moving. The ship is four feet above the ground. The door gunners will initiate some more new guys.

We all had to go through this process. The first jump from a moving chopper will always be memorable. The door gunners laugh as one of the grunts does a face plant into the wet rice paddy. My men and I laugh also. We knew that others laughed when we first jumped. My RTO, Craig, is walking toward me. "Hey, Sarge, the old man wants to see you."

"Thanks, Craig."

I hustled over to the CP, wondering as I briskly walked, what the captain wanted with me. I arrived to see the captain speaking to the new men. "Men, this is Sergeant Rodgers, known as Sergeant Rock. He has the third squad in Lieutenant Gibbons's platoon. Listen to Rock and he will keep you alive!"

We shook hands. The captain says, "Rock, is there anything that you want to tell them now?"

"Yes, sir!"

I noticed that all of the men had white nametags. "Every one of you, rip off those white nametags right now! The gooks will spot those a mile away!"

The men immediately started tearing off the tags.

The captain was smiling. "That was the very first thing that I noticed too. Men, by the way, don't salute me out here. The gooks always try to shoot officers first. Rock, you will not get any of these guys. I have assigned them to other squads."

"Yes, sir."

"OK, men, take off. I have to speak to the sergeant."

The captain calls for his RTO. The RTO hands the captain four envelopes. He holds them up in front of me. "You know what I have here, Rock?"

"No. Maybe DEROS orders?"

"No, it's not that good, but pretty close. These are R&Rs."

"Where to, sir?"

"Three to Hawaii and one to Bangkok."

"How come so many, sir?"

"One of these to Hawaii was for a soldier named Jeff Dugan. Dugan was going to meet his girlfriend in Hawaii. They were going to be married there. Here, Rock, you take Dugan's R&R to Hawaii!"

"No, sir, I can't do that. It would be weird. Give me one of the others!"

"Rock, every one of these were for guys that have been killed."

"I know, but I knew Jeff Dugan. It just doesn't feel right. Give me another envelope."

"OK, Rock, here ya go." He hands me the envelope.

I open the envelope. "Sir, the R&R is for a week from now. Will you be OK without me?"

"Yes, Rock, you deserve it. Are you going to meet your wife there? If you are, you had better write her today!"

"Yes, I will, sir. I better write her now!"

I wrote a quick note to my wife, Sue, that read, *"I am getting an R&R to Hawaii. I'll be there in seven days from today."*

I placed today's date on the envelope. I wrote the date on the paper. I addressed an envelope and sent it with a carrier heading for the rear. I returned to my squad.

"Hey, men, I am going to Hawaii!"

Emerald's eyes opened wide. "You are going to leave us, Sarge?"

Killer says, "When are you leaving, and when will you be back?"

279

"I'll leave in five days, then I will be back in about eight or nine days. Sergeant Lewis will be back soon, but until then, Eckert will take over. Men, get ready to move out. Eckert, you stay right next to me for five days. I don't want to lose any men while I am gone. I want you to tell me what you are going to do in every situation for the next few days!"

"OK, Sarge."

My radio sounds. "Move out!"

Craig looks at Eckert and me. Craig wants a response. I look at Eckert. "What are you going to do, Eckert?"

Eckert looks at Craig. "Tell them, 'Affirmatron, we are moving.'"

"That's it, Eckert, take command. You don't have to get on the horn yourself every time. All you have to do is act quickly and with authority in your voice. Craig is a good RTO. Be consistent with your commands and Craig will pick up on it. This will save you a lot of work. Now what are you going to do?"

"Tell the men to move out?"

"No, you have to assign point next!"

"Oh, yeah." Eckert calls Killer. "Killer, you assign point, but I want you in the rear today. I want protection from behind!"

Killer assigns point to White and moves to the rear of the squad. Eckert holds up his hand. "Move out, men, let's get it! Craig, make sure your antenna is down!"

"That's it, Eckert, good job."

"Hey, Sarge, are you looking forward to your R&R?"

"Man, I really am, but I worry about you guys. We have been in a lot of crap lately!"

"We are always in a lot of crap, it seems like. Hey, Sarge, where are we going?"

"We are going to the same place that we were going yesterday."

"Well, Sarge, if I am in charge, give me the map and show me where we are now!"

I handed him the map and showed him where we were going and where we were at the present.

"Do you think that it will be a quiet day, Sarge?"

"Nope. We will probably get in a firefight before the day ends."

"Are you ever afraid, Sarge?"

"Every day I am afraid!"

"Yep, me too."

We humped for another hour before we started to be shot at. We all hit the ground and started firing back. The fire was coming from our left flank, perpendicular to my squad. My radio sounds, "Blackhawk Three, can you see where they are?"

Eckert looks at me. "I can see them. Should I tell the captain?"

"You are in charge, Eckert. Do what you are supposed to do!"

Eckert looks at Craig. "Give me the horn, Craig!"

Eckert grabs the horn with authority. "Affirmative, I can call in fire support! I can see them!"

The captain got back on the radio. "Call it in and do it now!"

Eckert starts to call, "Fireball Five-Niner, this is Blackhawk Three Alfa, over!"

"This is Fireball Five-Niner, what can I do for you?"

"I need a shell at this grid."

Eckert gave him the coordinate. Fireball repeated the grid. "Affirmative, that is correct. Fire!"

"It is on the way!"

The shell hits very close to the enemy.

Eckert says, "From my position, add five zero meters and give me four rounds!"

The rounds hit right on target. Eckert is filled with excitement. "Now give me four rounds of VT and a five-zero spread!"

The rounds come in perfectly.

"Very good, Eckert! You did a great job!"

The enemy fire was now a thing of the past, at least for now. Eckert had listened and learned. Eckert looks up at me. "Thanks, Sarge. That was a lot of fun."

"It is fun, isn't it? I love it!"

"Sarge, now I can see why you like it so much. You are in complete control when you are calling in artillery, aren't ya?"

"Yep, you got it, Eckert!"

The radio sounds, "Blackhawk Three, who is Blackhawk Three Alfa?"

"It is Eckert. He called in the support."

"Tell him that he did a good job. Are we ready to move again?"

"Affirmatron."

We traveled another four hours before we reached our destination for the night. Eckert, without me saying a word, said, "OK, men, dig in. We will be here until morning! White, you assign guard duty!"

White says, "Consider it done, Acting Jack Eckert. I'll take care of it. What hour do you want?"

"I'll take whatever hour you give me."

"How about third?"

"That will work for me. I'll be over in a minute to help dig the foxhole."

White looks over at me. "Sergeant Rock, do you want first or last?"

"I'll take last!"

We started the nightly guard duty. We had another great night, with only mosquitoes and a few leeches biting us. Morning came and we started the same old thing again. Eat, check our ammo, assign point, move out, and cut through the jungle until we got shot at or reached our destination for the day.

For the next three days, we humped with only a few sniper rounds. No one was killed, and no one injured. This was very unusual for our company. This non-action gave me time to think about my R&R, going to Hawaii, and seeing Sue, my wife. We reached our destination for the day.

My good looking wife getting ready for Hawaii

We started to dig in for the night when Craig says, "The old man wants you."

"Thanks, Craig. See ya in a little while."

I reached the captain.

"Hey, Rock, things are quiet, so guess what?"

"What, sir?"

"When the choppers come in tomorrow, you get on one and go on your R&R."

"Sounds good, sir. I just hope that everything stays calm until I get back!"

283

"Well you know it won't, but enjoy yourself and tell Sue, your wife, *hello* for me!"

"Yes, sir!"

I walked back to my squad. "Hey, men, I will be leaving in the morning."

"You mean it, Rock?" Emerald said.

Killer responds, "Great, Sarge. You have a good time!"

Eckert says, "I'll keep the men alive, Sarge!"

"That is the main thing that I ask, Eckert; keep the men alive."

"You can count on me, Sarge. I'll have Killer help me."

"Yep, Sarge, I'll help the acting jack!" Killer said.

"Cool, men! Killer, I want to talk to you alone. Follow me."

We walked away from the rest of the squad. "Killer, I don't want you to shoot anyone but VC and NVA while I am gone. I am not joking. No more killing old men, women, or children! I, of course, don't actually know if you have committed any crimes, but just don't commit any!"

"What if the woman has a gun?"

"Then shoot her dead on the spot. I know that some women are VC. If she looks to be a Charlie, then shoot her."

"Rock, how come we call a VC a 'Charlie'?"

"It is simple. The new phonetic alphabet *V* equals *Victor* and *C* equals *Charlie*. So VC is Victor Charlie. We shorten it up and just say Charlie. Sometimes when I say gook it just means a VC, NVA, or a person that lives in Vietnam. When I think about it, saying gook is not a very nice thing to call another person. I think that we should start calling a VC either VC or Charlie. What do you think, Killer?"

"I still say 'Kill them all!' No, I am kidding. I will be a good boy while you are gone. Now let me see if I have my rules down pat. One, no killing anyone but a Charlie. Two, don't call a gook a gook. Three, kill a woman if she has a weapon. Four, do what the acting jack tells me."

"Yep, you have it. Now let's eat and pull guard."

The night went by really slowly for me. I was anticipating seeing my wife and visiting Hawaii. Morning came and Craig came up to me. "The old man says the choppers will be here in an hour, Sarge."

"Thanks, Craig. Hey, Craig, take my C-rations and divide them between the men! You help Eckert!"

"OK, Sarge. Can I have the pound cake?"

"Sure. You are in charge of my food."

We both laugh. I pour my rations out on the ground. The men and I eat breakfast and talk until the choppers start to come in.

The choppers are being shot at. The door gunners start shooting back. The first two choppers come in fast and the crew chief is kicking the new supplies off. I am a little worried because the first two choppers take off without even slowing down for me to jump on.

I look over at the captain. He is on the radio. The captain holds up two fingers and motions for me to get on the second chopper.

The choppers come in again. I run over to the second chopper and jump onboard. The door gunners are still firing at the snipers. We finally get away from the firing. The rest of the trip is uneventful. We land in Chu Lai.

I see Top outside his quarters. "Hi, Top, how are ya?"

"Better than you guys in the field. So, Rock, you are going to Hawaii, huh?"

"Yep, and I am looking forward to it!"

"I'll bet you are. In the morning, there is a chopper delivering supplies from Da Nang. They are going to go right back to Da Nang. When you get to Da Nang, find a plane going to Hawaii. You can figure it out. Now go and get some chow at the mess hall!"

I thought to myself on the way to the chow hall, *I have not had a real, hot meal in a long time.*

They were having meatloaf, mashed potatoes and gravy, yeast rolls, green beans, hot apple pie, and ice cream. I felt sorry for my men in the field eating cold C-rations. My stomach had shrunk so much that I could barely finish, but I was not going to pass up that apple pie.

I finished the meal and went to the supply tent where we stored our duffel bags. Chuck came running out. "I heard that you were coming in!"

"Man, Chuck, I thought that you were heading for the field. I would have come to see you first, before I ate, if I'd known that you were still here!"

"Don't worry about it. Here are your clothes. I laid them out for you yesterday so they would at least look ironed. I am going to the field tomorrow. How has it been this week out there?"

"Not bad, just a few gooks shooting, or I mean Charlies, shooting at us."

"Good. I'll see ya in a little bit. I've got to get this ammo ready to go."

He started loading cases of M-16 rounds into the back of a three-fourths ton truck.

"Do ya need help?"

"Nah, you take it easy. See ya later!"

I went to the tent barracks and got my stuff ready for the trip. It was getting dark. Night would be on us shortly. Chuck finally arrived with a couple of cans of ice-cold soda pop. "Sorry it took me so long. I had to fly to Delta Company."

"Did ya get shot at? Thanks for the soda!"

"Yes, but the gunners took care of it, and you're welcome."

Chuck and I talked for a few hours and then went to sleep. I woke up the next morning and Chuck was already gone to the supply tent.

I went to the supply tent and Chuck was getting his rifle and ammo ready to move out to the field. "Danny, tell your wife, Sue, *hi* for me. My ride is coming in. I have to go."

He gave me a man hug and took off for the incoming chopper. I headed for the mess hall. I figured that I would get one more hot meal before I headed out, and, besides, the choppers from Da Nang had not come in yet.

I started eating when I heard a commotion. More choppers were coming. I ran out of the chow hall and sprinted to the door gunner. "Did you guys come from Da Nang, and are ya going back there?"

"Yep. Are you the R&R guy?"

"Yes!"

"Hop in!"

We headed for Da Nang. We were not shot at even once that I could tell. We landed in Da Nang. I jumped off the chopper and headed for the airport.

I hopped a deuce-and-a-half and saw a few planes. I went to the terminal and showed my R&R packet. The sergeant pointed to the plane that I would be taking. "That's your plane over there, but it won't leave for an hour. You can leave your rifle and fatigues in the lockers. You can change to your dress clothes there too."

I walked out of the terminal. Reporters and cameramen from the United States bombarded me. I was still in my jungle fatigues. My sleeves were cut off, and I was as dark as a farm worker from the hot Vietnam sun. I had my M-79 grenade launcher with me, two bandoliers of ammo, the usual ammo belt, canteens, and regular hand grenades. One very pretty lady stuck a microphone in my face and a cameraman started filming. "Is this the attire for Vietnam?"

"Do you mean is this what we usually wear?"

"Yes!"

"Yep, this is what we wear, but some guys don't cut the sleeves off."

"Why do you?"

"Because it is so hot! But sometimes I leave the sleeves on for a while."

"What kind of a gun is that?"

"It is a grenade launcher called an M-79."

"Will you be willing to speak to my producer, my boss?"

"Yeah, but I only have thirty more minutes."

A man walks up to me. "Would you like to become a war correspondent for us?"

"What do ya mean? What would I have to do?"

"You would need to carry a mini camera and take notes. We would meet with you once a week right here and you would give us the real scoop about what is happening in the field."

"Well, I am going on R&R now, and I won't be back for a week."

"That's OK. We are here for a month or more. We will talk again when you return."

"OK, I'll talk to ya then. I have to get it all approved by the captain and all of that stuff!"

I walked over to the lockers. This could be a cool thing to do. In the past, the news people were always in the rear when the crap hit the fan. The news folks never really got close enough to see any real action.

I placed my weapon and fatigues in the lockers and changed to my Army dress clothes. I climbed the stairs to the plane and off we went, heading for Hawaii.

There were a lot of soldiers on the plane. Some were missing arms or legs, but many were in good health, as I was. I realized that I was really lucky. I started to speak to sergeants, lieutenants, and captains. Many were heading home to the States for good. Some were going on R&R to Hawaii. The plane was going to make a stop in Hawaii, and then continue to the United States. This made me wonder. Why couldn't a guy get an R&R to Hawaii, but actually jump on a plane and go to Houston, Texas, in the United States? The other soldiers and I talked for hours and hours about our adventures in the 'Nam.

I especially took interest in a sergeant from Delta Company who was speaking to a lurp guy. I overheard them talking about where they had been in Vietnam. I walked over to them. "Hey, guys, I heard you talking. I am in the 196th too."

The sergeant said, "Cool, what company?"

I answered proudly, "Company A."

"Do you mean the Killer Company?"

"What do you mean, 'The Killer Company'?"

"Company A has a lot of kills! What platoon are you in?"

"I am in the Third Platoon. I am the squad leader of the third squad."

"No way! You guys don't take prisoners; you guys cut the heads off!"

The sergeant turns to the lurp guy. "This is the squad that I was telling you about. They are mean!"

I started to laugh.

The lurp guy says, "What do they call you, Sarge?"

"They call me Sergeant Rock."

"No! You are Sergeant Rock? The leader of the Killer Squad?"

"Are you joking? Have you heard about us?"

"Yes, you guys cut heads and limbs off bodies. You guys break the necks of the enemy! You guys never take a prisoner!"

"No, that is exaggerated. Only one of my guys has cut a head off and that was because the VC was giving our position away."

"So, are you really Sergeant Rock?"

"Yep, that is I."

I was holding my chest out, for I was very proud of my guys in the squad. The lurp guy stood up and told everyone who I was. Some men had never heard of my squad, but many had. For the rest of the flight, guys were coming up to me and asking questions.

One guy asked me, "Are you going to write a book, Rock?"

I answered, "I don't know. I am sure that others have more to tell than I do, but maybe I will write a book someday."

The pilot came on the intercom and told us to take our seats. The pilot also said, "Men, we appreciate what you guys are doing for all of us. You soldiers that are staying here in Hawaii, have a good time. From the crew and me, we love you and God bless. We will be landing in ten minutes."

The plane had a perfect landing. My anticipation was enhanced, for the worse, by the amount of time it was taking to load us onto buses. Each bus held about twenty men. I was on the third bus. The trip to the base, where Sue was to be waiting, took fifteen minutes or so, but it seemed like two hours. The buses rolled up to a large holding area one after another.

My bus finally pulled up to the doors of the waiting room. I saw my wife and two other pretty ladies running out the door.

Sue saw me and came running. She dropped her luggage and her purse and jumped in my arms. She looked as pretty as I had remembered.

After lots of kisses and hugs, she says, "I want to introduce you to two great girls. They are both going to meet their men here. One is already married and the other is going to get married right here in Hawaii."

She grabbed my hand and led me to the ladies. "Danny, this is Shirley and Linda. Linda is waiting on her husband and Shirley is waiting on her boyfriend, Jeff. They are getting married here."

"Glad to meet you girls. Maybe we will all get together for a dinner or something."

"Sounds good," Linda said.

I could see in their eyes that they were both worried. They were wondering where their soldiers were.

Shirley says, "Here comes another bus. Maybe they will be on that one."

This was the last bus. I also hoped that their loved ones would be on the bus. The first guy off of the bus was Linda's husband. Linda ran to him, just as Sue had done when she saw me. Shirley was waiting and standing on her tiptoes to see her boyfriend.

The last soldier got off of the bus. Her soldier was not on the bus. Shirley started crying. Sue ran over to her. "Shirley, what's wrong?"

Sue placed her arm around Shirley.

"He is not here. He did not get off of the bus. Jeff is not here!"

I heard the name Jeff. I motioned for Sue to come to me.

I said, "Sue, did she say her boyfriend's name is Jeff?"

"Yes, I told you that a few minutes ago!"

"You probably did, but I was so glad to see you that I didn't pay attention to what you said. Go ask Shirley what Jeff's last name is, please."

Sue looked at me with a puzzled look. She walked over to Shirley.

"Shirley, what is Jeff's last name?"

With big tears in her eyes she says, "Dugan. Why do you ask?"

"I don't know. Danny just asked me to ask you."

Sue walked over to me. "It is Dugan, Jeff Dugan."

My face turned white. It was the guy that I knew. Jeff was the guy that had been killed and the captain had offered me his R&R. This was supposed to be a happy occasion for Sue and me. This was just another downside of Vietnam.

Sue was crying. She looks at my paled face. "What's wrong, Danny? What's wrong?"

"I knew Jeff. He is dead. He didn't make it. I need to talk to Shirley!"

I walked over to Shirley. I did not know what to say, but I had to say something. "Shirley, I need to talk to you."

She looks up at me. "Jeff is dead, isn't he? Did you know him well?"

"Yes, he is dead. I knew him pretty well. We were friends. I liked him. He talked about you a lot. He was a good soldier. Why don't you come with us?"

"No, you and Sue go ahead. I am going back to California tomorrow."

"Do you want to stay with us tonight?"

"No, I am fine. I already have a room, but thanks. Sue, come here and give me a hug!" She holds out her arms. "You take care of Danny. Maybe I'll see ya in California."

Sue hugs Shirley. "I will take care of him, and I am very, very sorry."

Sue and I turned and walked toward our hotel.

Sue started to cry and speak at the same time. "I feel so bad for her, but we can't let that spoil our time together."

"You know, you are right, Sue. Hawaii is beautiful. Let's make the best of it."

We stood at a corner and a lady was standing there with a cart of fruit drinks. The sign on the cart read, *"Free fruit drinks to service men."*

The lady gave us both cups. "We appreciate you soldiers. Now help yourself to pineapple, or any other fruit juice you want."

We started to drink. It was very good, the best that I had ever had.

"Thank you very much for the juice."

"You are welcome. Come back anytime for more."

We continue to walk toward the hotel when I see a sign for the drags. The sign reads, *"The South Pacific National Drag Races this weekend. American soldiers get in free."*

"Sue, do you want to go to the drags?"

My spirits were lifted.

"Sure, let's do it. Now you are feeling better about everything, aren't you?"

Sue knew how much I loved fast cars.

"Yes I am, Sue. Yes I am. Now let's get to the hotel."

Sue has a strange look on her face. I hear her say, "I am on my period."

I immediately say with no hesitation, "That is OK; I am used to seeing blood. Let's go to the room!"

Sue says, "What did you think that I said?"

"I thought you said that you were on your period!"

"No, I said that I *was* on my period. It stopped last night."

"That's cool, because we were going to do it anyhow!"

"You are gross!"

"No I'm not, I am just horny!"

We both laughed.

We arrived at the hotel and we got the room for half price. We stayed in the room for most of the night. The next morning, we ate breakfast and started walking.

I am in Hawaii with my wife Sue

We walked past the waiting area where Sue had met me the night before. Sue took off quickly and ran inside. It looked like Shirley was still waiting for Jeff. I felt terrible, but I did not go inside. I decided to let the girls talk. I saw hugging and crying, and then Shirley waved to me.

Sue walked out of the holding area. "Danny, do you know that Shirley waited there all night long for Jeff?"

"No! That is sad."

"She knows now that he is not coming."

"Sue, let's go ahead and make the best of the time that we have left. Agreed?"

"Agreed."

Everything in Hawaii was very cheap for service men. It was a great time. We surfed, made love, went to sea aquariums, made love, went to the beach, made love, and rented a car and toured the island. And to top it off, we went to the drags and met The Snake, Don Garlits, TV Tommy Ivo, Empie Inch Pincher, and The Mongoose, all drag strip racers. The time went by very quickly.

Thinking about going surfing

In Hawaii going surfing

I stayed in Hawaii for seven days. Sue and I had the time of our lives, but now it was time to return to the war.

We turned in our rental car and said goodbye at the airport. Sue was crying, and I also had a tear or two. A bus picked us soldiers up at the waiting area at the base. Sue and I kissed, and off we went toward our respective airplanes, Sue to Houston, and I back to more fighting in Vietnam.

The plane ride going back to Vietnam was much more somber than the one going to Hawaii. The plane was now full of new recruits fresh from AIT, plus the soldiers heading back to Vietnam after their R&R.

A few of the new guys could tell that I was a Vietnam vet and started asking questions. "Have you seen any action?"

"What is your job?"

"Have you killed anyone?"

"How many have you killed?"

"What kind of weapon is best?"

I thought to myself, *They don't know that I am* the *Sergeant Rock.* Then I thought further and deeper. *This was being conceited. Who cares if I am Sergeant Rock? After this Vietnam War is over, who will give a flying flip about Sergeant Rock?* I answered their questions with humility and dignity, trying to not give a lot of explanations.

"I am a squad leader. I have seen some action. I have killed a few. I don't rightly know how many I have killed. In my company, we can carry any weapon that is available to us — shotgun, M-14 or 16, M-79, M-60, or pistol. Right now, I carry a 79. Good luck, you guys. I want to get some sleep. I'll talk to you later."

"Thanks, Sarge!"

The men started speaking to other Vietnam vets. I was still awake when I heard my name mentioned.

"That is Sergeant Rock."

"It says Rodgers on his name tag. Why do they call him Rock?"

"Because he cuts off VC heads. He never ever takes a prisoner!"

"Is he mean?"

"Go ask him if he is mean or not!"

"No way!"

I laughed. I have never cut off a head; I take prisoners; and I am not mean, at least not to my own soldiers. I hear a few more comments, and I laugh again before falling asleep. Hours and hours go by before we reach Vietnam.

The plane lands and I start to disembark when I hear a few of the new guys. "Sergeant Rock, glad to meet ya. Maybe a few of us will land in your squad!"

"Maybe so. You guys take care, you hear!"

"Good luck, Sarge!"

I head down the stairs and walk to the locker.

Another squad leader is walking with me. "It is hard to get back into the swing of things here, huh, Rock?"

"It sure is. You know something, I really enjoyed Hawaii. How about you?"

"Oh, yeah, I loved it."

"I see by your patch that you are in the First Cav."

"Yep, the First Cavalry Division, tanks and all of that stuff."

"You guys are a great outfit. By the way, what is your name?

"It is Snow. I already know your name; it's Rock."

"No, not really. My name is Rodgers. Well, Snow, maybe we will meet up sometimes. Where is your unit now?"

"I don't know. We keep heading north toward the DMZ."

"Yeah, us too. I think we might meet up again."

We shook hands. "Good luck, Snow. Kill a few for me."

"You too, Rock. Later."

I kept walking toward the locker where I had stored my rifle. *What did I just say?* I thought. *Kill a few for me?* Becoming a sergeant in wartime had changed me. Before Vietnam, I was an easygoing, moral kid that loved to play games with my family and friends. I went to church every Sunday. Mom would say, "If you don't go to church, I will beat you to a pulp."

She, of course, was joking, but she and Dad did keep us five brothers in line. I met my wife Sue in church. We hit it off from the beginning. Our families went water skiing, camping, and a lot more events together. I raced my car, and Sue was there for every race. Sue and I were elected Queen and King for a Valentine's Day event we attended. Sue and I went together for four years before we got married. Sports were always a part of our lives.

My mom, dad, and Sue never missed a baseball game while I was in high school or college. I also played Little League baseball, football, and raced go-karts when I was younger. When I was twelve-years-old, I was having so much fun that I told my mom, "Mom, I never want to get any older. I am on the top of the world."

That was when I was a boy. I am still a boy, becoming a man faster than I want. There is now a big difference between the boy that I was and the man that I have become. When I get home, I hope and pray that I will never have to kill again. The locker was now just in front of me.

I opened it and pulled out my weapon and changed my clothes. I walked back out the door and heard a commotion. It was another news crew. When I looked closer, I realized that it was the same crew I had seen eight or nine days ago. They were interviewing another soldier when they saw me.

They came over to me quickly. "Sergeant Rodgers, can we speak to you again?" the lady said.

"Sure, I'll talk to you guys."

The pretty news lady says, "Will you speak to my boss again?"

"OK."

I think that she had told me earlier that her boss was also the producer of the show. The man came up to me. "Did you have a good time on your R&R?"

"Fantastic!"

"Great. So this is what I want to speak to you about. I want you to ask your commander if we can travel with you guys for a while. We want to give you a mini camera like this one." He holds up a small camera, but it looks sort of heavy to me.

I hold out my hand for the camera. He hands it to me. "Man, this thing feels heavy!" It felt like it weighed about seventeen pounds. "No, this is too heavy."

"What do you mean, too heavy? It is lightweight!"

"Yeah, if that was all that I had to carry! I have to carry C-rations and I think they weigh about twenty-eight pounds. My weapon weighs from six to eight pounds. My ammo weighs another six pounds. Then I have my hand grenades, canteens, and more. You guys don't know how hard it is to hump through the jungle with all of that weight on your body."

"We can pay you!"

I did not even want to know how much because the extra weight would kill me. Besides the weight that I normally carried, I sometimes carried bandoliers of M-60 rounds to help the machine gunner. "No. But I will ask the captain if you guys can tag along. You will need to send someone with me to get the answer, then return here to tell your crew."

"OK, I will go myself."

He walked over to tell his crew that he was going with me.

The producer returned. "OK, I am ready."

"Now just follow me and listen. Just do what I tell you."

"OK, Sarge."

We walked over to a chopper. I yelled to the door gunner, "Where are you guys going?"

"To Cam Ranh Bay. You need a lift?" the gunner answered.

"Yeah, but I need to go to Chu Lai. Thanks anyhow."

The gunner points toward the inside of the chopper and says, "What about him? Where does he think that he is going?"

I looked inside the chopper. The producer is sitting in the seat, ready to go. I grabbed his arm. "Get off, this is not for us."

He jumped off of the chopper. I looked at him with a frown on my face. "Don't ever do that again, Mister Producer. I told you to follow me, not jump ahead of me. Sometimes these choppers leave quickly! You may go some place you don't want to go to!"

"Yes, sir. It won't happen again!"

"Alright, don't let it happen again or I'll leave your butt behind. What is your name, Mister Producer?"

"My name is Steven."

"OK, Steven, we are going to find another chopper."

We ran to another chopper that was almost loaded with supplies. I asked the door gunner, "Where are you guys going?"

"To Chu Lai. Do you need a lift?"

"Yeah."

"OK."

I turned to Steven. "Let's help them finish loading! Grab some ammo!"

Steven immediately started grabbing the cases of ammo and placing them in the chopper. The chopper crew chief gave us a thumbs up to say thank you. Then he motioned for us to climb aboard.

I hopped on and Steven jumped on after me. I looked at Steven and noticed that he had a big, wide grin on his face. He felt like he was now one of the boys. The chopper took off, heading for Chu Lai.

Steven leaned over toward me. "Will we be shot at, Sarge?"

"We will be heading south, so maybe, but probably not."

Suddenly, we hear a *ping* sound. It was a sniper bullet hitting the inside of the chopper. The door gunners open up on full automatic. Steven jumps so bad that I thought he was going to fall out of the chopper. The sounds of the M-60s didn't bother me this time because I knew they were going to be fired.

The firing stopped. I tapped Steven on the shoulder. "Pretty loud, huh?"

He nodded his head yes and grabbed at his ears. We continued our journey, heading for Chu Lai.

We landed in Chu Lai near the supply tent. A sergeant came out to meet us, but it was not Chuck. Chuck must have gone back to the field, as he had said he would before I left for Hawaii. "Hey, men, how are you doing?"

"Good, Sarge. Where is Top?"

"He is at the CP."

"Thank you, Sarge. See ya later."

I walked to the CP. Top was on the radio. "Here he is now, sir. I'll tell him, out. The captain says that he is glad you're back. How are you, Rock?"

"I am great, Sarge. How about you?"

"I am better than the guys in the field. We lost a few while you were gone."

I immediately started to wonder if the deaths were any of my guys.

"What platoon? What squad, Sarge?"

"No, Rock, don't worry, it was not any of your men. Who is the civilian with you?"

I was relieved that the guys killed were not my guys. I felt bad for the guys that got killed, but my men were special to me.

"This is Steven. He makes movies."

Top held out his hand for a handshake. Steven does the same.

Top looks at me as he asks, "What do you want to do, Steven?"

"I want Sergeant Rodgers to take me to see his captain and ask if he will allow us to film the truth."

"Has Rock told you about how much action our company sees?"

"Sort of, but not really."

"Steven, you let Sergeant Rock tell you about what to expect, and after that, I'll let you go to the field and ask the old man."

Top walked back into the CP tent.

Steven starts to speak, "How much action are we talking about? Why do they call you Sergeant Rock? The *old man*! Who is that?"

"We have seen a lot of action."

I told him about January ninth and a few more of our battles.

"Why do they call you Rock?"

"A guy named Killer gave me that name. I have a very good squad. They get a lot of body count."

"And the old man! What does that mean?"

"The old man is slang for our leader, the captain."

"How dangerous do you think it will be if we go with you?"

"It will be bad at times, and I cannot protect you guys all of the time. Some of you may die. Now that you have heard what's going on, do you still want to go?"

"Heck yeah!"

"OK! I'll go in and tell Top."

I turned to walk to the tent.

"Rock, why do they call him Top?"

"Because he is the Top Sergeant. You cannot get any higher. By the way, Steven, don't call me Rock. Call me Sergeant Rock or Sarge. My men call me Sergeant Rock."

I spoke to Top and he gave approval for Steven to go and speak to the captain. On my way out of the CP, Top asks, "Did you tell him about what you guys have been through?"

"Yes I did, and I told him that we could not protect them. How long do you think they will last?"

"They will want to come home after the first two-day-long battle."

"Yeah, I think so too."

I walked out and told Steven. He was elated, overjoyed, and excited.

"Man! Steven, don't get too excited because we still have to get approval from the captain!"

"You mean the old man?"

"Yeah, but don't call him that. He knows that we call him the old man, but we don't call him that to his face."

"OK, I'll remember that, Sarge!"

Top sticks his head out of the tent. "You guys will be on the next chopper."

"Thanks, Top."

"You guys be safe! Good luck, Steven." He goes back into the CP.

I look at Steven. "OK, Steven, we will get on the chopper and head for the field. If the captain says you guys can film, he will probably furnish you with a chopper to pick up your guys and equipment. Is that pretty little girl that interviewed me going to be coming with you?"

"Yep, she is. She is cute, isn't she?"

"Yep."

I hear the choppers coming in. "Listen to that sound. That sound always means something good is going to happen. At least that is what it means when we are in the field."

"I hear it too."

"Now follow me and don't do anything that I don't do!"

"OK, Sarge."

The choppers are starting to get closer. We move toward the LZ. Steven is staying right behind me. I ask the door gunner if they are going to our company in the field. He confirms. I notice that this chopper had rockets attached to either side. We usually rode a chopper called a "slick." This one was a gunship. I couldn't remember if I had ever flown on a gunship. I hoped that the ship would fire a few rockets. That would be cool.

I yell to Steven, "Get on!"

I jump onboard with all my ammo and weapon. Steven had nothing to carry. I gave him a bandolier of ammo to carry. I did not need help carrying the ammo, but I knew that he would love to be part of all this.

He grinned and slung the bandolier over his head and placed it on his shoulder. The choppers took off for the field and away from Chu Lai. We were heading north again.

We traveled for a few hours before the gunner tapped me on the shoulder. He held up five fingers. I turned to Steven. "We will be there in five minutes! Don't jump off until I jump!"

He holds up a thumb. He understood!

Suddenly the gunners start firing. The chopper makes a big, sharp right turn. I can see tracer rounds coming toward us. There are a lot of tracers. For every tracer round I see, there are probably five to seven rounds in between.

The rockets from our chopper start firing straight at the incoming fire. Explosion after explosion is hitting the target. I can now only hear one door gunner shooting his M-60. I look to my right and see that one gunner has been shot.

The chopper starts jumping and moving erratically. Smoke is coming inside the ship. The pilot and co-pilot are working frantically to get the chopper to fly straight. We are in real trouble.

Steven is looking at me with eyes wide open. I look back at him and motion with my hands to pray. I say a prayer for the chopper to get as far away from the enemy as possible before crashing. The pilots have got the gunship moving away from the enemy. We travel for five more miles or so, in a semi-straight line.

The chopper is hitting trees. The rockets start firing. This is an attempt to get rid of all of the ammo. I know now that we are going to crash for sure.

The chopper hits more trees. Branches are coming inside the area where we are sitting. I wished that I had put on a seat belt. It was too late now, for we were going down. The door gunner hands Steven four M-16s.

When a gunner gets out the M-16s for the crew, it means that the ship is definitely going to crash. Steven does not know what to do with the weapons. He looks at me. I motion for him to squeeze the weapons tight.

The chopper hit a couple more large trees, turned on its starboard side, and started falling to the jungle floor below. Finally, the chopper stopped.

I looked to see how many were hurt. To my surprise, no one was hurt seriously, except for the door gunner that was shot earlier. Even he only had a flesh wound. The pilots were moving quickly, but I noticed something I had never seen before.

Both pilots reached between their legs and pulled out a holstered .38 revolver. I never saw anyone carry a weapon between his legs like that. We started to help each other get out of the port side of the chopper. Steven was scared, but he was not wounded.

I held my hands together to make a step for Steven to climb out. He had already placed three rifles with slings over his head and held one in his hands. He looked like a true infantry grunt.

"Steven, you go first, then help the rest of us out!"

"OK, Sarge."

We pushed the wounded gunner out next, then the crew chief. The pilots and I helped the other gunner get out, and then we helped each other out.

The pilots were excited. "Man, that was hairy, huh?"

They were looking at Steven and me.

I looked at Steven and laughed. "How did you like that, Steve-O? That was excitement and a half. Something to tell your grandkids, huh?"

"Heck no, that is something to tell the public in America! That was mind-blowing, electrifying, heart-stopping, and I really do mean almost heart-stopping!"

"Were you scared, Steven?"

"Oh, yeah, I was afraid. Were you, Sarge?"

"Yes I was! Very much so!"

The pilots and gunners were laughing, even the wounded gunner.

I looked at the pilots. "Hey guys, why do you carry your pistols between your legs and not on your side?"

They both started talking at the same time. "The seat is sort of bullet-proof and we wear a vest that is supposed to be bullet-proof, but our nuts are in the open. Maybe, just maybe, a bullet at our nuts will bounce off of the pistol!"

"Makes sense to me. By the way, getting us out of there was a great job. How many times have you guys been shot down?"

The pilot says, "Five times!"

The co-pilot says, "Four times."

One of the gunners says, "Six for me, but I have been here in the 'Nam for eleven months!"

I say, "This is only my second time being shot down, and I hope it is the last!"

We hear the other choppers coming in for a landing.

The pilot says, "You guys get on another chopper, and it will take you to your company. We are only a few miles away. We are going to stay here and dismantle the ship. Then we will blow it up."

He holds out his hands toward Steven. "Hand me the 16s, and thanks. Are you a reporter?"

"Yes, I make movies and news stories."

The pilot says, "Put this crash in your story. It was fun, huh?"

"Not fun to me!"

We all laugh.

I say to the guys, "OK, thanks for the ride."

The co-pilot responds, "Maybe the next ride will be smoother!"

We both laugh. "You guys get on that slick."

Steven and I head for the chopper. We jump onboard and the ship takes off. A few minutes later, I see blue smoke on the ground. The chopper comes in closer to the ground and we jump off. I motion for Steven to stay low. "Don't get your head too close to the blades. The chopper is not level, so the blades are closer to the ground on this side."

I motion a *thank you* to the gunners and pilots. The bird takes off. They will probably go to the downed chopper for support.

Every VC and NVA in Vietnam would like to get a hold of a gunship. Steven and I see my squad in the tree line.

I take off running toward them. They are glad to see me. I am glad to see them also.

Killer asks, "How was Hawaii?"

Emery says, "Did you see your wife?"

White says, "How was the surf?"

"Wait a minute, guys. I will tell you all about it. Where is Sergeant Lewis?"

Eckert hangs his head. "He is not with us, Sarge."

I am worried. *Did he get killed?* I thought. I looked at all of the guys. "What do you mean he is not with us?"

The guys are looking at the ground.

Emerald says, "You had better go to the lieutenant's CP, Sarge!"

"OK, and by the way, this is Steven. He makes movies. You guys get acquainted."

I start walking toward the CP. I look back and the guys start laughing. "You guys know that I thought Lewis was dead?"

"Yeah, we are sorry, Sarge."

"I'll see you guys when I get back!"

CHAPTER 16

Chuck Becomes Platoon Sergeant

I arrive at the lieutenant's CP, and to my surprise, I see Chuck on the radio. "Hey, Chuck, what's happening?"

Chuck gives me a hug. "Hey, Danny, glad to see you!"

"You too, Chuck. Do you know what the guys in the squad told me?"

Chuck started to laugh. "Yeah, they told you that I wasn't with them anymore."

"Yeah, you idiot! I thought that you were dead!"

Chuck laughed harder. "Forgive me, Rock. It was Killer's idea."

"I'll pay Killer back someday. So what are you doing up here on the lieutenant's radio?"

"Well, you know that Erickson got killed, and you were gone on R&R, so I am platoon sergeant until we get another one."

"That's cool, Chuck. I am proud of you. Way to go!"

"Thanks, Rock. How come you are all scratched up? Your arm is bleeding!"

"Man, Chuck, it was hairy. I was scared to death. The first chopper that I was on got shot down. It was a gunship. I have never ridden on a gunship before. I thought that Steve and I were going to buy the farm!"

"Really? I bet it was exciting. Was it as exciting as it was on January ninth?"

"No, but it was pretty eventful. I'll never forget it. So where are we going next, Platoon Sergeant?"

"We are heading toward Hill 348. Our new E-7 platoon sergeant will be flying in."

"That is cool. That is where our mortar platoon is, isn't it?"

"Yeah, that's right. Maybe we can get a stand down."

I shook my head. "I hope so. The men need at least a few days out of the field."

The lieutenant came up to Chuck and me. "Hi, Rock, I am glad to see you. Did you have a good time?"

"Yes, sir, I had a great time!"

"That is fantastic, Rock! Guys, I have some good news and bad news."

Chuck and I look at each other. We are both thinking that the trip to Hill 348 has been cancelled. I say, "What's up, sir?"

"My time is up. I am heading home when we get to Hill 348."

Chuck says, "So we won't be seeing you anymore?"

I could not resist saying, "So what is the bad news, sir?"

The lieutenant starts laughing. "Rock, you are still an a-hole!"

"I know, sir, but I am only messing with you. We have been through a lot together, haven't we, sir?"

"Yes we have, and if it weren't for you and Lewis, I would not have made it over here!"

Chuck gets a grin on his face. "Yeah, you are right, sir. We saved your butt!"

"Shut up, Lewis. You are an a-hole too! OK, guys, we are staying here tonight. We are going in the direction of the Hill tomorrow."

I turned and started walking toward my squad.

"See ya, Chuck! See ya, sir."

"Later, gator!"

Gibbons says, "Later, Rock. I am really glad you are back."

"Thanks, sir."

I arrived at my squad to see them laughing.

"You guys are something else! You had me worried."

They started walking toward me. Killer says, "We are sorry, Sarge."

Emery says, "Did you really think that Lewis was dead? It was Killer's idea!"

I answered, "I sort of did. I thought that maybe he was wounded or something like that. You guys did a good job of acting."

Emerald says, "Yeah, and when we were hanging our heads, we were laughing!"

"I'll pay you all back one day!"

The men gathered around. I shook hands with all of them. We talked about my R&R for thirty minutes. Then Killer noticed the blood on my arm.

"How come you are bleeding, Sarge? We are not in the bush."

I gathered the men together so I could tell the story of the chopper crash only once more. I told the story, leaving out the severity of the crash for the sake of Emerald.

Eckert says, "Sarge, that is the second time that you have crashed in a chopper."

"Yep, and I don't want any more crashes!"

Emery asks, "Are we here for the night, and where are we going tomorrow?"

"Yep, we are here for the night, and we are heading to Hill 348 tomorrow. It will take us a few days to get there."

Eckert is looking at me. I say, "What?"

He says, "Do you want me to still be in charge since you are back?"

"Yep, for tonight. I'll be back in swing tomorrow!"

"OK, Sarge! White, how about setting up guard?"

"On it, Sergeant Eckert!"

I looked at Eckert. "Was White being a smart-butt when he called you Sergeant Eckert?"

"Oh no! He always calls me Sarge. We get along great! As a matter of fact, all of the men and me get along great. They have given me respect ever since you left."

"Man, Eckert, that is great. You must be doing it right! Good job!"

"Thank you, Sarge!"

We spent the night in the rain. It poured all night long. Morning came and the rain let up slightly. I'll be glad when I can get back home and not have to get up at 4:30 in the morning. I look at Killer. Something is on his face.

"Killer, look at me!" He turns his head toward me. "You have a leech on your right cheek!"

Killer reaches for his insect repellent in his helmet band. "These leeches are like one of my girlfriends. She hangs around all night, then she tries to suck the blood from me!"

Killer squirts the leech with the mosquito spray and looks at me. "Sarge, look at your left arm!"

I look at my left arm and I see that a leech has made its way into one of my wounds from the helicopter crash. "Man, this is going to hurt!" I know that when I squirt the insect spray at the head of the leech, it will go directly into my open wound.

Killer says, "That is going to hurt. Are you going to cry?"

"No I am not, but I think that I will get Doc to put some alcohol on it first!"

I walked over to where Doc was starting to eat breakfast. "Hey, Doc, how are ya?"

"Good, Rock. I was just going to come to see you about your wounds from the crash. Let's see them!"

I showed Doc my arm with the leech in the wound. Doc looks at the arm. "What the heck? Is that a leech?"

"Yep!"

"I need to put some alcohol in the wound before we hit it with insect repellent. We cannot leave the head in the wound.

OK, put your arm on my leg and hang on. This is going to hurt!"

I placed my arm on Doc's thigh and he poured the alcohol into the wound. This was hurting, but not as much as I had expected.

Doc grabbed hold of the leech with some forceps. He gently pulled the leech as he poured more alcohol into the wound. This time it did hurt as much as I had previously expected. To my surprise, the leech released.

Doc lifted the leech up close to his face. "Yep, the head and all. The alcohol worked as well as insect repellent!"

"Thanks, Doc."

"No, Danny, you are not done yet. I need to clean up the wound."

I showed him my arm again, and he poured more alcohol in it and placed some bandages on it.

"How is your wife?"

"She is great. How is your mom, and your brothers and sisters?"

"They are good too."

Doc and I sat and talked about our families for a half hour.

I went back to my men and we started to eat breakfast. I opened my canned ham and hot chocolate mix. After opening the can of ham, I noticed that I didn't have any heat tablets. I looked at White and noticed that he had a great flame going under his can of beans.

"Hey, White, do you have any heat tablets?"

"No, but I have plenty of C-4. You want a stick?"

"No, just a half of a stick!"

I placed the C-4 below my can of ham and my metal canteen cup, and lit it with a match. I knew that C-4 would burn for a long time by just setting a match to it. White was our demolitions guy and our tunnel rat. He always had plenty of C-4.

Making a meal with C-4 explosives

"Thanks, White. Did you blow anything up while I was gone?"

"No, but I am ready when the time comes!" He patted his bag that held the C-4.

"See ya, White. We will move out in ten minutes!"

We ate breakfast, packed up, and loaded bandoliers of ammo.

"Men, be sure your weapons are on safety. We are moving out!"

Eckert handed me my map. "Here ya go, Sarge. Glad to have ya back."

"Glad to see you too, Eckert."

I looked at my map. It looked to me that it would take two days to get to the Hill if we did not run into trouble.

"Alright, men, we are moving. Eckert, assign point!"

Eckert says, "Raymond, do you still want point?"

Usually I did not want the machine gunner to pull point because he had to have another man close to him. The second man had to carry the gunner's extra ammo.

"Yes I do, Eckert!"

Raymond started moving toward the front, with White a few meters behind him.

Eckert continues to command, "Killer, you go behind White. Sergeant Rock, do you want to go after Killer?"

"Sure."

Eckert says, "The rest of you men fall in behind me. I'll be behind the sarge!"

We started to move. We traveled for a half hour when Eckert asked me, "What do you think about Sergeant Lewis being platoon sergeant?"

"I think it is great. He will be a good one."

"Yep, and he won't be in the rear every time the crap hits the fan either!"

"Yep, you're right. I guarantee you that Chuck will be up here with us during a firefight. He loves to be in the action!"

"Hey, Sarge, I have a question."

"Shoot!"

"Does it bother you that the lieutenant made Lewis the platoon sergeant instead of you?"

"Sort of, but not really. Gibbons likes Chuck a lot, and besides, I was on R&R. Gibbons would have made Chuck platoon sergeant even if I would have been here."

"I don't know about that, Sarge. Gibbons was asking about you the whole time that you were gone."

"Is that a fact?"

My radio sounds, "Blackhawk Three, this is Cherokee Three, over!"

"This is Blackhawk Three, go!"

"In 500 meters, there is going to be a small village across the rice paddies. There is a report about VC activity there."

"Are we going to attack the village?"

"Only if we get fired upon. Our platoon will get on line, cross the paddies, and check out the village."

I did not like crossing a rice paddy while being in the open, with no place to hide if we got shot at. We had to approach many villages like this because of the women and children living in the villages. In the past, we would get intelligence that VC were in a village, but when we made a surprise attack, we found no sign of VC. Maybe this was going to be a non-VC village.

We traveled the 500 meters and saw the village. I looked to my right side and saw Chuck. "You didn't think that you were going to get in a firefight without me, did you Danny?"

Chuck is ready to go

"You know, Chuck, I was just telling Eckert that you would be right here fighting beside us if the crap hits the fan!"

We both laugh.

"Gibbons says for you to take charge getting across the rice paddy."

"Alright!"

I get on the horn. "Blackhawk One, Two, and Four, my squad will cross first. Once we get across, we will give you fire cover. Bring your squads across but only after I give you the word, over!"

Each squad leader acknowledged with, "Roger, over."

I replied, "Roger, out."

I gathered up my men. "Are you guys ready? White, you and Raymond stay in the middle next to Lewis and me. Emerald, you stay next to me. Killer, you get on the right flank. Eckert, you go left. The rest of you fall in, but keep your distance! Remember the saying, 'If you are too close to each other, one round will get you all!' OK, let's move out!"

I immediately see a gook moving around in front of the village, but he is too far away for me to see if he has a weapon. He does not see us.

We move a little closer, and I see that he is carrying a rifle. This is going to be a long shot. I have to be accurate. I am carrying my M-79 grenade launcher. If I miss, I may wound or kill children. I decide not to take the chance. I only want to kill the VC.

"Emerald, give me your M-16 for a minute!"

He hands me the rifle. I aim the rifle. I hold my breath and squeeze off a round. I hear another shot at almost the same time as my round goes off. My round hits the VC and he goes down.

I look at Chuck and he is jumping up and down. "I got him! What a shot!"

"What do you mean you shot him? I shot him!"

"No you didn't, Rock. I shot him. He went down as soon as I pulled the trigger!"

"Yeah, that is because I shot him. I really mean it. He fell as soon as my bullet hit him!"

"No way, Danny!"

"Yes way!"

We both start laughing. "Let's get to the village before they start shooting at us!"

I hand Emerald his M-16. "What do you think, Emerald? Which one of us shot the guy?"

"I think that you did, but ask Emery. He was next to Sergeant Lewis!"

"Hey, Emery, be honest. Who shot the gook?"

"I think it was Sergeant Lewis, Sarge!"

"Ah, you are full of it, Emery. I'll bust you down to private first class if you mess with me!"

Emery and I laugh very hard. He knows that I am only joking with him.

Emery says, "OK, Sarge. In that case, it was your bullet that shot the VC." He laughs.

"That's better, Emery!"

We moved to the edge of the village. I got on the horn and told the other squads to advance. Once the other squads were across the paddies, I told them to check out the village for other VC.

"Chuck, let's go check out the Charlie!"

Chuck says, "Yeah, let's go check out the VC that I shot!"

"Yeah, right, you mean that I shot!"

We walked over to the VC lying on the ground. To our surprise, he was still alive. His rifle was lying near his feet. I pulled the rifle farther away from him. I examined the VC for a wound. I wanted to show Chuck where I had shot him. Chuck says, "Look there, he is shot in the arm!"

"Yeah, but getting shot in the arm wouldn't make him fall!"

I checked out the Charlie further and found that he was also shot in the side.

"Look here, Chuck, another hole. We both shot him!"

We laughed hard.

Chuck says, "You know, Rock, we both made a long shot for an M-16 rifle!"

"Yes it was, Chuck, but now I need to kill him!"

I didn't want to kill him, but he was bleeding to death just lying on the ground.

I said a prayer asking God to forgive me for what I was going to do. "Give me your rifle, Chuck!"

Chuck handed me the M-16. I held the rifle barrel against the man's head. He opened his eyes and our eyes met. I took my safety off and placed my finger on the trigger. A grandmother and a lady about twenty-five years old came out of a hooch with two kids, a boy and a girl, around eight or nine years old.

They all knelt next to the man that I was going to kill. They looked up at me, begging me not to kill him. I couldn't understand them, but I could tell that they were praying. They were praying harder than I had ever seen people pray before.

If I let the VC live, he would shoot at us later once he got healthy. If I kill him, it would make his family very sad and they would hate us GIs even more. I looked up at the heavens. "God, please tell me what to do, please!"

I paused. Thoughts were running through my head. There were too many *what ifs* for me to consider. I was in the moment, and at this moment, I was going to let this man live.

I put the rifle safety back in the lock position and pulled the rifle away from the head of the Charlie. I could see the relief in the VC's eyes.

The ladies started hugging and kissing me. The two kids grabbed my hands and hugged me around the legs. I showed them where he was shot. It looked like the bullets had passed through his side and the back of the arm.

I pointed at the side of the man. "Give him aid, patch him up."

They could not understand my words, but they knew that I was telling them to take care of their loved one. I pulled away from the man and stood up.

The women started kissing me again. This was the first time that I had ever felt good about not killing a VC. I handed the rifle back to Chuck.

"Chuck, do you think that I did the right thing?"

"Yep, I would have done the same thing. But we are going to keep his weapon."

"OK, let's keep checking the village, Chuck."

We checked out the village and found no more VC. The lieutenant walks up to Chuck and me. "Was it a Victor Charlie that you shot? Who shot him?"

I answered, "Both of us shot him!"

"Is he dead?"

"No, but the way that he was bleeding it will not take long for him to die."

Chuck looked at me and winked. We knew that the VC was not bleeding as much as we had told the lieutenant.

I think the lieutenant knew something was up, but he never said anything more about it. "Rock and Lewis, let's move 'em out. Let's get away from this village before we find trouble!"

"Yes, sir, let's go!"

We gathered the platoon and moved out, heading for Hill 348.

We had no more action for the rest of the day. The captain radioed the platoon leaders and told them that we would be shutting down for the night in three hours. After three hours, we found a place to bivouac. We made a perimeter and dug in for the night.

I did not trust that the VC did not know we were here. I think that we should have a mad minute and call in a little artillery. I walked toward the lieutenant's CP. I was going to suggest a mad minute.

On my way to see Gibbons, I passed by the captain. "Hey, sir, how is it going?"

"Great, Rock. Where are you headed?"

"To see Gibbons. I think we should have a mad minute."

"Well, why not ask me?"

"Because of the chain of command and all of that stuff."

"So what do you want me to do?"

"Well, sir, since we saw a VC village today and we have not been shot at today, I think we should call in artillery after we have a mad minute."

"OK, Rock, we will do it. I'll radio you guys when you get back to your squad."

"Thanks, sir. I'll feel much better."

I turned and headed back to the squad.

"Men, we are going to have a mad minute!"

The men were elated.

The captain announced on the radio, "Mad minute in two minutes!"

Chuck came up to me. "I am not missing a mad minute for all of the tea in China!"

He locked and loaded his M-16. He placed six magazines on a rucksack. I took out eight rounds of grenades for my launcher and placed them on my rucksack. The captain's voice came over the radio. "Fire!"

The men loved it. Chuck was standing up, shooting a complete magazine at a time, moving his rifle from side to side to spread out his bullet pattern.

I was shooting my grenades up and over the trees. I was shooting into the trees. As fast as I shot a round, I would load another. I shot canister rounds. I shot regular grenade rounds. I even shot a red smoke grenade.

My men were shooting their weapons just as fast as Chuck. We heard, "Cease fire! Cease fire!"

The next thing we heard was artillery being called in. It was hitting on all four sides of us. I felt much safer now. I knew my men felt the same way.

We pulled guard all night long without a single incident. I wish I could say that I slept like a baby, but that didn't happen here in Vietnam. Morning came and we did the typical morning duties — eating, talking, checking weapons, and loading the gear on our bodies.

We moved out again toward Hill 348. Twice on our way, we were stopped because snipers were shooting at us. This was not a big deal. Unless someone was shot, we hardly ever spoke of snipers. We humped the rest of the day until we could see the Hill.

We walked through the opening in the concertina wire. The radio sounded, "Halt! Everyone stop!"

I wondered what was wrong. The captain's RTO came up to me.

"Sergeant Rock, the captain says to stay in line going through the wire because it is mined just inside the perimeter!"

"Thanks. We will stay in line."

I looked at the men. "Stay in line! There are mines at the wire! Pass it on!"

The men understood as they passed along the command. We made it to the center of the Hill. The mess hall was still open.

The captain said, "Drop your sacks and eat a hot meal."

We started to go inside and, of course, waited in line. Waiting in line was no big deal for a hot meal.

While I was waiting, Chuck came up behind me. "Hey, Rock, let's eat!"

"Yeah, man, let's eat!"

"Danny, our new platoon sergeant will be here in an hour."

"Oh, yeah! Maybe he will be better than the last one."

"Danny, do you remember the platoon sergeant we had before Erickson?"

"Yeah, he was alright."

"Maybe this new guy will be as good as he was!"

We finished eating and went outside. "Hey, Chuck, no guard duty tonight, huh?"

"Yep, that is cool!"

Chuck, the squad, and I sat around and talked about the new platoon sergeant. We wondered what he would be like. *Would he be a coward? Would he be brave? Would he be a leader? Would he be ignorant of the ways in Vietnam?* The chopper landed in the prepared LZ.

After a short period, we walked over to Gibbons. "Sir, where is he?"

"He has been off of the slick for a little while. He should be here by now. Go check on him, Lewis!"

"Yes, sir!"

Chuck started walking toward the LZ. We heard a loud boom, then another. We all hit the ground.

I look at Gibbons. "What's happening, sir?"

"I don't know. Let me get on the radio!"

The lieutenant gets on the radio. We did not hear any more blasts and did not hear any shots being fired, so we stood up.

The lieutenant says, "Some idiot walked right up next to the wire and stepped on a mine. Lewis, you and Rock go find the new platoon sergeant!"

"OK!"

"Chuck, on our way to get the sergeant, let's go by the blast and find out what happened."

We walked up to where the blast took place. We could only see fragments of a soldier.

I asked the men pulling guard, "What happened here?"

"Sarge, you won't believe it. A staff sergeant jumped off of the chopper, came up to us, and said something like, 'Is that concertina wire tight?' He started to walk out near the wire. We all yelled at him to stop. He kept walking and blew himself up! There are little pieces of him all around. It is gross!"

"Was he the only sergeant on the slick?"

"He was the only guy that got off of the chopper. Was he a friend?"

"No, I think that he was supposed to be our platoon sergeant!"

Chuck and I looked at each other with our mouths opened. "Let's go and tell Gibbons, Chuck!"

"Let's do it. I can't believe it!"

We arrive at the lieutenant's CP. Gibbons looks up at us. "So where is the sergeant?"

Chuck says, "As Rock and I were just told, 'You won't believe it!' That was his explosion! He walked too close to the wire and blew himself to pieces!"

"Is he hurt bad?"

Chuck says, "Hurt bad? He was blown to bits. We told you that there was nothing left of him. Only little pieces!"

"Man, guys, that is terrible. Lewis, I guess you will have to stay at platoon sergeant for a while!"

"OK, but I want you to put me in for E-7, sir."

"Oh, yeah, Lewis? You want to skip E-6 and go right to E-7, huh?"

"Sure, why not?"

"The new lieutenant will be here soon. I hope he is smarter than the sergeant!"

I looked at Chuck. "Sir, I think that the sergeant was trying to show the guys on guard that he was a higher rank than they were. What do you think, Chuck?"

"I agree with Rock, sir. He would not have made a good leader!"

"Men, you guys find a place to sleep. No guard duty tonight!"

"See ya, sir."

"Sir, I am going with Rock and the squad for the night. Is that OK with you?"

"Sure, we are not doing anything, but if we get hit, come to the CP. I'll be with the captain."

I walked over to the squad. "No guard tonight! You guys find a place to sleep but don't wander off too far!"

The men all agreed.

Chuck had a strange look on his face. "Hey, Rock, let's give Gibbons a going-away party!"

"A going-away party?"

"Yeah, we can make our cupcakes!"

"Alright, we will need two ammo cans for the oven and C-4 and heat tablets for a slow cook."

"We have the ingredients in our C-rations! Hey, Rock, what do you think about building him a big chair out of sand bags?"

"You mean like a throne?"

"Yeah, like a throne!"

"Man, Chuck, you must love the guy!"

"No, not really. Once he started to pay attention to what we told him, he was OK!"

"Yeah, I guess you are right. I'll send you a few guys to build the chair."

Chuck and I making cupcakes for the Lieutenants departure

Craig walks up to me. "Sarge, the old man wants you."

"Thanks. Tell him I am on my way."

I arrived at the captain's CP, and he is talking to Steven, the movie guy. "Hi, sir! What do you say, Steven?"

The captain says, "That was something about your new platoon sergeant. I have never seen anyone killed so fast in Vietnam. How long was he on the ground? Like two minutes! He had to be a dud!"

The captain was answering his own questions.

"You are right, sir, and another thing, the guys on guard told him not to go near the wire!"

"Yep, too bad. Rock, on another matter, what do you want me to do with this guy?"

"Didn't he tell you what he wanted?"

"Yes, he wants to bring a news crew and stay with us for a month. We cannot give them any weapons because they have not been trained! What do you think we ought to do?"

"Let them have at it, sir!"

The old man looks at Steven. "OK, Steven, you get on the next chopper and bring your crew back here! Now Steven, you listen up! We will only be here another day, then we are heading north again. So get your crew moving!"

"Thank you, sir, and thank you, Sergeant Rock!"

The captain says, "You are welcome, but see if you want to thank me later! Steven, I need to speak to the sergeant in private, so split, huh!"

Steven walked away with a big smile on his face.

"What's up, sir?"

"You know Gibbons will be leaving in a few days, right?"

"Yes, sir!"

"What do you think about Lewis being platoon leader until the new lieutenant gets here?"

"Oh, man, sir. He would make a good one. He has been a good platoon sergeant, so why not move him on up to leader?"

"You won't get your feelings hurt if I do it?"

Feelings was not a word we used very often in Vietnam. The captain and I knew that saying the word *feelings* was just a tongue in cheek thing.

"No! If Chuck has any questions, he will just ask me. But really, truly, I think he knows everything that I know! However, it will hurt my feelings if you didn't consider me for the job."

"I did. I considered you for platoon sergeant but you were on R&R. I considered you for platoon leader, but I felt like Lewis would think that he was not doing a good job if I made you leader over him."

"You did the right thing, sir. Chuck has a good head on his shoulders."

"Yes he does! Rock, have you heard that this Tet Offensive thing is getting worse and worse?"

"Yes, sir, I have, but you will keep us alive, sir!"

I turned and walked to Steven.

"Hey, Steven, you take care, huh!"

"Affirmatron, Sarge!" He grinned, for he was now picking up the lingo. "Thanks again, Sergeant Rock!"

"Thank me in a month. Tell your crew to keep their heads down!"

I went back to my squad. They are spread out, speaking to other soldiers. "Eckert, go and get the guys!"

"On it!"

Eckert takes off. He returns with the guys in five minutes. "Here they are, Sarge!"

"Men, we will be here for another day or two. I want two or three of you to build a sand bag chair for Gibbons!"

Killer says, "For Gibbons? I thought that you didn't like the guy!"

"Yeah, you're right, but he is OK now. And besides, he will probably leave tomorrow afternoon. Sergeant Lewis wants to throw him a party. Lewis and I are going to bake cupcakes."

The guys respond, "Cupcakes! I am in!"

Killer says, "Let's get started. Do you want a back on the chair?"

"Yeah, like a throne!"

The guys took off.

Killer looked back at me. "Where do you want this king throne built?"

"Go to the CP and speak to Chuck. He will tell you where to build it."

This is hard to believe. Not long ago, we were fighting to stay alive and now we are planning a party! I see Craig walking toward me.

"The captain wants you and Sergeant Lewis at the CP."

"Thank you. Did he say what for?"

"No, Sergeant!"

I walked over to Chuck's position.

"Chuck, the captain wants us!"

"What for?"

"Don't know. Let's go!"

We reach the captain's CP. He is shaking his head in disgust.

"This has been a crazy, crazy day! Do you guys know who Williams is?"

"Not really. He is in the mortar platoon, isn't he?"

"Yes! He received a 'Dear John' letter from his girlfriend or wife and he left the perimeter. He is an idiot!"

I look at Chuck then back at the old man. "So what do you want us to do? We don't want to go outside the perimeter alone!"

"No, you guys get in the chopper and go in circles around the perimeter for an hour. If you don't see him, then just come on back."

"Did he take food or his rifle?"

"No. Like I told you, he is an idiot!"

Chuck and I jumped on a chopper. We verified that the pilot knew what the plan was and we took off. We traveled around the perimeter, even going ten miles away from the perimeter, for over an hour. We came back in to Hill 348. The chopper landed.

We walked to the CP. "Sir, no luck. He probably is dead by now!"

"Yep, you're right. Good try, guys. See ya."

"See ya, sir!"

Chuck looks at me. "What a day, huh, Rock? What a day!"

"Yeah, this is really crazy. If I ever do write a book, I am going to put this story in it. But you watch, I'll bet that this guy, Williams, will come back in, just a-strolling like nothing ever happened!"

Chuck says, "If he does come strolling in, I'll probably shoot him myself!"

"See ya, Chuck! Have a good night at your CP. Maybe it will be quiet tonight."

Chuck finds a place to relax, war is heck

CHAPTER 17

Lieutenant Stephen Watkins

I walked over to where my squad was located. Eckert asked, "Was that you and Sergeant Lewis in the chopper?"

"Yes! This idiot named Williams got a 'Dear John' letter and walked right out of the perimeter with no rations, water, or weapon."

"Did you find him?"

"No! You guys gather round!"

White says, "We are not going to go looking for him, are we, Sarge?"

"No, forget about Williams. We won't have to pull guard again, but I want you guys to stay close. Find a bunker or foxhole to get in for protection!"

I heard a commotion near our CP.

"Killer, come with me!"

Killer and I walked to the CP. "Hey, Chuck, what's all of the talking and commotion about?"

Chuck shakes his head. "The 'Dear John' guy just walked right back into the perimeter. He didn't know the password and was almost shot. The captain has him at his CP now."

Chuck looks at Killer. "Hey, man, how is it going?"

"Good, Sarge. This is like a holiday, not having to pull guard duty."

"Man, yeah, I love it. These mortar guys have it made!"

I look at Chuck and Killer. "I love it too. We could get spoiled in this place. Well, we will see you, Chuck. Come on, Killer, let's go."

Killer and I arrived back to see the guys in the squad heading for bunkers and foxholes. I said, "You guys take care, you hear?"

"We will!"

"You too, Sarge!"

The night started very quietly. At ten o'clock, the perimeter started to be attacked by what appeared to be six VC.

Killer and White ran up to me. "Hey, Sarge, can we go to where the action is?"

"No! These guys can handle it. You guys go back to your bunker!"

White says, "We are not actually in the bunker. We are sleeping behind it."

"Alright, go to where you were, but stay out of the line of fire!"

The firing continued for ten minutes, then artillery was called in, and the rest of the night was quiet.

Morning came and it was time to eat breakfast. I went in the mess hall and noticed that most of my guys had already eaten. I saw Chuck coming from the kitchen. He was carrying a bag of something. "Hey, Chuck, what do you have there?"

"It is flour, sugar, and yeast for our cupcakes."

I laugh. "I don't know nothing about cooking, but I don't think that we need yeast for cupcakes!"

"OK, we will forget the yeast. I have the ammo cans ready for baking. When you get finished eating, come on over to bunker number twenty-seven."

"OK. Get the cans warm ahead of time!"

I ate breakfast and traveled to bunker number twenty-seven. Chuck and I baked for two hours, making cupcakes and pudding for the whole squad and Lieutenant Gibbons. Once we were finished baking, I sent Killer and Emerald to find Gibbons and bring him to his throne. The big sand bag chair actually looked really good. It had a high back and armrests. The lieutenant arrived and we ushered him to his throne. We sat him down and served him a cupcake and pudding. He was quite pleased with the squad showing how much they liked him.

Gibbons stood up with his cup of Kool-Aid that we had made for him. He held the cup up high and said, "I know that I was a complete a-hole when I arrived, and you guys could have just let me be killed, but you didn't. Even though I acted very badly, you guys took me under your wing and protected me, both from the gooks and the captain. I also apologize to Sergeant Rock for busting him down to a private. He showed me how the cow ate the cabbage very quickly. I reinstated him within two days. Thanks to all of you guys. I hope your next platoon leader will listen to Lewis and Rock!"

The squad held up their cups. "Cheers."

We took a drink. Chuck and I looked at each other, not really knowing what to say. Chuck says, "We will be sorry to see you go, sir. Even though you were a big a-hole."

The lieutenant laughed. "Does anyone else have anything to say?"

Killer stands up. "Sir, do I have permission to speak freely?"

"No you don't, Killer. You are an a-hole too!"

The lieutenant and Killer laughed. We sat around and talked about our adventures in Vietnam for an hour. The lieutenant ate all of his cupcakes and pudding. They were both, actually, very good. We heard the sound of a chopper coming in.

The lieutenant stands up. "That's my ride coming in."

He shakes hands with all of the guys. He gives Chuck and I hugs and heads to the chopper. "Good luck, guys. Don't get killed, and be sure and kill a lot of them!"

Chuck and I walk Gibbons to the skid. When we arrive at the chopper, we notice that it is full. There are two soldiers and a camera crew aboard. They start to disembark.

I hear my name. "Sergeant Rock, Sergeant Rock."

It is Steven, the moviemaker news guy.

"Hey, Steven, you made it back."

"Yep! Which way to the captain?"

I direct him, "See ya, Steven, and good luck."

Chuck and I watch as Gibbons gets on the chopper and it flies off. The two soldiers are still standing in the same place. I look at them. "What's up with you two?"

One of them answered, "We are from Delta Company. We are waiting to be sent back. We are to stay with your company for a while."

"Alright, what are your names?"

"I am Allen."

"I am Henning."

"Let's go see the captain!"

Chuck says, "Rock, I am going back to my CP."

"OK, Chuck, I'll see ya later."

Henning and Allen watch as Chuck walks away. "What does he mean his CP, and did he call you Rock? Are you the leader of the Killer Squad?"

"The lieutenant that just left was our platoon leader. We don't have a new one yet. Sergeant Lewis is the temporary platoon leader. I am Sergeant Rock. Sergeant Lewis is a team leader in my squad."

Allen says, "Sarge, does your squad really cut off all of the heads of the NVA and VC after you shoot them?"

"No, those are just rumors. Let's go see the captain."

We walked up to the captain. I waited for the captain to get off of the horn.

"Sir, these are the two men from Delta Company."

"How do you do, men?"

"Fine, sir."

The captain shakes their hands. "Rock, take these guys to your platoon leader. We are going to keep them for a while."

"Yes, sir. Let's go, men. See you, sir."

We walked over to Chuck's CP. I looked at Chuck. "Sir, the captain says we are to keep these two for a while."

"OK, Rock. Do you want to take them into your squad?"

331

"Sure. Let's go, guys."

We cross the hill to my squad. I introduce the men to the squad. We sat and talked, but to our surprise, Henning was one of these guys that had done everything and could do anything in life. According to him, he was the best thing on earth.

I asked Allen, "Does Henning always brag on himself like this?"

"Yes, all of the time. No one likes him. He is a jerk!"

When my squad and I would have the time to just sit around and talk, we would invariably talk about cars. I had a 1965 Super Sport with a 409 cubic-inch motor and a four-speed transmission. White had a Corvette. Chuck was going to buy a Corvette if he got home alive, and Eckert had a GTO.

Sue & her sister Jeannie in front of my 409.
Notice she has the racing slicks on the car.

We started talking about our cars. White says, "Hey, Sarge, do you think a 409 motor will fit in my Corvette?"

Henning says, "Do you have a Corvette, White? I have two of them. I have a fast back and a convertible."

White say, "You have two Corvettes?"

"Yep, two!"

I don't believe Henning, but I answer White's question. "Your Corvette probably has a 327 or 283 in it now. If you put a 409 in it, you would probably have to change the motor mounts and beef up the front suspension, because I think that the 409 weights more than 850 pounds."

Eckert says, "Sarge, do you think my GTO would support the 409?"

"No, not really. You would have to do the same thing as White."

Henning says, "Yes it will, because I have a 409 in my GTO!"

The guys are saying, "You are full of it, Henning!"

I am getting a little tired of his lies now, so I decide to dig in further. "Henning, did you get the GTO straight from the factory with that 409 in it?"

"Yes, I did."

"What year did you get it?"

"I got it in 1967."

"Um."

I knew that the last 409 to be installed in a car was in 1965. The 396 cubic-inch engine came out in 1964 or 1965. When I ordered my 409, Chevrolet asked me to change my order from a 409 to a 396. I said no way. We went on to talk about other things.

No matter what we spoke about, Henning had done it before and, of course, more of it. The guys were getting very mad at him. They did not like him.

Chuck came up to me and whispered, "Do you think that anything Henning says is true?"

"Not really, but I have an idea. We are going to say that one of the men has six horses that are very rare. The kind of horses will be nonexistent. In other words, the name of the breed of horses will be something like 'Oshan Rebel stallions,' or something like that. Chuck, you take Henning away from the men, then bring him back in five minutes!"

"OK. Henning, come with me. I need to talk to you!"

When Henning walked away, I gathered up the men. "OK, guys, you all think Henning is full of crap, right?"

Killer replies, "Yep, but the word starts with an *S* and ends with a *T*."

Eckert says, "We don't like the guy. Do you think that he is full of it, Sarge?"

"Yes I do, but we will run a test!"

White says, "What kind of a test?"

"Do any of you own any horses?"

Emerald replies, "I have two horses!"

"What breed are they?"

"They are just roping horses, you know, like quarter horses. They are real good horses, but they are not good enough to race or anything like that."

"OK. When Henning gets back, I will start talking about horses and you say that you have six Oshan Rebel stallions."

"What! There is no such horse that I know of called an Oshan Rebel stallion!"

"That is the point. If Henning is lying, then he will say that he owns some too."

The men start laughing and agree to the plan. Chuck and Henning come back to our location. Chuck says, "What are you guys talking about now, Rock?"

"Oh, we were just talking about riding horses. How about you, Chuck? Do you like riding horses?"

"Oh, yeah, I do!"

I look at Emerald. "Hey, Emerald, don't you have horses?"

Emerald holds his head up. "Yes, I do. I have six Oshan Rebel stallions. They just won trophies at the horse show in Kentucky!"

I nodded my head up and down. "Man, that is cool. I'll bet that you are proud of them, huh?"

Before Emerald could answer, Henning interrupts, "I have horses too!"

"You do?" I say. "What kind are they?"

"They are what Emerald has, Alton Rebels."

"Do you mean, Oshan Rebel stallions?"

"Yes!"

"How many do you have?"

"I have twelve, and I won $50,000 with them last year."

The guys went bananas on him. I heard comments like, "Don't talk to me again!" "You are full of it!" "You are not worth a bullet to shoot you!" "Just stay away from us!"

Killer jumps to his feet. "Come on, men. Let's get away from this guy before I kill him with my bare hands!"

Chuck, Henning, and I are the only men in the group now.

I look at Chuck. "Hey, Chuck, will you go see what the men are doing? I want to talk to Henning."

Chuck replies, "I will, then I have to go back to the CP!"

I start to talk to Henning. I want to find out why he lies so much. "Henning, do you know who the guy named Killer is?"

"Not really. Do you think he would really kill me with his bare hands?"

"Killer is the guy that cut the head off of a VC. So don't mess with him!"

Henning looks at me with his eyes wide open. "Can I ask you something, Sarge?"

"Sure!"

"No one ever likes me. Even when I was in Delta Company, I had no friends."

"Well, let's talk about that, Henning. Why do you think that they don't like you?"

"I don't know. I try to fit in, but it never works."

"Do you think it could be that you exaggerate a little? I mean, like overstating the truth?"

Henning got on the defensive. "No! Everything I say is true!"

"Stop right there, Henning! You are lying about lying. No one needs to lie about what they have done. We are all different people and all of us have done different, interesting things! You don't need to exaggerate."

"But Sarge, I don't have anything interesting to say about myself!"

"OK, tell me about yourself with no lies, and I guarantee you that I will find something interesting about you."

"Alright, here goes, but I am really dull. I was an average student; I have two brothers and a sister. I don't race cars. I have a crummy pickup. I am bad at baseball. I don't like football. I hate golf. I am not an actor. I have been hunting only once."

By this time, I was thinking that maybe he was dull. Everything that he hated or couldn't do, I either loved it or I was able to do it.

"Henning, is there anything at all that you can do or that you like to do?"

"Well, Sarge, I have a bow!"

"A bowl of what?"

"No, not a bowl. I am talking about archery. You know, like a bow and arrow!"

"You mean archery?"

"Yes, Sarge. I have a fifty-five pound, sixty-four-inch re-curve bow!"

I was amazed about how fast he said the sentence. Maybe he was telling the truth this time. I looked at Henning. "Are you for real? Are you telling the truth?"

"Yes, sir, Sarge, but that is not interesting to anyone!"

"Yes it is! It is interesting to me. Did you know that there is a group of guys, right here in Vietnam, that go out with their bows and arrows and kill VC?"

"No, but that would be cool!"

"Hey, Henning, one time in high school gym class we had to shoot a bow. I only had a thirty-five or forty pound bow. When

I shot the arrow, the string hit me in the left arm and, man, did it hurt!"

"Yep, you didn't have an arm protector, did ya?"

"No, what is that?"

"It is a protector that fits on the inside of the arm. I like to use leather. Were you any good, Sarge?"

"Are you kidding? My first shot, I almost killed a guy running on the track!"

We both laughed. "I was pretty bad too, at first, but not that bad."

"You see, Henning. You have something interesting to say and you don't have to lie about it. Now when people ask you questions, just listen and answer the questions like you just did. You will start getting friends. Now I want you to go find the guys, but don't say anything. Just listen!"

I saw Chuck walking back from his CP. "Hey, Chuck, anything happening?"

"No, not yet! What were you doing with Henning?"

"Oh, he says he doesn't have any friends. I've been talking to him about exaggerating."

"Yeah, he doesn't have any friends because he lies so much. Did you tell him that?"

"Yep, I did!"

"Hey, Danny, have you ever thought about all of the things that we have to be as leaders over here in the 'Nam?"

I start laughing. "What do you mean?"

"Well, we have to direct the men. We have to be teachers. We have to tell the men that all is well when we are scared to death ourselves. We cannot show pain when we are hurting, and now you have to be a shrink."

"Yeah, Chuck, that is called being a leader. Here come the men. Let's see if Henning has made a change."

The men are shooting the bull as they get near us. Emery says, "Is the new lieutenant here yet? I don't know why Sergeant Lewis can't just stay as platoon leader. He is doing a great job."

I reply, "I want Sergeant Lewis to be right beside me when we are in a firefight. However, if we don't have a good lieutenant that knows what he is doing, I want Chuck as platoon leader."

I lean over and whisper to Chuck, "Get Henning away from here for five minutes, will you? I want talk to the guys about Henning again!"

"Sure, Rock. Henning, come with me!"

I look at the men. "Hey, men, I have had a long talk with Henning. Now don't say anything. He says that he does not have any friends."

The men start talking.

"No, now shut up for a moment! I talked to him about his exaggerations."

Killer blurts out, "Exaggeration? He lies about everything!"

"Yeah, I know, but he says he has changed. Now again, why do I want all of you to get along in my squad?"

The men start answering, "So we are a well-oiled machine during a firefight!"

"So we can fight the enemy and not each other!"

"Yes, so here comes Henning. Just give him a chance!"

The men and I start talking about just anything that pops into our heads. Before long I say, "Did you guys know that we have a unit that goes out with bows and arrows and shoots VC?"

My hope was that Henning would join the conversation without saying that he killed a thousand VC with one arrow.

Killer says, "Man, I wouldn't want to be in that unit. I don't even know how to shoot a bow."

Eckert says, "I shot a bow once with a thirty pound test, and it cut my arm when the string hit it!"

To my surprise Henning was just listening. I said, "Yeah, I had an archery class in high school and the string kept popping my arm too. That hurts a lot. Henning, don't you have a bow?"

"Yes, I have three, but the one I like the best is my fifty-five pound sixty-four inch re-curve!"

Emery responds, "That's a lot of pounds. Is it hard to pull back?"

Henning answers, "Oh, man, it was at first. The first time that I shot it, I pulled the skin right off my arm!"

"You mean from the string?"

"Yeah. I had to wear an arm protector for a while!"

The men and Henning talked about wood bows, fiberglass bows, arrows, and arrow lengths. They even talked about what makes a good feather on an arrow. They talked for an hour. Henning had an honest answer for every question. Henning was making friends without lying. My guys were giving him some slack. It was time for chow. The men headed for the chow hall. Chuck and I stayed, behind discussing the men.

Henning came up to us. "Sergeant Rock, thanks. I will try to keep my exaggerations down."

I looked at Henning and shook my head. "No, no, no, no. You stop lying altogether. As a matter of fact, you tell the guys that you were sorry about your exaggeration about the horses and the two Corvettes. That is the only way you will get respect from the guys."

"I'll do it, Sarge. Thanks again."

We hear the chopper coming in. Chuck says, "That could be our new lieutenant!"

"Yep, let's go see."

Chuck and I walk toward the LZ, past the captain's CP. The captain says, "Hi, Rock, hi, Lewis!"

"How ya doing, sir?"

"Good. Your platoon leader is on the chopper. Bring him to me, will you?"

"Yes, sir."

A tall officer jumped off of the chopper with his rucksack and his M-16 rifle. He saw Chuck and me and came up to us. This officer was very observant, for he noticed our drawn-on sergeant stripes. We would take a felt pen and draw our sergeant stripes on our sleeves. "Sergeants, would you direct me to your captain's CP?"

"Yes, sir, we will take you there. I am Sergeant Rodgers and this is Sergeant Lewis. I think that you will be our platoon leader!"

"Really? My name is Stephen Watkins, Lieutenant Watkins."

He held out his hand for a handshake. We shook hands and walked to the CP. The captain shook hands with the lieutenant. "Have you met Sergeant Lewis and Sergeant Rock?"

Watkins looks around. "No, sir, I just met Lewis and Rodgers!"

"Sergeant Rodgers is Sergeant Rock!"

"Yes, sir, I met them both."

"You will be in their platoon, or I mean you will be the platoon leader!"

"So Sergeant Lewis and Sergeant Rock are squad leaders?"

"Yes, and if you want to stay alive, you will listen to them!"

Watkins looked at Chuck and me. "Yes, sir. I will. I'll really pay attention to what they have to say."

The captain says, "Rock and Lewis, you guys gather up all of the men in the platoon. I want to speak to the lieutenant first, before he meets the men."

"Yes, sir!"

Chuck and I take off. The old man starts speaking to Watkins. "Our company has been through a lot. We have lost a lot of men. The platoon that you will be in charge of has a lot of kills. Sergeant Rock's squad, by themselves, has more kills than the rest of the company!"

"Why do you think that is, sir?"

"Rock has his men thinking all of the time. He has them working as a team. They want the body counts. No one over here wants to pull point. Sergeant Rock's men thrive on pulling point. Rock pulls point sometimes himself!"

340

"Really, Captain? Is this the company that cuts heads off of the VC and NVA and never takes a prisoner?"

"Lieutenant, this is the company. But much has been exaggerated. We are the company with the great number of body counts, and I plan to keep it that way. So go and meet your platoon and pay attention!"

"Yes, sir!"

Watkins heads for his new platoon. Chuck and I have gathered up the men. "Hey, Chuck, do you think Watkins will be as bad as Gibbons was when he first got here?"

"No way. I liked Gibbons, but he was terrible when he first arrived!"

Eckert says, "I see him coming! Oh, boy, another new recruit we have to train!"

Killer says, "He will probably start spouting his mouth off, giving us orders right away!"

Watkins gets closer to us. "Men, my name is Stephen Watkins. I am a lieutenant. I have not commanded in combat before. I will learn more from you men then you will ever learn from me. You give me respect and I will give it in return."

The men said, "Yes, sir!"

Watkins went on to say, "Before too long I will know your names and a little bit about you. We will be leaving in the morning, heading north. Let me ask you something. Who is the most likely man to take my place if I get shot?"

Killer responds, "Either Sergeant Rock or Lewis."

"Yes, sir, either one of them could take over," Eckert said.

"OK, men, I hope to be a good leader, but it will take me awhile. I will pay attention. Now I want to talk to the squad that they call 'the Killer Squad.'"

Sergeant Mac, another squad leader, says, "That would be Rock's squad, but we are just a few behind him!"

White responds quickly, "Sergeant Mac, you guys are twenty body counts behind us, according to the last count!" White has a big grin on his face.

Mac says, "Maybe so, but we are gaining on ya. See ya, Rock. Good to meet you, sir. I think you will be a good leader."

Killer makes a last comment before Mac leaves. "Brown noser!"

Everyone laughs, even the new lieutenant.

The lieutenant speaks. "Killer Squad, sit down. Let's talk! OK, men, what are your names? I'll find out where you are from later."

The men started introducing themselves. "Emery."

"Emerald."

"White."

"Eckert."

"Allen."

"Henning."

"Killer."

"Raymond."

"Why do they call you Killer, Killer?"

I did not want Killer to speak too much, so I said, "I'll answer that! Killer cut off a VC's head after being in country for two weeks!"

I didn't want to tell the lieutenant about the dull bayonet.

"You cut off a head. Was he dead?"

Killer answered, "Sort of. I had to do it because he was giving our position away."

I wanted to change the subject. "White is our demolitions guy and tunnel rat."

"So you like to blow things up, huh, White?"

"Yes, sir, I love it!"

"How many of you guys like to pull point?"

Everyone said they did, except for Emerald.

"Emerald, you don't like pulling point?"

"Not so much, sir! I like the body counts, but I prefer to not pull point. But I will do it when it is my turn."

"OK, guys, take off for a while, except for Lewis and Rock."

The guys did as the lieutenant directed them. The lieutenant turned to Chuck and me. "What's up with Emerald? Everyone else is gung-ho. He seems to be more reserved."

I answer, "We have to push Emerald a lot. He is much better than he used to be."

"Sergeant Rock, can I keep Sergeant Lewis with me for a while as my RTO, if it is OK with him? What do you say, Lewis?"

Chuck replies, "Sir, if it is OK with Rock, I'll do it for a while. But I am an E-5 sergeant, not a Spec-five."

"You can keep your stripes. I only want help in leading this platoon. What do you say, Rock?"

Reluctantly I said, "OK, sir, I think that we will continue to have a great platoon. I can see that you will listen and learn."

"You bet I will. I don't want to get anyone killed and I don't want to be killed. Thanks to both of you. Lewis, do we have a CP?"

"Yes we do. I'll take you there now. See ya, Danny."

"See you guys later, Chuck. Later, sir."

"Bye, Sergeant Rock!"

I motioned for my men to return. "Hey, guys, I think Watkins is going to be just fine."

Killer says, "Will he listen?"

"Yep!"

Emery asks, "Do you really think that he will actually, actually listen to you?"

"We will find out tomorrow because we are heading out back in the bush."

Eckert comments, "I remember how much of a hard time we had with Lieutenant Gibbons. Do you remember when he busted you, Sergeant Rock?"

"Yes I do, Eckert. Thanks for reminding me, you joker!"

Emerald says, "Man, Sarge, when you were busted and refused to call in artillery, I was afraid. I wanted you to call in artillery so bad I could taste it. I was really scared. Are you going to refuse to call in firepower again?"

"Not unless Watkins busts me to private!"

All of us started to laugh very hard. We were still laughing when the new lieutenant and Chuck walked up. The lieutenant gets a grin on his face. "Are you guys laughing at me, Sergeant Rock?"

"Oh, no, sir, not at all. We were talking about the time that our old lieutenant busted me down to private and I refused to call in artillery until he made me a sergeant again!"

With a big grin and a chuckle he says, "He busted you to private? Why?"

Killer interrupts, "Because Gibbons knew nothing, and he wouldn't listen. Gibbons was going to get us killed!"

Eckert says, "And another thing, the captain called on Rock directly and Gibbons didn't like it."

White started laughing. "Sir, here is the whole story!"

White went on to tell the complete story, adding in a few of his own opinions about Lieutenant Gibbons.

Watkins says, "Man, that is a cool story, and I'll tell you what, Sergeant Rock. I won't bust you down to private unless you shoot at me!"

We started rolling on the ground with laughter. We could not stop laughing. Everyone was making comments that made us laugh even harder.

The lieutenant was also laughing hard. He was one of the guys now. We would protect him at all costs. He was going to be alright. Our laughter started to slow when the lieutenant asked, "What can I expect men? I mean, what can I expect for a daily routine?"

Eckert replied, "Sometimes we will fight for two weeks straight, night and day, but sometimes we will go for three days with no one shooting at us!"

Killer remarks, "You will see plenty of your friends die. You will see many other soldiers dead. We even watched the NVA burn our men to death with flamethrowers!"

Emerald speaks up, "We also went fifty-seven days without fresh clothes or good water when the supply depots were blown up!"

Watkins's eyes are wide open. "Wow, men. We don't hear all of that in the States!"

I look at the lieutenant. "Did you hear about our company on January ninth, sir?"

"Sort of. Didn't ya lose a lot of men?"

"Yes, sir! At eight o'clock, we had 143 men, and by ten o'clock, we only had seventeen. Some came in during the night, but it was only a handful. I get sick even thinking about it."

"I'll bet you guys, I mean your minds, will never be the same, huh, Rock?"

"Yes, sir. We will never forget what we have already been through."

"Now, let's talk about day-to-day stuff, starting tonight."

"OK. During a regular night away from this hill, we will dig a foxhole and pull guard after we set up a circular perimeter."

Killer adds, "And if it rains, we will get leeches. They will get in your hair, in your ears, and even in existing wounds. Just ask Sergeant Rock!"

Watkins says, "Is that right, Sergeant Rock?"

"Yes, sir. You cannot even feel them until they get heavy from sucking your blood. One got into a small wound I had the other day. I didn't even know he was there."

"How often does it rain?"

Emery responds, "Parts of the year, it rains day and night. We are never dry!"

The lieutenant looks at Allen and Henning. "How come you two are not saying much?"

Allen says, "We are from Delta Company; they don't have enough men yet to rebuild."

"Were you guys around when the NVA torched your company?"

"No, sir, we were not. Thank God. And I really mean it, thank God!"

Henning says, "Sir, we will also get mosquitoes every day and night, so keep plenty of insect repellent in your helmet band!"

The lieutenant stood up. "Well, thanks, men. I think we are going to have a great platoon! I'll see you guys later. I am going to visit with the other squads, and then I'll go see the old man."

The lieutenant walks away. My squad starts talking about how much they like this new lieutenant. I lean over and tell Chuck, "This guy is going to be great. I like him. He could be the finest officer that I have ever met."

Chuck says, "I agree. I hope he learns fast. I think that he will, though, don't you?"

"Yep!"

I look at my men. "So what do you guys think?"

Their comments were all favorable.

"OK, men, we will be leaving this hill in the morning, so go and get plenty of ammo. Get your canteens filled today and load up on C-rations!"

Chuck stands up. "I better get to the CP. I'll tell Watkins that you will have your guys set up and ready to go in the morning."

"Thanks, Chuck. We will see ya tomorrow."

Morning came and my squad was the first squad to be up. We had already gone to the mess hall and started eating before the other platoons and squads woke up. I finished eating a hot meal and walked out of the mess tent.

I saw the lieutenant and Chuck walking into the mess hall. The lieutenant sees me and motions that I come to him. "Rock, I want to meet with you right after mess, OK?"

"Yes, sir!"

"By the way, Sergeant Rock, Lewis says that you wouldn't mind if I call you Rock instead of Sergeant Rock!"

"No, sir, I don't mind...as long as I can call you Stephen."

Of course I was just joking. We all start to laugh.

The lieutenant says, "OK, but only when the other men are not around."

We laugh again.

I gather the men. "Men, we are going to move out soon. I want each of you to clean your weapon! I am going to see the old man."

I moved quickly to the captain's CP.

The captain was packing his backpack. "How do you like your new platoon leader, Rock?"

"Great, sir. He listens. He is going to be a great one. Where are we going, sir?"

"Guess."

"Not north again?"

"Yep."

I shake my head. "If we keep this up, we will be at the DMZ."

"Yep, that's the plan. Take out your map and I'll show you."

The captain and I went over our plan and the route we would be taking for the next three days. I returned to find the lieutenant speaking to my men. "You wanted to speak to me, sir?"

"Yes. The old man says to go over everything with you concerning the map." He pulls out and unfolds his map.

I look at his map. "OK, sir, show me where you think we are right now."

He points his finger at the marking on the map. "Right here at 348."

"Right, and did the captain tell you where we were going?"

"Yes, he told me, but did not show me on the map."

"Sir, show me where we are going."

To my surprise, he knew exactly the location we were heading.

"Good job, sir, very good! Now, we will be going in and out of the bush, you know, the jungle, so every time that we come out of the jungle get a bearing, such as a mountain, a hill, a river, or something like that. And keep your compass ready. Did the captain tell you that we would probably be in another firefight tomorrow or the next day?"

"Yes he did, Sarge. Would you mind getting us started, so I can do it right the next time?"

"Sure, I will."

I looked at my men. "Hey, guys, do we want point?"

Eckert says, "Does a bear have hair? Let's get it!"

I turn to Watkins. "Sir, now you call in and tell the captain that we want point. He will be happy to give it to us, because no one wants point except my squad or Mac's squad."

"OK."

The lieutenant gets on the radio. "Annihilator Three-Three, this is Cherokee Three, we are ready to move out. Over."

"This is Annihilator Three-Three, I want Cherokee Three and Blackhawk Three to come to my CP!"

The lieutenant turns to me. "What's up, Rock?"

"I don't know, sir, but we better get up there!"

As Watkins and I turn toward the captain's CP, we hear the sound of a chopper coming in. We arrive at the captain's CP. I see that the old man is looking at the chopper. "What's up, sir?"

"Your buddy, Steven, and the camera crew are coming back. When they get here, you explain the ropes to them!"

I laugh. "What do ya mean, *my* buddy? Steven told me that he would make you famous, sir!"

"He will make me famous, alright, but we will probably all be dead trying to protect his butt!"

"I will tell him to keep his guys away from your CP. But sir, I thought the camera crew was already here?"

"They went back to get resupplied!"

The lieutenant is puzzled. "A camera crew is going to be with us, Sergeant Rock?"

"Yeah, but after a week or so of fighting, they will probably leave!"

The captain says, "OK, Rock, the chopper has landed. Bring the camera crew to me!"

"Yes, sir!"

I head out for the LZ. Steven and crew are unloading. They are now wearing fatigues, combat boots, and a few of them are carrying .45 pistols. They even have helmets. "Hi, Steven! Man, you guys and the girl look like soldiers now. Do you have C-rations?"

"Yeah, we are ready!"

I pointed at his weapon. "Do you know how to shoot that thing?"

"No, not really!"

We laugh.

"OK, let's go to the CP!"

We arrive at the CP. The captain starts to set out the filming crew's rules. "Steven, you keep your crew toward the rear of Lieutenant Watkins's platoon! You need to get camouflage on your cameras, and be careful of your camera lenses, because they will show a reflection in the sunlight and give away our position! Your crew can get as close to the action as you want, but only if the lieutenant or Sergeant Rock lets you. Do you understand my rules?"

"Yes, sir!"

The captain says, "OK, Lieutenant Watkins, you have five minutes before we move out! Set up your rules for the camera crew, and then move out. You guys have point!"

"Yes, sir! Let's get back to the platoon, men."

We took these newbies to the rest of the men. My guys saw the pretty girl and stared in awe. Killer says, "I was wondering when I was going to get a new comforter for my bed roll."

The lieutenant looks at the men. "None of that, guys! Rock, what rules should we give them?"

"I think that the only rules would be for them to be quiet while we are humping, and to stay down in a firefight!"

"Did you guys hear that, Steven?"

"Yes, sir!"

"Alright, Steven, take your crew to the rear of the fourth squad. Sergeant Rock's guys have point. Are you ready, Rock?"

"Ready, sir. Men, who wants point?"

I knew that the lieutenant would love the reaction of my men!

"I want point!" Killer says.

Eckert responds, "I want it!"

Now we hear from White. "No, no, no, it is my turn!"

The lieutenant is shaking his head from side to side. "I can't believe it. No wonder you guys get so many kills. Your guys are hungry, Rock!"

I look at my men. "I would put my men up against any men in Vietnam. They are great. OK, White, you have point. Let's get it!"

Watkins is on the radio. "Annihilator Three-Three, we are ready to move out! Over."

The reply comes. "Move out and good luck!"

The lieutenant looks at me. "Now what, Rock?"

"You now tell the other squads the order of travel. Do you want me to show you this time? It is easy."

"Yes!"

I get on the horn. "Blackhawk Four, you follow Blackhawk Three. Blackhawk Two, you follow Blackhawk Four. Blackhawk One, you bring up the rear. The camera crew will follow you, out!" I turn to Watkins. "From now on, sir, try to set up the order ahead of time so the captain does not hear us on the radio!"

Chuck looks at Watkins. "I'll help you, sir!"

The company moved out with my squad pulling point. We travel for a little more than an hour before we get fired upon by two snipers.

We hit the ground and start firing. White runs back to me. "I saw where they were firing from!"

"Cool. Is it too far for the 60?"

"No, that would be perfect!"

I turn to Raymond. "Raymond, follow White and go get 'em!"

Raymond and Allen jump up and move to the front very quickly. Raymond has the gun and Allen has the ammo. Raymond yells, "We will get 'em, Sarge!"

"I know that you will!"

The lieutenant is now next to me. "What's happening?"

"Just a few snipers. Raymond will get them. You need to call the captain and tell him we have it under control."

The lieutenant calls the captain, then asks me, "What do we do now, Rock?"

"We keep moving until we get shot at again, but there is something that I need to warn you about."

"What is that, Rock?"

"The VC and the NVA sometimes will snipe at us just to find out how much firepower we have, then they will hit us again later."

"So why don't we just call in artillery?"

"A couple of reasons. Two snipers ain't jack, and if we called in artillery, it may scare maybe a dozen or more NVA or VC away. Our job is to find them and kill them, not scare them away."

"Makes sense to me."

The lieutenant was learning quickly. War is sort of like baseball. You may know how to hit and catch, but if you don't know the ins and outs of the game you will never win. In baseball, you need to know what pitch to steal on. With a three and zero count, what will the pitcher throw you? There is a lot more to baseball then catching, throwing, and hitting.

I hear the M-60 firing. Then, after a hundred or so rounds, it stops. Raymond comes back. "It is done. We got both of them!"

The lieutenant stands up. "Way to go, Raymond!"

Allen says, "You should have seen Raymond! He was great! Man, he knows how to handle the Pig!"

Allen pats Raymond on the back. The lieutenant turns to me. "I should tell the captain we got them, huh?"

"Yep, he will love two more body count! I am going to tell the guys to move out again, sir."

"Alright, do it."

We traveled another hour before the crap hits the fan. We hit the ground. Machine guns, AK-47s, and grenades were firing at us. The firing was coming from an opening to the right of the path that we were traveling on. This was not a few snipers; this was serious.

The firing was being directed directly toward our platoon. This was an ambush, and we walked right into it. This was going to be hard to get out of. The lieutenant comes crawling up next to me. "This is more than snipers, huh, Rock?"

"Yes it is, sir. Let me take charge for now with your permission!"

"You got it!"

"We have to get as much firepower going in their direction as they are putting on us!"

I look at my RTO. "Craig, hand me the horn! Blackhawk One, on my go, you guys hit them from the right flank! Blackhawk Four, you guys hit them from the left flank! Blackhawk Two, you help on the right flank. We are going to charge up the middle. Don't do anything until I give the go, but get in position now!"

Raymond is up next to me. I look at Raymond and Allen. "We are going up closer to see if they are buried in. Sir, you tell the old man what we are doing!"

I look at my men. "All of you stay low and follow me."

We stay low, crawling through the mud until we get to a small berm before the opening. I see a machine gun nest with a very small opening in it. The gun is blazing away. There are two men throwing grenades on either side of the bunker. There are two NVA lying on the ground, pumping lead at us from their AK-47 rifles. It seems like there are a few more NVA firing at us, but I cannot see their exact location. *Is this going to be the day we die?* We must wipe them out quickly, before they kill someone in our company.

I get back on the radio. "My squad is going to rush them! We don't want to be killed, so keep them pinned down! Right flank, open up!"

I look over the berm, and the NVA are directing their fire toward their left. I get back on the horn. "Left flank, open up! Right flank, keep firing!"

Our left flank opens up. The enemy start firing to their right. They are now firing to the left and the right. I take my M-79 grenade launcher and start firing round after round. Killer asks, "Now, Sarge?"

"No, not yet! Raymond, hit 'em with the 60!"

Raymond opens up! I yell to my men, "Now fire! Fire! Fire!"

The gooks are firing like mad left, right, and forward. My guys are lying down, firing round after round! There is so much smoke and gun powder, it is hard to see the machine gun nest. I see an opening between the smoke and fire another round at the bunker. The round hits the opening in the bunker.

For a moment, the machine gun stops, but then it starts up again. I hit Raymond on the back. "Keep firing at the machine gun! You are better than he is! Now prove it!"

Watkins hits me on the shoulder. "When are we going to charge?"

I answer, "Right now! Men, get up and start moving forward!"

I jump to my feet and the men do the same. We get on line and start firing like it is a mad minute. We move forward, zeroing in on the machine gun. I yell, "Keep the gunner pinned down! Don't let up!"

Although I am still worried about being shot myself, I take a moment to see if anyone else is shot. I look at my men, and they are dead serious about taking this position. I look to my right and I see the lieutenant and Chuck firing magazine after magazine. Raymond is standing with the M-60 machine gun. Allen, while feeding the ammo to Raymond, is still shooting his M-16. Eckert, White, Emery, Emerald, Killer, and Henning are steadily firing.

I am firing round after round from my grenade launcher. I reach for another round to load, but something is wrong.

My arm is burning. I cannot reach the new round. My arm is bleeding. My muscle is not responding. My adrenaline starts to kick in. I try to load my weapon, but my arm is moving slow.

The burning slows and my arm starts working again. I am hurting, but I am able to reload my M-79. I cannot stop firing now, for we need the firepower. I keep firing and reloading. Another of my rounds lands directly in the machine gun nest. The machine gun falls silent, but we can still see movement in the bunker.

Killer yells, "I'll get 'em!"

He charges the bunker and sticks his rifle into the opening. He turns the rifle quickly and swiftly from side to side, firing off a complete magazine!

Eckert runs up to the front of the bunker and throws a grenade into the bunker opening. The explosion makes fire come through the hole in the bunker. We hear screams coming from the bunker. Eckert says, "I guess they won't kill anyone today!"

White says, "This bunker may be open at the top!"

He grabs a grenade and throws it over the top of the bunker. I hear the explosion. White throws another grenade. I hear another loud sound and an explosion. White lifts his head up. "That one was just in case they were still breathing!"

The men are jubilant. They were triumphant again, and as far as they knew, none of our men were hurt. The men are jumping up and down.

I say, "OK, men, make sure that you police up the weapons and check out the bodies! Give me a body count!"

The lieutenant is shaking his head. "Man, Rock, that was exciting. Do you guys do that a lot?"

"No, not really! We try not to charge the enemy, but this time we couldn't call in artillery because they were too close to us!"

Watkins sees the blood flowing from my arm. "Rock, you have been shot!"

"Yeah, I guess so, but it doesn't feel like it broke any bones! Sir, you better tell the captain that we killed them, but hang on a second!"

I turn to Killer as he comes from the top of the bunker. "How many, Killer?"

"Eight, Sarge. We killed eight!"

The men started rejoicing again.

"Sir, tell the captain eight."

Killer sees my arm. "Are you shot, Sarge?"

"I think it may be shrapnel!"

"Let me see!"

Killer twists my arm slightly. "Does that hurt when I do that?"

"What do you think, you idiot?"

I jerked my arm back and grabbed it. I was only messing with Killer, because it did not hurt as bad as I pretended when he twisted it.

"No, Killer, it does not hurt that much! I think it is shrapnel, not a bullet."

"I'll go get Doc!"

The lieutenant was off of the radio after speaking to the captain. "I told the old man that you were shot. He is on his way over here."

Doc arrived. "Let me look at it, Sarge."

He takes a bottle of alcohol from his bag. "Now I am going to pour this on your arm to clean up everything, so I can see what's going on."

"Alright."

The captain arrived. "Hey, Rock, you guys did a great job! Now what is wrong with you?"

"Doc is checking it out now."

The captain gets closer to my arm for a better look. "What is it Doc, a bullet or shrapnel?"

"It looks like two pieces of shrapnel, sir. I am going to have to pull them out right now, or he will get gangrene. They are deep."

"Can we just send him to the rear?"

"I don't know! It would probably be alright, but I know that infection will set in quickly."

The captain says, "Well, Rock, it looks like you have a Purple Heart."

I am a little shocked. I never thought that I would receive a Purple Heart medal. "Sir, I thought that you had to be near death to receive a Purple Heart?"

"No, you just have to be in combat and get hit by enemy fire, and that is exactly what you did. I will put you in for a Purple Heart today. Actually, all of your squad should be awarded Bronze Stars!"

The captain continues, "Well, Rock, it is up to you. Do you want to go to the rear and see a doctor with antiseptics so your pain will be less, or have our Doc yank the shrapnel out right now?"

Killer says, "Oh, give him an aspirin and see him in the morning. He will be OK."

I laugh. "No, sir, just let Doc pull it out, and I know that Doc won't yank it out. You won't, will you, Doc?"

"No, I won't. Do we need to hold you down? Because it is really going to hurt. I sure wish we had some whisky!"

"I don't drink, Doc."

"No, it is not for you. It would be for me because I am nervous."

I laughed.

Doc continues, "The metal is in the muscle near the bone. Your arm is really swelling up now. I better move fast."

The Doc started digging. I was starting to feel pain. It was like having a root canal when the dentist hits a nerve. He would hit a piece of the shrapnel with his forceps, and it would shoot pain through my body, all the way to my toes. This was really hurting now, but I could not let my guys know how badly.

"Can you wait just a minute, Doc? I just want to catch my breath."

"Yes, but I am almost there."

After thirty seconds or so I say, "OK, Doc, go ahead."

Doc pulls out a small scalpel. "I have to open the wound up a little, so I have room to work."

"Man, Doc, alright, do it!"

The pain was excruciating when he made the first cut into my flesh. My fingers were now swelling up. Beads of sweat were popping from my forehead. I was feeling sick to my stomach. I am now wishing that I would have gone to the rear and had a surgeon pull the shrapnel out.

Doc says, "I have a hold on one of them!"

He gently pulls it out. It is a piece of metal three-quarters of an inch long. "Now I need to get the next one, Danny."

"OK, Doc, you are doing just fine. Doc, I need to throw up."

"No, just take some deep breaths!"

I took some breaths. "OK, go!"

The Doc digs in again. Emerald starts to vomit, and the other guys start to laugh at him.

Raymond says, "Just stop watching if you are going to get sick!"

I look at the men. "You guys leave him alone!"

My pain is still intense, but it is not getting worse. I feel a slight pull in my arm. The Doc has removed the second piece of shrapnel. I immediately feel better.

The captain says, "Good job, Doc. I am going back to the CP. Tell me when we can move out! Are you OK, Rock?"

"Yes, sir, thank you!"

Doc starts looking in his bag. "I am going to pour more alcohol on it and gauze and bandage it. This will hurt a little bit." He pours the alcohol on my open wound. It only slightly stings.

Doc holds up the piece of shrapnel. It is about the same size as the other one. "Can I hang onto these for a while?"

"Yeah, but why? I want them back before you leave."

"OK. I want them because I am keeping the bullets and shrapnel that I pull out of the guys I save. I have twenty-seven bullets and a lot of metal."

"Thanks again, Doc. You are the *man!*"

"I'll see ya later, Danny!"

Watkins is checking his ammo. "Man, guys, my adrenaline was flowing so much. That was great!"

Killer replies, "Yep, mine was too, sir! It was great, huh?"

"Yes, yes, yes. I could not believe how you guys worked together to take out the bunker!"

I counter, "Yes, sir, but if the rest of the platoon had not kept firing from the flanks, we would have been killed. You have inherited a great platoon, sir!"

"Yes I have, Rock. You guys are the greatest, and we got eight body count! But Rock, you have a chance to get out of the field. Why don't you go to the rear?"

"It isn't because I want to be a hero or anything like that. It is because I worry all of the time about the men. There will be a time when I will go on another R&R, but not now."

The lieutenant just nods his head.

The camera and news crew is running up to us. Steven says, "Tell me all about it, Sergeant Rock!"

"Where were you guys during the action, Steven?"

"We were hiding! No, not really; we were trying to get in camera position, but it was too confining."

He sees my bandages. "Are you shot?"

"No, just some small shrapnel."

I told Steve about the event. He was amazed that we had not been killed.

The lieutenant says, "Don't be amazed, because it was well orchestrated. Sergeant Rock and the men knew exactly what they were doing! Steven, take your crew to the rear again!"

"Yes, sir!"

Steven and the crew took off. When the camera crew was out of hearing distance, the lieutenant speaks, "Rock, you and your squad are the bravest men I have ever seen."

"Well, thank you sir, but I'll tell you something! This is called a squad leaders' war, but to me, it is a squad and platoon leader war. We only did what we had to do to stay alive. I was very afraid."

"Yeah, but charging a bunker like that. You guys didn't even hesitate."

"All I can tell you is this: good people working together make good things happen. But remember this, sir. I was scared, but I tried not to let my men know it."

CHAPTER 18

Black Guys Can Fight

The captain gets on the radio. "Good job, men. We have another eight, so that is ten for the day!" The captain, as always, was talking about body count.

The lieutenant says, "I guess the old man is happy about the count."

"Yes, he is. He always gets happy when we don't lose men and we nail a few gooks."

Chuck, now the lieutenant's RTO, says, "Rock and sir, the captain wants to see you two."

I say to Watkins, "I wonder what he wants, Stephen."

The lieutenant grins.

"I am just kidding, sir. But I do wonder what the captain wants with us, sir."

"Yeah, me too, Rock."

When we arrived at the captain's CP, we noticed that he was speaking to the higher ups. I asked his RTO to whom he was speaking.

The RTO says, "He is talking to majors and generals. They say that there is an underground hospital right here in the area!"

The captain says, "Roger, out! Hey, Rock, do you still have your tunnel rat in your squad?"

"Yes, sir, it is White!"

"There is supposed to be an underground hospital close to this area, so let's find it!"

"You know what, sir?"

"What?"

"I think that it would be right under the bunker where the machine gun nest was, or close to it. The NVA and VC were fighting very hard. I would bet they were fighting so hard because they wanted time to get others out of the hospital. I suggest that we start looking for tunnels right where our little battle took place."

The captain thinks for a moment. "You may be right. Let's check it out."

"Yes, sir, we will get to it!"

I turned to the lieutenant. "Is that alright with you, sir?"

"Whatever you say, Rock!"

"Let's go and get our tunnel rat, White!"

"Does he really like going in tunnels?"

"Yes, sir, he is crazy! I get claustrophobic in tight spaces, and besides, if a Charlie is in the tunnel, he will probably kill the tunnel rat."

"I guess some guys love the adrenaline, huh?"

"Yep! White and Killer are adrenaline addicts."

"I think that you are an adrenaline addict too, Rock."

"Yeah, maybe, but not as bad as those two. And how about Raymond? He is just bad to the bone with the M-60!"

"He is, isn't he?"

The guys are waiting on my instructions. "Men, we are going to search for tunnels. When you find one, let me know so we can send the rat down it!"

I turned to Watkins. "I don't like this part because sometimes we will find a tunnel, or just a hole in the ground, and it will be hidden with a camouflaged top. The top will just slide over, then when the gook gets back in the hole, he pulls the cover back over the hole."

"I don't think that I will like this part either."

I say to White, "You take charge of the tunnel ratting, huh?"

"Yes, Sergeant!"

Killer is the first to find a hole, but it is just that, a hole. White checks it out anyhow. He pulls the cover back very slowly, watching out for booby traps. "Nothing in this hole, Sarge!"

Henning is moving very slowly, slightly poking the ground with his rifle butt. "Here is another one, White!"

"OK, I'll be right there!"

The tunnel rat checks out another hole with the same results.

Raymond excitedly says, "Here, here, over here! This is something for sure!"

White runs to the opening. I can tell by his excitement that he has found something good.

White is taking off his rucksack. "This is the one, Sarge. I am going in. I wish that I had a .45."

"Do you want me to get the captain's?"

"Nah, that would take too long."

"Wait a minute, White. I'll grab the camera guy's pistol!"

"That would be good!"

I ran over to Steven. "Steven, we need your gun!"

Steven immediately goes for his .45. "What's up, Sarge? Can we film? Can we get closer?"

"Yes, follow me, but stay back!"

We take off toward White. "Here you go, White!"

I threw him the weapon. "Don't forget to take a few grenades and come right back out!"

"OK, I'm going in!"

I motion for Raymond to keep his eyes open. Raymond gives me a thumbs up. I tell the men to keep their eyes and ears open.

The men are still searching and watching. We see two VC running. They jump behind a berm and start firing at us. Raymond jumps to his feet with the Pig and starts firing. He is shooting burst after burst, relentlessly. He charges the Charlies, showering a hail of bullets, uncompromisingly. I fire a grenade, but it looks like I am too late. The VC are dead.

Raymond is standing over the berm and the gooks. I nudge the lieutenant. "Now watch this!"

Raymond opens up his M-60 with a burst of about thirty rounds into the body of the enemy.

"Does he always do that, Rock?"

"Yes, sir. He knows that they are dead, but he takes no chances."

White sticks his head out of the tunnel. "What the heck was that all about, Sarge?"

"Just a few VC. We are OK!"

"Come up here, Sarge and sir, and look at this!"

He is holding up a 50-caliber machine gun. We run up to the opening.

"Man, White, where did you get that?"

"There is a whole room full of guns and ammo. Send Eckert and Killer down here to help me pull 'em out!"

"OK!"

I turn to Killer and Eckert, who are already running toward White. "You two jump in the hole and see what White has found!"

White sticks his head back out of the tunnel hole. "Eckert, bring my 16 with ya!"

I turn to tell the lieutenant to let the captain know what is going on. He has already told the old man about the two more body count and the cache that we have found.

The lieutenant is looking perplexed. "Is this a good find for us, Rock?"

"Oh, yeah, but it depends on how much more we find!"

I point to the entry of the cache. "Look there, sir." Eckert is pulling out ammo cans, AK-47s, radios, phones (land lines), and grenades.

"Yes, sir, this is a good find. Don't radio this to the captain because it may give our position away if any gooks are listening. Tell him in person."

Killer jumps out of the hole. "Rock, Rock, White found another room. He wants you to come and look at it!"

Hesitantly I say, "Alright, but I don't like crawling in tight spaces."

The lieutenant says, "When I get back, I will get in there with you, Sarge!"

"Sounds good!"

I climbed into the tight hole. My shoulders were hitting either side of the opening, but once I went down four feet or so, the tunnel started to open up where we could walk stooped over. Another ten feet of walking, and we entered a large cache room.

White says, "This was where we found the guns and stuff, but now look in that room."

I walked toward another small opening. "In here?"

"Yes, look through the opening!"

I looked through the small opening and saw a very large room.

"Follow me, Sarge!" White immediately crawls through the tunnel to the room. Reluctantly, I follow him through the tunnel. The tunnel is tight again, but after six feet, I end up in a very large room.

The room is about 800 square feet, or the size of a four-car garage. The room is lit with candles that are still burning. Somehow there is light coming in from above. This is daylight coming from the sun.

I hear a commotion. It is the lieutenant. "Wow, what is this, Rock?"

I look to the right and there is a stainless steel gurney with dried blood on it. I look to my left and I see a table with gauze, bandages, and various surgical instruments. I say to White and the lieutenant, "This is a hospital, and it has been used recently. Do you guys see the light coming in from above?"

"Yeah."

"Well, that would be a perfect place for Charlie to drop a grenade on us. Let's get out of here. Take the instruments, White!"

We head for the tunnel. We pull our way back to the other room. Eckert and Killer are still in the cache room.

"Let's get out of here, men!"

We scrambled out of the small tunnel. I was glad to be above ground again.

The lieutenant asks, "Rock, should we blow it up?"

"Oh, yeah, of course! White, you blow it up!"

"I am going to use a claymore, maybe two!"

"OK, do what it takes!"

White and Killer start rolling out the cord for the claymore.

Watkins touches me on the shoulder. "Do you mean a claymore mine?"

"Yes, sir!"

"Do you think that it will collapse the hospital?"

"Oh, no, it will just mess up the openings. Do you want to get in good with the captain, sir?"

"Sure, but how?"

"Write down the grid coordinates where we are right now and suggest to the captain that we call in artillery when we leave the area. This way, we would be sure we were going to destroy the hospital."

The lieutenant takes off for the captain's CP when he hears the blast from the claymore. The lieutenant jumps. He looks back and grins.

I hear a voice behind me. It is Allen. "Hey, Allen, what do you think about all of this?"

"Are you guys just crazy or what?"

"What do you mean?"

"I am only joking about you guys being crazy, but I was scared a little."

"Just a little?"

"No, actually a lot!"

"Allen, we will be here a few more minutes, so tell me something about yourself! What did you do in the States?"

"I was going to college, and I was in a band. What kind of music do ya like, Sarge?"

"I like rock 'n' roll, fifties and sixties."

"What groups do you like?"

"Oh, man, a lot. I like the Mamas and the Papas, the Beatles, Buddy Holly, Elvis, Beach Boys, Jan and Dean, Janis Joplin, Big Brother and the Holding Company, the Animals, Rolling Stones, and a lot more."

"Yeah, me too. I like all of them."

"Do you know a lot about the lyrics of the songs?"

"Yeah, pretty much. Why?"

"Well, there is a song that the Mamas and the Papas sing, and by the way, Michelle Phillips is hot!"

"Yeah, she is, isn't she?"

"Anyhow, the song says something like 'McQuinn and McGuire trying to get a hire, down in L.A., you know where that's at?' Then it says, 'In a coffee house, Sebastian sat; after every number they would pass the hat. No one's getting fat except Mama Cass. What is the meaning of all of that?' I like the song!"

"The song is called 'Creeque Alley.'"

"'Creek Alley'?"

"Yeah, it is spelled C-R-E-E-Q-U-E. 'Creeque Alley.' Basically, the song is about how the Mamas and the Papas got started. Mama Cass, I think her real name was Cass Elliot. Anyhow, the song says 'Zal and Denny working for a penny, trying to get a fish on the line.' Denny is Denny Doherty. He joined up with John Phillips. The first verse of the song says, 'John and Mitchy were getting kind of itchy.' John is John Phillips, the writer of the group. Denny convinced Cass to join the group."

"That's cool, but when did Michelle join?"

"I think that she and John were the two original members. You know where the song says, 'John and Mitchy'? I think that Mitchy is Michelle. I also think that Zal and Sebastian formed the Lovin' Spoonful!"

"Thanks. Now I can enjoy the song even more! Hey, Allen, do you think that even one of these guys gives a flying flip about all of the stuff we have been talking about?"

"Yeah, maybe, but it helps if you play an instrument. I play the guitar, both bass and rhythm."

"That's cool. I play the drums and a little piano. My dad plays the piano and the saxophone. My brother, Dwight, plays the saxophone too. Dwight is really good. We have written a lot of songs together."

"Really?"

"Yeah, I would just tell my brother what I wanted, and he would write the notes out!"

Doc walks up. He has been listening to us.

"Hey, Doc, how are ya?"

"Good, how are you? How is the arm?"

"It is still swollen, but I'll live."

"I like jazz and rock 'n' roll. I play the piano, the harmonica, and the guitar. I also sing."

"So does Allen. He plays guitar. If we get out of here alive, we need to start a group. My brother Dwight will join us!"

"That would be cool. What do you think about it, Allen?"

"I am for it. I know producers and all of that stuff!"

Doc reaches out his hand toward me. "Let's see it!"

He starts to examine my arm when he notices my empty ammo bandoliers. "Man, Rock, you guys used a lot of ammo, didn't ya?"

"Yeah, but I can see that you are running low too, Doc!"

"Yes I am, but wasn't that fun?"

"I thought medics were supposed to be sort of quiet. You know, wear the white ambulance cross and all of that stuff."

"Heck yeah, if you don't want to fight. I love to fight, and besides, these VC and NVA use the white or red cross for a target. The rules of war say don't shoot at medics."

"Maybe that coward, Erickson, should have been wearing a cross. That would have given him a reason to stay in the rear!"

"Yeah, he gave black men a bad name!"

"But no matter how bad he was, Raymond and you make up for him."

"Thanks, Danny."

"Raymond is awesome. He charged two VC a while ago and killed them both. And you know the Pig weighs a lot!"

Killer joins in. "He is amazing! I would put him up against anybody. And you, Doc, I have seen you shoot carrying your doctor's bag, C-rations, and, at times, you have carried M-60 ammo."

Eckert speaks up. "OK, Sarge, now listen to this! We have a black man carrying the M-60 and doing a remarkable, amazing job. We have a black man, Doc, who is a great doctor and fights like a caged tiger. We had a black platoon sergeant who probably only shot his weapon twice until he got killed. I would say that Doc and Raymond's good things outweigh one crumb bum, don't you, Sarge?"

"I am very proud to know these two. All I can say is *black men can fight!*"

Doc travels a short distance to where Raymond is listening to what we have been saying. "Raymond, you have made me very proud. Erickson gave us black guys a black eye, so to speak. I am proud to be your brother, Raymond."

"Same here, Doc. You keep up the good work too! And don't steal my body counts. You shoot a lot!"

They both laugh.

"No I won't, Raymond. See you guys later."

Doc heads back to the CP.

The lieutenant says, "We are moving out, Sarge, in five minutes!"

"Yes, sir, but we are going to need ammo before too long."

"Yep, there is a village coming up with a spot to make an LZ."

"OK. Emery, take point and let's move out now!"

"Affirmatron, Sarge!"

The men start to move out. One by one, they pass me. I am checking each man out to be certain he has ammo. Allen passes me and I smell a strong odor. It is not a body stink odor. We all stink. The odor is different. He is smoking something. I grab his shoulder. "Allen, I don't know how they did it in Delta Company, but we don't smoke pot over here in our company! Where did you get it?"

"From a gook, selling it in a village! Man, Sarge, it was cool!" Allen's speech was slurred, and he was speaking very slowly.

"Allen, you are an idiot. I ought to put you on point and let you get shot! You disgust me!"

"Yeah, that would be cool, Captain Rodgers, sir. Give me point. I will save us all from the enemy."

"You are stupid, Allen! Have you got any more pot?"

"No sir. All of my Mary Jane is used up, none left. When will we be to the next village?"

"Don't even think about it! No more marijuana. Do you want me to ask the men if you are capable of fighting with us?"

"I don't want to fight, Sergeant, sir. I want to love!"

"You are messed up, Allen!"

He straightened up his body and saluted. "No I ain't, Sarge! I am just sleepy."

"You stay near me all day, you piece of crap!"

We start to move out. It is a very, very hot day. This is one of the hottest days that we have had. We have to cut in and out of the triple canopy jungle with our dull machetes. Once we get out of the bush we are in the open most of the time, with the sun baking us. The humidity is terrible. I pass the word for the point man to hold up for five minutes.

Craig says, "The captain says guys are dropping out. We need to take a break every ten minutes!"

"Tell him that we are breaking now and we will start taking more breaks."

I take a drink from my canteen. I don't drink very much. I am feeling sick. I notice that most of the men are drinking half of a canteen of their water at one time.

My radio sounds, "Move out!"

We move out again. We are getting hotter and hotter. The sun is cooking us. Sweat is covering every inch of our bodies.

Some people have said many times that Vietnam gets up to 135 degrees. I don't know if the temperature gets that hot, but it sure seems like it today. It is time for another break.

We continue to hump and take breaks. I am feeling very weak. I sure hope we don't get in a firefight now. After four hours, we reach the village. I am feeling really bad. I have stopped sweating. This is bad. I should be sweating like a pig. I walk up to Emery at point. "Hold up, Emery. I am going to see Watkins. Trade weapons with me for a while."

I hand Emery my 79. I walk over to the lieutenant's position. "Sir, we are at a village. We are going in to check it out!"

Chuck says, "Can I go with Rock, sir?"

"Sure, go ahead, Lewis! You just want action!"

Chuck and I head toward the village. Chuck sees that I am pale. "What's wrong with you, Danny?"

"Oh, man, Chuck, I am sick."

"I think that you got too hot. You have heat stroke."

"Don't tell my guys."

Chuck and I made it to the village and we immediately see a VC running. We both start firing. The Charlie runs into one hooch, then another. We spray the hooches with a full automatic burst from our M-16 rifles.

From the first hooch, a Mamasan came walking up to me, crying and pointing at her rear end. Chuck says, "Danny, you take care of her. I'll get the VC!"

Chuck knew that I did not feel like chasing a Charlie.

"Thanks, Chuck."

I look at the lady. She is pointing at her butt and crying. I look closer and see that she has been shot in the rear, but the bullet went clean through to the other side of one of her cheeks. This was very similar to another time in Vietnam when we accidentally wounded an innocent bystander. I walked her over to the captain to ask if we could give her a lift out to a hospital.

Doc looked at the wound and told the captain that the wound would heal on its own.

Chuck washing up a ladies wound

The captain looks at me. "Rock, the choppers are coming in with supplies, ammo, and cold soda pop. What in the world is wrong with you? You look like crap."

"I don't know, sir. I am just weak, and I keep throwing up."

"You have heat stroke, Rock! You have not been drinking enough water! We have ice-cold soda coming. That will help you out. You go in that hooch and lay down on the cold ground. Where is your buddy, Lewis?"

"He is chasing a gook in a hooch."

"Is he alright?"

"Yeah, Chuck will either kill him or bring him to you!"

Chuck is walking toward the captain's CP with the VC in front of him. Chuck has his rifle pointing directly at the VC's head. "Here is one for you, sir!"

"Cool, Lewis! Is that the one that you were chasing through the hooches?"

"Yes, sir!"

The captain grinned. "So you got the VC, and Sergeant Rock got the Mamasan?"

Taking a small break. Chuck waiting on a chopper with supplies

They both laughed and looked at me. I was too sick to laugh. I went into the hooch. The floor was very cold. Somehow, these Vietnam people could take this claylike mud and make a floor with a basement. I noticed that the floor was very clean. I lay back on the cool, clean floor.

I fell asleep until the choppers started coming in. The choppers had ammo, C-rations, and to my surprise, I saw metal trashcans completely filled with ice and soda pop. I cannot remember even once when we got ice-cold soda pop. The captain says, "Men, every man can have two sodas. Tell your men!"

The men started filing in and reaching into the cold, cold water, pulling out two sodas each.

It was my turn, but I was so sick I could barely make it over to the trashcans to get my cold drinks. I was not going to pass up this opportunity, for it may never happen again in this horrible place.

I stuck my hand deep in the cold, icy water and took out two Cokes. I sat on a large rock. I thought about saving the Cokes for later, but they would just get hot. I opened one of the Cokes and took a drink.

As fast as I swallowed, I threw the Coke up. Every drink I took made me vomit. I finally finished the first cold Coke, vomiting at every swallow. I started on the second cold Coke. Every sip I took in came right back up. If nothing else, maybe this would help cool off my insides, if I could ever get any to my stomach.

The captain says, "If we could get a medal for being sick, I think that you would get one, huh, Rock? I saw that you tried to drink all of your Cokes."

"Yes, sir, I am pretty sick."

"Well, suck it up. We are moving out."

"Yes, sir, I'll go and tell my men."

"Rock, I need you to get Raymond up here before we move out."

"Yes, sir. What's up?"

"I need to ask him about prisoners."

I slowly walked over to my squad. "Raymond, the captain wants you!"

"For what?"

"I don't know, but I'll go with ya."

Raymond and I walked to the captain. Raymond says, "Yes, sir?"

"Raymond, good job today, and every day, but there is something that I need to ask you."

"Shoot, sir! Just ask me anything."

"Alright, Raymond, listen up. You know that the higher ups are asking why we don't have many prisoners. So I am asking you this. When you shot those two VC today, could you have taken them prisoners?"

I spoke up, "Sir, Raymond has already talked to me about that."

"I want to hear the story from him, Rock."

"Yes, sir."

Raymond explains, "I shot both VC, but when I ran up to them, they both had their fingers on the triggers of their AK-47s. They were both alive and moving. They rolled over toward me. They would have shot me if I hadn't shot them first."

"Acceptable answer. Thanks, Raymond. I guess you are right, Rock. Black men can fight!"

CHAPTER 19

I Receive a Kit Carson Scout

The captain places his hand on my shoulder. "Sergeant Rock, you are a mess. You are sick, your arm is swollen and bleeding, and you look like crap. This will make you feel better."

"What, sir?"

"We are flying in an interrogator to ask the VC a few questions. This will give you a little more time to rest. You just stay up here with me. Your men don't need to see ya in this shape."

"Thanks, sir!"

I head back to the cool floor of the hooch.

"Chuck, will you tell the men that we will be here for a while?"

"Yeah. Go and lay down, Rock."

After about fifteen minutes, a chopper arrives. A small Vietnamese man jumps out. He has fatigues on, just like we are wearing. He walks up to the captain. He speaks to the VC prisoner and then speaks to the captain again. The captain is shaking his head *no*. The small guy goes back to the VC. It is a one-sided conversation. The VC is not talking. The captain is heading my way.

He arrives at the hooch. "Rock, in a few days, you will get a Kit Carson Scout. We are going to get two of them. I will give one to you and the other to another squad."

"Is that what the little guy is? A Kit Carson Scout?"

"No, not really. He is an interrogator. They say that he gets the VC and the NVA to talk."

The interrogator is walking the VC over near the waiting chopper. The interrogator sets the gook on top of a berm and places the VC's legs out in front of him. The interrogator is talking, but the VC is not responding. The interrogator places his foot on the ankle of the VC and turns the foot and ankle on its side. The interrogator then shoots the bottom of the VC's foot where the arch is located with his M-16 rifle. The interrogator then holds the rifle at the VC's knee.

The gook says a few words. I can see by his body language that the interrogator is not happy. The interrogator throws the VC in the chopper and then jumps in himself. The chopper takes off.

I can hear the chopper in the distance. I can barely see the chopper as it climbs higher and higher in the sky. The chopper flies around for ten minutes, and then I can see it returning.

The chopper starts to come in. "Sir, do you think he got any information from the VC?"

"Probably. The guy's good."

The chopper lands, but there is no VC on board. The captain says, "Come on with me, Rock." We walk up to the chopper and see the interrogator is getting off of the skid. He has a big grin on his face.

The captain says sharply, "I guess that you got no info, huh? Where is he?"

The interrogator reacts quickly. "Of course I did. Did you really doubt me?"

The captain and I are puzzled. The captain looks at me, then at the interrogator. "OK, then, where is the VC?"

"Sir, he told me what I wanted to know, but he didn't give it to me fast enough. He tried to escape in midair."

"You mean that you shoved him out of the chopper at 2,000 feet up?"

"No, like I said, he tried to escape."

The interrogator was sticking to his story. He was not going to debate or argue the subject.

I turned to the captain. "Sir, this may not be right, throwing a VC from a flying helicopter. No wonder this interrogator is getting a reputation for getting info from the enemy."

"Yep, sometimes I wish that we could just throw all the NVA and VC off a chopper. By the way, Rock, how are ya feeling?"

"A hair better. On another thought, sir, why didn't we get any fresh water?"

"Because we have a river coming up soon."

"Did you have anything to do with that, sir?"

"Do you mean not ordering water?"

"Yes, sir."

"No, I ordered it, but a higher up says we did not need it yet. Sometimes they are just stupid up there."

"Yeah, just let them come out here for a week!"

"You are right. Go and tell your guys we are moving in five. I am going to give you guys a break from point. I'll give it to another squad."

"We can handle it, sir."

"Nope, you guys take a break."

"You're the boss, sir."

"See ya, Rock."

I get my men together. "We don't have point today. I think the old man is giving it to Mac's squad."

White and Killer at the same time say, "Mac's squad? We cannot let them catch us on the body count, Sarge."

"Unless we run into a battalion, he won't stand a chance."

Emery looks weary. "Sergeant Rock, I drank all of my water. I thought we were going to get some on the resupply. I am thirsty."

"I'll give you a little of mine, Emery. The rest of you guys ration your water. We won't get to the river for four hours."

Emery says, "Can I have a swig now, Sarge?"

"Yeah, give me your canteen."

I poured the water from my canteen into his canteen. "Now, that is all that you are going to get from me."

"Thanks, Sergeant."

We started moving out, with Mac's squad pulling point. The weather was unbearable. The thorns in the back-up bushes were harsh. Chuck and some of the other guys call these bushes Wait-a-Minute bushes, because you had to stop and move backward to free your arms, hands, or legs from the thorns on the bush. This day was excruciating, hard, and tormenting.

Although the point guys are warning us about the bushes, our men keep getting into them. I was wondering about Chuck, because he had the skin that would get infected very easily by these thorns.

Emery gets into a bush. "I hate Vietnam!"

"Yeah, me too, Emery!"

"Sarge, how are you holding up? You have a bleeding arm, you are sick, and you look like crap."

"I feel better than I did an hour ago, even though this is tough. By the way, what about your buddy, Emerald? Is he getting any better?"

"He is not as afraid as he used to be."

"You, yourself, have come a long way, Emery. You have learned a lot. Everyone trusts you on point and they know that you can become a leader one day. Maybe you will become a squad leader when I go home, huh?"

"That would be great, Sarge. But I really don't want the responsibility. I would feel bad every time I lost a man."

"Yeah, you're right about that. Every time I lose a man, I get sick to my stomach. What are your plans when you get home?"

"I am going to get married to the prettiest girl ever."

He pulls out a creased picture and holds it up to me. She was really pretty.

"Man, Emery, she is pretty. Is she blind?"

"No, she's not *blind*!" He looks back at the picture. "Why? Does she look blind to you?"

"No, but if she wants to marry you, she must be blind."

We both laugh.

"You know what, Sarge? No matter how bad we have it, we can find something to laugh about."

"What else will you do back in America?"

"One thing I won't do is hunt anymore. It would not be a challenge anymore. We hunt over here, but the ones being hunted shoot back."

"Yeah, you are right. I used to love to hunt. So what else will you do?"

"I got very good grades in college, so I will continue school and become a doctor. My dad works very hard to put me through school. My older brother and sister both went to college. They are business majors. I have one of the best families ever."

I could see tears coming from his eyes.

"So if you got drafted, that meant that you skipped a semester of college?"

"Yeah, I went to work to save enough money to help pay tuition. That didn't work out so good; I got drafted. Isn't that what happened to you?"

"Yeah, exactly. I wanted to go to college and buy my 409 Super Sport car. So I took six months off, away from college, to make some money. I was also playing baseball in college."

"Will you go back to school?"

"Oh, yeah, I want to be a dentist."

"Well, then we both have to take pre-med subjects for a while. Maybe we will take some classes together."

"Yeah, maybe. You have heard me talk about Boomerang One-Three or Three-Three or Seventeen — I cannot remember his number — haven't you?"

"Yeah, your chopper pilot friend."

"Yes, his name is Terry Waggoner. Anyhow, he is going to be an optometrist, so we were both taking pre-med classes together too."

"Has he ever given us a lift?"

"I don't really know, but probably not. He is down south around Chu Lai. His base camp is called Bear Cat or something like that."

We are talking and humping through the hot humidity. I have to stop talking because it is taking too much out of me. I am running very low on energy and water.

I see that Emery has drunk all of his water. "Emery, do you want a drink of mine?"

"Yes."

"One drink. I have enough for three more swigs."

We travel another thirty minutes, taking a break after every ten minutes, and we finally reach the river. The lieutenant comes up to me. "We will be here for an hour. The old man says to take turns pulling guard while we take baths and fill canteens!"

"Yes, sir!"

The small river looked great. The water was clear and cold. The water was moving over rocks and sand, very similar to our rivers in California.

I gather my squad. "Men, we will fill our canteens and take baths here. We will have two squads pulling guard and two in the river."

All of the squads were drinking water from the fresh, clear, clean water and filling their canteens. We were supposed to take turns, but I could not blame the men for wanting water.

The lieutenant spoke to me. "I better get control of these guys, huh?"

"Yes, sir, you had better have two squads pull guard!"

"OK, men, out of the river! Sergeant Rock and Sergeant Mac, you guys get your squads in the river first."

I had a plan for what I was going to do in the river. First, I was going to drink lots of water. Second, I was going to fill my canteens. Third, I was going to take off my fatigues and wash them. Fourth, I was going to wash my body. And fifth, I was going to wash my stinky, reeking, and foul-smelling towel.

Watkins was doing as we were. "Hey, Rock, is this clean water unusual?"

"Oh, yes, sir, very unusual!"

I got in the water, boots and all, and started drinking water. I made sure that no one was upstream from me when I started filling my canteens. I was kneeling in the water, talking to the lieutenant, and did not notice Freeman and another man from Mac's squad upstream from us.

Freeman came over to Vietnam at the same time that Chuck and I came to this horrible place. Freeman was a joker. He was like Killer as far as his ability to make us laugh. Freeman was six-foot-four and as strong as a horse. In basic training, he would leave base when he was not supposed to, get drunk, and somehow get back on base and not get into trouble. Now this joker was upstream from me, but he was being very quiet. He was naked, just sitting in the water with a bar of soap.

I decided to move a little bit to the right so I would not be directly in line with Freeman. I started filling my canteens again with the fresh, cool water.

I looked down at my canteens as I held them under water and I saw a large, brown, long piece of crap. I jumped back and grabbed my canteens. Killer and Emery were yelling, "Watch out! Get out of the way! Freeman, you are stupid!"

Freeman starts to laugh. "That was a good one. I hope you guys didn't get any of my crap or pee in your canteens!" He gets up on his knees. "Now it is time to wipe!" He takes his hand and flushes his butt crack out with the same water that we want to drink.

I look at Freeman, now laughing his head off. "You are gross! You are bad!"

Freeman responds with a big grin, "Don't forget about the pee!"

"What?"

"The pee. I always pee before I crap!"

"Disgusting!"

I look at my now-full canteens and decide to dump all of the water out and start over.

The lieutenant says, "Is he always like that?"

"Yes he is. You never know what to expect with him, but he is not afraid of anything. He is really a good man."

I finished washing my clothes and towel, then swam a little in the refreshing water. The men were doing the same. The lieutenant is on the bank of the river, getting dressed. I walk over to him. "Do you want me to tell the guys to get out?"

"No, give them a few more minutes."

The lieutenant could see how hard we worked in Vietnam. He could also see that we were always worried about being killed. He was a very smart guy; I hoped that he would not be killed here in the 'Nam. He was going to be a great leader.

"Sir, are you getting used to this place yet?"

"Yes, but can we ever get used to this? Rock, I know that I have asked you this before. Do you think you will be the same when you leave here? I mean that I have only been here a short while, and I have seen killing, both enemy and our men. I have seen that we cannot trust any village. Our living conditions are horrible. We hump up and down mountains in extreme heat. Our clothes are never dry. Then we run across a great river and a guy craps and pees in our water!"

"No, I don't think so, sir. Before you came over here, we saw our own men get burned to death. We have seen our guys with missing legs and arms. We have seen a man that had been shot eleven or so times and he lived. We have had a man get a bullet through his cheek and it was in his mouth. Our future platoon sergeant was blown to bits. I have been in two helicopter crashes myself. I am worried and nervous all of the time about losing my men. My arm still hurts from the shrapnel. Now Freeman craps in the water. I don't think that I will ever be the same. And do you know what I think the big thing is, sir?"

"No, what, Rock?"

"Fear! I cannot show fear when I am scared. Sometimes I am so afraid that I shake. On January ninth, I shook so hard that I thought the NVA were going to hear my teeth chatter."

"Do you mean by not showing fear, not showing your men that you are afraid?"

"Yeah. Emerald would go ballistic if I showed him how scared I was sometimes. But don't get me wrong. I have confidence in my men and I am not afraid to fight any gook or any man. Don't worry; I will be the first to lead any attack for you at anytime. I am just not as brave as the rumors say that I am."

"I am glad we are a team, Rock. Get the guys out of the river."

"Thanks, sir. OK, men, out of the water before Freeman takes another dump!"

Emery comes up to me. "I am going to kick Freeman's butt, Sarge."

"OK, go ahead."

Emery is five feet, seven inches tall. Freeman is a very big man. He walks up to Freeman, who is now getting out of the water. "I want to talk to you, Freeman!"

In a deep, deep voice, Freeman says, "Yes?"

Emery sees the height difference between himself and the guy that he plans to beat up. Emery changes his mind and says, "That was funny, Freeman!"

"Yeah, it was, wasn't it Emery?"

The lieutenant and I start to laugh. I say to the lieutenant, "You see, sir. You did right."

"What do you mean, Rock?"

"When Emery said that he was going to beat up Freeman, you just let him go over to him. You didn't stop him. Gibbons would have made a big deal about it. The men, with all of their stress, need to sometimes get things off of their chests."

"Yeah, I agree, but if they would have started to fight, I would have stopped it."

"Yeah, me too."

My squad and Mac's squad moved out of the river and started pulling guard for the other squads. The other two squads and the balance of the company now took their turn in the river. After an hour, we started to move out toward our new destination, called Small Baldy.

Craig says, "The lieutenant says we have point if we want it."

"Cool, who wants point?"

Allen says, "I do!"

He hands me a small plastic bag discreetly. "No more, Sarge. I won't smoke anymore pot! Can I take point?"

I look at the bag. It is his stash of pot. "OK, Allen, take point!"

I take the pot out of the bag and sprinkle it on the ground as I continue to walk forward. I look behind me and see Killer pretending to pick up the marijuana from the ground. He, Emerald, and White are laughing and looking at me. They want to be certain that I see them pretending to pick up the pot.

Emery, now in front of me, starts laughing too. "Hey, Sarge, how did you like that river?"

"It was great, huh? Just like some of the rivers and streams that we have in California."

"Did you laugh when Freeman pooped in the water?" Emery starts to laugh.

"Yeah, but not at first. I was filling my canteens just downstream when I saw his log floating. I was only two feet from him."

"Oh, no, for real?"

"Yeah, for real!"

"I like Freeman. How come he isn't in our squad? Didn't you want him?"

"Yes I did, but he was just placed with Mac."

"I am glad that I am with you, Sarge. I write home about you."

"You do?"

"Yes. As long as I am with your squad, I am safe. By the way, my mom keeps telling me to tell you *hello*."

"You tell her *hi* for me too. Moms are very important."

The company keeps moving in the direction of Small Baldy. We are traveling next to the river that keeps winding in and out of villages and small hills. We travel for two hours when we hear the dreadful sound of enemy mortars. *Pop! Pop! Pop!*

The good thing about mortars is the time frame in which we have to take cover. There is a delay from the time that the mortar is fired until it hits. We can hear the mortar sound coming from our left. I tell the men to get next to the river. We jump next to the river and take cover beside a berm. The berm is four feet tall; therefore, we must get on our knees to move. We are now being fired on by AK-47s. This is going to be a battle.

The mortars are being fired at us from the left. The rifles are being fired at us from the left. We are pinned down between the weapons and the river. Relentlessly, the enemy firepower was trying to kill us. Their mortars were off course, and a lot of them were falling in the water. I hoped that they did not start trying to shell us. Three or four direct shell shots would wipe us all out.

Chuck comes up to me. "Man, Danny, this is bad!"

"Yeah, it is real bad, Chuck!"

All of a sudden the firing stops. Chuck comes closer. "Do you think they have gone?"

"No way. I think that they are just waiting for something to shoot at."

Chuck takes his helmet off. "Danny, I have an idea."

"Yeah, what?"

"You know in the cowboy western movies how a guy puts his hat on his pistol and he holds it up to see if anybody shoots at it?"

We both start laughing.

"Yeah, try it."

Chuck places his helmet on his rifle. He slowly lifts the helmet up over the berm. Immediately, the bullets start flying. The helmet is spinning like a top on top of his rifle. We laugh again.

"Well, does that answer your question, Chuck?"

The firing starts up again. It is getting more intense. We are going to have to get on top of the berm and start firing back. We must locate the enemy's position so we can call in artillery support.

I pass the word to get on top of the berm. Chuck and I are the first men on top. We are firing our weapons like mad. The rest of the company is now firing. The enemy's rounds are hitting beside us, in front of us, and behind us. I yell to the lieutenant. "Sir, call in firepower! Do you know the coordinates?"

"Yes! What do you think we want?"

"One for location! Then lots of VT!"

The lieutenant calls in the firepower. The artillery starts to come in, but the bullets are still firing. I yell to Watkins, "Shell 'em! Shell 'em! Call in shells! They are dug in!"

The lieutenant calls in more artillery. It sounds like the firing is slowing down. Suddenly, I hear White yelling, "Doc, Doc, over here!"

I take off toward White. I have to dive in the mud. My hands and arms are buried up to my elbows. I pull my hands out of the mud. My brand new watch is missing. I have no time to retrieve it. I run to where White is yelling, dodging the incoming fire all the way. I see White behind the berm. "What is it, White?"

"It's Allen, Sarge. He is in bad shape! He has been hit bad, real bad!"

I lean down over Allen. "Man, Allen, I am so sorry!"

Allen can barely speak. "I am getting cold, Sarge."

"You hang in there, Allen, just hang in there!"

Doc arrives and checks over Allen's wounds, then he stands and says to me, "If you want to talk to him, do it now. He won't last long."

I leaned over Allen. "How ya doing, buddy?"

Very faintly he says, "Not good, Sarge. I am going to die."

"I am so sorry. Allen, listen to me the best that you can. I have seen many guys die; some are Christians and some are not. Do you believe in God?"

"Yes I do. You showed me how to do it. I am sorry I couldn't have been a better point guy for ya."

"No, you did great, Allen. You did great."

Allen did not answer. I look up at Doc. Doc says, "Let me look at him."

I stand up and Doc leans over. Doc checks him out further. "He is dead, Danny."

The enemy is still shooting at us, but we are sort of tucked away behind the berm. Killer comes running up to us. "Doc, it's Emery! He has been shot!"

Doc and I run to Emery. He is lying on the ground with his arm and leg twisted as if they were broken. I am thinking to myself, *Not Emery, not Emery. He has so much to live for!*

Doc examines Emery, and then like he did with Allen, he stood up and told me to talk to him now because he didn't have long to live.

"Doc, did he break his arm and leg?"

"No, they were just twisted, but he has been shot several times. He will probably die real soon."

I leaned down next to Emery. I picked his head up and laid it in my lap. Emery says, "I hurt, Sarge!"

"I know, Emery, but you don't die on me!"

Killer is now crouching over us. "Don't you dare die on us, Emery!"

I pull Emery closer to me. I have his head close to my chest. "Emery, don't die. Your pretty girl is waiting for you to marry her. You will make a good doctor. Your hard working dad and mother need you. Your brother and sister need you!"

Emery is now fading away. "Don't let your stomach hurt, Sarge!"

Emery remembered what I had told him about my stomach hurting every time I lost a man. He was worried about me getting an ulcer.

"We need you, Emery! Someone needs to take over when I go home!"

"I will be going home shortly. I will see Jesus soon, Sarge. Thanks for giving me your water. Thanks for pulling me out of the back-up bush. Thanks for teaching me. Thank you for –"

He did not finish. He stopped speaking. Emery was dead.

I grabbed him and pulled him tighter and tighter to my chest. "I am sorry, Emery. I am sorry for being such a bad squad leader!"

I rocked back and forth with him, praying for him. "I need you, Emery. We all need you!"

I was holding and rocking with one of my dead brothers in war. I had tears that were not going to dry for a while.

Doc places his hand on my shoulder. I did not know it at the time, but I had been rocking Emery for more than ten minutes. Doc says, "He is gone, Danny. Let me check him out."

Slowly I stood up. We were still in the middle of a firefight. My sorrow switched to rage. Again, I wanted to kill every NVA and VC in sight.

Killer comes up to me. "Let's get them, Sarge! Let's kill every gook that moves!"

"Sounds good!"

I run over to the lieutenant. "Sir, can I finish up calling in the firepower?"

"Yes, sir, Sergeant Rock! Yes, sir!"

Watkins could see that I was serious. At this time, it did not matter to me if he wanted me to call in the artillery or not. I was going to do it!

I get on the horn. "Fireball Five-Niner, this is Blackhawk Three. Let's go!"

"This is Fireball. Where have you been, Blackhawk Three?"

"I have been away. Now let's kill some NVA, VC, and anything else that moves!"

"Let's do it!"

"They are dug in, so give me some of those bunker buster shells! The same coordinates, but spread them out at twenty-five meters! Give me twelve of them now! Give me something that will go deep into the ground!"

"We don't have a bomb or shell like that, but I'll give you the best that we have!"

The rocket shells started coming in, one after another. In my opinion, this was not enough.

I jumped back on the horn. "This is not good enough! Get off the pot and get some help! Get the Navy gunships!"

The firepower started pouring in. Double rounds started hitting. I was using a lot of money, but I was determined that on this day, no more of my men would be shot. My radio sounded, "How was that, Blackhawk?"

"Now you have it. Do we have any air support available?"

"Yes, you want it?"

"Send it!"

Within five minutes, two jet fighters were shooting and rocketing the area. When the planes left and the smoke cleared, there was nothing left but flat ground. The enemy was dead.

My radio goes off, "Blackhawk Three, come to Annihilator!"

"On the way!"

I arrived at the captain's CP. "Yes, sir?"

"Rock, you called in a lot of artillery!"

"Yes, sir, but they killed Allen and Emery."

"Yeah, and you really liked Emery. He was a good man."

"He was a very good man, sir. A very good man!"

"Rock, today was just a sample of what we can expect of days to come. I have ordered tanks to help us for a week. They are on the way right now."

"That will be great."

"Also, two choppers will be coming with supplies and ammo, and, of course, to lift out Emery and Allen. We have two more wounded guys too."

"Sir, I want to trade this 79 for an M-16!"

"Sure, talk to my RTO. He will send the order in for ya."

"Thanks, sir!"

I started to walk to the RTO.

"And Danny, I am sorry about Emery and Allen. I know that Emery meant a lot to you. Doc told me how you took it! Don't you remember the rule over here? Don't get too close to your men!"

"I know, sir, but when my guys save my life over and over again, I cannot help getting close to them."

"Yeah, I really do know what you mean. That is how I feel about you, Danny."

The captain never called me Danny. I was honored.

"Thank you, sir."

I started to walk toward my squad. The captain grabbed my arm. "Rock, what will you do if Lewis gets killed?"

"What?"

"Lewis is your closest friend, isn't he?"

"Yes, sir."

"I just don't want you to fall apart if he gets shot."

"I won't, sir. I think that I could handle it."

I arrived at my squad. "Men, we will be getting help from tanks in a little while, and choppers are coming in to pick up Emery and Allen and the wounded."

"Who got wounded, Sarge?"

"I don't really know, but I don't think it was from our platoon."

The tanks started rolling in. The tanks got on line, side by side, facing the direction of the enemy. There were ten tanks in all. This was a welcome site. In the distance, we could hear the *pop, pop, pop* of the Huey helicopter blades cutting through the air.

The choppers land, and the gunners start throwing off our supplies. We start picking up the supplies, and I see the two black body bags. Killer says, "I'll get 'em, Sarge!" Killer picks up the bags and takes them to Doc.

Doc says, "Are you going to help me, Killer?"

"Yes."

By this time, all of my men were back. Eckert says, "We are all going to help, Doc."

Doc is surprised. "Man, you guys really must have liked Emery and Allen."

White replies, "We liked Emery. We didn't know Allen that good."

I was proud to see my squad sticking together again. The captain's RTO came up to me, holding a brand new M-16 and plenty of bandoliers of ammunition. "Here is the weapon you ordered. Let me have your M-79."

I reached for the 16 and handed him the 79. "Thanks."

"Sure, Sarge."

I helped the men load the bodies into the body bags and carry them to the waiting choppers. We gently loaded the bodies of Allen and my friend, Emery, on the chopper. The choppers took off, and we all stood there in silence, watching until the helicopters were no longer in sight. Henning says, "Emery was a very good man, huh, Sarge? And I think Allen was pretty good too."

I was still staring in the direction of the choppers, wondering what would happen next. I answered Henning, "Yes, they were both very good men."

I could not help from wondering about me letting Allen pull point. *Was he high when he was leading us? Was it just a coincidence that we were hit by the NVA? Maybe he was just doing a poor job at pulling point?* Nevertheless, it was a squad leader's responsibility to know these things! I turn and start walking back to the lieutenant's CP.

On our way to the CP, Emerald says, "I think we will be safer traveling with the tanks. What do you think, Sarge?"

"Yeah, the gooks will be shooting at the tanks, primarily."

The lieutenant is listening. "Is that right, Rock? They will be shooting at the armor and not the infantry?"

"Only in general. We have to watch for bullets and shrapnel bouncing off the tanks and hitting us. The NVA and VC still shoot at us, but they would rather capture a tank than kill one of us!"

"So how do we know where to send the men? I mean, how many men to each tank?"

"Just tell the men to pick out a tank that they like and to stay with that tank during a firefight. I am going over to the tank guys, sir. I'll see what's happening over there."

I walked up to the tank guys and noticed that they were eating and just taking it easy. I also noticed their arm patches. These guys were from the First Cavalry. These guys were mean, gnarly, and terrific. They also took no prisoners, according to their reputation.

I approached one of the sergeants. "Hi, I am Sergeant Rock. I know that you guys have a very large division, but have you ever heard of a guy named Snow?"

"Yeah, he is right over there!"

The sergeant points to Snow. I walk up to Snow and he turns around. "Sergeant Rodgers, I was just talking about you. I was going to ask if you were with these guys."

One of the other guys that Snow was talking to looks at me. "Is this Sergeant Rock?"

He sticks out his hand and we shake hands. Snow replies, "Yep, this is Sergeant Rock. We met coming home from Hawaii on our R&Rs. Hey Rock, why don't you have your squad travel with us? You know, near our track?"

"Yeah, that would be cool. Thanks."

I turned to go back to the lieutenant when Snow says, "Sergeant Rock, where were you guys getting hit from?"

I pointed in the enemy's direction. "Over there!"

"Alright, that will be our first objective. If we get one shot from them, we will wipe them out. That will be fun, huh, Rock?"

With a big grin on my face I said, "Gnarly, dude! Let's do it!"

"Hey Rock, I didn't know you were a hippie! Far out, dude!"

We both laughed. We knew that neither of us was a draft-dodging hippie. Not all hippies were draft-dodgers, and not all draft-dodgers were hippies. I certainly hated the draft-dodgers. Although I was not a hippie, I had a lot of friends that leaned that way.

I arrived back at our CP. "Sir, we should put our platoon with tanks four and five. I know the commander."

"OK, let's do it! Men, pass the word! Stay with tracks four and five!"

I go over to my men and notice that Henning, White, Killer, and Emerald are carrying on a conversation about Indians. The men are listening to Henning intently. I overhear Henning say, "Can you guys just imagine how hard it would be for an Indian to kill a cowboy with their homemade arrows?"

The men were saying, "Yeah, it would be a real lucky shot it seems."

As I listened to all the men talk, what was important to me was the change that Henning had made. He was not lying about everything. He was getting along well with men that hated him not long ago. I walked closer to the men. "Sorry to interrupt, but we are fixing to move out."

Killer laughs. "Don't you mean *going* to move out, Sarge?"

"Yeah, going to move out, and I am fixing to beat your butt!"

Killer was correct, the word should be *going* not *fixing*, but I was born in Texas, and all of my life, everyone around me said *fixing* or *fixin'*, in lieu of *going*. We all had a chuckle.

Killer says, "Which tracks are we going to be with, Sarge?"

"Four and five. Remember the tank guy I was telling you about?"

"The one you met on R&R?"

"Yeah! He is the boss of the whole group. We will be with him."

"Cool, Sarge."

We started walking to get in our positions near the tanks.

Killer says, "You know something, Sarge?"

"No, what?"

"I think that you ought to keep Henning. I hated the guy at first, but now he is alright."

"I'm glad he has toned down, but Delta Company is building back up, and they will need him back next week."

"Man, he won't like that. He says he likes it here and that you are his psychiatrist."

"I don't know. I think he will be OK now if he just listens before he speaks."

"You know that you are my shrink too?"

"What do you mean?"

"Since our talks, I have not killed a single person unless they are trying to kill me."

"I guess I am your shrink then. Back to Henning; he needs to go back to Delta Company."

"Maybe so, but we need men too. Let's keep him."

"I wish I could."

We had now reached the tanks. "We are ready, Commander Snow! By the way, what rank are you, Snow?"

"Sergeant Rock, I am a captain."

"What? Sorry, I mean, sir?"

"Yes, I am Commander Captain Snow."

"I am sorry, sir, I did not mean any disrespect, honest!"

"I know. I spoke to your captain and he told me all about you and what your company has been through."

"Sir, what do you call the guy who drives the tank?"

"The driver."

"What rank would he be?"

"Oh, he could be anywhere from a Spec one to Spec four. Why do you ask?"

I laugh. "I just wanted to know if I was qualified."

"Oh, your rank more than qualifies you. OK, you guys just fall in behind us unless we need your help."

We started moving out. We felt powerful behind these tanks. The tanks got on line side by side. They headed in the direction of the area where the enemy had been, or should I say, hopefully had been.

The tracks arrived at the enemy location. We had done a good job knocking out the NVA. There was nothing left but craters in the ground from the artillery. The tanks stopped, and Captain Snow came out. "Wow, you guys blew these guys away. Did you lose many men yourself?"

"We lost two, and two or three wounded."

"Maybe we can keep ya from losing anymore, huh?"

"Hope so."

"Hey, Sarge, you guys are probably tired of walking, aren't ya?"

"Yeah, so are you going to say, 'Then run a while'? I have heard that joke."

"No. After this little village, we are going to be on a smooth road, so you guys can jump on."

"OK!"

The tanks finally got onto the road and stopped. There was not enough room for all of the company to ride at the same time, but my squad found a seat. I found a hard, hard seat beside the turret and alongside the 105 mm gun. I was on the port side of the 50-caliber. We traveled for about thirty minutes. I was getting sleepy. I strapped my canteen and ammo belt to a holder loop on the tank, and then I strapped it to my ammo bandoliers. This would keep me from falling off the tank and getting run over if I actually fell asleep.

It was hard for me to believe, but several of us fell asleep on the tanks. We would hit a bump, and I would wake up and immediately fall back to sleep. We traveled until almost dark. The lieutenant came up to my tank. "Sarge, we are going to put up a perimeter with the tanks."

"Do you think we should dig in?"

"What do you think, Rock?"

"Yeah. The guys won't like it, but we'd better do it."

I motioned for White and Eckert to come to me. "After the tanks set up their perimeters, we need to dig foxholes."

White says with a Mexican accent, "We don't need no stinking foxholes. We have tanks!"

"I know, but we will need them for stray bullets if the tanks get hit, and what about mortars?"

White replies, "Oh, yeah, I didn't think about mortars. Let's dig in, guys!"

The men started digging two foxholes. The ground was soft and muddy from the rain. I take my turn in the foxhole. The lieutenant walks up to me. I am still in the hole, digging. "Rock, there is going to be a squad going out on an LP tonight."

"It's not us going on a Listening Post, is it, sir?"

"Nah, it is a different platoon. Why, did your squad want to go?" He laughed.

"No, not really. And besides, we are already dug in. Our foxholes are almost done."

Night came and, in general, we heard very little sounds from the surrounding area. Far, far away, ten miles or more, we could see a firefight that lit up the sky like the Fourth of July.

As my men and I talked about the days to come, Captain Snow came up to us. He had a canteen cup of soup and some crackers. "Hey, Rock and men, how are you guys? How did you like the ride?"

"Man, sir, I couldn't believe I fell asleep sitting on the tank!"

"I know. The steady rumble is humdrum."

"Have a seat, sir. Sir, how do you drive one of those things?"

"Just like a large tractor with tracks, with two hands. If you want to go left you pull back on the left lever and so on. Rock, have you ever driven a track machine?"

"No, only a tractor."

"OK, follow me to my tank. I am going to give you a lesson."

"Sure, let's go!"

Man this was going to be good — a captain showing a sergeant how to drive a tank. We arrived at his tank. "OK, Sarge, hop in the top hole."

I jumped on the tank and climbed through the turret. It was dark and cold. "Now turn on the switch for light!"

I found the switch and threw it. The lights came on. "OK, Rock, now turn that switch on, then that one."

He pointed at the direction of the switches. This was cool. I stayed in the tank for twenty minutes, moving forward and backward, turning right and left. When I finished my lesson, I was convinced that I could drive a tank.

"Sir, is an APC (armored personnel carrier) the same as a tank? I mean, do you drive it the same?"

"Yep, the same."

"OK. Now I am ready to shoot the gun!"

I am only joking, but I would really like to fire at least one shot. "Maybe, Sarge. If we get a chance, I'll let you shoot a round or so."

I climbed out of the tank. "Thanks for the lesson, sir."

"You're welcome, Rock. Rock, have your men ready for tomorrow!"

"Why? What have you heard?"

"We are going to hit a load of crap tomorrow. We have been through these areas before, and it is no picnic!"

"I'll tell the men. I am glad you guys are with us."

I went back over to where my men were. The men were eating C-rations. Henning was right in the middle of the group. This was my chance to give him a little credibility. I looked at the men. "Have you guys set up guard yet?"

Eckert says, "No, not yet, Sarge. Do you want me to do it?"

"No, let Henning set it up."

Henning replies, "Me?"

"Yeah, you."

"OK, so what do I do?"

"Come on now, what do you think? First of all, you count the men."

"Alright, let's see. We have Emerald, White, Eckert, Killer, Craig, Raymond, and you, Sergeant Rock. That is seven."

Killer says, "Haven't you forgotten about someone?"

"Well, let me see again. Emery is dead. Allen is dead. Sergeant Lewis is with the lieutenant. So no, I haven't forgotten anyone."

"You dope. You didn't count yourself!"

We all start to laugh.

"Oh, yeah, myself, so that is eight. OK, Sarge, what guard do you want?"

"Give me last."

Henning started to tell each man which guard they had.

Eckert says, "Henning, now you have something else to tell us."

"What would that be?"

"The time. How long will each man pull duty before he wakes up the next guy? Now, turn to Sergeant Rock and ask, 'What time are we getting up'?"

Henning turns to me. "What time are we getting up, Sarge?"

"A half hour before daybreak. Five-thirty."

"OK, we will start guard at seven-thirty, so that is ten hours. Ten hours divided by eight men is one hour and fifteen minutes each. Now let's get to it!"

We laugh.

"That's it, Henning, take charge!"

The men and I continue to talk while eating our C-rations. Henning opens up a can of peaches with his P-38 can opener. Killer says, "I'll give you my pound cake and $2 for your peaches."

Eckert says, "That sounds a little cheap to me, Henning."

"What do you offer, Eckert?"

Eckert turns to me. "Nothing, but tell him about Warmont, Sarge."

"Oh, yeah, Warmont! He paid a guy $35 for a can of peaches."

"Sounds good to me. I'll sell mine for $30!"

"No, Warmont was crazy."

"What happened to him?"

"All I know is that he got fragged in a foxhole while pulling guard. He fell asleep on every one of his guards."

"Sounds like friendly fire killed him to me."

Killer and White immediately say, "We all hated him, so it couldn't be friendly fire. He had no friends!"

I look at Henning and turn my head toward Killer and White. "I still wonder about that grenade that killed him. Was it ours or the enemy's?"

Henning jumps up. "I, for one, won't be falling asleep on my guard period time frame!"

We all give a big chuckle.

We start pulling guard. Craig and I are monitoring the radio. We hear that a squad is going out on patrol. They are going to their LP. Everything is quiet, so I decide to lay out my canteen-ammo-belt pillow and lay down. I sleep for two hours before I hear incoming rounds.

I sit up and grab my rifle. The incoming rounds appear to be just a few AK-47 rounds, but the tanks open up like it is the end of the world. For seven or eight minutes, the tanks are firing the 105 guns, the 50s, and M-60s. Us grunts have not fired a round, but we are now in our foxholes. The firefight is over. The tanks stop firing. When the smoke has cleared, I hear the radio, but it is inaudible.

"What did they say, Craig?"

"The squad that was on LP got a man killed!"

"They were supposed to be listening, not engaging in battle!"

"They weren't. It was friendly fire. A tank shot them!"

"Them?"

"Yes, one man killed and two wounded."

"Oh, man! Somebody just made a big mistake! Either the squad was not where they were supposed to be or a tank just blew it! I'll find out in the morning from the captain!"

The balance of the night was quiet. After I pulled my guard, I woke all my men up and walked over to the captain's CP. "What happened last night, sir?"

"A man was killed!"

"I know, but how? Was it from the tanks?"

"Yes, it was a 50 that got him!"

"Was the squad in the location that they were supposed to be in?"

"Yep, it was simply a mistake by an individual tank."

"You know something, sir? If the squad leader told the tank commander that his squad was going to be in front of the tank, then the tank guys should have never fired a shot!"

"I agree, Rock, and I am going to write it up just like it actually happened, but I don't want to tell the camera crew everything, if you know what I mean."

"Yes, sir!"

I walked back to my squad. I explained to them what had happened. As my men and I were talking, we heard the chopper come in to lift out the dead and wounded.

Craig came up to me. "The chopper is going to drop off a glad bag and then come back."

Henning and the men are listening to Craig. Henning says, "What is a glad bag, Sarge?"

"It is a body bag." I really never liked calling a body bag a glad bag, but sometimes I did.

The chopper came in and picked up the dead and the wounded. I walked over to Snow, the tank commander. "Sir, what happened last night?"

"I am still trying to find out the real story. Tank Six says that the squad leader never told him that they were going to be in front of him. The squad leader says that he told the tank commander where he would be. It's a bad deal for sure."

"I am glad it wasn't you that killed one of our men."

I continued my walk to the squad.

It was time to move out. "Men, get in your same positions behind the tracks, as you were yesterday!"

We traveled with the tanks for four hours before we started getting fired upon from a village.

One of the tracks fired a blast from its 50-caliber. In return, all heck broke loose. We could see twenty or more NVA or VC firing at us. We started hearing the mortars being fired.

I yelled to my men, "Get ready, men! This is going to be a bad one!"

The tanks started to get on line. They were lined up abreast with forty meters between the tanks. I commanded my men to line up between the tanks.

We were now set to go to war with this village. I could see the bullets bouncing off of the tanks' steel skin. Craig, Henning, Killer, and I were between two tanks, numbers four and five, while the rest of my men were between other tanks. The tanks were now firing full automatic with their 50s and M-60s. Snow holds up his hand and motions for the tanks to move forward.

In unison, the tanks move forward. There was too much noise to hear the mortar sound, but we could see the rounds exploding. The bullets and shrapnel were bouncing off of the tanks. Commander Snow holds up his hand again and every tank fires its 105 big gun. Again and again, the big guns fire.

The tanks are moving forward. The large guns are shooting large holes right through the village. The 50-calibers are constantly ripping up everything in sight. The M-60s are blasting full ammo belts at the enemy. My men and I are between the tracks, firing on full automatic with our M-16s, M-60s, and M-79s. I look around to check out my men.

Henning is too far forward. He is not on line as he is supposed to be. He goes down. He tries to stand, but he is shot again. Killer and Craig run to his aid. I can see by the way they are carrying him that Henning is dead. The firing continues.

The tanks are pulling closer and closer to the village. There is not one moment of silence. The ground-pounding of the tanks and the big guns pulverizing the village are killing our eardrums. I guess this is why the Army gives us earplugs, which we never wear because we lose them. Our ears finally received a break when the tanks and our company reached the village. There was no village left, only a few burning remnants of hooches. Bodies of dead NVA and VC were scattered all over the place. But now it was time to see how many of my men were dead.

I walked over to Killer, Craig, and Henning. "Killer, is he dead?"

"He is dead, Sarge!"

"Go check on the rest of the men and bring them to me, please."

Killer takes off. Craig is on the horn.

I leaned over Henning and looked at Craig, who is still on the radio. "How many dead, Craig?"

"Two dead including Henning and two wounded. We have choppers coming in for ammo and glad bags. By the way, the captain says the camera crew will be up here to talk to you."

Steven and the camera crew arrive at my location. "Hi, Sergeant Rock. Man, you guys go through a lot. Some of my crewmembers want to go home. I want you to keep writing down what you can and maybe sometime in the near future we will meet up again. Did you lose a man today?"

"Yes, we lost Henning. Are you going home too, Steven?"

"Yes, me too. Wasn't Henning one of the guys from Delta Company?"

"Yes, he was. He was going to be a good soldier."

"OK, Sarge, we will be going now. Keep making your notes!"

"I will."

We shook hands, and the crew took off, heading for the incoming choppers.

The choppers dropped off our new ammo supply and picked up the camera crew members and Steven. The choppers also picked up Henning, another dead soldier, and two wounded men.

As we watched the choppers take off, Killer says, "I guess that Delta Company won't get any men back from us, Sarge."

He was speaking of Allen and Henning. Both men were given to me for safekeeping, so to speak. I felt like I let Delta Company down. By the time I leave Vietnam, I will probably let a lot of people down. I just hope death doesn't come with it!

The captain has always told the new men, "If you want to stay alive over here in Vietnam, listen to Sergeant Rock."

I don't know why he kept saying that because, in my opinion, I was losing a lot of men.

Speaking of death, I hear my radio. It is body count time. Everyone is talking body count. I never actually knew the exact body count for the day, but I know that it had to be a very good one. The tank guys received ninety-five percent of the body count. The word came down to move out.

The tanks and our company started moving out. I told my men to get in the positions that they were in before the little battle at the village.

Five more hours and we arrive at Small Baldy, our original destination. The tanks pull in and set up the perimeter in a big circle.

The lieutenant walks up to me. "Rock, we lost another man today. I hope we don't lose any more for a while."

"Yeah, me too, sir. Do you want us to set up like we did yesterday? I mean the perimeter and all of that?"

"Yep. The captain wants us to go on an LP tonight. Do you want to go? He also wants us to get a man on Small Baldy KP (kitchen police, cleaning pots and pans)."

"KP?"

"Yep, KP!"

"No, sir! Not one of my guys are going on KP! These guys, on this hill, get shot at once every three weeks! They sleep in bunkers, eat hot meals, get fresh water to drink, and even get to take showers! We get shot at every other day! No! No! No! We ain't pulling KP! You can bust me down to private! Lieutenant Gibbons busted me once, and you can bust me again! I'll talk straight to the captain if you want! The captain is full of crap if he wants us to pull KP!"

"I get the point, Sergeant Rock. I'll relay your concerns to the old man!"

He walked away. My guys were listening. Each of them told me that they backed me all of the way. Killer says, "Look at it this way, guys: if we get put in the guard house, we will be out of this mess altogether!"

White says, "That's the ticket. Let's all refuse KP!"

I spoke up, "No, it won't come to that, I am sure. The lieutenant will smooth things over with the captain, and he will never know about this little problem. But we will have to do the LP tonight."

Emerald is astonished. "You mean in front of the tanks?"

"Yes, but I'll talk to Commander Snow and tell him exactly where we will be. I will also tell him not to fire a shot, especially from the 105."

"It will still be dangerous."

"Yeah. As a matter of fact, I'll go over and talk to Snow right now."

I travel the short distance to where Commander Snow is located. "Hey, Commander, how is it going?"

"Great, but again, I am sorry about your man."

"He was not in my squad, but thanks anyhow. We need every man we can get. We are always short."

"I have warned all of my guys. That won't happen again. It will never happen again, I guarantee it."

"OK, sounds good, because my squad is going out tonight, and we will be right in front of you."

"Just let me know when you guys are heading out. I will warn all my units."

"Sir, how accurate is the big gun?"

"You mean the 105?"

"Yeah. I mean yes, sir."

He picks up the binoculars and starts searching through the hills and mountain. "I will find something to shoot at in a minute. There, I found something." He points toward a faraway mountain as he hands me the binos. "Do you see that gook walking up the mountain?"

"No, I don't see anything."

"Raise the binos up higher. He is two miles away, maybe more."

I finally locate the gook moving up the hill. "I see him. Why?"

The big gun starts to move. "Now keep your binos directly on him."

I thought that he was going to shoot the 105 over the gook's head to scare him.

"OK, he is still going up the hill. I can see him."

"Now watch close."

Snow yelled, "Fire!"

The 105 shell hit the gook dead on. A direct hit blew the man to pieces. "Now how about that, Sergeant Rock? Are we accurate or what?"

The man did not even have a weapon. I was astonished that a person could do that to another. This was another time in Vietnam

405

that I got sick in my stomach. *How could a tank commander be so shallow about death?* "Sir, I thought that you were going to shoot over his head, at a tree or rock or something!"

"No, then you wouldn't see the accuracy of the gun!"

"But he didn't even have a weapon, sir!"

"He didn't? Oh, sure he did!"

Snow turns to one of his men. "You saw a weapon, didn't you?"

This was not a question. It was leading for an answer of *yes.*

The questioned man answered, "Of course, sir. I think that he was carrying two weapons."

In my opinion, this was murder. I had not seen a weapon. Maybe the gook could have been carrying his weapon in front of him when I was viewing him walking up the mountain, but I don't think this was a feasible answer to my own question. I didn't trust Snow any longer.

"You see, Rock. He had weapons!"

"Maybe, but I did not see one!"

I turned and headed back to my squad. My men were questioning me about what the firing was all about. I told them what Snow had done. Their mouths were opened wide as they heard the story. Even Killer had qualms about killing a man like that. My guys liked to kill, but they all had reservations about killing this way.

Emerald speaks out. "Do you think he was a VC? Do you think that he could possibly have had a weapon, Sarge?"

"I just don't really know. He could have been a VC and he could have had a weapon, but I sure didn't see one."

Raymond says, "These guys may be good, but I don't like being in front of them at night."

"Yeah, you are right. Just what would happen if another firefight broke out? They may forget about us and start opening up. I don't like it either!"

Emerald has anxiety. "What are we going to do, Sarge?"

"OK, men, here is what we will do. I am not going to tell the captain, but I think I will tell the lieutenant in case we need to be rescued."

"Tell him what, Sarge? Are we not going on a LP?"

"We are going on an LP alright, but we are only going to be about fifty feet in front of Snow's tank. That way, even if they open up, the rounds will go over our heads."

Eckert says, "Sounds cool, Sarge."

"OK, I am going to see the lieutenant. Be back in a minute."

I walk to Watkins, but I see Chuck first. "Hey, Chuck, how are ya?"

"Cool, Danny."

"Hey, what do you think Watkins would say if I told him that we were not going as far out on LP as we are supposed to?"

"After you yelled at him and the captain about KP duty, I don't think that he would say a word."

"I didn't really shout at him. I just was mad about the KP thing."

"Yeah, he agreed with you."

The lieutenant walked up to Chuck and me. "Hi, Rock, what's up?"

"It's about the KP tonight. I mean, the LP tonight."

We all started to laugh. "What about the LP tonight?"

"Well, here goes. The tank guys killed a guy the other night, and I think that they killed an unarmed gook a while ago."

"Was he really not armed?"

"The commander says that he was carrying a weapon, but I didn't see one."

"It is tough on the mind over here, isn't it, Rock? Sometimes we don't know what to do."

"Yes, sir."

"So go on. What do you want to ask?"

"We are going on LP, but we are only going out fifty feet from the tanks' perimeter."

"You mean you only want to go out a little more than fifteen meters?"

"Yes, sir. We don't trust these guys. They are great, and I really like them, but tonight I want to do it my way. I am not going to get my men killed by friendly fire."

"OK, Rock, but I don't know anything about it. Understand?"

"Yes, sir. You know nothing about it."

"Sergeant Rock, off of the record, if I would have said no, would you have done it anyway?"

"Yes, sir."

Chuck started to laugh hard.

The lieutenant is laughing. "Lewis has told me a lot about your previous lieutenant and you."

"Well, don't believe him, for I was always a perfect soldier with Gibbons."

We all start to laugh again. "See you two in the morning."

The lieutenant places his hand on my shoulder. "Be sure and tell the tank commander where you guys will be tonight."

"I will. Thanks."

As I strolled back to the men, I started thinking about how the lieutenant actually did care about his men. I just wished all commanders and officers would care for us like he cared.

I saw the men chatting, but someone was missing. It was Henning, the reformed liar. I don't know why I missed him, but I did.

"OK, men, it is dark enough. Let's go!"

We headed to Snow's tank. Snow was standing outside the tank. "Hey, Sarge, you getting ready to move out? Here, let me get my map, so you can show me exactly where you will be."

"No need. We will be right over there."

I pointed to a small berm just forty feet away from the tank.

"You mean, right there?"

"Yep!"

"Well, then, I guess that you will be too close for us to shoot ya, huh?"

We chuckled.

"OK, men, let's go!"

We walked about twenty steps, and I said, "OK, we are here. Who wants first guard?"

Killer says, "Here? Our LP is here?"

"Yep!"

"Alright."

We set up guard duty and took turns at listening. At 3:30, the tanks started opening up with the big guns. The noise scared us so bad that Emerald said he peed his pants. After five minutes the firing stopped. I don't think Snow's tank fired a single shot. The night continued in calm.

Morning came, and we went back inside the perimeter. When we passed Snow, I said, "Thanks for not firing last night. What was that all about, sir?"

"Oh, it was just a few VC on the war path. They were a mile or so away."

"Good! See ya, sir!"

We walked over to the lieutenant. "Sir, we made it back."

Watkins laughs. "It must have taken you hours to come back in from your LP position."

"No, only thirty seconds."

We are all laughing.

I turned to the men. "You guys go eat! I'll see ya later!"

The lieutenant is on the horn. He gets off and turns toward me. "Your Kit Carson Scout is coming in shortly. The captain wants you now."

"OK. Is he mad about anything, sir?"

"No, he just wants to talk to you about the scout."

I saunter over to the captain. "You wanted me, sir?"

"Yes, Rock. How was your LP?"

I took a big swallow. "My LP, sir?"

"Yeah, how did it go?"

"Oh, great. No problems, sir."

"Good! Your Kit Carson Scout is on his way. There will be two of them. You are going to get one and Sergeant Mac will get the other. You get to choose first."

"What are we supposed to do with them? Can they speak English?"

"They will help us track both VC and NVA. They can speak English a little. I will give you a book for translation."

"So I am going to get a gook and a book, huh, sir?"

"Yep, that is the gist of it. Here comes the chopper now."

The chopper lands and two small-statured men unload. The captain says, "*Can cuoc?*"

The two men pull identification cards from their pockets and hand them to the captain. The captain turns to me and says, "Rock, this is Long, and this is Dong."

I hold out my hand for a handshake. I receive a very wimpy handshake from each of them.

"So which one do you want, Rock?"

"Well, since all of my brothers' names start with the letter *D*, I guess I will take Dong!"

"OK, you got him. Here is your book. Send Sergeant Mac to me, please."

"OK. See ya later, sir."

As Dong and I walk toward the men, I say, "So your name is Dong, huh?"

"No, just Dong, not Dong Huh!"

"What did you say?"

"My name is Dong!"

"That is what I said, Dong!"

"Yes, my name is Dong, not Dong Huh!"

"Oh, I see what you are saying. When I finish a sentence with the word *huh*, it just means *Is that right?* or *Do you agree?*"

This was going to be a long year, trying to explain everything to Dong.

Dong says, "Your name is Sergeant Wock?"

"No, not Wock. It's Rock!"

"Otay, Wock, no sergeant!"

"No, no, no. It is Sergeant Rock, not Sergeant Wock. And the word is *OK*, not *otay*!"

"OK, Sergeant Rock!"

"Now you have it! Now shake hands with me."

I stick out my hand and he places his limp, washrag grip hand in mine. "No, that is weak. Shake it hard. Squeeze it harder."

I showed him again. Dong grabs my hand and makes a manly shake. "How is that, Sergeant Wock?"

"Good! And it is Rock. Oh, just forget it for now."

"We hunt VC now?"

"No, but very soon."

"Today?"

"Yes, today we will hunt for VC, today."

I was not sure about this new venture with Dong, the Kit Carson Scout, but only time would tell.

CHAPTER 20

Silver Star and Purple Heart

Our company, along with the tanks, moved out. As usual, we were heading north. We traveled up and down small hills and middle-sized mountains until two o'clock, when my radio sounded, "Blackhawk Three and all the Blackhawks, come to the CP!"

I headed for the captain's CP. The captain was speaking to all of the lieutenants and Chuck. Watkins sees me. "Sergeant Rock, we have a new platoon sergeant coming in on a chopper in a few minutes."

"I guess I will get Chuck back, right?"

"No, Chuck will take over squad one. The squad leader of squad one will DEROS."

"Cool! Chuck can certainly handle it."

"Anyhow, the tanks will be leaving for a while."

"How come? Man, sir, it sure was better with them!"

"Yep, I know, but they are going to pick up some APCs. We will see them in a week or so."

"So where is the new platoon sergeant?"

"Do you hear the chopper? That should be him."

The chopper lands and dumps off more ammo and rations. An E-7 sergeant jumps off of the slick. He is about six feet tall and 200 pounds. He is asking the men near the chopper something. The guys unloading our supplies point toward the lieutenant.

The sergeant walks up to the lieutenant and shakes hands with him. "Sir, I guess I am your new platoon sergeant! My name is Hammond."

"Pleased to meet you, Sarge. This is Sergeant Rock and Sergeant Lewis. Sergeant Lewis is our present platoon sergeant."

Hammond shakes hands with Chuck and me. "Have you guys seen much action over here?"

The lieutenant jumps in quickly to answer the question. "Yes, we have seen a lot of action. If you are smart, you will listen to Lewis and Rock. That is what I did, and I am still listening to them."

I reply, "No, sir, you are doing great. I don't think that you need anymore help."

"No, that is not true, Rock. Everyone over here needs help."

"Yep, I guess you're right, We all need help."

Chuck says, "Good to meet you, Sergeant Hammond."

"You too, Sarge. And you too, Sergeant Rock!"

I turn and tap Chuck on the shoulder. "This will be cool! Fighting side by side again, huh?"

"Yeah, it won't be long for my squad to catch your squad on the body count!" He laughs.

"Yeah, right. We would have to stop firing a shot for a whole month for your squad to catch us. Even Mac's squad is twenty or more behind."

"Did you like being hooked up with the tanks, Danny?"

"Heck yeah. I felt a lot safer. How about you?"

"Yep, me too."

The tanks started to move out. They went one way, and we went another. Snow gave me a thumbs up when he passed me. I did the same.

"Hey, Rock, how long do you think it will be before we get shot at again?"

"Oh, maybe a day. But do you mean a firefight or just being shot at?"

"Yeah, a firefight."

"Still, a day, or twenty-four hours from now. Why? Are you looking for body counts?"

"No, I am just so tired of fighting. I can't sleep. I keep getting rashes from worry, and the Wait-a-Minute bushes are killing my skin!"

"You know what, Chuck?"

"What, Danny?"

"I would give up all of our body count and never want to kill a VC or NVA again if we could spend the rest of our time here in Vietnam with no more shooting."

"Man, I agree. This place is rough on us!"

The company started moving out. Another platoon and squad were on point for the day. I took the last position in my squad, and Chuck took the first position in his new squad. This way we could talk, and in case of a firefight, we could fight side by side.

We traveled for a few hours before we started getting a few sniper rounds. We took care of the small problem quickly. We traveled for another five hours and the crap hit the fan. Rounds were flying at us from the left. We hit the ground and started opening up, but the incoming firing didn't stop. I could hear grenade launchers, M-60s, and rifles firing. These guys were not letting up. We started firing back the best we could, but they had the advantage.

Surprise was one of the best advantages that we could have in the 'Nam! We had a great disadvantage this time. Every time that we fired a shot, we would receive five in return.

I yelled to Chuck, "Come over here! Craig, bring the radio over here!"

Chuck crawls up to me. "What do you think?"

I listen for a moment before I speak. "Chuck, I don't hear AK-47s, I hear 16s!"

"Yeah, me too!"

"I am going to crawl on top of the berm for a better look. White, give me your binos!"

I get on top of the berm and pull out the binos.

I look through the glasses and I can see American soldiers. I jump off the berm quickly. I run to the radio when Chuck says, "What is it, Rock?"

"It's our guys! We are fighting our own. It's another company!" I grab the horn. "Cease fire! Cease fire! Cease fire!"

I ran to the lieutenant. "Sir, it's our own men! This has happened before, sir!"

"What should we do?"

"You need to tell the captain to get to the higher ups and tell them that we are fighting a friendly company!"

The higher ups were commanders that directed all of the companies. Sometimes the companies would overlap the areas of defense or sometimes a company commander would not actually know his exact location. Hence, two companies in the same area!

The lieutenant gets on the horn and talks to the captain and explains the situation. The firing slows down, but they are still shooting. They must realize that if we are not shooting back, we are friendly. I hope they don't charge us!

Ten more minutes pass, and all of the firing stops. Craig says, "Listen, Sarge, they are on our channel!"

I run to the radio and monitor it. The captain of the other company was speaking to our commander. The other company was Company C from another unit.

The captain radioed, "All men, stop firing. Company C is coming to our location!"

Company C arrived. The whole company divided up, and we ate dinner together — their company and ours. Two squads from Company C walked up to my squad. The squad leader and I shook hands and started to laugh.

Chuck came up to the squad and said, "Man, I thought that we bit the bullet. I thought that we were goners."

The squad leader says, "What company is this, anyhow?"

Chuck answered with pride, "Company A."

"Company A? The Killer Company? The company that cuts the heads off of every NVA and VC they kill? You guys have a lot of kills!"

"Some of that is not true."

Killer says quickly, "Yeah, sometimes we cut the heads off while they are still alive!"

I say, "In general, a lot of what you have heard is simply rumor."

We talked for a while, eating as we spoke. Craig says, "The captain says that we are going to stay here for the night!"

"Both companies?"

"Yes, both companies!"

I turn to my men. "We are staying here! Make a perimeter and dig in!"

Kane, the squad leader, says, "Do you guys dig in every night?"

"Just about!"

Kane turns to his men. "Dig in, men. Hey, Rock, how far apart should we be?"

"I think that we should just make a long trench and put the dirt in front and behind the trench. That way we will get protection and won't have to dig so deep."

"Yeah, that sounds cool."

After we set up the perimeter, I showed the men what we were going to do. I grabbed my entrenching tool. "OK, men, let's go!"

Kane looked at me strangely. "Do you help dig too, Sergeant Rock?"

"Of course, don't you?"

"No, I let my men do it!"

"I always help my men dig. We are a team. I would put my life on the line for any one of them, and they would and have done the same for me! I don't dig because I have to. I help dig because I want to. These guys are my brothers."

Killer says, "You don't always help, Sarge!"

"What do you mean? I always help!"

"When you got shot in the arm, you didn't help!"

"You idiot, I couldn't hold the shovel!"

"I know. I am just messing with you!"

Kane says, "You got shot, Sarge?"

"No, it was shrapnel!"

"Did you get a Purple Heart?"

"Yep, and I hope it is the last one too!"

Kane looked over his shoulder at his men. "I guess that I better help them. They will want me to pull point next! You don't pull point duty, do you, Sergeant Rock?"

Eckert speaks up. "Sergeant Rock pulls point, and every other thing we do! We would die for him! Sergeant Kane, how many kills do you guys have?"

"Do you mean the company, or our platoon?"

"Neither. I mean your squad! How many body count does your squad have?"

"Oh, we have a lot!"

All of my men stop digging. They are listening now to every word.

Kane continues, "We have ten!"

My men start to laugh. Killer says, "Ten?"

Kane sheepishly says, "Yes, ten. Does your squad have more than that?"

Killer picks up his helmet and hands it to Kane. "You see the stars?"

"Yes!"

"There are forty-two stars on the cover. Each star represents a kill!"

"Wow, that is a lot. Your squad killed over forty men?"

Killer grabs his helmet. "No, Sergeant Kane, those are just my kills alone! Our squad has killed over 200!"

Kane's eyes open wide. "Two hundred? How many have you killed, Rock?"

"Well, let me think. We don't count the ones we kill with artillery. We have killed hundreds and hundreds more with artillery. I have killed at least twenty-two that I have shot directly, where I got to keep their IDs and such. Most of them didn't have identification cards, but a few had a little bit of money!"

"That means that you guys are always in the crap!"

"Yep!"

We spent the night taking turns at guard duty. This was really cool because with this many men, each guard lasted only thirty minutes. The quiet night rolled along.

Nothing happened the entire night. This was really refreshing. We had no rain, no leeches, and water to drink. The night, however, did offer a lot of mosquitoes and high humidity. But what the heck. With a great night like this, I could put up with a few mosquitoes.

Morning came, and the captain told us that we would be traveling with Company C for a while. We packed up our gear and headed out. We traveled for three hours when the captain wanted to meet with the platoon leaders, platoon sergeants, and squad leaders.

Chuck and I met up and walked to the captain's CP. When we arrived, we noticed that not only were our company's leaders were with the captain, but Company C's leaders were speaking to him also. I looked at Chuck. "Something bad is up!"

The captain says, "It looks like everyone is here! Men, we are working with Company C in an effort to take over an NVA and VC village. Other companies have lost a lot of men trying to take this fortress. But we are going to do it! We are going to hump for three or four hours, and then we will take over the village."

This sounded simple enough to me, but nothing here in Vietnam was that simple.

I asked, "Sir, will the armor division be helping us?"

"Yes and no! For now, we will only get help from APCs. They will have 50s and 60s mounted! So tell your men to get ready!"

Chuck and I head back to our squads. Chuck says, "This sounds pretty bad. Do you think it will be as bad as January ninth?"

"No way, but I'll bet it is going to be a bad one!"

"Yep, me too!"

Both our companies started heading out. Within one hour, the APCs met us. Each track had five men or more inside. Some tracks had a 50-caliber mounted and some had M-60s. Some of the APCs had both. Usually, the APCs were available to us to carry men, but this time it looked like they were ready for battle. I sure wished that we had the tanks back with us! The tracks and us grunts moved forward, getting closer and closer to, possibly, our day of reckoning.

My squad was on point, with Chuck's squad following. Killer gives us the halt sign. Both companies stop. Killer walks back to my location.

Killer whispers, "The village is just around the corner. I can see NVA on guard. There are a lot of them."

I get on the horn and tell the lieutenant and the captain what we had found.

The captain says, "We are sending the tracks and the infantry in at the same time!"

Killer is intently listening. "Rock, we have a quarter of a mile of open rice paddies to cross before we get to the village!"

"Sounds like fun, huh, Killer?"

Killer knows that I am being facetious. He knows that I am as worried as he is.

Emerald is almost crying. "Are you afraid, Sarge?"

"No, not even a little bit. We have tanks, I mean tracks, with machine guns, and I am sure that we will call in fire support!"

I was afraid, but, as always, I could not tell the men.

Chuck is standing beside me. "Well, here goes, Danny. It's been nice knowing you."

"You too, Chuck."

We are generally joking, but deep down, we realize that this may be the last time we see one another.

Chuck gives me a hug. "Are your mom and dad still praying for us?"

"Yep, every night at nine o'clock."

The tracks move out quickly down the small path. They get on line, but before they can fire a shot, the NVA start unloading on us.

The captain gives the command, "Ground troops, get on line with the tracks!"

The tracks and both companies get on line. Bullets, mortars, and rockets are hitting all around us. We are only 500 feet or so into the rice paddies. I tell Craig, my RTO, to stay close so I can give commands and, of course, hear the captain's commands.

The captain gets on the radio. "Pull back! Pull back!"

The tracks put it in reverse and pull back, shooting their machine guns as they retreat. The artillery starts to come in from our support team.

We are now in the tree line again, but the enemy is still pounding us with rockets and mortars. We wait for thirty minutes and start to advance again.

The tracks move out, heading for the village. Our men are between the tracks, shooting at anything that moves. The sound is earth-pounding. The ringing in our ears is almost unbearable. This is like a war movie that will never end! The mortars are hitting the APCs. The mortars and rockets are hitting all around us. The tracks are firing round after round from their 50s and 60s. More and more bullets and shrapnel are bouncing off of the skin of the tracks. My radio sounds off, "Pull back! Pull back! Pull back!"

This time, we had made it halfway across the rice paddy. If we had gone more than halfway, we would have been at the point of no return!

The tracks started pulling back. Again, they were running in reverse and firing forward as we retreated. Craig hands me the horn. "This is Blackhawk Three, go!"

The lieutenant's voice is on my radio. "Come see me when we get back to safety!"

Craig says, "What did he want?"

"He says to see him when we are safe. I don't know why he couldn't wait until we got to safety to tell me that."

"I think he is just worried!"

"Yep, you are probably right, Craig!"

I take a quick scan of my men. They are backing up and firing forward, the same as the tracks are doing. We finally get to the safety of the tree line.

I run to the lieutenant. "Sir, you wanted me?"

"Yes, yes, yes. This is a bad one, huh, Rock?"

"Yes, sir, it is! What are we going to do next?"

"We are going to regroup and do it again, but this time we are going all the way!"

"We better go all of the way this time, because if we get any deeper in the rice paddy and have to stop, we will be wiped out. We have to make it to the village!"

The tracks and us grunts regroup. My radio goes off, "Men, get on line! We are moving again! Attack, but stay with the tracks! Do not get ahead of the tracks!"

We move out, firing our weapons steadily and rapidly. The tracks are firing quickly and changing gun barrels briskly. The tracks that have the M-60s are firing twenty round bursts. This is too long of a burst. The barrels are getting too hot. They should be firing seven round bursts and allowing five seconds between bursts. The machine guns are jamming up. Changing barrels takes time.

If I were running the M-60, I would probably be firing as fast as I could also. In past firefights, I would get wrapped up in trying to save my life and forget about letting my rifle have a break. I would fire until it got so hot that it jammed. I motioned for Raymond to watch the jamming. He acknowledged me with a head nod and an OK sign. We were now halfway in the rice paddy field again. Halfway is not good enough this time. We must get to the village. The NVA were defending their position with immense control and power. We were slowly advancing again.

We were now three-quarters through the rice paddy. I started to feel a little better about our chances. The APC that we are charging with starts to move faster and faster. It is getting hard for us to catch up. We are having to run faster and faster through the thick mud. We are firing as we run toward the enemy. The rice paddy dikes are tripping us. It is hard to keep our eyes on the enemy and watch our next step. We are constantly tripping and falling in the deep mud and water. The track makes it to the edge of the village. It is in tall grass and bamboo-like trees and bushes.

Something is wrong! The track stops. The guns are not firing, but this does not stop the enemy. There are no timeouts in a battle. The NVA are firing as hard as ever. We have to make it to the edge of the village and get into the tall grass and bamboo.

One more big charge and my squad can have a little bit of cover from the enemy fire. I yell, "Charge! Charge!"

My men jump to their feet. Again, our guns are blazing! We make it to the edge of the village and hit the ground. The motionless track is to our right side. Our artillery firing and shelling stops.

Something is terribly wrong. Chuck crawls toward me. "Something is wrong!"

We look behind us and see no tracks or soldiers! We look to our left and see nothing; no men but my squad, and no tracks.

I yell to Craig, "Find out what is happening!"

Craig yells back, "They retreated! The whole company pulled back!"

We are now in enemy territory with five men and a track that isn't moving. The rest of the company is behind the tree line in safe territory.

I am mad. "Craig, give me the horn!"

I get on the radio and yell, "What the heck are you idiots doing, leaving us out here in the open?"

The lieutenant gets on the radio. "You men, come back! Retreat! Come back to tree line!"

The enemy fire was getting stronger and now it was directed directly at us. My squad was pinned down. I motioned for Chuck to come closer. "Chuck, I am going to the track to see if the guns are working!"

"Yeah! Let's all go!"

Chuck yelled at the men, "Follow us, men!"

We headed for the track, jumping and diving, trying not to be hit by the incoming rounds and shrapnel.

This was another of those moments in the 'Nam when I thought that this would be all over for my men and me. There was no way that we were going to get out of this situation alive. I kept praying as I ran toward the track.

I finally arrived at the track with Chuck close behind. I jumped up on the APC to see if the guns were working. I looked around inside the track for ammo and, to my surprise, I saw four men. Two of the soldiers looked almost dead and the other two were able to talk, but they were shot up too bad to do much of anything but whisper.

One of the wounded looked up at me. "Help us, help us!"

I did not know how we were going to help, but I said, "We will help you guys. We're going to get you guys out of here!"

Craig jumps on top of the track. "The captain wants to know what we are doing. He says for us to get out of here!"

"Tell him that we are not leaving these guys in the track! He better send us some help, fast!"

Craig gets back on the radio and then he responds, "The captain says that he cannot send any help to us right now!"

This makes my blood boil! I jumped out of the track. "Killer, you go to the front and keep firing! Craig, you stay close to the track and keep firing! Where are Emerald and Raymond and the rest of the men?"

Craig says, "Raymond and Emerald are on the other side of the track. I don't know where the other guys are, Sarge!"

We are missing White and Eckert. *Are they dead? Are they wounded?* I must take care of my immediate task, and that is to try my hardest to save the lives of my men and myself. Chuck, of course, is trying to do the same. We must do something, and do it now!

"Chuck, jump on the 50. We will take turns! I'll change out the barrels and feed ammo for you!"

"Cool, Danny!"

Chuck and I loved to shoot the 50-caliber machine gun. Chuck got behind the 50 and let it rip. He was a maniac. I fed him belt after belt of ammo. He was firing so fast that the barrel turned white-hot. It was too hot to touch with my bare hands. The jammed gun needed to be restarted. I looked for a glove, but I could only see a rag. I grabbed the rag, placed it on the white-hot barrel, and pulled it off. I reached for another barrel and quickly stuck it on the gun. Chuck continued to fire. I yelled to Chuck, "My turn! My turn!"

Chuck jumped down onto the track floor, and I jumped to the top of the track. I started firing as quick as I could. Chuck was feeding me ammo until the gun jammed. The barrel was white-hot again. I glanced down to see what Chuck was doing.

I was on top of the track in the open, and not firing a weapon. The enemy was now concentrating on capturing the APC. This would be a great trophy for the NVA. The firing by the enemy was now getting hotter. Mortars are now hitting the track and all around us. A piece of shrapnel hits my right hand near my thumb.

Chuck does not know that I am now wounded. "My turn to shoot!"

"OK, coming down!"

I jump to the floor of the APC, and Chuck jumps behind the 50. I start feeding the ammo belts to Chuck. I have so much adrenaline in me; I cannot feel the pain in my hand. Chuck again is firing hard. He is not letting up. He cannot stop for a second because the enemy is now in the trees and bushes within fifty feet of us. The enemy wants this APC really bad. The barrel is getting hot and the gun jams.

I reach for another barrel and the rag to pull the scalding barrel from the gun. I cannot find the rag. Chuck yells, "Come on, Danny! We are getting overrun!"

I don't have time to remove my shirt and use it for a hot pad to remove the barrel. I must act quickly. I have no other choice but to remove the barrel with my bare hands. With my bare hands, I reach for the barrel and twist it off. I install the new barrel in a matter of seconds. I feed the ammo to Chuck as he fires away.

The new barrel is getting hot again and jams. I change the white-hot barrel out time after time. My hands begin to bleed but they are cauterized quickly. The scorching, searing heat from the barrels keeps the blood from flowing from my hands.

I don't know how much more we can take. I move inside to the driver's seat. I pull the wounded, almost dead driver out of the seat. To my marvel and amazement, the motor is still running. I pull one of the levers and the machine moves. The track is still able to move.

I yell to Chuck, "Did you feel that?"

"Yeah! Can you drive it?"

"Yes, but I'll get Craig to drive and I'll feed you ammo!"

I pulled myself over the top of the tank. "Craig, come in here!"

Craig climbs in. "Sarge, the lieutenant wants you!"

"Tell him to shut up!"

"What?"

"Tell him to shut up, now!"

Craig gets on the horn. "Blackhawk Three says to *shut up!*"

I grab Craig. "Can you drive this thing?"

"No!"

"Well, you are going to learn!"

We moved to the driver's seat. "Just work these two levers and move that thing for the accelerator!" I pointed to the levers. I pointed at another lever. "I think that that is reverse. Figure it out!"

I moved back to help Chuck with the gun. The barrel was sweltering again and jamming after every shot. I changed the barrel and Chuck started shooting again. The APC started moving. This gave me an unbelievable feeling inside. *Could this be possible? Are we going to get out of this event alive?* My mother has always said, "Prayer changes things!" No one could say that I was not praying, for I was praying hard! The track started moving erratically.

I did not care how it moved, just as long as it moved away from the enemy. Craig finally got the track headed toward the rest of our company. Craig must have figured it out because we were moving faster now. I jumped on top with Chuck. "Hold on tight, Chuck. Craig doesn't know what he's doing. Don't get thrown off!"

I looked in the direction of our company, and I could see that the other tracks were now firing at the village. I looked back at the village and I could see our artillery support coming in again. Chuck was still firing, and we were now in the middle of the rice paddy.

I saw Raymond, Emerald, and Killer doing a good job of keeping up with the speed of the track. I yelled to Craig, "Stop!"

Craig stopped the APC. I yelled to the men on the ground, "Get on, men! Get on!"

Killer, Emerald, and Raymond jumped in the track.

"OK, Craig, get moving!"

The track takes off. Chuck loses his balance and almost falls off. The rest of us are getting tossed around in the tank like rag dolls. This rough ride is of no consequence compared to death. The track finally arrived at the defensive perimeter the company had set up. My palms were hurting from the burns, and my right hand was hurting from the shrapnel.

My discomfort quickly dissipated as I thought about the whole company leaving my squad in enemy territory. I was enraged, fuming, and infuriated! I jumped out of the track and ran to the lieutenant. Watkins stuck out his hand for a handshake and said, "Am I happy to see you!"

I did not shake his hand. I started yelling, "You have got to be the worst lieutenant in the Army! You and the old man are the stupidest pieces of crap I have ever seen! Neither you nor him deserve your bars! Why would you leave us to die out there in no-man's land? Look at my hands! Look at the shrapnel in my hand! Look at the blisters!" I held out the palms of my hands and showed them to him.

"Sarge, you just saved the lives of four men! You guys could have come back and just left the track and the soldiers in it, but you didn't!"

"Do you really think for one minute that Chuck and I would leave wounded men to the gooks to be tortured?"

"Please, calm down, Sergeant Rock. I am going to go and speak to the captain!"

"Fine! I am going to find out where the rest of my guys were!"

I hurriedly walked to Eckert, White, and my Kit Carson Scout, Dong. "Where in the heck were you guys?"

Eckert replied, "Everyone was pulling back. We thought that our squad was pulling back too!"

White joins in, "Yeah, Sarge, everybody was running backwards, retreating. You know us. We would have stayed with you all of the way, even if we thought that we were going to die. With all of the explosions and noise and smoke, the guys on our left were pulling back. You guys were on the other side of the tank, or I mean the track, so we lost contact! It will never ever happen again!"

I turned to Dong. His eyes were really big. "Dong, you had better keep up with me from now on! If I get killed, you get killed! You got it?"

"Yes, Sergeant Wock!"

"It's Rock! It's Rock! It's Rock! Not Wock!"

Eckert says, "I'll teach him, Sarge."

The Doc arrives. "Let's see your hands, Danny!"

I held out my hands with the palms up.

"Man alive, Danny. How did you get these burns and blisters? Let's see the back of your hand! What is this?"

"It's shrapnel."

"So how did you get the burns?"

"The 50 gun barrels. I was switching out the barrels, and we lost the rag that we were using, so I had to use my bare hands."

"Was it painful?"

"I was so afraid of the gooks taking the APC and killing us, I didn't even think about the pain! Maybe I did think about the pain for a second, but when we saw the NVA in the bushes close to us, all that I thought about was feeding Chuck the ammo and changing out the barrels! Man, Chuck was great!"

"Here is some ointment for your hands. I'll wrap them up, but first I need to pull out the shrapnel from the back of your hand!"

Doc turns my hand over and starts pulling small pieces of metal from my hand. I flinch, but the pain is far less than the pain I felt when he pulled out the shrapnel from my arm!

"You are lucky that this shrapnel didn't break any bones."

"Yeah, I am lucky about that."

"OK, I'll wrap your hands now. Are they hurting?"

My palms were hurting really bad, but my men were all watching Doc and me. "No, not much. I'll live."

"Yeah, right, Danny."

Doc finished wrapping. He stood up. "That is the best that I can do for ya."

"Thank you, Doc. I appreciate you."

Doc left to check on other patients.

The lieutenant returns. "Sergeant Rock, have you calmed down enough so we can talk?"

I was still mad and really did not want to speak to him or the captain. "Yeah, I guess so, sir."

"I spoke to the captain and he said that you guys deserve a medal for what you did."

"We only did what any soldier should have done. We saw the wounded and decided to try to save them. If I would have left those guys behind, I could not live with myself. And besides, the track had a 50 that was working, so it gave us some more firepower."

"Well, anyhow, the captain is going to try and get you and Lewis the Medal of Honor, and he is going to try to get medals for your other men too."

Chuck overhears the conversation. "The Medal of Honor? I thought that the Medal of Honor was mainly for men that were heroes, or got killed trying to be heroes. Like a guy jumping on a grenade to save his men."

"Yeah, you are right. But in this case, you were told to come back and leave the track. The captain didn't know that there was anyone in the track alive. Rock, you will also earn another Purple Heart!"

"Really, another Purple Heart?"

"Yep, another Purple Heart. Now you and Lewis are tied, but neither of you try to beat the other one, huh?"

"Yeah, I will go for that idea. I don't want to be in a contest for Purple Hearts."

"OK, men, I have to go see what is next! We have got to take this village!"

Chuck and I start talking. Chuck says, "A Medal of Honor? Did you hear that, Danny?"

I had never thought about medals. I did not even know the level of medals, but I did think that the Medal of Honor was one of the best. I did not know the difference between a Bronze Star and a Silver Star. "Yeah, that would be great, Chuck, but don't count on it!"

I looked around at the men. "OK, men, get ready! Load up! We're going after the village again!"

Watkins returns. "Lewis and Rock, the old man says that you guys will be getting Silver Star medals, not Medal of Honor medals. I am not sure why, but it has something to do with you being alive!"

I looked puzzled. "Sir, I am not going to get killed in order to get the Medal of Honor!"

We all laugh.

"Yes, you are right. Get a smaller medal and stay alive. And besides, a Silver Star is right up there with the best!"

"But, sir, what about the guys that were on the ground, and Craig, inside the track with us?"

"The captain says that you and Lewis will get Silver Stars and the rest of your men that were with you will get Bronze Stars."

"That will be really great, sir. Now let's go and capture that village!"

CHAPTER 21

Chuck Saves My Life

Chuck says, "Hey, Danny, with all of this going on, why do you think the lieutenant and the captain are talking about giving us medals? Why can't they wait until we are not fighting?"

"I think they just want us to be at our best."

"You mean because you yelled at them for leaving us out there in the open to be killed?"

"Yeah, I think they are worried about us dropping back and not fighting as hard, because we are afraid they will pull back on us again. Maybe the medals are just something to keep us going. You know, like a dangling carrot."

Chuck laughs. "We probably won't receive our medals because we will be dead after this assault on the village."

I also laugh. "You are probably right, Chuck! Well, let's get the men moving. Chuck, do you hear that?"

"Yeah, that sounds like tanks."

"Yeah, to me too. We'll take that village now."

The tanks and the tracks get on line. "Man, Chuck, will you look at that?"

The tanks and the tracks looked great. They reminded me of fire-eating dragons. They were ready to go. They were ready to fight.

Chuck acknowledges, "We are going to win this battle now for sure, Danny!"

My radio sounds, "Blackhawks, come to Annihilator!"

Chuck and I and the rest of the squad leaders headed to see the captain. Before the captain said a word, I said, "Sir, why don't we just call in a bunch of artillery then attack the village?"

"That is exactly what we are going to do. We are not going to fail today. Failure is not an option here. Set your men up next to a tank, not a track! Now let's move out!"

We turned and walked toward our squads. "Why does he want us next to the tanks and not the tracks, Danny?"

"Probably because of the tanks' firepower. But, if we think about it, I think that I would rather be next to an APC. The NVA want to stop a tank before stopping an APC."

I really did not know why the captain wanted us to be next to the tanks. I had learned a long time ago to not ask questions, unless I thought the command would kill my men or me. We got on line with the machines. Our firepower support started coming in, round after round, pounding the enemy fortress. The tanks and tracks started moving forward. I saw Commander Snow. He saw me and motioned for us to come next to him. We moved closer to his tank. I gave him two thumbs up.

Snow's machine opened up, firing the 50. He gave the command for all of the tracks to start firing. He gave the command for the tanks to start firing the 105s. The sound was overwhelming — rockets firing, explosions, guns firing, the infantry firing grenades, M-60s, and M-16s. Finally, we have more firepower going out than coming in.

We crossed the rice paddies without a single pause. When we arrived at the village tree line, we kept firing. The tanks were relentless with their 105 big guns. The 50s were cutting down trees and hooches. Every M-60 on the tracks was firing. Finally, we were going to wipe out these guys.

The enemy was on the run. Every time an NVA or VC would move, a shot would chase them down. This was a great feeling, to be in command after trying so hard to take this village. However, the village was not completely taken. We had to do more. The tanks and APCs moved forward twenty to thirty meters at a time. The more movement forward, the less incoming fire we were getting. Over and over again, the tracks and the tanks moved forward, until finally only a few rounds were being fired at us.

We had learned from past experiences that just because the firing has stopped, it does not mean that the entire enemy was dead. The VC and the NVA would jump in holes and underground bunkers. They were very good at hiding. It looked as though the fighting was over, at least for now. My radio sounds, "Blackhawk Three, come to Cherokee Three, over!"

"On my way!" I hurried to the lieutenant. "Yes, sir!"

"Rock, we have a tank stuck in the paddies!"

"Are there any men in the tank?"

"Yes, but they are OK."

"So what do ya want me to do? Do you want me to take my squad out there so you can leave us again?" I was still mad about the company leaving us out in the open.

"No, we are not going to let that ever happen again! I want your squad to go out and secure the area around the tank until the tank guys can free it."

"OK, sir, but no monkey business. You just remember that there are probably thirty VC still hiding in holes!"

"Yep, I know. We are going to be searching the area."

"I'll get my guys ready!"

I walked toward my squad. On my way, I saw lots of bodies. All were enemy bodies. I saw mortars, guns, ammo, and a few big guns. I met up with my squad and told them what we were going to do. Chuck came up to us and asked, "What did Watkins want, Danny?"

"He wants my squad to pull guard in the paddy so they can get the tank out of the mud. The tank is really deep in the mud!"

"Man, Rock, haven't we done enough? Why doesn't the captain get someone else to pull guard?"

"I don't know, but if anything weird happens this time I am going to be mad! Keep an eye on us, Chuck. I am going to be on point." I turn back to my men. "OK, men, let's go! Now I am going to go first. Keep spread out with more space between us than usual!"

I wanted the extra space so we would not all be in the rice paddy at the same time if the crap hit the fan. I started to move from the back of the village toward the front. I did not know it, but Chuck was moving adjacent to me, fifty meters away and to my right. He was tracking me. I was now almost at the high weeds and trees at the front of the village. I could not see the tank because of the thickness of the bushes. I was getting a little worried because I was now in the bush by myself. I wanted to get out of the bush fast.

I did not notice the three VC that had come out of a hidden hole. They were moving toward me. I was struggling to get out of the bush. The VC were getting closer and closer to me. They were now just fifteen meters behind and to the right of me. They lift up their weapons and get me in their sights. I hear a scream. "Danny, get down!"

I jump to the ground and I hear a burst of shots from an M-16 rifle. I look in the direction of the yell and the sounds of the weapon. I see three dead VC. Then I see Chuck. My friend has saved my life. Chuck starts rolling over the bodies while I am still on the ground. He is checking to be certain that they are dead. I jump up and hurry over to Chuck. "What happened?"

Chuck wipes the sweat off of his forehead. "Man, Danny, that was close."

"So how did they get on me?"

"They must have come out of a hole. They saw you and started tracking you. I started tracking them. I was hoping that you would see them and start shooting so we could get them in a cross fire. Where are the rest of your men?"

"I told them to stay a long distance apart. So keep talking. What happened before you killed them?"

"I was being very quiet, but still keeping up with them. They were like cats sneaking through the bush. Anyhow, they raised their rifles to shoot you. I yelled at you so they would turn toward me. When you ducked and they turned, I opened up. It worked out perfectly. If you hadn't hit the ground before I opened up I might have shot you. It was cool!"

I looked at Chuck with amazement. Chuck was not even supposed to be here. He saw that my situation may be dangerous and decided to act.

I walked close to Chuck and gave him a hug. "Thanks, Chuck. You are the man!"

"Any time, Rock. We are in this together. Now let's get that tank unstuck!"

I was so proud to have a friend like Chuck. He had an instinct, a feeling when something might be dangerous. He was very smart about war, and I was glad to have him near me in battle. I looked at Chuck. "I guess that by you saving my life, you will want my pound cake from my C-rations, huh?"

"Are you kidding? I want your pound cake and your peaches for a month!"

We laugh hard.

"OK, Chuck, you got it."

I would do anything for this man, and I do mean man! Chuck and I started speaking to each other on the very first day we met at basic training. We hit it off quickly. We laughed at the same things and had equal morals. He would always say that he was the bad guy and I was the good guy, because he cursed a little and I did not. We were like brothers.

"What is your squad supposed to do?" Chuck asked.

"We are just going a little into the rice paddy to keep the gooks away from the tank."

We finally got to the edge of the rice paddy. By this time, all of my men were with me. I was happy to have all of my squad together.

Killer says, "I see three dead gooks, Sarge. Did you get 'em?"

"No, Sergeant Chuck Lewis did, just before they got me."

"Way to go, Sergeant Lewis. Hey, Sergeant Rock, look at the tank. Do you think he will get out?"

435

I turned and looked at the struggling tank moving back and forth. "Man, Killer, I don't know. It is really deep. Craig, what does the radio say?"

"They are going to send out another tank to pull it out."

"Oh, boy, now we are going to have two tanks in the open instead of one."

The second tank came out of the village running wide open. The second tank hooked a large towing cable to the first tank and started pulling. The second tank was pulling so hard that it started to get stuck. The pulling stopped. One man jumped out of the second tank and unhooked the tow cable. The first tank was now buried very deep.

The men from the buried tank started to take off guns and unload ammo. They were taking everything that they could off of the dead, useless tank in the mud.

Eckert says, "What's happening, Sarge?"

"They are going to abandon the tank."

"You mean leave it so the gooks can get it?"

"Man, I hope not."

The men from the stuck tank climbed aboard the second tank, and the second tank headed toward the village. We watched closely as the second tank slowly moved through the paddy back to the village, trying not to knock any men off. We looked back at the stuck tank, and to our surprise we saw NVA and VC climbing in the tank. They somehow had managed to get behind the tank, out of our sight. I could not tell how many they had, but I could see at least five. I yelled to the men, "Men, look at the stuck tank! There are gooks climbing inside!"

My men and I start shooting. We are hitting the tank, but it appears as though the enemy is safe behind the strong steel walls of our American-made machine! The second tank reached the village perimeter, and the turret slowly turned. The big gun on the tank moved slowly until the stuck tank was in their sights. One more slight move to the right, and all heck broke loose.

The big gun was opening up on the stuck tank. The 105 shells from the tank were bombarding the stuck tank round after round! I actually did not know if they were shooting 105 rounds or larger, but I did know that the rounds were not smaller than the 105s.

I looked at Chuck. He was as amazed as I was that we would blow up our own tank. "Chuck, are they firing 105s?"

"Yep, I think so! Man, Danny, they are blowing the tank to pieces!"

"Yeah, and what about the gooks inside?"

We both laugh. Chuck pats me on the back. "I guess they met their Waterloo, huh?"

"Yep, even John Wayne couldn't save those turkeys!"

Craig brings me the radio horn. Craig says, "The old man says for the leaders to come to the CP. He has good news."

I get on the horn. "This is Blackhawk Three, go!"

"All Blackhawks come to Annihilator!"

"On my way!"

I rushed over to the CP, stepping over and avoiding dead enemy soldiers. I saw a neatly laid-out stack of AK-47 rifles.

Chuck was beside me. "Man, this is a mess, Danny. The flies are already swarming."

Chuck, Mac, and I walked up to the captain. The lieutenant was speaking to the old man. The captain turns toward us. "How are your hands, Rock?"

"I'll live, sir!"

"OK, men, here is the good news!"

We all listened intently.

"First of all, you guys all did a great job. I haven't figured out the body count yet. I have to figure out how many the tanks killed and how many we killed!"

I looked at Killer as I spoke to the captain. "Let Killer count them, and he would say that we killed ninety percent!"

"Oh, I can't do that. I am thinking thirty percent for us and sixty percent for the tanks."

I scratch my head. "But, sir, that is only ninety percent!"

"Well, I know, but you have to realize that Killer will say that he killed ten percent by himself." We all laughed. The captain really liked Killer. Some people say that Killer put the captain on the map, so to speak.

The captain continued, "We are going to be lifted to the next zone. And, as always, heading north! The choppers will be here in a few minutes with ammo. They will drop off supplies then return and pick us up. The LZ will be between the blown-up tank and the village tree line."

I liked how the captain laid out the plan. I could never tell if he was afraid. If he was afraid, he never showed it. I don't think anyone over here in the 'Nam was completely free of fear.

The captain says, "Go ahead, men! Get your guys ready!"

"Yes, sir!"

Chuck, Mac, and I headed out to meet up with our squads.

Mac speaks, "Hey, Rock, I heard that you almost bought the farm. Did ya?"

"Heck yeah. Chuck saved me. He shot three of them!"

"Cool, Chuck! You guys are really close. OK, I'll see ya later."

Mac walked toward his squad.

Chuck says, "I like Mac."

"Yeah, me too. Hey, Chuck, how did the saying *'Bought the farm'* come about? You know, like when you get killed, people say 'he bought the farm.'"

"Believe it or not, I know the answer."

"Shoot, tell me. I have always wondered."

"OK. Back in the thirties, when people took out life insurance and died, their insurance policy could pay off the farm. So you get the phrase because when you die, you bought the farm."

"I never knew. You are so smart."

Jokingly, Chuck says, "Yeah, I know. Hey, Danny, I hear slicks."

"Yeah, me too."

The choppers start to come in after some squad throws out green smoke and the pilot acknowledges it. The gunners throw out ammo. There are M-60 rounds, M-16 rounds, hand grenades, and M-79 grenade launcher rounds. This is a welcome sight because I am a little low on ammo. I still had a bandolier that was seventy-five percent full, but this would be used up quickly in a firefight.

We received our ammo and got ready for the next pass of the slicks. I look at the men. "Take all you can, because we won't hump today!"

I was heavy with ammo. My men were loaded down with lots and lots of grenades and rifle rounds. I looked at Chuck. He was also loaded down.

Chuck's M-60 carrying guy was loaded too heavily. Chuck saw that he was struggling. "Here, give me two belts of your rounds."

"Thanks, Sergeant Lewis."

"You are certainly welcome, Oli. You are certainly welcome."

He was quoting the comedy movies of Laurel & Hardy. In a way, it was strange to me how we can make jokes when we all knew that we might not even make it through the day. In America, people would say, "Just take it a day at a time!" Over here in Vietnam, we would say, "Just take it an hour at a time!" I looked at Raymond, my M-60 guy, to be sure that he wasn't too heavy.

White and Eckert had belts of M-60s placed over their shoulders. They usually took care of Raymond. The M-60 belts can get very heavy. I see Craig running toward me.

Craig is on the horn. "Hot LZ! Hot LZ!"

"What?"

"We are going to be landing in a hot LZ!"

I yell to my men, "We will be lading in a hot LZ, men! So be careful! Here come the choppers! We will be on three and four! Let's get it!"

Chuck runs up to me. "Which slicks does my squad usually get on?"

"Usually one and two, left. The left side, first and second, but check with Mac. Make sure you aren't all trying to get on the same slick!"

"OK!"

Chuck takes off running. We all start heading for the rice paddies where the LZ is located. The slicks will come in fast. This is not a hot LZ any longer, but with all of the crap we have been through, they won't take a chance of landing.

I take one more glance at my men, then I decide to tell Dong to stay with me. I look at him and notice that he is only carrying one bandolier of ammo and his M-16 rifle. "Dong, go get an M-60 belt of ammo from White, and carry it!"

"Yes, I do!"

"Stay close to me when we get on the chopper!"

"Yes!"

The choppers came in, and they were moving fast. "Let's go, men!"

My men knew the routine that I required of them. They knew where I wanted every man and what chopper I wanted them to jump on. We jumped on the choppers, helping each other, pulling and tugging each other while the choppers were still moving, until we were in the slick.

I looked back to be sure that Eckert and his men were loaded. I see Eckert pointing at the chopper in front of mine. I look in the direction of his pointing. Chuck is having a hard time getting in the slick. He has loaded himself down with so much weight that it is hard for him to get in. He is standing on the runners and trying to sling his leg up. The chopper is speeding up and moving higher and higher. We start to laugh.

But then Chuck slips and his legs are on either side of the skid-landing rail. Our laughter turns to horror. Chuck is losing his balance. He is getting farther away from the body of the chopper. The chopper is going higher and higher and faster and faster. I want to help him, but I am helpless!

I see an arm coming out of the chopper, then another one. One arm grabs Chuck's rucksack and the other grabs his hand and arm. He finally gets his footing back on the skid-rail. One more strong pull from the men inside the chopper, and Chuck is inside. This was scary.

I thought to myself, *What a way to die.* This was no laughing matter. I look at my men and we start laughing anyhow. Chuck was in a bind, but he was not killed. This was a relief. I look at Chuck's chopper, and he sticks his head out, looking back at me. He has a big grin on his face. I give him the thumbs up sign. He acknowledges with one thumb up and laughs. He sticks his head back inside. I do the same. Our choppers are now moving at full speed.

We move along at the chopper's maximum speed for forty-five minutes before we get almost scared to death by the door gunners' machine guns firing. Every time the gunners open up with their M-60s, the sound hurts our eardrums. Again, I wished that I had done a better job of keeping up with my earplugs. I would get earplugs when our C-rations came in. I, as many other men, would put them in our pockets or install them in our helmet cover's elastic band. But during a firefight, we would lose them.

We cannot worry about earplugs now, because we all knew that we were going to be dropped off in a hot LZ. In just a few minutes we would be fighting for our lives again. I looked at Emerald and, as usual, he was as white as a ghost. I could not blame him for being afraid. I was afraid myself, but, as usual, I cannot show fear. The door gunners continue to shoot.

I look ahead and I can see the landing zone. We are going to be dropped off in the middle of the enemy. There is a large rice paddy ahead and the enemy is firing at the choppers from both sides. We can see the tracer rounds coming at us.

I know that tracer rounds are used every fifth to seventh shot; therefore, a lot of shots have already been fired by the time we see the tracer. The door gunners also have tracer rounds. There are so many bullets leaving the choppers and so many bullets coming toward the choppers that some must be hitting head-on. I don't know why I think about things like that at a time like this, but I do. The slicks come in fast and hard. I can hear the bullets bouncing off of the metal of the choppers.

As usual, the door gunners want us to jump out as fast as we can. They would prefer that we jump out at six to seven feet above the ground. My men knew from the past that jumping out of a speeding chopper from six to seven feet above the ground could be the cause of a broken leg or arm. How would we survive a firefight with a broken limb?

The slicks moved closer to the ground. The choppers were closer to the left of the rice paddy tree line than the right. When the slicks were at an elevation of four feet, we jumped off. The whole company was now firing at the left tree line. We had to take the tree line and get to safety. The choppers were still firing.

We were getting fired at from the rear and from the front. The choppers moved higher and turned around. They were now returning to fire again at the enemy to our rear. This was really helpful to us grunts, because now the enemy fire at our rear was being directed toward the choppers. The enemy fire was intense, now directed at us, on our side of the paddy.

We would open fire on the enemy and then hit the ground. We would jump to our feet, start firing, and move forward. We did this rapidly, again and again. On our next assault I could see NVA and VC. Craig hands me the horn. The captain says, "All of you, listen up! On our next assault, we are taking the tree line! Ready, ready, ready...Attack! Attack!"

The whole company jumped up from the leech-infested, wet rice paddy and started firing. We were now winning the battle. We finally made it to the tree line. The NVA and VC that were not dead were running away from us!

The captain directed me to call in artillery in the direction of the runaways. I did so, and for a moment after the artillery had come in, it was quiet.

My radio sounds, "Platoon One and Two, do the body count! The rest of you, pull security!"

I look at Chuck. "Man, Chuck, were you worried about getting on the chopper?"

"Was I? I really didn't think that I was going to make it! Did you see how I was struggling?"

"Yes I did! I was really worried! That would have been some way to die, huh?"

"If I would have died like that, I would want you to tell the people back home something different!"

"Like what?"

"Tell 'em that I jumped on a grenade to save my whole squad!"

We both laughed.

"And if I die before you, tell my family how I died, and tell them that I never almost fell out of a chopper like you did!"

"Oh, shut up!"

Our radios sound, "All Blackhawks come to the CP!"

We hurried over to the captain's command post. The captain says, "Men, we didn't lose anyone, thank God, but we killed a lot of NVA and VC. Good job! We will dig in for the night here. Tomorrow, we will take over the enemy's position across the rice paddy. I have been told that they are dug in deep!"

In the past two battles, I felt as though we called in artillery too late. Sarcastically, I say, "Sir, do you think that we can call in some firepower this time before we go in?"

"Yes we will, smart-butt! The reason that we have not been getting fire support is because of this stupid Tet Offensive thing! The NVA have really built up their forces. They are stronger than ever. We are fighting gooks all over South Vietnam, and the artillery support bases and the Navy have been busy. You men get your men dug in deep. I will be calling in fire support off and on during the night. Sergeant Rock, if I get tired directing firepower, I'll let you know and you can take over!"

"Yes, sir!"

"Now make a good perimeter and be ready. Tomorrow will be a rough day!"

CHAPTER 22

Two-Week-Long Battle

I tell my men how important tonight and tomorrow will be. I have a bad feeling about tomorrow. My men are digging in and they are staying low to the ground.

"That is it, men! Keep low!"

I look to my left and I see that Dong is standing up with his clothes off. He has a pair of white, Army-issued boxer underwear on. I grab him and push him to the ground. "What are you doing, you idiot? You're going to give our position away!"

Dong is surprised by my intensity. "No VC, Sergeant Wock! No VC!"

"What are you talking about?"

"VC and NVA are in tunnels and hiding. They not come out 'til morning, Wock!"

"Dong, you just do what I tell you to do!"

"Yes, Sergeant, I will do!"

"Why were you standing up?"

"I was airing out clothes. No water, I use air to clean!"

"Well, they still stink!"

"Yes, Sarge!"

"OK, now start digging! I am not mad at you, but don't do that again!"

"What is 'mad,' Sergeant Wock?"

"It's angry."

"Angry?"

How can I explain angry to him? "OK, Dong, look at me!" I smiled and had a pleasant look on my face. I said, "Happy!" Then I made a mean face and got in his face with mine and said, "Mad or angry, huh?"

"OK, Sergeant Wock, I know!"

I looked in the book that the Army had given me when they gave me Dong, but I found no reference to angry or mad. Maybe the rest of the night would be less confusing!

The night started out quiet. After we dug our foxholes, my men and I started talking about all of the crap that we have been going through. White, while opening up a can of C-rations, says, "Sarge, I know that I have asked you this before, but do you think that we will ever see home again? I don't feel that tomorrow is going to go right! What do you think?"

I didn't feel that things were going to go well either, but I couldn't tell White that! It was time to play psychiatrist again. I had to get White's mind off of our possible demise in the upcoming battle.

I turned toward White. "Yes, of course! We will wipe these gooks out in four hours! Hey, what are you looking most forward to when you get home?"

"Well, Sarge, first of all, even if it only takes us four hours to win the battle, that is four hours they will be shooting at us!"

I sort of laugh. "Yeah, but just shoot and stay down!"

"Sarge, when I get home, I am going to start racing my Corvette. I think about home every day now. I think about family, friends, and girlfriends. But first of all, I am going to see a doctor!"

"A doctor?"

"Yeah, I think that my jaw is still broken from when you beat me up!"

We both start laughing.

"I did not beat you up. I just hit you in the face a few times. Did you learn a lesson?"

"Yes I did. I will never grab another man's weapon and run with it again!"

Again we both laugh.

"You know, White, it is funny now, but it wasn't funny then! You have turned out to be a great soldier. You and I have been through a lot together, huh?"

"Man, have we! Do you remember when I took the whole case of grenades on an LP?"

"Yes I do! We were supposed to just go to the site and listen, but you threw grenades all night long. The captain was very, very mad at me."

"Yep, and you didn't squeal on me either! Do you remember the smell of Proud Mary?"

"Man, how can I forget? You stuck her in her private parts with your bayonet and she deflated. What a smell! I had to lie next to that dead body for a long time. But you know what?"

"What?"

"I would rather lay next to Proud Mary for a whole day than fight the NVA like we have been for four hours!"

"Yes, me too! Maybe tomorrow won't be as bad as we think, huh, Rock?"

"I hope you are right, White. I hope you are right!"

Deep down I knew that the next few days were going to be bad. I never could figure out exactly how Chuck and I knew when it was going to be a fierce battle or just a routine shoot and capture. Maybe some artillery will help us make a long fight into a short one!

We bombarded the enemy's stronghold on and off all night long. The captain would call in the support for a few hours, then I would take over. Needless to say, neither of us got our much-needed sleep. Morning finally came.

We ate our C-ration breakfast as we checked out our weapons and loaded ourselves with ammo. My men were somber. No one was talking about cars. No one was talking about loved ones. No one was talking about home.

Killer stands up and starts to sing, "Please, Mister Custer, I don't wanna go! Please, Mister Custer, please don't make me go!"

Killer was singing a song from 1960, and this finally broke our quiet, somber mood. We all started to sing, "I had a dream last night about the coming fight. Somebody yelled attack, and there I stood with an arrow in my back. Please, Mister Custer, please don't make me go!"

By this time, we were getting a little loud. Lieutenant Watkins came up to me. "Man, Rock, you guys are in a good mood, huh?"

"Not really."

I motioned for Watkins to come closer. "I am really worried, sir. We have to cross the rice paddy in the open even before we get to the enemy."

"Yeah, but we have not had any incoming fire all night. Maybe they left and went home." He laughs.

"Yeah, right."

I did not believe for one minute that these guys had gone home. When the NVA started to fight, they really fought. They will fight to the end.

"Rock, the old man wants us. Go and tell Lewis and Mac. I am going to the CP."

"Yes, sir."

I head over to grab Chuck and Mac. "Hey, men, the old man wants us."

Mac says, "He is probably going to give us some glad bags."

I smile. "No body bags today. Let's just kick their butts and be done with it! Let's go see the captain."

We walked up to the captain. He turned. "Hey, men, let's get this over quick! Platoon One will take the left flank. Lieutenant Watkins, take your guys up the middle, and the rest will take the right flank! We will call in artillery as we cross the paddy. We will charge in five minutes. There will be no questions. That is the way we will do it. I want to have this thing done by noon!"

We all answered, "Yes, sir!"

We took off, heading for our squads.

Mac says to Chuck and I, "Are you guys scared?"

Chuck says, "Of course we are, but remember what Rock told you!"

"What's that, Lewis?"

"Don't let your men know that you are afraid!"

"Oh, yeah, I won't. But sometimes it is hard, huh, Rock?"

"Yeah, tell me about it. OK, men, good luck!"

I am now within hearing distance of my squad. No one is saying anything. There is no singing, only heavy breathing. I look at Emerald and, as usual, he is white with fear. "Emerald, just stay close to me! Craig, you make sure the radio antenna is turned down! Raymond, you make sure your ammo carriers are close to you. We are going up the middle!"

The men started to move around, getting in fighting position. My radio goes off, "Let's attack, men!"

The artillery starts to come in, and us grunts start to move quickly toward the rice paddy. We get a few meters into the rice paddy and we are not getting any incoming fire.

We get to the middle of the paddy, and still no one is shooting at us. We are now running toward the tree line. We are three-quarters of the way deep into the rice paddy, and still no one is shooting at us!

Maybe the lieutenant was right. Maybe the NVA decided to just go home. Wouldn't that be nice, to have no fighting today! We finally made it to the tree line with no resistance. The captain holds up on the artillery. Maybe he feels that the enemy has gone.

I actually knew that the captain was cautious. He knew, as I did, that the gooks could be waiting in holes and tunnels.

Once we made it to the tree line, we were in a medium blend of bush, bamboo, and trees. We cautiously moved deeper into the bush. Once we moved 200 meters into the bush, things changed.

Explosions, whistling rounds, and shrapnel were just a few of the sounds we were hearing. The NVA and VC were hitting us with rockets, mortars, bullets, and grenades. We jumped to the ground quickly and started returning fire. Craig hands me the radio. "It's Annihilator!"

I grab the horn. "This is Blackhawk Three, go!"

"Can you see 'em? Can you call in support?"

"No, but I can get close with firepower!"

"OK, do it!"

"On it!"

"Fireball Five-Niner, this is Blackhawk Three, over!"

"This is Fireball Five-Niner, how have you been Blackhawk Three?"

Fireball Five-Niner sometimes did not realize that when I called him, it was because I was in dire need of help. I usually did not have time for chitchat.

"I am doing just fine, thank you, but we need help quick!"

"Ready to go. What's your location?"

I gave the grid to Fireball.

"OK, Blackhawk, I got it!"

"Give me a location round!"

"On the way!"

The round came in, but I could not tell if it was one of the NVA or ours. There was just too much noise and smoke for me to be able to see or hear where the round hit.

Fireball is back on the air. "How did you like it, Blackhawk?"

I had to think of something quickly. I could not call in artillery not knowing where it was hitting. One misplaced round could kill a lot of our guys. I decide to get a round high in the sky for a marker round.

"Fireball, I could not tell. So send me a high marker round! Send me one Willy Peter!"

This was also dangerous because when white phosphorus hit the skin of a living creature, it continued to burn until it had burned through the body. Water would not extinguish it. If I called the Willy Peter in on top of our own forces, it would be disastrous. However, if the first round that I called in did not hit us, then neither would this one.

"Willy Peter on the way!"

The round hit far up in the sky. It was far right of where I needed the round.

"Send me one shell left, five-zero-zero!"

"Left 500, on the way!"

The round dropped near perfect to the location that I wanted it.

"Fireball, that is good! Now walk 'em left!"

The shells started coming in one right after another. But the incoming rounds from the enemy did not quit. We advanced forward slightly. Every time we moved a little forward, we had to also move back slightly. Finally, we could see the NVA. They were dug in deep. They had a fortress.

We fired our weapons every time we saw movement, round after round and burst after burst from the Pig. Raymond, with the M-60, was using up a lot of ammo. If we didn't take over the enemy position by tonight, we would be dangerously low on ammo.

I told Raymond to fire short bursts. I saw Killer firing on full automatic. I ran over to Killer. "We are running low on ammo! Spread the word to fire semi-auto and shoot what you are aiming at!"

"OK, I'll tell everyone!"

Killer takes off to do as I had told him.

I get back on the radio. "Fireball Five-Niner, this is Blackhawk Three, over!"

"I am ready! How are they hitting?"

"Good! Now from my position, drop five-zero!"

"Here it comes!"

The rounds hit closer to our location, but it was also right on target.

"Perfect! Now give me six VT!"

"Here it comes!"

"Great! Keep firing!"

The shotgun shells were coming in strong and fast, but we were still getting incoming fire.

My radio goes off, "Blackhawk, this is Annihilator. Do you want me to take over fire support?"

"Can you see 'em now?"

"Yes! Do you want me to take over?"

"Yes! Go ahead!"

The fire support continued. Our support was coming in on the NVA. And the NVA fire support was dropping on us! We started to advance about fifteen feet forward. For every foot of advancement, we seemed to use twenty rounds each. Our ammo was disappearing. We had been fighting for seven hours now. The day was now starting to get darker. I felt a relief because the night usually brought a slowdown of fighting. We could not see the enemy and the enemy could not see us.

We fought for another hour, and as I had hoped, the fighting slowed. Craig came to me. "We are to make a perimeter and dig in for the night."

"Thanks, Craig. Sounds good to me. As long as we keep artillery support hitting 'em."

"Yeah, me too, Sarge."

"Craig, you pass the word to the guys on your right, and I'll pass the word to the rest."

"OK." He takes off.

"Craig, Craig, tell the guys to come down here!"

"Got it!"

The men cautiously move to my location. "Men, we are going to dig in for the night, so start digging! Dig two holes, and dig 'em deep!"

White says, "I am ready for that!"

Killer says, "Being in a hole is much safer than being behind a bush almost in the open!"

A few more single rounds whiz past our ears. We all hit the ground.

Emerald says, "I thought the captain said we were going to kick these guys' butts in a few hours!"

Eckert, while digging, asks, "Sarge, do you think that these guys are as tired as we are?"

Before I had a chance to answer, Raymond says, "I hope that they are as tired as we are, and I hope that they are running low on ammo."

I answer both questions. "I hope they are getting tired, and I don't think that they are low on ammo. But, usually, the night brings a little quiet."

Craig is handing me the horn. "I hope it is quiet. Sarge, it is Cherokee."

"This is Blackhawk Three, go!"

"How are you guys doing on ammo? Never mind. Not over the air. I'll come to you!"

The lieutenant was getting smarter and smarter. The Army had taught us to never give the enemy too much information. The enemy may be monitoring our transmissions. We didn't need to tell the NVA that we were low on ammo.

Watkins walks up to me. "How's your ammo, Rock?"

"Man, sir, we are dangerously low!"

"Yeah, so is everyone else!"

"Sir, here is what we can do in the morning. A chopper can come in, or maybe two choppers behind us at the rice paddy, and drop off ammo!"

"I have already spoken to the old man, and that is his plan exactly!"

"Man, he must be really smart!"

We both laugh.

The lieutenant takes off. "Take care, Sergeant Rock!"

"You too!"

I took my turn at digging, and then we sat next to the foxhole, finally getting a chance to eat our C-rations. As I opened up my bread in a can, I said, "Now men, we will start getting a few rounds shot at us tonight, so what are you supposed to do? I know that you guys really know, but we can't afford a mistake tonight. White, tell us."

"We don't want to shoot back!"

"And why do we not want to shoot back?"

Killer, like a school kid, raises his hand. "I know, I know, I know!"

"OK, pupil Killer, give us the answer, please!"

"Because if we fire back, the hot gases emitted from our rifles' flash-compressors at the end of our weapons will make a highly visible flame that will penetrate the dark, humidity-filled air, and give away our position!"

"Why can't you just say that the flash will give away our position?"

"Sarge, you have always told us to explain our comments well!"

The whole squad starts laughing.

"OK, men, let's pull guard! Set it up, Killer! I hope it will be reasonably quiet!"

The night, as expected, had a few incoming rounds, but my men held fast. Every once in a while, a rocket would hit near us, but the gooks' aim was off. No one was killed, at least not tonight. It was still dark when we started to get ready for the next day. We grabbed a bite to eat and loaded down with what ammo we had left.

With only a small amount of ammo, our goal was to sit tight and wait for our supply of ammo. Then we would attack again. We could see a glimpse of sunlight coming through the trees. The light made it easier for the NVA to zero in on us. In just minutes, all heck broke loose. We were being shelled and mortared and shot at. The NVA were relentless. This could be the day that we die. I was glad that we had dug deep foxholes.

We were in the foxholes, looking at the direction of the enemy. Emerald yells, "They are coming! They are coming! Sarge, they are coming!"

I could see the NVA advancing and shooting. "Hold your fire until you have a clear shot!"

We started to fire one shot at a time. We were knocking off a few of the enemy, but more were coming. The enemy's shooting was increasing. Rounds were flying. I hear a yell to my left. One of my men is slumped over the foxhole. I hear, "Medic, medic! Doc, over here! It's White!"

Doc, as usual, put his own life on the line to save another. He runs to White, ducking and diving, trying to stay away from the incoming fire.

I yell to my men, "Give Doc some cover!"

Doc is working on White. He abruptly stops. I could see that White was dead. I heard, "Doc, Doc, medic!"

Doc took off to save another life. Again, he was running, avoiding bullets, shrapnel, and falling trees. The NVA were getting closer. With the enemy getting so close, our ammo would be depleted soon! I heard the choppers in the distance. This was a welcome sound. The choppers kick out our ammo supply. We now have a large problem. The ammo is so far away from us that it will be dangerous to retrieve. The enemy is still advancing. I am down to two magazines of ammo. Killer comes up to me, crawling on his stomach. "Sarge, I am almost out of rounds! Is someone going to bring the ammo to us?"

"No, we have to get it for ourselves!"

Two rounds come in and almost hit Killer!

"I'll go, Sarge!"

Before I could say a word, Killer took off! We kept firing one round at a time, being very careful. Raymond has only fifty rounds for his M-60 machine gun. Ten more minutes, and I see Killer. He is so loaded down, he can barely walk. He looks like a Christmas tree that is covered with bandoliers and belts of M-60 ammo. He collapses at the back of our foxhole. We distribute the ammo quickly. Once Killer has unloaded, he grabs his rifle and one bandolier and heads back out to bring us more ammo.

We start firing more rounds at the enemy. Momentarily, the NVA stopped advancing. Killer returned with more ammo.

Again, we distributed the ammo. Killer unloads and starts to take off again. Eckert says, "Wait, Killer, I'll go with you!"

"Cool, let's get it!"

Over and over, Killer and Eckert bring us ammo. I look to my right and left and I see a few of the men from other squads getting ammo for their men. We start really firing hard at the enemy again. Craig is on the radio. Craig leans over. "We have plenty of ammo now, and more is coming!"

We continue to fight for two more hours before we move forward thirty feet. We fight for the rest of the day and we are able to advance another thirty feet. Night is falling. We are looking forward to night and hopefully a rest. The evening was starting to turn darker, and as it did last night, the firing slowed.

We dug in again with basically no changes except for one. We had more ammo to pick up. Killer approached me. "Sarge, I am going to go and get us more ammo."

"Killer, you are the man."

Eckert says, "I'll go with him, Sarge."

"OK."

Raymond is listening. "Me too."

"No, we may need you here in case they take a run at us. We need you and the Pig to be ready."

Dong is listening. "I go, OK, Sarge?"

"Yes, you go too, Dong."

They all take off. I have forgotten about White. "Wait, guys, wait. Will you three take White over to the LZ please? Tomorrow, we will get a glad bag for him."

Killer nods his head up and down. "Sure, Rock. How many more did the company lose?"

"Only five more, but none from our platoon."

"Cool. Let's go, guys."

Killer was a very brave guy. He did not hesitate to secure more ammo when we were low. The three men returned. I looked at Dong. "Do you think that they will attack tonight, Dong?"

"No, no attack. NVA and VC sleep. They may attack tomorrow."

"OK, thanks, Dong."

Dong handed me all of the ammo that he was carrying. Killer and Eckert place their ammo on the ground. "You guys divide up the rounds and take some to Raymond. After that, dig in."

The night was very similar to the night before, except for a few rockets being shot at us. We would retaliate with four of our own artillery shells for every one that we received. Morning came, and we grabbed what we could to eat.

No one really felt like eating, for we were worried about the day to come. The lieutenant walked up to me. "Sarge, in an hour or so, more ammo will be coming."

"Great. I guess we can load White, huh?"

"The old man has another platoon to load the bodies. I know that your squad likes to take care of their own, but the captain wants us right here."

"OK. Thanks, sir."

"Good luck today, Rock."

The lieutenant was very worried.

"You too."

We fought hard for the next seven days, moving forward ever so slightly. Killer stayed very close to me the whole time. Time after time, Killer would run to the rear to give the rest of us ammo. We were finally getting closer to the enemy.

On the ninth or tenth day, Killer runs and dives next to me. "Sarge, I am going over to the left. Cover me!"

"You will be in the open! Just stay here!"

"I can see better lying in the open! I promise, I will be OK!"

"Alright, but if you get killed, I will never speak to you again!"

We both laugh.

"Ready?"

"Yes. Go!"

I stand up and open a full burst from my M-16 rifle! Killer is running and jumping to the ground. I take another magazine and cram it in my weapon. I open up with another full automatic burst until the magazine is empty. I can feel and hear the rounds from the AK-47s flying by me. Killer is now where he wants to be.

He is lying down in the prone position. He is being very smart, popping off semi-automatic rounds. He is adding more to his body count. Finally, even Killer was running low on ammo.

Killer motions to me that he is going for ammo. I motion for him to hold up for a moment. I jump up and run over to Raymond with the Pig. "Killer is going for ammo! Open up when I give you the word!"

"OK, Sarge!"

I run back to my position. I look at Raymond, then at Killer. "Go! Go! Go!"

Raymond and I open up, firing on full automatic! Killer stands up and runs to the rear, where the choppers have left the ammo. Killer comes back with our ammo, and we distribute it again. We fight for another two hours, and night falls. We have now fought for twelve days. Craig walks toward me. "The old man wants the leaders to his CP!"

"Thank you, Craig!"

I start toward the CP when Chuck catches up to me. "Man, Danny, I am getting tired!"

"Yeah, me too!"

"Hey, Rock, have you seen much of our new platoon sergeant?"

"Yeah, I see him every now and then. He is fighting pretty good!"

We arrived at the old man's CP. "OK, men, we are going to get help tomorrow from two more companies, C and D! So dig in again for the night. Everybody take off, except for Sergeant Rock and Lieutenant Watkins."

I wondered what the captain wanted with me. "What's up, sir?"

"Heck fire, Rock. Our artillery is not doing the job, so what do you think?"

I actually had to think for a moment. "I think that we should call in lots of Willy Peter and burn the gooks up! Maybe we won't penetrate into the bunkers, but anyone outside the bunker will be burned to death!"

"I like that, Rock. Good idea."

"But sir, listen. The wind must be blowing away from us or to the left or right!"

"Right, because of the smoke. We won't be able to see."

"Right. The Willy Peter will burn up everything above the ground. Lots of smoke."

"OK, see you guys in the morning!"

"Yes, sir!"

The lieutenant and I left, heading for our men. Watkins approaches me. "Rock, I am so tired. I have only been getting an hour of sleep a night, and the days are hot! I am getting worn down!"

"I would say 'Welcome to Vietnam,' but you have already been here long enough. I am getting very tired too, sir."

"Have you guys ever fought a battle this long, Rock?"

"No, I don't think so."

"I hope we finish them off tomorrow. Our men are tired."

"Yep, maybe with the extra help, we will!"

The night was a typical night for this battle. Morning came and we started the routine again. I listen to my radio for any sign of Charlie Company or Delta Company to help us. All I hear is, "Two more men down! Two more!"

When is this long nightmare going to be over? I guess the nightmare could be worse. The last four men that were killed were not my guys. We advance twenty feet and hit the ground. Raymond is close to me. I run over to Raymond. Eckert is next to Raymond, feeding him ammo. "Let's see the glasses, Eckert!"

Eckert hands me the binoculars.

"Raymond, I am going to spot for you!"

"OK!"

I look through the glasses. I can see the enemy's faces. They are dead tired. Some of them take a shot, and then lay their heads on their arms. These men are as tired as we are! "OK, Raymond, fire a shot at that yellow bush!"

Raymond fires.

"Move right four feet!"

"How is that?"

"Move right two feet."

"How's that?"

"Fire! Fire! Move left and right! Cool, you got three of 'em!"

"Well, keep spotting for me, Sarge!"

"No, I can't. Eckert, you spot. I have to get to the radio!"

I run back to the radio.

Craig says, "Go to the CP!"

"Which one?"

"The old man's!"

I arrive at the CP. The captain is loading his rifle and checking his .45 pistol. "Charlie Company is going to hit them from the right flank, and Delta Company will hit them from the left. In a little while, we will have air support!"

"Sounds good, sir!"

"Yes, Rock. Now let's get 'em!"

The fight continues with Charlie and Delta companies moving slow but sure. We fight for another three hours when all of a sudden our artillery stops!

Emerald crawls up next to me. "What is going on? Are we losing?"

"No, we are winning!"

"Then why did our artillery stop?"

"We are going to get air support!"

"Air support?"

"Yes! In just a few minutes, you will see jet airplanes!"

Four jet planes started to come in. They were firing something like 50-calibers from the front, and then they would fire rockets once they reached their targets. This was wonderful. I was feeling good!

Again and again the jets would take a run. On the last run, one of the jets did a victory roll. Chuck says, "Man, did you see that, Danny?"

"It makes you proud to be an American!"

Night was falling again. Even if the jets had more ammo, it would be too dark for them to find their targets. As usual, we dug in and did our usual prep work for the night. Maybe tomorrow it will be over. Another night dragged by. We received hardly any sleep again. Our nerves were shot. Morning came, and we got ready for the day.

Craig says, "The captain says that we won't move out until it gets a little lighter!"

"OK, thanks, Craig!"

I walked over to Eckert, "Let me see your glasses. I want to see what the gooks are doing!"

I looked through the glasses. The enemy was barely waking up. They were dragging. They looked sick! I handed the glasses to Eckert. "Look at those guys. They look sick!"

"Man, they are as weary as we are. We will win the battle today!"

"I hope so, Eckert. They just don't have the support that we have. We should knock them out today. Now make sure you guys have plenty of ammo. It is going to be another rough day!"

We start to move out. Immediately, our artillery is falling on the enemy, but I know that retaliation is inevitable. Sure enough, we start getting incoming rockets and mortars and, of course, plenty of AK-47 rounds. We were now getting help from Charlie Company and Delta Company.

Charlie Company was charging hard from the right, and Delta Company was charging from the left. We were going up the middle. We finally started making headway with our forward

461

movement. We could now see more and more movement from the NVA and the VC. The artillery that the enemy was firing at us was diminishing! Instead of advancing twenty to thirty feet at a time, we were able to advance fifty feet before holding back slightly.

The routine was to move forward fifty feet, stop, take cover, and open up while in the prone position. We did this over and over again. The enemy's artillery support finally stopped all together. This was a welcome sight! Two and a half hours later, we moved right on top of the enemy. I could see a few of the NVA and VC running toward the rear of their position. A few had escaped, but many were dead. The captain gave the body count detail to another platoon.

Usually, I wanted to know the body count, but today, I just didn't care. I was worn out.

I took off my helmet and sat on it, looking around at all of the dead bodies. I thought to myself, *What if there was a war and nobody came?* This was a quote I had heard before.

Killer walks up to me. He takes off his hardhat and sits down beside me. "What are you thinking about, Sarge?"

"Oh, just about how many men die and that they probably don't want to fight any more than we do! I bet these dead gook guys were as drained as we are now."

"I agree with you somewhat, but doesn't it seem to you that the NVA and the VC are vicious?"

"Yep."

"I guess that we won another battle, huh, Sarge?"

"Yeah, but wouldn't it be nice to win a battle without losing any of our own men?"

"Yes it would, Sarge. Yes it would."

Craig approaches me. "The captain says that we will get sixty percent of the body count and Charlie and Delta companies will take the rest. Also, we are moving out in fifteen. Man, Sarge, I was hoping to rest and maybe get a night of good sleep. I am tired!"

"I am too, and so is everyone else."

We start to move out. My men are grumbling. They are exhausted. Charlie Company is on the far right and Delta Company is on the far right of them. They don't seem to be as tired as we are.

Craig hands me the horn. "Watkins wants us to stay on the far left when we move out!"

"Man, that is the way the NVA ran off to!"

"What do you want me to tell him, Sarge?"

"Just tell him, 'Roger, out'!"

We started moving out, moving in and out of the jungle and the rice paddies. I took a quick glance at my map. "Hey, Chuck, look here."

Chuck walked up to me. "What you got, Danny?"

"If we stay on this course, we will run across this river." I pointed at the map.

"Yeah, fresh water!"

"Spread the word!"

Three more hours, and my squad arrived at the bank of a river that was approximately 200 feet wide. It was a coincidence when the captain told the company to take a ten-minute break.

"Fill your canteens, men! The water looks good! I'll pull guard!"

My men fell down, exhausted, at the bank of the river. Some were sticking their heads completely in the cool, clean, refreshing river water. We were finally getting a break from the fighting.

I was waiting for my turn in the water. I watched intently all around us while taking quick glances at my men. The men were too tired to make noise or frolic in the river. I glanced to the other side of the river. I saw soldiers. They were doing as we had done, collapsing on the bank, exhausted. To my surprise, the soldiers were not Americans! They were NVA soldiers!

I quietly and slowly walked toward my men. "Men, don't move quickly, but there are seven NVA across the river."

My men looked at the enemy and the enemy looked back at us. The enemy calmly and peacefully pointed at us.

"What do we do, Sarge?" Eckert said.

"Nothing right now. I just don't want to fight anymore today."

"Me neither."

"Men, just keep filling your canteens, but be ready!"

The NVA were doing the same. They did not want a fight today. They had one man on guard and the rest were filling canteens and sticking their heads in the river. They definitely could see that we were their enemy. I decided to offer a sign of acknowledgement. I raised my right hand and waved it once. The soldier on the other side of the river did the same. I now felt a little more comfortable. I truly did not want another fight today!

Killer quietly says, "Do you want me to grab the Pig and kill them all, Sarge?"

"No, don't make a move. I don't think we will fight them today. Maybe we will all live to fight another day."

"OK, you are the boss."

The NVA filled their canteens, stood up, and slowly started to move out. The soldier on guard looked back at us one more time. He made a gesture with his hand and a slight head tilt forward as if to say *thank you*. They disappeared into the bush.

I watched the jungle that they went into, hoping that they did not come back out shooting!

Raymond says, "Sarge, that was weird, huh?"

"It was, wasn't it? They were just too worn out to fight!"

"Do you think we will run across them again today, tonight, or tomorrow?"

"No! If they keep walking in the direction that they are going now, they will not have any trouble for a while! But I do need to warn the rest of the company, in case they start going right!"

"Are you going to tell the old man?"

"Yep, right now! Hand me the horn, Craig!"

I start talking. "Annihilator Three-Three, this is Blackhawk Three, over!"

"This is Annihilator Three-Three, go!"

"We have just seen possibly seven gooks. They were heading north. We could not get a shot off in time."

"Roger. We will be on alert!"

Eckert is checking out his weapon. "Hey, Sarge, that was strange! Do you think that their morale is as low as ours?"

"Yep. I am so glad that we didn't get into another firefight!"

"Hey, Sarge, I guess that you will take one of these R&Rs coming down, huh?"

"What do you mean? Did you hear something?"

"Yep! Craig says some are coming to us. You pass up a lot of R&Rs. How come?"

"Oh, it is just because of all of the crap our company goes through. I am just afraid that you guys will all get killed if I am not here to help out!"

"Yeah, but if you go and get some rest, you will be an even better leader!"

"You know something? You may be right. I won't take one now because of the morale of the men, but in a few weeks, maybe I'll take one."

We traveled another half mile when we heard a lot of shooting. We hit the ground quickly. This was an automatic reflex because we had done it so many times before.

The firing was coming in front of and to the right of our location. I glanced at Craig. "What's up?"

"It's the NVA guys that we saw filling their canteens. They must have turned right and walked right into the rest of our company or Charlie Company!"

The radio sounds, "We got seven! They were NVA. We killed all of them!"

I looked at Craig. "Did our guys kill them or Charlie Company?"

"Our guys. I actually feel bad for those guys, and I don't know why!"

"I do too. I think it is because we know how bushed that we are, and they were just as exhausted. Their morale was at an all time low, just as ours is now! I think that I just didn't want them to be killed today. Tomorrow, I may feel differently, but today I wanted to give them a break!"

"This is a crazy war, huh, Sarge?"

"Yes, and I am getting sick of fighting! I am tired of being wet from the humidity. I am tired of being wet from the rain. I am tired of being cold at night. But don't tell the rest of the guys that I am complaining!"

"No, I won't. I feel the same way. How cold and hot is it actually here in Vietnam?"

"Actually, it only gets to about 103, but with the humidity, it feels like 135 degrees, especially in the bush."

"How cold does it get?"

"Oh, I have been told that it only gets down to fifty degrees, but when we are wet, and the wind is blowing, it feels like thirty."

"If it wasn't for C-4 to keep me warm, I think I would freeze!"

CHAPTER 23

Campfires at Night

After taking the body count of the seven NVA, we moved out again. The whole company was dragging. Not many of us were speaking. It was just too much of a drain on our bodies to speak unnecessary words. Charlie and Delta companies had now departed, and our company was on our own again.

I felt better having the other companies around, but I knew that it wouldn't last forever. The wind was starting to pick up. The rain was falling again. The temperature was falling quickly. We had no jackets or coats; they were just too heavy to carry. This made for an even lower morale. Night was starting to fall, but there was still a little daylight left.

Craig says, "Sarge, I am freezing! Do you think that I am getting sick?"

"No, I am cold too!"

Craig is speaking on the radio. "This is Blackhawk Three X-ray, go!"

"Send all of the Blackhawks to the main CP, go!"

"Roger, out! Sarge, the old man wants you leaders!"

"Thanks, Craig. See ya in a minute!"

I walked slowly with Chuck and Mac toward the captain's CP. "How are you two holding up?"

"I am dead!" Mac replies.

Chuck places his hand on my shoulder. "Danny, do you remember when we went fifty-seven days without clothes or any clean water?"

"Yeah, that was pretty bad!"

"Well, I am more drained now than then!"

"I know what you mean!"

We arrived at the old man's CP. "Sir, you wanted us?"

"Guys, I am going to let you guys do something that I have never done before! The whole company's morale is down! Are your men cold?"

"Yes, sir, all of my men are very cold. So are Sergeant Lewis's and Mac's men. So what's your plan, sir?"

"Fires!"

Mac, Chuck, and I say, "Fires?"

"Yes, campfires so we can warm up! We are deep in the bush, and if we just start small fires, maybe we will be safe! Besides, if we don't do something to warm up, we won't be able to fight if we are hit. The men's spirits are at an all time low. Tell your men to find some firewood before it gets too dark. Build small fires. Men, we are taking a big chance, so be alert. If we get hit, cover the fires fast!"

"Yes, sir!"

Mac, Chuck, and I walked back to our squads.

Killer says, "What's going on now, Sarge?"

"Gather firewood! We are going to build small fires!"

"Fires? It is almost dark. What about giving away our position, Sarge?"

"Just keep the fires low!"

Eckert jumps in with a comment. "I don't care. I am going to dry my clothes and get warm. I am also going to warm up my canned ham and anything else that I can eat from my C-rations!"

The men laugh. By the mention of a small fire, the men's spirits started to pick up. Very small things like this make a difference when you feel like you can't go on. In the United States, small things that we just took for granted were very important here in the 'Nam!

My men were gathering wood and stacking it in several piles. Raymond brings in a stack of tree limbs. "How do you want to do this, Sarge?"

"OK, now dig a hole for the fire deep enough so the enemy cannot see the flame!"

"Sounds good, Sarge!"

We were too exhausted to dig foxholes for protection. This decision could be costly. I had never let my men spend the night without a foxhole except on an LP or ambush.

"OK, men, get some kindling in the hole with a little C-4 and light it!"

The fire started. We could feel the heat rising from the fire pit. The first thing that I did was pull out my poncho liner and dry it out. My clothes started to dry as I moved around. The fire was getting hotter. I took my metal canteen cup and mixed a combination of turkey, ham, and bread. I then placed it near the fire on a couple of rocks I had found. I looked around and saw more fires. I could see the silhouettes of soldiers on the other side of the perimeter. This was very dangerous, but the men didn't care. I said a prayer that we would not get hit tonight.

After an hour or so of heat, I told the men to set up guard duty and get some sleep. Eckert set up the guard. I was assigned last to pull it. I pulled out my poncho and my now-dry poncho liner and placed my head on my makeshift pillow. I still thought that sleeping between a couple of hand grenades and a few canteens on an ammo belt was strange. But as I looked around, I saw that most of my men were doing the same.

We started pulling guard, and everyone, including myself, fell fast asleep. Each man on guard would keep the fire going. As each man pulled his turn at guard duty, he would dry out his poncho liner and poncho. The night continued with no incidents. This was a relief. We had a calm night with no killing. We had dry clothes. We had a little sleep. I could not believe how much better I felt than yesterday.

Craig says, "Man, what a great night! The captain wants you."

"Thanks. Tell the men to eat a hot meal! I'll be back."

I walked to the CP; the captain was on the radio. Watkins was also near the captain. The captain looked up at me. "Rock, how did you sleep?"

"Man, sir, great. I was tired."

"Well, we won't be building any more fires, huh? That was taking a chance."

"So what is on the agenda for today, sir?"

"There is a VC village that we will take a look at."

"How far away is it, sir?"

"Fifteen miles or more."

"Fifteen miles?"

"Yep, but we will be lifted in an hour. We have to get to the LZ. OK, take off and tell your guys to get ready."

"Yes, sir!"

I turned and headed for the squad. The men were eating. Craig says "Now what, Sarge?"

"No, Craig, it isn't all bad. We are going to be lifted to check out a VC village."

Killer speaks up with a mouth full of food. "Where is the LZ?"

"It's not too far away, but we need to be there in an hour, so load up your gear. Get ready for a ride!"

We moved out and located a good LZ. The choppers came in and we jumped aboard. The choppers flew over the area where we had been fighting. I looked out and I could see the devastation from the battle that we had won.

We flew for a while before the door gunner tapped me on the shoulder. "Hot LZ! Hot LZ!"

I told my men to get ready for the coming fight! The skids were getting closer and closer to the hot LZ. The gunners start firing and, as usual, this hurts our ears and startles us. We get lower and lower, and the door gunners are trying to make us jump while we are eight feet above the ground. I motion to my men to go when I give the word. When we reach an elevation of four feet, I yell, "Jump! Jump now! Now!"

We jump and roll and start firing into the tree line. We are getting fired upon, but it is a very small amount of incoming fire. We make it to the tree line without any of my men getting shot. Once we moved away from the LZ and deeper into the tree line, we set up a perimeter. The captain summoned the leaders to his CP.

I walked over to where Chuck and Mac were talking. "Hey, guys, the old man wants us!"

Mac looks up and sees another squad leader walking toward us. "What's up, Wyman?"

"I wanna go home, that's what! How you guys doing?"

I notice that Wyman has a pin from one of his grenades pulled out a little. I reach up to adjust and close it. "We are doing as good as expected in these conditions. What are your men saying?"

"Complaining every step we take. How about my other grenades? Are the pins tight? I got caught in the bush!"

"Turn around. Let me look!"

I checked out his equipment. "You're good. Let's go!"

We arrived at the CP and the old man was on the radio. I looked around and saw that only our platoon was represented at the meeting. I saw the lieutenant speaking on his radio and our platoon sergeant, Hammond, listening intently.

I walk up to Hammond. "Are you tired yet, Sarge?"

"I am really, really tired, but I got some sleep last night, so I feel a bit better! How about you?"

"The same as you. What is everybody talking about on the radio?"

"It looks like our platoon is going to go into the VC village and clean it out!"

"How far is it from here?"

"The lieutenant says three and a quarter klicks!"

Both the captain and Watkins are now off of the radio. They walk up to Chuck, Mac, Wyman, and me. The lieutenant says, "Men, we are going to go into the VC village!" He pulls out his map and points to a spot. "Right there, a little more than three klicks."

Wyman sits on his helmet. "Just our platoon is going in?"

The captain walks closer. "Yes, only your platoon. I don't want to get too many platoons in the small village. Just get in there and get rid of the VC!"

"Yes, sir!"

I am getting aggravated. I am full of questions. *Why does our platoon get the dirty work again? Why can't we just rest for another day? How many more men will we lose today? Why does our company continue to stay in the field while others get a stand down?*

I decide to speak. "Sir, when are we going to get a stand down?"

"I have been working on that!"

"So how long will it be?"

"Basically, Rock, they say we have not lost enough men to go to the rear."

"That is ridiculous! That is stupid, sir!"

"I agree! So get your men together and let's move out!"

I am still angry. "Sir, why don't you just call in artillery and blow the VC village off of the map?"

"Because of the women and children living in the village!"

"So we are to go into the VC village and kill the VC and not wound or kill a child or woman?"

"Yes, but if the Mamasans are younger than forty, watch out. They may be VC!"

"Yes, sir!"

We turned and headed to our squads. My men were talking to Emerald, trying to calm him down. His nerves were shot. I place my hand on Emerald's shoulder. "What's wrong, buddy?"

"I don't know, Sarge. I think that we are going to die!"

"No we aren't. Why do you think that?"

"Sarge, just look around! White is dead. Allen is dead. Emery is dead. Henning is dead!"

I was trying to calm Emerald when Killer says, "Don't forget about our old platoon sergeant, Erickson, and those two guys Jacop and… What was the other guy's name?"

I look at Killer with dismay. "You're not helping. The other guy was Johns! I am going to get Doc."

I took off toward Doc's location. He was bandaging a soldier's foot. He saw me and stood up. He shook my hand briskly and slapped me on my back. "How are you doing, Danny?"

"Good, but Emerald isn't!"

"Is it his nerves again?"

"Yeah. He is pretty bad this time!"

"You know, he is one guy that should be sent home. He is not faking it, is he?"

"No, he isn't!"

"OK, let's go."

Doc grabs his bag and walks with me toward Emerald.

"How is your family, Doc?"

"They all say to tell you *hi*!"

"Same back to them, huh? You really tell them!"

"I will. You knew that my brother got married and the other one, his wife had a kid!" He pulled a picture out. "Look at that new kid. He looks like his uncle. He is good looking, huh?"

"Do you mean you?"

"Yeah, I mean me! He looks just like me!"

"Let me see that picture again."

Doc holds the picture up again. I look at it closer. "Yep, that is a good looking baby, but he must look like one of his other uncles!"

We both have a hearty laugh.

"When we get back home, Rock, you will come over to my house and meet all of my brothers and all of the kids!"

"I can hardly wait!"

Doc looks at Emerald and gives him some pills. "This will help calm your nerves, Emerald!"

Doc pulls me to the side. "Watch him close, Danny. He is in bad shape!"

"OK, I will. See ya later, Uncle Doc."

Emerald took the pills and said that he started to feel better.

"OK, men, let's move out! We have point. Which one of you wants it?"

Killer was first to accept it.

Craig says, "How far is it to the village, Sarge?"

"A little over two miles. Spread the word!"

I motion for Killer to come closer to me. "The village is only two miles straight ahead. Just before you get there, stop, and we will hit it with everybody!"

"You mean, come back and get you before going in?"

"Yep!"

We moved out with little or no struggle through the bush. We traveled on and off of a path that led to the village. Killer knew to watch for booby traps on the trails. He was a great point man. We finally made it to the outskirts of the village.

Killer runs back to me. "Sarge, there are three VC just hanging around by the entry!"

"Do they have weapons?"

"What?"

"Do they have guns?"

"Yes they do!"

"OK, spread the word. Tell everyone to hold tight. I am going to see Watkins!"

I took off in a hurry! I reached the lieutenant. "Sir, we are at the village. There are three VC with weapons at the entry!"

"Are they pulling guard?"

"No, I think they are just hanging around talking!"

"Good. I think that we should hit them by surprise from the left and chase them to the right. What do you think, Rock?"

"Yeah, that's good. I'll get us moving!"

"Good luck. We will be right behind ya!"

I ran back to the front. "OK, men, on my go, we will surprise them!"

The men nodded their heads in acknowledgement.

"Are you ready? Go! Go! Go!"

We all took off toward the village. As expected, the VC took off, heading through the village. They fired a few shots at us and we fired back. Chuck and I started chasing a VC through the village. The VC ran into a hooch. Chuck and I sprayed the hooch from left to right with full automatic from our M-16 rifles.

We cautiously approached the hooch just in case we had not killed the VC. Chuck says, "I'll peek around the entrance. You keep me covered! If I hit the ground, you open up!"

"You got it!"

Chuck slowly peeked around the corner. There was no one in the hooch. I looked at Chuck with a puzzled look on my face. "I'll go and get Dong!"

I ran to Dong. "Dong, we chased a gook into the hooch, but he isn't there now! Where is he?"

"He probably in bomb shelter!"

"Oh, yeah, a bomb shelter." I recalled that some of these hooches have underground bunkers.

"Yes, they have underground bunker."

"Thanks, Dong!"

I ran back to Chuck. "Chuck, Dong says the VC is probably hiding in an underground bomb shelter."

"Oh, yeah, I didn't think about that. Let's go inside and see if there is an opening for a shelter."

We crawled very slowly, taking turns aiming our rifles to protect the other one. Chuck stops and points at an opening. The opening was just large enough for a man to crawl through. I take out a grenade and Chuck does the same.

I am lying to the left of Chuck. I pull the pin from my hand grenade and hold it up for Chuck to see. Chuck looks at my hand to be sure my fingers are clinched around the grenade's release handle. Chuck pulls the pin from his grenade and holds on to the release handle firmly. We motion to each other that we will throw both hand grenades in the bomb shelter's opening on the count of three.

I look at Chuck and hold one finger up, then two, then three. We throw the grenades into the opening and take off running out of the hooch. The blast and concussion is very loud. The earth is blowing out of the hooch walls. A small fire is spreading on the straw-like walls.

"Well, Chuck, I guess he won't be shooting at us anymore!"

"Yep, we did good Danny. We did good!"

"Chuck, did you hear that?"

"Yeah, what is it?"

"Get ready to shoot!"

We moved to the entry of a hooch and waited with our rifles ready. We could see movement coming out of the bomb shelter opening. Amazement came over our faces. A little kid about three years old came out of the hole. Chuck and I looked at each other with our jaws dropped. We heard more movement coming from the hole.

Again, we raised our rifles, aiming toward the opening. The next person to come out of the bomb shelter was a girl, about eight years old.

"Man, Chuck, what is going on? They should be dead!"

We heard more movement coming from the hole. I looked at the two kids. They had dirt all over them and traces of white powder from the grenade explosion. They were crying. The kids were standing in one spot. I could tell that they were waiting on another to come out of the shelter. We heard even more movement.

Just in case we had to shoot, I motioned for the children to move out of the way of fire. The sounds I heard next led me to believe that the next person coming from the shelter was larger than the kids.

Again, we pointed our rifles at the opening. A Mamasan appeared. As soon as she was completely out of the shelter, the two children ran to her arms. They were all shaken up. Their bodies were trembling with fear. They were holding their ears. I have never felt so sorry for people in all of my life. I was in tears as we led them out of the hooch. How could they possibly survive the two hand grenades' shrapnel? How could they survive the concussion? I didn't like this situation. The Mamasan was too old to be a VC. But now it was time to locate the VC.

Chuck and I started to go back in the hooch when the Mamasan says, "Viet Cong dead!"

"Chuck, I am going to get Dong to interpret!"

"I'll watch the hole!"

I brought Dong to the hooch. "Dong, find out how they survived! And what about the VC?"

Dong started asking questions, but I could tell that the Mamasan was having a hard time hearing. Dong was persistent. Dong turned toward me. "VC is dead!"

"OK. Find out why they are not dead!"

Dong walks over to the Mamasan and children. Again, they were speaking in Vietnamese. They were moving their hands, explaining to each other how the bunker was constructed. Dong walks back to me. He explains to me in his broken English how the Mamasan had dug a secondary bunker below the first one. This made sense to me. This was the only way that they could have survived the discharge of shrapnel coming from our grenades!

"OK, Dong, but what about the VC?"

"VC dead!"

"Go in the tunnel and make sure!"

"Yes, I go!"

I wished that White were here because he loved to go into tunnels and dark places. I hated it! Although Dong had never given me a reason for not trusting him, he was still a gook. I was not completely sure that he would tell me the truth about the VC.

I turned to my men. "Who wants to go with Dong and check to see if the VC is dead?"

Killer and Raymond stand up. "We will go!"

"OK, good, but wait a minute! Dong, ask Mamasan if anyone else is in the tunnel or bunker!"

Dong asks the Mamasan and then says to me, "Mamasan says no one else but dead VC in bunker!"

"Alright, men, but be careful."

Killer says, "Don't worry, Sarge!"

Killer is the first to the opening in the bunker. Killer takes out his M-16 and fires from side to side into the opening on full automatic. He goes into the opening, deeper into the ground. He fires another full automatic blast. I cannot see him. I am waiting for another blast from an AK-47, but it never comes. Killer comes out from the underground bunkers with a big Killer grin on his face. "The VC is definitely dead now!"

"Good job, Killer. Did he have a weapon?"

"Yeah, but it was all broken and twisted!"

"Alright, Dong, I want you to tell the Mamasan and kids that I am sorry!"

Dong and I walk up to the Mamasan and Dong starts talking. Dong looks up at me. "Mamasan says she forgives you. She says that she hates the VC, but there is nothing she can do when they come to her village!"

"Tell her again that I am sorry."

I place my arm around her and give her a hug. Next, I reach in my rucksack and pull out two candy bars. I get down on my knees and motion for the children to come to me. I give both of them a candy bar and give them a big hug. "I am sorry, kids. I am sorry."

The children hug me back. The older child looks up at me. "Thank you. Don't cry, GI, don't cry!"

I must have had a tear coming from my eye. "Thank you for worrying about me."

I gave them an even bigger squeeze. Craig is standing next to me. "You like kids, don't you, Sarge?"

"Yeah, I guess I do."

"How many kids are you and Sue going to have?"

"I think that I want three! How many do you want?"

"I want a basketball team, five. Isn't that what your mom had?"

"Yep, all boys too!"

"If we make it home, I'll start working on my team! Sarge, the captain says we are moving out, but he wants the leaders to the CP first."

"On my way!"

Chuck is walking toward the CP. "Hey, Sergeant Rock, that was sort of exciting, huh? Man, am I glad we didn't kill the kids and Mamasan!"

"Me too, Chuck."

We arrived at the captain's CP. The old man looks at us. "Hi, Rock. Did you get the VC that you were chasing?"

"Yes, sir, we did. No problem!"

"Alright, good. We did our job. Next, we are going to Big Hill One. Below the hill there are supposed to be NVA and VC. We are to get some intelligence from the VC that we capture!"

The lieutenant has his mouth open. "Capture? We are supposed to capture them now?"

"Yes, I have been getting in trouble. The higher ups say that we never take any prisoners!"

I shake my head in dissatisfaction. "That's because the gooks are trying to kill us. They fight us so hard that we don't get a chance to capture them. It is kill or be killed!"

"I know what you are saying, but our reputation of cutting off the enemy's heads and never taking a prisoner is still in their heads!"

"Yes, sir, I understand!"

"When we get to the hill, we will be resupplied. I will send squads out to capture prisoners. You guys had better get me some prisoners so we can interrogate them! You understand?"

We all answered, "Yes, sir!"

"Now, we are going to hump it hard so we can get to the hill tonight! Let's get it!"

CHAPTER 24

Who Drowned My Prisoner?

We arrived at Big Hill in the afternoon. Chuck walked up to me. "Hey, Danny, I think our old friend Baby Bird is here."

"Yeah, where is he?"

"Don't know, but he is in the mortar platoon. Hey, guess what?"

"What?"

"We are going to get mail. I hope your mom is going to send cookies and Kool-Aid."

"Yeah, care packages. That would be cool."

Craig is approaching. "Hey, Sarge, we are going to get mail tomorrow. I hope your mom is going to send a care package. The captain wants you and Sergeant Lewis."

Chuck and I walk to the old man's CP. The captain looks up. "Hey, men, we will be here for tonight and tomorrow, but I have good and bad news for you two."

I take a deep breath. "OK, sir, let's have it."

"The good news is we will get mail tomorrow. The bad news is that you guys are going out to capture me a VC. There is a lot going on at the bottom of the hill. The higher ups want some intelligence. So Rock, take your squad and Lewis and capture a gook! I mean a VC!"

"When do you want us to leave?"

"Leave after mail call in the morning. Tonight, divide your men and help pull guard duty!"

"Yes, sir!"

Chuck and I walked away.

Chuck pats me on the back. "We are getting the shaft again, Danny."

"Yep, again. Let's go and tell our men."

I walked up to my men. "Hey, men, you have already heard that we are getting mail!"

Killer stands up tall and straight. "We have already heard about getting mail and that's good. Now what is the downside of us being on the hill? I know that we will be cheated in some way or another."

"Yep, you are correct. We are going down the hill to capture VC!"

"Capture? Capture? What do you mean, capture? We don't capture. We kill!"

"Yep, the old man is getting heat. So we are going to get a prisoner tomorrow! So that is that! Now you guys divide up and pull guard!"

"I know that this is not your doing, but I just think some other squad should go out once in a while!"

Eckert says, "Killer, I thought that you loved to get the body counts!"

"Yeah, I do, but sometimes even I want a break!"

Eckert laughs. "Yeah, me too."

Chuck is heading my way with an old friend. "Hey, Rock, look what I found!"

Chuck had found Baby Bird. I placed my hand out for a handshake. "Hey, Baby Bird, how have you been?"

Baby Bird gave me a big hug. "OK. After January ninth, I had my nose sewn back on and stitches in my chest and back."

"Man, Bird. I didn't know about your chest and back! Did ya get out of the field?"

"Yeah, for two days. I got a Purple Heart."

"That's cool."

"How have you and Lewis been doing? Have you and Lewis seen much action?"

Writing a letter when I see baby bird

Chuck says, "Baby Bird, we have lost so many men it is unreal!"

"But neither of you have been wounded?"

Chuck laughs. "We have received two Purple Hearts each! And both of us have received a Silver Star!"

"No fooling?"

"No fooling, Baby Bird, but we don't want a chance to get any more medals."

I am listening. "You got that right, Chuck."

Baby Bird says, "Let's go and get some hot food, huh?"

"Let's go," Chuck said.

We ate a hot meal from the chow hall and found a place to share in the guard duty. The night was quiet, just like I wanted it to be. No incoming or outgoing rounds.

Morning came, and we could hear the choppers coming in. We were looking forward to hearing from home. All of the men gathered around the supply sergeant who brought the mail.

Names were being read. Baby Bird received a letter from his wife. I received a care package from my mom and dad and my wife. The care package had cookies, Kool-Aid, and letters from my wife, mom, and dad.

My letters said that they were praying for me every night at 9 p.m. Sue's letter said that she had towed my 409 Super Sport car from Sparks, Nevada, to Houston, Texas. She had towed it behind my brother's car. I guess she towed my 409 because it used more fuel to operate than my brother's car. She went on to say that they had rented a tow bar and hitch from a U-Haul dealership. All of my family was now living in Houston. My men are eyeballing my care package.

Craig looks in my box. "What did we get, Sarge?"

Killer and Eckert move in. "Did your mom make some of those great persimmon cookies?"

"Yes she did!"

I started to pass out the cookies. Killer, Craig, and Eckert tell me to tell my mom *thank you.*

Baby Bird returns. "Hey, Danny, sorry to hear about your 409 Super Sport!"

"What do you mean?"

"Sue totaled it!"

"No. No, you heard it wrong. She towed it from Sparks or Reno to Houston."

"Man, Danny, my wife usually knows what she is talking about, and she says that Sue was crying when she told her about the wreck."

"When did it happen? According to your wife?"

"A couple of weeks ago."

"Well, thanks for the information, but I sure hope that you are wrong."

"Yeah, me too. I know how you love that 409. That car is fast and good looking too."

Chuck is listening. "Do you think that Sue would total your car and not tell you about it?"

"Yes. My dad and mom probably told her not to tell me because I would worry."

"Well, did it work?"

"Heck no, I am worried to death! Did you know that I washed underneath that car? It was so clean under the engine that you could eat off of the oil pan!"

Chuck laughed. "Man, I wouldn't want to be Sue right now."

Craig says, "Too bad about your car. The lieutenant wants you!"

"Thanks!"

I headed for Watkins. "Sir, you wanted me?"

He pulls out his map and I did the same. "Here is where the enemy VC are supposed to be. The old man wants you guys to go and capture a VC!"

He points to the location. I place my finger on a spot on the map. "Here?"

"Yes, there. Try to get in and out quick!"

"I still don't know why the whole company can't go there and capture a lot of VC!"

"Yes, I understand your point. The higher ups say that if we go in there with too many men, it would lead to a big battle."

"I understand, but I still don't like it. I'll tell you what, sir. If we can capture a gook or two, we will do it. But if my guys are in danger, we will kill every VC that we see!"

"Rock, just try to bring back a live VC!"

"I'll try."

I walked away, heading toward my men. My guys were getting ready. "Emerald, go over to the supply tent and pick up a little bit of rope so we can tie up a prisoner."

"On it, Sarge!" He takes off running.

"Men, it may be hairy, so watch Emerald. That is why I sent him to get the rope, so I could talk to you guys. His nerves are shot."

All of the men said that they would keep him safe. Emerald returned with the rope. "Here it is, Sarge."

"Thanks. You hang on to it. OK, men, let's move out!"

We started to move out with Eckert on point. We humped down the hill and through the bush for three hours before reaching a creek. The creek had large boulders and rocks at the bottom. It was two to three feet deep. We had a hard time keeping our footing. Although the creek was only 150 feet wide, it took us a while to forge across. Every one of us had fallen in the water once or twice by the time we reached the bank on the other side.

Killer is soaking wet. "At least the water is cool! How much farther do we have to go, Sarge?"

"At least another three hours! The next three hours will be tough because we will be in the bush."

We humped for three hours before Eckert halts us. Eckert slowly walks back toward me. He was not in a hurry, but he was whispering to the guys to be quiet.

He reached me. "Sarge, there are three VC eating lunch just ahead. If we are quiet, we can capture all three."

I walked up the path to get a better look. The VC were eating. Their rifles were about ten feet away from the log that they were sitting on. I quietly walked back to the squad. I motioned for the men to gather around in a small huddle. "Craig, make sure the radio is turned way down low."

"OK."

"Chuck, what do you think about taking half of the men and hitting the VC from the side? I'll take the others and go straight at them. The gooks are sitting on a log. Their weapons are ten feet away from them."

"Yeah, that will work. What if I throw a grenade to the right of them for a diversion?"

"No, I think that we can surprise them and maybe capture all of 'em."

I start tapping men on the shoulder. "Killer, Emerald, and Craig, you guys come with me. The rest go with Sergeant Lewis. Chuck, you guys don't fire until we spring. Don't shoot them unless they shoot or run."

"Got it."

I turn to my selected men. "OK, guys, let's go. We are going to sneak up to the opening, then jump in the opening and capture the three VC."

We cautiously crept to the opening. The VC were still eating and talking. We jumped into the clearing, but instead of surrendering, the VC went for their rifles.

Chuck and his guys fired warning shots, but the gooks kept reaching for their rifles. We kept yelling, "Stop! *Dung Lai! Dung Lai!*"

The VC grabbed their rifles and started shooting at us! We opened up on full automatic. The battle did not last long.

When the skirmish was over, two VC were dead and one was wounded. I looked at the wounded VC. "This one only has a wound in the leg. This is our prisoner! You guys check out the others. They may be playing possum!"

Killer and Eckert move toward the dead VC.

I look at Chuck and his men. "Raymond, find something to wrap up the VC's wound!"

"OK!"

Chuck is pointing his finger at the dead VC. "Look over there, Danny!"

I look. They have both been turned on their back. They both have flowers stuck in their nose passages.

I stand and walk to the dead VC. "Killer, what is this? Which one of you guys stuck the flowers, weeds, and dirt up the nose of the gooks?"

Killer, with a big grin on his face, says, "Sarge, they are just pushing up daisies! You know, like when you are dead!"

"I know how the saying goes!" I shake my head. "Did you cram that stuff in their noses, Killer?"

"Oh, no, Sarge. They must have done that when they hit the ground!"

"Well, you and Eckert clean it out, and I mean now!"

"Yes, Sergeant. We will!"

I never knew if they had actually put the dirt and flowers in the VCs' noses, but it was something that Killer would have done.

Raymond walks up to me. "Sarge, the gook is bandaged, but when he stands up, it starts to bleed too much!"

"Alright, all of you guys build a stretcher to carry the gook! Craig, get the captain on the horn!"

All of the men are complaining about building a bamboo stretcher in this hot, humid weather. Just a few days ago, the weather was making us cold. Now it was sweltering hot.

Killer walks over to the VC. "Sarge, do you mean that we are going to tote this guy all of the way up the hill?"

"That is what I said! Now build the stretcher!"

Chuck has a frown on his face. "Rock, does the captain really want us to carry this guy up the mountain? That will kill us."

"I don't like it either."

Craig hands me the horn. "It's the old man."

"This is Blackhawk Three, go!"

"You have a prisoner, huh?"

"Yes, but we have to build a stretcher. He is wounded!"

"OK, but get him here fast! And don't let him die!"

"Roger, out!"

The men built the bamboo stretcher. They have done a pretty good job. "Now load the VC on the stretcher and tie him down so he doesn't fall off!"

We now had to start the long hump through the bush, over the river, and up the mountain. The humidity and heat were almost unbearable. Our fatigues were soaked with sweat.

"Men, we will take turns carrying the stretcher. Raymond, you and Emerald start out first!"

Raymond grumbles, "I think we should kill him now."

"What did you say, Raymond?"

I really understood perfectly what he had said.

"Sarge, I just said that this is a wonderful day to be carrying a VC up a mountain!"

"Yeah, right! Let's get it. Move out!"

We started out trying to stay on paths as much as possible. Within a quarter of a mile, Raymond and Emerald had to take a break. I could see that this was going to be hard. My radio sounds off.

Craig hands me the horn. "It's Annihilator!"

I knew that the captain was going to ask if the prisoner was OK.

"This is Blackhawk Three, go!"

"How is the prisoner?"

"He is fine. We have him on the stretcher!"

"Are ya sure he can't walk?"

"Affirmatron!"

"Roger, out!"

I decided to take a turn at carrying the VC. "Lewis and I will take over for a while!"

Chuck grabbed one end, and I grabbed the other. We started out, and to my surprise, it was harder than I had expected, trying to maneuver in and out of the bush.

I looked forward and I could see that Chuck was struggling. "Chuck, let's show these guys what we can do. Let's carry the stretcher for a half mile!"

"Are you kidding?"

"No!"

"OK, let's get it!"

After carrying the gook the half mile, we were worn out. "OK, Craig, give me the radio and you carry for a while. Dong, you grab the other end."

I start to think about us getting hit by other VC. *What if my prisoner got killed before we reached the captain?*

"Dong, get the VC to tell you where the NVA and VC's stronghold is!"

"What is stronghold?"

"Where they are camped, or where the base is!"

"OK, I ask!"

Dong starts speaking to the VC. The VC turns his head away from Dong. This infuriates Dong. He grabs the VC's wounded leg and squeezes it. The VC stiffens up with pain. He starts to speak. I cannot let Dong torture the prisoner.

"Dong, stop! Dung Lai. Don't do that. What did he say?"

"He said to kill him. He not going to say nothing!"

"Let's go!"

My radio sounds off again, "Blackhawk Three, this is Annihilator Three-Three, over!"

"This is Blackhawk Three, go!"

"How is the prisoner?"

"Same as before. He is fine!"

"Is he bleeding much?"

I look at the VC's wound. "No, he is not bleeding much!"

"What is your ETA?"

"Oh, man. It is very hard humping with the stretcher. I guess four hours or longer!"

"Get here ASAP! And keep him alive!"

"Roger, out! Men, let's go!"

Dong and Craig pick up the stretcher.

I place the radio on my back. "Chuck, you watch out back here! I am going to the front to pull point!"

"If you are pulling point, be sure and keep the antenna down! Eckert and Killer will relieve Dong and Craig in a little bit!"

"Roger."

I went to the front to pull point. I felt sorry for all of my men. We humped for another half mile. I halted the squad for the change over and relief of the stretcher carriers. I walk back to the VC and look at him. He looks like he feels better than ever.

Eckert and Killer are starting to relieve Dong and Craig. Craig says, "Here, Sarge, give me the radio!"

"Was it hard carrying the VC?"

"Very hard, Sergeant Rock, very hard!"

The captain's voice comes over the radio. Craig hands me the horn.

"This is Blackhawk Three, go!"

"How is the prisoner doing?"

"Better than ever!"

"Great. See ya soon!"

Craig is listening intently. "Man, Sarge, the old man really wants to interrogate this gook, huh?"

"I guess he does. He has called fifty times to check on his health! Maybe not fifty, but a lot!"

Eckert and Killer start moving out with the stretcher. I move forward to the point position. I hear water running ahead. We make it to the river before the captain calls again, asking how the prisoner is. I tell the old man again that the VC is in good shape.

I start to cross the river. I try to find a portion of the river that is not too rocky and is only three feet deep. I find a good place to cross. We start to cross the river one at a time, watching out for the enemy. I hear a commotion toward the rear of the squad. I run back to the middle of the river. Killer has a big smile on his face and the stretcher is empty.

Killer points downstream and says, "He tried to escape!"

My prisoner was floating face down in the water!

"What do you mean, he tried to escape? You drowned him, didn't you? Raymond, see if he is dead."

Raymond moves slowly downstream toward the floating body.

Killer, with a smirk on his face, says, "Would I do that, Sarge?"

"Yes! You would!"

My prisoner was dead. I knew deep in my soul that Killer had held the VC underwater until he drowned. Killer was just tired of carrying the stretcher and the VC and decided to kill him. I had to dig further trying to get Killer to admit it.

"So, Killer, you say he tried to escape, huh?"

"Sure, Sarge. He tried to slide off of the stretcher and swim like a fish. He thought that we wouldn't notice that he was gone!" He laughs.

I look at Eckert. "What happened, Eckert?"

"I am not sure, Sarge. I was in the front!"

Eckert and Killer were great friends; I knew that Eckert would not squeal on Killer. I look back at the VC, and I notice that the ropes that held him on the stretcher were still tied to his legs and wrists.

"Killer, how did the prisoner untie both legs and both wrists then slip off the stretcher without you noticing?"

"All kinds of strange things happen over here in the 'Nam, Sarge!"

"OK, let's say that I believe you. How did he die?"

"Oh, I have the answer to that! He couldn't swim!"

All of my squad laughed.

Chuck moves closer to me and whispers, "You have to admit that that last comment was funny."

I whisper back, "Yes, but don't tell Killer."

I again stare at Killer. "So you will not admit that you killed him?"

"No, I wouldn't do that!"

Raymond approaches me. "Yep, the prisoner is dead!"

"Thanks, Raymond."

"What are ya going to tell the captain, Sarge?"

"I don't know. I just don't know!"

I walk up to Chuck and quietly said, "Do you, deep in your heart, think Killer drowned the gook?"

"Yep, he probably did, but he will never admit it! Oh, man, here comes your RTO!"

Craig says, "The captain wants to know how the prisoner is doing!"

"Tell him I will call him back!"

"OK. Annihilator Three-Three, this is Blackhawk Three X-ray. Blackhawk will check and call you back!"

Chuck shakes his head and looks at Killer. "Killer, you have really got us in trouble. What are you going to tell the captain, Danny?"

I look at Killer. "Killer, I am going to save your butt!"

The captain calls for me again. "How is the prisoner?"

I had to tell the captain something that would protect Killer if he had actually killed the VC. I also had to protect the captain from the higher ups. I had to try and protect myself. How could I have lost the prisoner? I decided to answer, "The prisoner is bleeding bad now!"

The captain was very agitated. "What?"

"He is bleeding!"

"You keep him alive and get back to my CP, quick!"

"Roger, out!"

Now what was I going to do?

"OK, Killer and Eckert, you guys keep carrying the stretcher. I want to show it to the captain, just in case he does not believe we had a prisoner. Alright, men, let's move out."

We humped up the mountain for another hour before the captain calls again, "How is my prisoner?"

"He is very, very weak!"

I could hear the disappointment in his voice. "Do what you can to keep him alive!"

"Roger, out!"

We traveled another half-hour when I decided to call the captain. "Annihilator Three-Three, this is Blackhawk Three, over!"

"This is Annihilator, over!"

"I am sorry to tell you that the prisoner is dead!"

"I Roger that, but you get your butt in here ASAP. I want to talk!"

"Roger, out!"

We humped for another hour and a half before I could see the top of the hill. Chuck walked up to me. "Do you want me to go with you to face the music, Danny?"

"No, I will do it alone, but thanks!"

When we reached the perimeter, the first person I saw was the lieutenant. "Rock, what happened? The old man was ready to interrogate the prisoner. He flew in interpreters and all that stuff!"

"Ask the other guys. I better go see the captain!"

"Good luck!"

I somberly walked to the captain's CP. "Sir, I am back!"

"What the heck, Rock!"

"All I can tell you is that he died!"

"But you kept telling me that he was fine."

"I guess that he was worse off than I knew!"

"Where is the body?"

"We left it near a river where the gooks could see him and bury him."

"Something just doesn't sound right to me, Rock!"

"All I can tell you is that he is dead, sir!"

"Well, you caused me some pain with the higher ups, but there is nothing we can do about it now! I still think that there is more to the story! OK, take off!"

"Yes, sir!"

"Oh, by the way, I have R&Rs that were supposed to go to some of our men that have been killed. I want you to take one!"

"I don't think so, sir!"

"OK, but think about it, alright?"

"I will."

I turned and walked back to the lieutenant. The lieutenant had just finished up talking to my guys. He sees me, and right away he says, "Do you think Killer killed your prisoner?"

I was not going to squeal on Killer because I actually had no proof that he drowned the VC. "What did the other guys say?"

"You know your squad; they would never come right out and tell on a comrade!"

"Did you ask Killer, directly?"

"Yes!"

"And what did he say?"

"He said, 'Would I do that?'"

"And what did you say?"

"I just said that I hoped not."

"Yeah, that is all that I got out of him too. I am going to talk to him again!"

I walked over to Killer. He was eating and joking with the guys. "Hey, Sarge, sit down and take a load off! You look serious. What did the old man say?"

"Come over here. I want to talk to you alone!"

We both walked away from the men, far enough so no one could hear. "Killer, the captain was really mad at me. I let him down. He had already told majors and generals that he had a VC to interrogate!"

"I am sorry, Sarge. Do you want me to go and tell him what I did?"

"I thought you said that he tried to escape and you had nothing to do with his death!"

"Oh, yeah, that's right! Sarge, if you really thought that I killed the gook, would you tell on me?"

"You are one of the best soldiers in the company. You are braver than most men, and you are afraid of nothing. Remember when you kept running back and forth getting ammo for us? No one else had the nerve to take the chance. You do what I tell you to do without question. So I guess that I would not tell on you. But please, please don't put me in that situation again!"

"Yes, Sergeant, I'll try harder! By the way, my mom and dad say *hi* and they want you to write them."

"Tell them *hi*, and I will write them back."

"Tell your mom that the cookies were delicious!"

I look around a bunker and see Baby Bird approaching. "OK, Killer, go on back to the squad. I need to talk to Bird!"

"See ya, Sarge."

"See ya, Killer! Hey, Bird, how ya doing?"

"Cool, man, cool."

"You sound like a hippie."

"Danny, have you thought any more about your 409?"

"Yes I have, and you know what?"

"What?"

"I am going to take an R&R to Hawaii!"

"I have heard that you guys can get all of the R&Rs you want because you lose so many guys!"

"Yeah we do. We'll see you later. I am going to go and tell the captain that I want one of the R&Rs!"

"See ya, Danny, and, again, I am sorry about your car!"

"Thanks."

I started toward the CP when I saw Mac heading in that direction. "Hey, Mac, how are ya?"

"Great. I am getting an R&R thanks to all of the guys that have been killed!"

"Yeah, me too. Where are you going?"

"Hawaii."

"Me too!"

"Are you going to meet anybody there?"

"Nope!"

"Me neither!"

We arrive at the CP. The captain stands up and says, "I guess that you two have decided to take the R&Rs?"

"Yes, sir!"

"Where do you want to go?"

We say at the same time, "Hawaii!"

"OK!" He looks at his RTO. "X-ray, give them the Hawaii R&Rs!"

"Thank you, sir!"

"You're welcome. A chopper will pick you up in the morning and take you to Da Nang. The rest of us are going down the hill to a stand down for three days, so this is a good time for you two to go on R&R!"

CHAPTER 25

My Second R&R

I didn't sleep very well because I was anxious to be going on R&R. I was pleased that my men were going to be on a stand down for a few days. With them being on stand down, I could relax, knowing that they would not be in danger.

When I woke up, Emerald was standing beside me. "What's up, Emerald?"

"Are you really going to leave us, Sarge?"

"Yeah, but only for a week or so. I am going to Hawaii."

"Are ya meeting your wife there?"

"Nope, I am not!"

I was still a little hacked off about her wrecking my 409!

"Sarge, I am worried. We are only going to be on stand down for three days!"

"Alright, go get the men and bring 'em here to me!"

"OK." He headed off toward different bunkers and foxholes, gathering the men. After ten minutes, he returned with the guys.

Killer says, "What's up, Sarge?"

"Men, you guys all know that I am going on R&R! When I am gone, Eckert will be in charge and Sergeant Lewis will help him."

Eckert speaks up. "That will be cool! Sergeant Lewis and me get along great!"

Killer says, "Don't you mean Sergeant Lewis and *I*, Eckert?"

The men and I laugh.

"OK, Mister English Teacher. Sergeant Lewis and I get along well!"

Killer nods his head up and down. "There you go, Eckert. If you are going to take Sergeant Rock's place, you have to know the proper form of English!"

"Yeah, right!"

I look at Emerald and he has a grin on his face. "You see, Emerald, you will be in good hands while I am gone. Men, I will see you when I get back. Now be sure and keep your heads down! Don't let Emerald worry about a thing!"

They all told me to have a good time. I quickly ate at the mess hall and met up with Mac. "Are you ready to go, Mac?"

"Yep, I am ready."

"Let's go and tell Watkins that we are leaving!"

"Sure."

I walk up to the lieutenant. "Sir, we are leaving in a minute, so see ya in eight to nine days."

"You guys have a great time! But there is a small change of plans!"

"What?"

"Oh, don't worry! The chopper will take you to Chu Lai first, and then you will both go to Da Nang for the plane to Hawaii. Just drop off your gear and weapons with the supply sergeant! I guess the captain forgot about you guys having to go to Chu Lai before going on R&R, huh?"

"Yes, sir."

The slick came in and Mac and I jumped aboard. As we rose above the trees, my men were waving. I waved back. We were now heading for Chu Lai.

After a long trip, we arrived in Chu Lai. We placed our weapons and our fatigues in our duffel bags. We pulled out our dress uniforms and put them on.

"Mac, are ya ready?"

"Yeah, but as I remember, we used to store our weapons in Da Nang when we went on R&R, didn't we?"

"Yep, we did. And I felt better having my M-16 or weapon with me as long as I could!"

"Yeah, me too!"

"Hey, Mac, let's go and see Top!"

We walked over to the CP and walked in the door of the tent. "Hey, Top, how are ya doing?"

"Oh, man, guys, glad to see ya!"

Top gave us a big hug.

"Good to see you too, Top!"

"I am monitoring the radio all day long. You guys have been in a lot of crap! I am glad that you decided to take a break and go on R&R. You too, Mac!"

Mac says, "You are right, Top. We are worn out!"

"You guys grab a bite in the chow hall. Your slick will be here in an hour."

He shakes our hands.

"See ya, Top."

"Have a good time!"

We ate a good, hot meal again and waited for the chopper. The chopper arrived and took us toward Da Nang. The door gunner tapped me on the shoulder. He yelled, "We have to refuel!"

I nod my head *yes.*

Mac asks, "Where are we, Rock?"

"I don't know!"

"I thought that you always knew where we are at!"

"Not unless I have a map!"

After refueling, the chopper started back up and we took off for Da Nang. We landed in Da Nang without any incidences. I leaned over toward Mac. "Isn't it good to get in the air and not be shot at, Mac?"

"It really is, Rock, but I am always watching the ground for a flash from a rifle!"

"Yeah, me too!"

"Hey, Rock, how many air combat assaults have we been on?"

"I know for certain that it has been more then twenty-seven!"

"I think that it has been more like thirty! Hey, Rock, which plane is going to Hawaii?"

I looked at the airstrip, and there were six planes lined up side by side.

"After we land, let's go to the building over there!"

The chopper landed, and we walked toward the buildings. I could see an E-7 sergeant with a clipboard in his hand.

The sergeant looked up at us. "Where are you men going?"

Mac says, "Hawaii."

He points to a plane on our right. "That's your flight there. It will leave in an hour."

"Can we get on it now?"

"Sure. Have a good time, guys."

"Thanks, Sarge. Hey, Rock, do you wanna go to the PX first just to look around?"

"Yeah, I want to see what a watch costs."

"That's right. You lost yours in a firefight."

We looked around inside the PX. We didn't buy anything. However, we noticed that they had some great prices. After a half hour, we decided to get on the plane.

We boarded the plane along with a lot of other soldiers going to Hawaii. Mac and I sat in the same row. I sat by the window, and he sat in the aisle seat.

As we sat there, I started to think about my 409 Super Sport car. I had worked so hard, saving the money for a down payment, and now it may have been wrecked. I just sat there thinking and thinking.

Mac looks over at me. "What are ya thinking about, Danny?"

"I am thinking about my car!"

"Nothing you can do about it here in Vietnam!"

"You know something, Mac, you are right! So guess what?"

"What!"

"I am going home to Houston!"

"What, you mean AWOL?"

"No, I am coming back. I just want to see my car. I don't really know if it is totaled or not!"

"How are ya going to do that?"

"When the plane lands, I will take the next plane from Hawaii to Houston!"

"Man, I'll bet your wife and your mom and dad will be surprised!"

"Yep, they will be!"

After hours and hours of travel and another stop, I guess to refuel, we landed in Hawaii. The plane approached the gate. I reached out my hand toward Mac. "Well, see ya, Mac. You have a good time here in Hawaii." We shook hands.

"I will, and you have a good time in Houston. Do you think you will have any trouble getting on the plane?"

"Not if I keep my uniform on!"

The airlines were really good to us Vietnam servicemen. They let us fly any place we wanted for a really cheap price.

I found the departure board and found a flight leaving for Houston in thirty minutes. I only had a small duffel bag with me, so I knew that thirty minutes would be plenty of time to board the plane.

I walked up to the line of people waiting to buy tickets. A lady behind the counter told me to come to the front of the line. As I walked toward the counter, one couple said, "Sergeant, thank you for fighting in Vietnam for us!"

I stuck out my hand and the man and woman grabbed it. I replied, "You're welcome, and thank you."

Another twenty- or twenty-one-year-old guy said, "I tried to go, but the Army said I was 4-F!"

"Thanks for trying, but it is really getting dangerous in the 'Nam. You may be lucky!"

I walked a little farther, and I saw a young couple with hippie-looking beads, sunglasses, and colorful clothes. They mumbled something at me as I passed by. I stopped and said, "What did you say?"

The girl replies, "He said you were a piece of crap for going and killing people!"

I moved in closer and got in his face. "Do you always let your chick do your talking for you?"

He holds his head back. "Here is what I think of you servicemen!"

He starts to make a sound in his throat. He is gathering up a load of saliva so he can spit on me.

I moved in even closer to him. "If you spit on me, I will beat your butt from one end of this airport to the other!"

He took a big gulp and swallowed his spit. He was now worried about what I was going to do next.

I grabbed his arm and squeezed it tight. "You are probably a draft-dodging, draft card and flag-burning piece of crap who loves Jane Fonda!"

The other people in the line started to clap and say, "Way to go soldier!"

The hippie and his friend said nothing more to me.

I placed my duffel bag on the counter. The lady behind the counter had a big grin on her face. "Way to go, Sergeant, they needed that!"

I turned and looked at the hippies. "You know, I have a lot of friends that are hippie-like people, and they don't hate soldiers. I don't understand some of these people!"

"Well, those two have bad attitudes. Sergeant, are you going to Houston?"

"Yes I am!"

"OK, the plane is full, but don't worry because you will be on it when it leaves!"

Soldiers were supposed to fly standby, unless you met the right counter lady or guy; they would let us on first.

"Thank you."

"Now, guess who will not make the flight?"

I laugh. "The hippie couple?"

"Yep. That will teach them to mess with us, huh, Sarge?"

I laugh again. "Thank you so much. You are great!"

"We love you guys, Sarge, and thanks from all of us at the airlines. Now grab a seat in first class."

"First class?"

"Yep, first class!"

I grabbed my boarding pass and duffel bag. "Thank you."

"You are certainly welcome."

I boarded the plane and sat in the first seat that I found in first class. I had never flown on a regular commercial jet airliner. I flew on a troop-carrying plane when I flew to Vietnam, but it was not luxurious like this one.

As the balance of the passengers boarded the plane, they gave me favorable comments about what I had told the hippie. The passengers got settled and we took off.

The trip to Houston was really pleasant. The stewardess kept giving me V8 juice and any other drink I wanted (except alcohol). I also had a great meal. I don't know how they made it, but the steak was great. I was treated like a king. We started our descent toward the Houston airport.

The stewardess came up to me. "Sergeant Rodgers, we were glad to have you aboard."

"Thank you!"

"When we land, the captain and co-captain want to say something to you!"

"OK."

We landed and pulled up to the gate. Many passengers were passing by me as I waited to meet the pilots. A lot of the passengers were giving me accolades as they passed. The pilot's cabin door opened.

The two pilots held out their hands for a handshake. "We are glad to have you aboard, Sergeant!"

"Thanks to all of you. I really appreciate how you treated me."

"It was our pleasure, Sarge. Do you live here in Houston?"

"Yes, sir, I do! Actually, my mom and dad live here. I was drafted in California."

I grabbed my duffel bag and headed for the nearest telephone booth. I called the phone number and I could hear the rings. *What if no one is home?* I would have to stay in the airport for hours.

Dad answered the phone. "Hello, this is Vic."

"Hey, Dad, how are ya?"

"Dwight? Where are you?"

"No, it isn't Dwight!"

"Duane, is that you?"

All of my brothers and my dad had the same voice. Even I could not tell one from the other.

"No, it's not Duane!"

"Danny…Is it Danny?"

"Yes, sir!"

"Are you calling from Vietnam?"

"No sir, I am at the airport in Houston!"

"You're joking! Are you really?"

"Yes, sir."

"OK, what airline? We'll come and pick you up right now! Are you home for good?"

"No, just on R&R. I am supposed to be in Hawaii."

I gave Dad the airline information.

"We are leaving now. See ya in an hour!"

I waited outside the airport, sitting on a bench. Many people spoke to me; others stuck their noses up at me. Some of the passersby stopped to shake my hand. Some folks asked me if I knew certain soldiers. Many people didn't realize how many soldiers were in the 'Nam. I didn't know any of the soldiers that they asked about. After an hour, I heard a car horn.

I looked up and saw my mom and dad's station wagon. Sue was the first one out of the car. She ran up to me and gave me a big kiss. My brothers were next to shake my hand. I hugged Mom and shook hands with Dad. Everyone was speaking so much and so fast that I could hardly understand what was being said.

One thing I could understand was that they were happy to see me. Dwight says, "Give me your duffel bag. I'll put it in back!"

We climbed into the car and everyone started talking. Dad says, "One at a time. I am going first! Son, will you get in trouble for being here in Houston when you are supposed to be in Hawaii?"

"No, sir. As long as I get back to Vietnam in a week!"

"Are you still wearing two bullet-proof vests?"

I could not tell him that it was just too hot to wear one flak jacket, let alone two. I decided to sort of avoid the question.

"No, sir. It is too hot to wear two vests!"

Duane starts to laugh. "Danny, you know that piece of skull that you sent me?"

I laugh. "Yeah!"

"Well, I took it to school and a guy thought that it was a cookie and he tried to take a bite out of it!"

"Oh, man, that's bad!"

The rest of the family starts to *ooh* and *aah*.

Sue hugs me again. "I am so glad to see you!"

"I am glad to see you too. I'm glad to see all of ya!"

As we traveled the hour back to the house, everyone was talking and laughing. It was good to be home again. We started making turns in the subdivision, getting closer to the house. Before we made the last turn, everyone got quiet.

We made the last turn and I could see the house. I could also see what looked like a car under a car cover. I stared intently as we passed the car and turned into the driveway. Sue started crying.

I jumped out of the car before it even stopped moving. I walked over to the car cover and lifted up a corner. The car looked terrible. "Dwight, please help me take off the cover!"

"OK, but don't kill anybody!"

Everyone was out of the station wagon now, looking at me and holding his or her breath. Mom was holding Sue as she cried.

Dad was just waiting to see what I would do when I unveiled my 409!

Dwight and I took off the cover and I was flabbergasted, stunned, and shocked. My beautiful 409 cubic inch engine, four speed Chevrolet Super Sport car was completely squashed! It looked like a pretzel. If I had only been able to afford to keep up my insurance payments, everything would be fine.

I got paid very little being in the Army, and Sue's allotment was only $95 a month. My car payment was $65 per month and Sue's wedding ring was $14 per month. That didn't leave much left over for insurance or anything else.

I said, "Well, I guess that Baby Bird was right!"

Dad places his arm on my shoulder. "We didn't want to tell you because we figured that you had enough to worry about in Vietnam. How did you find out?"

"My friend Baby Bird told me. His wife told him in a letter."

"You mean all the way over in Vietnam, a friend of yours knew about it?"

"Yes, sir!"

"Sue has been crying every day since it happened!"

"How did it happen?"

"She and Dwight were towing it and the tow bar slipped and fell down on one side. It was raining, and they lost control. Don't be too mad at Sue!"

"OK, Dad."

I walked toward Sue and gave her a big hug.

She hugged me back. "I am so sorry! I am sorry! I love you!"

"I love you too. Let's go in the house!"

Dwight is still holding an end of the cover. "Danny, do you want me to cover it up?"

"Yeah, thanks, Dwight."

Dwight looks at Duane. "Hey, Duane, grab the other end!"

"OK!"

We went in the house and started talking about things in general. Dwight and Duane started to ask about Vietnam. Dad says, "Maybe he doesn't want to talk about Vietnam! Do ya, Danald?"

I hadn't had anyone call me "Danald" since I left home and went to college. Dad still remembered how I liked to watch "Daniel Boone" when I was a kid.

"No, Dad. I don't care if they ask me questions!"

Denis and Doug joined in with Dwight and Duane. They asked me questions for an hour about everything. "How many men have you killed?" "Do they die quick?" "Did it hurt when you got wounded?" "How does it feel to win a Silver Star?" "What do C-rations taste like?" "What is the difference between a VC, an NVA, and a gook?"

Dad finally said, "OK, boys, enough. Let your mom and me have a chance! OK, son, what is Killer like, and how about Chuck?"

Duane asks, "Did Killer really cut off a VC's head?"

I answer, "Killer and Chuck are the bravest men I have ever met. Yes, Killer really did cut off the head of a VC!"

Mom says, "We still pray every night for you and I know that you will come home to us again. Tell Chuck and Killer that we pray for them and all of the boys over there!"

She started to cry. I stood up and gave her a big hug and kiss. "Thank you, Mom. I love you, and I'll be back home soon!"

I didn't tell her, but I actually wasn't sure if I would make it back home alive.

Mom stands up. "I am going to make you a spice cake with white icing!"

"You remembered that I like spice cake, huh?"

"Yep!"

I walked over to Sue and gave her another hug. "I love you."

"Are you still mad at me?"

"No! I know that you didn't do it on purpose. Let's just stop talking about it."

"I love you, Danny."

"I love you too, Sue."

My brothers started laughing at our conversation. I started laughing also. I had some great brothers. We could laugh at anything. The brothers were constantly playing jokes on each other. This joke playing came from my mother, for she was the biggest prankster of all.

Mom says, "I am fixing hamburgers for lunch. We will eat something good for supper. Is that OK with you, Danny?"

"Yes, ma'am, anything but C-rations."

"Are C-rations that bad?"

"No, not really. For canned food, they are OK. I just get tired of eating them!"

We talked for a while before Mom served the hamburgers. Each one of us was served a bun with the meat already on the bun. Mom knew that the boys were big eaters, so she made a large plate of hamburgers and placed them on the table in case we wanted seconds. She also placed the tomatoes, mayonnaise, lettuce, cheese, and catsup on the table. I hated catsup.

Dwight picks up the bottle of catsup. "Here, Danny, let me fix your hamburger for you!"

I grabbed my hamburger and pulled it away from the table. "Get away from me with that stuff!"

Dwight loved catsup.

I put a little bit of mayonnaise, lettuce, and tomatoes on my hamburger. I bit into my hamburger, but something was wrong. The meat was too tough. I couldn't tell Mom because I didn't want to hurt her feelings. I turned the hamburger around and tried to take a big bite from the other side. It was just too tough to eat. I looked up at Mom, and she and Dad started laughing.

Mom had stuck a rubber hamburger on my bun. The rest of the family started laughing. I was laughing very hard.

I looked at all of them. "It's good to be home."

For the next five days, I had a great time. Sue and I acted like newlyweds every night and day. It was great being with the family again, but now it was time to head back to the 'Nam.

On the sixth day, all of the family went to the airport with me. Everyone was crying. Sue and Mom could hardly release their grips on me. I gave everyone hugs, and kissed Sue and Mom. I headed for the airline counter.

I had already called to find out when the plane would be leaving for Hawaii. The lady at the ticket counter was very gracious. "Your plane has been delayed, Sergeant Rodgers!"

"Thank you!"

I took the boarding pass and walked to the gate. I sat in the waiting area for more than an hour before getting on the plane. Finally, we took off for Hawaii. Again, I was allowed to sit in the first class section. I was treated very well.

A stewardess leaned over me. "Soldier, are you going to Vietnam, or will you be staying in Hawaii?"

"I will be going to Vietnam."

"Is this your first tour to Vietnam?"

"Yes. Actually, I am supposed to be there now. I took an R&R to Hawaii and decided to go to Houston."

"You did? That is pretty unusual, isn't it?"

"Yeah, I guess so."

"Do you want me to check the flights to Vietnam for you?"

"Yes, ma'am."

"I think you will go to Tokyo first, then to Vietnam. I'll go and check it out."

She turned and walked toward the front and looked in a book that contained the flight schedules. After looking at the schedules, she opened the door and walked into the pilot's area. She was inside the cockpit for three to four minutes before returning. "Sergeant, we have a small problem."

I look up at her. "We do?"

"Yes, we land at two o'clock in Hawaii, and the plane for Tokyo, then Vietnam, takes off at 2:05. Do you have any luggage to pick up?"

"No."

"That is good. When we land, you had better hurry. I will call for a golf cart to pick you up!"

"OK, thank you very much!"

I was starting to worry. What if I missed the plane? Would my company think I had gone AWOL?

The stewardess came by again. "Can I get you some more Snappy Tom, Sergeant?"

"Yes, please. If I miss the plane to Vietnam, when will the next one be?"

"Not for three days."

"Oh, wow!"

I was worried for the remainder of the trip. The pilot's voice came on the loud speaker. "Please take your seats; we will be landing in five minutes."

I asked the stewardess, "What time is it?"

"Almost two."

"Thanks."

I have never been so anxious for a plane to land. We landed, and the plane taxied up to the gate. Before the plane stopped, I grabbed my duffel bag. I did a quick handshake with the crew and ran down the ramp. A golf cart was waiting. I looked at the driver. "Is this for me?"

"Are you going to Vietnam?"

"Yes, sir!"

"Then this is for you! Let's go! It is a long way to the gate!"

I was sure that the driver broke the speed record for golf carts in an airport. We arrived at the gate, and I saw several men and women standing at a closed door to the ramp.

I jumped off of the cart. "Thank you, A.J. Foyt! You should drive a racecar!"

"You are welcome, soldier."

I ran over to the closed ramp door. One of the ladies says, "You are too late, soldier!"

"I have got to get on that plane!"

"Come with me and look at this!"

We walked over to the adjacent window. I could see the plane moving away from the gate. I could see the ramp being pulled away from the plane.

I looked back at the two men standing at the closed door. "I am supposed to be in Vietnam in the morning or I will be AWOL. I can see the plane right there! Isn't there anything you can do?"

The lady says, "No, we cannot do nothing!"

She had just given me a double negative, but now was not the time for a grammar lesson. One of the men picked up the phone, and then he started speaking on his radio. The plane stopped and the rolling ramp started to move out. The plane started moving in toward the ramp.

The man says, "Soldier, you made it, but hurry it up! And I mean run down that ramp!"

"Yes, sir, and thank all of you!"

I shook his hand.

"Good luck, Sergeant!"

The ramp door opened, and I ran down the ramp to the plane. To my surprise, I could see the outside of the plane. The door of the plane was not opened. I could see through the glass in the door. A stewardess was turning a wheel-like apparatus, trying to unlock the airtight pressure door.

The door finally opened, and a very lovely stewardess was standing in front of me. She reached out her hand. "Have you ever felt like you almost missed a plane?"

I shook her hand. "Yes, ma'am, this one!"

She releases my hand. "Don't call me ma'am. We are probably the same age!"

The other stewardesses laughed.

"OK, I won't!"

I looked around and saw many other soldiers heading back for Vietnam. I turned to the pretty stewardess. "Where do you want me to sit?"

"Where do you want to sit?"

I look around and saw that no one was sitting in first class. "Right here, in front!"

"You got it!"

"Thanks, ma'am!"

"Don't call me ma'am!" She pointed at her nametag. "Julie. My name is Julie!"

"OK, Julie. I'll call you Julie!"

Before I could sit down, the plane jumped and Julie fell into me. I could tell that she did it on purpose.

Julie looked in my eyes. "I am sorry, Sergeant Rodgers."

"That's OK."

I decided to see if Mac was on the plane. He probably had already left for Vietnam. If he hadn't, I would get him to move up to first class and we could tease Julie together.

"Julie, can I walk to the back and look for someone?"

"Sure, and bring him back up here if you want!"

I walked to the rear and checked every seat. Mac was not on the plane. I returned to first class. I found a seat by the window that I liked and sat down. The plane engines started to roar.

We lifted off and within minutes, Julie walked down the aisle. "Can I sit here next to you?"

I looked around and I could see plenty of empty seats. "Sure, but don't you have to work or something?"

"No, I am deadheading. I am just watching and learning!"

"So you won't get in trouble for just sitting?"

"No, the crew is training another stewardess now. They told me to take it easy. Are you from Houston?"

"Not really. I am from California. I was going to college when I got drafted."

"I am from California too!"

"Yeah, where?"

"Bakersfield."

"I am from Porterville, fifty miles away."

"It's a small world, huh, Sergeant Rodgers?"

"It sure is, Julie."

"Since we are almost neighbors, can I call you by your first name?"

"Sure. It is Danny!"

Julie and I talked for an hour or so about things in general. She started telling me about her personal life and asking me things like what kind of food I liked. She asked me what kind of movies I liked. She asked me what kind of girls I liked. I was getting tired of answering questions, and she could see it in my face.

Julie looks at me. "Are you getting tired, Danny?"

"Yeah, pretty tired."

"Me too. I'll get you a pillow."

She stood up, opened the upper compartment, and handed the pillow to me.

"Thank you, Julie."

"You are welcome, Danny."

I placed the pillow behind my head and fell asleep fast. I was very tired from all of the stress and running around while trying to make my flight.

I slept for two hours before I started to wake up. I could feel pressure on my shoulder and I could feel something on my right hand.

I slowly opened my eyes. Julie had her head leaning on my shoulder and her hand lying on top of my hand. I now could see that Julie wanted more than just conversation. Julie was a beautiful girl and any guy would be glad to have her as a girlfriend. But I was married to a beautiful girl myself.

I moved slightly so she would wake up, but instead of waking, she snuggled closer to me. I moved again. She woke up and sat back in her seat. "I am sorry, Danny. I must have been tired too."

"Julie, do you have a boyfriend?"

"No. Do you have a girlfriend?"

"Yes and no."

"What?"

"I have a wife, and I am really happy. Sue is a great girl."

"Are you mad at me?"

"No, I am flattered that a fine girl like you would be attracted to a guy like me."

"You are a very nice guy and good looking too. Can I give you a kiss on the cheek before I go?"

"Sure, but you don't have to go. I like talking to you."

"Thanks, Danny. I will just keep sitting here then."

"What kind of guy are you looking for, Julie?"

"One with a sense of humor who likes cars, cares about me, goes to church, and is a leader, not a follower!"

I start to laugh.

Julie says, "What's wrong? Am I asking too much from a guy?"

"No, that's me. I have a sense of humor. I have a 1965 Super Sport with a four-speed and a 409 cubic-inch engine. I care about people. I am a Christian and go to church. I am a squad leader in Vietnam."

"But you are taken. Are you sure that you are a happily married man?" She laughs.

"Yep, I am very happy. I plan to be married to Sue for the rest of my life. We want three kids."

"I think Sue is lucky. Does she know it?"

"I don't know if she is lucky, but she tells me that she loves me all the time."

We spoke about Vietnam for the remainder of the trip to Tokyo. We landed in Tokyo, refueled, and picked up more servicemen.

The soldiers started boarding the plane. Julie was standing at the entrance and directing the men to their seats. Every man looked at Julie in awe.

One man started to sit next to me. Julie tapped him on the shoulder. "You can't sit there. That is my seat."

The soldier looked at me with a smile. I looked at him and shrugged my shoulders as if to say, "I don't know why she wants to sit next to me!"

Every soldier on the plane would be happy to have Julie sit next to him. Even though I was married, I felt good that she chose me to sit next to. The airplane's jet engines started revving up.

The plane pulled away and headed for the takeoff strip. Julie sat down. "We are almost on our way, Danny."

"It looks like it."

"I'll bet you hate to go back to Vietnam, huh?"

"Yeah, it is getting bad over there. This Tet Offensive thing just keeps going on. The NVA and VC are stronger than ever! We fight them almost every day!"

"When I watch the news, it says that the North Vietnam soldiers are not coming to the south. Is that true?"

"No. That's what NVA stands for, North Vietnam Army, or sometimes they're called NVR, North Vietnam Regulars."

"What is the difference between a VC and an NVA?"

"Training and good equipment."

"So the NVA gets better guns and stuff like that, huh?"

"Yeah, they have helmets like we do and fatigues and all of that!"

"Where is your base camp?"

"Well, we really don't have a base camp. We store our duffel bags in Chu Lai. Once our company left Chu Lai, we never went back. I had to go to Chu Lai to get my clothes and duffel bag before going on R&R."

"Do you get scared?"

"Yep, lots of times."

"Are you afraid every day?"

"No, only during a firefight."

"Do you want to change the subject?"

"Yes."

"OK, tell me about your wife."

"Sue is a very pretty girl who looks great in a bikini. She is a very good water skier. She plays softball, ping pong, and is really competitive. But above all, she loves me very much. I love her and would do anything for her."

"Sue sounds like a real fine catch. Are you going to tell her about me and how I have been acting?"

"Maybe someday when the time is right. She is real jealous."

The rest of the trip to Vietnam went well. It was nice to talk to Julie. She talked about her high school in Bakersfield and the sports that she played. She played volleyball and liked to watch baseball and football.

"Hey, Julie, I played baseball for Porterville High and we played Bakersfield!"

"Yeah, I remember. Did you play third base?"

"Yes, I played third and the outfield. When I got to college, I played third most of the time. I even pitched a little, but I was too wild."

She laughed. "I am sure that I saw you in a game a few times. You played varsity and junior varsity, didn't you?"

"Yes, I played both."

The pilot announced that we would be landing in Cam Ranh Bay, Vietnam.

"Cam Ranh Bay? Julie, I left from Da Nang! Man, oh man, that is a long way from where my company is located. My company is in the northern portion of South Vietnam and we are going to land in the southern portion of South Vietnam!"

"Yeah, but didn't you say that you picked up your duffel bag in Chu Lai?"

"Yeah!"

"Well, Cam Ranh Bay and Chu Lai are both south of Da Nang, so wouldn't it be a shorter trip for you?"

"No. Cam Ranh Bay is a long way from Chu Lai. Da Nang is a lot shorter from Chu Lai! I will just hop a cargo plane and take it to Da Nang."

"Where is your company now?"

"They are probably at Hue or near the DMZ. We spent a lot of time in the Khe Sanh Valley. They could even be there."

"Isn't that the place you guys call Death Valley?"

"Yes it is. We have lost a lot of men there."

"We are about ready to touch down. Please be careful over here, Danny."

"I will, and it has been nice talking to you."

The plane landed, taxied for a few minutes, and stopped. Julie got out of her seat and stood by the plane exit along with the other stewardesses and pilots. They were telling each soldier to take care and be careful.

I stood up and took my duffel bag from the overhead compartment. I shook hands with both pilots and two of the stewardesses. I reached for Julie's hand and she said, "Can I give you a hug, Danny?"

"Sure you can."

She gave me a hug and a kiss on the cheek. The other soldiers were watching. One of the men looked intently. "What about us? Don't we get a hug?"

Julie immediately answered, "Nope, only one hug per trip!"

We all laughed. I turned around and looked at the crew. "I hope to see all of you again sometime. Thanks for everything!"

I knew that I had to hustle to get back to Chu Lai and then to my company. My R&R was over! Now it was time to take care of business again. My squad probably needed me!

CHAPTER 26

Chuck is Dead

Once I walked down the steps of the large plane, I looked back over my shoulder just to take another look. The airplane that I had been riding in was a really nice plane that made little noise.

The next plane I would be riding in would be a cargo plane that made plenty of noise. I would have to find a plane going to Chu Lai. I would be sitting in a steel or net seat. I would have to wear earplugs. I looked around at the buildings and I saw many Vietnamese in black pajamas, working.

Yes, I was back in Vietnam again. I walked over to a couple of cargo planes.

I saw a crewman loading C-rations. "I need a ride to Chu Lai. Are ya going there?"

"Yep, hop in!"

"Do you need help loading?"

"No, I am almost done, thanks!"

The crewman handed me a pair of earplugs. I grabbed a seat, and the plane took off. The rumble of the plane would have put me to sleep, but the seats were too uncomfortable. Finally, we landed in Chu Lai.

I hopped a deuce-and-a-half that took me to Top's CP. I walked over to see Top at the command post. "Hey, Top, I am back. How are ya?"

Top shakes my hand. "Good to see you, my friend! Good to see you."

"You too!"

"We have been in a crap load since you left!"

"Did we get to stay in our stand down?"

"Yep, but it was only for three days!"

"If I remember correctly, we were supposed to have a seven-day stand down a few months ago!"

"That was a bunch of crap! I don't think we will ever get a seven-day!"

"Have we lost any men lately?"

"Only wounded. Your guys need you. The old man calls every other day for you. I spoke to the captain, and he will give you sergeant E-7 if you will re-up for three months!"

"Nope!"

"But Rock, that would be great for you back in the States!"

"I would never make it back to the States!"

"What if I could get you an acting jack officer's position, like a lieutenant? I could make you a full, regular lieutenant in a few weeks!"

"You couldn't do that, could you, Top?"

"Danny, we can do anything over here in the 'Nam! We can do anything! Now are you interested?"

"Nope! The same thing; I wouldn't make it back to the States. Sorry, Top."

"I don't blame you! Now grab a bunk and jump a skid in the morning! Think about the officer's position!"

"See ya, Top."

As I located a tent with an empty bunk, I thought about Top's offer. The offer was great. I didn't really think that the captain and Top could give me the rank of lieutenant. It was nice to think that they thought I was worthy.

I didn't get much sleep, worrying about my men and the offer Top and the captain gave me. Morning came and I went to speak to Top. "Top, I am ready to go back to the field!"

"Your chopper will be here in an hour. Can I call you 'sir' now? Are you going to accept the lieutenant position?"

"No, Top, you can't. I am not going to stay over here for three more months! Not even if you made me captain."

"OK, Rock, I understand."

I hung around, talking to Top until the chopper came in. Top and I spoke about the war in general and our plans for when we went home.

I heard the skid. "There is my ride, Top. I guess I'll see ya later!"

Top grabbed my hand. "See ya later, Rock. Think about the offer!"

"I will!"

As I walked away, I thought to myself, *I don't think I would stay over here in the 'Nam for three more months even if I were offered President of the United States!*

I jumped on the chopper after it was loaded with supplies for the guys in the field. We took off heading for Khe San. I hoped that we were not going to be deep in the valley. I did not want any more of the area we called Death Valley.

We traveled for a while before the door gunner tapped me on the shoulder and pointed straight ahead. "Hot LZ! Hot LZ!"

Truly, I was back in Vietnam again!

My company was in a firefight, and we were going to land right in the middle. The door gunners started firing from both sides of the skid. Both gunners had long bungee cords attached to their guns so they could stand on the skid rails for a better aim.

The chopper came in fast. The gunners were busy, so I started unloading cases of C-rations. Other men from the company ran out to help me. As soon as the rations were unloaded, the slick started to take off. The gunners were still blazing the bush with their M-60s.

I jumped off the chopper and ran to the tree line. The first place that I ran to was the captain's CP. The rounds were still flying, so I stayed low.

The captain was on the radio, directing the platoons and squad leaders. He looked up. "Hey, Rock, glad to see ya!"

"Same here, sir!"

"These gooks have been fighting us on and off for a few days! They are dug in across the rice paddy."

"Are we going to attack?"

"No, I'm going to keep calling in fire support. These guys hit us at night sometimes, so be careful! Now get to your platoon."

"Yes, sir!"

I walked cautiously to the lieutenant's CP. "Hey, sir, how are you?"

"Great, Danny. I am sure glad that you are back! We are fighting both VC and NVA. They are hitting us at night then running!"

"Can't we see their flash?"

"No, they throw grenades. Now go see your men. Eckert has been doing a good job!"

"That's good."

The incoming fire started to slow so I was able to move toward my squad a little faster. However, I still kept low while I moved.

I decided to check in with Chuck before seeing my guys. When I saw Chuck, he was lying on the wet and soggy ground with his rifle in the ready position. I tapped him on the back. "Hey, Chuck!"

"You're back! Glad to see you. Did you know that after our short, three-day stand down, we have been fighting ever since?"

"With these guys?"

"No, but we have been fighting somebody every day. Sometimes it is only for an hour or so! I am ready to go home!"

"Me too. I am getting tired of all of this!"

"How was Hawaii?"

"I don't know. I didn't see much of it."

"What?"

"I went to Houston!"

"No way!"

"Yep way. I jumped on a plane from Hawaii to Houston!"

"Did you see your 409?"

"Yep!"

"Was it OK?"

"Yes, if you like accordions!"

"Was it smashed up that bad?"

"Yep."

"Did you kill Sue?"

"I wanted to kill her at first, but it was an accident!"

"How long did it take you to stop being mad?"

"I stopped being mad right away, but I pretended to be mad so I would get a little every night!"

Chuck started laughing really hard. "You are the man, Danny. You are the man!"

"Yeah, I had a good time with Mom, Dad, and my brothers."

"How was your trip back to Vietnam? Did you have to change planes a lot?"

"Yeah, but listen to this! I met a stewardess that was hitting on me!"

"For real?"

"Yes, she laid her head on my shoulder and held my hand while she was sleeping. She was off duty so she could do what she wanted."

"What did she look like?"

"She could be a model. She was very good looking!"

"Did she kiss you?"

"Yes, she did, but it was only on the cheek!"

"Are you going to tell Sue?"

"Oh, maybe someday. Probably in about forty years."

Chuck grins. "I am going to tell her as soon as I see her!"

We both laugh.

"Chuck, are we going to stay here tonight? I see that foxholes are already dug."

"Yep, I think so, but be careful. These guys throw grenades at night!"

"Yeah, that is what the lieutenant or the captain told me! See ya; I am going to my squad!"

The incoming fire was now next to nothing. I hustled to my guys. "What's happening?"

All of my squad was very glad to see me. We started talking, being careful not to be nonchalant about the possibility of incoming rounds or even an enemy attack. The artillery was slowing enough where we could speak without yelling. I looked at Eckert and noticed that he was checking the ammo for Raymond's Pig. He was being a good squad leader, watching over everything.

I looked at Emerald, and as usual, he was shaky.

"Hey, Eckert, how has Dong been?"

"He has been just fine. I am starting to understand him better, but the other scout named Long is sort of weird. He acts like he is hiding something!"

"I noticed that about him too. I am glad that we got Dong!"

I reached over Dong's shoulder and pulled him closer, then pretended to hit him in the stomach with my fist.

Dong says, "Thank you, Sergeant Rock!"

"Cool, Dong! You said Rock and not Wock! Dong, what is the deal with Long?"

"I not know. He come from another part of Vietnam!"

"Men, I am going over to Sergeant Lewis's squad. See ya in a bit."

I went back to Chuck's location. "Hey, man, guess what?"

"What?"

"Top offered me E-6, E-7, or a lieutenant's position if I would extend over here for three months."

"Well, that would be great in the States, but over here, you would be dead before you could get your bars."

"You are right, but anyhow, I don't think he could really do it, do you?"

"I don't know about that because Top knows his crap."

523

"Oh, well, I will never know because when my turn is up, I am going back to the States!"

"I guess since your 409 is totaled, you will get a new car, huh, Danny?"

"Yeah, I will probably get a '68 Camaro or maybe an El Camino. Are you still wanting to get a Corvette?"

"Heck yeah! I can hardly wait. I want a hardtop convertible. You know, one that you can take the top off!"

"Do you think we will be stationed at Fort Ord?"

"I hope so. Wouldn't it be cool if we could both be stationed in California, right back where we started? That would be neat, huh? Danny, are you going to live on base?"

"No. Sue and I will probably get an apartment."

"I guess I will live on base."

"Nope. We won't have it. You are going to live with Sue and me! We will have a great time living by the ocean and all of that. We will get an apartment in Monterey, Carmel, or Seaside."

"Yeah, and I'll get a girlfriend, and we will all walk on the beach and build fires at night."

"I have an idea for you, Chuck."

"Yeah, what?"

"You can start dating that Jane Fonda chick."

"You mean the protester that hates us soldiers?"

"That's the one. With your charm, she will love all of us soldiers!"

"She is too old for me."

"Yeah, but she is cute."

"How old is she anyhow?"

"Well, let's see. She was born in 1937, so she is probably around thirty. Did you know that her mother committed suicide?"

"No. How do you know so much about her?"

"Because I like her dad. Jane just does not know what is really going on over here. So every time I want to read about Henry Fonda, Jane is in the story."

"Do you think that you would want to meet her?"

"Yeah, but only if she would listen."

"I'll bet she drives a Corvette, huh?"

"Yeah, she probably has one for every day of the week."

"Enough about Hanoi Jane."

"When we drive in downtown Carmel, we will take your Corvette so we look cool, huh?"

"We would look cool in your Camaro or El Camino too! We would look cool in any car!"

We both laughed hard.

"Hey, Danny, be careful tonight. I have a feeling that they may hit us."

"OK. Thanks for the warning."

I went back to my squad, and we started pulling guard. Sure enough, a few incoming grenades were thrown every so often. We would wake up and run to a foxhole for cover. I heard an explosion nearby. I heard a loud groan. Someone yelled, "Medic! We need a medic!"

I ran to where the groans were coming from. It was Chuck. Chuck was in the foxhole, pulling guard, when an incoming grenade dropped right on top of him.

Doc was already near Chuck. "Man, Danny, he has a lot of blood coming out of his back!"

Chuck is lying partially in and out of the foxhole. "Hey, buddy, how are ya?"

"I really hurt more on my back than any place else. Danny, I am getting weak and cold. I squeezed the claymore trigger, but it didn't go off."

"You are getting weak because you are losing blood, but Doc is fixing you up."

Doc says, "Roll over for me a little, Chuck!"

Chuck didn't move.

"Wake up, buddy! Wake up!" I said. I slapped him a few times in the face. Finally, he woke up.

Chuck looked at me. "Danny, I hurt."

"Move over, Doc. I want to see his back!"

Doc moved over so I could see. "Give me your flashlight, Doc!"

I shined it on his butt and back. I checked out his back for wounds, but all I could see was a lot of blood. I took a fresh piece of gauze from Doc and wiped the blood off. I saw wounds in his back. The blood was still coming out through the bandages.

I handed the flashlight back to Doc. "Do what you can, Doc!"

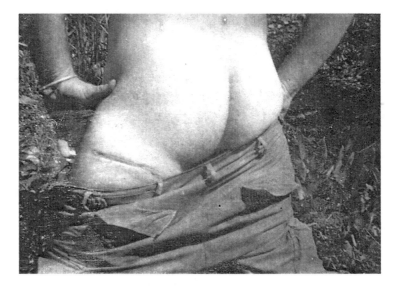

*Chucks butt wound-leg. Notice the infections
on his back from the jungle bushes*

Doc was almost finished taping the compressed bandages to Chuck's wounds when Mac walks up. "Doc, I've got another man down."

"OK, I'll be right there!"

Mac smiles and facetiously says, "It is good to be back in Vietnam, huh, Danny?"

"Yeah, right!"

"Where did Chuck get it?"

"In the back."

"The back?"

"Yep, but it won't stop bleeding!"

"Too bad it was not his butt!"

"Yeah, we could make lots of jokes about it! But this one is no joke!"

"It is that bad, huh?"

"Yeah, it is pretty bad. He will have to go back to the rear and get the shrapnel pulled out!"

"Well, let me know when you hear something. I am going back to my squad."

I did not sleep a wink the rest of the night. Killer, Eckert, and I took turns watching Chuck. We wanted to be sure that he kept breathing. I could see a glimpse of sunlight coming over the horizon.

Now we could get Chuck and the other wounded men on choppers and send them to the rear.

I ran back over to Chuck. "Chuck, I am going to see Watkins to find out when we will lift you out!"

With a whisper, Chuck said, "Thanks, Danny, but don't look so worried. I'll be alright."

He was still very, very weak.

"Be right back, Chuck."

I hurried over to the lieutenant. When he saw me, he stood up quickly. "How is Chuck, Danny?"

I think this was the first time the lieutenant had ever used our first names together in the same sentence. In some way, I thought that this was an expression of how much he cared for both of us.

"He is weak and still bleeding."

"OK, get him on the chopper fast when it lands!"

"Yes, sir! I am going back to Chuck!"

I hustled back to Chuck. Emerald was leaning over Chuck. "Is he going to be alright, Sergeant Rock?"

I could not let Emerald know how worried I was about Chuck. "Yes, he will be OK, but we need to get him back to the rear."

The choppers came in and landed. Two were for security guard and one was to pick up our wounded. Killer and I help walk Chuck to the chopper. Chuck was still groggy when he lay down in the seats. The skid started revving.

The slick took off, heading for somewhere in the rear. Chuck mustered up enough energy to give us a wave. I gave him two thumbs up.

"Killer, Chuck says he tried to set the claymore off but it didn't blow! Let's go and find out why!"

"Yeah, let's go!"

We walked back to Chuck's foxhole. "Now, Killer, start tracing the cord to the claymore, but let me disconnect it first!"

Killer started walking down the claymore line. "I found the problem, Sarge!"

"What ya got?"

"A broken line. It wouldn't go off because the electric charge couldn't go to the claymore mine!"

"I guess that the shrapnel cut the line, huh?"

"Yep, that is what I think too."

"Hey, Killer, do you notice anything new?"

"Oh, yeah, it is quiet. I guess the enemy has moved on, or what is left of them."

"Yeah, the old man shot them up pretty bad with a lot of artillery."

"How many men did we lose last night, Sarge?"

"Doc says four wounded, plus Chuck!"

"I'll bet that you are feeling real bad about Sergeant Lewis, huh?"

"Yep, real bad. I hate it over here!"

Craig sauntered up to me, being very solemn. "Watkins wants you in the CP, Sarge. I am so sorry to hear about Lewis."

"Thank you, Craig. We all made a good team."

"The best."

I ambled over to the lieutenant's CP, very somber myself. "Yes, sir."

"Hey, Rock, in a little bit, we are going across the rice paddy to get a body count. After that, we are heading in the direction of the DMZ."

I was still feeling very low about Chuck. He had been wounded twice before, but this time it seemed worse.

I hung my head and answered, "Yes, sir. Just let me know when we are going to move out."

"Don't you get down or I'll kick your butt! We need you up and ready!"

He made me laugh a little.

"OK, sir, I won't!"

"Oh, by the way, Rock, we have a Shake and Bake coming in tomorrow!"

"Oh, boy, another Shake and Bake! See ya later, sir."

"Later."

My men were waiting on me. Eckert says, "What did Watkins say? This is quite a conundrum, huh, Sarge?"

"Yes, but this is no riddle and the answer is not a pun."

Killer laughs at Eckert. "Where did you learn big words like that, Eckert?"

"In my college consortium brotherhood council."

"You're full of crap!"

Now we were laughing again, thanks to Killer and Eckert.

"So what did Watkins say?" Raymond asks.

"He says we are going to cross the rice paddy today and count the bodies. After that, we will head out in the direction of the DMZ. Tomorrow, we will get a Shake and Bake."

Killer, Eckert, and Craig all groan in unison.

Emerald asks loudly, "What is a Shake and Bake, Sarge?"

Killer answers, "Most of the time, it means trouble!"

Eckert joins in, "We have seen one that was good until he got killed!"

I spoke up, "Emerald, a Shake and Bake is a private or corporal that has been put through Non-Commissioned Officers' School really fast, and when they come out, they are an E-5 sergeant, ready to be a squad leader!"

"You mean an E-5 like you?"

I started to answer when Killer says, "Not an E-5 like Rock, not exactly!"

Emerald tilts his head. "What do you mean, 'Not like Rock'?"

"Which sergeant would you want to follow into battle? A seasoned Vietnam veteran or a Shake and Bake fresh from the States?"

"I would want to follow Sergeant Rock!"

"There you go!"

My men are looking at me. "OK, men, let's go. Eckert, you did a good job, I have been told!"

"Thanks, Sarge. Good to have you back."

We moved out carefully through the rice paddy. We received no retaliation. Maybe we had killed most of them. When we reached the tree line and the bush on the other side of the paddy, we saw lots of tangled and twisted trees, bushes, and bodies.

I was glad when the body count was assigned to another platoon. I was so engrossed in thinking about my buddy Chuck that I did not hear how many NVA or VC were killed.

After an hour, maybe longer, we moved out. We did the typical travel, in and out of the bush, until we found a location near a small river.

I looked at Craig. "This would be a cool place to set up for the night, huh?"

"Hey, Sarge, the old man says that is what we are going to do. We are going to dig in here."

"OK, thanks. Men, we will make a perimeter here, so let's dig in!"

We dug our foxholes and most of the guys were quiet. Killer says, "Sarge, we know that you are feeling bad about Lewis, but you have still got to lead us. Don't worry about digging tonight. I'll take your turn!"

"Give me that shovel, Killer! Thanks anyhow! Emerald, set up guard duty!"

Emerald set up the guard and we ate our C-rations. We talked a little, then tried to get a little sleep. No one shot at us, nor did they throw hand grenades at us. However, when your best friend has been wounded from incoming fire the night before, you tend to sleep light.

When morning came, we ate and moved out. We were heading for the LZ to meet up with the Shake and Bake. We arrived at the LZ and set up security for the chopper.

Craig approaches. "The lieutenant wants you to bring in the chopper!"

"OK, what is his sign?"

"Boomerang One-Three."

I got on the horn. "Boomerang One-Three, this is Blackhawk Three, over."

"This is Boomerang One–Three. Will you be landing me?"

"Affirmatron."

"I am ready."

I threw out a grenade of blue smoke. "What do you see, Boomerang?"

"I see blue smoke."

"You are correct. Affirmatron on the blue smoke."

The chopper landed and the Shake and Bake jumped off. He had a brand new rifle and brand new fatigues and boots. His fatigues looked like they were even pressed. His freshly made nametag said his name was Brooks.

I knew that as soon as Killer and the other guys saw him they would start laughing. I hustled over to my guys. "Men, don't laugh at the Shake and Bake. He may be your squad leader when I leave or get killed!"

I walked back to speak to the Shake and Bake. I stuck out my hand for a handshake. "Brooks, how are you?"

531

"It is Sergeant Brooks to you, soldier."

I laughed.

"What are you laughing at?"

"You just remind me of a guy named Gibbons and a guy named Brock."

"What is your name, soldier?"

"My name is Rodgers!"

"You should say, 'My name is Rodgers, Sergeant!'"

"No, I won't be saying it like that today!"

"What do you mean, soldier? Don't you have any respect?"

"Yep, for some people."

"Take me to your platoon leader, soldier!"

"OK, Brooks, follow me!"

"I told you to call me Sergeant Brooks!"

"And I told you no!"

We arrived at the lieutenant's CP. "Sir, this is the new Shake and Bake."

Watkins stuck out his hand for a handshake. "How are you, Sergeant?"

"I was just fine until I met this guy, Rodgers!" Brooks looks at me. "He has no respect for his superiors! He won't even call me Sergeant!"

The lieutenant starts to laugh. "He gives me respect!"

"Sir, I want Rodgers to call me Sergeant!"

Watkins turns toward me with a grin and chuckles. "Are you going to call Brooks Sergeant?"

"No, sir, not today, but maybe someday."

"Well, there you have it. If Rodgers doesn't want to call you Sergeant, then no one is going to make him call you Sergeant."

"What do you mean, sir?"

"Go ahead and tell him, Danny."

I looked at Brooks. "I am a sergeant also."

"If you are a sergeant, where are your stripes?"

"I left them on the battlefield."

"So what is your name?"

"My name is Rodgers, but most people call me Sergeant Rock."

"You are Sergeant Rock? Top in Chu Lai told me all about you. I am sorry. Top told me to listen to you and Sergeant Lewis. I am sorry."

"The first thing that you need to do is lose the attitude."

"What do you mean?"

"In the States, soldiers are forced to give respect to their superiors. Over here, you have to earn it."

"I'll listen and learn. By the way, I saw the dead guys and the wounded guys from yesterday. They were brought in on a chopper. Were you guys in a big battle?"

"Not too big! Did you see Sergeant Lewis?"

"No, there were three men left in Chu Lai that were wounded. The other two were dead and the helicopter took them someplace else."

"Did you speak to the three wounded guys?"

"Yes."

"And none of them were Sergeant Lewis?"

"Lewis was not in that group."

"How sure are you that Chuck is dead?"

"Chuck?"

"Yes, Sergeant Chuck Lewis. Is he dead?"

"Yes he is. Sorry, Sergeant Rock."

"OK. Follow me to the captain."

We arrived at the old man's CP. "Sir, this is the Shake and Bake."

"Glad to meet you, Sarge."

"Same here, sir. Why does Sergeant Rock call me 'Shake and Bake'?"

"Because you were made a sergeant so fast. You know, like quick food. You shake and bake it."

"I am as good of a sergeant as Lewis was and as good as Sergeant Rock is now!"

"No you're not! I think you are an idiot. You will probably be killed within a week. I am giving you Sergeant Lewis's squad. But you don't make a move until Rock tells you to. Now go over and introduce yourself to Lewis's squad. Danny, stay here for a minute!"

"Yes, sir."

"I am hearing rumors about Lewis being killed. Man, I know that he was bleeding bad, but I thought he would make it!"

"What does Top say?"

"He says that if he didn't return to Chu Lai, he was dead."

"That is just bad, sir."

"Yeah, it is. You have lost a lot of friends over here, haven't ya, Rock?"

"Yeah, but none as close as Chuck. We lived in California in two towns that were very close to each other. We got drafted at the same time, went to basic training together. We took AIT together. We sat next to each other on the plane that brought us to Vietnam. We even convinced a sergeant to change our orders to come here to this company."

"Are ya going to be alright, Danny?"

"Yes, sir. I just want to do my time and go home. I am feeling sick in my stomach. See ya, sir."

I started thinking about all of the good times Chuck and I had before Vietnam and here in the 'Nam. Chuck and I could talk for hours. There was just something special about our relationship. Chuck could make me laugh at the drop of a hat. We liked the same type of girls, baseball, football, guns, fishing, and much, much more. My throat started to swell, and I was trying to hold back the tears. I thought that Chuck and I would be friends for life. This was not the way that I wanted to become a man.

I walked back to my squad. I was so mentally drained that I could have walked through a minefield and not even noticed.

Killer was the first to see me. "Sergeant Rock, we are very sorry about Sergeant Lewis. He was one of the best."

Eckert says, "He was a great leader and someone you could trust in a firefight."

Raymond is listening. "Sarge, what do you think of the Shake and Bake?"

I grin. "He told me to call him Sergeant Brock, or I mean Brooks!"

"Wasn't Brock that sergeant who couldn't call in artillery and tried to get you in trouble?"

"Yep, and Brooks is very much like him!"

"So he will take over Sergeant Lewis's squad, huh?"

"Yep, but I hope he listens, because there are at least two men in Lewis's squad qualified to be a squad leader. They won't take any crap from him!"

Emerald and Killer are whispering to each other. I look at them. "What are you two whispering about?"

Killer says, "Emerald is worried about your well-being."

"You mean, am I going to be able to lead?"

"Yes, Sergeant. We can see it in your eyes. It looks like your fire is gone."

CHAPTER 27

DMZ Behind the Wall

Had I lost my fire? Had I lost my determination to lead? Had I lost my resolve? I thought about all of the American and Vietnamese soldiers that were killed. I thought about the men that were missing arms and legs. Now here I am with two Purple Hearts, but my wounds did not leave me with missing legs or arms. I have to suck it up and keep leading my men.

Doc comes to my location. "How are ya holding up, Danny?"

"It is tough, Doc."

"Yeah, I know what you mean. The old man wanted me to check you out."

"You know, Doc, we are not machines. It seems like the higher ups, and even the captain, want us to forget about everything else that happens and kill. Man, Doc, I am getting tired of seeing death, and I am getting tired of killing!"

"Danny, it wouldn't be so bad if your friends were not the dead ones."

"There is something else, too."

"What's that?"

"I think that I have changed. I liked to hunt before I came over here, but now I don't think I would like it so much."

"Yeah, I know what you mean. I liked to hunt too, but I probably won't hunt anymore when I get home. Why do you think that is, Rock?"

"It is because we are use to hunting prey that shoots back at us! Hunting deer or rabbits or birds will not be a challenge for us anymore."

"That's it. I couldn't put my finger on it before, but that is it. There will not be a challenge."

"You know something else, Doc?"

"What?"

"Believe it or not, I still love guns and knives, and I will continue loving them back in the States. Why is that?"

"It is because your gun is your friend. Over here, the difference between life and death is your weapon. So, psychologically, you love that rifle!"

"Yep, you are right. Thanks for the talk!"

"OK, Danny, now you keep your spirits up. I am really, really sorry about Chuck. He was the best. I am going back to the captain to tell him that you are fine."

Craig walks up to me. "Sarge, we are moving out again in ten."

"Thanks, Craig. Get the men together. I want to talk to all of you men."

"OK!" He takes off, then returns with the men. "Here they are, Sarge."

"OK, men, who do we have left? We have Emerald, Eckert, Killer, Raymond, Craig, Dong, and me!"

Killer says, "Don't you mean *I*?"

I started to answer when Eckert says, "He already said your name, Killer!"

We all laughed.

"OK, Killer. You are right. I should have said *I* instead of *me*."

"Just trying to keep your education going, Sarge."

"Thank you for that stimulating insight! Men, we have got to pull together now harder than ever. We are heading to the DMZ. I don't think we will make it all of the way to the DMZ today; at least, I hope not. You guys are the best, so let's stay tight. Raymond, do you have an ammo carrier?"

"Yes, Killer and Eckert."

"OK, let's move out!"

Emerald moves closer to me. "We don't have point, do we?"

"Not today, Emerald. Not today."

The travel was hot and muggy. After a half hour, all of us were drenched with sweat. Each of us stunk. The body odor was overwhelming. This odor was nothing compared to the stench we had when we went fifty-seven days with no fresh water. Each of us had a green towel that we used to wipe the sweat from our faces. The towels were wet with sweat; therefore, they were useless to wipe your face. We needed some rain badly. We traveled two more hours before the hot, humid wind started to pick up.

I could see the dark clouds heading in our direction. The rain started to fall. This was a welcome sight. We could now let the rain rinse out our clothes. Craig is on the horn. He turns toward me. "The old man says we are going to rest for fifteen."

"Cool! Alright, men take a break!"

I took my grungy towel and hung it on a tree limb so it would get completely soaked by the rain. I took off my shirt and did the same. I looked around and all of the men were doing likewise.

Every five minutes, I would reach up and ring out my towel and shirt. The rain was now falling very hard. Finally, we were getting a break from the hot, scorching, sultry weather. I decided to grab a can of bread. When the men saw me opening my bread with my P-38, commonly known as a John Wayne, they grabbed what they could from their C-rations.

The rain was now coming down so hard that I had to eat my canned bread fast because it was getting wet, and I hated wet bread. It was time to move out again.

Most of my men ate as they humped, eating very fast. We humped for another two hours before stopping for the night, just short of the DMZ. My men were still soaked from the rain and the sweat, but now the stench was gone.

The rain started to lighten, and I instructed my men to dig in for the night. Killer grabbed a can of turkey. "Who wants to trade ham for turkey?"

Dong stands. "Me, I trade."

They swap cans.

Killer says, "Dong, do you have any of that chocolate cocoa package stuff?"

"Yes!"

"I'll trade my cigarettes and gum for your cocoa."

"OK, I trade."

Killer is looking through his rucksack. He finds what he is looking for and walks over to me and shows me. He holds out a package of hot chocolate mix and Oreo cookies.

"Sarge, it is time!"

I knew what he wanted; however, I said, "Time for what?"

"I have been here for six months!"

"So?"

"You and Sergeant Lewis said that you would teach me how to make your chocolate pudding!"

"You're right. OK, I will, but you need pound cake too. And before I show you, we need to dig our foxholes!"

"Then you will teach me?"

"Yep, but I won't show everyone, only the guys who have been here six months!"

"What about Shake and Bake?"

"Nope, not him."

Doc, as he had promised, came over to me. "Hey, Danny, what's going on?"

"Hey, Doc, not much. I am going to show Killer how to make chocolate pudding after we dig in."

"Yeah, he has been here six months, hasn't he? Can I watch again too? My pudding never tastes as good as yours."

"Sure. I am going to teach Emerald too!"

Doc looks at Emerald. "Hey, Emerald, Rock is going to show you how to make his pudding in a little bit!"

"For real, Sarge?"

"Yep, come over here! Doc and I want to talk to you!"

Doc knew that I wanted Emerald to be in on some conversation with his superiors, so he could build his confidence.

Doc says, "How ya doing, Emerald?"

"Good, Doc."

"What are you looking forward to when you get home?"

"My family and horses."

"Oh, yeah, Danny told me that you were a cowboy!"

"Yes, I love my quarter horses."

"Emerald can rope too, Doc!" I said.

Doc says, "I am impressed. Are ya any good?"

"Actually, without bragging, yes. I am pretty good. Hey, Sarge, remember that guy that said he owned some Oshan Reds?"

We all start to laugh.

"Yes, but the name was Oshan Rebel stallions, I think."

"Yeah, that was it. What was his name?"

"His name was Henning."

Doc joins in, "He was the guy that had to have more things than anyone else, wasn't he?"

Emerald says, "That's the guy! Doc, what are you looking forward to when you get home?"

"Being a great uncle. My brothers and sisters have kids, and some of them are brand new."

"That's cool. Well, I better take my turn at digging."

I stood up. "Me too." I grabbed an entrenching tool.

Doc stood up. "Me too, I'll help!"

This was a really nice offer. The men respected Doc. This was just another way that Doc showed he was willing to help. We finished the digging, and we sat back down near the foxholes. Doc wipes the sweat from his brow. "Danny, will you really come and meet my family when we get home?"

"Heck yeah! If your mom is as good of a cook as you say she is, I will probably stay a month."

Doc pulls out his latest letter from his mom. "Here, Rock, read this!" He points to the second paragraph.

The paragraph said, *"Be sure and ask Sergeant Rock, or Danny, what he likes to eat. Tell him that I love him and I pray for you both every night."*

"Man, Doc, that is cool. OK, here goes: does it have to be black food?"

"Black food? What do ya mean?"

I start laughing. "You guys like collard greens and poke salad and all of that stuff."

"Are you kidding? I hate all of that stuff!"

"Alright, here is what I like. I like fried okra, fish, steak, mashed potatoes and gravy, and almost all vegetables. I like ham, turkey, and Mexican food. I hate catsup."

"Me too. I like all of that. Man, Danny, with all of this talk about food, I am getting hungry again!"

"I stay hungry all of the time. Everything we eat, we burn it off!"

Killer and Emerald walk up to me. "OK, Sarge, let's cook!"

"OK, here is what you need: C-4, two tin cups for cooking, Oreo cookies, water, pound cake, and hot chocolate mix. You guys go and get all of that and come back over here."

Killer sees the Shake and Bake walking toward us. "Here comes trouble, Sergeant Rock."

"Stick around, Killer. Let's see what he wants."

Brooks approaches. "Sergeant Rock, I have a question!"

"What is your question, Brooks? And by the way, over here sergeants of equal rank usually just call each other by their last name."

"So do you want me to call you Rodgers or Rock?"

Killer replies to our conversation. "Rodgers? You had better call him Rock!"

"Was that your question, Brooks?" I said.

"No, no. I have seven men and not even one of them likes me!"

Doc stands. "You have to gain their respect. They want to depend on you in battle. You have to become one of them!"

I stand. "Did you help them dig your foxhole?"

"Heck no, I am a sergeant and sergeants don't dig with the grunts!"

Emerald looks at Brooks. "Sergeant Rock digs with us every night, and he pulls guard. He pulls point, and he carries ammo for the Pig."

Brooks stares at me. "Do you really do all of that, Rock?"

"Yep, every sergeant in this platoon helps dig. Watkins even digs."

"The lieutenant digs foxholes?"

"Yep."

"Man, I don't know what to do now."

"Here is what you better do, and I mean right now. Your squad had one of the best squad leaders, Sergeant Lewis. So you go back to your men, be humble, and tell them that you are sorry for being an a-hole. You get one of your guys to show you what to do. Offer to let one of your men set up guard, and above all, take a guard yourself. If you have any questions, just come back over here and see me or any of my men!"

Brooks hung his head. "Thanks, guys!" He turns and walks away.

Killer sits down. "OK, let's cook!"

Emerald does the same, and Doc watches and listens.

I start talking. "Crumble your cookies, put them in the cup, and add water a little over halfway. Put the first cup on a rock, leaving space for C-4."

Killer says, "How long do we cook it?"

"Just hold on and listen. Now, let the Oreo cookies and water sit for ten minutes. Pour the hot chocolate mix in the other metal canteen cup and pour water in it three-quarters full. Now, get rocks for another stove. Start the C-4 and place the hot chocolate water mixture on the C-4 until it boils, or almost. Now, bring the Oreos and water to an almost boil."

Emerald says facetiously, "This takes longer than my mom's cooking!"

Doc tilts his head. "But it is worth the wait!"

I continued, "After they boil, or almost boil, take them off to the side and let them sit for another ten minutes. Take the pound cake and crumble it and place it in with the cookie mixture. Now place the hot chocolate into the Oreo and pound cake mixture. Add a little water and place it back on the C-4. When the mixture starts to boil, remove it quickly and let it sit for another ten minutes, stirring a few times, and you are done. The secret is the ten minute waiting between the stages."

Killer and Emerald complete their cooking.

Killer says, "I have let it cool for about eight minutes. I can't wait any longer!"

Emerald is more patient. "Should I stir it again, Sarge?"

"It depends on how thick you want it. Yeah, give it another stir."

After another few minutes, they both begin to give me acclaim. "Sarge, this is great!"

"Better than I have ever tasted!"

"Thanks, guys, but I think the reason that you guys like it so much is because we never get anything like it."

"No, Sarge, it is really better than I get at home! What do ya think, Doc?" Killer asked.

Doc replies, "Give me a taste, Emerald!"

Emerald gives Doc a bite. "Yep, it is better than Mom's."

I raise my eyebrows. "Don't you dare tell your mom that, Doc!"

"No, I won't."

"After this war, or when we get back home, you can come visit my family. My mom is the best cook ever. Just like your mom, Doc."

Doc stands up. "Yeah, I really want to meet your mom and family. You know what, Danny?"

"What, Doc?"

"I think that you and I will be friends for the rest of our lives."

"I do too, Doc."

"I'll see you later, Danny. I need to get back to the CP. We will probably get into a lot of crap tomorrow. What do you think?"

"Yep, we probably will! Every company that gets near the DMZ runs into crap."

"Be careful."

"You too."

We start to pull guard when Dong moves closer to me. "Hi, Sarge, how you?"

"I am OK, Dong. How are you? What's up?"

Dong looks puzzled. "What's up?"

"Yeah, what's up means 'what do you want?' So what's up, Dong?"

"Tomorrow we fight a lot, yes?"

"Yes, probably. Do you like Vietnam?"

"I love South Vietnam. I hate VC and NVA and the North Vietnam!"

"Dong, you are a good Kit Carson Scout!"

"Thank you, Sergeant Rock."

"Alright, now get some sleep so you can pull guard and stay awake!"

"I not sleep on guard never!"

"I know. You are a good soldier. See ya tomorrow!"

"OK, see ya."

We had a peaceful night. However, as always, we could hear distant explosions and shooting as another company fought off the enemy. Morning came, and we got ready to move out.

We moved again in the direction of the DMZ. It was another hot, searing day. We had no rain so far. We traveled for four hours before we started to encounter incoming fire. The firing started to get heavier. We needed a place for cover, and we needed it quick.

I spotted a block and brick wall just ahead. "Take cover behind the wall!"

My squad ran up to the wall.

We were in a good position for a battle. The NVA were in the bush straight in front of us. There was a rice paddy between our position and the enemy's. The wall was thick enough where we could lay our weapons on top for a steady aim. The wall was long enough to protect all of my men. The wall was tall enough for us to sit behind it, and our helmets would not be exposed to the enemy. I had never felt so combative and comfortable at the same time. I looked to see how the rest of the company was doing.

The other squads and platoons were firing from behind trees, bamboo, and berms. My eyes and Doc's met. He shook his head from right to left as if to say, "Oh, boy, not again."

Doc was lying on the ground behind a berm, firing at the enemy. On this particular day, my squad was lucky.

Being lucky is a relevant term. The wall protected us; therefore, we were lucky. We had not made it to the DMZ yet, but we must be close. The incoming fire was getting intense, enhanced, and heightened. My squad was firing at the enemy at a blistering pace.

I, too, was firing fast and furious when I noticed something that would change this battle. The enemy was not wearing helmet covers. Therefore, as they moved through the trees and bushes, their helmets would shine.

The fervent, scorching, broiling hot sun was working in our favor for once. Our helmets were covered with a camouflaged cover so they would not shine in the sun. The slits in our helmet covers made it easy to place twigs and small tree branches and bush greenery into them. This technique would hide our silhouettes.

I yelled at my men, "Cease fire! Cease fire!" My squad stopped immediately.

Killer runs to me. "What's wrong, Sarge?"

"All of you, look over the wall at the enemy, but hold your fire for a minute."

My guys looked over the wall.

"OK, men, keep looking for a shiny reflection. These guys are not wearing helmet covers!"

Eckert says, "I see one! Look, he is moving from right to left!"

"I see him too!" Raymond proclaims.

"Me too," declare Killer and Emerald.

The rest of the men had now spotted what I hoped would be the downfall of these NVA.

"Now, when you see a shining helmet, you take the shot. Put your rifles on semi, not full. Place some branches in your covers."

We started firing at the shiny helmets, but now we had a small problem. Sometimes, four or five men would shoot the same gook.

"OK, men, take a breather. I want you to wait until they get in the open before firing. We are going to take turns, one at a time, on the wall."

Killer blurts, "Me first!"

The incoming fire was slightly lightening up. "OK, I want the rest of you to start eating lunch."

Eating lunch during a battle was unusual, but I had a plan to help Emerald. I looked at Eckert as he opened a can of C-rations. "Eckert, what do you think about me putting Emerald on the wall to build his confidence?"

"I think it is a good idea. We will be right here for support."

I look at Emerald. "Emerald, you are not going to eat?"

"No, I can't eat at a time like this!"

"Nothing to worry about. We have got this one in the bag."

I reach over and grab Killer's leg. "Killer, take a break. Emerald is taking over!"

Emerald turns toward me. "Me?"

"Yes you! Now get up there! Don't shoot until they are in the open!"

Hesitantly, Emerald moves in position. Killer opens a C-ration can as he grins and looks at me.

Emerald declares, "I see one, I see one!"

I reply, "Then kill one! Then kill one!"

My men start to laugh!

Emerald looks at me. "He is getting closer! He is in the rice paddy!"

Killer announces, "You better kill him before he joins us for lunch!"

"He is closer, Sarge!"

"You kill him now!"

I motion to my men to get ready in case Emerald fails at his duty!

Emerald fires. "I got him! I got him, Sarge! I got him!"

All of us jump up to look over the wall. Sure enough, he had killed the NVA.

I tap Emerald on the leg. "Great shot, but the next time, don't let him get that close to us. One hundred feet is just too close!"

"OK, Sarge. Here comes another one!"

Emerald fires and kills another.

"Here comes another one, Sarge! But I am going to let him get to the middle of the rice paddy before I blow him away!"

All of us start laughing hard. Finally, Emerald has become a soldier. It has taken a long time for him to come around, but maybe, just maybe, he can stay alive after I DEROS and become a dependable member of the squad.

Emerald again proclaims, "I see another gook!" He fires. "I got him!"

Killer taps Emerald on the leg. "Give me your helmet and I'll put some kill stars on it for you!"

Emerald reaches for his helmet and then stops. "Are you crazy? We'll do that later!"

Again, we all laugh.

"OK, men, take your turn. Raymond and Eckert on top. Emerald, come down!"

Emerald had a grin on his face as wide as Texas. He immediately started to open a C-ration. "Man, Rock, that was great. You made me do that by myself to teach me, didn't you?"

"Yep, and you are a pretty good shot too!"

"Sarge, I am sorry for being such a coward!"

"Well, you are not a coward any longer. Besides, I never thought that you were a coward. I just thought that you were overly scared."

"We will never be the same, will we, Sarge?"

"No, I don't think that we will ever be the same."

The incoming fire is coming again, quickly and ferociously. I look over at Doc and I see that he is being summoned to take care of wounded soldiers. He is trying to carry the wounded to the rear for safety by himself. I must help him.

"Eckert, I am going to help Doc. You guys stay here at the wall!"

Eckert nods his head. "Be careful!"

I take off running toward Doc, dodging and jumping behind anything I can find for cover. "Hey, Doc, do you need some help?"

"Heck yeah. I have three wounded that I need to carry back here to the rear!"

"OK, let's go!"

We took off for the battle in front. We grabbed the first wounded soldier and took him to the rear. Doc stopped his bleeding, and we headed for the next man. Again, we headed for the front. I reached down and grabbed the wounded soldier's legs and Doc grabbed his arms. We headed back toward the rear. The rounds were coming in, knocking limbs off of trees and bouncing off the bamboo.

When we were about halfway, Doc stumbled and fell to his knees. I said, "Let's go, Doc! Let's go!"

I dropped the soldier in order to help Doc to his feet. Doc grabbed me and said, "Danny!"

"Doc, what's wrong?"

Doc fell to the ground.

"Danny" was the last word that would ever come from this fine human being. Doc had been shot through the head by an NVA. I carried Doc to the rear and gently placed his lifeless body on the ground.

Seeing my friend lying on the ground made me think of different things. I thought of not being able to meet his family. I thought about eating his mother's okra. *How would his mother take his death?* I had to finish what Doc would have wanted me to do.

I had to bring the other two wounded soldiers to the rear. I must have been in some sort of a daze because I carried the soldiers to the rear by myself with no effort. I placed one soldier over my shoulder and carried him to the rear and gently laid him on the ground. I went to the next soldier and did the same. I carried him to the rear. As I placed the soldier on the ground, I wondered what could be worse than another dead friend. The incoming rounds were now coming in stronger than ever. I needed to get back to my squad.

I heard yelling and a great deal of commotion from the other squad leaders. It appeared that we were being overrun. I could see many more NVA attacking us through the rice paddies. I ran and jumped next to the first squad I saw. I landed next to Deven, a very good squad leader from another platoon. "Are we being overrun, Deven?"

"No, but you wouldn't believe what just happened!"

"What?"

"You know that Kit Carson Scout named Long, don't you?"

"Yes!"

"He thought that we were being overrun by the NVA and the VC. He ran out in the rice paddy holding up a white flag. When he got to the center of the paddy, he turned around and started shooting at us!"

"What?"

"Yeah, he started firing at us. I opened up on full auto and blew him away! Don't you have the other scout in your squad?"

"Yes I do! Man, that is bad!"

"You better keep an eye on him!"

"Yeah, you are right. I think he is OK, but now I am worried!"

I stayed next to Deven, shooting at the enemy in the rice paddy. Once the NVA and the VC started to retreat, I headed toward my squad. As I ran back toward my squad, I now thought about Dong. *Had he done the same as Long? Was he a traitor? Did I misread him? Did I fail to see that he was a VC?* I arrived back at the wall.

My men were on the wall, including Dong. I was relieved to see Dong killing the enemy. Someone was missing, though. It was Emerald. I run to take my place on the wall next to Killer. As I arrive next to Killer, the firefight starts to wind down.

"Killer, how has Dong been doing?"

"He has about three or four kills. Why?"

"Long, the other scout, turned traitor and started shooting at us!"

"For real?"

"Yes, for real. Deven killed him!"

"Sarge, there is something else that you won't like!"

"What is that, Killer?"

"Emerald got it. He is dead. He is right over there!" Killer points to the bushes. "We placed his body at the left end of the wall."

I walked over to Emerald's still, lifeless body and said a prayer for him. I walked back to Killer. "Man, Killer, he was just becoming a real good soldier!"

"Yeah, you should have seen him, Rock! He was shooting right and left and forward. He was a real good shot. He was getting into it. He even bet me a dollar that he could shoot the next guy coming into the rice paddy before me! Now what about Dong? Should we keep an eye on him?"

"Yeah, for now! I am going to tell him and see what he says about Long."

I stroll over to Dong. "How is it going, Dong?"

"I am good, Sergeant Rock!"

"Long turned traitor and started trying to kill us!"

"Him did?"

"Yep, he did!"

"Long I not know. I did not like him. He came from another village. I go now and kill him dead. I will pull his heart out!" Dong starts to walk away quickly.

"No! Dong, wait! He is already dead. Deven killed him!"

"That good. Now I go tear his heart out!"

"No, he is in the middle of the rice paddy!"

"Sergeant Rock thinks Dong is VC too?"

"No I don't. You are a good soldier!"

Craig is coming toward me. "Sarge, the captain is going to blast them with artillery. Then we are going to cross the paddy for a body count. After that, we will have choppers with supplies and to load our dead men! The old man and Watkins want to know what you think."

"Tell them the plan sounds good."

I was getting to a point where I really didn't care what we did next. The artillery started to fall. Relentless explosions were hitting the enemy. Once the firepower stopped, we crossed the paddies and started to get a body count. Our platoon pulled guard while another tallied the enemies' dead bodies.

As we pulled guard, Killer and I talked. "Sergeant Rock, how many of our guys got it?"

"I don't know. Doc would always come over and tell me!"

"What do you mean *would*? Don't you mean *will* tell you?"

"Oh, you don't know?"

"Know what?"

"Doc is dead."

"Man, Sarge, that is real bad! I thought you and Doc would be friends forever. Now you have lost Chuck, Doc, and a lot of other guys that you would have been lifelong friends with!"

"Yep, Chuck and I and Doc would have stayed buddies forever."

"Well, Rock, I guess that you only have me left, so you better keep me alive!"

"Yep. I will be happy to meet your family after we leave this place. But I am worried about you!"

"Worried about what?"

"I think that you may get in an argument at a bar or someplace, and then you will just kill the guy!"

Killer laughs. "No, Sarge. I only kill people that try to kill me. I can fist fight with the best of them!"

"OK, now I am not worried so much, but be careful when you get home!"

"Don't worry, Rock, I promise not to kill more than four or five when I get home!" He laughs, then says, "Here comes Craig."

Craig says, "The lieutenant wants you."

"Thanks, Craig. Tell him I am on the way!"

I arrived at Watkins's CP. "Yes, sir, you wanted me?"

"Yeah, Rock. Craig told me that Emerald ate it and Doc got killed too."

"Yeah, Doc was a good friend, and Emerald was really coming around."

"This war is brutal. Well, I have some good news."

"Can there be any good news after all of this, sir?"

"Yeah, I know what you mean. We are going to Hill 881 or 882 or 883. I don't remember the number. We are going there for a special dinner."

"I think it is 881, but I am not sure either. That is good news! I'll go and tell my men. See ya later, sir!"

I hustled over to where my men were located. "Men, we are going to eat a special dinner at Hill 881."

My squad was ecstatic, delighted, and thrilled. With all of this death surrounding us, we could still get excited over a hot meal.

The word came down that we were moving out in five minutes, but we needed to load the dead and the wounded in the choppers first. It was going to be a hard hump getting to the hill, but it would be worth it. I heard the skids coming.

"Killer, do you want to help me load Emerald and Doc?"

"Of course I do, and so do the rest of the guys!"

"Alright, let's go!"

We gently and respectfully loaded Doc and Emerald into the chopper. As I saw Doc for the last time, I started to choke up.

Killer looks at me. "Are you going to cry, Sarge?"

It was hard to hold back the tears. "No, I guess not, but I am sure tired of seeing death."

"Me too, Sarge. Me too."

We moved out with the sun beating down on us. Within five minutes, we were drenched in sweat. We were moving quickly so we could be at the hill by dark. Hopefully, we could get a good night's sleep before dinner tomorrow.

Killer is walking behind me. "Sergeant Rock, of all things, I never thought that what I would be doing is humping in the hot sun, going over mountains, to have a chance to eat a good meal."

"Man, Killer, that was a long sentence."

Killer laughs. "I hope we have ham and turkey."

"Yeah, me too. I hope we have dressing and hot yeast rolls. Oh, yeah, and gravy."

Eckert says, "Don't forget about candied yams or sweet potatoes."

"Eckert and Killer, you guys are making me hungry. Get out your machetes. We are going to run into some jungle crap."

The bush is getting thicker now. The big wet leaves are dropping leeches on us. The ground is very wet. I look down at my boots and see about twenty small leeches crawling up my pant leg. I reach up for the insect repellent that is attached to the outside of my helmet cover. I spray my boots and legs with the repellent, and the leeches drop off. "Men, look out for the leeches!"

Each man is going for his repellent. Some men had leeches already on their skin. These were harder to remove because if we pulled too hard, the head would be left behind.

Killer was pulling a leech from his head. "Sarge, would you squirt some repellent on my head?"

I grabbed his repellent and hit the leech with a large squirt. "It is coming off."

"Sarge, I hate, hate, hate this place. Why would anyone want to live here?"

"Yes, I wonder that myself, but don't say that to Dong. He says Vietnam is number one. I don't know why North Vietnam wants to take over South Vietnam. I just don't understand it!"

"Me neither!"

It was getting close to dark when we reached the hill. We humped up the steep incline until we reached the top. We walked through the perimeter and past the men pulling guard.

Craig brings me the radio. "The lieutenant says to spread out and find a place to sleep tonight, and no guard duty for us. Do you want to speak to him?"

"Yes." I grab the horn. "Affirmatron, I have the message, go!"

"That is all, out!" The lieutenant hung up the receiver.

"OK, men, find a place to relax for the night!"

My squad found a place near the wall of a mortar squad. We pulled out our C-rations and ate our dinner (or *supper*, if you are from the south).

The squad was talking about how much they were going to enjoy the special dinner tomorrow.

Killer stands up. "I am going to ask these guys in the mortar squad what will be served for the dinner."

We laugh. Killer walks over to the mortar guy and starts speaking to him. Our eyes are all on him as he returns. "So what did they say, Killer?"

"Man, Sarge, we are going to have everything — mashed potatoes, gravy, yams, turkey, stuffing, ham, salads, yeast rolls, green beans, iced tea, and a lot more!"

Raymond says, "I am not going to eat breakfast tomorrow. I'll wait for dinner!"

All of my men said, "Me too!"

We slept as well as could be expected with the rain coming and going during the night. I woke up my men. "Killer, Eckert, Craig, wake up!"

Killer grumbles, "OK, Sarge, I am awake."

"Eckert, go and be sure Raymond and Dong are up, please."

Killer stands and stretches. "Do you smell that, Sarge?"

"Yeah, it smells like turkey in the oven. It is making me hungry. I am going to eat some Cs."

"Eat some C-rations, you say? I am not eating a thing until the dinner. Actually, it will be served at noon, so it will be lunch time."

"Yeah, I get headaches if I go too long without eating. Oh, yeah, men, let's pretend it is Christmas! Merry Christmas, men!"

Each of the men said, "Merry Christmas to you too, Sarge!"

Raymond and Dong arrived. "Morning, Sarge."

"Merry Christmas, Dong and Raymond! Merry Christmas!"

"What?"

"Since we are getting a special meal, we are pretending it is Christmas."

"Same to you, Sarge!"

"OK, men, in the Christmas spirit, we are going to give each other gifts!"

Killer looks surprised. "Yeah, right. What can we give? Grenades, bullets, a sweaty towel?"

Eckert inquires, "Yeah, what?"

I grab my rucksack and reach inside. "C-rations! Each of us will give our best Cs to one another. Give one can each to each man, and do it in the Christmas spirit. We will open gifts in ten minutes!"

I walked up to the CP area and grabbed a whole box of fresh C-rations. I placed them on my shoulder and walked back to the squad.

I started sorting out the C-rations. I picked out the ones that I liked the best to give away. I selected pound cakes, peaches, and hot chocolate mix. I selected lima beans and ham for Dong. I did not really like lima beans and ham very much, but Dong loved them.

I gave Killer and Eckert my two pound cakes. I gave my peaches to Raymond and Craig. I gave my hot chocolate mix and, of course, my lima beans and ham to Dong.

The men started giving me my gifts. Eckert gave me a can of ham. Raymond gave me pound cake. Craig gave me his Oreo cookies and hot chocolate mix. "Here, Sarge. This is so you can make your pudding."

"Thank you, Craig."

Dong handed me pound cake. "Merry Quishmas, Sergeant Rock!"

"Thank you, Dong, and it is *Christmas*, not *Quishmas*."

"Christmas, huh?"

"Yes, Christmas!"

Killer stands up proudly and hands me a can of lima beans and ham. "I picked out the best gift from my rucksack that I could find for you, Sarge!"

I stare at the can in amazement.

Eckert says, "Killer, you know Sarge hates lima beans and ham!"

Killer starts laughing and hands me his pound cake, Oreo cookies, and hot chocolate mix. "I was just joking, Sarge!"

"Well, thank you, Killer. This means a lot to me."

This unselfish act that Killer had just done made me feel even more proud of him. Killer loved to make the pudding that I had taught him to make, and now he was giving it to me.

"You are welcome, Sergeant Rock. Hey, Sarge, what would you have given Sergeant Lewis if he were here?"

"Peaches and pound cake. Chuck loved peaches and pound cake."

"I miss Sergeant Lewis."

I got choked up. "Me too, Killer. Me too."

We look up and see the lieutenant coming. He has a disturbing look on his face. As he gets closer to us, we immediately stop talking and stand up.

Watkins looks at us. "Men, I have some bad news! The old man needs to find a platoon to pull an LP today!"

I can feel my temperature rising. "So we were chosen, huh? Sir, you had better get that straight right now! We aren't going! Our platoon gets all of the crap!"

"Please calm down, Sergeant Rodgers!"

The lieutenant had called me Rodgers instead of Rock. He was getting formal, so I decided to start calming down before I got into trouble.

"OK, sir, I am calm. How did you let this happen?"

"Here is exactly how it happened. The captain called me to his CP and told me that one platoon would have to go on a listening post. He asked me if I wanted our platoon to go and I said 'No! N-O. No!' Then he gathered all of us platoon leaders together. He placed our platoon numbers in a hat and drew out a number. Unluckily, it was our platoon."

"Do we get to eat dinner first?"

"No, you have to go now."

Killer yells, "This is bull crap, sir! This is a bunch of bull crap!"

"I agree with you, Killer. It is crap. I don't know how we manage to get all the crap details."

I pull out my map. "Where are we supposed to go, sir? And how long do we stay there?"

He pointed at a place on my map. "You take your squad here. I'll show Brooks and the others where to go. You are to stay out until tomorrow afternoon."

"OK, men, get your crap together! Sir, save us some food!"

"I'll try."

We put our rucksacks and ammo on our tired, worn-out bodies and headed down the hill. Each man was grumbling as they walked. On the way to our location, we saw Delta Company coming up the hill. This infuriated us even more. Delta Company would eat our special dinner. After an hour and a half, we arrived at our listening post. The rain started to pour from the sky.

"We are here, men. Talk quietly. Keep the noise down. Try to stay dry, guys."

Trying to stay dry in this hard rain was impossible.

Killer pulled out a piece of acetate and covered his head. The rest of us took out our ponchos and put them on our already-wet bodies. The men that had not eaten yet started to open their C-rations.

We would open the cans with our P-38s and place the opened cans under our ponchos. We would pull the ponchos up and above our heads, making a tent. Now we could eat under the ponchos, avoiding the rain.

The rain and dirt were now mixing together to make thick mud. Our butts were getting wet and muddy. After an hour of this rain, we were in six inches of mud. We took off our helmets and used them for seats. We were supposed to be on an LP, but with all of the noise the rain was making, we could not hear a thing.

"Men, keep a good watch because we can't hear anything!"

I was disgusted with my company, the higher ups, and the whole entire Army.

Raymond shakes his head. "Sarge, do you think there will be any dinner left for us?"

"No I don't. Delta Company will eat our dinner."

"Man, Rock, I am getting wet. I am miserable."

"Yep, all of us are miserable. We will go back to the hill in the morning."

We took turns at guard while the rest of us dozed. The day finally turned to night. The rain continued into the night. I was awake when Killer took his turn at guard. "Sarge, do you think we will see anything?"

"No. I think Charlie is too smart to be out in this terrible weather. Sometimes I think Charlie fights when he gets good and ready."

"Me too."

During the night, we were getting sit-rep calls about every half hour. Finally, the sun started to rise. The rain stopped, and it was time for us to head back up to the hill.

"Men, get ready. We will move out in five. Hand me the horn, Craig!"

Craig handed me the microphone. "Cherokee Three, this is Blackhawk Three, over!"

The lieutenant answered, "This is Cherokee Three, go!"

"We are heading back up the hill, go!"

"No, I have more bad news. Your squad is to pull another LP at a new location!"

Again, I was getting angry. I paused and said nothing.

"Blackhawk Three, are you there?"

I still didn't answer. "Craig, talk to him and find out where the idiots want us to go!"

Craig starts talking on the horn to Watkins. When he is finished, he says, "Watkins says he is real sorry! He told me where we are to go and pull the LP!"

"Yeah? How far is it?"

"A lot of klicks."

"More than five miles?"

"No, but it is more than six klicks."

"OK, men, gather around! I am again tired of all of this crap the company gives us. Do you guys remember the hooch with the chickens and pigs around it that we passed on the way up to the hill?"

The men said, "Yeah!"

"Well, that is where we are going to pull our LP!"

Eckert stands up. "That would be cool, Sarge!"

"OK, men, I hope you all had a Merry Christmas. Now let's get it!"

Killer puts his rucksack on his back. "Maybe our pretend New Year's will be better!"

CHAPTER 28

Eckert Has Two Weeks Left

We travel an hour or so and arrive at the small hooch with the chickens and pigs. I motion for the men to gather around me. "Men, we may not have a good meal, but at least we can get in the hooch and be dry!"

Eckert laughs. "Hey, Killer, do you remember the last time we stayed in a hooch?"

"Yes I do! That is when I cut the VC's head off! Hey, Sarge, get Dong to talk to them to find out if they are VC affiliated!"

Eckert laughs. "Affiliated, huh, Killer? That's a word I have never heard you use!"

"Well, Eckert, I am quite educated, you know!"

All of us start to laugh.

"OK!" I turn to Dong. "Find out about these people. Are they VC?"

"I find out, Sergeant Rock!"

Dong starts to ask questions. After five minutes, he comes back to where the rest of us are standing. "They not VC! They hate VC!"

"So you think we will be safe, Dong?"

"Yes, we be safe! These people will fix us good dinner. I told them about us missing our good dinner on the hill."

Raymond looks at Dong. "What will they cook? Monkey?"

"Monkey? No, they cook chicken!"

"Chicken! That sounds great, huh, Sarge?"

"Yes, that sounds great!"

The Papasan started to chase a chicken, but the chicken wouldn't cooperate. Killer aims his rifle. "I'll get him!"

Papasan says, "No shoot! I get!"

I look at Papasan and start to laugh. Papasan is chasing the chicken with a large knife like a machete. Dong is starting to help chase the chicken.

"Dong, should we help chase the chicken?"

"Yes, we help!"

"OK, men, start chasing the chicken toward Papasan."

We started chasing the chicken when two more chickens started to run. We were running and tripping, trying to catch these birds. Every time we got our hands on a bird, it took off. We were laughing so hard that we forgot about all of the sorrel we had had in the past few months.

Finally, we chased the chickens into a pen that the Papasan had built. While Papasan and Mamasan made dinner, we sat and laughed about chasing the birds. A little laughter went a long way in building our spirits. We started to smell something.

Killer stands. "Do you guys smell that?"

I stand. "It smells like barbecued chicken, just like home!"

Raymond says, "Yes it does!"

Eckert sniffs. "Just think, I will be home in two weeks and one day. I am going to eat all kinds of great food! You had better keep me alive, Sarge!"

"Eckert, I will do my best. Let me see your helmet!"

Eckert handed me his helmet. The helmet cover had numbers written on it from thirty to one with the word DEROS after the one. The numbers from thirty to fifteen had been crossed out. Many soldiers would keep up with their scheduled departure from Vietnam this way.

I looked at his helmet. "Two weeks to go, huh, Eckert?"

"Yep, only fourteen more days. Hey, Sarge, I forgot again. What does DEROS stand for? I know it means we are leaving, but I forget."

"It is an acronym."

"An acronym? What is an acronym, Sarge?"

"An acronym is a word formed from the first initial of other words or syllables. For instance, 'RADAR' is an acronym of 'radio detection and ranging.'"

"OK, so what is DEROS?"

"DEROS stands for 'date of expected return from overseas.'"

"Man, Rock, I can never remember that."

"Don't worry about it, because half of the time I can't remember what it means either. Hey, men, that chicken smells good, huh?"

"The old man said it would be ready in a half hour."

After a half hour, the Mamasan and Papasan started bringing out the food. They brought out some sort of white, wafer-looking things shaped like potato chips, but thicker. They also gave us plenty of rice and, of course, the main dish, chicken. Everything tasted great. The chicken was a little tougher than the chicken at home, but it was still very tasty. My men ate and ate until they were stuffed.

After the meal, we all shook hands with the man and hugged the woman. We gave them both some of our extra C-rations. Dong also handed C-rations to our hosts. He spoke to the very nice people for five minutes before returning to speak to me.

"Sergeant Rock, Papasan say it is OK for us to stay here all night!"

"Cool, and your English is getting very good, Dong."

"Tank you!"

I started to correct his language but decided not to at this time. Dong had come a long way since he was given to me. "Here comes your X-ray, Sarge."

I turn around and see Craig. "The lieutenant wants to meet up with us tomorrow at 1000 hours. He will have the rest of the platoon with him by then."

"Tell him affirmative."

I now had a small problem. We were not where we were supposed to be. Therefore, we would have to move out early in the morning. I gathered the men. "Men, we will meet up with Watkins and the rest of the platoon in the morning, so we will leave here early, at sunrise. Eckert, assign guard duty!"

"Yes, Sarge!"

Eckert started assigning guard. "Do you want last guard, Sarge?"

"Yep, fine."

The night came and so did the rain. Papasan had built a good hooch. We stayed dry all night. We also did not encounter any enemy fire. At four in the morning, Killer woke me up by placing his hand on my shoulder, and this startled me. "Sarge, it is your turn."

"OK, thanks. Anything happening?"

"Nope, all is quiet."

I pulled my guard and ate my C-ration breakfast while on duty. After my guard duty was complete, I woke up the men. "Guys, eat and let's go. We have to be there before the lieutenant."

We humped through the boonies for two and a half hours before making it to our correct destination. "OK, men, spread out and don't shoot our guys. They will be here in about two hours."

After an hour, Craig hands me the horn. "Watkins wants you, Sarge."

"Thanks, X-ray Craig!"

"You are welcome, Sergeant Rock!"

We both laugh.

I get on the horn. "This is Blackhawk Three, go!"

"We will be coming in within ten minutes. Don't shoot us!"

"Affirmatron. We will not engage you, over!"

"Cherokee Three, out!"

I turned toward the men. "OK, men, they are coming in!"

The lieutenant was the first to come up to me. He was pulling point. He stuck out his hand. "Hey, Rock, are you still mad at me?"

"No, sir. I was really mad at everybody above your rank!"

"Yeah, I know!"

"So what now, sir?"

He pulls out his map and shows me our new destination. "Do you guys want point?"

"Yes, sir. We will take it. Sir, I noticed that you were pulling point when you got here. What did Shake and Bake think about it?"

"He couldn't believe it. Brooks kept asking me 'Why?'"

I turned to my men. "Let's move out. Killer, you have point!"

"Great, cool, fantastic. That will be copasetic!"

Eckert laughs. "What the heck does copasetic mean, Killer?"

"I am not sure, but it means in agreement, and I will kill more Charlies than you!"

"Yeah, right. I will be right behind you, so don't miss!"

"OK, move out, men!"

Watkins starts to laugh. "Your squad is something else, Rock! I am going to the end of our line to check on the other squads! I'll be back in a little bit!"

We traveled in and out of the bush. When I felt it was safe, we would travel on paths around and over hills and steep inclines. After two hours, Killer had the platoon stop.

Killer came back to my position. "Sarge, there is a wooden gate blocking our path! I didn't touch it because what is a gate doing on a small path like this?"

"Yeah, it doesn't make sense. It could be setting us up for an ambush!"

"So what do you want to do?"

"I want our squad to drop back and go up the mountain on the left. Then we will fire a grenade and shoot the gate to be certain no booby traps are on the gate!"

"OK, sounds good! Man, Sarge, this could be bad. We can't go over the mountain on either side because it is too steep!"

"Yeah, and we can't go through the gorge because it is too steep. Watch everything, because this is the perfect place for an ambush! The only way for us to go is past that barricade, the wooden gate!"

Craig says, "Watkins wants to know what you are going to do! I already told him what was going on and why we halted!"

"Tell him we are going to shoot a 79 at it."

Craig gets on the horn. "We are going to shoot a grenade at it, go… Sarge, the lieutenant says 'Do it!'"

I look around for the 79. "Eckert, shoot a round at the gate!"

"Here goes!"

Eckert fires a round that hits just to the right and slightly above of the barricade. We did not hear a secondary explosion, which would indicate a booby trap.

"Eckert, fire another round!"

"OK." He fires another round that hits the bottom of the gate, but the gate did not fall and, again, we did not hear a secondary explosion.

Eckert stands up. "Alright, Sarge, let's go. I don't want to be sitting here and get ambushed. I only have two weeks left in Vietnam, and I don't want to be killed now! Can I take point and knock down the gate? Or maybe I can just open it!"

"Yeah, go ahead, and take Killer with you. We will stay here until it is cleared."

Eckert and Killer carefully hiked down the steep cliff to the path around the mountain. We could see them clearly as they climbed the path and headed for the gated barricade structure.

Eckert was the first to arrive at the gate. Killer was fifty meters behind, pulling guard. I watched as Eckert looked under and over the gate. He methodically looked at each end of the gate for trip wires. He looked at me and gave me two thumbs up.

Eckert reached over the gate and started to pull a handle to release the barricade. The gate exploded in his face with such a force that it blew his helmet deep into the rocky gorge. Eckert's body lifted off the ground with such a force that he landed ten feet away from the gate.

"Oh, man, Craig, not another death! Move out, men! Craig, tell Watkins what is going on! Let's get it!"

We hustled down the cliffs and up the mountain to the path. When I arrived, I saw Killer holding Eckert's head up. "Killer, is he dead?"

"Not yet, Sarge!"

I leaned down over Eckert. His face was bleeding from the shrapnel. "Eckert, can you hear me?"

To my astonishment, he could speak. "I can hear you, Sarge, but I can't see! Sergeant Rock, I am blinded! I am blind! I only have fourteen days left, and I can't see!"

I took his shredded towel and started to wipe the blood from in front of his eyes. "Is that better?"

"No, Sarge, I can't see!"

I looked closer at his eyes and could see metal shavings in and around his eyes. "Eckert, we will have to airlift you out, but there is no LZ. We are going to have to hump for a while. Craig, give me the horn! Can you walk?"

"I think so!"

I got on the radio. "We have a wounded man! We need a dust-off!"

The reply came back, "Give me the name!"

I started to give the name phonetically. "Echo, Charlie, Kilo, Eckert… Oh, heck! His name is Eckert!" In my haste, I did not use the phonetic alphabet correctly. Instead of saying "echo" for the second *e*, I said Eckert.

Watkins replied, "I got it, but we have no landing zone. Can he walk or be carried?"

I looked at Eckert and he nodded his head yes. "Yes, he can walk. I'll find an LZ on the map and head out!"

"Roger, out!"

"Men, let's get it! We have a ways to go before the LZ!"

As we made our way toward the LZ, I started to think about how much I liked Lieutenant Watkins. He has been the best platoon leader we have ever had. He did not ask a lot of stupid questions. When he gave me an order, he had already thought it out before directing me. When he gave me an order, it was more like a request. He would always sit down and talk to me at night concerning anything of importance that we would be doing the following day.

I never acted like I had all the answers, for I did not have all the answers. We would put our heads together in thought, and if he really wanted to do something a certain way, I agreed. Sometimes, if it wasn't too dangerous, I would let the lieutenant have his way, knowing that he would come to me later and say that he was wrong. This is the only way an officer can learn. If I had shot down every idea that he had, he would think that I wanted to be the platoon leader. Watkins and I had a great relationship, and I was not going to ruin it by acting superior.

Craig says, "Watkins is coming up to travel with you."

"OK, thanks, Craig."

Lieutenant Watkins came up to me quickly. "Hey, Rock, how bad is Eckert?"

"I think he is blind. We need to get him a lift-out quick."

"Right. Have you found an LZ yet?"

"Yes, sir, but we need to get moving."

"I am going to hang around with you for a while."

"OK, sounds good. We have not talked in a long time. Eckert, you hang on to Raymond. Killer, you take point. Keep your eyes open, but move fast. We have got to get Eckert out of here."

We started to move toward the gate that had just exploded. "Killer, be careful going through the gate!"

"I will, Sarge, thanks."

Killer stopped at the gate and placed the butt of his M-16 rifle on the ground. He carefully dragged the rifle on the ground from side to side, looking for more trip wires. He placed the rifle barrel over the top of what used to be a gate and moved it very slowly from side to side. He also did the same on each side of the area where a few pieces of wood were still standing.

Killer turns around. "All clear, Sarge. All clear!"

Watkins taps me on the shoulder. "Did you teach him that?"

"Yes, sir, I did. I have taught all of my guys how to look for trip wires. But actually, White had a big part of it. He was very smart about locating trip wires and explosives."

Eckert is listening to us talk. "I bet if White would have been checking the gate, it would not have blown up. White was great about that kind of crap."

"I don't know; it was just a freaky deal."

"What did I miss, Sarge?"

"I think that a trip wire was inside the bamboo, and when you lifted the latch, it pulled the pin on the grenade! How much are you hurting, Eckert? Can you see anything?"

"I can only see a little light from my right eye, and yes, my face hurts."

Raymond is listening to our conversation. "Eckert, your face has always hurt me!"

We laugh.

Eckert groans, "Don't make me laugh, Raymond. It hurts!"

We started to move again. The lieutenant and I talked about many things as we walked.

"You know something, sir?"

"What, Rock?"

"I think you and I make a good team!"

"You don't know how much that means to me. The other day, Lieutenant Daniels asked me how I knew so much in so short of a time."

"What did you tell him?"

"I simply said 'Rock and Lewis.'"

"Thanks, sir, but the real reason why you are so smart about this jungle fighting is that you listen! I just wish that Chuck could be here to see how you turned out."

"Yeah, me too, Rock. Rock, I didn't even look at the map. How far before we will be at the LZ?"

I laughed. "You didn't look at the map? And I was bragging on you so much!"

We chuckled.

"I know what you are saying, but I have you. We are safe with you leading us."

Again, we laugh.

"We will be at the LZ in two hours. When we are close, I'll let you know so you can call in the dust-off. How long have you been married, sir?"

"A year and two months and two days!"

I laugh. "You mean a year and two months and two days and six hours and twenty-seven minutes and thirteen seconds!"

We laugh.

"No, I don't have the marriage pinned down that good, but you are close!"

"I want to meet your wife some day. Is she good looking?"

"Man, yeah! I saw the picture of your wife in that bikini and she is good looking too. I bet you miss her. I hear that she likes wrecking your car."

"Yep, you should see it. It looks like an accordion."

"I knew it. I knew it!"

"What?"

"You went home on your R&R, didn't you, Danny?"

Again I laugh. "Yes, sir."

"Well, good for you. You must have steel balls to take that chance."

"I don't know about that, but I wanted to see my 409 bad."

We continued to travel until we reached an area close to the LZ.

"OK, sir, you can call for the dust-off now."

The lieutenant got on the horn and started giving coordinates. He paused. "Hey, Rock, give us the coordinates!"

I laughed and gave the grid to the lieutenant.

Watkins noticed my laugh and he smirked. "You smart-butt. You are right. I should know where we are at all times, even if I do have you close by!"

The chopper came in, and we gently loaded Eckert. "See you later, I hope, Eckert!"

"Are you making fun about the seeing part of your goodbye?"

"Oh, no, Eckert. I am sorry."

"I am only kidding, Sarge."

"You smart-butt, get out of here!"

The chopper took off, carrying a very good man to the hospital.

Watkins came up to me. "Do you think he will be able to see again, Danny?"

"Man, I don't know. He looked pretty bad, didn't he?"

"Yes, he did! OK, Rock, here is where we are to go next." He pointed to a spot on his map. I took out my map and a grease marker and marked the spot.

"OK, men, let's get it! You take point, Killer!"

We humped for two hours before we started being shot at. Killer started firing on full auto. I ran up to Killer and hit the ground. "What do you have, Killer?"

"There are two bunkers on the right with four to six gooks in 'em!"

"We have been through this scenario before, haven't we?"

"You are using big words again, Sarge! But you are right! The last time we charged bunkers, you got shot!"

"You know, that is what I like about you, Killer! Even in a dangerous situation, you find something to laugh about! But we better take care of business and kill some gooks! Raymond, you get the Pig up here! Killer, keep them pinned down. I am going to tell Watkins what is going on!"

I hustled to Watkins. "Sir, we have four to six gooks in bunkers!"

"How many bunkers?"

"Two!"

"Sounds like we have been here before, huh, Rock?"

"Yep, very similar!"

"What do you want to do, Rock?"

"You send a squad up the hill to the right of the gooks. We will start firing, and you send another squad up and to the left of the gooks!"

"OK, but I am going to stay with you just like we did before! Are we going to charge them?"

"Yeah, but only once the squad on the right starts drawing their fire!"

"OK, give me a minute to tell the others what to do!"

Watkins moves out quickly. "I'll be up at the front helping Raymond and Killer!" I turn to Dong and Craig. "Let's get up there and help!"

We started to move toward the front when the Shake and Bake ran up to me. "Rock, what do you want my squad to do?"

"When we stand up and attack the bunkers, you guys take off down the path and move up to the left of the bunkers!"

"OK!"

"I'll wait for the squad on the right to start shooting. Then we will move in and attack!"

I waited for the squad on the right to open up. As soon as they started shooting at the enemy in the bunkers, we stood and attacked. With a fury of bullets, and with the Pig on full auto, we moved forward. I looked to my right, and the lieutenant was right next to me. I looked behind me to be certain that Shake and Bake's squad was doing their job. They were moving down the path and turning to be on the left of the bunkers. This was going to be the perfect attack.

Shake and Bake's squad started firing from the left at the enemy. My squad and Watkins moved forward. Watkins was firing his rifle on full auto. He looked up at me and grinned. He loved to be in combat.

His love for combat turned to hate when he got shot in the ribs. I ran over to him quickly. He was on the ground, trying to get up. He says, "I got it in the side and the shoulder."

"You stay down. I'll be back!"

We moved closer to the bunkers. Now we could throw grenades in the bunker openings. After five more minutes, the battle was over. As usual, I turned to Killer for clean up. "Killer, you make sure we have no more incoming from the bunkers!"

"I am on it, Sarge!"

Killer ran to each bunker and threw another grenade in them. I watched carefully as Killer looked inside. "All is clear, Sarge!"

"Way to go, Killer!"

I ran back over to Watkins. "Oh, man, sir, how bad is it?"

"It is pretty bad. I don't think even Doc could patch this one up!"

"Move your hands away from your side. Let me see!"

"What does it look like to you?"

"I can't tell if the bullet went through or not! I'll call in for a dust-off!"

"Man, Danny, I don't want to leave you guys. I really don't!"

"I don't want you to leave either, but I don't want you to die out here!"

"OK, Sergeant Danny Eugene Rodgers. I am so sorry I could not finish the year with you!"

"It is OK, sir. We did a lot of good stuff together, didn't we?"

"We sure did!"

I radioed for the chopper, and within thirty minutes we had the lieutenant picked up and heading to a hospital.

Killer walks up next to me. "It looks like the body count is five. They were too messed up to tell for certain. How was Watkins?"

"He was bad. I think the bullet is still in his stomach or side."

"Are you going to take over as platoon leader?"

"I don't know. I better go and see Hammond!"

Hammond generally stayed low-profile. The lieutenant never spoke about him to me. Or should I say very often? I never received a command from him. I arrived to see Hammond on the radio.

"Sergeant Rock, how are you doing?"

"Good, Sarge! You know that is a lie. I feel real bad for the lieutenant!"

"Me too. So what do we do now? You know I am supposed to take over as platoon leader. But I know, without a doubt, that the lieutenant would want you to take over. So I won't get in your way. You should take over!"

"I have a better idea! You become platoon leader, and I will help you in every way that I can. I think the lieutenant would want us to work together, don't you?"

"Yeah, I guess you are right, but you won't hold a grudge if I do take the position?"

"Only if you get us killed!"

We both laughed.

"Rock, did you ever wonder why I never gave you orders?"

"Yeah, I have wondered about that! Why?"

"Because the lieutenant always wanted to talk to you directly. He said that you and Lewis had saved his life many times."

I had a puzzled look on my face. "Really?"

"Yes, he liked you two like brothers."

"That's cool. I liked him too."

"Well, Rock, what is our next move?"

"Pull your map out, and we will be sure we are on the same page, so to speak! You and I should get together and go over our maps every day before we start humping. Remember this: always, always –"

Hammond didn't let me finish.

"I know. Watkins told me that you told him to 'Always, always know where we are on the map at all times.'"

"I think we are off to a good start, Sergeant Hammond."

"Me too, Rock. I will try to be a good platoon leader. I have heard that this Tet Offensive thing is even getting worse."

"Yep, I think that we are in for a big battle soon."

CHAPTER 29

The Big Battle

Our platoon heads out and meets up with the rest of the company. Sergeant Hammond, our new platoon leader, calls me on the radio. "Annihilator Three-Three requests a debriefing from both of us!"

"I'll meet you at your CP!"

"Affirmative, I'll wait on you."

I hurry to Sergeant Hammond's CP. "Are you ready to see the old man, Sarge?"

"Not really. I don't speak to him much."

"Well, get used to it now that you are a platoon leader. Let's go."

We walked to the captain's CP. "Hi, sir."

"What's happening, Rock and Sergeant Hammond?"

I answered his question. "Killing, being killed, long days, no fresh water, leeches, stinky clothes. Should I go on?"

"I get the point, Rock. What about you, Hammond?"

"Ditto, sir."

"Yep, I know it is very tough over here. Wouldn't you like to have Jane Fonda over here for a week?"

"I sure would!" I said.

"Sergeant Hammond, how do you feel about commanding the platoon?"

"If Rock will help me, I think I can do it."

"What do you think about it, Rock?"

"Hammond will be just fine."

"Alright, now tell me how Eckert and Watkins got it!"

We explained to the captain how the two good men almost bought the farm.

"Rock, do you realize that you only have about thirty days until you DEROS?"

"Yes, sir, I do."

Hammond says, "What? I don't know if I can learn everything in thirty days!"

"Rock will teach you. Just listen."

"I will, sir, I will."

"OK, men, this Tet Offensive crap is bad. We have the NVA on the ropes. If the bureaucrats back home would quit playing politics, we could wipe these guys out. Needless to say, we have a lot of battles coming up."

"Yes, sir, we'll be ready."

"I wish we could put Jane Fonda inside the barrel of a 105 and shoot her straight across the DMZ to the enemy."

I laugh. "You know, she would probably fit. She is real cute."

"Yep, but she is too old for you. Guys, keep up the good work. We will be short-handed for a while. See you two later."

"Later, sir."

I watched Hammond very closely for the next two weeks. I only had to correct him on a few items of command. One item was his map orientation to our surroundings. The other item was determining when we had snipers or when it was going to be a battle. After another week of us being sniped at, he was well-versed in sniper fighting.

I was now feeling comfortable enough that he could take over when I left for home. I started to train Killer to take my place. Killer and I would have long talks about squad leading.

"Killer, I am going to request that you get a sergeant's rank before I leave. I want you to take over my squad leader position."

"I will take over your position, but no one can take your place. Why don't you take that officer's position that Top offered you? You would only have to stay for three more months."

"First of all, I am not sure if I could really get the officer's position. Another thing is, I have been here almost a full year, and I am ready to go home!"

"Being with you, Rock, and Sergeant Lewis was great. It was like you two were our fathers and all of us were your little kids. You two protected us and you taught all of us how to protect ourselves."

"Well, thanks for the pep talk, but I am still going home in two weeks."

Craig says, "I wish you would stay too. The old man says to bivouac here for the night."

"Thank you, Sir Craig!"

"Welcome, Master Rock!"

We both laugh.

"OK, men, dig in!"

Killer is the first to start digging. "Man, Sarge, it was sure a lot easier digging when we had a lot of men in the squad!"

"Yes, and it will be harder on us pulling guard. We have less people. Killer, set up guard!"

"OK, let's see: one, two, three, four, and a half," he said as he looked at Dong.

"I not a half, Killer!"

"I am only joking you. Man, you were great behind the wall. You killed a lot of 'em!"

The rain started to fall, and the night began. We had no contact with the enemy, but we could hear firefights in the distance.

I didn't get much sleep, for I was thinking about how these men would get along without me. I also thought about home. I thought about how it would be to become a lieutenant. Maybe I could push Top and the captain a little and become a captain myself. The still night became morning. I walked over to my men and woke them up. "Let's go guys! Eat your wonderful breakfast and we will move out!"

We moved out, and within thirty minutes we were engaged in a small battle. We had the VC pinned down in a small village.

"OK, men, we are going to attack, but if one gook fires a shot at me, I will shoot you myself. I only have thirteen days left!"

The men laugh and start shooting. Everything went textbook. We had a perfect assault. After the body count (seven) was made, we moved on. Within fifteen minutes, we were engaged again.

For the next twelve days, this scenario kept happening. It was like we were being set up and drawn into something bigger, but I didn't know what!

On the thirteenth day, the day I was supposed to go home, the crap hit the fan again! Mortars, rockets, grenades, and rifle rounds were flying. This was going to be a big one.

Trees and bamboo started to fall and fly through the air. The captain radioed me. "What do you see?"

"Nothing. We are getting hit hard. We will move closer!"

"Move out, men! We need to locate the gooks!"

We moved in closer to the enemy. I called the captain. "Annihilator Three-Three, we need fire support!"

"Call it in! You know what to do!"

I started to call in the artillery. Round after round, I called in, but the enemy was doing the same. We were firing our weapons, and the enemy was doing likewise. We were running low on ammo. I called the captain on the radio. "We need ammo and right now!"

I knew that I should not have said that over the airway, but I could see that soon we would be in a bind.

"I am ahead of you! The choppers are on the way!"

We moved a little more forward, and we could see a bunker in front of us. There were many more bunkers that I could see on my right and left. We were shooting round after round.

Raymond runs up to me. "Sarge, I am running low on ammo!"

Killer runs up to me. "Sarge, me and Dong will go get us some ammo, OK?"

"OK, sounds good, Killer. Thanks, Dong!"

I hear a couple of choppers coming in, with the door gunners blasting away. As the two men ran away toward the chopper, I couldn't help but think how lucky I have been to have a brave man like Killer on my side. I was very proud of Dong also, for he was truly on our side. He was not a VC.

Craig says, "The old man wants you!"

I lift up the horn. "This is Blackhawk Three, over!"

"Blackhawk, a chopper will be here to pick you up in fifteen!"

"I'll be ready!"

What a time for me to be leaving! I thought. We are in a large firefight, and we are running low on ammo.

Killer and Dong arrive with the ammo for the Pig and for our rifles. "Sarge, here you go!"

He hands me the bandoliers of M-16 ammo. "Sarge, we have got to knock out that bunker!"

"I agree! Let's do it! Men, concentrate on the bunker right in front of us!"

We attacked by running and diving, each of us covering one another like a well-oiled machine. These men of mine were great! We got close enough to the enemy in the bunker to throw grenades, but no matter how hard we tried, we couldn't hit the opening in the bunker. We needed to be a little closer.

Killer rolled over and over until he was beside me. "Sarge, I am going to crawl closer so I can throw a grenade into the hole!"

"I don't know about that, because you will be in the open for too long!"

"That is the only way we can get 'em!"

"No, just wait! I'll figure out something!"

"See ya, Sergeant Rock!" Killer took off for the bunker.

I yelled, "Give him cover! Give him cover!"

We started to open up directly on the bunker, firing everything we had through the bunker opening. We had to keep the enemy pinned down while Killer was making his move!

Killer finally reached the bunker and threw a grenade directly into the opening. He jumped to the ground, covering his head with his arms and hands.

Within a split second, the grenade came flying out of the hole! It came right back out of the opening and landed adjacent to Killer, lying on the ground. The grenade exploded next to him.

The enemy had thrown Killer's grenade back at him. I could tell immediately that Killer was dead. These dirty, no-good NVA had killed one of the bravest men I had ever known. We had to get to the bunker before we were all killed.

It took us another five minutes to kill the three or four NVA in the bunker. Once we made sure they were dead, I ran over to Killer's body.

I turned him over to be sure that he was actually dead. Killer was dead for sure. His own grenade tore up his body! The last lit ember in my body was out. I had nothing left but gray and ashes. The firefight had slowed, but we were still fighting.

Craig ran up to me. "The captain says your chopper is coming in right now!"

The chopper came in, but it was receiving too much fire. It came in quickly and lifted right back off. Craig runs back up to me again. "Sarge, the chopper is coming back in one minute. You better get on it fast!"

"OK, Craig. You tell the men goodbye!"

"You tell them! They are right here!"

Raymond, Dong, and Craig all gave me a hug goodbye. They had tears in their eyes, as did I!

"Sarge, here it comes again!"

"See you guys. I am gone!"

I took off running toward the chopper, but I was pinned down by enemy fire. The chopper waited for thirty seconds and took off. My men started firing, giving me cover support.

Craig came running up to me. "Sarge, the officer in the chopper says if you don't get on this time, you won't get out of here for a week!"

"OK. See ya, Craig!"

The chopper started to come in again. I took off for the slick, but the rounds were coming in fast and furious, and, again, I had to stop! The chopper was now hovering.

The rounds were still flying, but I had to get on the chopper. It was now or never. I ran and jumped and hit the ground. I rolled on the ground trying to dodge what I couldn't even see. All I had to do now was get past a break in the large, four-foot-tall berm, and I would be to the chopper.

I took off running again, but the chopper started to lift before I got to it. The officer in the chopper looked directly in my eyes. He saw how close I was and he motioned for the chopper pilot to go back down.

The skid came closer to the ground, and I ran hard and jumped inside. My legs were still hanging out of the chopper as we took off. The door gunners were firing at a furious, feverish, and rapid pace. The officer sitting in the chopper grabbed my hand and pulled me inside.

I could see by the stars on his collar that he was important. I yelled to him, "Thanks, sir!"

He was on the radio, directing the troops. He held up a finger. "Hold on a second!"

The rounds from the enemy were hitting the chopper! The brass cartridges from the M-60s were hitting the inside of the chopper as we turned to get away from the enemy!

The officer was talking into his headset when the chopper made an abrupt turn to the left, then made a circle, climbing a little higher. I could see that he was directing the company toward the enemy's stronghold.

The officer turned toward me and told me to pick up a set of headphones. I placed the headset on my head after removing my helmet. "Yes, sir!"

"Did you know that you almost missed your ride?"

"It was close, wasn't it?"

"Yes it was, and if you hadn't gotten on when you did, no telling when you would be picked up! What is your name, Sergeant?"

I decided to give him my real name because he wouldn't know who Sergeant Rock was. "Rodgers."

"Your name is Sergeant Rodgers?"

"Yes, sir!"

"Are you the Sergeant Rock with the Silver Star and two Purple Hearts and all that stuff?"

"Yes, sir!"

He reached out his hand for a handshake. "It is a pleasure to meet you, Sergeant Rock!"

I shook his hand. "Thank you, sir! It is a pleasure meeting you too!"

"Rock, when we get to Chu Lai, I want to talk to you further!"

As our chopper left the battlefield, I could see the artillery coming in right on top of the enemy. This officer had done his job.

"Good job, sir!"

"Yeah, that ought to fix 'em!"

We finally made it to Chu Lai. The skid landed and the pilot turned off the engine. The rotor slowly stopped, and all was quiet. I took off my headphones, and the general did the same.

The general turned toward me. "So you are going home in a few days, huh, Sergeant Rock?"

"Yes, sir, I am! By the way, do you know General Westmoreland?"

"Of course. Have you met him?"

"Yes, sir, I think I have, but it was a while back."

"OK, Rodgers, enough of the chit chat! I have been talking to Top and he says you won't re-up for three more months. We really need you, and I can guarantee you a rank of lieutenant!"

I start to shake my head.

He says, "Well, you have three days before you can get out of here, so think about it, OK?"

I quickly counted the days to DEROS in my head. I did not have three days. I had one left!

"Yes, sir, I will, and thank you for the offer. If I did decide to do it, could you really make me an officer?"

"Without a doubt. Here in Vietnam, if we have the need, we can do it. I think you would make a fantastic platoon leader!"

"Thank you, sir!"

I jumped out of the chopper and hurried to Top's CP. Top was listening to the radio. He looked up and gave me a big hug. "How are you, Rock? Boy, it was sure bad to hear about Killer and Doc! Did you know that I had to look up Killer's real name?"

"It was Rydser, Mike Rydser. He was going to take my place as squad leader. He would have been great."

"Yeah, I looked it up. So how are you?"

"I am ready to go home tomorrow. That is how I am. What are you doing? What is happening in the field?"

"I think we have it under control now. The fight that you just came from almost got out of control, but after the artillery strike, we wiped them out. You will have to stay here for a few more days because I won't have your paperwork ready. Did the general talk to you?"

"Yep, he did."

"Rock, would you help me for a few days?"

"Sure, doing what?"

"Every day, we have to take the three-quarter ton truck thirty miles to deliver supplies. Hanks was driving it, but now he has to get on the deuce-and-a-half. Go over and talk to Hanks."

"OK. See ya, Top."

"Good to see you again, Rock."

I walked over to the small motor pool. I see a guy standing next to a large two-and-a-half ton truck. "Is your name Hanks?"

"Yes it is, Sarge! How can I help you?"

"Top says that I am supposed to help you on deliveries for the next few days."

He looked surprised. "Really? A sergeant is going to take my place? What is your name, Sarge?"

"I am Sergeant Rock."

*I am in Chu Lai getting ready to take a small
supply truck to a bad area*

"Sergeant Rock? For real?"

"Yeah. Why are you surprised?"

"Because Top always talks about you and Lewis. I was sorry to hear about Sergeant Lewis. He was your closest friend, wasn't he?"

"Yes he was, but why were you surprised that I was going to drive your three-quarter ton?"

"Because it is dangerous. We have lost two drivers already!"

"How come?"

"There is an area between the villages about ten miles out that is wide open. Nothing but rice paddies on each side of the road. Every day, going and coming, we get sniper fire. Just look at my truck!" He points his finger at several bullet holes in the truck.

"Wow, that does look dangerous!"

"Yeah, but nothing like the danger that you are used to! That is why I was surprised. I didn't think that anyone but a private would be making the run!"

"You mean you think you are easily replaceable?"

"Yes, Sergeant, something like that. I am very much surprised that Top is sending the Rock. Can I ask you a personal question, Sarge?"

"Sure, go ahead."

"Have you actually cut off twelve gooks' heads all by yourself?"

I laughed out loud. "No, actually, it was twenty-four!"

"For real?"

"No, I am just kidding. I never cut off any heads. A guy in my squad, whom we named Killer, cut off one head, and the rumors started."

"Well, the guys around here like the rumors! Every one of us wants to go to the field with you guys!"

"Good talking to you, Private. I am going to see Top!"

I saw Top outside of his quarters. "Hey, Top, are you trying to get me killed with a day left in country?"

Top grins. "No, but I have got to get these supplies over to the village every day. Did Hanks say he was still getting sniped at? I don't have anyone else to send, but if you won't go, I will understand."

"I'll take it. I hope that truck has a V8 with a 409 cubic inch engine in it. He said that he was still getting sniped."

Top laughs. "No, I think it is a four cylinder."

"Alright, I'll take it."

"OK, Danny, thanks. Grab a bunk and I'll see you in the morning. The truck will be loaded by 0800 and fueled up!"

"I'll be ready. See ya, Top!"

"See ya, Rock!"

I went to the chow hall for a hot meal. As I was eating, many men gathered around to speak to me. These were men that had to stay around Chu Lai, working at the base camp. Without these guys, we wouldn't have ammo, C-rations, water, or clean clothes.

One soldier asks, "I feel like I need to be in the field. My job back here is not important compared to what you do, Sergeant Rock."

I looked at all of the guys. "No, you are wrong! I mean this for all of you. You guys are very important! You men are great!"

We continued to talk about the field. We spoke about Proud Mary, the VC that would run through hooches, when I shot the Mamasan in the rear, January ninth, the Tet Offensive, and my Silver Star and two Purple Hearts. We spoke about the NVA torching our men. We talked about all of the fine men I had lost, including my best friend in Vietnam, Chuck Lewis. And, of course, we spoke for an hour about Killer and how he got his nickname.

One soldier asks me, "Sergeant Rock, how does it feel to be respected as a great leader with a reputation for not taking any prisoners?"

I had not thought about my reputation in a long time. Much of my reputation was due to Killer! Reluctantly, I answered, "I never think about it much, but I do know that I get a lot of respect now."

"Are you really friends with lieutenants, captains, and generals?"

"I have been very close to our platoon leaders and pretty close to our captains. I wouldn't say that I was a friend with the captains, and I only get respect from generals. I wouldn't say that I had a general as a friend."

"I hear Top talking about you a lot!"

"Yeah, I like Top too. He gives me great respect! But you know what?"

"What?"

"When I get back to America, I won't be jack crap! No one will care!"

We could have talked for two more hours, but I was getting tired. "OK, men, I have got to get some sleep! See ya!"

"Nice talking to you, Sergeant Rock," each of them said.

I went to the barracks and found a cot that looked empty. There was no equipment under the bed, so I took it. Other men started to come in and grab their cots. Many of these men were the guys that I had been talking to in the chow hall.

I was almost asleep when a soldier I had never seen before bumps my cot. "You are sleeping in my bed!"

"Your bed?"

"Yes, get out!"

I sat up and noticed that he was a private. I had my shirt off; therefore, he could not see that I was a sergeant and outranked him. "Why do you say this is your cot, man?"

"Because I sleep here every night!"

"You know what, soldier?"

"What?"

"I will move to another cot under three conditions! One, you apologize for kicking my bunk! Two, you apologize for waking me up. Three, say that you are sorry for telling me to get out!"

"Do what?"

Really calmly I said, "If you don't give me those three things that I want, you won't get your bed back, and I will kick your butt in the morning!"

By this time, everyone in the tent was sitting up or standing. One of the men that I had been talking to addressed the private. "Do you know whom you are trying to get out of your bunk?"

"I don't care who he is!"

"It is Sergeant Rock!"

"Sergeant Rock?"

"Yep, the sergeant from the field!"

The private looked at me. "I am sorry, Sarge. I am sorry. You keep the bunk for as long as you need to!"

He walked away. I lay back down and tried to sleep. I could hear the private and the other men whispering.

"Why didn't you guys tell me that he was Sergeant Rock? If I had gotten in a fight with him in the morning, he would have cut my head off. I have been told that he never takes a prisoner, and he just simply kills everyone he fights. You guys should have told me. Why didn't you?"

"Because we wanted to see how far you would go before he kicked your butt! I understand that his buddy Sergeant Lewis wouldn't have been so calm, cool, tranquil, unruffled, and serene. Lewis would have jumped up and killed you immediately."

"Was Sergeant Lewis the sergeant that got killed?"

"Yep, when the chopper came in, the wounded stayed here, and the dead went to Da Nang or somewhere like that."

"You better apologize to the sarge again in the morning. You know that he and Top are tight, don't you?"

"Yeah, and I will."

I listened and thought about all of the men that I had lost. I dozed off, and then I would be startled by a slight noise and wake up. I thought about the truck run that I would be doing in the morning. *Would I be killed on the day that I was supposed to DEROS?*

Morning came, and I grabbed a quick breakfast. I walked over to Top. "I am ready, Top. What is the cargo that I will be carrying?"

"You will be carrying M-16s and ammo."

"You get my papers ready. I'll be back this afternoon."

"Good luck, and Danny, again, I am sorry about Lewis."

"How did he look the last time that you saw him?"

"I didn't see any of the dead. The chopper unloaded the wounded and took the dead to Da Nang. Sorry, Rock."

"Yep, me too."

I hurried over to the motor pool. "Hey, Hanks. Is the truck ready?"

"Yes. Now be ready for snipers at mile ten."

"OK. You know, what we need is a high speed rear end in this truck!"

"Yep, you are right, but then what about the mud? We need the low gears for torque."

"You are probably right."

I jumped in the truck. The truck was nothing more than a three-quarter ton Jeep pickup with rails in the back and a tarp to hide the cargo.

"See ya tonight or this afternoon, Hanks!"

"Be careful!"

I took off up the mine-swept road to the hard-packed dirt highway. The road was so bumpy that I could only drive forty-five miles per hour most of the time.

I had my M-16 and six bandoliers of ammo strapped down in a holder. I kept looking at my rifle to be certain that it stayed in place. I was eight miles out, and I was getting nervous about what was to come.

I started to think. *With all of the crap that I have been through, why was I worried about a few snipers?* I was now nine miles out from Chu Lai.

I started to hear rocks hitting the fenders of the truck, but I was not running over any rocks. What was the noise I was hearing? I realized that I was being shot at. I threw the truck into third gear and mashed the accelerator pedal completely to the floor. The truck took off. I shifted the truck to the highest gear that I could find and kept smashing the accelerator pedal!

The truck was hitting mud puddles and bumps in the road. It was bouncing from one side of the road to the other. The motor was winding to its maximum. I didn't let up. I kept pursuing my destination. I would blow the engine up and fight the VC before I would let them have the cargo aboard. I finally reached the eleven mile mark.

I was now out of the range of the snipers. I slowed down as I drove the truck through villages, but I was very much aware that I might be shot at again. I started to look over the inside of the truck. I noticed that I had a bullet hole in the windshield!

I did not like this duty with only a few days left in country. I really appreciated the guys in the rear even more after this episode.

I finally reached my destination. As the men unloaded my cargo, I examined the truck. I had six new holes in the fenders and the body of the truck, plus the one in the windshield.

One of the soldiers unloading my cargo said, "Looks like Charlie wanted your M-16s and ammo! You have new holes in the truck! Why do they have a sergeant driving, anyhow?"

"Yeah, I got shot at around the nine mile marker. I am driving because Hanks is on the deuce-and-a-half for a while. I only have one more day before my DEROS. Actually, I am supposed to leave today!"

"And they have you on this stinking detail, huh? Well, take it easy going back!"

"I will. I think that I'll drive full blast all the way back to Chu Lai!"

"No, don't worry, Charlie is smart. He knows you will be empty, no cargo going back. You won't be shot at!"

"I hope you are right!"

"OK, Sarge, you are unloaded. See you tomorrow, or maybe not!"

"I hope that I am on a plane heading for home tomorrow!"

I took off for Chu Lai. When I reached about twenty miles away from my delivery point, my senses were heightened. Even though I was told not to worry, I was worried. I goosed the truck to sixty, keeping my eyes open for any flash from a rifle that I may see.

I did not get shot at, and I arrived at Chu Lai without another incident. I pulled the truck into the motor pool. "Here you are, men. Here is your truck!"

Hanks rubs his hand over the new bullet holes. "Looks like Charlie wanted you bad!"

"Charlie wanted the ammo and guns, not me! I'll see ya, Hanks. I am going to see Top, then eat!"

"See ya, Sergeant Rock!"

I strolled over to the CP. The general from the chopper was coming out. "Sergeant Rock, you go in there and listen to that! We need you!"

I walk in and see Top intently listening to his radio. "Man, Rock, listen to this!"

I started to listen to the transmissions. "We need more firepower! Give us some help, please!"

In the background, I could hear rockets going off, exploding. I could hear machine gun fire, and I could hear the rounds being fired from the M-16s. This was a very bad battle. I listened with frustration. I heard, "Annihilator Three-Three, this is Blackhawk Three X-ray. We are being overrun!"

Then the transmission stopped. I looked at Top. "Top, that was my RTO, Craig, talking! All of my guys are being killed! They are getting wiped out!"

"Delta Company is going to give them a hand, but I think it is too late!"

I hear another transmission. "This is Cherokee Three. We need help, and we need it now!"

I look at Top. "Top, that was Sergeant Hanna; he took Lieutenant Watkins's place!"

"Yeah, I know!"

"OK, Top, you get me on a chopper and get me back out there! The general wants me to go, and if I don't, I will feel like a coward for the rest of my life!"

"You ain't going, Danny! It won't do any good! You would just get yourself killed. You would be killed as soon as you got off of the chopper! So what is the use? I am not letting you go!"

"But Top, something needs to be done! What can I do? I feel like a coward!"

"Rock, I want you to think about it! You have done your time. You have been through much more than a lot of soldiers. When the general sees you again, you tell him just what I have told you!"

I hung my head. "OK, Top."

Top placed his hand on my shoulder. "Day after tomorrow, you will be heading home."

The door opens. It is the general. "Have you two been listening to all of that crap on the radio? They are wiping us out! I have been listening from my quarters! Man, how long will it take for Delta Company to get there?"

Top says, "They are on their way."

The general places his hand on my shoulder. "What do you think, Rock?"

"It's bad, sir."

"So are you going to become an officer and go back out for three months?"

"You know, sir, I have done my time. Everyone that I have gotten close to has died. I feel bad, and I sort of feel like a coward, but do you really think I can get out there in that battle and save anyone?"

"No, Rock, not really. If you go out there now, you will be killed as soon as you jump off of the chopper. But if you stay here in Vietnam for three more months, you can become an officer. I am going to need help rebuilding the company. I will not send you back out until the battle is over."

"There you go again, sir. You are making me feel like a coward when you say you won't send me out until the battle is over. I don't mind fighting, but I mind dying!"

"Yeah, Rock, I know what you are saying, and to tell the truth, when my tour is up, I am going home too. Don't worry about it. You go home and enjoy your family. I'll find out where you will be stationed next and come see you."

Top turns to the general and me. "Sir, you and Rock have made the right decision. Rock, it has been a pleasure knowing you. I will have a chopper here day after tomorrow to take you to Da Nang. You have to hop a freight to go to Cam Ranh Bay. You hop on a jet going to America!"

"Oh, man, Top, you don't know how good that sounds!"

"Now, I have one more favor to ask of you!"

"It isn't that thirty mile sniper run, is it?"

"Yes it is. I need you to ride shotgun for Hanks in the morning! The snipers are getting too close. We cannot afford to lose a shipment! Will you do this last thing for me, Danny?"

"OK, but only if I can grab any weapons that I need from supply!"

"OK, anything that you want!"

The general shook my hand. "Thanks, Sergeant Rock. I'll see ya in America!"

"Yes, sir, see you then!"

I turned back toward Top. "I am going to the supply tent, then to see Hanks!"

"Cool!"

I decided to talk to Hanks first. I walked over to Hanks and told him I was going to get some more firepower for our trip tomorrow morning. He was grateful for the help. Next, I walked in the supply tent and spoke to the supply sergeant.

"I need an M-60, a thousand rounds of ammo, a grenade launcher with twenty rounds, and three more bandoliers of M-16 ammo!"

"What are you going to do, win the war by yourself? I will have to get the approval from Top!" The supply sergeant picked up the horn. "Top, I have a guy here that wants an M-60 and a 79!"

Top replied, "That is Sergeant Rock. Give him a missile if he wants it!"

I thought to myself, *A missile?*

"Yes, Sergeant!" He turns toward me. "Why didn't you tell me that you were Sergeant Rock?"

"You didn't ask, and besides, I am not as important as you guys act like I am."

"OK, Sergeant Rock, I will have it for you ASAP."

"Thanks, Sarge. By the way, throw in a LAAW."

"You want a rocket?"

"Yep."

He laughed. I received the arsenal and headed for my bunk in the tent. This equipment was very heavy. I decided to grab a different cot than I had the night before. The private that had said I was in his cot would be happy to know that I chose another.

I placed the Pig, the 79, the LAAW, and the ammo below the cot. Next, I went to the chow hall and ate a hot meal.

After the meal I went back to the barracks. The men wanted to talk and ask questions again. After a few hours, I told the men that I had to get some sleep.

Morning came too quickly. I grabbed a light breakfast and headed to the motor pool. Hanks was looking over the truck. "Well, Hanks, are you ready to go?"

"Yep, Sergeant, I am ready!"

"OK, I want you to go over to the barracks. I have to pick up something."

"OK."

We drove over to the barracks and parked in front of the opening. I ran in and brought out the Pig, the ammo, and the balance of my small arsenal.

Hanks raises his eyebrows. "Cool!"

I say, "That's not all!"

I ran back in the barracks and brought back the M-79 and the ammo, plus the bandoliers of M-16 ammo.

"OK, Sarge, we will have something for them now!"

"Alright, Hanks, let's go!"

We headed out for the dangerous thirty-mile trip.

I leaned over toward Hanks. "Yesterday, I started getting shot at around the nine mile mark!"

"OK, one mile to go!"

I placed the M-60 through the side window of the truck. I hooked up four belts of ammo, one after another.

Suddenly, I saw flashes from rifle fire. I opened up immediately with the Pig. I took the M-79 and fired two rounds. Then I got back on the Pig. I looked at Hanks and he had a big grin on his face. He had the accelerator pedal to the floor. The truck was flying. He was up on the wheel like a NASCAR driver. I had the Pig out of the window opening, firing in the direction of the snipers. I grabbed the 79 again and fired three rounds simultaneously.

I got back on the M-60 and looked again at Hanks. We both started to laugh. We drove another mile at full speed, and then started to slow down. We were out of danger.

"That was a kick, huh, Sarge?"

"Let's go back and do it again!"

"No way!"

We both laugh.

"Hanks, stop right here!"

Hanks stopped the truck. "What's up, Sarge?"

"I am going to walk back to the corner of the tree line and hit them with the LAAW!"

"Right on, Sarge. Right on!"

I walked through the village and found a place where I could see where the VC were firing. I could see movement, but they could not see me.

I opened the fiberglass launcher and lifted the sight glass. I had the enemy in my sight. I looked behind me to be certain no one was directly behind the LAAW. I fired. It was a direct hit! I said, "Alright!" Then I ran back to the truck.

"Hey, Sarge, what do you think about letting me light them up on the way back? They won't be shooting at us, but we now know where they shoot from!"

"Sure, that would be cool! I'll bet that you have never fired a Pig over here, huh, Hanks?"

"You mean an M-60?"

"Yeah, a Pig, an M-60! We have plenty of ammo left, so why not!"

"Thanks, Sarge!"

We made our delivery and headed back toward Chu Lai. I drove, and Hanks manned the weapons. When we arrived at the sniper point, Hanks says, "Slow down!"

He starts to fire on full automatic with the Pig. Quickly, he grabs the M-79. "Stop right here!" Hanks jumps out of the truck and fires six rounds in the direction where the enemy had been.

He jumps back in the truck. "I don't get to fire an M-79 either!" I laugh. "I see that!"

"Thanks, Sarge. Can I shoot some more?"

"Yeah, but let me get moving first!"

Hanks kept firing the Pig until we were almost out of ammo. We arrived in Chu Lai.

Hanks jumped out of the truck quickly. "Thanks, Sergeant Rock! That was a rush!"

"Hanks, will you take all of this ammo back to supply?"

"Sure!"

"You better clean the weapons first!"

"OK, I will! I am going to tell the rest of the guys first! Good luck going home!"

"Thanks, Hanks."

I hurried over to see Top to tell him goodbye. He gave me one last hug and gave me my papers.

The rest of the day, I spent getting my duffel bag ready and saying goodbye to the men at the base. I ate a good meal and tried to sleep, but all I could think about was going home.

I will be going home soon. I hope

The sun came up, and I was ready to eat. My chopper came in and took me to Da Nang. I located a cargo plane that was going to Cam Ranh Bay and jumped aboard.

Once the cargo plane landed, I looked around for a jet and saw one sitting near the runway. Only one more step and I would be heading away from this horrible, horrible place called Vietnam!

CHAPTER 30

DEROS and the Trip Back Home

I looked around for someone in charge of the plane. When I saw a couple of soldiers coming out of a building, I decided to head in that direction.

I stopped the men. "What do we do now?"

"Are you going home, Sarge?"

"Yeah!"

They point at a building. "You just go in that building and see the staff sergeant."

"OK, thanks."

I walked into the building and see a sergeant that I had seen before. "Hi, Sarge, do you remember me?"

"Heck yeah. You and another guy begged me to let you go to the same company a year ago."

"Yeah, you are right. Here is my paperwork. Now I am going home."

"How about your buddy?"

"His name was Lewis, but he didn't make it."

"Oh, man, Rodgers, I am sorry to hear that."

"Hey, Sarge, do you keep up with the wounded and stuff like that?"

"Sometimes. Why? Who are you wondering about? I know I should say *whom* are you wondering about, not *who* are you wondering about!"

"I get *who* and *whom* mixed up too! His name is Eckert. He came in blinded. Do you know anything about him?"

"I remember his name, but once I sent the paperwork off, I never heard anymore."

"So he flew back home?"

"Yes, but I don't know if he was still blind when he got back home."

"What about Chuck Lewis?"

"I don't recall seeing his name. I only take care of the wounded. If he isn't on my list, he is probably dead."

He handed me back my DEROS papers.

"Thanks anyhow."

"Rodgers, you better go and get changed into your Army dress clothes."

I went to the dressing area and changed from my jungle fatigues to my dress clothes. Next, I walked across the tarmac to the plane. Several men were getting on the plane. I got in line and climbed the steps. I handed one of my papers to a stewardess. I looked around for Julie, the stewardess that I had met coming back from my R&R. It would have been nice to see her again. I looked toward the rear of the plane and was surprised that the plane was almost full. I thought that with all of the men that had been killed, the plane would be only half full. I took a seat.

I stopped a stewardess. "I am surprised that the plane is almost full!"

"It will be full by the time we leave. We run two to seven days behind until there are enough men to fill the plane."

"Do you know who Julie is?"

"Oh, yeah, she was on a plane last week. Do you know her?"

"I met her coming back from R&R. I came from Houston to Hawaii, then to Tokyo, then to Vietnam. She sat beside me from Tokyo to Cam Ranh Bay."

"Yep, she was just learning. She told me about you."

"Really? Was any of it good?"

"Oh, yeah. She really liked you."

"Yeah, I liked her too."

I heard a voice from the rear. "Rock, Rock, Danny, Rodgers!"

I turned around and saw Freeman. I put my hand out for a handshake. "Freeman! How are you? You made it!"

"Yep! I made it! What about Lewis? Where is he, Danny?"

Very somberly I said, "He didn't make it."

"Man, Danny, you guys were tight. I am sorry to hear it. Can I sit up here by you?"

"Sure you can."

More men start to board the plane. I look around and see that every seat is taken.

The plane starts to rev the motors. The men explode with anticipation. I cannot hold back my excitement and, like the others, I yell out. The plane starts to move, and we yell again. After five minutes, the plane rolled in position to take off down the runway.

The engines rev up even faster and louder. The pilot gets on the radio. "Are you ready, men?"

Every man, including myself, yelled, "Yeah! Let's go!"

"OK, men! Let's get the heck out of Vietnam and get you brave guys home!"

The plane starts to move. It picks up speed. It is running down the runway faster and faster at a blistering pace. It hits full throttle and starts to lift. We yell again.

Finally, we are leaving the 'Nam and heading back home! The men are still hooting and hollering. Once we reached a very high altitude, the men settled down.

Freeman turns toward me. "I was the first to get on the plane, and I saw every man. There are not many of us left. I only saw a few familiar faces."

"Yeah, I know. We lost a lot of men."

"Yep, we did."

The plane traveled for hours, taking us closer to America. We sat back in our seats and started to fall off to sleep. But every time I dozed off, some soldier would yell out something. I just laughed. The men and I were very, very excited about returning home. Suddenly, the plane jumped erratically.

I thought that it was just turbulence. The captain came on the radio. "Men, fasten your seatbelts. It may get bumpy."

I could tell from the inflection in his voice that something was wrong. He came back on the intercom. "We are having difficulty with the number three engine."

Freeman and I are sitting by the wings of the plane; therefore, we can see all of the engines. Freeman and I, at the same time, look out the window.

Freeman grabs my arm. "Difficulty? Difficulty my butt! The thing is on fire!"

"Man, Freeman, it is on fire! Wouldn't that be something to be over in Vietnam for a year and not be killed, and now we are going to be killed in an airplane crash?"

"Don't even say that! I am scared!"

"Yep, me too!"

The captain gets back on the intercom. "Men, we are going to try to make it to Tokyo and get the engine fixed."

I look at Freeman. "Did you hear what he said? He said we are going to try to make it to Tokyo!"

"Yeah, what does he mean *try to make it*?"

"I don't know for sure, but I'm going to say a prayer!"

I looked out the window, and the engine was still on fire and pouring out a lot of smoke. Suddenly, the plane leaned over on its side and started plummeting down! The pilot came on the intercom again. "Hold on, men, hold on!"

The plane was still losing altitude. I leaned over. "Say a prayer, Freeman!"

"I am! I am! I have been!"

Finally, the plane stabilized. The pilot came back on the intercom. "Sorry about all of that, men, but we will definitely be landing in Tokyo!"

After a few more long and scary hours, we looked out the window and the fire was gone from the engine, but it was still billowing smoke. Another hour, and we touched down in Tokyo.

The landing was rough, but not nearly as bad as we had expected. The captain got back on the intercom. "Well, men, how did you guys like that for excitement?"

We hollered, "Alright! Good job!"

The stewardess came on the intercom. "Men, we will be here for I don't know how long to get the engine repaired. You men may disembark if you would like and go in the terminal. But stay in the terminal. Don't buy any large items, and don't go downtown!"

The men groaned. Freeman looked at me. "Let's go, Rodgers!"

"You mean downtown Tokyo?"

"Yeah, I want to buy something!"

"I have never been to Tokyo. OK, let's go!"

We stood up, and when we did, two more men did likewise.

"Hey, Freeman and Rock, can we go too?"

I looked at Freeman and shrugged my shoulders. "Sure, why not? Let's go!"

Only a handful of us stood up to leave the plane.

When the stewardess saw us, she said, "Now remember, don't buy anything from the airport because we don't have any room in the plane, and we are carrying cargo in the cargo bays!"

The four of us walked into the airport terminal. The terminal had kites, lanterns, pots and pans, and all kinds of stuff for tourists to purchase.

Freeman says, "Let's grab a cab and go downtown or uptown, whatever it is, but let's go!"

The four of us jump in the cab and I say, "Let's go to Tokyo, please!"

The driver says "OK, we go!"

We make the trip to town and start looking at stuff. My plan was to just see Tokyo, but Freeman's plan was to buy something! We walked around for a half hour, going in and out of buildings and small canopies. Then Freeman says, "I found it! There it is!"

He had found an electric guitar. It was a beautiful white guitar with gray trim. The price was $7! I looked at Freeman and reached for the guitar. "Seven dollars for this? You've got to be kidding me! Man, I am going to buy one too!"

"I didn't know that you played a guitar!"

"I don't, but for $7 I'll learn how to play!"

We laughed. I picked out a red one with a lever on it for vibrating the notes. It was cool! On my way to the checkout counter I saw a blue lacquered floor tom-tom drum that was the same color as the set I had at home. I also saw a pair of drumsticks at a very cheap price.

"Now, there is something that I do know how to play, Freeman. I have been playing the drums for ten years! I wonder how much it is."

I ask the clerk how much it was, and she told me $11. For only $11, I had to have this tom-tom! I gave the clerk the money for the drum, the guitar, and a pair of drumsticks.

Freeman was right behind me with two electric guitars. The other two men that had followed us also bought drums and guitars.

Once we had all been checked out with our merchandise, we looked at each other and started to laugh.

Freeman says, "Well, so much for not buying anything, huh, Rodgers?"

"Yeah, what are they going to do, send us back to Vietnam?"

We beckoned for a cab and loaded our goods. On our trip back to the airport, we could not stop laughing, anticipating the trouble that we would be in when we got back on the plane! We arrived at the airport terminal and jumped out of the cab. The driver opened the trunk and we started pulling our wares out. I grabbed my guitar and drum and stuck the sticks in my pocket. Freeman reached for his two guitars and a large vase that he had bought for his mother. The other two men had guitars and some sort of Japanese ironworks that went on a wall in a house.

We went into the airport, struggling to hold on to our goods. Other soldiers were sitting in the terminal, watching us as we moved toward the stairs that led out of the terminal. I heard comments like "I thought they said for us to stay in the terminal!" and "They told us not to buy anything!"

Before we reached the terminal, we heard a voice on the intercom. "Soldiers, your plane is ready now. Please start getting aboard."

I looked at Freeman. "We could have missed our flight, Freeman!"

"Oh, they would have waited on us, and especially the famous Sergeant Rock!"

"Yeah, right. I am not jack crap now. I am simply Sergeant Rodgers."

"Not to me! You'll always be Sergeant Rock to me, and if you write a book, will you put me in it?"

"Yes I will! I'll put you in it concerning this little Tokyo adventure and when you pooped in the river!"

"Oh, no, not the crapping in the river thing! Your readers will think I'm gross!"

"Well, you are gross!"

"Yeah, I guess I am!"

We both started to laugh hard.

"Hey, Rock, do you think Lewis would have gone with us downtown?"

"Oh, yeah. He would have been the first guy out of the airport!"

We walked over the tarmac to the stairs leading up to the plane. Many men are in front of us. The four of us look at each other, and, again, we start to laugh.

I glance at Freeman's vase. "We are in so much trouble! I cannot even see your face because of those fake weeds coming out of that jug!"

"It is not a jug! It is a *vahhz*!"

We reach the top of the stairs and start to enter the plane. The stewardess's eyes widen. "You can't bring all of that aboard. We have no room!"

Again, we start to laugh! Freeman says, "We will just hold everything in our laps!"

"No, you can't do that!"

We hear the plane's engines starting up!

Another stewardess walks up to the first stewardess. "What is the problem? The door is still open and the captain wants everyone seated so we can take off!"

"Look at all of the extra stuff these guys have bought! We have no room in the cargo bay!"

"Yeah, I see, but we are not going to hold up this plane to open the cargo doors! The captain would kill us! Close the door!"

We are still standing in the entryway while the door is closing.

The stewardess looks at us and shakes her head. "I don't know what we are going to do with you guys! OK, just put your stuff in the restrooms for take off! Do it quickly!"

I looked at her. "Thank you!"

She grinned. "You're welcome."

The plane started to move and shift on the tarmac, heading for the runway.

"Alright, men, take your seats!"

We sat down and started looking at each other. We begin to laugh very hard. Our laughter turned to an ecstatic, jubilant roar as we left Tokyo and headed for America again.

After hours and hours and hours, a stewardess came on the intercom. "We will be landing in Hawaii for a short time. Please do not leave the airport terminal!"

Again, we look at each other and laugh.

Freeman says, "What do you think, Rock?"

"No way. I am not leaving the airport again!"

The plane touches down and taxies close to the terminal. As the plane stops, we unbuckle our seatbelts and stand up.

Again we hear the intercom. "Men, remember. Do not leave the terminal!"

A stewardess walks up to us and says, "Not you four! The captain says that you four are to remain on the plane!"

Freeman looks surprised. He looks at me and points. "Do you know who that is? That is Sergeant Rock!"

The stewardess raises her eyebrows. "The captain doesn't care if he is Sergeant Boulder or Sergeant Mountain! He says to keep you four on the plane!"

Freeman looks at me. "I guess you are right, Rock. You ain't jack crap over here!"

"I guess that none of us are jack crap over here!"

CHAPTER 31

Christmas in July

While many of the men went into the terminal, our little group of four stayed on the plane. Many other men stayed on the aircraft also.

Freeman leaned over. "You know, we can go into the terminal if we really want to, and they couldn't do anything about it."

"Yeah, but let's just be cool about it."

"Alright, but I am going to get bored."

The front cabin pilot's door opened, and the pilot came back to where we were huddled. "So you guys are the men that are breaking all of the rules, huh?"

I answered, "I guess we are, sir."

"Well, don't worry about it. The first time that I came to Tokyo, I bought all kinds of crap. My wife hated everything that I bought her."

My group laughed.

"Have you guys seen much action?"

I look at him. "Yeah, this Tet Offensive thing is bad, but there are probably men that have seen more action."

Freeman joins in. "Yeah, but I'll bet not many. We have seen men with their guts blown out. We have seen missing legs and arms. Rock, tell him about the time you went back to identify bodies, and tell him about the boots too!"

"OK. Do you want to hear it, Captain?"

"Yes, by all means tell me. We have over two hours to wait here."

"One of our men got killed, so I was told to go to Da Nang to identify the body. I got a lift into Da Nang and located a big, tent-like barracks. I went in and told the guys what I was there for, and I gave them the name. While I was waiting, I started looking around, and there were twenty to thirty boots lined up against the inside of the tent wall.

"I picked up a boot for a closer look, and I noticed that it was stuffed with dirt and grass, or at least it looked like dirt. When the guys came back, I held up a boot and asked 'Why do you guys put dirt in all of these boots?'

"Calmly, a soldier said, 'It is not dirt, it is a foot.'

"I dropped the boot. 'What?'

"'Yeah, sometimes a foot comes in. That is extra. Once, we received six bodies and fifteen feet. On this day, we had three more feet than we needed. It is very hard to keep up. When the next load of soldiers comes in, we always check for feet first, then we make sure we don't have two right or two lefts. We know that we don't always get the correct feet with the bodies, but we really do try, Sarge!'

"I asked, 'OK, so where is the body I am supposed to identify?'

"'It is over here.' He lifts up a blanket and shows me the body.

"'Yes, that's him!'

The pilot says, "Man, that is quite the story!"

"No, we are not to the good part yet!"

"There is more, Sarge?"

"Yeah, so I go back to my unit, and more men get shot. After two weeks, I go back to Da Nang to identify two more bodies.

"Again, I walk into the large tent. I give the men in charge the names I am looking for. While I wait, I get closer to the boots, but this time I don't touch anything.

"A soldier comes up to me and tells me that I need to look at five bodies. I look at the first two, but I don't recognize them.

I look at the next two, and I recognize one soldier. Now, here comes the surprise! I look at the next body, and it is the same body that I identified two weeks ago! I turned to the guy. 'I identified this soldier two weeks ago!'

"'Oh, man, that means we sent the wrong body to the wrong parents or funeral home!'

"I left shaking my head!"

The pilot has his mouth open. "You mean they sent the wrong body home, and to the wrong place?"

"Yes, sir."

"Wow!"

"Sir, how many trips a month do you make to Vietnam?"

"Quite a few. I also pick up the dead and the wounded."

"Do you keep a list of the bodies and the wounded?"

"Sure do. Every man and woman!"

"Do you have the lists with you now?"

"Yeah, who are you looking for? I'll go and grab the list." He returned shortly. "OK, give me the last name."

"The first one is Lewis, Chuck Lewis."

He looks at two lists. "No, he isn't on the deceased or the wounded."

"How about Eckert? E-C-K-E-R-T."

"Yeah, I have Eckert. He was having trouble seeing."

"How about Lieutenant Watkins?"

Again he fumbles through his papers. "Yep, I have Watkins. He is in a hospital right here. He is not dead."

"Captain, I know that we are restricted to the plane, but can I go and pay him a visit?"

"Yes, if you promise not to buy anything!" He laughed.

"I promise!"

"You better be back in two hours!"

"I will!" I took off to track down a cab.

The taxi took me to the hospital. I asked a lady at the information desk to find Lieutenant Watkins.

"Do you have his first name?"

"Yes, it is Lieutenant! No, I am only joking. I think it is Steven or Stephen."

"Yes, here he is. Are you a relative?"

I paused for a minute. "Yes, I am his brother!"

I did not come all of this way to be sent away because I was not a relative. So I told a little lie.

"Yeah, right! And you don't know your brother's first name?"

"I am heading home from Vietnam, and I know that he would be glad to see me. I will be leaving in about an hour!"

"OK."

She handed me a piece of paper with the room number on it, and then she whispered, "Brother my butt."

I ran to the elevator and went to his floor. I located his name on the side of the door. I heard talking coming from his room, but I decided to go in anyhow.

I walked into the room. His wife was sitting next to him on the bed. I knew it was his wife from pictures that he had shown me.

He looked up. "Sergeant Rock! Come here and let me give you a hug!"

I walked over to him and gave him a man hug.

He looks at his wife. "Honey, this is the guy I have been telling you about! Danny, this is my wife, Kristy!"

"Glad to meet you, Kristy. So, sir, how are you doing?"

"From now on, just call me Steve. I am great. I will be out of here in three days!"

"So what was your damage?"

"The bullet hit two ribs and hit some organ in my back. But I hurt more from the shrapnel than the other wounds."

Kristy says, "Yeah, it was touch and go for a while. The bleeding wouldn't stop. So you are the famous Sergeant Rock? Steve does nothing but tell me how many times you have saved his life."

"Yeah, but he has saved mine a few times too! You have a great man there, Kristy."

"I know. He is the best."

The lieutenant started to speak. "Kristy, this is the bravest guy I have ever known. He attacked a bunker straight on, got shot in the arm, and never went down. He never lets up. He taught me everything, him and his buddy, Lewis."

I was getting embarrassed. "Actually, I did not get shot by a bullet. I think it was from a grenade, but it did hurt. When you are attacking, you can't let up. Steve listened so well that he was easy to teach."

"Nevertheless, Danny, thank you."

"You are welcome, sir."

"Not *sir* anymore, Sergeant. You just call me Steve."

"But you just called me Sergeant again!"

"Yeah, I did, huh?"

All of us laughed. We talked for another forty-five minutes, and then it was time for me to leave. I said my goodbyes and headed back to the plane.

When I arrived at the plane, I spoke to the pilots and the men about Lieutenant Watkins's injuries. We were ready to fly again after another half hour of delays.

The plane took off, heading for the next stop in California. Freeman starts to chat. "Where are your new orders sending you next, Rock?"

"To Fort Ord in California."

"Yeah, me too. Isn't that something? We're both were living in California, but we get shipped to Washington, then to El Paso, then to Louisiana, then to the 'Nam! What will you be doing there?"

"The orders say COMM GRP. I think that is committee group. I will probably be teaching the trainees something."

"I am going there too. I am going to drive a truck."

"That's cool."

"How long do you have off before you have to be there?"

"Two weeks. I am going to Houston first, where my family lives now, then I'll report to Fort Ord. Freeman, you better be on time when you report, or they may send you to the 'Nam again!"

He laughs. "I will go AWOL before going back to Vietnam!"

We talk for a few more hours before landing in Los Angeles. The plane pulls up to the gate and slows. Freeman, as usual, not doing what he is supposed to, stands up before the plane stops completely.

He sticks out his hand. "Sergeant Rock, I'll see you in two weeks!"

"See ya then, Freeman!"

He takes off for home.

After thirty minutes the plane takes off for Houston. Two and a half hours later we land in Houston. I am getting excited about seeing my family. When the plane stops, I thank the stewardesses and the pilots. I grab my duffel bag and disembark from the plane. I hurry down the runway and into the terminal.

Before I could see my family, I heard my name being called. I looked in the direction from which I heard "Danny" being called, and I saw a magnificent sight! My family was all here — Dad, Mom, Dwight, Duane, Denis, Doug, and my wonderful wife, Sue. Sue came running up to me, yelling, "Danny!"

I received kisses from Sue and my Mom. I shook hands with Dad and my brothers. They were all jubilant about seeing me. My brothers were asking so many questions that I could not keep up with the answers.

The excitement continued until we arrived at home. Before we pulled into the driveway, I saw something out of the ordinary. The whole house was decorated for Christmas. There were reindeer in the front yard, pulling Santa Claus in a boat. Every tree was decorated with foil. The windows had fake snow on them. There were decorations all over the exterior of the house. I looked up at the roof and saw more decorations on the roof and chimney! Someone had done a fantastic job.

I looked at Mom and Dad. "Christmas in July! This is great!"

Dad says, "We knew that you had spent Christmas in the mud in Vietnam, so we decided to give you one here!"

"Oh, man, Dad and Mom, this is great!"

Mom hugs me. "You can thank all of your brothers too! They all helped!"

"Thanks, Dwight, Duane, Denis, and Doug! You guys are cool!"

We walked into the house, and I had another surprise! The whole house was decorated with Christmas decorations, including a Christmas tree. I looked under the tree and there were many presents.

Dad says, "They are all for you, Danald!"

Everyone is gathered around the tree in the living room. Dad grabs the camera.

Mom hands me a present. "Open this one first."

"OK. Thank you."

I opened the present, and to my surprise, it was an Army metal mess kit. Everyone starts to laugh.

Dad says, "We thought we would get you one of those to remind you of all of the good times that you had in Vietnam."

Everyone laughed again.

"No, I don't think that I will have to have anything to remind me of the good times, because there weren't any! On the other hand, things could have been worse."

Mom starts to cry. "We are just thankful that the Lord brought you back to us, son."

Dad says, "Amen! Now open the rest of your presents."

After I had opened all of my presents, we had a great lunch. It was just like Christmas dinner.

As we ate lunch, many conversations were going on at the same time.

Dad says, "What are your plans, son?"

"My next duty station is in Fort Ord, California. I have to be there in two weeks. After I get out of the Army, I will enroll in school again and become a dentist. There is a place called University of the Pacific, I think. It is a dental school, I think."

"Will you and Sue live on base or find an apartment?"

"If it is cheap enough, we will live in Seaside, Monterey, or Carmel."

Mom stands up. "If you are almost through eating, I want to give you something."

"I am through. It was great."

Mom walks over to a small desk and picks up two letters. "These are for you. They are from Killer's mom and dad."

"Killer's mom and dad?"

"Yes. Wasn't his real name Mike Rydser?"

"Yes ma'am."

I opened the first letter and in it Mrs. Rydser asked me exactly how Mike died. Everyone was quiet in the room as I read the letter.

I looked at the family. "She wants to know how Killer died."

Duane asked, "Did she actually say *Killer* in the letter?"

"No, she said *Mike*. I don't know if he ever told them that his nickname was Killer."

"How did he die?"

"He threw a grenade in a bunker, and the gooks threw it right back out. It landed right next to him. I guess I'll open the other letter."

The second letter asked again about his death, and if he was actually dead. She asked if I actually saw his body.

"In this letter, she wants to know if I actually saw his body, and if he is really dead."

Dad places his hand on my shoulder. "Son, I am sorry. Do you think that you will ever be the same?"

"No, sir, I don't. Tomorrow, I will write to them, but today let's just have fun."

We played board games, "Password," watched TV, and ate Mom's great desserts and delicious cooking for the rest of the day. It was a great day!

The day turned into night. I took a shower and climbed into some comfortable clothes. We stayed up very, very late, but now it was time for Sue and I to enjoy each other's company.

Sue reached out and gently placed her hand in mine. We slowly walked into our bedroom and turned off the lights.

I was ready to jump into bed with my beautiful wife. I took off my clothes quickly and climbed into bed. I was ready to go! Sue was not ready to go quite so quickly.

Sue turned on a dim light and stood in the center of the bedroom in her bathrobe. Very, very slowly she started to untie her robe. I sat up in the bed, my eyes wide open.

She didn't know how much this was teasing me. She slowly dropped the robe from over her tanned shoulders. My mouth dropped open. She was wearing nothing but a pair of very small yellow panties.

I could not take my eyes off of my wife's perfectly-shaped hourglass body. She looked at me and slowly took off her panties and gently threw them in my face. She slowly climbed on top of the bed, moving slow like a panther in the night, looking for her prey.

I was her prey alright, for I was not going to put up a fight. I was her capture and she was the captor. We made love for more than an hour. We rested and started over again. It was wonderful to be home! We finally fell asleep. Sue had her head resting on my chest the whole night long.

I kept waking up all night long, having nightmares of Vietnam. Finally, morning came.

It was time for me to look for a new car! I was the first one up, followed by Mom, Sue, and Dad. My brothers were next to join us in the kitchen.

Dad pours himself a cup of coffee. "Do you want me to go with you and help you make a deal on a new car?" Dad had worked for an auto dealership. Therefore, he knew exactly what the cars cost and the mark ups on them.

"Yes, sir! That would be cool."

"OK, after breakfast, we'll go to a few Chevrolet dealerships."

The whole family sat at the table, eating breakfast together. Mom says, "How did you sleep, Danny?"

"Not too good. I had lots of dreams."

Sue looks at Mom and Dad. "I think there is something wrong with him. He doesn't dream; he has nightmares! He groans and jumps in his sleep a lot."

I look perplexed. "Really?"

"Yes, and you grabbed my arm a few times, and it hurt!"

"I am really sorry!"

We finished breakfast, and Dad and I headed out. We went to a dealership with several 1968 Camaros on their lot.

"I like this one, Dad. It has a big motor and a four speed!"

We found a salesman, but we could not make a deal. We drove to another dealership and found another Camaro.

"This one has chrome on the motor, a four speed, and positive traction. I like it better than the other one. Let's go in, Dad, and try to make a deal!"

"Let's go in."

I found a salesman and after an hour of heated negotiations, he said, "I will have to take this offer to my boss!"

He stood up and walked over to his manager.

"Dad, I am getting nowhere with this guy. Do you want to take a shot at him?"

"Sure."

The salesman returned and made me an offer. I felt like it was still too high.

Dad looks at the potential contract with all of the figures on it. Dad writes a figure on a piece of paper. "This is what we will pay, and this is our final offer."

"I'll go back to the boss and show him."

Dad leans over. "How bad do you want the Camaro, Danald?"

"Pretty bad, but not all that bad."

The salesman returns. "Here is what we can do. We are only $100 off of making a deal."

Dad says, "No deal." We stood up.

"Do you mean that you are going to walk out of here over $100?"

"Yep!"

The salesman was so mad that he jumped to his feet and tore up the contract right in front of us. We walked to Dad's car. We climbed in and sat down. We looked at each other and busted out laughing.

Dad says, "I guess he did not like our offer."

"I guess he didn't."

We laughed again. We located another dealership, and as we drove onto the lot, I saw a 1968 El Camino. "Man, Dad, look at that one!"

"I thought that you wanted a muscle car or a Corvette!"

"That is sort of a muscle car, but I bet it is a slush box, and I don't want that."

"What do ya mean, *a slush box*?"

"Oh, a slush box is an automatic transmission. You know, where the liquid transmission fluid slushes through the torque converter."

We walk over to the El Camino. I look inside for the gearshift lever, and I see that it is on the floor. It is not a four speed, but it is a Muncie three speed. I open the hood and see lots of chrome.

"Dad, this is a 327. This will work! Let's go in and try to deal!"

"OK, Danald. Maybe we won't get thrown out this time!"

Dad had a great sense of humor. We walked into the showroom, and Dad says, "We would like to speak to the manager!"

The manager walks up to us. "Hi, gentleman. What can I help you with today?"

Dad looks the manager straight in the eye. "You have an El Camino out there, and we want to buy it for $150 over your cost, including your General Motors hold back!"

A hold back is sometimes called flooring. The car company gives money back to the dealership.

The manager says, "Are you going to resell it?"

"Oh, no! It is for my son here. He just got back from Vietnam."

"I have a son that has just gone to Vietnam."

"Yeah, we prayed every night for Danny to come home to us."

"Well, Danny, do you really want that El Camino?"

"Yes, sir, I do."

"Then it is yours."

"For real?"

"For real. Let's just sign the paperwork, and you'll be on your way!"

In less than five minutes, we had made a great deal. I drove the El Camino home, and I loved every minute of it. It was very fast and handled well!

We walked in the house and Mom had another fine meal ready for us.

"Hi, Mom. Something smells good. I am going to write Killer's parents before I forget!"

I knew that I wouldn't have forgotten to write to Mr. and Mrs. Rydser, because their sorrow was constantly on my mind!

I was changed now, mentally, after the year in Vietnam. I was more resilient and tougher. But I still had a soft heart for people that had lost someone in Vietnam.

When I finished writing the letter, I just sat there and wondered. *Whatever happened to Craig, my RTO, Raymond, the brave guy that carried the Pig, and Dong, my Kit Carson Scout?* I also was thinking about Chuck and Lieutenant Watkins.

Sue walked up to me and placed her hand on my shoulder. "What are you thinking about?"

"Oh, nothing."

I knew that the more that I told the family about Vietnam, the more they would worry about me. I even wondered myself if I could cope with other people. Only time will tell.

"Supper is ready. The boys and your mom love the new car."

"Yeah, me too."

I walked into the kitchen and Mom had a big glass of tea ready for me.

I took a big drink, but something was peculiar. There was nothing wrong with the tea, but as soon as I took a drink, I thought about Vietnam. This had happened to me every time I drank water, or any liquid. Every time I placed anything to my lips and swallowed, I thought about going without clean water for fifty-seven days. I would also think about the hot, stinky, rice paddy water that we had to drink. Maybe this would go away someday.

Mom says, "What are you thinking about, son?"

"It is strange, Mom. Every time I take a drink of water or tea, I think about Vietnam. Your tea is still great, Mom."

"Thank you."

Sue and I spent another week with the family before it was time to head to Fort Ord in California. We did not have much to load in the back of the El Camino because we had very little clothes and no furniture.

My brother, Denis, shook my hand. "Don't wreck the El Camino because I want it when you get something else!"

The whole family gave us hugs and kisses, and we waved goodbye. Sue and I were heading for our next adventure in the U.S. Army!

CHAPTER 32

Life After Vietnam

Sue and I drove my brand new El Camino from Houston to California. I noticed on the trip that I would get very agitated at other drivers. This disconcertment with the other drivers was bothering Sue. "Danny, that guy just forgot to put on his blinker!"

"If he does it again, I'll pull him over and show him what a blinker is for!"

"Danny, you are getting too excited over nothing!"

"You know, you are probably right."

I didn't tell Sue, but I was noticing that I would get mad very easily. I was not like this before Vietnam. I had better learn to control my temper.

We finally made the trip to California, but before driving to Fort Ord, we stayed a day visiting Sue's family in Cotton Center.

Sue asked me if I would mind taking her sister with us, for a week or so, to Monterey. I told her that I would not mind a bit. I liked Renee.

Visiting time was done, and it was time for me to get to Fort Ord and find out what I would be doing. "OK, Sue and Renee, are you ready?"

Renee grabs her suitcase. "This is all I am taking, Danny."

I reached for the small suitcase. "Here, let me have that."

"No, I can get it, but thanks anyhow."

"No, you don't understand. I don't want you to scratch my truck."

620

We laughed. I placed the suitcase on top of a blanket in the bed of the El Camino. We said our goodbyes and headed for Fort Ord. During our trip, my temper got the best of me again. I was ready to fight over the smallest detail!

I noticed Renee looking at me. "What's wrong, Renee?"

"I knew you before you went to Vietnam, and you were sort of mellow then."

"Yeah, I know. I don't know what is wrong with me. I don't sleep. I have nightmares, and I think about the men that I lost."

"I bet that you think about your friend…what was his name again?"

"Chuck Lewis. Both of us would probably have been stationed at Fort Ord."

We finally arrived at Fort Ord. I go through the front gate and go to a place called Committee Group. "You girls stay here. I am going to find out what I will be doing."

I walk in the door and see a private typing. He does not acknowledge that I am there. I wait another thirty seconds. "Don't you see me standing here, Private?"

"Oh, sorry, sir. I didn't realize that you were an officer!"

"I am not an officer. I am Sergeant Rock, or I mean, Sergeant Rodgers!"

"When you yelled at me, I thought you were an officer! So how can I help you, Sarge?"

I handed him my papers. "Here are my papers. What do I do next?"

"I will be right back!" He took my papers into the next room. He was gone for about five minutes.

The private and a top sergeant came out of the room. The sergeant held out his hand. "Hi, Sarge. I see that you were awarded the Silver Star and two Purple Hearts. So that would be a Purple Heart with Oak Leaf Cluster."

"Yes, Sergeant, but I don't know what all of that *Oak Leaf Cluster* is all about."

"It was started by President George Washington. You also received something from General Westmoreland. Have you ever met him?"

"Yes, I believe I have. So what will I be doing, Top?"

"Here at the Committee Group, we teach trainees that are heading for Vietnam."

"So what do you want me to teach?"

"I want you to teach the trainees how to zero their weapons and teach them the positions for fighting."

"You mean like the prone, standing, and kneeling positions, and all of that?"

"Yeah, and you will teach camouflage and target detection. How does that sound to you?"

"Man, Top, that sounds great! I know all about that stuff! How many men will I train per week?"

"From 250 to 500."

"Wow! Will there be anyone to show me how to do the classes?"

"Yeah, his name is Sergeant Beckem! You need to drive over to shooting range number three and talk to him. You will start Monday morning!"

"OK, I will. Thanks, Top."

I walked briskly to my El Camino truck. I was stoked! Of all of the jobs the Army could have put me on, they put me on this one! This was absolutely the best job I could hope for! Maybe I could show the trainees how to save some lives!

I stuck my head through the window. "Guess what? I got the exact job I wanted!"

Sue smiled. "What's that?"

"Teaching men how to shoot and camouflage!"

"Really?"

"Yeah, and I don't need a book for that. I have real life experience! We are going to the rifle range to meet a sergeant."

We drive to the rifle range. I park the car in front of a set of steps that go to a few buildings on a hill. I walk up the steps, and

I can feel the ocean air and the ocean aroma. Once I reach the top of the steps, I see a berm of sand running the whole length of the range. I look over the berm and in the distance, I could see the ocean. Wow. This was great.

I walked into the building and saw a staff sergeant. "Are you Sergeant Beckem?"

"Yes I am, and who are you?"

We shook hands.

"I am Sergeant Rodgers. I guess I will be teaching here."

"Yep, you will! I am retiring soon."

"Really? How long have you been in?"

"Twenty years, and I don't want another tour in 'Nam!"

"I hear you there! Will you be teaching me how to give the classes before you go?"

"Oh, yeah, I won't leave for two weeks! I'll show you what to do with the extra ammo and all of that. I'll be with you every step of the way until you can give the classes as good as me. Did you just come back from 'Nam?"

"Yes."

"What did you do over there?"

"I was a squad leader."

"What unit were you in?"

"The 196th!" I was very, very proud to say the 196th.

"The 196th?"

"Yep!"

"Oh, man, Sarge, you were in the Tet Offensive and all of that stuff. You guys were in a lot of crap. I don't know how you made it back!"

"I prayed a lot!"

We both laughed.

"OK, be here at 5:30 on Monday! Oh, and here, take this helmet liner."

He handed me a black shiny helmet liner with a white band and the words *Committee Group* written on it.

"Thank you, Sarge. I'll be here Monday, early!"

I ran down the steps to my car. I jumped in the El Camino. "I start Monday at 5:30 in the morning!"

Renee says, "Did you like the sergeant?"

"Yeah, he seemed cool. OK, we had better look for an apartment, huh, Sue?"

"Yep!"

We drove around for a few hours, and we finally found an apartment that was affordable, in Seaside! It was furnished with some decent furniture. Everything was clean and sanitary, and it smelled fresh. I paid the deposit to the manager.

After taking care of our new living quarters, we decided to drive around and see more of Seaside, Monterey, and Carmel. I could not believe how nice the beaches were and how pleasant the weather.

"Well, what do you girls want to do next?"

"Let's go bowling!" they both declared.

We drove to the bowling alley. After renting shoes, we found bowling balls and started to play. I kept watching a guy that kept looking at Sue. I was getting angrier and angrier. I was getting furious.

The guy walked up to the counter to get a drink. I took off after him. I was going to rip this guy apart. Sue and Renee took off after me! They were three paces behind me when I reached the guy.

I got up in his face. "What are you doing looking at my wife?"

"Which one is your wife?"

I pointed to Sue. "This one!"

"No, I was looking at the blonde!" He glanced at Renee. "Honest, I was looking at the blonde! I think she is cute. Don't get me wrong, I think your wife is cute too, but I could tell that she was yours!"

"Oh, man. I am sorry!"

"Sure, OK."

Sue looks astonished. "Man, Danny, what is wrong with you?"

"I don't know. I wanted to kill that guy! OK, let's go."

We climbed in the El Camino and started to talk. "I am sorry. I just get too angry."

Sue says, "That guy outweighed you by twenty pounds!"

Renee utters, "How much do you weigh, Danny?"

"Two O-three."

"And you're six foot two?"

"Yep."

"How much did you weigh when you went in the Army?"

"I weighed 165 pounds and had a thirty-two-inch waist. Now I weigh 203 and still have a thirty-two-inch waist. Must be good eating, huh?"

"Yeah, right. C-rations will make you gain weight every time!" She grinned.

We make it back to our new apartment, and Sue decides to take a shower. I look at her. "Do you need any help?"

"If you want to."

"No, I'll stay out here and visit with Renee."

Renee and I are talking when we hear a loud scream. I run to the bathroom, and I see lots of blood in the shower, running down the wall and at the bottom of the tub!

"What happened, Sue?"

"It is my leg. I cut a big gash out of it!"

"How?"

"The porcelain soap holder is broken and it made a six-inch gash in my leg! Take me to emergency right now!"

"Let me see it!"

She showed me her thigh.

"I don't see bone! You will be alright!"

"No, I won't be alright! It is six inches long!"

"Let me look again."

I took another look. "It is five inches long. Not six. I have seen a lot worse, and we never got a stitch! We are not going to the hospital!"

I bandaged Sue's leg and watched it very closely for the rest of the weekend.

Monday morning came, and I met Sergeant Beckem at the rifle range. He taught me how to give the class, and after a week, he turned it over to me.

I started speaking to the trainees. "Men, this class will save your lives. I have just returned from Vietnam, where I was a squad leader. I lost three squads. And in the last one, only three men were left. They also got killed when I left the 'Nam!"

Six hands went up.

"Put your hands down for now! When we get through, I will let you guys ask any question that you want to! OK, men, I was in your shoes once. I know how sleepy you get, sitting here in the sun with the cool ocean breeze blowing. *So don't fall asleep!*"

The men jumped. I started to show them how to set their sights on the rifle. Then I started to show them some of the battle positions. I looked up and saw two trainees with their eyes closed. I screamed, "Wake up!" and they jumped.

"OK, you two, come up here on the platform!"

They climbed down from the bleachers and walked up to me.

"Men, I asked you not to fall asleep, so here is what we are going to do! Sergeant Beckem taught me this! Have you guys ever heard of the Army's dying cockroach position?"

"No, Sergeant!"

"OK, lay on your backs!"

They both lay on their backs.

"Now, put your feet and hands up! Reach for the sky!"

The rest of the trainees are laughing hard.

"Now for the rest of the day, no matter where you are, when I yell 'Raid!' you jump in the dying cockroach position! You got it?"

I only did this for a little humor.

"Yes, Sergeant!"

By the time I was finished teaching my lesson, I had four more dying cockroaches. I decided to open the class for questions. I knew that the first question would be "How many men have you killed?"

"OK, men, how many of you have questions about me or the lesson?"

Two hundred hands went up!

"Many of you will have the same question, so when it is answered, put your hand down until later. OK, if you are going to ask how many men that I have killed, drop your hands!"

One hundred hands dropped.

"I have killed twenty-two or more with a weapon, and hundreds and hundreds where I have called in artillery! The twenty-two were gooks that I confiscated the IDs from. I believe that I shot many more, but they were too far away to get a good body count!"

The men started to ask more questions. "Have you ever found any money on the enemy?"

"Yes!"

"How much?"

"The most that I ever found was a $1.27 or $1.37! One of our men found $1,200 on a guy he killed!"

"Which one is harder to fight, a VC or an NVA?"

"An NVA, North Vietnam Army, or NVR! R is for regular. They have the same equipment as we do!"

"Have you ever been wounded?"

"Yes, twice, but my company couldn't afford to get me out of the field!"

"Have you won any medals?"

"Yes, a Silver Star and two Purple Hearts!"

"Did you lose any good friends?"

I started to count out loud. "One, two, three, four, five, six, seven... Oh, heck, about twelve close friends. And twelve or fourteen guys I liked well, and about four that I didn't like!"

"We have been told that some guys that are a-holes, especially officers, can be shot by their own men! Is this true?"

"Yes, absolutely, but I won't go into detail on that one!"

Many, many more questions were asked, and I answered each one. After the question session, I instructed the men to get into the pre-made foxholes.

I climbed into the tower. "The firing line is ready! Men, lock and load three rounds into your weapons and keep your weapons up and down range!"

The men loaded their rifles.

"Now aim at the silhouette target and try to hit the bull's eye!"

The shots were fired.

"Now squeeze off the next two rounds and take your time!"

The next two rounds were fired.

"OK, men, place your weapons on safety and leave the weapon in the foxhole. Climb out of the foxhole!"

The men climbed out of the foxhole and waited for my next command!

"Men, do not run, but quickly move down range and check out your targets!"

The men took off quickly. Now it was the time to see if the cockroaches were paying attention! I yelled, "Raid!"

Six men hit the ground and turned on their backs with their legs and arms reaching for the sky! The whole company was laughing, including the cockroaches!

"OK, men, good job! Get on your feet! Check out your targets!"

I heard someone in the background coming up the stairs to my tower. "Sergeant Rodgers, I am Sergeant Burns!"

"Hi, how are ya? I'll talk to you as soon as I get out of the tower!"

"OK!" He descended back down the steps.

Once I closed the firing line, I closed the tower and climbed out.

I saw Sergeant Burns snooping around my papers in my office. "What can I do for you, Sergeant Burns?"

"I just got out of the sergeant's school. You are supposed to train me on how to teach the classes."

"Have you been to Vietnam?"

"No, I actually just got out of school!"

"So you are a Shake and Bake, and you are going to teach these men about shooting, camouflage, and target detection, and you have never been to Vietnam?"

"Yes! You don't have to go to Vietnam to teach that stuff, do you?"

"It sure helps! Well, start listening to my classes and learn!"

For the next three days, I trained and taught these trainees. The next morning a new group would be coming in with another 250 privates.

As usual, I met with the trainees' drill sergeant. This drill sergeant had been to Vietnam; therefore, we had a mutual respect toward one another. I told him what we would be doing for the next three days. The drill sergeant told me how many sick calls he had. I could then deduct the amount of ammo that we would not be using.

The drill sergeant moved closer. "Sergeant Rodgers, we have a celebrity with us today!"

"Yeah, who?"

"We have an Osmond Brother with us."

"You mean the Osmond Brothers that sing on 'Andy Williams'?"

"Yeah."

"What kind of a guy is he?"

"He is OK. He doesn't give me any trouble."

"That is good. Sometimes celebrities act up."

"Not this guy. He does anything that I ask him to do."

Sergeant Burns walks up to me. "How many do we have today?"

"Two hundred and fifty-seven!"

"OK, I'll get 'em in the bleachers. What were you guys talking about? I heard you say celebrity."

"Yeah, an Osmond Brother."

"Alright!"

Burns takes off. After another five minutes I finish talking to the drill sergeant.

"Do you mind if I stick around for a half hour?"

"No, I don't mind. It will be good to talk to someone that has been to Vietnam during the Tet."

I see Burns with a trainee. Burns is yelling at him at the top of his voice. "I don't care what kind of a celebrity you are! I don't care if you are the president! You are going to clean my coffee pot so clean that it looks like chrome!"

The trainee hustles to the coffee pot and takes it out of the building. Sergeant Burns has a big grin on his face.

I look at Burns. "Is that Osmond?"

"Yep."

"What did he do wrong?"

"He didn't do anything."

"So why are you yelling at him?"

"Just because I am a sergeant and he is a private."

"Burns, this is my range, so leave him alone! If you get shipped to Vietnam and try that crap over there, one of your own men will kill you!"

"OK, OK, don't get so excited. I was just having a little fun!"

"You Shake and Bake guys are all alike. You don't know crap, but you try to overcome what you don't know by yelling at the privates! I'll take care of Osmond! You have to earn the respect of the men! I want you to watch and listen to my class very closely today! I will have their respect in the first ten minutes of the class!"

"That is because you tell them that you have been to Vietnam!"

Before I could answer, the drill sergeant says, "Burns, do you know what they called Sergeant Rodgers in the 'Nam?"

"No, what?"

"Sergeant Rock!"

"No way!"

Burns looks at me. "Do you mean to tell me that you and Sergeant Lewis are the guys that cut the heads off of your prisoners?"

I answered, "That's us, Sergeant Lewis and I! Lewis was worse than me though! He would cut them off before they were dead! Now Burns, go and get the guys into the bleachers!"

"Yes, Sergeant!"

I turned to the drill sergeant. "You know that I was just messing with Burns."

"No, I didn't. I thought that you and Lewis really did do that!"

"No! I had one guy in my squad that cut the head off of a VC, and after that, the rumors started! We called him Killer after he cut the head off."

"Where are Killer and Lewis stationed now?"

"They are both dead. I am going to see what is going on with the celebrity, Osmond. See you later, Drill Sergeant!"

I go over next to where Osmond is filling the coffee pot with water. "How are you, Osmond?"

"Fine, Sergeant! I am good! I am trying to hurry!"

"Hey, Osmond, take it easy. Sergeant Burns is a jerk."

"Yes, Sergeant! I mean, OK, Sergeant! I don't know what I mean, Sergeant!"

"OK. Quit yelling!"

"Yes, Sergeant."

"For the next few minutes, just talk to me like I am not a sergeant."

"OK, Sergeant."

"No! Don't even say Sergeant after every sentence."

"OK."

"So, you are an Osmond Brother. How do you like singing on the 'Andy Williams Show'?"

"I love it. Andy Williams is a great guy!"

"How do you like the Army?"

631

"Believe it or not, I like it."

"You do. Why?"

"Because I am treated like everybody else. No one gives me special favors, and I can just be myself. I don't have to impress anyone. As long as I do what I am told, the drill sergeants stay off my back. I have had to clean the latrines, but it was along with some other guys. We just laughed together and did our jobs."

"Well, the yelling and all of that will be easier as you go. Don't you have a few younger brothers or sisters?"

"Yeah."

"What are their names, and how old are they?"

"Donny is ten and Marie is eight."

"I think that I have heard of Donny. Do they ever sing with you brothers on 'Andy Williams'?"

"Not really, because they keep goofing up!"

I start to laugh. "I think that I have heard Donny sing, but I don't think that I have heard Marie. Can she sing? I mean, does she sound good?"

"Oh, yeah, God has given all of us Osmonds the ability to sing. Andy is putting on a special deal where we will all sing together. Say a prayer that Donny and Marie don't goof it up too bad!"

We laugh!

"I will! Do you think the Army will let you out for the show?"

"I hope so. If not, they will have to do it without me."

"Do you think that you will be sent to Vietnam?"

"I don't know, but if I am, I will do my best over there!"

"I'll pray that you don't have to go."

"Thank you, Sergeant Rodgers. Are you a Christian?"

"Yes, I am a Christian, but not a Mormon. I am a Baptist. You better finish up and get into the bleachers. My classes will be the most important classes that you will ever need if you get shipped to the 'Nam!"

"Yes, Sergeant!"

He finished his work and ran to the bleachers. We finished the training day and I marched them off of the range and down the hill to where their drill sergeant would march them back to their barracks.

I saw my wife, Sue, driving up in my El Camino. Sue stops and parks the car. She is looking at the men and me.

I turn to the men. "Attention!"

The men snapped to a perfect posture.

"Men, we are going to march over to my car or truck, and when I give you the command you will say very loudly 'Hi, Sue!'"

The men chuckled. We marched right up next to the car. Sue was getting embarrassed because all of the men were looking straight at her.

"OK, men, I will give you a three count. One, two, three!"

The men yelled, "Hi, Sue!"

The yell was quite impressive. They did a good job.

"Great job, men! I appreciate it. Now I will give you back to your drill sergeant. You men did a good job today, and we only had five cockroaches! See you all tomorrow!"

Sue was sunk down in the seat. I walked over to her. She sits up a little taller. "You idiot, that embarrassed me to death!"

"It was all in fun. By the way, how is your leg?"

"It is going to leave a big scar. I should have had stitches, but oh, no, I had to listen to you. You have been to Vietnam and you have seen a lot worse, but from now on, if I get hurt, I am going to the doctor!"

"Man, OK, OK. Sorry I asked. Let's go home. I am hungry. Are we having beans again?"

"Yep, beans again. But I made chili beans out of the beans we had last night!"

"You know, once I get out of the Army and become a dentist, I am never going to eat a bean again!"

We laugh, and I give her a kiss. We drive to our apartment. We eat our beans, and afterward, we walked down to the beach.

"Sue, did your trip to Porterville or Cotton Center with Renee go alright?"

"Yeah, Renee had a good time!"

After the stroll on the beach, we return home and watch a little television then go to bed. Again, I have lots of nightmares. I am so exhausted that I am happy when morning comes, so I can get out of bed!

Sue drives me to the range at five o'clock. For the next few days, I teach again until it is time for the next group of trainees to come to the range. I go through the same routine at the apartment every night.

I wake up, and Sue has my breakfast ready. "Danny, are you getting tired of teaching yet?"

"No, not at all. These guys need what I am teaching them."

Sue and I drive to the range at five o'clock, but there is a Jeep parked in front of the steps going up to the shack. There is a man sitting on a bench outside the building.

I turn to Sue. "Wait here until I find out what he wants and who it is."

I walk up the long walkway and address the guy sitting. I see he is a colonel. I stand at attention and salute. "Sir!"

He salutes back. "At ease, Sergeant Rock, at ease!"

"Yes, sir. How do you know I am called Sergeant Rock?"

"Do you remember the general that was on the chopper when you were lifted out of 'Nam?"

"Oh, yes, sir, I do!"

"He is a very good friend of mine! He was telling me about how you had to fight your way onto the chopper!"

"Yes, sir, that was scary!"

"Well, he asked me to come and see you. I have been checking, and you have been doing a good job running the range!"

"That is because Sergeant Beckem taught me so well!"

"Sergeant Beckem is a very good teacher! OK, I am prepared to give you sergeant E-7 if you re-enlist!"

"You know sir, you and the general and even General Westmoreland are fine men! But there are so many a-holes in the Army, I can't stand it. So I am getting out!"

"That is what the general and Sergeant Beckem said that you would say! I really do know what you mean about the a-holes. Well, I tried!"

He walked away. "Nice car, Rock!"

"Thank you, sir!"

I waved at Sue, telling her everything is alright! She drove away.

The next groups of trainees were marching up to the parking area below. I hustled into the shack to get my paperwork ready. My ammo was being delivered at the same time I was working.

The truck driver handed me a clipboard. I counted the cans of ammo and signed the paperwork. "Thanks. See ya tomorrow."

The trainees were standing at ease in the parking area. Their drill sergeant started to climb up the steps. I could hear his steps as he got closer to my office. As usual, I walked out of the shack to meet the drill sergeant.

But this time it was different. Meeting this drill sergeant would change my life for the better. My life would be enhanced!

The drill sergeant finally reached my office. I looked at the drill sergeant's face. "Chuck! Chuck! Is that really you?"

He got closer and he grabbed me with the biggest hug ever. "Danny, it's me! I thought that you might have been killed!"

"Chuck! I thought that you were dead for months! Man, oh man, I am glad you are alive!"

I sat back down. "Chuck, give me a minute to catch my breath." I turned around in the chair and started crying. I bowed my head. "Thank you, God, for bringing Chuck back home."

I turned back around and I could see that Chuck was crying also.

Chuck, with a grin, says, "Oh, quit it. We are a bunch of babies."

"I am so happy, Chuck. I thought we would never see each other again."

"Yeah, me too. I tried to find out if you were alive, but I couldn't remember the name of Sue's parents. And I think that your mom and dad moved to Texas!"

"OK, Chuck, tell me what happened the last time that you left the field! Top couldn't give me any information!"

"When I left the field, the chopper took me to Hill 348!"

"So you never went to Chu Lai?"

"No! Some of the wounded went to Chu Lai and the dead to Da Nang. I got off at Hill 348, so the guys that were wounded even worse could get on the chopper!"

Sergeant Burns walks in the shack.

"Burns, this is Sergeant Chuck Lewis!"

"Sergeant Lewis, the guy that cut off heads even worse than you and Killer did?"

"Yep, this is the guy!"

Chuck's eyebrows lifted.

"I thought he was dead, Sergeant Rodgers!"

"Yeah, me too, until five minutes ago!"

Burns sticks out his hand for a handshake. "Glad to meet you, Sergeant Lewis!"

"Same here, Sergeant Burns!"

"Sergeant Rodgers, do you want me to get the trainees in the bleachers?"

"Yeah, thanks, Burns!"

Burns walks out of the shack.

Chuck says, "What did he mean about me cutting off heads?"

"Well, he is a Shake and Bake that thinks he knows everything, so I let him believe that we did all of that stuff just to shut him up."

"I can tell by his starched new clothes that he is a Shake and Bake! Man, Danny, it is good to see you again!"

"OK, so what happened after Hill 348?"

"I was shipped to Da Nang. They took care of my wounds, but then I caught malaria!"

"You caught malaria?"

"Yeah, can you believe that? With all of the crap that you and I went through, now I thought that malaria was going to kill me!"

I start to laugh. "OK, so what happened next?"

"I thought that I would never get out of the hospital in Da Nang! But then one day, a captain doctor came in and asked me when I was supposed to be going home!"

"You mean DEROS?"

"Yep! I told him 'day after tomorrow!' He looked at my chart and he said, 'Young man, you have been busy! You have three Purple Hearts and a Silver Star, and now malaria!'

"He turns to the nurses and says, 'Let's get this kid home!'

"I could not have heard any better words, even though I was very sick. I thought that I was dying, but I wanted to die in America!"

"So then what?"

"I was shipped to Letterman Hospital in San Francisco! I had to stay there for a few weeks. They also found out that I had blood poisoning. I couldn't be on active duty, but they did let me go home a few days a week. Then I would return back to the hospital. I tried to find you, but I couldn't, as I have already told you."

"Was the blood poisoning from all the shrapnel?"

"I think partly, but I think it was all of those stupid Wait-a-Minute bushes! The ones that you call back-up bushes."

"Maybe, but you must have five pounds of shrapnel in your body."

We laugh. "So then what?"

"Then I got orders to Fort Ord as a drill sergeant."

"Are you a good one, or are you the kind that just yells a lot?"

"No, I don't yell much, and I think I am a good one. When I tell some of the stories about you and me, the men don't move a muscle."

"Hey, Chuck, I better teach the class. Can you stick around or do you have to go back to your company?"

"No, I can stay here. I would stay here with you even if I was supposed to go back!"

We both laugh very hard.

"That's my buddy, Chuck. We are on our way to getting into trouble together again!"

I walked on the stage platform. "Men, I am Sergeant Rodgers. I am Sergeant Lewis's friend!"

A trainee quickly raised his hand. "Are you Sergeant Rock?"

"That is I!"

The men started clapping and whistling.

"Why? Has Sergeant Lewis been saying bad things about me?"

"No, Sergeant, not bad things about you. He has been telling us about some of the stuff you guys went through in Vietnam! He doesn't talk about it much, but other sergeants have told us about you two!"

"Well, that is cool! OK, men, we are going to have fun today, but everything that I will be telling you will be for real. What I teach you will save your life!"

The training day ended, and Chuck and I can talk again.

"Man, it is good to see you, Danny!"

"You too, Chuck! Why don't you come and live with Sue and me?"

"I better not, because I almost have to be right there in the barracks in case anything happens. You know like a fight, a fire, or something like that. But tell Sue that I am going to spend so much time with you guys, she will think that I live in your apartment!"

"That will be just fine with both of us! Do you talk to the trainees very much about the stuff we went through in the 'Nam?"

"No, not really, but other sergeants have told them about us. So let's go over the guys that have been killed."

"OK."

"How about Killer?"

"Dead."

"Craig, Raymond, and Dong?"

"I was listening on the radio when they got overrun. So they are probably dead."

"How many got killed after I left?"

"Well, let's see." I started to think. "Emerald, Doc, Eckert blinded, White, Henning, Allen, Emery, Erickson, Warner, Roberts, Jacop, Johns, Marsh, Byron, and there were a lot more."

"Some of the guys you mentioned got killed when I was in the field. How about Lieutenant Watkins? I guess he got it in the big battle, didn't he?"

"No, no! He is in Hawaii wounded, but he is probably home by now. I stopped by the hospital. He looked good."

"Man, Danny, that's great. I really liked him. Hey, Danny, have you ever noticed how many times we say 'man' before we say our sentence?"

"Man, Chuck, I never noticed."

Both of us laughed hard.

"I guess we both have a little hippie in us."

"Chuck, do you ever wonder why we made it, and so many others got killed?"

"I believe that your mom, dad, and your family praying for us every night at nine o'clock saved us!"

"Yep. Just think about our adventure in the 'Nam."

"Yeah, let's go over it, Danny."

"OK, we almost got killed on January ninth when we lost over 100 men! We met Killer, the joker, and you got your first Purple Heart! We watched the lurp guys after Killer cut the head off the VC!"

"Don't forget about Lieutenant Gibbons busting you to private," Chuck says, widening his eyes.

"Yeah, that was funny! Then we went fifty-seven days with no fresh water or clothes. I had to lie beside Proud Mary."

"Danny, do you remember how good things were at Cam Ranh Bay? Then we went to Da Nang, and all heck broke loose! What about the men that made us mad? They got killed!"

"That is the way it seemed, Chuck. Every guy that made us mad got killed or wounded! Then you saved my life. You received two more Purple Hearts and a Silver Star!"

"You received two Purple Hearts and a Silver Star too, Danny. You and I saved a lot of lives, didn't we?"

"Yes we did, Chuck, and you know something else?"

"What?"

"If it was possible for someone to take our Vietnam adventure away from us and give us a million bucks, I wouldn't take it! On the other hand, I wouldn't take a million dollars to do the exact same thing again!"

"Man, me neither, Danny! Again, I really do believe that your family's prayers saved us!"

I placed my hand on Chuck's shoulder. "I know it was! It was divine intervention from God that brought us home."

"Danny, do you ever think that we will really know why God spared us?"

"Maybe. God must have a plan for us."

The End

Chuck at a fire support base

My brothers playing with NVA Bayonets I sent them

Dad, Mom Duane, Denis and Doutg

Author Dan Rodgers

CPSIA information can be obtained at www.ICGtesting.com
Printed in the USA
LVOW12s1245181013

357543LV00001B/2/P